Pitt Series in Policy and Institutional Studies

The Moral Dimensions of Public Policy Choice

Beyond the Market Paradigm

John Martin Gillroy and
Maurice Wade, *Editors*

University of Pittsburgh Press

Pittsburgh and London

Published by the University of Pittsburgh Press, Pittsburgh, Pa., 15260
Copyright © 1992, University of Pittsburgh Press
Eurospan, London
Manufactured in the United States of America

Library of Congress Cataloging-in-Publication Data

The Moral dimensions of public policy choice : beyond the market paradigm /
  John Martin Gillroy and Maurice Wade, editors.
      p.   cm.
    Includes index.
    ISBN 0-8229-3697-6. — ISBN 0-8229-5463-X (pbk.)
    1. Policy sciences—Moral and ethical aspects.   I. Gillroy, John
  Martin, 1954–   .   II. Wade, Maurice L.
  H97.M67   1992
  320'.6—dc20   91-27052
                                                                      CIP

A CIP catalogue record for this book is available from the British Library.

Contents

Preface

WITHIN THE growing literature on the analysis of collective decisions, an area of critical concern—the normative political analysis of public policy—has received only isolated and unsystematic treatment. This anthology is meant as a first step in the eventual codification of options, arguments, and methods within this developing discipline.

Normative political analysis[1] is just that. First, it is *normative* in recognizing that "ought" questions motivate both dissatisfaction with the present state of public affairs and hopes for different and "better" policy in the future. It is *normative* in that every policy presupposes an underlying moral argument that justifies it and requires some ethical principle(s) that will act as a standard of evaluation.

The subject is *political* because it is concerned with how metaphysical principles become positive law, with how the theoretical and the practical meld into the sociopolitical reality every person faces, and with how that "reality" can be shaped and directed by collective decisions. Its premise is that policy is the attempt to solve a collective action problem—that is, to find ways to synthesize a "public interest" from individual wants and needs and to coordinate strategically rational actors toward cooperative solutions to joint problems.

Normative political analysis is concerned not with personal moral questions—"Why ought I to do A rather than B?"—but with political-moral questions—"Why ought we to use the powers of the state collectively to do A rather than B?" In other words, the normative analysis of public policy is not concerned with one's personal virtue but rather with how the individual, as citizen or policy maker, rationally justifies the use of state power to achieve one goal instead of another. The ethical principles of concern to the normative analysis of public policy are those that address the ethics of the policy itself.

In addition to this distinction between personal morality and normative politics, normative political analysis also distinguishes between politics and economics. This volume will suggest that the state and its function in the production and distribution of collective goods is distinct from the market's function in the production and trade of private goods. Our contentions are three:

1. The market and the state are two distinct entities with different moral foundations supporting distinct ends and means for accomplishing those ends.
2. The political person is more complex than her economic counterpart (homo economicus) and the role of citizen is irreducibly distinct from the role of consumer.
3. Although individual preferences are important in determining the proper nature of collective life, public policy ought also to recognize distinct types of value that do not function as subjects of instrumental economic preferences but may take moral priority in policy judgments.

Public policy analysis is, and has long been, the purview of economics. Its assumptions, methods, and essential principles, which were originally developed for the analysis of markets, have come to dominate the formulation, evaluation, recommendation, and implementation of public policy. However, policy analysis is essentially the normative exercise of defining and recommending that which is "socially better." Part I of this collection therefore examines the comprehensive nature and inherent normative assumptions of the economic approach to policy analysis. The essays in Part I suggest that the principle of efficiency, when applied outside the market and used as a comprehensive decision standard for public affairs, requires an underlying connection to deeper ethical principles, such as utility or respect for individual moral autonomy. This connection cannot be successfully established. The essays in Part I allow readers to examine the normative claims and limitations of cost-benefit methods and to establish in their minds the limited role efficiency plays in judging the ends of policy choice.

Part II brings together essays suggesting the serious need, given the claims established in Part I, for a coherent alternative to the economic approach to public policy. To begin the search for alternatives, we have assembled essays that suggest that the realm of public decision is distinct, both strategically and normatively, and that policy argument can be grounded on utility or autonomy when these are treated as distinct principles prior to, and independent of, efficiency. Having the resources to distinguish what is necessary to a normatively sophisticated policy argument, the reader should be able to synthesize and apply it to specific policy contexts outside this anthology.

No policy is value-free. Every public choice is based, explicitly or implicitly, on normative premises that are crucial to its practical effectiveness and to how this "effectiveness" is defined and evaluated. In assembling this volume, we therefore looked for essays that not only contained rigorous theoretical argument but also applied this argument to concrete policy issues. We believe it is important for the reader to understand that the theoretical enterprise informs practical application and is not antithetical to it.

Accordingly, when this volume focuses on duty and responsibility, it is ultimately interested in the duty and responsibility of actual citizens and policy makers as manifested in ethically sound policy argument that attempts to match normatively responsible means to morally justified ends. We have tried to bring together essays that, collectively, examine the limitations of the market paradigm in policy analysis and provide the building blocks for an important, coherent, and distinctive approach to public policy and its normative analysis.

Our investigations proceed on the basis of two premises:

1. Public policy seeks to solve collective action problems. Its task is to get strategically rational individuals to cooperate and coordinate their individual acts to solve joint problems.
2. The normative dimension of policy is the most essential component of any analysis. This means that collective choice is not limited to the empirical aspects of policy but also concerns the normative arguments that justify and promote one set of means or ends rather than another. We are concerned with the ethical values and moral principles that are contained in the policy argument, that direct its formulation and implementation, and that act as the standard of evaluation and accountability.

NOTES

1. We first ran across this description of the enterprise in (Hamlin and Pettit 1989, 1).

Acknowledgments

THIS ANTHOLOGY reflects the experience of both editors and of many of our colleagues in political science, philosophy, policy studies, public administration, and law. We would like to thank all of the contributors, especially the many colleagues who sent us course syllabi or other suggestions that contributed to our ultimate selection of essays.

A special thanks must go to Paul Churchill for his unique contribution to the genesis of this anthology and for his continuing friendship. In addition, we would like to acknowledge Mark Sagoff, Stephen Elkin, Douglas MacLean, and Mark Petracca for providing the encouragement and advice needed to bring this project to completion. We also wish to thank Trinity College for financial assistance and especially the Dean of the Faculty, Jan Cohn, for her help.

We would also like to express our debt to Bert Rockman and Fred Hetzel of the University of Pittsburgh Press for their willingness to take on this project and to Nancy Fleming and Jane Flanders for their conscientious editing of the manuscript.

We dedicate this volume to Margaret and Janet.

THE MORAL DIMENSIONS OF PUBLIC POLICY CHOICE

PART I

Efficiency in Policy Analysis

Introduction

BY CONSIDERING the role of the principle of efficiency in public sector deliberations and posing a series of questions related to the essays in Part I, this essay attempts to help the reader understand the ramifications of cost-benefit methods in policy analysis and their normative implications. There are many controversies that we hope will be better illuminated by the viewpoints presented here. Our specific task is to examine the principle of efficiency and to determine its adequacy as a basic normative standard of policy choice.

A common assumption of those who make public policy decisions is that a good standard for policy choice is "efficiency": the condition of obtaining the most benefit for the least cost. The idea finds its natural home in the economic ideal of the market which, as a competitive field for the free exchange of goods between individuals, allows each person to satisfy his or her preferences in such a way as to give that person the greatest freedom, personal autonomy of choice, and utility of outcome. The principle of efficiency is the basic standard of market decision making.

Routinely, however, efficiency has also been used as a standard for public decision making. In Part I, we focus on this established practice of using efficiency as the primitive principle of policy argument. We proceed on the basis of four assumptions:

1. Outside the market context, efficiency can be discussed either as cost-effectiveness analysis, which judges only the most efficient *means* to policy ends, or as cost-benefit methods, which use efficiency to judge both the means and the ends of policy choice.
2. Although efficiency is a sufficient "economic" primary decision standard to

5

judge the ends of a competitive market, it requires additional "moral weight" to judge ends outside of markets.
3. Two possible sources of this moral weight are contained in the concepts of utility and autonomy, both of which underlie market assumptions.
4. The use of cost-benefit methods rather than cost-effectiveness analysis implies that their use not only produces the most efficient outcome but simultaneously satisfies the additional moral requirement of providing for the utility and/or autonomy of the individuals involved.

The purpose of this section of essays is twofold. We explore the contention that a *moral* justification for the use of cost-benefit methods exists. We also explore whether such a justification is based in either a consequentialist concept of utility or a nonconsequentialist concept of individual autonomy, which is implied by the search for efficiency but carries more ethical weight than the strictly rational economic arguments for preference aggregation. We will argue that, although it is used as a standard of public policy argument, cost-benefit method has no moral grounding in either utility or autonomy. In effect, we will contend that using efficiency as a comprehensive principle to shape the means and ends of a public policy—as is done with cost-benefit analysis—is an illegitimate use of the principle of efficiency outside its proper context. This conclusion limits efficiency solely to the consideration of public *means,* promoting cost-effectiveness analysis over cost-benefit methods and initiating the search for independent moral standards and ethical arguments for the assessment of public ends (the subject of Part II).

Pareto and Kaldor Efficiency: A Primer for Policy Analysis

To understand the use of the principle of efficiency in policy analysis, one must begin with the basic concepts that define efficiency in a market and determine how the demands (for a standard of choice) from the public sector and the market differ. The principle that motivates and defines welfare in a market context is efficiency, and the means to efficient allocation is trade. The market is the framework of trade, and it defines the terms of exchange, considering only the desires of each individual and a free interplay of supply and demand for goods.

Trade proceeds between individuals until each person is satisfied that no further trade will make one party better off without making the other one worse off. This efficiency condition, called *Pareto optimal efficiency,* is the rational standard by which different allocations are judged within markets. It is a noninterpersonal standard in that satisfaction is an individual subjective judgment. It is an outgrowth of the ordinal preferences of each person who ranks states of affairs in isolation and in terms of the initial endowment of goods with which one begins to trade.

One allocation outcome is said to be Pareto superior to another when an exchange can be made so that everyone is indifferent ($p^0 I p^1$) between the status quo and the new outcome, while at least one person (i) strictly prefers ($p^1 P_i p^0$) the new allocation to the status quo. The allocation is said to be Pareto optimal or rational, and therefore efficient, if no further trades can be made without someone being made worse off.

> *Pareto superiority:* $p^0 I p^1$ for all, while for at least one individual, $p^1 P_i p^0$.
> *Pareto optimality:* No allocation p^* exists that makes anyone in p^1 better off without making someone else in p^1 worse off.
> (Where p^0 = status quo; p^1 = new allocation; and p^* = a third alternative)

The problem with Pareto optimality is that more than one point of optimality can exist at a time, depending on the initial endowments that the traders had before transactions started. One can assume that distributions of the amount of a good between traders can vary and that each redistribution gives the traders a different status quo point (bundle of goods in certain quantities) from which to begin trade (w_i). Each of these status quo points will find a distinct Pareto-optimal point at which trade will be stopped (w^*). One can be faced, therefore, with a series of Pareto-optimal allocations that assemble along what an economist calls a *contract curve,* a series of points at which no Pareto-superior moves are possible and agreement to stop trade can be made. This Pareto frontier will correspond to the range of possible distributions between the traders of initial endowments, where each original distribution of the total quantity of goods will render a single Pareto-optimal point on the frontier. Pareto efficiency will therefore reflect and maintain any initial asymmetries in the allocation of entitlements as initial endowments.

Cost-benefit analysis, as a technique by which government can set policy and remain faithful to market norms, is justified first and foremost as a set of criteria that allows the "efficiency" of the free market to be "mimicked" in centralized decision making. However, cost-benefit analysis concerns a choice problem with a difference. Traditionally, the Paretian efficiency standard has rendered a series of Pareto-optimal points (w^*) on a contract curve, and the social-choice dilemma involves finding a normatively acceptable means of choosing between these points (Feldman 1980).[1]

Cost-benefit evaluation is an attempt to use economic technique, in place of formal market bargaining or price setting, to locate a Pareto-optimal policy alternative—that is, to find the contract curve in the first place. In this case, the individual status quo points are off the contract curve at the point of initial endowment for each player (w_i). The job of the

policy maker using cost-benefit technique is to find an alternative allocation for each individual (w^*) that is Pareto-superior to the individual's
present position, or at least *potentially* so.

In many ways, this is a more interesting and all-encompassing social-
choice dilemma because it does not assume that the Paretian standard has
already been decisive in presenting and defining the public-choice options
to the political decision maker. It leaves evaluation options open, so that
cost-benefit methods can make a case for why the policy it recommends
should be considered superior. This situation also shows the comprehensive nature of the cost-benefit test, for it assumes that it is sufficient both
to locate the contract curve and then either to recommend this "efficient"
allocation as public policy or to deny its value as a collective-choice option. In this way, cost-benefit method makes the case for both efficiency
(finding the contract curve) and normatively optimal social choice (choosing between points on the contract curve).

The social-choice problem addressed by cost-benefit criteria, however,
is such that it is not the case that any one policy alternative is going to
satisfy the demands of the Paretian efficiency standard by making all
individuals it affects either indifferent to, or better off in, the new proposed allocation. The reality of policy making is that there will be welfare
winners and losers as a result of any collective decision. In addition, most
choices will be irreversible, in that once a path is chosen it will be hard or
impossible to switch back to an alternative that was passed over. In any
case, after a policy choice is made, a large, and real opportunity cost will
be incurred by the welfare losers that will make the new status quo more
attractive to the winners than other options that have already, for other
reasons, been discounted.

Because of the existence of both winners and losers, as a result of
policy choice, the definition of efficiency must be altered, and the case for
finding the contract curve must be supplied by a weaker set of requirements than Pareto superiority. The substitution welfare economists supply
is the Kaldor criterion, which is the effort to efficiently maximize wealth
through choosing the policy alternative that maximizes net benefit over
cost incurred.

The introduction of the Kaldor test as a Paretian substitute contends
that, as long as the gain to the winners in a policy choice outweighs (in
welfare terms) the losses of those who do not benefit, a situation is created
where the winners could, through transfer of wealth, compensate the
losers while still surpassing their position at the former status quo point. In
other words, the maximization of total wealth creates a situation where
everyone's welfare could be potentially improved to Paretian standards: *a
potential Pareto improvement.*

Policy makers use cost-benefit evaluation to find the Kaldor-efficient
allocations that maximize net social benefit over incurred cost. It is their

attempt to maximize social welfare in a policy decision. Richard Posner (1983, 60) recognized this process as "wealth maximization" based on Kaldor-efficiency criteria. Necessary to wealth maximization is the ability of decision makers to value the costs and benefits involved with each alternative in order to judge which will increase the welfare of more individuals, producing the net benefit of Kaldor efficiency. The valuation of goods, services, and surplus, which contributes to the welfare or wealth of the individual, is subject only to personal evaluation in line with one's preference order and must be translated by the policy maker to judge the net social benefit of any policy. "The most important thing to bear in mind about the concept of value is that it is based on what people are willing to pay for something rather than on the happiness they would receive from having it" (Posner 1983, 60).

The translation of valuation into *willingness to pay,* and then to an aggregated quantity that can be read by a policy maker, takes place in the following fashion. One begins by assuming that for each proposed policy alternative, each individual has a money valuation that corresponds to the individual's willingness to pay for, or to avoid, a certain outcome. This valuation can be represented as v_i. If an individual benefits from a policy alternative (the net benefits being more than incurred cost), then her v_i will be positive and will reflect the monetary amount she is willing to pay to get that policy choice enacted. If the net effects indicate that, in terms of personal welfare, the policy will cost her more than it will bestow benefit, then her v_i will reflect the amount she will suffer, and its value will be less than zero.

The task of the policy decision maker is to collect and add these subjective valuations, producing an aggregate V, so that the collective net benefit will be reflected in a sum greater than zero, $(\Sigma v_i > 0)$, while net cost, on the aggregate, will be shown in a sum that is less than zero, $(\Sigma v_i < 0)$, which would be enough for rejection of the policy on Kaldor-efficiency grounds.

Therefore, to recommend policy (x) over policy (y), the efficiency-oriented policy maker must be able to have access to tools for two processes. First, he must be concerned with the subjective valuations of all persons affected by the policy; second, he must strive to calculate the dollar equivalent of these effects on the welfare of individuals. All measures of welfare must be converted into the common currency of money, which attests to their fungibility and instrumental value to the end of efficient allocation. Those commodities that do not have a market price must be given a shadow price that reflects their opportunity cost and individual willingness to pay for each marginal unit.

Overall, however, the principle value distinction supported by markets is that the production of benefits and their efficient allocation are of paramount importance, while questions of distribution are less critical. Economists justify this priority on the supposition that efficiency is a "rational" and objective quantum that can be mathematically calculated and judged, independent of any ethical considerations. But is this argument, which may be a strong one for real competitive markets and the standard of Pareto superiority, less satisfying when it concerns public policy choice? In the policy context, centralized decision making by government replaces real individual choice (which generates supply and demand in the market), with abstract individual valuations and the need for an aggregation rule to define societal preference. In addition, the Kaldor criterion, not Pareto, has become the standard of efficiency.

Kaldor, like Pareto, is "indifferent to questions of distribution." But as Brian Barry notes, a difference also exists.

> The criterion of Pareto superiority as a necessary condition of something's counting as an improvement is, in one sense, strongly concerned with distribution. For it obviously has the implication that no gain, however large, to one person can counterbalance an uncompensated loss, however small, to another. But it is at the same time in another and more important sense sublimely unconcerned with distribution inasfar as it provides no basis on which to assess the status quo against which Pareto superiority is to be measured. (See chapter 13)

Where Kaldor, like Pareto, is deficient in the second instance, Kaldor also loses the benefit of the stronger sense of uncompensated loss, for now any large gain can be recommended in policy if the *possibility* of compensation exists.

Kaldor has a bias toward producing economic benefits as large as possible, without even the "uncompensated loss" protections of the Pareto criterion. The purpose of cost-benefit analysis, then, is to substitute for a rational Pareto criterion by maximizing benefit over cost, where the emphasis is on the production of wealth with little or no concern within the analysis for who benefits and who pays the costs.

In public policy, therefore, the work of the decision maker trying to allocate efficiently is as abstract and general as an economist might say the effort to distribute in a market must be. At this point, a general question arises. Given these drawbacks, why would a market standard of efficiency be recommended as the primary basis on which to judge collective policy choices? The answer lies in the argument for the primacy of efficient allocation, which makes a distinction between the "moral low ground" (preferences are being satisfied efficiently) of the rational justification of cost-benefit evaluation and the argument for a deeper ethical basis for efficiency as a policy standard that grants market procedures the "moral high ground" in the public debate (the proper ends of policy are being obtained). Essentially, monetary cost and benefit figures (these less than unambiguous efficiency results) are the outcomes of a market process (real or mimicked) built on the human "ethical consensus" that important social values are better promoted by markets than by any other mechanism.

First, it is contended that the prescriptive capability of market efficiency lies only in an ethical consensus that supports a society's value system.

> Although we can agree that ethical beliefs change over time, . . . at any given time some ethical consensus is to be found in any viable society. And if there is to be a normative economics, from which prescriptive propositions and policies can be derived that are applicable to a particular society, then it cannot be raised on any presuppositions that do not accord with whatever ethical consensus remains in that society. (Mishan 1981, 17)

Second, it is assumed that markets derive support from a more stable and timeless "ethical consensus" that recognizes and promotes basic moral principles that are universal and necessary to the flourishing of all individuals.

Cost-benefit method, therefore, holds a position of priority in the evaluation of policy as both a morally sanctioned and formally rational technique (Leonard and Zeckhauser 1986). Efficiency is all that policy makers must concern themselves with to ensure that the basic moral principles of their constituents are simultaneously promoted. If a decision maker using Kaldor can find a way onto the contract curve, he or she will also have found a policy that maximizes personal welfare or utility and/or has the ethical ramifications of respecting individuals and their choices to seek their own ends. It is not surprising, then, to see that efficiency is a standard that holds great power in policy choice and evaluation. The argument from the "moral high ground" adds power to the initial contention that allocation is a more rigorous process than distribution, while allocation can also be said to respond to an "ethical consensus" based on moral principles that are necessary to individual and collective well-being, independent of distributive concerns (Posner 1983, chapter 3).

The methodology of cost-benefit procedure involves a comprehensive process that attempts to judge both the means and ends of alternative public policies. Unlike cost-effectiveness analysis, which attempts to judge only the most efficient means to policy ends that have been arrived at on the basis of other than efficiency standards, cost-benefit analysis aspires to judge not only the most cost-conscious means to policy ends but also the efficiency of the ends themselves.

The ethical consensus for maximizing allocative efficiency is combined with the belief that efficiency supports deeper moral ends so that cost-benefit methods can act as a comprehensive approach to policy judgment. Kaldor efficiency, remember, competes against other policy principles such as equality (Okun 1975) and is not justified in terms of them, as it would have to be were its practitioners aware of its lack of "moral weight." The power and popularity of cost-benefit procedures lies in their comprehensive nature and their use as the critical and central consideration in policy decision making.

Without its comprehensive nature and its capacity to judge public ends, cost-benefit methodology is reduced to cost-effectiveness analysis, and the need for independent arguments for the selection and justification of policy ends becomes critical. Because of their comprehensive nature, cost-benefit methods require a stronger normative dimension than their purely economic counterpart (cost-effectiveness analysis) in order to claim the "moral high ground" in the public-choice sphere and set the ends as well as the means of the policy agenda.

Those who recommend cost-benefit methods as a basis for policy decision making either believe they carry moral weight from some kind of "ethical consensus" outside of markets or incorrectly apply them in this sphere. In the first case, the question relates to the source of this moral weight (the content of the "ethical consensus") and, in the second case, to the possible argument for Kaldor efficiency outside of markets without such normative grounding.

Part I of this anthology suggests the discussion of three areas of questions related to the use and normative roots of cost-benefit methods in policy analysis.

1. The first question relates to the uniform application of the cost-benefit test and looks at two essays that attempt to apply Kaldor efficiency to questions of atmospheric environmental-risk policy. Both essays are comprehensive treatments of the regulator questions, with policy recommendations made at the conclusion of the analysis. Does each begin with the same assumptions? Do they reach the same policy recommendations? Why or why not?

2. The second question for discussion regards the implicit normative structure of cost-benefit (Kaldor) methods. A basic foundational dichotomy for normative argument within policy studies exists between consequentialist and nonconsequentialist moral theory, specifically between ethical utilitarianism and some form of Kantian moral theory that relates to the freedom or autonomy of the individual (Bobrow and Dryzek 1987, 108–16; Majone 1989, 142). What is the ethical consensus? How can it be defined? Is the point of cost-benefit methods simply to find the "rational" policy alternative or is there a deeper ideological structure to the argument for "efficient" public policy? What is the content of this "ideology"? Is it utilitarian in character? Does making this ideology explicit affect the use of the "efficiency" argument in policy choice? What is that effect?

3. The last group of essays in Part I directly addresses the role of utility and autonomy as a normative basis for cost-benefit arguments. Can utility or autonomy provide the normative foundation as implied in the search

for efficient policy outcomes? Is there a basis for cost-benefit methods in utilitarian moral thought? Even if there is, does one need nonconsequentialist principles to support consequentialist decision making? Can the freedom of the individual in trade (his or her market autonomy) provide a nonconsequentialist basis for the use of cost-benefit methods in choosing public ends? Are moral rights important to public policy argument? Can one discuss rights as part of policy choice without a concept of the "self" as "holder" of those rights? Does the use of efficiency criteria take adequate account of the capacities and potential creation of the human self? Can it have a nonconsequentialist foundation without such an account?

We invite the reader to join us in the examination of efficiency as a basis for policy choice.

NOTE

1. For all references in this introduction, see the complete Bibliography, which follows the Epilogue at the end of this volume.

1   Benefit-Cost Analysis of Environmental Regulation: Case Studies of Hazardous Air Pollutants

John A. Haigh,
David Harrison, Jr.,
Albert L. Nichols

REGULATING TOXIC CHEMICALS is highly controversial, yet it promises to be a major task confronting an industrial society. Increasing attention to toxic substances reflects in part recent growth in the number and quantity of man-made chemicals. As controls over the conventional pollutants take effect, toxic substances move to center stage in the political arena. This increased attention also stems from the fact that many of the statutes and regulatory procedures developed for the conventional pollutants are ill-suited to the new substances.

The Administrator of the Environmental Protection Agency, William Ruckelshaus, has urged Congress to reconsider the present statutory framework for regulating toxic air pollutants.[1] EPA may shift its regulatory strategy from the identification of specific control technology and evaluation of the industry's ability to afford controls[2] to a strategy that weighs the trade-offs between control costs and risk reduction.[3]

This article evaluates alternative methods of integrating benefit-cost considerations into the regulation of toxic substances. The use of benefit-cost considerations in this context is highly controversial and widely debated. The debate, however, has incorporated little or no reference to specific decisions made by environmental policy makers.[4] Proponents of benefit-cost analysis point to the general virtues of explicit evaluation of benefits and costs. Critics, on the other hand, stress the philosophical difficulties involved in making judgments about life and death[5] or the practical difficulty of estimating the costs and benefits of control.[6] These broad debates do not consider what is at stake in particular circumstances and, indeed, whether those who assess the scientific evidence very differently might find much common ground in actual regulatory decisions. This article

15

attempts to fill that gap by considering three toxic pollutants—benzene, coke oven emissions, and acrylonitrile. All three pollutants are currently considered targets for control under section 112 of the Clean Air Act.[7]

This article focuses on the ideas that benefit-cost principles can help to identify regulatory alternatives and that benefit-cost analysis can yield widely accepted policy recommendations despite large uncertainties in many parameter estimates. Critics caricature benefit-cost analysis as a mindless toting up of costs and benefits, but benefit-cost principles are more properly viewed as a framework for exploring opportunities to in-crease health and other benefits or reduce unnecessary costs. The crucial concept is *marginalism*. Given an existing regulation, benefit-cost analysis identifies marginal changes that increase benefits more than costs, or decrease costs more than benefits.[8]

Critics argue that the data on benefits and costs of regulatory alterna-tives are simply too uncertain to use risk assessment or benefit-cost results in policy making.[9] In some cases, however, all plausible estimates of the parameters lead to the same policy recommendation. Thus, the results in such cases remain robust with respect to uncertainty. Two of the three case studies evaluated in this paper fall in this category.[10] Uncertainty, there-fore, should not serve to dismiss out-of-hand benefit-cost analysis in envi-ronmental regulation.

Part I of this article discusses section 112 of the Clean Air Act, which provides the framework for regulating the three case-study pollutants.[11] Part II presents the three case studies and includes an analysis of regula-tory alternatives for the three pollutants.[12] Part III summarizes the uncer-tainties in calculating regulatory benefits, and the effect of those uncertain-ties on policy recommendations.[13] Finally, Part IV outlines the overall conclusions derived from examining the case studies.[14]

I. Regulatory Controls

A. *Section 112 of the Clean Air Act*

Section 112 provides the statutory authority for regulating "hazardous" air pollutants emitted from stationary sources.[15] That section reflects the need to regulate hazardous pollutants outside the complex framework of ambi-ent standards, state implementation plans, and new source performance standards established for the more ubiquitous "criteria" pollutants.[16] The Act defines a hazardous air pollutant as one "to which no ambient air quality standard is applicable and which in the judgment of the Adminis-trator causes, or contributes to, air pollution which may reasonably be anticipated to result in mortality or an increase in serious irreversible, or incapacitating reversible, illness."[17] Section 112 requires the EPA Adminis-trator to establish a list of hazardous air pollutants and, within 180 days of listing a substance, to set emission standards for sources "at the level which . . . provides an ample margin of safety to protect the public health."[18]

The language of section 112 emerged as a compromise from the House-Senate conference committee on the Clean Air Act amendments of 1970.[19] The House bill proposed basing national emission standards for hazardous air pollutants on technological and economic feasibility.[20] In contrast, Senator Edmund Muskie and his supporters in the Senate favored a zero-discharge requirement, which would have applied to fewer pollutants than the House bill.[21] The final language of the section, however, refers neither to technological feasibility nor to zero discharges.[22] This suggests that, while the conference committee expected health considerations to determine standards, it did not expect health protection to require the absolute elimination of all hazardous emissions.

B. Dilemmas in Implementation

EPA's regulatory activity under section 112 over the past thirteen years has been modest.[23] Emission standards have been promulgated for only four substances: beryllium, asbestos, mercury, and vinyl chloride.[24] The EPA has listed three additional substances: benzene, radionuclides, and inorganic arsenic.[25]

Both EPA and the environmental groups monitoring the agency's actions under section 112 have concentrated on pollutants suspected of causing cancer.[26] The focus on carcinogens creates a dilemma for the agency because many scientists believe that there are no thresholds for carcinogens—no exposure levels short of zero that are risk free.[27] Thus, a strict interpretation of section 112's requirement to provide "an ample margin of safety" would require zero-discharge standards, tantamount to banning the listed substances.

Such a strict interpretation of section 112 could be impractical. Many substances subject to regulation under section 112 are important industrial chemicals. Zero-discharge limitations on these substances would lead to numerous plant closures and the loss to consumers of many valuable products.[28] Consequently, EPA has avoided a strict interpretation of section 112 and instead has proposed standards requiring the degree of control achievable with the "best available technology" (BAT).[29] Standards promulgated by the EPA for asbestos and vinyl chloride illustrate the agency's dilemma and its eventual decision to base control requirements on technological feasibility.

In 1971, EPA proposed standards for asbestos because of its link to a form of cancer known as asbestosis.[30] Public comments on the proposed standards revealed no scientific doubt about asbestos hazards, but also stressed the importance of asbestos to the economy.[31] Although the EPA maintained that the final standard "was not based on economic consider-ations"[32] and that "the overriding considerations are health effects,"[33] the preamble to the standard acknowledged the dilemma:

> EPA considered the possibility of banning production, processing, and use of asbestos or banning all emissions . . . into the atmosphere, but rejected these approaches. . . . Either approach would result in the prohibition of many activities which are extremely important; moreover, the available evidence relating to the health hazards of asbestos does not suggest that such prohibi-tion is necessary to protect public health.[34]

The effect of this dilemma on EPA action is indicated by the fact that the agency did not even adopt this compromise standard until 1973 (well beyond the 180-day limit), and then only after a court order.[35]

The language of the vinyl chloride standard, promulgated in October 1976,[36] provides an even clearer indication of the adoption of a technology-based approach. In the proposed regulation, EPA interpreted section 112 as allowing it to set standards:

> that require emission reduction to the lowest level achievable by use of the best available control technology in cases involving apparent nonthreshold pollutants, where complete emission prohibitions would result in widespread industry closure and EPA has determined that the cost of such closure would be grossly disproportionate to the benefits of removing the risk that would remain after imposition of the best available control technology.[37]

Thus, although section 112 mentions only health effects, and a literal reading might require that all emissions of nonthreshold pollutants be banned, the EPA developed an accommodation that bases control on technological feasibility.

EPA did not identify guidelines for listing substances under section 112 in its standards for asbestos or vinyl chloride. Asbestos and vinyl chloride presented clear cases of proven carcinogens, but over fifty other sub-stances are identified only as potentially hazardous air pollutants.[38] In contrast, many toxic water pollutants were listed (and a schedule for developing regulations established) in 1976 as part of a consent decree with the Natural Resources Defense Council.[39]

Environmental groups became dissatisfied with the slow pace at which the agency was listing substances and promulgating standards under sec-tion 112.[40] In November 1977, the Environmental Defense Fund (EDF) filed a petition requesting that EPA establish the terms of the vinyl chlo-ride agreement as a generic approach to the regulation of all carcinogens.[41] Finally, in October 1979, EPA proposed a cancer policy entitled "Policies and Procedures for Identifying, Assessing, and Regulating Airborne Sub-stances Posing a Risk of Cancer."[42] Although the proposed policy was never promulgated, a review of its provisions provides an indication of the procedures that evolved over the first decade of section 112's existence.

C. Cancer Policy

The most important features of the EPA's proposed "cancer policy" involved the criteria for listing substances and the criteria for setting standards for source categories.[43] The proposal established a relatively low hurdle for listing; EPA would list any substance having a high probability of carcinogenicity unless there was no evidence of a significant threat of ambient exposure from emissions by stationary sources.[44] Upon listing, a set of generic regulations including maintenance, storage, and "housekeeping" requirements would immediately apply to sources emitting the substance.[45]

For each listed substance, the EPA would prepare detailed estimates of health effects and use those estimates to set priorities to develop emission standards for individual source categories posing the most imminent threat to the public health.[46] The emission standards would, at a minimum, require BAT controls. The procedures for determining BAT do not involve risk assessment. Quantitative risk estimates would, however, be employed in the standard-setting process if they showed that the residual risk after BAT controls was "unreasonable." In such a case, EPA would impose tighter controls.[47]

In sum, EPA's record in implementing section 112 has consisted of much study and little regulation. The proposed cancer policy did create a methodology that would have allowed vastly greater listings, but would also have severely limited EPA discretion in setting specific standards for listed substances.[48] In the last several years, the EPA has continued to analyze potential section 112 pollutants, but has not listed any new substances, nor proposed new standards for substances previously listed, nor promulgated standards proposed earlier.[49] The following statement made by David Patrick, the chief of the Pollutant Assessment Branch in the Office of Air Quality Planning and Standards at EPA, illustrates the concerns of the agency:

> All have perceived that a literal interpretation of section 112 would not preclude open-ended control requirements or the possibility of zero emission goals, regardless of the control costs. Given this potential and the apparent lack of flexibility regarding the removal of substances from the list of hazardous pollutants or the exclusion of source categories from control requirements, the Agency has also been reluctant to list pollutants as hazardous without some reasonable assurance that subsequent regulations would convey health benefits that are not grossly disproportionate to the costs of control.[50]

D. Recent Congressional Debate

In the current debate on reauthorization of the Clean Air Act, environmental groups have criticized EPA's review process as "slow and repetitive."[51] The Environmental Defense Fund has urged Congress to: (1)

adopt a generic method for listing airborne carcinogens; (2) list the thirty-seven substances now under study; and (3) require that EPA develop a systematic regulatory approach that includes literature reviews, periodic reports, and time limits for action.[52] In contrast, the Chemical Manufacturers Association (CMA) advocates modifying section 112 to allow EPA to regulate only those substances that pose a significant risk to health and to consider social, technical, energy, and economic consequences in setting standards.[53] Finally, EPA Administrator Ruckelshaus advocates a regulatory strategy that is based on the balancing of many factors including the nature of the risk posed by a substance and the cost of eliminating or minimizing it.[54]

The eventual result of this debate over section 112 cannot yet be determined. Thus far, however, sentiment in the House seems to favor swifter, more aggressive regulation of airborne carcinogens. In August 1982, the House Energy and Commerce Committee voted in favor of an amendment requiring that, in each of the next four years, EPA review 25 percent of the thirty-seven substances discussed earlier.[55] The amendment would create a presumption in favor of listing; each of the thirty-seven substances would be listed automatically unless EPA determined that it was not hazardous.[56] If this provision, or a similar one, is enacted. the pace of regulation under section 112 should reach substantially higher levels than ever before.

II. The Case Studies

A. Steps in Estimating Benefits

These studies estimate the benefits of pollution control standards by tracing the links from emissions to exposure to risk. The purposes of the analysis are either to estimate the dollar value that affected parties place on the reduced risk or to use the risk estimates to calculate the implicit cost per statistical life saved. The steps used, presented schematically in figure 1, apply in assessing the benefits of controlling virtually any dangerous pollutant. The following discussion provides a general overview of the calculations associated with each step in the context of regulating airborne carcinogens.

The change in emissions due to regulation is the most straightforward of the calculations that produce benefit estimates.[57] For each plant, the EPA estimates the emissions with and without controls in place.[58] The difference between these two estimates equals the emissions reduction attributable to the regulation imposed.

Emissions reduction estimates are converted into more meaningful estimates of exposure reductions by calculating an "exposure factor" for

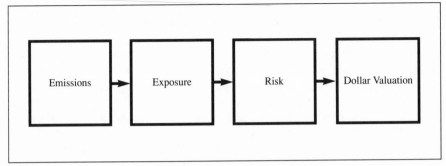

FIGURE 1.   Steps in Estimating Benefits

individual plants.[59] The exposure factor indicates the amount of exposure caused by a unit of emissions from a particular source.[60] Both the dispersion pattern of emissions and the population pattern in the area surrounding the plant contribute to calculating this factor.

In many cases, EPA estimates emissions dispersion using a "model plant."[61] For a given level of emissions, the dispersion model uses meteorological data to generate estimates of average annual pollutant concentrations at various distances from the source. The estimated concentrations are then combined with plant-specific population data to estimate total exposure levels for a given level of emissions.

Exposure levels are expressed in terms of "$\mu g/m^3$-person-years," which is simply the average annual concentration (in micrograms per cubic meter) multiplied by the number of people exposed and the period of exposure.[62] This summary measure of exposure provides sufficient information to predict total risk under certain conditions.[63] Dividing the exposure level by the total level of emissions gives the exposure factor, expressed in terms of $\mu g/m^3$-person-years per kilogram emitted.

Reduced exposure is translated into reduced risk using the unit risk factor for the particular pollutant. A unit risk factor represents the risk of cancer posed by exposure to one unit of a substance—measured as the risk of cancer per $\mu g/m^3$-person-year.[64]

Each of the three case studies used unit risk estimates prepared by EPA's Carcinogen Assessment Group (CAG). The CAG unit risk estimate measures the increased probability of cancer resulting from exposure to 1 $\mu g/m^3$ for a lifetime.[65] This figure divided by seventy equals the risk of cancer per $\mu g/m^3$-person-year. In applying epidemiological data, the CAG employs a procedure that assumes that risk remains proportional to dose at low levels of exposure.[66]

Over the past decade or two, a substantial literature has accumulated on the issue of valuing reductions in risks to life.[67] Economists agree that the appropriate criterion is "willingness to pay."[68] The principle is a simple one: an individual values each benefit just as much as the amount he would be willing to pay to secure it.

Inferences drawn from actual behavior provide the best estimates of willingness to pay. Many studies have estimated willingness to pay for reduced risks to life based on the wage premiums associated with occupational risks.[69] Bailey has reviewed several empirical studies, adjusting them for consistency.[70] His estimate covers a range of $170,000 to $715,000 per life saved, with an intermediate estimate of $360,000 in 1978 dollars, or approximately $500,000 in 1982 dollars.[71] Other studies, however, have estimated much higher wage premiums for occupational risks, with the highest estimates in excess of $5 million per life saved in 1982 dollars.[72] Thus, the published estimates from wage studies range from several hundred thousand dollars to several million dollars per statistical life saved.

Many of the calculations in this article forgo the final step of placing a dollar value on lives saved and presenting a single net benefit result. However, estimates of the reductions in lives saved and the implicit cost per statistical life saved are presented. These results are then compared with reasonable estimates of the value of this risk reduction to determine if the regulation is likely to pass a benefit-cost test.

B. The Case Studies

Benzene, coke oven emissions, and acrylonitrile are all high-priority section 112 pollutants. Benzene has been listed formally[73] and regulations have been proposed,[74] and recently reproposed, for several source categories.[75] Coke oven emissions and acrylonitrile are included in a list of thirty-seven substances the EPA is currently evaluating.[76] The health risks of and control options for these pollutants are well documented.[77] Although the following case studies use a common underlying methodology to estimate the benefits of controls for all three pollutants, the empirical details of the methodology vary considerably with each pollutant.

This section presents the results of benefit-cost analysis in each of the three case studies. The next sections suggest two approaches as alternatives to uniform BAT standards: (1) modification of the uniform standards to increase net benefits and (2) differential standards based on exposure levels around individual plants.[78]

1. MALEIC ANHYDRIDE (BENZENE) CASE STUDY[79]

Maleic anhydride plants emit benzene, a major industrial chemical used in making nylon, plastics, insecticides and polyurethane foams.[80] A 1977 study by the National Institute of Occupational Safety and Health showed an abnormally high incidence of leukemia in workers exposed to benzene while employed at two plants in the rubber industry.[81] Following this study, the EPA listed benzene under section 112.[82]

In April 1980, almost three years after listing benzene, EPA proposed an emission standard for maleic anhydride plants that use benzene as a feedstock.[83] The BAT standard called for an emissions reduction of roughly 97 percent from uncontrolled levels.[84] A majority of the plants, however, already had installed controls of 90 percent or better, probably in response to state regulations directed at hydrocarbons or the hope that the benzene recovered would pay for the controls.[85] As a result, the proposed BAT standard was expected to reduce full-capacity emissions by less than 90 percent, from 5.6 million kilograms per year to just under 0.5 million kilograms per year.[86]

The costs of implementing the proposed standard were estimated at $2.6 million per year in 1982 dollars.[87] These costs are quite affordable to the maleic anhydride industry, whose total sales grossed $142 million in 1979.[88] The cost estimates are meaningless in isolation, however; they can be judged appropriately only in relation to the benefits they secure. As estimated, the proposed regulations would have reduced exposure by 3.6 million $\mu g/m^3$-person-years and saved 0.4 lives annually.[89]

2. COKE OVEN EMISSIONS CASE STUDY[90]

Coke, produced by distilling coal in ovens, is essential to the production of iron and steel. In 1978, U.S. plants produced approximately 44 billion kilograms of coke.[91] Epidemiological studies of coke-oven workers show that emissions from the coking process increased the risks of lung, trachea, bronchus, kidney, and prostate cancers.[92] Although the toxic elements include gases and respirable particulate matter, most attention has focused on the polycyclic organic matter (POM) contained in coal tar particulates.[93]

Coke oven emissions are released from numerous fugitive sources, including leaks and imperfections in the ovens. Charging emissions occur when coal is added to the ovens at the beginning of the coking process. Door leaks are the result of imperfect fits between the ovens and the doors through which the finished coke is later removed. Finally, imperfect seals on the lids and offtakes on the tops of the ovens create topside leaks.[94]

If the EPA listed coke oven emissions under section 112, the Agency would probably specify standards similar to the following as BAT: 12 percent of doors visibly leaking; 3 percent of lids visibly leaking and 6 percent of offtake systems visibly leaking; and sixteen seconds of visible emissions for each charging.[95] EPA estimates suggest that only thirty-seven of the fifty-four identified coke plants would have to increase control efforts to meet these standards (and some of those plants already meet one or two of the three potential BAT standards).[96] EPA estimates annual control costs for those plants at $24.5 million.[97]

Plant-specific emission estimates indicate that coke oven emissions would fall by 289,000 kg/year and exposure would fall by approximately 819,000 $\mu g/m^3$-person-years if the above BAT standards were imposed.[98] Coke oven emissions are very potent carcinogens; this relatively slight reduction in exposure would save an estimated 10.6 lives each year.[99]

3. ACRYLONITRILE CASE STUDY[100]

Acrylonitrile is an important industrial feedstock, employed primarily in the production of chemicals used to make a wide range of common products including rugs, clothing, plastic pipes, and automobile hoses.[101] Almost a billion kilograms of acrylonitrile were produced in 1981.[102] Extensive evidence indicating acrylonitrile's carcinogenicity exists.[103] Specifically, epidemiological studies have associated acrylonitrile with respiratory cancers.[104]

While EPA has neither listed acrylonitrile nor proposed specific regulations, EPA contractors have identified available control options that could reduce emissions by at least 95 percent from uncontrolled levels.[105] All thirty existing plants, however, already have implemented some type of controls. Thus, potential BAT standards would only cut annual emissions from 3.6 million kilograms to 0.5 million kilograms, a reduction of slightly less than 87 percent.[106] Uniform controls would create an estimated annual expense of almost \$29 million in 1982 dollars.[107] Reduced exposure to acrylonitrile, just over 450,000 $\mu g/m^3$-person-years, would avoid only one case of cancer every five years (0.2 lives per year).[108]

C. Analysis of the Best Available Technology Standards

Table 1 summarizes the results of the BAT standards analyzed. Controls on coke oven emissions produce much greater health benefits than do controls on the emissions of benzene or acrylonitrile. BAT controls on coke ovens would result in almost eleven fewer cases of cancer each year, compared to reductions of 0.4 cancer deaths for maleic anhydride benzene controls and 0.2 cancer deaths for acrylonitrile standards.

The final line of table 1 presents the most relevant figure in measuring the cost-effectiveness of the three control standards—the value placed on saving a life that is necessary to justify incurring control costs. To justify acrylonitrile controls on benefit-cost grounds, the value of a statistical life would have to be at least \$144 million, an implausible figure from virtually any perspective.[109] The cost-effectiveness figure for benzene, \$6.5 million, also is larger than the range of plausible estimates. Controls on coke oven emissions are the most attractive of the three BAT options. To justify the coke oven emissions standards on benefit-cost grounds, the value of a life saved must be equal to or greater than \$2.3 million. That value does fall within the range of the published benefit estimates. Nevertheless, all three

TABLE 1
Benefits and Costs of BAT Standards

	Benzene[a]	Coke Ovens	Acrylonitrile
Annual Costs and Benefits			
Control Costs ($1000)	2,577	24,511	28,988
Number of plants	8	37	31
Reduced Emissions (1000 kg)	5,059	289	3,112
Reduced Exposure (1000 $\mu g/m^3$-person-yrs)[b]	3,646	819	455
Lives Saved[c]	0.4	10.6	0.2
Cost-Effectiveness			
Emissions ($/kg)	0.51	84.8	9.3
Exposure ($/$\mu g/m^3$-yr)	0.71	29.9	63.7
Lives saved ($1 million/life)	6.5	2.3	144

Notes:
   a. Estimates are based upon the 1980 proposed standard for maleic anhydride plants.
   b. Exposure reductions are calculated by aggregating the concentration changes for people at different distances from each plant. For example, if 1000 people have their exposure reduced by 10 micrograms per cubic meter ($\mu g/m^3$) in a given year, exposure would be reduced by 10,000 $\mu g/m$-person-years.
   c. Lives saved are calculated by multiplying the exposure reduction by a unit risk factor that measures the increased probability of contracting cancer as a result of exposure to 1 $\mu g/m^3$ for one year. For example, if exposure is reduced by 1,000,000 $\mu g/m^3$-per-years for a carcinogen that increases the risk of cancer by 1.5 $\times$ 10^4 for each $\mu g/m^3$-per-year, a total of 15 statistical lives would be saved. (Note: this article assumes that all cancer cases result in premature death.)

BAT options would fail a conventional benefit-cost test based upon a value of $1 million per life saved.

Table 2 indicates two principal reasons why the cost-effectiveness of control varies so greatly among the pollutants. First, the carcinogenic potency of coke oven emissions is much greater than for acrylonitrile or for benzene.[110] Second, coke oven emissions affect many more people than do the other pollutants. Fugitive coke emissions occur at ground level rather than from stacks, and coke plants tend to be located closer to large population concentrations."[111] As a result, a kilogram of coke oven emissions causes three times the exposure that a kilogram of benzene emitted from maleic anhydride plants does and over seventeen times the exposure that a kilogram of acrylonitrile does.[112] Because of these two factors, a reduction of one kilogram in coke oven emissions produces a risk reduction roughly 500 times greater than for either of the other cases.[113]

Together, tables 1 and 2 indicate that concentrating only on the cost per kilogram of emission reduction provides a misleading measure of the relative attractiveness of the three BAT standards. A kilogram of coke oven emissions is much more costly to control than a kilogram of either acrylonitrile or benzene. The marginal benefit of controlling coke oven emissions is so much larger, however, that coke ovens are far more cost-

TABLE 2
Risk and Exposure Information for the Three Cases

	Benzene[a]	Coke Oven Emissions	Acrylonitrile
Unit risk factor (deaths/ $\mu g/m^3$-yr)[b]	1.1×10^7	$\dfrac{1.3}{10^8}$	4.4×10
Total population exposed	8,080,000	25,948,000	8,457,000
Population within 1 km	27,550	90,193	7,138
Average exposure factor ($\mu g/m^3$-person-yrs/kg)[d]	0.721	2.83	0.146
Risk per kg of emissions	7.9×10^8	$\dfrac{3.7}{10^8}$	6.4×10^8

a. Estimates are based upon the 1980 proposed standard for maleic anhydride plants.
b. See foootnote c, Table 1.
c. Population within 20 km of all plants.
d. The exposure factor is calculated by dividing the reduced exposure by the reduced emissions. For example, the calculation for coke oven emissions is: 819,000 $\mu g/m^3$-person years divided by 289,000 kg, which equals 2.83.

effective objects of regulation. This comparison gives the most compelling reason for formally evaluating the benefits of toxics control. It is impossible to target controls where they provide the greatest health benefits without considering relative carcinogenicity and relative exposure factors.

D. Analysis of Alternative Standards

Benefit-cost criteria assist policy makers in evaluating regulatory alternatives beyond uniform BAT standards as well. This section analyzes two alternatives for each pollutant: (1) a relaxed uniform standard; and (2) a set of differential standards that would be more stringent for plants located in more densely populated areas than for plants that cause less exposure.

Choosing the appropriate degree of control is a common issue in pollution regulation.[114] Controls should be tightened as long as the marginal benefits exceed the marginal costs. Negative net benefits at one control level do not imply that regulation is undesirable at all levels, because a less stringent alternative may provide positive net benefits.

Pollution control regulations can also be targeted to specific firms.[115] The EPA and other regulatory agencies typically develop regulations for broad source categories. Section 112 is typical; the BAT standards apply to all plants within the source category. This approach ignores the fact that plants located in high density areas affect many more people and produce much greater exposure reduction for the same amount of emission control.[116]

Table 3 summarizes the application of these alternative regulatory

TABLE 3
Benefits for Alternative Strategies

	Benzene[a]	Coke Ovens	Acrylonitrile
Percentage of BAT Results			
Relaxed Uniform Standard[b]			
Benefits	94	80	62
Costs	57	61	29
Differential Standard[c]			
Benefits	96	81	60
Costs	37	33	18
Cost per Life Saved (in $1 million)			
Relaxed Uniform[b]	3.9	1.8	64.2
incremental BAT	41.6	4.7	274.
Differential[c]	2.5	0.93	42.1
incremental BAT	80.4	8.3	286.
Net Benefits ($ million/year)			
BAT	−2.2	−13.9	−28.8
Relaxed uniform	−1.1	−6.4	−8.0
Differential	−0.6	0.5	−4.9

a. Estimates are based on data available to EPA when the standard was proposed.
b. Defined as:
  maleic anhydride: 90 percent
  coke ovens: doors only
  acrylonitrile: AN monomer and nitrile elastomer plants
c. Defined as:
  maleic anhydride: 97 percent control for plants with exposure factors greater than 0.6
  coke ovens: doors and topside for plants with factors greater than 2.0
  acrylonitrile: BAT controls for AN monomer and nitrile clastomer plants with exposure factors
    greater than 0.2

strategies to the three pollutants. Alternatives that target controls on the high-exposure plants are referred to as "differential standards." Both the relaxed standards and the differential standards reduce costs much more than they reduce benefits. The cost-per-life-saved estimates, however, are still quite high. In fact, the only alternative that yields positive net benefits at a value per life saved of $1 million is differential standards for coke oven emissions. The other alternatives result in net losses ranging from $0.6 million for differential standards for maleic anhydride plants to $28.8 million for the BAT standards for acrylonitrile plants.

The wide range in net benefits demonstrates the need for more detailed analysis of alternative regulatory strategies for the specific pollutants. In addition, the details of estimating the benefits and costs of alternatives differ considerably among specific pollutants. Since the analysis of the effect of uncertainty presumes a familiarity with the derivation of the estimates, a more comprehensive description of the case study results is presented below.

1. Benzene

Of the five maleic anhydride plants that would need new control equipment to meet a 97 percent control standard, two already achieve 90 percent control.[117] Therefore, the marginal cost of increasing control efficiency in these plants by 7 percent is quite high. EPA would save a substantial amount of money with little change in benefits by relaxing the standard to a 90 percent control level. The estimated exposure reduction is only 6 percent lower than at 97 percent, but costs fall 43 percent.[118] The cost per statistical life saved drops to $3.9 million, a substantial improvement over the BAT proposal. The cost per statistical life saved of BAT standards rises to $41.6 million when 97 percent controls are compared to 90 percent controls. Therefore, unless the value of a statistical life saved is taken as greater than $41.6 million, the stricter standard is unjustified.[119]

A uniform standard of 90 percent control improves cost-effectiveness by screening out plants for which the proposed standard has little impact on emissions or exposure. Differential standards, which set tighter requirements for plants with high exposure factors, offer a more ambitious and controversial way of increasing efficiency.[120] In extreme form, differential standards based on exposure factors lead to plant-specific standards. Limited categorization is a more practical approach. The eight plants emitting benzene, for example, could be split into four "high-exposure" plants and four "low-exposure" plants.[121] A regulation requiring 97 percent controls on only the high-exposure plants, and no additional controls on the other plants, yields 96 percent of the benefits of the proposed uniform standard at 37 percent of its cost.[122] The differential standard also surpasses the uniform 90 percent alternative, achieving slightly greater benefits at 71 percent of the cost.[123] Thus, even a crude, two-level differential standard significantly improves the cost-effectiveness of benzene standards.[124]

2. Coke Oven Emissions

The EPA could improve the cost-effectiveness of BAT controls on coke oven emissions by eliminating controls on some sources of emissions.[125] Controls on charging are substantially less cost-effective than those for doors or topside leaks.[126] Eliminating the charging standard reduces costs by 29 percent, but cuts benefits by only 9 percent. Controls on door leaks are the most cost-effective component of the BAT standard, with a cost-effectiveness ratio of less than $1.8 million per statistical life saved. By imposing BAT standards solely on door leaks, the EPA would cut costs 39 percent while retaining 80 percent of the benefits of the complete BAT standard.[127]

A total of fifty-four plants would be subject to BAT control requirements, but seventeen plants currently meet the requirements.[128] The exposure to coke oven emissions varies widely across the remaining thirty-seven plants, with the exposure factor ranging from a low of 0.58 to a high of 5.93.[129] The wide range in exposure factors offers an opportunity to increase efficiency by restricting the standard—or portions of it—to plants with relatively high exposure factors. Of the thirty-seven plants, twenty-one have exposure factors greater than 2.0 $\mu g/m^3$-person-years/ kg.[130] A regulation imposing the door and topside standards only on those plants yields 81 percent of the benefits at only 33 percent of the cost of the uniform BAT standard.[131]

3. ACRYLONITRILE

The thirty plants currently emitting acrylonitrile can be divided into four source categories: AN Monomer, acrylic fiber plants, nitrile elastomer, and ABS/SAN resin plants.[132] The cost-effectiveness estimates vary widely among these source categories. A regulation restricting the BAT standards to the two most cost-effective source categories, the nitrile elastomer and AN monomer plants, would yield 62 percent of the benefits of the complete set of standards at 29 percent of the cost.[133] The average cost per life saved, however, would still be over $64 million.[134] Controls on even the most cost-effective category, nitrile elastomer plants, yield a cost per life saved of almost $48 million. Thus, none of the BAT standards for controlling acrylonitrile emissions can be justified on benefit-cost grounds.

EPA model plant data indicate that a flare to control column-vent emissions from AN monomer plants would reduce emissions about 76 percent below uncontrolled levels at a cost of less than $0.032 per kilogram of acrylonitrile.[135] Using the average exposure factor for those plants of 0.248 $\mu g/m^3$-person-years/kg, the implicit cost per life saved would be under $290,000, a relatively modest sum.[136] All of the AN monomer plants, however, already have such flares.[137] This fact affords at least one indication that manufacturers have already installed those control devices that are least expensive.

As in the other two case studies, widely varying exposure factors offer opportunities to improve cost-effectiveness by limiting standards to high-exposure plants.[138] Regulations restricting BAT standards to AN monomer and nitrile elastomer plants with exposure factors greater than 0.2 $\mu g/m^3$-person-years/kg, for example, yield 60 percent of the benefits of the complete set of BAT standards at only 18 percent of the cost.[139] The most cost-effective plant, however, has a cost-effectiveness ratio of approximately $18 million per life saved.[140] Thus, although differential standards substantially improve the cost-effectiveness ratios of acrylonitrile controls, they do not yield benefits commensurate with the costs of control.

E. Summary

The results of the three case studies indicate that uniform technology-based controls have vastly different net benefits depending upon the pollutant and the source category. The implicit cost per life saved by BAT standards varies by a factor of almost 100 among the three pollutants. Moreover, in each of the three cases, alternative standards yield higher net benefits than BAT for any plausible value of risk reduction. For two of the three cases, however, even the most cost-effective standards considered fail any reasonable benefit-cost test. In the third case, coke oven emissions, regulation produces positive net benefits for a value per life saved of $1 million only by relaxing the control standard and restricting it to high-exposure plants.

These conclusions must be viewed as tentative, for they do not take into account the substantial uncertainties associated with estimating the benefits of controlling airborne carcinogens.

III. Uncertainties in Estimating Benefits

The benefit estimates discussed in the case studies employ point estimates of parameter values based on EPA data. Most of the estimates, however, are highly uncertain; the plausible range for the unit risk estimate in each case covers several orders of magnitude. Critics argue that such uncertainties render quantitative analysis too unreliable to guide policy. The key issue, however, is not whether the estimates are precise—clearly they are not—but how robust the conclusions are in the face of substantial uncertainties and potential errors. Part III [of this article] evaluates each of the four steps in benefit estimation, beginning with the estimation of emission reduction. It addresses both the generic problems and specific examples from the case studies for each step. Additionally, it considers the potential importance of noncancer control benefits that have not been quantified.

A. Uncertainties in Estimating Emissions

In theory, estimating emission reductions involves nothing more than monitoring the pollutant source before and after control, and subtracting the results. Despite this apparent simplicity, estimates of the reduction in emissions are far from precise. Several sources of uncertainty, common to the vast majority of regulations likely to be considered under section 112, arise in measuring emissions. In the case of coke oven controls, emissions estimation may be the largest source of uncertainty in estimating the benefits of regulation.

The uncertainties in estimating emissions and emission reductions are particularly great at the level of individual plants. The EPA bases its emission estimates on a model plant and projects them to actual individual sources using a limited number of plant-specific factors.[141] In each of the three cases, for example, EPA assumed that all plants within a given category had the same uncontrolled emission rate. In reality, however, plants are likely to vary widely. An EPA contractor estimated that maleic anhydride plants vary by a factor of three in the amount of benzene that is not converted in the manufacturing process, and that would thus be emitted in the absence of controls.[142] Nitrile elastomer plants emitting acrylonitrile show a similar range.[143]

Another factor creating uncertainty in model plant projections is the lack of adequate knowledge about the effectiveness of existing controls. Although many plants already have emission controls of some kind, due to state regulations, Occupational Safety and Health Administration (OSHA) standards, or economic self-interest in recovering valuable feedstock or by-products, the EPA has made only rough estimates of the effectiveness of such controls.[144]

Finally, model plant estimates do not consider the effects of varying production levels on eventual emissions. Emissions depend on both the emission rate and the percentage of plant capacity used.[145] Few plants operate at full capacity; thus, benefit estimates must be adjusted downward to compensate for actual production levels. This problem is most severe when control techniques are capital-intensive because control costs are then fixed across all production levels while benefits vary directly with production levels.[146] Therefore, the EPA model plant projections may be highly inaccurate predictors of emission reductions at actual plants.

Even if emission estimates are accurate at the time they are made, they may not provide reliable projections of the impact of a proposed regulation. The effects are most dramatic in the case of maleic anhydride plants, where all of the uncontrolled plants identified by EPA when the regulation was proposed have since closed, switched feedstocks, or installed controls.[147] In the case of coke ovens, the depressed state of the steel industry suggests that additional plants may close over the next few years.[148]

Emission estimates are likely to be most uncertain when each plant has multiple "fugitive" sources (such as leaking doors), as the coke oven case illustrates. An EPA contractor presented minimum and maximum estimates, which vary by a factor of 11 for door leaks, 6.4 for topside leaks and over 300 for charging leaks.[149] The results for coke ovens presented in Part II [of this article] use a simple average of the minimum and maximum estimates.[150] Substitution of the maximum estimates reduces the cost per life saved by less than a factor of two. Use of the minimum estimates, however, increases the cost per life saved by more than a factor of six for the BAT standard.[151]

Uncertainties about emissions appear to be most important for coke ovens because: (1) the uncertainties are much greater for coke ovens than for either of the other cases; and (2) the coke oven decision is the "closest" one, with cost-effectiveness ratios in the plausible range. Even with the maximum emission estimates, however, it is not clear that the uniform BAT standard yields positive net benefits.

These results suggest that it would be useful to narrow the range of estimates of emissions from coke ovens, particularly if the tentative decision was to proceed with regulation. A plausible benefit-cost case for the BAT standard is possible only if actual emissions are in the upper end of the estimated range.

B. Uncertainties in Estimating Exposure

The dispersion models used by the EPA to predict pollutant exposure contain pervasive uncertainties. In particular, critics question the reliability of these models at substantial distances from sources and their ability to predict concentrations indoors, where individuals spend most of their time.

Dispersion models for toxic air pollutants combine source characteristics, like the height and velocity of releases, with meteorological inputs, including wind speed, direction, and turbulence.[152] Although the methodology is straightforward, the accuracy of these dispersion models is uncertain. Model accuracy is difficult to evaluate empirically because, in many cases, measured ambient concentrations at a particular location are hard to relate to emissions from the individual sources modeled.[153]

The accuracy of the models deteriorates as the distance from the source increases.[154] As a result, dispersion modeling usually is not carried out more than thirty kilometers from the source plant.[155] In theory this truncation introduces a bias, understating total exposure levels. Concentrations at greater distances, however, are typically very low, making the resulting bias very minor as well.[156]

Dispersion models are designed to predict outdoor concentrations, but most people spend the vast majority of their time indoors. Recent studies of "indoor air pollution" suggest that concentrations of pollutants indoors may be very different from those outdoors.[157] Many of these studies, however, have involved pollutants that have indoor as well as outdoor sources.[158] Pollutants emitted solely by outdoor sources will have equal or *lower* average concentrations indoors than those outdoors.[159] Therefore, the use of outdoor concentrations to estimate exposure levels may overstate the benefits of the regulations.

Another source of uncertainty arises from the failure to use plant-specific data in estimating exposure from individual plants. Exposure levels around a particular plant critically depend on whether prevailing winds blow toward or away from densely populated areas. Variables like stack height, exit velocity, gas temperature and local meteorological data also affect actual exposure.[160] None of the case studies, however, used such plant-specific data to calculate exposure factors.[161]

Finally, EPA estimates implicitly assume that individuals spend all of their time close to their homes; the population data are based on place of residence.[162] This assumption is accurate for children who attend nearby schools, or for nonworking adults who spend most of their time at or near home. It may, however, create larger inaccuracies for adults who work far from their homes. To the extent that concentrations where people work are different from those at home, the exposure factors will be inaccurate. Plants located in areas where more people work than live create higher than estimated exposure levels, but the opposite occurs if plants are located in areas where more people live than work.

Uncertainties about the exposure factors used in these case studies have not been quantified. The uncertainties are greatest, however, at the level of individual plants, because of the failure to use plant-specific values for any parameters other than population.[163] No systematic sources of upward or downward bias are apparent in the case study exposure estimates.

C. Uncertainties in Estimating Risk

Estimating the unit risk factor is the most uncertain step in analyzing carcinogens. Evidence of carcinogenicity typically comes from either high-dose animal studies or from epidemiological studies of workers exposed to relatively high concentrations of the substance. All three of the case studies described above relied on epidemiological evidence of carcinogenicity as the primary basis for risk assessment.[164] Thus, none involves the difficult and controversial task of extrapolating carcinogenicity from animals to humans.[165] Risk estimates in the case studies did, however, require substantial extrapolation from high-dose to low-dose exposure.[166]

The problem of extrapolating from high-dose data to low-dose exposures arises because neither epidemiological studies nor laboratory experiments with animals are capable of detecting low-level risks.[167] Several mathematical models have been developed to perform the necessary extrapolations.[168] Unfortunately, neither current theory nor empirical evidence provides unambiguous support for any one model.[169]

Most regulatory agencies, including the EPA, use the "one-hit" model or a variant of it.[170] That model assumes that cancer can be induced by a single "hit" of a susceptible cell by a carcinogen. Thus, the model does not yield a threshold below which there is a zero risk of cancer. At low exposure levels, the predicted risk is proportional to the dose; if the relevant dose is 1,000 times lower than that at which the risk was measured, for example, the estimated risk is also 1,000 times lower. Because of this property, the "one-hit" model is often called the "linear" model.

It is difficult to tell how much of the linear model's popularity is due to scientific belief in its accuracy as opposed to a value judgment that decision makers should be conservative in the face of great uncertainty. In any event, most scientists accept the linear model as providing an upper-bound estimate of cancer risk.[171]

The other models commonly used in estimating cancer risk are convex at low doses; as the dose is reduced, risk falls more than proportionately.[172] Given the same data, these models all predict smaller low-dose risks than the linear model.[173] In fact, when the extrapolation from measured risk covers two or more orders of magnitude, as typically happens in EPA regulation, the other models' estimates may be treated as zero because they are so much lower than the linear model's projections.[174] Thus, regulations to reduce low dose exposure to environmental carcinogens must rest on a belief that the linear model has a significant probability of being correct.

Ideally, experts could assess the probability that each of the possible models is correct, and then use those probabilities to compute an expected dose-response function. Unfortunately, such assessments are not available. If they were, it is likely that the expected dose-response function would be approximately linear at low doses, because the nonlinear models predict such small risks that the linear model component would dominate so long as the probability assigned to the linear model's correctness was nontrivial. Note, however, that the unit risk factor for the expected dose-response function would not be as large as that estimated by the linear model alone; the estimated risk would equal approximately the pure linear estimate times the probability that the linear model is correct. Thus, while it may be reasonable to assume that the expected benefits of control are proportional to the reduction in exposure, estimates of reduced mortality in this article are probably too high, perhaps by a substantial margin, because they rely exclusively on the linear model.

Even if one accepts the linear model, controversies about the interpretation of epidemiological data make the unit risk estimates uncertain. Exposure levels in epidemiological studies often cause the greatest difficulties because the exposures typically occurred many years earlier when few measurements were made.[175] The controversy surrounding the CAG's risk estimate for benzene illustrates this problem and others that can arise in interpreting epidemiological studies.[176]

The CAG based its unit risk estimate for benzene on data from three epidemiological studies.[177] In each case, it had to make assumptions about exposure and other factors. Many of these assumptions have been criticized for overstating the risk.[178] Two EPA analysts, for example, concluded that the CAG risk estimate was too high by a factor of four.[179] An occupational physician testified that the CAG estimate should have been lower by more than a factor of ten.[180] The differences between these estimates and the CAG's are particularly startling because they were based on the same studies and model.

Disputes about the appropriate dose-response model and the interpretation of highly imperfect epidemiological studies make it impossible to develop unit risk estimates for any of the three substances that can be defended rigorously. The unit risk estimates used in Part II [of this article], however, probably reflect an upward bias, primarily because they were derived solely from the linear model.[181]

To the extent that the unit risk factors are too high, the expected benefits of controls are overestimated. Revising those estimates downward reinforces the earlier conclusions that benzene and acrylonitrile controls are not cost-effective.[182] It also reinforces the conclusion that uniform BAT standards on all three sources of emissions from coke oven plants would not be cost-effective relative to less stringent regulations.[183]

D. Uncertainties in Valuing Risk Reduction

Critics of the use of benefit-cost analysis to evaluate environmental policy often focus on the difficulty of assigning a "value to life."[184] The empirical studies of wage premiums for occupational risk cited in Part II [of this article] cover a wide range, from several hundred thousand to several million dollars per life saved. Even that wide range, however, is sufficient to reject BAT standards for maleic anhydride plants and for all four types of plants emitting acrylonitrile. It is also sufficient to indicate cost-beneficial modifications of the coke oven regulations, though not sufficiently precise to determine if more limited regulation of coke ovens is justified.

Several objections can be raised to the use of wage premium studies to value risks reduced through environmental regulation. If workers are not fully aware of the risks they run, wage premiums will not reflect the workers true willingness to accept risk in exchange for higher pay.[185] In addition, dangerous jobs tend to be filled by individuals willing to accept risks for lower compensation.[186] Thus, even if the wage premium studies accurately measure trade-offs acceptable to workers studied, they may underestimate the general population's willingness to pay for reduced risk.

Despite these criticisms, some simple examples suggest that the higher end of the range of values estimated by the wage premium studies is more likely an overestimate than an underestimate. If the value per life saved is $5 million, for example, the government should impose auto safety regulations that cut the risk of traffic fatalities in half as long as the control cost per new car is less than $12,500.[187] With that same value per life saved, a family of four with the median yearly income should be willing to give up about one half of that income in order to face the average overall death rates that prevailed in 1975 rather than those from 1970.[188]

A more fundamental philosophical objection is based on the distinction between voluntary and involuntary risks.[189] Individuals are free to choose their jobs (and their cars). In contrast, people, as individuals, have little choice about the quality of the air that they breathe. Society should be willing to pay much more to avoid such involuntary risks, the argument continues, than individuals would spend to reduce hazards over which they have personal control. Supporters of benefit-cost analysis reply that it makes little sense for the government to make fundamentally different trade-offs than individuals would when confronted with similar private choices.[190] Decision makers, however, may be especially concerned about distributional implications if the risks are unusually large and concentrated among a small group of individuals.[191]

Two factors suggest that, in general, a lower value should be ascribed to lives saved through the regulation of environmental carcinogens than to many other public choices involving risk. First, cancer is disproportionately a disease of the elderly, so each life "saved" represents relatively few additional years of life.[192] Regulatory programs should be evaluated in terms of years of life saved, not total lives saved.[193] This suggests that the value per life saved should be lower for evaluating regulations to control carcinogens than for analyzing other programs, such as highway safety, that prevent the deaths of younger people.

The second factor is the substantial delay between control expenditures and reductions in risk due to time lags between exposure to carcinogens and the onset of disease. Conventional benefit-cost analyses discount streams of benefits and costs to reflect the time value of money. Economists differ as to whether discounting should be applied to health benefits.[194] Most theoretical discussions support discounting,[195] but in common practice the timing issue is ignored.[196]

Discounting reduces the relative value of saving lives through control of environmental carcinogens, because the benefits of reducing exposure are realized many years after the costs are incurred. At a discount rate of 5 percent, for example, a twenty-year time lag reduces the value of risk reduction by 62 percent compared to an immediate risk reduction, say through improved fire protection.[197]

The valuation of risk reduction remains uncertain and highly contentious, with little prospect for agreement on any particular dollar value for saving a life. The problem is at least as much one of ethics and politics as it is one of science and the interpretation of empirical evidence. EPA, however, cannot avoid making trade-offs between protection and control costs, whether it does so explicitly or implicitly. Fortunately, precision may not be very important because many decisions are correct over wide ranges of values. Moreover, it is possible to narrow the range presented earlier by reducing the high end. Values much in excess of $1 million per life saved appear difficult to justify, particularly for airborne carcinogens for which the benefits are delayed and the lives saved are relatively short.

E. Unquantified Benefits[198]

EPA's procedures almost certainly overstate the cancer-reduction benefits of controlling hazardous air pollutants. By focusing solely on cancer in its quantitative estimates for section 112 pollutants, however, the EPA may miss other important health and environmental benefits.

Many carcinogens, including the three considered here, have also been associated with noncancer health effects at relatively high doses.[199] For most of these noncancer effects, however, scientists generally accept the concept of zero-risk thresholds, and current environmental exposures appear to lie far below the relevant levels.[200]

Chromosomal damage—mutagenic effects—may be an exception, as scientists are less willing to assume that such effects have thresholds.[201] All three of the case study pollutants appear to cause chromosomal damage.[202] None, however, has been associated with birth defects, and analyses by EPA's health experts emphasize mutagenic evidence as corroborating the carcinogenicity of the substance, rather than as a separate concern.[203]

The "conventional pollutant" benefits associated with controlling some hazardous air pollutants may be more significant. States have regulated benzene and acrylonitrile to help meet the ambient standard for ozone.[204] Coke ovens have been regulated to meet the particulate ambient standard.[205] In addition, controls on section 112 pollutants may also control other pollutants. If maleic anhydride plants use incineration to control benzene emissions, for example, they would also reduce carbon monoxide, a "conventional" pollutant covered by an ambient standard.[206]

Occupational exposure represents still another potentially important omitted benefit category. Some controls designed to reduce emissions to the ambient environment also reduce the exposure of workers. This effect is most likely to be significant when the emissions are from low-level, fugitive sources, as is true of coke ovens. If the sources are elevated stacks, as with maleic anhydride plants emitting benzene and the acrylonitrile plants, environmental controls are unlikely to have much impact on workers.

The importance of these omitted benefit categories varies widely across specific regulations. In the three cases discussed, they do not affect the basic conclusions for maleic anhydride plants and acrylonitrile, primarily because the cancer benefits are so small in those cases and the only potentially important omitted benefits appear to be those associated with conventional pollutants. To the extent that such benefits are important, benzene and acrylonitrile are probably best addressed by the framework established for other conventional pollutants—state implementation plans for existing sources and new source performance standards for new ones.

The omitted benefit categories are more troubling for the coke oven case, primarily because it is a closer decision on the basis of cancer reduction benefits alone. The quantitative significance of the additional benefits from reduced worker exposure and reduced particulate emissions cannot be evaluated, but it seems unlikely that they would be sufficient to justify the uniform BAT standard over the alternatives of a less stringent uniform standard or a differential strategy targeted at high exposure plants.

F. Summary

Huge uncertainties pervade estimates of the benefits of regulating airborne carcinogens. As a result, the figures presented in Part II [of this article] must be viewed with a strong dose of skepticism; they may well be in error by orders of magnitude. These uncertainties, however, do not alter the major conclusions of the case studies.

The clearest conclusions emerge for the four source categories emitting acrylonitrile. The cost-effectiveness ratios for emission controls were ten or more times higher than the plausible range of values for risk reduction.[207] Nothing in this section has suggested that benefit estimates err by that margin.[208]

The calculations for benzene emitted from maleic anhydride plants gave a substantially narrower result, although the estimated cost per life saved was still in excess of $6 million.[209] Several factors suggest that an accurate estimate of the expected cost-effectiveness ratio would be substantially higher. They include: (1) the general issue of the appropriate dose-response model;[210] (2) evidence that the CAG overestimated the linear model's risk factor;[211] and (3) a significant rise in the cost per life saved when the estimates are adjusted for less than full capacity operation.[212]

The most ambiguous results arise in the case of coke ovens, although a BAT standard for charging emissions almost certainly would fail a benefit-cost test.[213] Whether the uniform door and topside standards generate positive expected net benefits remains in doubt. Two issues raised in Part III [of this article], however, weigh against those standards: (1) the likelihood that the pure linear model overestimates the expected risk;[214] and (2) the evidence suggesting that a value on risk reduction much in excess of $1 million per life saved cannot be justified.[215] In fact, it is unclear whether even differential standards limited to high-exposure coke plants would yield positive net benefits. Such standards, however, unquestionably represent an alternative superior to uniform BAT standards.

G. Postscript

Recent developments reinforce our conclusions regarding benzene emitted from maleic anhydride plants and cast further doubt on the wisdom of imposing standards on coke ovens. After the maleic anhydride standard was proposed in 1980, five important changes took place: (1) four plants shut down; (2) two plants converted to n-butane, apparently in response to higher benzene prices; (3) the largest plant installed controls and began to convert all of its capacity to n-butane; (4) an additional plant was "discovered"; and (5) EPA reduced the BAT standard to the equivalent of 90 percent control.[216] As a result, had the standard been imposed, it would have applied only to the newly discovered plant, a small one located in a lightly populated area, and the estimated health gain would have been to prevent approximately one case of cancer every 300 years.[217] Citing those minimal potential health impacts, the EPA withdrew the proposed standard for maleic anhydride plants in early 1984.[218]

More recent estimates from the EPA indicate that coke oven plants also pose a smaller threat than estimated earlier. Data in a recent EPA report suggest that the BAT standards would save less than five lives per year, in contrast to over ten lives per year estimated on the basis of the earlier data. The newer EPA estimates rely on higher emissions but much lower exposures, based on newer modeling using meteorological data for each plant.[219] Even more recently, the CAG lowered its estimate of unit risk and the EPA learned that additional plants have shut down, so the estimated annual reduction in cancer cases has fallen to about two.[220] It thus appears that coke ovens are no longer a "close" case; although no cost estimates are available for the closed plants, the estimated cost per case avoided for the BAT standards must be well in excess of $5 million.

IV. Findings

The three case studies illustrate many of the problems and uncertainties involved in estimating the benefits of environmental regulation. Although benefit-cost analyses of such regulations can never be very precise, these studies suggest that quantitative assessments of benefits can provide valuable information to regulators interested in improving the efficient use of society's resources. In this part, some of the lessons from the case studies are summarized, first with respect to section 112 of the Clean Air Act and then with respect to the more general use of benefit-cost analysis to evaluate strategies for regulating health-threatening pollutants.

A. Section 112

In dealing with "hazardous air pollutants" covered by section 112 of the Clean Air Act, the EPA has consistently followed a technology-based approach to regulation. The "generic" policy proposed in 1979 would have formalized this approach in an attempt to speed up and routinize the process of listing and regulating such substances.[221] More recently, some members of Congress have suggested forcing EPA regulation of section

112 pollutants by giving the agency a deadline for making decisions on a list of thirty-seven substances.[222] The BAT approach to regulation is flawed because it implicitly treats airborne carcinogens as a homogeneous class. The case studies indicate that airborne carcinogens are a very heterogeneous class, with wide variations in benefits (and costs) across substances and source categories.

1. HETEROGENEITY

Even within a small sample of three pollutants studied, the risk-reduction benefits from controlling emissions vary enormously because of differences in carcinogenic potencies and in exposure patterns. Each kilogram of coke oven emissions, for example, causes about 500 times as much cancer risk as a kilogram of acrylonitrile or a kilogram of benzene emitted from a maleic anhydride plant.[223] Regulatory analyses that focus on the feasibility and affordability of controls ignore these critical differences.

The cost per unit of risk reduction also varies greatly across the three cases, differing by a factor of more than 100 between coke plants and the least cost-effective acrylonitrile category. These wide variations suggest that a policy of applying BAT standards to *all* sources emitting airborne carcinogens imposes higher than necessary costs to achieve *any* given level of overall risk reduction. Individual substances and source categories must be considered on their own merits, taking account of potencies and exposure levels as well as technology and affordability.

2. MODEST BENEFITS FROM CONTROL

The desirability of strict regulations on airborne carcinogens is easily overstated. In both the benzene and the acrylonitrile cases, for example, a small number of sources emit millions of kilograms of proven human carcinogens each year. Moreover, the controls being considered are eminently affordable: their costs are estimated at less than 2 percent of total sales.[224]

The case studies show, however, that only modest health benefits are likely to result from the regulations. BAT standards for both acrylonitrile and maleic anhydride plants would have a combined effect of avoiding less than one cancer death per year. The coke oven standards would provide substantially larger benefits, but even in that case the gain in public health seems rather modest for standards that apply to a major industry on a nationwide basis.

Of course, it is not certain that all section 112 regulations would yield similarly small benefits. The case studies, however, cast doubt on the proposition that control of airborne carcinogens will lead to major reductions in the nation's cancer burden. The fact that the pollutants considered here have been assigned relatively high priority by EPA reinforces this skepticism.

B. The Role of Benefit-Cost Analysis

1. EVALUATING PROPOSED REGULATIONS

Existing methods of quantitative assessment may not yield clear answers as to the cost-effectiveness of regulations in all, or even most, cases. Many of the components in benefit estimation are highly uncertain. Because the final estimate typically is a multiplicative function of these individual components, the overall level of uncertainty is extremely high. Nonetheless, robust conclusions often can be drawn to help regulators avoid imposing some regulations for which the benefits are far smaller than the costs. Benefit-cost analyses may also identify regulations that clearly provide positive net benefits, although none of the instant case studies identified such a regulation.

2. IMPROVING REGULATIONS

Most discussion of benefit-cost analysis focuses on its role as a "test" for proposed regulations. Benefit-cost analysis is even more useful, however, as a tool for designing regulations. In all three of the case studies, less stringent controls yielded most of the benefits of the BAT standards at far lower cost. Although none of these modified uniform standards resulted in clearly positive net benefits, all were more efficient than the original BAT standards. If benefit-cost principles were applied early in the regulatory process and used to guide the selection of control options for detailed analysis, even larger gains could be realized.

The case studies indicate that regulatory efficiency is maximized by exploiting marginal differences in the benefits of control among sources. These differences arise primarily because of differences in population densities around plants; the public health benefits of controlling emissions are far larger in cities than in lightly populated rural areas. In all three cases, restricting standards to areas where the marginal benefits of control are relatively high led to impressive efficiency gains over uniform standards.

3. INFORMATION REQUIREMENTS AND DELAYS

If they are to be useful to decision makers, analytic techniques cannot rely on data that are unduly expensive or time consuming to obtain. Analysis is not free; it consumes scarce resources that could be put to other uses and may cause delays in an already lengthy regulatory process. Fortunately, a great deal can be done with information that is already collected by EPA. Also, a sharper set of decision criteria should speed up rather than delay the regulatory process. Note that the technical data for all three case studies were based on information developed as part of EPA's BAT strategy for controlling hazardous air pollutants. Thus, performing the kinds of analyses presented in this article should not significantly increase either the costs or the delays of the regulatory process.

For relatively close decisions, such as the coke oven case, additional information could prove useful, particularly in four areas: (1) cost and emissions estimates for a wider range of control options; (2) more plant-specific data for exposure estimates (as were recently developed by EPA for coke ovens); (3) estimates of noncancer benefits, particularly those associated with conventional pollutants (such as ozone and particulate matter); and (4) development of techniques for estimating the expected level of cancer as well as the "plausible upper bound" now used by EPA.

Adoption of benefit-cost principles could reduce the amount of information required to regulate in many cases. Current efforts, for example, typically include studies of the "economic impact" of regulations, attempting to predict their effects on plant closings, product prices, and the like. Such impacts are of second-order importance relative to the direct benefits and costs of control. Application of benefit-cost principles in allocating agency resources may also reduce the costs of analysis by leading to the curtailment of the regulatory process before large expenses have been incurred to gather data. The acrylonitrile case provides an excellent example; some crude analysis early in the regulatory process—based on the unit risk factor, existing levels of control, and average exposure factors— probably would have indicated the minimal potential benefits involved and consequently eliminated the need for detailed analysis of control technologies and costs.

C. Conclusion

Pleas for the use of benefit-cost analysis in environmental decision making are commonplace. This article contributes to the discussion by illustrating how benefit-cost techniques might be employed to evaluate individual regulations, to identify promising alternatives, and to evaluate the robustness of regulatory choices relative to uncertainties. Although the case studies reviewed here assess particular regulations for airborne hazards, the conclusions regarding the usefulness of benefit-cost principles apply more generally.

Over two dozen federal statutes require the regulation of toxic or hazardous substances.[225] Some of these explicitly call for a balancing of benefits and costs,[226] while others use a "reasonableness" standard that would permit such an analysis.[227] Those statutes that explicitly permit the consideration of only health effects tend to deal with food products or common consumer items.[228] Thus, a benefit-cost analysis, although not applicable to all situations, could be applied far beyond the Clean Air Act.

The advantages of benefit-cost principles must, however, be put into perspective. A benefit-cost analysis of an environmental program is not a substitute for good science or good judgment. To the contrary, explicit estimation of health risks, and the amount that controls will reduce those risks, provides a context for incorporating both science and judgment into regulatory decisions. Cruder rules based solely upon evidence of carcinogenicity or technological feasibility of control hide the real choices involved in regulating health-threatening substances.

NOTES

This article, first published in *Harvard Environmental Law Review* 8 (1984): 395–434, is reprinted by permission of the *Harvard Environmental Law Review*, copyright © 1984, and by the President and Fellows of Harvard College.

Financial support for this article was provided by the U.S. Environmental Protection Agency under Cooperative Agreement CR-809802–01–0 with the Energy and Environmental Policy Center, John F. Kennedy School of Government, Harvard University; Harvard School of Public Health, Interdisciplinary Programs in Health, U.S. Environmental Protection Agency Grant #CR-807809; and the Alfred P. Sloan Foundation Program in Environmental Health.

Although the research described in this report has been funded by the agencies listed above, it has not been subjected to their peer and administrative reviews, may not reflect the views of those agencies, and no official endorsement should be inferred.

1. See Statement by W. Ruckelshaus, Administrator of the EPA, Before the Subcomm. on Oversight & Investigations of the House Comm. on Energy & Commerce 10–11 (Nov. 7, 1983) (listing the specific problems experienced in implementing section 112) [hereinafter cited as Statement by Ruckelshaus].

2. Id. at 20.

3. See W. Ruckelshaus, Administrator of the EPA, Science, Risk and Policy 10 (June 22, 1973) (speech to the National Academy of Sciences). See also W. Ruckelshaus, Administrator of the EPA. Risk in a Free Society (Feb. 18, 1984) (speech at Princeton University); speech by J. Cannon, EPA Asst. Administrator for Air and Radiation, to the Natural Resources Law Section of the American Bar Association (Mar. 10, 1984).

4. See, e.g., Crandall, "The Use of Cost-Benefit Analysis in Regulatory Decisions," in *Management of Assessed Risk for Carcinogens,* 99–107 (W. Nicholson ed. 1981) (defending the general applicability of benefit-cost analysis to regulatory decision making); Harrison, "Cost-Benefit Analysis and the Regulation of Environmental Carcinogens," in *Management of Assessed Risk for Carcinogens,* 109–22 (W. Nicholson ed. 1981) (evaluating the advantages of using benefit-cost principles in regulating carcinogens); Ashford, "Alternatives to Cost-Benefit Analysis in Regulatory Decisions," in *Management of Assessed Risk for Carcinogens* 129–37 (W. Nicholson ed. 1981) (discussing the general limitations of benefit-cost analysis in regulatory decision making).

5. See. e.g., S. Kelman, *What Price Incentives?* 27–88 (1981) (summarizing the ethical concerns involved in using the market for pollution control); Kelman, "Cost-Benefit Analysis and Environmental, Safety, and Health Regulation: Ethical and Philosophical Considerations," in *Cost-Benefit Analysis and Environmen-*

tal Regulations: Politics, Ethics, and Methods, 137–54 (D. Swartzman, R. Likoff, & K. Croke eds. 1982).

6. See, e.g., Ashford, note 4 above, at 129–37.

7. 42 U.S.C. § 7412 (Supp. V 1981). Although this article provides background information on the provisions and history of section 112 to place the specific case studies discussed in context, its analysis is not restricted to regulatory alternatives permitted by the current statute. Thus. some of the alternatives that it considers might require statutory changes.

8. The technology-based standards that the EPA has promulgated provide a basis for evaluating the benefits and costs of those standards and for a detailed investigation of regulatory alternatives.

9. See, e.g., Hurter, Tolley, & Fabian, "Benefit-Cost Analysis and the Common Sense of Environmental Policy," in *Cost-Benefit Analysis and Environmental Regulations: Politics, Ethics, and Methods,* 92–99 (D. Swartzman, R. Likoff & K. Croke eds. 1982) (discussing the potential sources of uncertainty in comparing the benefits and costs of environmental programs).

10. See below, text accompanying note 109. See also below, table 1.

11. See below, notes 15–56 and accompanying text.

12. See below, notes 57–140 and accompanying text. A more detailed analysis of these case studies has been presented in an earlier manuscript. Haigh, Harrison, & Nichols, "Benefits Assessment and Environmental Regulation: Case Studies of Hazardous Air Pollutants" (July 1983) (unpublished manuscript available upon request from the authors).

13. See below, notes 141–220 and accompanying text.

14. See below, notes 221–228 and accompanying text.

15. 42 U.S.C. § 7412 (Supp. V 1981).

16. [I]t is urgent that Congress adopt new clean air legislation which will make possible the more expeditious imposition of specific emission standards both for mobile and stationary sources and the effective enforcement of such standards by both State and Federal agencies. . . . Therefore, particular attention must be given to new stationary sources which are known to be either particularly large-scale polluters or where the pollutants are extrahazardous.

H.R. Rep. No. 1146, 91st Cong., 2d Sess. 5, reprinted in 1970 *U.S. Code Cong. & Ad. News,* 5356, 5360–61.

17. 42 U.S.C. § 7412 (Supp. V 1981).

18. Section 112(b) provides that:

(1) A) The administrator shall, within 90 days after December 31, 1970, publish (and shall from time to time thereafter revise) a list which includes each hazardous air pollutant for which he intends to establish an emission standard under this section.

(B) Within 180 days after the inclusion of any air pollutant in such list, the Administrator shall publish proposed regulations establishing emission standards for such pollutant together with a notice of a public hearing within thirty days. Not later than 180 days after such publication, the Administrator shall prescribe an emission standard for such pollutant, unless he finds, on the basis of information presented at such hearings, that such pollutant clearly is not a hazardous air pollutant. The Administrator shall establish any such standard at the level which in his judgment provides an ample margin of safety to protect the public health from such hazardous air pollutant.

Id. § 7412(b).

19. H.R. Rep. No. 1783, 91st Cong., 2d Sess. 10–12, 45–47, reprinted in 1970 *U.S. Code Cong. & Ad. News,* 5356, 5378–79.

20. The relevant section provided that:

(a) For the purpose of preventing the occurrence of significant new air pollution problems arising from or associated with any class of new stationary sources which, because of the nature or amount of emissions therefrom, may contribute substantially to endangerment of the public health or welfare, the Secretary shall from time to time by regulation, giving appropriate consideration to technological and economic feasibility, establish standards with respect to such emissions . . . . (b) Such emission standards shall provide that—

(1) If such emissions are extremely hazardous to health, no new source of such emissions shall be constructed or operated, except where (and subject to such conditions as he deems necessary and appropriate) the Secretary makes a specific exemption with respect to such construction or operation.

(2) In the case of other emissions, any new source of such emissions shall be designed and equipped to prevent and control such emissions to the fullest extent compatible with the available technology and economic feasibility, as determined by the Secretary.

H.R. Rep. No. 1146, 91st Cong., 2d Sess. 35 (1970).

21. Bonine, "The Evolution of 'Technology-Forcing' in the Clean Air Act," [Monograph No. 21] 6 *Env't Rep.* (BNA) 7 (July 25, 975). The Senate report indicated its determination "that existing sources of pollutants should meet the standard of the law or be closed down, and in addition, that new sources should be controlled to the maximum extent possible to prevent atmospheric emissions." S. Rep. No. 1196, 91st Cong., 2d Sess. 2–3 (1970). Later, however, the report says that "[i]n writing a relatively restrictive definition of hazardous agents, the Committee recognized that a total prohibition on emissions is a step that ought to be taken only where a danger to health, as defined, exists." Id. at 20.

The bill provided in part that:

(a) (1) The Secretary shall, within ninety days after the enactment of this section and from time to time thereafter, publish in the Federal Register a list of those air pollution agents or combination of such agents which available material evidence indicates are hazardous to the health of persons and which shall be subject to a prohibition or emission standard established under this section.

(2) Within one hundred and eighty days after the publication of such list, or revision thereof, the Secretary, in accordance with section 553 of title 5 of the United States Code, shall publish a proposed prohibition and a notice of a public hearing within thirty days. As soon as possible after such hearing, but not later than six months after such publication, the Secretary shall promulgate such prohibition, unless, based upon a preponderance of evidence adduced at such hearing, he finds within such period and publishes his finding—

(A) that such agent is not hazardous to the health of persons; or

(B) that a departure from such prohibition for stationary sources will not be hazardous to the health of persons.

(3) If the Secretary finds under paragraph (2)(A) of this subsection that such agent is not hazardous to the health of persons, he shall immediately publish an emissions standard in accordance with the procedures established under section 114 of this Act.

(4) If the Secretary finds under paragraph (2)(B) of this subsection that a departure from such prohibition for any stationary source will not be hazardous to the health of persons, he shall immediately promulgate an emission standard for such agent or combination of agents from any such stationary source to protect the health of persons.

Id. at 95–96.

22. See above, note 18.

23. See generally Doniger, "Federal Regulation of Vinyl Chloride: A Short Course in Law and Policy of Toxic Substances Control," 7 *Ecology L.Q.* 497, 565–85 (1978); Currie, "Direct Federal Regulation of Stationary Sources Under the Clean Air Act," 128 *U. Pa. L. Rev.* 1389 (1980) (generally discussing regulatory activity under section 112).

24. 40 C.F.R. §§ 61.20–.34, 61.50–.55 (1979) (promulgating emission standards for asbestos, beryllium and mercury); 40 C.F.R. §§ 61.60–.71 (1979) (promulgating emission standards for vinyl chloride).

25. 42 Fed. Reg. 29,332 (1977) (listing benzene as a hazardous air pollutant); 44 Fed. Reg. 76,738 (1979) (listing radionuclides as a hazardous air pollutant); 48 Fed. Reg. 33,112 (1983) (listing inorganic arsenic as a hazardous air pollutant).

26. See Statement by W. Ruckelshaus, Administrator of the EPA, Before the Subcomm. on Health & the Env't of the House Comm. on Energy & Commerce 10 (Mar. 29. 1984) [hereinafter cited as 1984 Statement by Ruckelshaus].

27. See Industrial Union Dept. v. American Petroleum Inst., 448 U.S. 607, 624 (1980).

28. 1984 Statement by Ruckelshaus, above, note 26, at 13.

29. As discussed in more detail below, a "generic" policy proposed in 1979 would have formalized the agency's implicit policy of requiring, at a minimum, BAT controls for sources emitting pollutants listed under section 112. See below, text accompanying notes 43–50.

30. 40 C.F.R. §§ 61.20–.25 (1971).

31. 38 Fed. Reg. 8820, 8822 (1973).

32. Id.

33. 40 C.F.R. §§ 61.20–.25 (1971).

34. 38 Fed. Reg. 8820, 8822 (1973).

35. Id.

36. 40 C.F.R. §§ 61.60–.71 (1976).

37. 40 Fed. Reg. 59,534 (1975).

38. 44 Fed. Reg. 58,642, 58,643 (1979).

39. Natural Resources Defense Council v. Train, 8 Env't Rep. Cas. (BNA) 2120 (D.D.C. 1976).

40. See, e.g., Doniger, above, note 23, at 565–85 (discussing the politics underlying EPA's promulgation of a vinyl chloride standard).

41. See Doniger, above, note 23, at 584.

42. 44 Fed. Reg. 58,642 (1979). The proposal was part of a larger effort by the Carter administration to develop regulatory policies for carcinogens. A controversial cancer policy proposed by the Occupational Safety and Health Administration (OSHA) preceded the EPA document, see 45 Fed. Reg. 5002 (1980). In addition, the heads of the four major regulatory agencies dealing with carcinogens had formed the Interagency Regulatory Liaison Group. That group had a mandate to develop a greater scientific consensus on cancer risk assessment procedures. Id. at 58,647. Finally, in 1979 EPA was developing regulations on benzene emissions under section 112 to be used as a prototype for the procedure the agency was elaborating in its generic policy. Indeed, when the White House Regulatory Analysis Review Group selected the EPA cancer policy for review, the agency suggested that the group use benzene as an indicator of how the policy would be implemented. See Nichols, "The Regulation of Airborne Benzene," in *Incentives for Environmental Protection,* 148 (T. Schelling ed. 1983).

43. See 44 Fed. Reg. 58,642 (1979).

44. Id. at 58,654.

45. Id. at 58,648. See also 44 Fed. Reg. 58,662–70 (1979).

46. 44 Fed. Reg. 58,642, 58,654 (1979).

47. Id.

48. See above, text accompanying notes 45–47. See also Harrison, above, note 4, at 112–13.

49. See [14 Curr. Dev.] *Env't Rep.* (BMA) 1109–11. But see below, notes 216–220 and accompanying text (discussing the recent developments in regulation under Section 112).

50. See D. Patrick, Air Toxics: Regulation and Research 3 (Apr. 6, 1982) (speech presented at the Air Pollution Control Association [APCA] Conference, Houston, Tex.). See also Harrison, above, note 44, at 112–13 (critiquing EPA's proposed cancer policy).

51. D. Doniger, Statement on Behalf of the National Clean Air Coalition, Before the Subcomm. on Oversight & Investigations of the House Comm. on Energy & Commerce 10 (Nov. 7, 1983).

52. Doniger, above, note 23, at 579–84.

53. [11 Curr. Dev.] *Env't Rep.* (BNA) 1026 (1981).

54. 1984 Statement by Ruckelshaus above, note 26, at 14.

55. [13 Curr. Dev.] Env't Rep. (BNA) 491 (1982).

56. Id.

57. But see below, notes 141–51 and accompanying text (discussing the uncertainties inherent in this analysis).

58. See Office of Air Quality Planning & Standards, U.S. Envtl. Protection Agency, Benzene Emissions from Maleic Anhydride Industry—Background Information for Proposed Standards, table 1–5 (Feb. 1980 draft) [hereinafter cited as Benzene Emissions Background Information].

59. If a plant with an exposure factor of 0.6 $\mu g/^3$-person-years/kg reduces its emissions by 1 million kilograms, for example, exposure falls by $0.6(1,000,000) = 600,000$ $\mu g/^3$-person-years.

60. See Nichols, above, note 42. at 187–88.

61. See, e.g., Benzene Emissions Background Information, above, note 58, at E-8.

62. Thus, for example, 1000 people exposed, on average, to 10 $\mu g/^3$ for one year generate 10,000 $\mu g/^3$-person-years of exposure, as do 10,000 people exposed to 1 $\mu g/^3$.

63. Such risk is independent of how total exposure is distributed across the population if risk is proportional to exposure. See below, notes 164–171 and accompanying text.

64. The risk of getting cancer obviously varies with the carcinogenicity of the substance. See below, notes 164–183 and accompanying text (discussing the difficulties of extrapolating from low to high doses).

65. CAG considers a lifetime to be seventy years; hence, in this study the CAG's estimated exposure factor is divided by seventy to obtain an annual estimate. See, e.g., Carcinogen Assessment Group, Office of Health & Envtl. Assessment, U.S. Envtl. Protection Agency, Carcinogen Assessment Group's Final Report on Population Risk to Ambient Benzene Exposures 12 (1977) [hereinafter cited as Final EPA Benzene Assessment].

66. Id. at 2.

67. See, e.g., Zeckhauser, "Procedures for Valuing Life," 23 *Pub. Pol'y* 419 (1975); Graham & Vaupel, "Value of a Life: What Difference Does It Make?" 1 *Risk Analysis,* 89 (1981).

68. See Schelling, "The Life You Save May Be Your Own," in *Problems in Public Expenditure Analysis,* 127, 142–58 (S. Chase ed. 1968). Schelling is generally credited with being the first to argue that willingness to pay for risk reduction is the appropriate conceptual approach to valuing "life saving." A slightly different formulation, which should yield virtually identical results when dealing with small risks, is to ask how much money an individual would have to receive to forgo the benefit.

The technical terms for these two measures are "compensating variation" (CV) and "equivalent variation" (EV). In general, when discussing risk reductions, EV (how much money an individual would have to receive to be willing to go without the risk reduction) will exceed CV because of income effects. For small changes in risk, however, the differences between the two measures will be negligible.

69. See Thaler & Rosen, "The Value of Saving a Life: Evidence from the Labor Market," in *Household Production and Consumption,* 265–301 (N. Terleckyj ed. 1976); G. Blomquist, *Valuation of Life: Implications of Automobile Seat Belt Use* (1977) (Ph.D. dissertation, University of Chicago); A. Dillingham, *The Injury Risk Structure of Occupations and Wages* (1979) (Ph.D. dissertation, Cornell University).

70. See M. Bailey, *Reducing Risks to Life,* at app. 35–45, 52–66 (1980).

71. Id. at app. 66 (Bailey's estimates are based on Thaler & Rosen, above, note 69; Blomquist, above, note 69; and Dillingham, above, note 69).

72. See Viscusi, "Labor Market Valuations of Life and Limb: Empirical Evidence and Policy Implications," 26 *Pub. Pol'y,* 359 (1978).

73. 42 Fed. Reg. 29,332 (1977).

74. 45 Fed. Reg. 26,660 (1980).

75. 49 Fed. Reg. 8386 (1984).

76. D. Patrick, above, note 50, app. on "Section 112—The Process and Status."

77. See, e.g., Office of Health & Envtl. Assessment, U.S. Envtl. Protection Agency, Health Assessment Document for Acrylonitrile (Mar. 1982) (draft) [hereinafter cited as Acrylonitrile Assessment Document].

78. See below, notes 114–40 and accompanying text.

79. Maleic anhydride plants convert benzene into maleic anhydride—a crystalline cyclic acid anhydride used chiefly in manufacturing resins and modified drying oils. The primary source of data for this case study is Benzene Emissions Background Information, above, note 58. For additional sources, see Nichols, above, note 42.

The analysis is based on data available to EPA when it proposed the standard for maleic anhydride plants in April 1980. Since then, however, several new developments have led EPA to propose the withdrawal of the proposed benzene control standards. See below, text accompanying notes 216–18.

80. See S. Mara & S. Lee, Assessment of Human Exposure to Atmospheric Benzene 21 (May 1978) (report prepared by SRI International for U.S. Envtl. Protection Agency) [hereinafter cited as Human Exposure to Benzene].

81. See Infante, "Leukemia in Benzene Workers," 2 *Lancet,* 76 (July 9, 1977). See also Nichols, above, note 42, at 149–50 (summarizing the studies of benzene's health effects).

82. 42 Fed. Reg. 29,332 (1977). After listing the pollutant, EPA commissioned studies of benzene emissions. See PEDCo Environmental, Inc., Atmospheric Benzene Emissions (Oct. 1977) (report submitted to U.S. EPA) (EPA-450/3–77–029) [hereinafter cited as Atmospheric Benzene Emissions]; S. Mara & S. Lee, Human Exposures to Atmospheric Benzene (Oct. 1977) (report prepared by Stanford Research Institute for U.S. EPA); Human Exposure to Benzene, above, note 80. These studies provided a rough idea of the relative amounts of pollution contributed by different types of sources. See also Nichols, above, note 42.

83. 45 Fed. Reg. 26,660 (1980). EPA developed an emission standard for maleic anhydride plants first, because more than half of all estimated emissions from chemical manufacturing plants came from the eight plants that used benzene to produce maleic anhydride. See Atmospheric Benzene Emissions, above, note 82, table 1.2.

84. The standard limited existing plants to 0.3 kg of benzene emitted per 100 kg of benzene input. 45 Fed. Reg. 26,669 (1980).

85. See Benzene Emissions Background Information, above, note 58, table 1–5.

86. 45 Fed. Reg. 26,660, 26,661 (1980).

87. Id. at 26,666. See also Benzene Emissions Background Information, above, note 58. For the two plants that had 90 percent controls, however, the cost estimates assume that they would need all-new control equipment; no credit is given for possible adaptation of existing controls. All of the cost estimates are for carbon absorption controls, which the EPA estimates indicated would be the lowest-cost control technique (including a credit for benzene recovered), and all assume 100 percent capacity utilization.

88. "Facts and Figures for the Chemical Industry," *Chemical and Engineering News,* 26, 31 (June 13, 1982). The costs estimates included credits for the benzene recovered.

89. See Haigh, Harrison & Nichols, above, note 12, at 25–28.

90. The primary sources for the coke oven emission case study are: Emission Standards & Eng'g Div., Office of Air Quality Planning & Standards, U.S. Envtl. Protection Agency, Preamble and Regulation for Coke Oven Emissions from By-Product Coke Oven Charging, Door Leaks, and Topside Leaks on Wet-Coal Charged Batteries 1 (Mar. 1981) (draft) (Research Triangle Park, N.C.) [hereinafter cited as 1981 EPA Draft Coke Oven Regulation]; Office of Air Quality Planning & Standards, U.S. Envtl. Protection Agency, Coke Oven Emissions from By-Product Coke Oven Charging, Door Leaks, and Topside Leaks on Wet-Coal Charged Batteries—Background Information for Proposed Standards (July 1981) (draft) (Research Triangle Park, N.C.) [hereinafter cited as 1981 Background Information]; Carcinogen Assessment Group, Office of Health and Envtl. Assessment, U.S. Envtl. Protection Agency, Carcinogen Assessment of Coke Oven Emission (Feb. 1982) (draft) (EPA-600/6–82–003) [hereinafter cited as EPA Coke Oven Assessment]; and Research Triangle Institute, Cost Estimates of Meeting the Potential EPA Regulation Affecting Coke Oven Emissions from By-Product Coke Oven Charging, Door Leaks, and Topside Leaks on Wet-Coal Charged Batteries (Apr. 1983) (computer printout) [hereinafter cited as 1983 Research Triangle Cost Estimate].

91. See 1981 Background Information, above, note 90, at 3–2.

92. See, e.g., EPA Coke Oven Assessment, above, note 90, at 108–12.

93. Id. at 54–63.

94. 1981 EPA Draft Coke Oven Regulation, above, note 90, at 4.

95. Id. at 4–5.

96. A detailed breakdown of the status of individual plants is not available. The cost data supplied by the Research Triangle Institute, the primary EPA contractor for the coke oven analyses, includes positive entries only for those plants that are expected to require controls if standards are promulgated. Personal communication from Phillip Cooley of Research Triangle Institute (Aug. 1983).

97. 1983 Research Triangle Cost Estimate, above, note 90. EPA's emission and cost estimates are stated in terms of 1982 dollars and assume current compliance with existing state and OSHA regulations. Id.

98. Haigh, Harrison & Nichols, above, note 12, at 32–34.

99. EPA Coke Oven Assessment, above, note 90, at 144–63. See also below, table 1.

100. The acrylonitrile case study relied on data assembled from several sources, including Click & Moore, Emission, Process and Control Technology Study of the ABS/SAN Acrylic Fiber, and NBR Industries (Apr. 1979) (report prepared by Pullman Kellogg for the Office of Air Quality Planning & Standards, U.S. EPA, contract 68–02–2619); Key & Hobbs, Acrylonitrile (Nov. 1980) (report prepared by IT Enviroscience for the Office of Air Quality Planning & Standards, U.S. EPA); Energy & Envtl. Analysis, Inc., Source Category Survey for the Acrylo-nitrile Industry (July 1981) (draft report prepared for the Office of Air Quality Planning & Standards, U.S. EPA, under contract 68–02–3061); Radian Corporation, Locating and Estimating Air Emissions from Sources of Acrylonitrile (Dec. 1982) (draft report prepared for Office of Air Quality Planning & Standards, U.S. EPA); Carcinogen Assessment Group, Office of Health & Envtl. Assessment, U.S. Envtl. Protection Agency, The Carcinogen Assessment Group's Carcinogen Assess-

ment of Acrylonitrile (Feb. 1982) (draft) [hereinafter cited as EPA Acrylonitrile Assessment]; B. Suta, Assessment of Human Exposure to Atmospheric Acrylonitrile (Aug. 1979) (report prepared by SRI Int'l for U.S. EPA) [hereinafter cited as 1979 Assessment of Exposure to Acrylonitrile]; B. Suta, Revised Assessment of Human Exposure to Atmospheric Acrylonitrile Using Industry Supplied Emission Estimates (1982) (report prepared by SRI Int'l for U.S. EPA); and personal correspondence from B. Suta (Aug. 1982) (data on exposure to acrylonitrile emissions) [hereinafter cited as Suta Data on Acrylonitrile].

101. Energy and Envtl. Analysis, Inc., above, note 100, at 3–1.

102. "Facts and Figures for the Chemical Industry," *Chemical and Engineering News*, 30, 37 (June 14, 1982).

103. EPA identified three epidemiological studies; seven lifetime laboratory studies with rats; several mutagenicity studies with bacteria, drosophila (fruit flies), and rodents; chromosomal studies of humans; and numerous metabolic studies. Carcinogen Assessment Group, Office of Health & Envtl. Assessment, U.S. Envtl. Protection Agency, Health Assessment Document for Acrylonitrile 101 (1982).

104. See EPA Acrylonitrile Assessment, above, note 100, 1, 63–67.

105. See Key & Hobbs, above, note 100, ch. V, at 1–4, ch. VII, at 1–3 (discussing such control systems).

106. These calculations of emission reductions are based on "current" emissions in U.S. Envtl. Protection Agency, Summary of Acrylonitrile Emission Estimates and Production Capacities (Jan. 1983) (draft) (tables provided by R. Crume, Office of Air Quality Planning & Standards), and on model-plant controlled emissions in Key & Hobbs, above, note 100, ch. V, at 1–4 for AN monomer and in Click & Moore, above, note 100, at 61–64. See also Haigh, Harrison & Nichols, above, note 12, at 36–38.

107. The control costs are estimated from model plant data in Key & Hobbs, above, note 100, at table VI-2, and new plant data in Energy and Envtl. Analysis, Inc., above, note 100, at table 5–5 for AN monomer and in Click & Moore, above, note 100, at table 6–1, for the other categories. All costs have been updated to 1982 dollars using the GNP implicit price deflator. See also Haigh, Harrison & Nichols, above, note 12, at 36–38 and table 2.11.

108. See Haigh, Harrison & Nichols, above, note 12, at 36–41. Exposure factors were estimated using dispersion modeling results and plant-specific population data provided in Suta Data on Acrylonitrile, above, note 100.

109. See above, notes 67–72 and accompanying text.

110. See below, table 2 (indicating carcinogenic potency with unit risk factors). See also above, notes 64–66 and accompanying text.

111. See below, table 2 (comparing population figures across the three case studies).

112. Id. (comparing average exposure factors across the three case-study pollutants).

113. Id. (comparing risk per kilogram of emissions across the three case-study pollutants).

114. E. Stokey & R. Zeckhauser, *A Primer for Policy Analysis*, 139–42 (1978).

115. See Harrison & Nichols, Benefit-Based Flexibility in Environmental

Regulation (Apr. 1983) (Discussion Paper Series, Kennedy School of Government, Harvard University) (discussing the general advantages of these differential standards and an evaluation of potential obstacles). The potential policy considerations that might arise in imposing different standards on different plants, including equal protection issues and problems arising from regulations that encourage businesses to locate new plants in less populated but generally more pristine areas, lie beyond the scope of this article.

116. The maleic anhydride plant located in St. Louis, for example, accounts for approximately 80 percent of the overall benefits. See Haigh, Harrison & Nichols, above, note 12, at 27.

117. See Benzene Emissions Background Information, above, note 58, at table 1–5.

118. See Haigh, Harrison & Nichols, above, note 12, at 28–29. Unfortunately, the EPA has not developed cost estimates for 90 percent controls. A conservative estimate of the net benefits of relaxing the standard results from assuming that 90 percent controls would cost just as much as those achieving 97 percent for the three plants that currently have no controls.

119. Id.

120. See generally Harrison & Nichols, above, note 115 (discussing the advantages of varying standards in response to inter-plant differences in the marginal benefits of emission control).

121. See Haigh, Harrison & Nichols, above, note 12, at 29–30.

122. Id.

123. Id.

124. Of course. the cost-effectiveness of the differential standards will vary with the categorization of the "high exposure" plants. Id. at 31.

125. Although the data available to the EPA permit consideration of the individual components of the BAT standard for coke oven emissions, it is insufficient to analyze alternative levels for the different sources within plants.

126. See Haigh, Harrison & Nichols, above, note 12, at 34–35.

127. Id. The door standard still does not yield positive net benefits, however, unless the value ascribed to saving a life is at least $1.8 million (based again on the CAG risk estimate). Id.

128. See id. at 16 (citing U.S. EPA, Draft Tables on Maximum and Minimum Emission Estimates from By-Product Coke Oven Charging, Door Leaks, and Topside Leaks on Wet-Coal Charged Batteries (Apr. 1983)).

129. See id. at 33 (citing 1981 Background Information, above, note 90, at app. E).

130. See 1983 Research Triangle Cost Estimate, above, note 90.

131. See Haigh, Harrison & Nichols, above, note 12, at 35–36.

132. Plants in the last three categories all use AN monomer as a feedstock. The largest feedstock use is acrylic fibers, employed primarily to manufacture rugs and clothing. ABS and SAN are both resins used to produce hard plastics for such items as pipes, appliances, disposable utensils, and packaging. Nitrile elastomer is a type of rubber used extensively in the automobile industry for hoses, gaskets, and seals.

Id. at 17–18. See also Energy and Envtl. Analysis, Inc., above, note 100, at 1–1 to 1–9.

133. See Haigh, Harrison & Nichols, above, note 12, at 39–40.

134. Id.

135. See Key & Hobbs, above, note 100, table VI-2.

136. See Haigh, Harrison & Nichols, above, note 12, at 39–40.

137. See Key & Hobbs, above, note 100, at app. F, at table F-1.

138. Another possibility is to consider less stringent regulations for the individual source categories. The EPA, however, has not analyzed such alternatives.

139. See Haigh, Harrison & Nichols, above, note 12, at 40–41. The estimated reduction in emissions from controlling those plants is 312,000 $\mu g/^3$-person-years, while the estimated control cost is $8.4 million.

140. Id. The estimated reduction in exposure from controlling that plant is 98,000 $\mu g/^3$-person-years, while the estimated cost is $800,000.

141. See Nichols, above, note 42, at 184–86.

142. Benzene Emissions Background Information, above, note 58, at 1–7. See also, Nichols, above, note 42, at 181.

143. See Radian Corporation above, note 100, at 43.

144. See, e.g., Benzene Emissions Background Information, above, note 58, at table 1–5 (presenting estimates of current benzene emissions from maleic anhydride plants).

145. Obviously, as capacity utilization declines, the production process uses less of the substance and therefore emits less of it.

146. Benefits are proportional to the amount of emissions reduced and the emission reduction is related to the production level. Hence, if production levels drop, so do total benefits. Because capital costs are fixed, the benefit-cost ratio also drops.

147. See below, notes 216–218 and accompanying text.

148. See U.S. Envtl. Protection Agency, Draft Tables on Maximum and Minimum Emission Estimates from By-Product Coke Oven Charging, Door Leaks, and Topside Leaks on Wet-Coal Charged Batteries (Apr. 1983) (provided by S. Grove, Office of Air Quality Planning & Standards).

149. See, e.g., 1981 EPA Draft Coke Oven Regulation, above, note 90, at 1. The charging standard under consideration for coke ovens, for example, sets an upper bound on the number of seconds of visible emissions during the charging cycle. Id.

150. See above, notes 90–99, 125–131 and accompanying text.

151. See Haigh, Harrison & Nichols, above, note 12, at 61.

152. See Benzene Emissions Background Information, above, note 58, at 4–11 to 4–17.

153. C. Miller, Exposure Assessment Modeling: A State-of-the-Art Review (1978) (report prepared for U.S. EPA) (EPA-600/3–78–065).

154. See Haigh, Harrison & Nichols, above, note 12, at 62–63.

155. See, e.g., 1979 Assessment of Exposure to Acrylonitrile, above, note 100, at table V1–5; Benzene Emissions Background Information, above, note 43, at app. E-8. The modeling for maleic anhydride plants was carried out only to 20 kilometers, which may distort comparisons with the other cases. Id. To check for possible bias, exposures for coke ovens and acrylonitrile were estimated using data carried out to only 20 kilometers and the results were compared with the original estimates. The comparisons were reassuring: the differences were only 9

percent for coke ovens and 11 percent for the acrylonitrile plants. See Haigh, Harrison & Nichols, above, note 12, at 63.

156. See, e.g., 1979 Assessment of Exposure to Acrylonitrile, above, note 100, at table VI-5.

157. See, e.g., Spengler & Sexton, "Indoor Air Pollution: A Public Health Perspective," 221 *Science,* 9 (July 1983) (compiling the various primary studies on indoor air pollutants).

158. Id. at 11.

159. Id.

160. Greater accuracy could be achieved by using more plant-specific parameters, some of which could be measured with very low decision costs. It would seem particularly easy and cost-effective, for example, to use local meteorological data.

161. See 1981 Background Information above, note 90, at app. E (extrapolating from Pittsburgh meteorological data to all coke oven plants); Benzene Emissions Background Information, above, note 58, at app. E, at E-8 (extrapolating from Pittsburgh meteorological data to all maleic anhydride plants); 1979 Assessment of Exposure to Acrylonitrile, above, note 100, at 26 (basing acrylonitrile results on generalized conditions rather than actual data from any particular area).

162. See, e.g., Benzene Emissions Background Information, above, note 58, at app. E, at E-6.

163. See above, notes 152–62 and accompanying text. See also Harrison, "Distributional Objectives in Health and Safety Regulation," in *The Benefits of Health and Safety Regulation,* 177–201 (A. Ferguson & E. LeVeen eds. 1981) (estimating exposure to automotive air pollution at work as well as at home).

164. See above, note 81 and accompanying text (benzene). See above, note 92 and accompanying text (coke ovens). See above, note 103 and accompanying text (acrylonitrile).

165. See E. Crouch & R. Wilson, *Risk/Benefit Analysis,* 64–68 (1982).

166. These studies often measured risk, however, at doses 1,000 or more times higher than the exposure levels affected by the regulation. Id. at 114–16.

167. Id.

168. See Nichols, above, note 42, at 164–70 (discussing the various models).

169. Id.

170. See, e.g., E. Crouch and R. Wilson, above, note 165, at 115.

171. In its preliminary report on benzene, for example, the CAG said that the linear model "is expected to give an upper limit to the estimated risk." See Carcinogen Assessment Group, Office of Health & Envtl. Assessment, U.S. Envtl. Protection Agency, Carcinogen Assessment Group's Preliminary Report on Population Risk to Ambient Benzene Exposures 1 (1977) (unpublished paper).

172. See Nichols, above, note 42, at 164–70.

173. See id. (providing equations for the various models and an example of their widely different predictions at low doses when estimated from the same high-dose data).

174. See id. fig. 7.2, at 168.

175. See Address by S. Lamm to the EPA in Washington, D.C. (Aug. 21, 1980) (testimony for the American Petroleum Institute at hearings on the proposed standard for maleic anhydride plants) [hereinafter cited as Address by

Lamm]; see also R. Luken & C. Miller, Regulating Benzene: A Case Study (Sept. 1979) (U.S. EPA unpublished paper).

176. See above, notes 80–89 and accompanying text (discussing the cost-effectiveness of benzene).

177. See Final EPA Benzene Assessment, above, note 65. Studies included: one of workers in two plants using benzene as a solvent to make a transparent film, see Infante, above, note 81, at 76–78: another of Turkish shoe workers using benzene-based adhesives, see Aksoy, "Leukemia in Shoe Workers Exposed Chronically to Benzene," 44 *Blood,* 837 (1974); Aksoy, "Types of Leukemia in Chronic Benzene Poisoning: A Study in Thirty-Four Patients," 55 *Acta Haematologica,* 65 (1976); Aksoy, testimony before Occupational Safety and Health Administration, Washington, D.C. (July 13, 1977); and the third of workers in chemical plants using benzene, see Ott, Townsend, Fishbeck & Langner, Mortality Among Individuals Occupationally Exposed to Benzene (Exhibit 154) (OSHA Benzene Hearings July 19–Aug. 10, 1977).

178. Critics have raised issues including the CAG's exposure estimates for all three studies, its inclusion of the deaths of two workers not in the original cohort of the Infante study, its failure to exclude workers exposed to other hazardous chemicals in the Ott study, and its estimate of the baseline risk in the Aksoy study. See Nichols, above, note 42, at 170 (summarizing the criticisms of the CAG study); Address by Lamm, above, note 175.

179. See R. Luken & C. Miller, above, note 175.

180. Address by Lamm, above, note 175, at 4.

181. See above, notes 170–75 and accompanying text. For benzene, several studies suggest further that the CAG has overestimated the linear model's coefficient. See above, notes 176–80 and accompanying text.

182. See above, notes 117–24 and accompanying text. See also above, notes 132–140 and accompanying text.

183. See above, notes 125–31 and accompanying text.

184. See, e.g., Doniger, above, note 23, at 518–19; Rodgers, "Benefits, Costs, and Risks: Oversight of Health and Environmental Decisionmaking," 4 *Harv. Envtl. L. Rev.* 191, 196–98 (1980).

185. See Raiffa, Schwartz & Weinstein, "Evaluating Health Effects of Societal Decisions and Programs," in *Decision Making in the Environmental Protection Agency* (1977).

186. Id. at 37.

187. As there are roughly 50,000 automobile-related fatalities each year, such a technology would save 25,000 lives annually. If the value per life saved is $5 million, then the value of the technology would be $125 billion. If we assume further that there are 10 million new cars sold each year, then the technology would be worth up to $12,500 per car. See Haigh, Harrison & Nichols, above, note 12, at 68.

188. See Bailey, above, note 70, at 45–46.

189. See E. Crouch and R. Wilson, above, note 165, at 85.

190. See, e.g., Zeckhauser, above, note 67, at 419.

191. For a general discussion on distributional effects of environmental regulations, see Harrison, above, note 163; Harrison and Portney, "Who Loses from Reform of Environmental Regulation" in *Reform of Environmental Regulation* (W.

Magat ed. 1982). See also D. Harrison, *Who Pays for Clean Air?* (1975) (discussing the cost and benefit distribution of federal automobile emission standards).

192. The death rate for the type of leukemia associated with benzene, for example, is more than 26 times higher among people aged 70 to 74 than among children aged 1 to 5. See Final EPA Benzene Assessment, above, note 65, at table 1.

193. Zeckhauser and Shepard argue that mortality benefits should be summarized in terms of the discounted number of "Quality Adjusted Life Years" (QALYs) saved. Their QALY measure adjusts benefits to include reductions in the quality of life due to disability, for example. See Zeckhauser & Shepard, "Where Now for Saving Lives?" 40 *Law and Contemporary Probs.* 5 (Autumn 1976).

194. See, e.g., Raiffa, Schwartz & Weistein, above, note 185, at 42–49.

195. See, e.g., id. at 49.

196. See, e.g., Page, Harris & Bruser, Removal of Carcinogens from Drinking Water: A Cost-Benefit Analysis (Jan. 1979) (Social Science Working Paper »230, California Institute of Technology, Pasadena, Cal.).

197. The equation for discounting is $B/(1+r)^x = PV$, where B is the benefit in current dollars, r is the discount rate, x is the number of years from today in which the benefit accrues, and PV is the present value of the benefit. In the example given, r equals .05 and $\times$ equals 20; the present value of the benefit today (PV) is 37 percent of B.

198. This article, and therefore this section, considers only human health benefits; no consideration is given to benefits related to reduced wildlife and plant damage from these toxic substances. See, e.g., Acrylonitrile Assessment Document, above, note 77, at 88–100 (describing the effects of acrylonitrile on plants, domestic wildlife, and aquatic organisms).

199. Office of Research & Dev., U.S. Envtl. Protection Agency, Assessment of Health Effects of Benzene Germane to Low-level Exposure 48–65 (1978) (EPA-600/1–78–061) (noting benzene's association with aplastic anemia and other serious blood disorders) [hereinafter cited as Health Effects of Benzene]; EPA Coke Oven Assessment, above, note 90, at 54–63 (noting the acute and chronic toxicity of coke oven emissions); Acrylonitrile Assessment Document, above, note 77, at 116–48 (noting the acute, subacute, and chronic toxicity of acrylonitrile).

200. See, e.g., Nichols, above, note 42, at 152 (benzene).

201. Id. at 162.

202. See Acrylonitrile Assessment Document, above, note 77, at 156–66; Final EPA Benzene Assessment, above, note 65, at app. 1–5; EPA Coke Oven Assessment, above, note 90, at 27–52.

203. See, e.g., Final EPA Benzene Assessment, above, note 65, at app. 1–5.

204. See, e.g., [3 State Air Laws] *Env't Rep.* (BNA) 521:0621, 521:0631–:0664 (1983) (Texas' regulation of volatile organic compound emissions); [1 State Air Laws] *Env't Rep.* (BNA) 346:0501, 346:0521 (1983) (Florida's regulation of volatile organic compound emissions).

205. See, e.g., [1 State Air Laws] *Env't Rep.* (BNA) 301:0501, 301:0513–:0515 (1982) (Alabama's restrictions on coke oven emissions); id. at 336:0501, 336:0512 (1984) (Delaware's restrictions on coke oven emissions); [2 State Air Laws] *Env't*

Rep. (BNA) 411:0501, 411:0516 (1982) (Michigan's restrictions on coke oven emissions).

206. 45 Fed. Reg. 26,660, 26,661 (1980).

207. See above, notes 132–140 and accompanying text.

208. Unless, of course, one favors a nonlinear dose-response model, but that would cut in the other direction.

209. See above, notes 87–89 and accompanying text.

210. See above, notes 167–175 and accompanying text.

211. See above, notes 176–180 and accompanying text.

212. See above, notes 145–146 and accompanying text.

213. See above, notes 125–127 and accompanying text.

214. See above, notes 167–175 and accompanying text.

215. See above, notes 67–72 and accompanying text.

216. See A. Nichols, *Targeting Economic Incentives for Environmental Protection,* 157 (1984).

217. Id.

218. 49 Fed. Reg. 8386 (1984).

219. See Office of Air Quality Planning & Standards, U.S. Envtl. Protection Agency, Coke Oven Emissions from Wet-Coal Charged By-Product Coke Oven Batteries—Background Information for Proposed Standards (Sept. 1983) (draft EIS) (Research Triangle Park, N.C.). This document does not calculate reductions in fatalities or exposure. It does, however, include estimates of unit risk and baseline emissions and cancer cases, from which it is possible to measure average exposure per unit of emissions. The document also gives estimates of emission reductions, from which reductions in cancer cases can be estimated.

220. Personal communication from Teresa Gorman, Office of Policy, Planning, & Evaluation, U.S. Envtl. Protection Agency, Washington, D.C. (Apr. 12, 1984).

221. See above, notes 43–50 and accompanying text.

222. See above, text accompanying notes 55–56.

223. See Haigh, Harrison, & Nichols, above, note 12, at table 2.1.

224. See, e.g., above, text accompanying notes 87–88.

225. Office of Toxics, U.S. Envtl. Protection Agency, Chemical Substances Designation (Dec. 1981).

226. See, e.g., Environmental Pesticide Control Act, 7 U.S.C. §§ 136b(b), 136a(c)(5) (1982); Federal Hazardous Substances Act, 15 U.S.C. § 1262(i) (1982); Toxic Substances Control Act, id. § 2605(c) (1982); Food, Drug, & Cosmetics Act, 21 U.S.C. § 346a(b)(1) (1982); Atomic Energy Act, 42 U.S.C. §§ 2022(a), 2022(b), 2114(a) (Supp. V 1981).

227. See, e.g., Poison Prevention Packaging Act, 15 U.S.C. § 1472(b) (1982); Hazardous Liquid Pipeline Safety Act, 49 U.S.C.A. § 2002(b) (West Supp. 1983).

228. See, e.g., Food, Drug, & Cosmetics Act 21 U.S.C. §§ 342(a)(2)(A), 348(c)(3)(A), 360(d)(1)(H), 376(b)(5)(B), 451, 601, 1031 (1982); Lead Based Paint Act, 42 U.S.C. § 4831 (1976 & Supp. V 1981). Other nonconsumer statutes also focus exclusively on health factors. See, e.g., Surface Mining Control and Reclamation Act, 30 U.S.C. §§ 1265(b), 1266(b)(9)(A) (Supp. V 1981), Marine Protection, Research, and Sanctuaries Act of 1972, 33 U.S.C. § 1412(a) (1976).

2 The Methodology of Cost-Benefit Analysis, with Particular Reference to the Ozone Problem

Ezra J. Mishan and Talbot Page

Introduction: State of Physical Problems

The ozone layer which mantles the planet is the result of an equilibrium process by which the natural disintegration of ozone into oxygen molecules is continuously being offset by the creation of ozone from the action of sunlight on free oxygen in the stratosphere. It is believed that this stratospheric ozone shields life on earth against biologically harmful ultraviolet radiation from the sun and helps to maintain the heat balance of the globe.

The initial threat to the ozone layer was seen as arising from the nitrogen oxide produced by supersonic flights. More attention today is paid to the threat posed by free chlorine atoms acting as catalysts in the destruction of ozone. The largest potential source of chlorine in the stratosphere comes from a class of chemicals designated as "fluorocarbons" (FC), or more formally as chlorofluorocarbons, and are derivatives of methane. The two most common of these are used as propellants in spray cans (or aerosols) and are known as $FC_{11}(C.Cl_2.F_2)$ and $FC_{12}(C.Cl_3.F)$. "Fluorocarbons" are also used as refrigerants and foaming agents.

A rough breakdown by use (not by effect) is:

spray cans	50%
refrigerants	30%
other	20%

In 1974 several scientific groups were led to the hypothesis that the introduction of chlorine compounds into the stratosphere could destroy ozone on a scale having potentially harmful consequences for life on earth. Since there is, as yet, no adequate model of the stratosphere, there is a major problem in the attempt actually to measure the magnitude of the effect of nitrogen oxide and fluorocarbons on the ozone layer. The problem is exacerbated by fluctuations in ozone concentrations which occur naturally and are large and frequent.

The length of time involved in the chain reaction catalyzed by a chlorine atom is currently believed to be at least 10 years. After production and use it may take scores of years for fluorocarbons to enter the stratosphere. (There appear that there are no natural sinks for fluorocarbons other than the stratosphere and a conservative assumption is that virtually all fluorocarbons, including refrigerants, eventually end up in the stratosphere.) Because of the long time delays involved, another 50 years may be necessary before scientists can reasonably be certain of the extent of the damage done to the ozone layer and of the range of ecological consequences. In his summary of the technical information on ozone depletion, Choi (1978) devotes 12 pages to critical areas of research currently being undertaken by agencies and universities in the United States.

In the meantime, the possibility that supersonic flights, and the use today of aerosols, refrigerant liquids, and other postwar products, will act to dissipate over time the ozone shield that protects life on this planet from solar ultraviolet radiation is one that is being taken increasingly seriously, at least in the United States. Inasmuch as a decision to reduce the extent of supersonic travel and to curb the production of suspect products in order to diminish the risk to which unchecked development of such activities would expose humanity entails costs and benefits, the problem ostensibly has an economic aspect. In particular, it may seem to lend itself to cost-benefit techniques.

In this instance, where the alternative under most consideration is that of curbing in some degree existing commercial activities suspected of causing ecological damage, the costs in question are believed to be those which arise from forgoing the benefits associated with such commercial activities. The benefits, on the other hand, would appear to consist of the reduction of the risk of ecological damage to which existing and future generations are exposed.

The Aims of the Present Paper

The present paper is to be regarded as a preliminary investigation into some of the more critical concepts which inform allocative economics with the object of determining the extent to which a cost-benefit analysis and related techniques can throw light on the ozone problem and so make an economic contribution to the decision-making process of society.

Within the broad field of welfare economics, a distinction is to be made between, on the one hand, the more ambitious and more abstract approach to social welfare comprehended by the notion of a "Social Welfare Function" (SWF) for society that has, somehow, to be derived from each individual's SWF and, on the other hand, the traditional principles of resource allocation closely associated with the development of neoclassical economics. Attention to the former approach has given rise to a mathematically sophisticated literature about the possibilities for deriving from individual ordering of alternative social states an ordering for society as a whole that meets a number of conditions deemed reasonable by that society. Furthermore, and more importantly for our purposes, this former approach may yield insights as to the nature of the problem of intergenerational equity. Intergenerational equity can be viewed as the problem of choosing "fair" rules of aggregation of interests or preferences across time, and we will discuss how the social choice literature is related to the ozone depletion problem in its equity aspects.

The former approach does not, however, lend itself to project evaluation in the sense that it does not seek, as do allocative techniques such as cost-benefit analysis, to produce figures that have an economic interpretation which figures may then be submitted as an economic contribution to society's decision-making process. As things stand at present only restriction to conventional allocative principles can yield specific figures which can be interpreted as meeting, or failing to meet, an acceptable economic criterion. Most of the economic analysis of the ozone depletion problem has been in terms of this latter approach and we will turn most of our attention to this approach as it applies to the ozone depletion problem.

There are, of course, many facets of a cost-benefit analysis that are fascinating in themselves and that would interest the informed public. But since there is broad agreement, at least among the theorists in the subject, about most of these facets, little purpose is served by expounding them in this paper. We have chosen instead to focus attention on the likelier points of controversy that will arise in the attempts of economists to apply cost-benefit and other allocative techniques to the ozone problem. The task we have chosen has impelled us to reexamine the fundamental concepts on which these economic techniques are raised and from which they derive their sanction.

If our conclusions are, in the main, correct they will act inevitably to weaken the faith that can be reposed in a cost-benefit analysis or, at least, to restrict its range of application. Such an outcome is obviously unwelcome to economists including ourselves. But we follow the logic of the arguments wheresoever it leads.

The facts of a cost-benefit analysis to which we address ourselves in this paper are five in number, to wit:

1. The implications of the concept of economic efficiency.
2. Conceptual problems of valuation.
3. The legitimacy of using the discounted present value method (DPV) in ranking public projects.

4. The question of intergenerational equity.
5. The treatment of risk and uncertainty.

These five headings are not arranged in order of importance but, being related to one another, they follow in logical sequence the arguments which we advance in the examination of one problem from observations made in our examination of earlier problems.

1. Implications of the Concept of Economic Efficiency

Since cost-benefit analysis is to be regarded as no more than an extension of the conventional allocative analysis to a proposed economic change, often in the form of a proposed project, it is as well to address ourselves at the start directly to allocative economics—to the criterion by which the economist compares one economic arrangement with alternatives, either in the small or the large.

The singularity of the economic method consists in the adoption of what we may refer to as the basic economic maxim: that the objective data for the economist are the orderings, or the subjective valuations, of the individual members of society, and nothing more. These subjective valuations are usually measured in terms of money; less frequently (and usually for theoretical purposes) in terms of some standard commodity or *numeraire*. What is more, these valuations are accepted by the economist as relevant data irrespective of the tastes of the individual or the current state of his information. Finally, the phrase "and nothing more" is appended to the above description of the basic maxim in order to obviate any "holistic" interpretation of the idea of social welfare. In other words, there is no abstraction such as "the general good" and no entity such as "the State" to be considered by the economist in addition to the welfare of the individuals who comprise society—a view that accords with the philosophic position sometimes referred to as methodological individualism.

Since, however, a large number of individuals are generally affected by any economic change, a further criterion is necessary for ranking the alternative economic situations. A criterion that would attract widespread support would be that of an actual Pareto improvement—one for which each member of society is made no worse off by the change and one or more members are actually made better off than before. But changes that meet such a criterion are unlikely to be common in the world we live in. If the economist adopted as his criterion an actual Pareto improvement as described above, the resulting allocative economics would countenance very few changes. Thus, bearing in mind that nearly all economic changes raise the welfare of some persons while lowering that of others, the criterion chosen by economists today, and indeed the criterion implicit in neoclassical economics, can properly be described as a *potential* Pareto improvement: a situation II is ranked above a situation I if, in a costless movement from I to II, the aggregate value of individual gains exceeds the aggregate value of individual losses. Indeed, the excess value of aggregate gains over aggregate losses arising from the specific change is commonly referred to as the social net benefit of that change, and this magnitude is taken to be the economic measure of the resulting change in society's welfare.

Assuming the social net benefit in question to be positive, the recommended change from I to II may be rationalized by the proposition that costless redistributions of the net gains can be envisaged which, were they implemented, could make each individual better off than he was in the I situation.

Clearly, a potential Pareto improvement—which we shall also refer to as the *Pareto criterion*—is consistent with a change that can make the rich richer and the poor poorer yet. For this reason, among others, there have been objections to its adoption, and proposals have been made to elaborate the criterion so as to guard against this contingency. Notwithstanding these objections and proposals, the standard allocative criterion employed by economists today is no more than this Pareto criterion. A change that is said to increase "economic efficiency" is nothing more than a change which meets the Pareto criterion—one, that is, which meets a potential Pareto improvement.

Since the weight of the argument to follow turns on this notion of economic efficiency, we spell out carefully its prescriptive implications. The term economic efficiency—when it is not being used by economists simply as a shorthand for $\Sigma v < 0$ (where the v's are individual valuations)— entails a norm by which alternative situations may be ranked. And since alternative economic organizations are agenda that affect the welfare of all members of society, the norm must be one that is acceptable to members of society. One way of expressing society's will with respect to alternative economic forms of organization is through the political process; in a democratic state through the voting mechanism. But the outcome of a political decision about a set of economic alternatives is not necessarily regarded by the economist as efficient. It follows that the norm of economic efficiency is distinct from, and independent of, an expression of the political will: indeed, that political decisions may properly be criticized by reference to the norms of economic efficiency.

Inasmuch as the sanction for the norms of economic efficiency to be adopted rests ultimately on its acceptability to the society in question, it cannot be grounded in any single individual's value judgment. And since, as indicated, it cannot be grounded either in the political will of that society, but has to be independent of it, the norms of economic efficiency have to rest on an ethical consensus—or what one of the authors has called elsewhere,[1] "a virtual constitution" that is deemed to be impervious to political fashions and the vicissitudes of political office. It is then wholly appropriate for economists to debate the nature of the relevant components of the prevailing ethical consensus in assessing alternative economic criteria or norms of economic efficiency. In contrast, debate about individuals' value judgments is a separate issue, and is set aside, for this paper.

Assuming, then, that there exists a consensus on which a norm of economic efficiency can be raised, it follows that it is independent of current expressions of the prevailing political will. Inasmuch as society's ethics transcends its politics (a society's politics of course is to some extent an expression of its ethics) the outcome of the norm of economic efficiency transcends the outcome of the political mechanism.

As indicated earlier, there may be little doubt that the adoption of an actual Pareto improvement—a requirement that the change actually makes "everyone" better off—as the norm of economic efficiency would be ethically acceptable to society. But if no less restrictive a norm were acceptable, the economist would have little allocative advice to offer society. Can we then assume the Pareto criterion on which all allocative propositions and recommendations are, in fact, raised is also ethically acceptable?

Although at first glance it is far from compelling, a belief that society as a whole would agree to abide by it can draw upon a number of arguments arising from notions about the actual operation of the economy; for instance, (i) that such changes which are, in fact, potential Pareto improvements do not generally have regressive distributional effects, (ii) that a progressive tax system, in any case, provides a safeguard against pronounced distributional consequences resulting from any economic change, (iii) that, over time, a succession of economic changes countenanced by this Pareto criterion will not have markedly regressive distributional effects and will, therefore, tend to bring about an actual Pareto improvement, and (iv) that a succession of economic changes that meets the Pareto criterion has a better chance of raising the general level of welfare than a succession of changes that meets any other criterion.

An acceptance of this distinction between the political and the economic does, at least, have the merit of assigning a role to the economist that is independent of the political process. Yet if the economist does in fact give primacy to "economic efficiency" over considerations of distribution, it is not necessarily because he accepts the Kaldor distinction (1939) between the economic efficiency aspect of a change and the distributional aspect which Kaldor declared to be a political issue upon which the economist, qua economist, had no particular competence to pronounce. Nor is it because the economist believes that economic efficiency takes precedence over considerations of distribution or equity. It is simply that, provided the economist is guided by the Pareto criterion, his craft enables him, from time to time, to come up with unambiguous results or with specific numbers. Concern with distributional changes, on the other hand, enables him to come up only with general statements and abstract theorems.

2. Conceptual Problems of Valuation

The problems grouped under this heading are:

    a. The uses of Compensating Variation (CV) and Equivalent Variation (EV) in measuring allocative changes.
    b. The use of distributional and other weights in a Cost-Benefit Analysis.
    c. "Intangible" externalities and "merit" and "demerit" goods.
    d. Doubts about the existence of the required ethical consensus.

a. The Uses of Compensating Variation (CV) and Equivalent Variation (EV) in Measuring Allocative Changes

Many cost-benefit studies, explicitly or implicitly, base their valuations on the CV concept (with respect to specific changes, the sums which individuals need to pay or to receive in order to restore their welfare to their original levels) rather than on the EV concept (the sums which the individuals have to pay or receive if, spared the specific economic changes, their welfares have to assume the level they would reach if they were actually exposed to those changes). And there are a few cost-benefit studies in which, unwittingly we presume, the authors have used CV for some valuations and EV for others.

It is now accepted that in a general analysis, one in which all prices change, apparently contradictory results can arise according as CV or EV is used. It is possible, that is, for the II situation, represented by a collection of goods, to yield a potential Pareto improvement compared with the I situation when based on the set of prices determined by the actual distribution of the I situation. At the same time, it is also possible for the original I situation to yield a potential Pareto improvement when compared with the II situation, when the comparison is based on the set of prices emerging from the actual distribution of the II collection of goods.[2] Associating CV and EV respectively with these two paradoxical results, the economist has either to decide in favor of CV or EV or else to reject any public project which does not meet the Pareto criterion when measured in terms both of CV and of EV. The latter policy appears the more prudent course, although it clearly favors the status quo inasmuch as the existing situation I is the one effectively adopted in all cases in which ambiguity precludes a ranking of I and II.

Generally, however, exercises in cost-benefit analysis are conducted within a partial equilibrium framework. Thus, the public project being contemplated is assumed to require so small a proportion of the economy's total resources that the prices only of the goods immediately under scrutiny are perceptibly affected by the alternative projects. For the usual size of such projects, the assumption is not unreasonable, and it enables the economist to circumvent the difficulties associated with the Second Best Theorem and the apparent contradictions, referred to above, that can arise whenever the alternatives being compared involve perceptible changes in many prices.

Nevertheless, even within a partial equilibrium framework contradictory outcomes can still arise when the calculations are done in terms of both CVs and EVs. Yet the contradiction arises for reasons quite different from those indicated above. The contradiction now depends upon the magnitude of the individual's response to the welfare effect of the change in question. Thus, wherever given changes in nonmarket goods or bads are valued differently by the individual according as the amount he is willing to pay for a good (or to pay for avoiding a bad) differs significantly from the amount he is willing to accept to forgo it, the EV calculation can differ from the CV calculation. A Pareto criterion based on the EV measure can be met by the change which is rejected when the same criterion is based on the CV measure.

The larger the environmental effects of a project, and the more substantial are the welfare effects on the people involved, the greater the likelihood that a project accepted on an EV test will be rejected on a CV test. It is particularly important, therefore, where environmental effects are large, that economists reach a decision on which test is to be adopted. Again, the prudent course to adopt may seem to be one of requiring both tests to be made, so effectively favoring the status quo. On the other hand, if there appears to be a consensus bearing on other factors, such as equity or conservation, economists may be able to justify their adoption of the one measure or the other according to the project in question.

The Use of Distributional and Other Weights in a Cost-Benefit Analysis

There [have] been a number of proposals to incorporate distributional weights or merit weights in a cost-benefit analysis. With respect to distribution, the weights are chosen to vary inversely with the income levels of the various groups affected by the introduction of the public projects. Such a procedure effectively transforms money estimates of compensating variations into *utils*. Thus a cost-benefit criterion that is not met in money terms might well be met when the calculation is translated into utility terms, and vice versa.

The particular weighting systems that have been proposed are of necessity arbitrary and all assume, not surprisingly, diminishing marginal utility of income. One method is that of adopting a particular form of the utility-income relation; for example, one that gives a constant elasticity of minus two with respect to income. Alternatively, the weighting system can be made dependent upon the political decisions taken in the past. A method of deriving such weights has been proposed by Weisbrod (1968) and rests on the assumption that all public projects which were adopted despite their failure to meet cost-benefit criteria over a period were adopted because of an implicit set of utility weights attached by the political process to the earnings of different income or regional groups. Another method of deriving these political weights is by a more direct approach to policy makers. Yet another method is that of calculating them from the marginal rates of income tax on the premise that the object of the existing tax system is to share the real burden of any increment of tax equally among all income groups.

Whether bureaucratically or democratically chosen, such parameters, purporting to represent "ultimate national objectives," will vary not only from one country to another. Within any one country they may vary from year to year according to the particular regime in power, or according to the composition of the legislature or, again, according to political fashions and the exigencies of state. Moreover, since it will soon become recognized, in any representative democracy, that some projects which would be accepted on one set of weights, or national parameters, would be rejected on another set, one may anticipate continued lobbying and political infighting, both by regional and other group interests, over the weights to be adopted. The resulting vicissitudes and conflict would go far to discredit cost-benefit techniques and, possibly, economists also. Choice of the "appropriate" discount rate, which can be viewed as specifying an intertemporal set of distributional weights, has been subject to political pressures in the evaluation of public works projects, for example.

Even if it were possible to secure permanent agreement within any one country on the set of *distributional* weights to be attached to the benefits and losses of different income groups, it could not be counted on to prevent the introduction of a project having a markedly regressive distributional impact. Of the projects that meet a distributionally weighted cost-benefit criterion some might well make the rich richer and the poor poorer if the beneficiaries were rich and many and the losers were poor and few. Such distributionally undesirable outcomes can be avoided only by separate consideration of the distributional impact of any contemplated project.

The proposal to employ politically determined parameters in project evaluation appears, on the surface, to be one arising from the modesty of the economist who overtly recognizes the limitations of his craft, and particularly, his inability to place a socially acceptable valuation on a variety of social phenomena that are influenced by an investment project and that alter people's welfare for better or worse. But it is a modest proposal which issues in more ambitious claims for the *resulting technique,* one that is then held to "integrate project planning and national policy."[3] For it purports to reduce to a single critical magnitude a variety of considerations, tangible and intangible.

In contrast, in the conventional (unweighted) valuations used in allocative techniques, the calculation of gains and losses is made on a purely economic principle; that is, by placing a value on them by reference only to the subjective valuation of the persons affected by the project. Thus, if the government calls upon the economist to undertake a cost-benefit study, it presumably expects him to employ economic principles and only economic principles. If for any reason the economist encounters difficulties in evaluating some particular social benefit or cost item, he has the option of leaving its calculation out of the analysis and making it clear that he has done so. If, instead, he attempts to derive a value for this social benefit or social loss by reference to values that are implicit in recent political decisions (assuming they are consistent) he is, in effect, presenting the government with a result that depends, *inter alia,* on the government's own preferences or valuations and not on those of the individual citizens whose welfare will be affected by the project. The government having referred the problem to the economist for a solution, the economist, by these means, surreptitiously hands it back to the government.

The government, if democratically elected, may of course claim to represent the nation. But it is hardly necessary to remind the reader that the ballot box can produce results very different from those of the market or those reached by an application of the Pareto principle. A majority may well vote in favor of the use of weights or parameters that would justify the introduction of *uneconomical* projects to be financed by the wealthier minority. Thus, if the present value of the cost of building a funfair for the community were $4 million and the present value of the maximum sums the members of the community were prepared to pay were equal to $3 million, the funfair project would not meet a cost-benefit criterion. But if a majority wanted the funfair built, it would not be hard to pass it off as a "merit good" so as to attach to each pound of a benefit a weight, say, of two. Alternatively, since the poor would visit the funfair more than the rich, while the rich, through taxes, would pay more than the poor, by judiciously weighting the expected losses and gains of rich and poor, a "utility" cost-benefit criterion could be met and, therefore, the funfair project pronounced economical.

Now there may be some good reasons why the community should have a funfair despite the fact that it cannot meet a purely economic criterion. These reasons could be brought out in public debate and the decision taken to build the funfair. But there is everything to be said for making it abundantly clear that the project does *not* meet an economic criterion. For by "doctoring" the method of evaluation so as to accommodate current political predilections, the economic facts are concealed from the public which is then misled into the belief that the proposal has the sanction of pure economic calculation, a belief that is likely to influence the course and outcome of any debate on the subject.

We should add in passing that while arguing for the exclusion of politically determined prices or parameters in project evaluation, no inconsistency is committed in simultaneously acknowledging the existence of political constraints. These do not offer to the economist arbitrary or noneconomic valuations of goods or bads. They act only to circumscribe the range of choices open to the economist. They can best be regarded as information on how the government is expected to act or react to a change in relevant economic circumstances. In accepting these constraints, the economist does not have to endorse the government's policy. Indeed, he may go on record as opposing it. In taking into account the expected actions and reactions of the government, the economist is seeking only to discover whether in these circumstances, the introduction of the mooted project will yet realize a potential Pareto improvement. In the endeavor to discover this, however, the economist may not also accept politically determined parameters or prices. He must restrict himself to *economic* prices—those arising from the subjective valuations of the persons whose welfares are affected by the project.

Once politically determined valuations are believed pertinent to some agenda, there is no obvious case for limiting the extent of political intervention for this purpose. If decision makers can attach weights to merit or demerit goods, why not also to the more ordinary goods on the argument that, as among ordinary goods also, some will have smaller social merit than others? If political decision makers may attach a valuation to accidents or loss of life, why may they not also attach their own valuations to a wide range of other spillover effects? And if so much can be justified there seems to be no logical reasons against going further, and having political decisions override all market prices and individual valuations.

There would then seem to be no reason why each and every investment project should not be approved or rejected directly by the political process, democratic or otherwise.

"Intangible" Externalities and "Merit" and "Demerit" Goods

Assuming the economist intends the term "economic efficiency" to have reference to an economic criterion that is independent of the political expression of society, and one therefore that can be sanctioned only by an ethical consensus, a question of consistency arises. Economic efficiency regarded as a normative criterion in this way requires that it be raised entirely on an "ethical base" as distinct from what we might call a "utilitarian base." Such a requirement, however, leads to some fundamental problems. For example, although we may continue to suppose that society, in its ethical capacity, accepts the Pareto criterion in ordinary circumstances, there can be circumstances in which society would reject it on ethical grounds.

The economist who ignores all exceptional circumstances of this sort, and continues to base his allocative recommendations entirely on the criterion $\Sigma\Delta v > 0$, is said, here, to be building his allocative propositions upon a "utilitarian base"; which is to say that he restricts himself to the utilities, or welfares, of the individuals affected as expressed in their own valuations (whether declared or inferred), without exception. If he does so, however, his recommendations may no longer claim to be grounded in the ethics of society and, therefore, they may no longer be applicable or relevant to that society. For example, a person B may be willing to sell himself into servitude for the rest of his life to person A for a sum that is smaller than the most person A is willing to pay him. Alternatively, a poor man B may agree to his being flagellated by a rich man A for a sum that ensures mutual gains. The bargain that could be struck in either case would, of course, meet the Pareto criterion: indeed, such bargains would effect actual Pareto improvements. Yet the economist who would, in consequence, recommend that the transaction take place, would be prescribing a course of action that runs counter to the prevailing ethical consensus in the West.

Clearly, if a normative allocation economics is to be a valid instrument, as it can be only if it accords with the prevailing ethics of society, it cannot be raised in all circumstances on a utilitarian base. Ultimately it has to be raised on an ethical base. Thus, in addition to the difficult problems of measurement, which the economist faces in deducing allocative propositions or in calculating net social benefits, he has now also to view his results in the light of his understanding of society's ethics. Adherence at all times to the Pareto criterion is therefore not enough.

But this is not all. This criterion subsumes the ethical validity also of the basic maxim. Yet there can also be occasions on which society would not regard adherence to the basic maxim as ethical either; it would refuse, that is, to be bound by the individual valuations that comprise the data of $\Sigma\Delta v$. The calculation of externalities in a cost-benefit analysis provides a useful example. Thus a distinction can be made between "tangible" external diseconomies, on the one hand, which cover the range of familiar pollutants that are commonly quoted for illustrative purposes in the economic literature, and on the other hand "intangible" external diseconomics which comprehend people's responses to a change where no physical discomforts are anticipated therefrom. A well-known example of the latter is that of the "interdependent utilities" hypothesis, in which each person's welfare is a function also, positive or negative, of the level of welfare or, by extension, of the income or possessions of others.

If a person B is expected to suffer as a direct result of the noise or fumes emitted by the automobiles of group A, the cost of the damage he sustains—as measured, say, by his expenditures directed to reducing the damage plus a minimal compensation for the residual inconvenience suffered—should indeed be entered into the $\Sigma\Delta v$ calculation of net social benefit. For it is reasonable to believe that such a cost would be endorsed as a legitimate item in measuring the social value of the project in question. In contrast, if the automobiles of the A group have no effect whatever on person B's health, and cause him no inconvenience, his welfare may yet decline in consequence only of his envy of the A group. If this be the case, it is reasonable to suppose that the considered opinion of society is wholly unsympathetic to his claim for compensation. Thus, if our allocation economics is erected upon an ethical base, as it should be, this distinction between "tangible" and "intangible" externalities—ignored in an allocation economics erected upon a utilitarian base—can be crucial in the economic calculation of net social benefit.

Clearly this sort of distinction between "tangible" and "intangible" effects is operative also in the field of public works and economic policy generally. If, for example, a project raises the incomes of a group of people, the additional income would be included among the positive benefits of the project. The fact that awareness of this group's material improvement would also cause resentment among members of another group may, in some circumstances, enter strongly into a political decision. But in its ethical capacity, society might well repudiate the idea of counting as costs the envy-claims of the latter group on a par with the claims, say, of financial losses or physical discomforts of some other group. It is possibly true that modern society is one in which the Commandment "Thou shalt not covet thy neighbor's property" is honored by individuals more in the breach than the observance. But if, as yet, society accepts the Tenth Commandment as part of its ethical code, the inclusion of envy-claims in a calculation of net social benefit violates the ethical consensus.

On reflection, however, it is manifest that we cannot stop here. If, in its ethical capacity, society is deemed to discountenance the envy or resentment experienced by people at the good fortune of others, to the extent of repudiating any claims arising from these "intangible" externalities in an economic calculation of net social benefit, consistency also requires that society's ethical position be extended to cover the individuals' valuations of market and collective goods also. For society may well have strong ethical reservations about the motives which impel people to buy certain goods—motives such as resentment, spite, hatred, exhibitionism, or merely a desire to keep up with the Joneses. Even where the motives are not deserving of censure, society may regard them with contempt enough, as being too petty or trivial, and rule that their reckoning be dismissed in any calculation designed to determine a reallocation of resources.

Doubts About the Existence of the Required Ethical Consensus

Allowing that a normative allocation economics is faced with the problem not simply of describing or calculating the money equivalence of the effects on the welfare of individuals arising from different economic changes but also with the problem of prescribing economic changes for a particular society, we reach the following conclusion. The economist, having to base his normative allocative propositions on an ethical consensus is also saddled with the task of determining the ethical judgments of society with respect to a wide range of possible transactions. Unless he is successful in his endeavors, society will (or ought to) ignore his economic recommendations or calculations. As a corollary, then, the economist will have no criterion of economic efficiency to juxtapose against a politically determined allocation.

Clearly, such a task is easier to discharge the lower the level of consumption in a society and the slower its pace of change. A society in which goods are scarce in a more literal sense, and in which the patterns of consumption and production are largely determined by tradition, is one for which the economist might prescribe with confidence in the belief that allocative propositions or calculations derived directly from a utilitarian base would be little different from those derived from an ethical base.

Within a modern growth economy, on the other hand, in which there is ample evidence for the allegation that the "Jones' effect" is growing, or that personal attire is increasingly exhibitionist, or that norms of taste are declining, or that much of the economy's outputs for mass consumption is increasingly trivial if not regrettable, the task of the allocation economist is not an enviable one. In such circumstances it can reasonably be contended that the ethical consensus to which the normative economist has to defer is itself breaking up. Wherever the consumption of some goods, or the indulgence of some commercially provided activities, are believed by some proportion of the population to be unworthy or degrading and, at the same time, are believed by others to be innocuous if not liberating, the task of the welfare economist becomes impossible.

Therefore, as commonly asserted, the so-called permissive society, the child of affluence, is becoming "pluralistic" in the sense that a traditional or dominant set of beliefs no longer exists; if the tendency is in the direction of each person "doing his own thing"—in effect judging his own activities and those of others in the light of his own privately constituted conscience—then the economist will no longer be able to vindicate his prescriptive statements.

Fragmentation does not, of course, have to proceed to the point where there is a multitude of groups each espousing a particular set of convictions about what is right or wrong, proper or improper. Suffice it that two or more groups differ markedly in their attitudes about the merits and demerits of the products and services of modern society.

For instance, it may be impossible to secure a consensus that more of society's resources should be diverted from their existing employment in order to make available increased outputs of pornographic literature or for "You're Welcome" flash signs for automobiles, or in order to extend the range of tobacco products regardless of expected consumer expenditure on these items.

Reflection on recent developments reinforces the suspicion that, in some respects, the consensus necessary for a normative allocation economics is dissolving. First, there appears to be a growing reluctance today among segments of the public—made explicit in debates between economists, lawyers, and sociologists—to accept without reservation the judgment of the market in the face of substantial expenditures on commercial advertising designed to influence the valuations placed on goods by the buying public. Secondly, there is now the question of rates of depletion of a large number of fuels and materials. Although prior to World War II, the question was one of limited concern to society at large, and of limited importance in economics, the current scale of resource consumption has made it a topic of growing concern to the public at the same time as it has become one of controversy within the ranks of economists themselves.

There can be little room for doubt that there is currently a deep division of opinion among informed members of the public, including economists, about the wisdom of current and proposed economic policies in these respects, which amounts also to a division of opinion about whether the valuations currently attributed to "finite" resources (either under existing economic arrangements or under "ideal" competitive arrangements) has any normative significance. Certainly, a number of reputable economists have argued that the existing valuations of fuels and minerals, and their current rates of consumption, cannot be justified by reference to any criterion that would exclude the opinions of future generations.[4]

Finally, there is a growing agreement that inasmuch as the untoward consequences of consumer innovations—one thinks in this connection of food additives, chemical drugs and pesticides, synthetic materials and a variety of new gadgets—tend to unfold slowly over time, their valuations at any point of time by the buying public (as determined by the market prices to which individual purchases adjust) may bear no relation whatever to the net utilities conferred over time. Indeed, the very pace of change today with respect to new models and new goods, it can be cogently argued, is such that it is no longer possible for the buying public to learn from its own experience to assess the relative merits of a large proportion of the goods coming onto the market. In consequence, society can have no confidence that the valuations of such goods have any *ex post* correspondence with people's subjective wants (whether socially approved or not) as to justify them, on the standard argument, as indicators of claims on society's resources.

Assuming this latter belief becomes so widely accepted as virtually to become unanimous, it follows that, for a growing proportion of goods, the subjective valuations, upon which the normative allocation economist has to depend, will no longer be indicative even of the overall subjective utilities of the buyers. On the other hand, the continuance instead of a division of belief about the extent and importance of this development must also act to prevent the would-be normative economist from invoking an ethical sanction for this use of these valuations.

Of course, on particular issues, the would-be normative economist may be able to speak with greater confidence than on others. He may have no hesitation in employing Dupuit's arguments in calculating the net benefits of a bridge, or of calculating the net benefits of a better system of food production or distribution in one of the poorer countries in the world—at least if he were willing to disregard the possible long-run effects associated with the growth of population. But for many of the public projects in an affluent society, even where they are designed to provide the population with lower cost inputs of different forms of energy or basic materials, the conscientious normative economist can no longer speak with authority. For he is amply aware that the values to be placed on such basic inputs are part of a highly controversial topic and, moreover, that such inputs are used in a wide range of items and gadgets about whose social justification the community may be deeply divided.

It follows that if the circumstances described above prevail, the more restricted conception of the role of the economist, as one whose task it is simply to describe the economic consequences expected to follow from the introduction of alternative projects of policies, may become the dominant one. And the calculations of Σv or of $\Sigma \Delta v$, currently used in allocation and cost-benefit analysis, then become no more than a convenient and popular method of presenting the economic effects expected from a proposed policy or project. Such net benefit aggregates, of course, no longer carry independent economic recommendation. They are of value only in so far as they are made use of by the political authority itself as an input into the decision-making process, an input to which any weight (including a zero weight) can be attached.

Terms such as (a) "increased economic efficiency" or (b) "an optimal position," whether used within a partial or general equilibrium context, might, of course, continue to be used by economists, though only as a sort of professional shorthand, respectively, for (a) an economic change for which $\Sigma \Delta v > 0$, or (b) an economic situation for which $\Sigma \Delta v \leq 0$, where the v's refer either to the individual valuation of all of the goods and bads experienced by members of society or else to any specified category of them. After all, there is no good reason why the economist should allow the elaborate structure of allocation economics to go to rust merely because there was no foundation in which to embed it. But if the economist wishes, at the end of his analysis, to be able to conclude that one project is better than another, he needs seek out a broader role by explicitly considering the normative base which ultimately leads to normative policy prescription; moreover, he must be explicit as well about his assumptions concerning the underlying ethical consensus, or lack of it. These observations apply particularly to the discussion and practice of discounting, which we turn to next.

3. The Legitimacy of Using DPV in Ranking Public Projects

The ingenuity and conviction with which some professional economists argue the case for the adoption of the device of discounting to the present the stream of net benefits (positive or negative) of a public project is understandable. Were the methods to be discredited, the expertise of the allocation economist might be significantly diminished. Only very recently has this device been challenged. Most of the controversy over the last two decades has turned, instead, on the question of the appropriate rate of discount to use; for instance, whether it should be the common rate of time preference, or the current yield in the private sector, or some other opportunity rate of return; whether it should be [a] weighted composite of such rates and whether it should be lower for public investment than the current yield in the private sector.

The observations that follow are grouped under two main headings; that above, where they are relevant within an *intra*generational context, and that which follows, where they are relevant within an *inter*generational context.

For methods of project evaluation that rest ultimately on a Pareto criterion, an unresolved difficulty arises if the lifetimes of the people in the community do not overlap at some point of time common to all of them during the period of the net benefit stream in question. Although there can be factors other than this, such as the growth of uncertainty about the magnitudes of costs and benefits to an intolerable degree after a certain date, the former consideration of itself is warrant enough for the introduction of a finite time horizon, extending from $t = 0$ to $t = T$ in a calculation designed to rank alternative public projects. (In the latter part of this paper, we will consider some of the fundamental aspects of intertemporal equation with the perspective of an unlimited number of generations.)

In order to avoid inessential elaboration, the practice common in the literature, of first setting aside the problem of uncertainty so as to focus on a critical part of the logic of investment criteria, is followed here, as is also the fiction that market values are equal to social values—in particular that the value of an outlay K on the public project is equal, not to the nominal sum transferred for the purpose, but equal to its opportunity cost.

Although the assumption of "full employment" is popular in the literature of investment criteria, it is of no great consequence. "Unemployment" can be dealt with by attributing lower opportunity costs in any project for which a proportion of labor (or other factors) comes from the existing pools of unemployment, while any employment multiplier effects are conceived to generate benefits. Nonetheless, it will be convenient to stay within the convention in this respect and, therefore, to go along with the usual assumption—inapplicable to instances of public projects designed to reduce the level of existing unemployment—that voluntary changes in current savings entail equal changes in private investment.

Let r be the rate of time preference common to all the individuals who are affected by and remain alive over the period in question by the public project, and let ρ be the yield on private investment.

Although it is not strictly necessary that the rate of time preference be common to all individuals in any evaluation of the benefit stream, it should be evident that if, say, all of the gainers from the project have a higher (weighted) rate of time preference than all the losers, or vice versa, the benefit-cost ratio will, in general, vary with the point of time chosen for the evaluation. Moreover, it is entirely possible that for the evaluation taken at, say, the terminal date the benefit-cost ratio would exceed unity at the same time as the evaluation taken at the initial date would show a benefit-cost ratio below unity. However, since our enquiry goes far beyond this possibility, we may suppose that any weighted rate of time preference is the same both for losers as for gainers or, simpler still, that r is the rate of time preference of all the individuals who are affected by the public project and remain alive over the period in question. The current yield on private investment is taken to be ρ, and for a number of reasons (of which the most obvious is the income tax paid on the return from investment) ρ is taken to be above r. Although there can be many different r's and ρ's (r_i for $i = 1, \ldots, n$, and ρ_j for $j = 1, \ldots, s$), and each r_i, ρ_j, can also be dated $t = O, \ldots, T$, an analysis conducted in terms of such generality adds only elegant complexity which may obscure the main lines of the argument. We shall therefore continue to regard r and ρ as single magnitudes, and not as vectors or matrices, except to comment on the proposals of others.

Writing $PV_a(B)$, then, as a shorthand for the Present Value of the stream of benefits (some of which can be net outlays, or negative benefits) when discounted at rate a, the four type-(a) criteria to be reviewed are as follows:

(1) $PV_r(B) > K_0$

(2) $PV_\rho(B) > K_0$

(3) $PV_\rho(B) > K_0$ where $p = \displaystyle\sum_{i=1}^{n} w_i r_i + \sum_{j=1}^{s} w_j \rho_j$ and $\Sigma w_i + \Sigma w_j = 1$

(4) $PV_q(B) > K_0$ $\rho > q > r$

Criterion (1), the staple of textbook instruction, is superficially plausible enough. If r is the common rate of time preference then the community is indifferent as between receiving the stream of benefits (B) = $(B_0, \ldots, B_T)$, and receiving its present value $PV_r(B)$. It is then convenient to rank the community's preference between any set of alternative investment streams, $B^1, B^2, \ldots, B^g$, each of which results from an initial outlay K, according to the relative magnitudes of $PV_r(B^1)$, $PV_r(B^2)$, $\ldots$, $PV_r(B^g)$. In particular, any project having a benefit stream that meets the (1) criterion tells us that the present value of that stream of benefits exceeds the present value of its costs and, therefore, represents a potential Pareto improvement for the community.

The rationale for criterion (2), treated in Eckstein's paper of 1957 and also advocated in Baumol's two papers (1968) and (1969), is no less plausible. For it suggests that if funds equal to K_0 are to be spent on a public project, the average yield from the project should be no less than the ρ per annum that the sum K_0 could fetch if it were placed instead in the private investment sector. If, over the period, the benefit stream yields on the average more than ρ, then the $PV_\rho(B) > K_0$ criterion is met, and there is a net gain from adopting the investment project.

Clearly, the (3) criterion is a generalization of (1) and (2) extended to cover all the different r's and ρ's in the economy. Since the weights, the w's, are the fractions of K contributed by the separable components of reduced consumption and of reduced private investment, the resultant weighted rate of return represents society's actual opportunity yield per dollar of investing a sum K in a public project. In general then, p will vary according to whether K is raised by tax finance, loan finance, or as a mixture of both. Although (3) was originally proposed by Krutilla and Eckstein (1958), it was advanced again by Harberger (1968) in connection with a rise in interest rates in response to government borrowing which is supposed to check both private investment and consumption. With such a weighted discount rate Harberger claimed (erroneously, as we shall see) that "the so-called reinvestment problem disappears" (p. 308).

The well-known Arrow-Lind paper (1970) produced criterion (4) as a modification of the popular (2) criterion, $PV_\rho(B) > K_0$ when, for their analysis, ρ can be taken as the highest actuarial rate of return corresponding, say, to the riskiest private investment. Accepting without criticism their argument that the risks associated with public projects, when divided among a large population of taxpayers, are felt by each taxpayer to be negligible—in contrast to the sense of risk apprehended by the private investor—a risk premium of $(\rho-q)$ can be attributed to the private investor. Inasmuch then as the investor is indifferent between the riskiest private investment at ρ and a virtual certain return of q on his money, a potential Pareto improvement is effected if funds are removed from this private investment, so forgoing ρ, and placed instead in public investment at a yield greater than q. Hence the proposed criterion $PV_q(B) > K_0$.

However, as they acknowledge in their reply (1972) to critical comments, the crucial assumption on which their criterion rested—that the set of public investment projects excludes opportunities in the private investment sector—did not receive explicit emphasis. And if the assumption is lifted, and the government, permitted to undertake private-sector investment, can avail itself again of the yield ρ, the $PV_\rho(B) > K_0$ criterion comes into its own again.

Although the (4) criterion is an interesting variation on the type (a) criterion, in other respects it is, as stands, subject to the fundamental criticism of this sort of criterion.

Since the demonstration that follows applies to any of the four criteria, we can use $PV_p(B) > K_0$ to represent the generic type.

Given the stream of benefits $B_0, B_1, \ldots, B_T$, the above criterion is explicated as

$$\sum_{T=0}^{T} \frac{B_t}{(1 + p)^t} > K_0 \ldots \tag{1}$$

By multiplying through by a scalar $(1 + p)^T$, we obtain the equivalent inequality

$$\sum_{t=0}^{T} B_t(1 + p)^{T-t} > K_0(1 + p)^T \ldots \tag{2}$$

which can be summarized as $TV_p(B)>(K)_p'$ where $TV_p(B)$ stands for the terminal value of the stream of benefits when compounded forward to T at the rate p, and $(K)_p$ stands for the terminal value of the outlay K_0 when it is also compounded forward to T and rate p.

If and only if $PV_p(B) > K_0$ does $TV_p(B) > (K)_p$: one form of the criterion that is, entails the other. But the latter form is more revealing. For it makes clear that in order for the criterion to be met, the sum of each of the benefits, $B_0, B_1, \ldots, B_t, \ldots$, *when wholly invested* and *reinvested to time T at rate p* must exceed a sum equal to K when wholly and continually reinvested at p to time T. Such a criterion is clearly applicable when *in fact* both the benefits and the outlays are to be used in exactly this way. If, however, they are *not* to be used in this way—and it is unlikely that they will be—then a criterion based on such a supposition can seriously mislead. Certainly this $PV_p(B) > K_0$ criterion is misleading when it is applied to public investment projects without information in each case about the actual disposal of the returns to the project, and without information about the uses to which the sum K_0 would have been put were it not used as initial outlay for the project.

To illustrate, suppose it to be the case that the initial outlay K_0 required by a particular public investment is to be drawn entirely from the private investment sector where it would otherwise have been reinvested at p to reach the value $(K)_p$ at time T, whereas the project's benefits are to be entirely consumed as they emerged over time. The value of these benefits will grow over time only at r, the rate of time preference, reaching a total value of $TV_r(B)$ at time T.[5] Now, if the sum $TV_r(B)$ is smaller than $(K)_p$, the project is rejected on a Pareto criterion. Society, that is, will be better off leaving the sum K in the private sector than employing it on the public project. However, since p > r, the hypothetical sum $TV_p(B)$ exceeds $TV_r(B)$ and therefore $TV_p(B)$ can exceed $(K)_p$. If so, the project is approved on the $PV_p(B) > K$ criterion even though it is rejected on a Pareto criterion.

Let us return now to the criterion $PV_r(B) > K_0$, regarded as a limiting case of the generic $PV_p(B) > K_0$ criterion. Its transformation into the $TV_r(B) > (K)_r$ form, however, enables us to appreciate immediately the sufficient conditions required for its valid application; namely, that all the returns from the project be wholly consumed as they occur and that the sum K_0 be raised entirely from current consumption. Similarly, transforming the other limiting case, $PV_\rho(B) > K_0$, into the form $TV_\rho(B) > (K)_\rho$ enables us also to appreciate at once that its Pareto validity is assured if, in fact, it is applied to a case in which the benefits, as they occur, are wholly invested and reinvested in the private investment sector at prevailing yield ρ until the terminal date T, and if the sum K_0 raised from the private sector would have been wholly invested and reinvested also at yield ρ until T.

Put otherwise, the correct terminal value of a project's benefit stream, and the correct terminal value of the opportunity cost of its outlay, are both functions of three vectors r, ρ, θ or, in the simplest possible case, of three variables, r, ρ, and θ, where θ is the fraction of any income or investment return that is reinvested in the private sector. In contrast a criterion $PV_p(B) > K_0$ makes the terminal value both of the benefit stream and the outlay a function only of p, whether p is equal to r, or to ρ, or to a weighted sum of r and ρ.

To anticipate a little, the above stringent conditions for the Pareto validity of the type (a) criterion are sufficient. They are not strictly necessary however. For instance, where the consumption-investment ratio is the same for all the benefits and also for the outlay, then a (b) type criterion can, as we shall see later, be reduced to the $PV_r(B) > K_0$ criterion.[6]

Such simplifications are very agreeable. But one can go further. Under the terminal value approach, there is no need to discount at all. All that matters are the relevant rates at which returns are to be compounded forward to T. Indeed, once this is done, the terminal values can then be discounted at r, or at ρ, or at any conceivable rate, without any alteration occurring in the ranking or in the criterion.

In order to complete this part of the critique, we must also reexamine criteria based on IRR, the internal rate of return. There is a seeming advantage in being able to use the IRR for ranking projects without reference to the prevailing yields or interest rates in the economy. Nonetheless, it is not possible to accept or reject projects on the basis of IRR alone. For this purpose, the IRR has to be compared with whatever is believed to be the relevant opportunity rate.

In fact, letting λ stand for the IRR, the internal-rate-return criteria corresponding to the DPV criteria (1) through (4) are (1') $\lambda > r$, (2') $\lambda > p$, (3') $\lambda > p$, and (4') $\lambda > q$.

As a ranking device, the IRR has fallen into disfavor among economists, chiefly because there can, in general, be more than one IRR for a given investment stream.[7] However, this is the less important reason. The more important reason is that, even in the common case in which all benefits are positive, the unique IRR calculated for an investment stream does *not* accord with the true average rate of return over time of the value of that stream. In fact, as conventionally defined, the IRR when used as a criterion has the same defect as the DPV criterion; namely, that a reinvestment rate is entailed that has no necessary relation to the actual rates involved in the particular case.

This defect follows from the standard definition of the IRR as that λ for which

$$\sum_{t=0}^{T} \frac{B_t}{(1 + \lambda)} t = K \quad .$$

For multiplying through by $(1 + \lambda)^T$ we obtain

$$\sum_{t=0}^{T} B_t(1 + \lambda)^{T-t} = K(1 + \lambda)^T \tag{3}$$

So explicated, (3) reveals the IRR to be defined as the rate which, when used to compound the benefits forward to T produces a terminal value equal to outlay K when this outlay is also compounded forward at that rate. The resulting terminal value of the benefits is therefore calculated on the implicit assumption that they are wholly invested and reinvested to T at the rate λ—irrespective, that is, of whether this calculated λ is less than r or greater than ρ. Since in any actual project, the disposal of the benefits depends upon behavioral and institutional factors, the actual terminal value of the benefit stream is, again in the simplest case, a function of r, ρ, and θ, and not, in general, of λ alone. In other words, before we can calculate λ as an average rate of growth of the initial investment K over the period to T, we must be able to calculate independently the actual terminal value of the benefit stream by reference to r, ρ, and θ.

A procedure that is free from the above defects is that proposed by Mishan (1967), one that transforms an investment stream, $-K_0$, B_0, B_1, . . . B_T into the stream $-K_0$, O, O, . . . , TV(B). Of the initial return B_0, the amount consumed cB_0 is compounded forward at the relevant rates of time preference, say r, to the terminal date T. The remaining amount sB_0 being divided among the different investment opportunities that are actually anticipated according to one of, say, two alternative political directives, either (1) each investment component is compounded, at its yield, to the following year when it is treated as a receipt along with any other income, or else (2) the investment component is taken to yield equal returns for all successive periods up to T, with the original investment component being included at T. Whether the (1) or (2) assumption is adopted, the sum resulting from the investment component at t = 1 is designated ΔR_1.

Thus at time t = 1, we have returns $B_1 + \Delta R_1$ to dispose of. Again the c proportion of this total $(B_1 + \Delta R_1)$ that is consumed at t = 1 is compounded to T at the rate r, the remainder being allocated among the various investment opportunities anticipated in consequence of the existing political and institutional constraints. Continuing in this way until T, the original benefit stream is transformed into its terminal value.[8]

A valid ranking of two mutually exclusive projects, X and Y, both of which may be rejected however, requires not only a common terminal date T but also a common initial outlay of K_0. This latter requirement is not restrictive. If, say, Y's initial outlay is 20 less than that of X, the 20 left over from the Y investment can be treated as generating a stream of returns in the private sector of the economy having a terminal value that is to be added to that of the Y stream of benefits.

As for the social opportunity cost of K_0 itself, this is allowed for simply by treating the stream of returns it would generate if left in the private sector, on a par with projects X and Y. For identification, we refer to this alternative as the "reference stream" Z. Using the same rules this stream compounds to terminal value TV(Z).

In this way we end up with three terminal values, TV(X), TV(Y), and TV(Z) from which to choose, all generated by initial outlay K_0. No further operation is required for ranking purposes. If both TV(X) and TV(Y) are less than TV(Z), neither public project is acceptable on a Pareto criterion.

If instead, say $TV(X) > TV(Y) > TV(Z)$, then $TV(X)$ is chosen on the Pareto criterion. Any further operation that is acceptable, say, reducing the terminal values to present social values, to present benefit-cost ratios, or to internal rates of return cannot alter this basic ranking.

Thus, corresponding present values for X, Y, and Z, are obtained simply by multiplying each of their terminal values by a scalar, $(1 + r)^{-T}$. Corresponding present value benefit-cost ratios are obtained by multiplying them by a scalar $(1 + r)^{-T}/K_0$. As for the corresponding IRRs, when defined in accordance with the basic concept of an average rate of increase over time of the initial investment K_0, and therefore as that unique value of λ for which $\frac{TV(B)}{(1 + \lambda)} T = K_0$, the resulting equations

$$\frac{TV(X)}{(1 + \lambda_X)} T = \frac{TV(Y)}{(1 + \lambda_Y)} T = \frac{TV(Z)}{(1 + \lambda_Z)} T = K_0$$

entails the ranking $\lambda_X > \lambda_Y > \lambda_Z$.

The Legitimacy of Using DPV in Ranking Intergenerational Public Projects

Extending the simplifying assumption that the time rate of preference r is common to all members of n successive generations that are affected by a public project, the condition under which it is Pareto valid to use DPV or CTV (Compounded Terminal Value) is the existence of a common point of overlap; that is, a point of time at which each person affected is alive.

This can be illustrated in the simplest case of two persons from different generations, each one being capable of making rational decisions for 60 years, whose rational lives overlap by, say, 20 years. Let person A be alive in this sense from year 0 to year 60, and receive a stream of benefits (positive and negative) that on balance raises his welfare. Let person B be alive from year 40 to year 100 and receive a stream of benefits that on balance reduces his welfare. Since r is the rate of time preference common to both, A's benefit stream can be transformed into an aggregate value of, say, 100 at year 0, or into an equivalent value of $100(1 + r)^t$ for any year t up to year 60. Inasmuch as he is indifferent as between all such sums $100(1 + r)^t$, for t equal to 0, 1, . . . , 60, such sums can be represented by a continuous line sloping upward from year 0 to year 60. Such a continuous line may then be interpreted as a time indifference curve, as shown in figure 2, with aggregate net benefit—whether on balance gain or loss—measured vertically on a logarithmic scale.[9]

If r is such that $1 is worth $2 in 20 years' time, person B whose stream is equivalent, say, to a net loss of 600 in year 60 is indifferent between this loss and a loss of 300 in year 40, and a loss of 2,400 in year 100.

As depicted in figure 2, at any point of time between years 40 and 60,

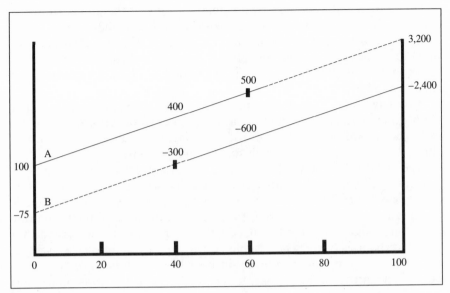

FIGURE 2

the values placed by persons A and B on their respective net benefit streams are such that the benefit-loss ratio is 4/3. This benefit-loss ratio, being greater than unity, meets a Pareto criterion (A's gain is such that, via costless redistribution, both persons could be made better off), without violating the basic maxim. Adopting this benefit-loss (or benefit-cost) ratio as criterion, discounting to year 0, or alternatively, compounding to year 100, simply multiplies numerator and denominator by a common scalar which, therefore, does not alter the benefit-cost ratio of 4/3.

It follows that if a common point of overlap exists among all individuals of the successive generations, the use of DPV or CTV is indeed Pareto valid. Per contra, if there is no common point of overlap then, since the basic maxim is no longer met, neither can be the Pareto criterion. There may well be a large number of overlapping generations over, say, a 1,000-year period. But in such a case there is no direct way of reaching agreement between all persons of those generations about their respective magnitudes of net benefits at some common point of time. If, for example, a third person, D, beginning his rational life in year 100, values the benefit stream conferred on him by the project at $1,000 in year 100, then he is certainly not indifferent as between $1,000 in year 100 and $1,000(1 + r)$^{-40}$—or $250—in year 60, since he was not alive in year 60. Nor, for that matter will person A be indifferent as between a net receipt of $800 in year 60 and a net receipt of $3,200 in year 100, since he will not be alive in year 100.

Hence, in a time context, the basic maxim requiring economists to accept as their data people's own valuations only of the goods and bads resulting from an economic change poses a problem whenever the time span of the project covers a number of generations. For each person's valuation is now dated over his rational lifetime, and there is no longer a common date at which each person's valuation can be directly compared and the algebraic sum of their valuations determined.

Two ways of getting around this difficulty have been proposed: (1) that of introducing such "externalities" as altruism or a concern for people yet to be born, and (2) that of introducing intergeneration interventions, either directly or through some institutional mechanism.

The first, (1), it is worth noting, is generally not resorted to in the conventional cost-benefit analysis. Even if incorporated, such externalities cannot be supposed to take such magnitudes as to justify extending the time rate of preference for each person to cover all the time prior to his birth and subsequent to his death. In any case, an admission that such externalities have to be assumed for the intergeneration case reveals the particularity of this recourse, since such externalities are "unnecessary" in the intrageneration case. In the latter case, it can be assumed, and often is, that each person is wholly a selfish being.

The second way around the difficulty, (2), is worth commenting on, if only because the conclusions drawn have been misinterpreted.

With respect to this second line of reasoning, let us consider in turn two possibilities; A, that of government agreements as between generations to transform an existing intergeneration stream of costs and benefits so that, in fact, net benefit comparisons can be made at a common point of time, and B, the use of market mechanisms, in particular investment opportunities for transforming an existing intergeneration stream into one that does, in fact, meet a Pareto criterion.

A. Government Agreements Between Generations

To illustrate the A case, let a situation involving three persons, X, Y, and Z be that depicted in figure 3 which clearly has no common point of overlap. Of course, the economist might choose year 60 for the comparison of the three persons. But since he has no warrant for reducing the -100 of person Z at year 80 to anything smaller (absolutely) than -100 in any year prior to his birth in year 80, he might propose to use -100 also in year 60. If he does this, the algebraic total for the three persons in year 60 comes to -10, and the project appears inadmissible. If, instead, he uses exactly the same procedure in choosing year 80—and therefore values person X's net gain of 60 in year 60 as equal to a gain of 60 also in year 80 (year 80 being 20 years after X's death), the algebraic total for the three persons is now plus 20, and the project would appear now to be admissible.

In this situation, the economist might envisage government interven-

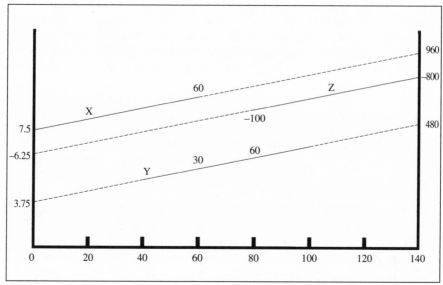

FIGURE 3

tion taking the following form: instead of X having 60 and Y having 30 in year 60 (Z not yet born), we could transfer 60 from X to Y. And this 90 now received by Y in year 60 is equivalent for Y to 180 in year 80. In year 80 we then transfer 100 from Y to Z. The net result is that X and Z are no better or worse off than before, while Y is better off by 80. A Pareto improvement has thereby been achieved.

Two comments will help us to interpret this proposed way around the problem. (1) If costless transfers were indeed possible then every hypothetical improvement could indeed be converted into an actual Pareto improvement. Whenever the Pareto criterion were met then, costlessly, every one would actually be made better off, all the conventional paradoxes would vanish, nobody would have a legitimate grumble, and we should live happily in a "first best" world. Nobody takes this easy way out in allocative problems in the context of comparative statics, and there is no warrant for taking such an escape route from the problem when chronological time, particularly generational time, is introduced.

(2) Some economists might want to argue, however, that (in our example above) allowing these transfers as between individuals over time to be hypothetical, then a test of hypothetical compensation is met—which is to say one of potential Pareto improvement. In consequence, if the use of DPV results in a net benefit, a Pareto criterion is met. But this reasoning is facile and misleading for two reasons.

First, in our example, X, Y, and Z were persons, whereas they ought to be generations of persons. For example, the positive gain of 60 for the X generation in year 60 has now to be conceived as an algebraic total, the excess of gains over losses for the X generation in year 60. Within the X generation, that is, hypothetical costless redistribution has already to be invoked to warrant our use of the positive gain of 60. Secondly, the *hypothetical* transfers as between generations X, Y,and Z can no longer be justified by reference to those considerations (i) to (iv) which were adduced for an existing generation earlier. These four considerations, it was there argued, might reasonably be held to give rise to an ethical consensus in favor of adopting a potential Pareto improvement by the members of a given generation, or of a society at a point of time. Among these considerations were the activities of the welfare state, via progressive tax structures and other instruments of redistribution, which tend to diffuse the net gains from a public project which meets a Pareto criterion among the members of that society. However, it can *not* be taken for granted that these or other considerations would operate to secure a consensus among the members of all successive generations involved that a public project which, via *hypothetical* intergeneration transfers, could show a net gain ought to be adopted.

The above two reasons for rejecting the proposed argument can be cast in different forms.

If the transfers envisaged were *not* hypothetical but actually took place, then no generation would, on balance, be left worse off and one or more generations would, on balance, be left better off. In that event, a potential Pareto improvement would be possible among the members of the one, or more, generations that, on balance, were left better off. Thus, only when actual intergeneration transfers of this sort take place, is the conventional Pareto criterion met.

When we now face the fact that the possible transfers described do *not* actually take place, but are hypothetical only, this case A line of reasoning, by which the use of DPV is to be justified, can be seen to meet a *hypothetical* potential Pareto improvement—or *potential* potential Pareto improvement. In sum, this A operation advanced by economists for favoring the use of DPV transpires to be one that can be split into two hypothetical transfers; one the familiar hypothetical redistribution among the members of an existing community or generation; the other, a hypothetical redistribution also as between the successive generations themselves.

B. The Use of Market Mechanisms

The introduction of investment opportunities gives rise to much the same reasoning and reaches the same sort of conclusions. Adopting the rate r as reflecting also the rate of return on current investment, the sum 60 received by person X in year 60 could be invested at r for 20 years to compound to the sum 120. From the 120 so accumulated, person Z can be paid 100. Thus Z is left as well off as he was without the project (as is the case also with person X who dies 20 years earlier), while person Y is left with 80 in year 80. And this result is believed to meet a Pareto criterion.

The correct interpretation of the above simple example follows that of the preceding example. However, what is involved can be brought out more starkly yet by adopting the somewhat extreme example used by Freeman (1977) in order to illustrate his assertion that, in project evaluation, it makes economic sense to discount to the present the value of damages expected to be borne by generations who will be alive many thousands of years from today. Thus, a colossal amount of damage, equal in value to $D, to be experienced in 100,000 year's time should, according to Freeman, be discounted to the present to equal, say, $80 today. If the immediate benefits of such a project are equal to $100, then the benefit-cost ratio exceeds unity and the project is to be regarded as economically efficient.

Freeman goes on to argue that the justification for this conclusion resides in the fact that if the $80 were invested today, and continually reinvested at the discount rate for 100,000 years, it would compound exactly to this sum $D. The beneficiaries from this sum $D would then be able exactly to compensate those destined to suffer the loss of $D, leaving a net gain of $20 for today's generation. According to Freeman, a potential Pareto improvement is thereby met, as required by economists.

Now with respect to the *hypothetical* time stream devised by Freeman, a potential Pareto improvement would indeed be met. But clearly this time stream is not the original stream that conferred a gain on the present generation and inflicted damages equal to $D on generations living 100,000 years from today. What his argument amounts to, therefore, is the sanctioning of an actual intergeneration project that, by recourse to investment opportunities, could be changed into a different intergeneration project, which different intergeneration project could then meet the conventional hypothetical compensation test. Since both a hypothetical project and a hypothetical compensation test are involved in his example, he also is, in effect, ascribing allocative virtue to an economic change that meets a *potential* potential Pareto improvement.

Extending the argument for illustrative purposes, if instead a colossal benefit equal to $B were to be conferred on some group that would be alive in 100,000 years' time by investing today the sum of $80, the project would also be approved on Freeman's logic if the discounted present value of this $B were equal, say, to $100. For although future generations cannot pass benefits backward in time to their predecessors, it is always possible for the existing generation to consume $100 of the existing capital stock which, were it not so consumed, could have compounded to $B in 100,000 years. Hence, if such action were taken, the generation alive in 100,000 years would also suffer a loss of potential value equal to $D, which loss would exactly offset the benefit of $B conferred on it by the project. Future gains and losses would thus cancel out, leaving only a loss to the present generation of $80 (equal to the outlay on the project) and a gain to it of $100 from consuming that much of the existing capital stock which otherwise would have been passed on to the future. This contrived *hypothetical* time stream would, therefore, also meet a potential Pareto improvement.

In general, then, by appropriate intervention at points of time over the intergenerational period, an original investment project whose stream of benefits and outlays occurring over the distant future can be discounted to yield a positive net benefit today is one that can also be converted into a hypothetical project that—by using the rate r as a means also of compounding sums forward to the terminal date—would indeed meet a potential Pareto improvement.

Again, however, there are now, in these examples, two sorts of hypothetically costless transfers involved, not just one. The first has reference to the sums assumed to be taken from earlier generations which are invested for the time necessary to produce an algebraic sum of benefits that is positive at some future date, say, the terminal year. The second has reference to the assumed redistribution of this positive algebraic sum among members of the community at that time so as to make "every one" better off. Since the DPV method espoused by Freeman in this intergeneration context is *not* being regarded as contingent upon an agreement, between governments of all generations involved, actually to invest the receipts of earlier generations with the object of presenting later generations with sums calculated to offset the losses they are to suffer, this imaginary transfer between generations is clearly as hypothetical as the subsequent redistribution of net gains among members of the community at any point of time.

Once more then, Freeman's use of DPV in an intergeneration context would realize *not* a potential Pareto improvement, as he claims, but a *potential* potential Pareto improvement. A consensus on the acceptability of the ordinary potential Pareto improvement among members of a given generation may be presumed to exist. Moreover, it can be assumed that at the time of completion of the change redistribution for actual Pareto improvement is feasible. In contrast, a consensus among members of all generations involved in the long-lived investment project may *not* be presumed inasmuch as there are no mechanisms which can be counted upon to diffuse the net benefits among this intergenerational community; nothing, in effect, to prevent later generations having to shoulder heavy burdens while earlier generations reap benefits. Moreover, the potential redistribution across generations becomes infeasible at the completion of the change if the compensating investment is not undertaken at the beginning of the change.

Bailey (1978) has suggested that the behavioral condition of hyperrationality, along with normal market mechanisms, ensure that a discounting approach leads to actual Pareto improvement across generations. This observation, depending on the plausibility of the behavioral condition, would tend, of course, to strengthen the ethical appeal of the discounting approach. We can illustrate the idea and our misgivings about it with a simple example.

Smith and d'Arge (1978) estimate the benefits associated with CFMs for the single use as a propellant for insect repellent sprays, for personal use in the United States, to be $5 billion (p. 32). Suppose for the sake of illustration that these benefits are concentrated in the first year (the "present generation") and after this first year there will be a perfect substitute at no additional market cost and with no environmental hazard, so that future benefits of CFMs, as a propellant for insect repellents, are zero. Suppose further that these CFMs released to the atmosphere remain latent, in manifest effect, for 100 years, but then in the 100th year there is a 1 percent chance of catastrophic effect in which the entire world population is destroyed. This last supposition is indeed somewhat extreme—it appears that scientists accept nonnegligible probabilities, of 1 percent or so, of enormous catastrophes associated with the continued growth, 10 percent or more worldwide, of CFMs—but no one is forecasting ultimate catastrophe from a single and minor use of CFMs over a limited period of production. Nonetheless, it sets out the decision problem more sharply to consider the illustrative case of an insect propellant which entails a 1 percent probability of ultimate catastrophe a century hence.

Under a discounting or type (a) criterion, the first step is to calculate the expected value of the potential loss. Assuming that the world population a century hence would be about 10 billion, and taking a value of life of $500,000,[10] the expected value of the potential catastrophe is $(0.01)(10^{10})(5 \times 10^5) = \$5 \times 10^{13}$ or $50 trillion, valued by those living in year 100.[11] Next this expected value is discounted back to the present at 11 percent, the rate recommended by Bailey (1978) for the ozone problem (p. 5), with the resulting present value of 1.5×10^9. This present value cost, $1.5 billion, is less than the present benefits of $5 billion, associated with the use of CFM spray repellents. In fact the benefit-cost ratio is 3.4 to one, in favor of the environmental gamble.

Some, including ourselves, will find this simple calculation and conclusion unsatisfactory, on the grounds that the advantage of a spray mosquito repellent over a lotion repellent is too trivial to justify the risk of an ultimate catastrophe. On the contrary, Bailey defends the methodology of this discount approach, on the grounds that the future would actually be better off under the gamble than without it. The idea is as follows: Suppose that CFMs are banned for the use of insect repellent spray. Present consumers would be faced with a decline of $5 billion in consumption. If they were hyperrational they would act to preserve their original consumption pattern, generating $5 billion worth of consumption through other consumption expenditures. With the aggregate consumption stream maintained intact, the $5 billion comes out of natural savings (Bailey [1978] appendix C, p. 9). Each year the consumption stream is maintained, so that this $5 billion is compounded forward as an investment forgone. Thus at the end of a century there would be, under the ban of CFMs, $(5 \times 10^9)(1.11)^{100}$ worth of less resource, compared with what there would have been without the ban. With the ban the future avoids the catastrophic risk, valued at $50 trillion, but also is $(5 \times 10^9)(1.11)^{100} = 1.7 \times 10^{14}$ or $170 trillion poorer in resources than it would have been without the ban. Thus, the argument goes, the future would actually be better off without the ban and with the ozone risk. For in the case of no ban in year zero, the future in year 100 could apply $50 trillion to life-saving programs, reducing the aggregate risk of early death as much as the ozone depletion increases the risk. This risk of ozone depletion being offset, the future would still have $120 trillion left over, and thus would be better off than if the present had banned CFMs for insect sprays and correspondingly reduced its investment stream. Moreover, the present would also be better off without the ban. With respect to its own consumption it would be indifferent, for by the hyperrationality assumption it would act to maintain its consumption stream intact. But because the ban requires compulsion, presumably the present is better off without the ban ([Bailey 1978] appendix C, p. 10). Thus the interests of the present and future harmonize. Both are better off without the ban than with it. And the decision not to ban is an actual Pareto improvement, compared with the alternative of the ban. If the discounted expected value of the risk had turned out to be more than the present benefits of the spray, and enough more to compensate the present for compulsive regulation, a similar argument could be constructed leading to actual Pareto superiority of the ban.

If hyperrationality (the assumption that the present acts to preserve its consumption stream intact) described the actual behavioral condition of the economy, we would be prepared to accept the above analysis and we would find the ethical appeal of discounting, at a rate equal to the opportunity cost of capital, (criterion type (a)(2)) greatly strengthened. Moreover, if hyperrationality were an immutable condition, there would be no conflict of interest between present and future. What is good for the present would also be good for the future and there would be no need to consider the problem of intertemporal equity. However, we find the condition of hyperrationality, which harmonizes the interests of present and future, to be implausible.

Consider that the U.S. GNP is growing at about 3 percent a year (without the ban). In a century we might expect it to increase about twentyfold (1.03^{100}), or to about 20 trillion. Thus it is not possible for the ban to reduce GNP by 170 trillion. The point is that it is possible for a marginal investment to grow at 11 percent for a few years, but it is not possible for it to grow at such a rate for many years if the entire economy is growing at a substantially lower rate. Over a long period, something must give and it appears that the assumption of hyperrationality must give. Otherwise it would lead us to believe that if hula hoops were banned in the 1950s the entire economy would be destroyed a century hence.

We can consider two other behavioral conditions which might be more plausible than hyperrationality, for the very long run. For the first, we assume that if CFMs for insect sprays were banned most of the reduction would come out of consumption and a little out of forgone investment. If forgone opportunities to consume and invest fall into the same pattern as consumer spending of income, we would expect about 90 percent to come out of present consumption and 10 percent out of investment (a "Keynesian savings rule"). Thus we take 10 percent of the $5 billion and compound that forward at 10 percent of 11 percent for a century. The resulting loss of investment resource a century hence is then $(5 \times 10^9)(.1)(1.011)^{100}$ or $1.5 billion. If the "Keynesian savings rule" describes the actual behavioral condition of the economy, it is clear that the interests of the future lie with the ban. From the perspective of people in year 100, the ban prevents the catastrophic risk valued by them at $50 trillion at a modest cost, to them, of $1.5 billion. Of course this is not the whole story. The present is somewhat worse off with the ban, as its consumption is reduced by $4.5 billion, and each "generation," or year, between zero and 100 is worse off by a somewhat lesser amount, somewhere on to the order of about $1 billion. The two possible paths, under the assumption of a "Keynesian savings rule," are depicted in figure 4. One entire path can be viewed as the intertemporal opportunity cost of the other. As can be seen, figure 4 indicates a conflict of interest between generations. The first generation is better off without the ban and the generation living in year 100 is better off with the ban.

The second behavioral condition is the polar opposite case of the condition of hyperrationality. For this condition we assume that the $5 billion comes entirely out of this year's consumption. Thus there is no effect of the ban except for reduced consumption the first year and reduced risk in the last year (fig. 5). While this assumption is no doubt unrealistic for major environmental regulations affecting consumer purchases, it has some plausibility for minor changes. For example, it would lead us to believe that if hula hoops were banned in the 1950s there would be no discernible effect on the economy a century hence. Similarly, if consumers were faced with the prospect of liquid insect sprays instead of aerosols it

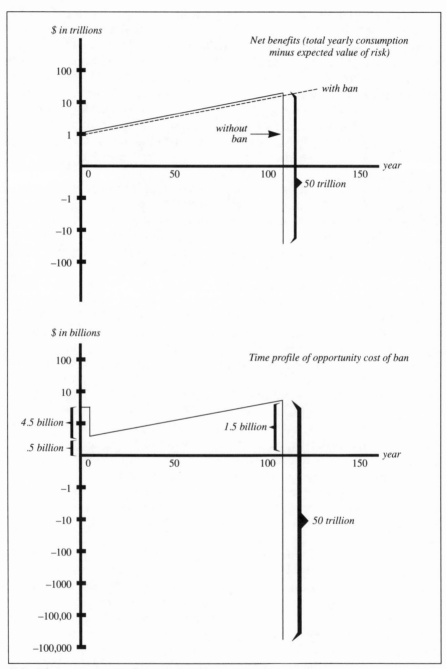

FIGURE 4. Keynesian Savings Rule Behavioral Assumption

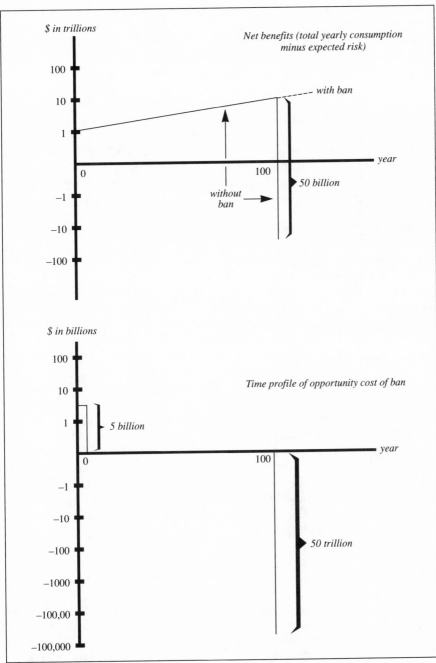

FIGURE 5. Behavioral Assumption that Cost of Regulation Diminishes First Period
Consumption Only

seems somewhat plausible that there would be no profound effect on the economy a century hence (except for the change in environmental risk). In fact it even appears conceivable that if consumers are faced with the slight extra exertion of liquid rather than spray insect repellents, the economy, 100 years hence, might actually be modestly stimulated. Thus, although this last behavioral condition is the polar opposite of hyperrationality, at least for minor environmental regulations it appears more plausible than hyperrationality, applied to the very long run.

The virtue of this last behavioral condition is its simplicity. It shows the conflict of interests between generations most starkly, and it may be the implicit assumption people have in mind when they reject discounting altogether and affirm that the present should not impose a 1 percent risk of ultimate catastrophe upon the future for a mere $5 billion benefit to the present.

However, this last behavioral condition appears to us to be less realistic than the "Keynesian saving" pattern, which is a mixed case lying between the two polar extremes. (As can be seen, the implications of the second two behavioral assumptions are not far different, as indicated in figures 4 and 5, compared with figure 6.) In the mixed case, discounting still has an important role, in defining intertemporal opportunity costs of one whole path, or intertemporal distribution, of consumption and risk burden.[12] In any case, once the behavioral assumptions are made explicit, it is useful to construct, as far as possible, the intertemporal distribution of costs and benefits with and without regulation. In doing so, infeasible implications, such as those derived by straightforward discounting at the short-term marginal opportunity cost of capital, for a century or more, can be avoided. In dealing with long time horizons discounting exercises depend critically upon the underlying assumptions and empirical conditions and it is easy to be led to nonsensical results.

For the ozone case and many others like it, with immediate benefits and long delayed costs, we believe that intergenerational conflicts of interest are an inherent part of the decision problem. In these circumstances, the economist is impelled to face directly the intergenerational distributional implications of such projects.

4. The Question of Intergenerational Equity

Since it is unlikely that a stream of returns from a public project having significant welfare effects on future generations will, in fact, be transformed via institutional mechanisms into one that can meet a conventional Pareto criterion, the question of intergenerational equity has to be faced squarely. Certainly if an ethical consensus is the basis of any adopted economic criterion, an intergeneration consensus for the use of DPV (or

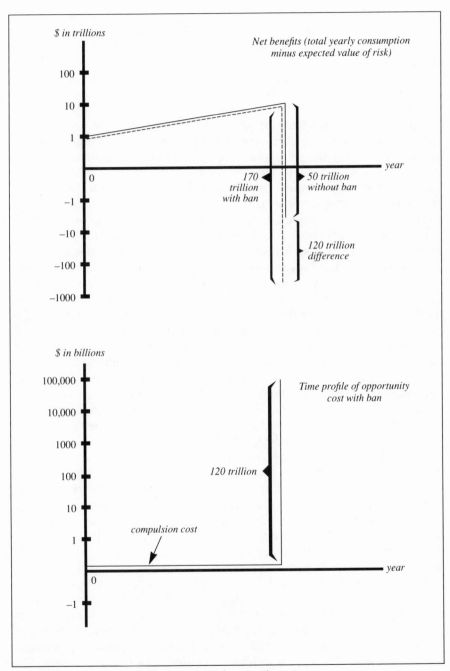

FIGURE 6. Hyperrationality Behavioral Assumption

(Note that this calculation implies that GNP in year 100 with the ban is less than zero.)

CTV) is unlikely, as indicated in the preceding section, since it would entail acceptance by later generations of smaller weights being attached to their valuations—whether of benefits or losses—than to the valuations of earlier generations.

Thus, although the economist does, from time to time, extend his conventional maximization techniques even so far as to resolve the problem of distribution over generational time, unless the results of his chosen set of assumptions—whenever the exercise is not merely taxonomic—yields a distributional pattern over time that accords with that to which our present society believes is just—for all the affected generations—his conclusions will, or should, go unheeded. However, one cannot suppose the economist to be wholly uninfluenced by what is held to be just and proper in this respect. For the results of much of the economic literature on the subject of an optimal distribution of the product over generational time conforms with the popular belief that a just distribution is one that yields constant per capita income over generational time—at least, whenever the populations of successive generations remain unchanged. A somewhat different version of this idea is that the means for future well-being be at least as good as our own, thus focusing our attention on the future condition of the resource base and its ultimate renewability, and the portfolio of catastrophic risks that are passed from one generation to another.[13]

The appeal of an equal division among all members of a community of the fruits of their collective efforts rests ultimately on a philosophical view, or rather an interpretation of the world or, in the last resort, a factual judgment; namely that the material success of a person depends predominantly or entirely on factors outside his control—these being, primarily, his endowments of ability and character, the family that rears him, the social environment in which he grows, the people he happens to meet, and the events that overtake him. A contrary interpretation of the world, one that regards such factors as minor influences and believes that personal deficiencies are personally remediable, would explain differences in income between persons (within a unified economic area at least) as arising, in the main, from differences in personal decisions about the efforts and sacrifices to be made over the span of their lives.[14] Those who believe that differences in income arise chiefly from such causes are not likely to accept an equal sharing of the society's product as a just distribution. They would tend rather to support the dictum, "to each according to his work."

The observations in the preceding paragraph, however, are germane to the distribution of the product within an existing society at some point of time, or over some short period of time. The case is different when we are to consider distributions over generational time, comparing the average real income or consumption in one generation with that in another. For whatever be our view of the fundamental factors explaining differences in existing incomes, we are likely to agree that an equal per capita real consumption for all generations is an eminently fair arrangement. Even if we take what seems today to be the less popular view, that one's income is primarily the fruit of one's effort, it is the average income of each generation, not the distribution within it, that is at issue. For, making the minor assumption (which can always be modified) that the average effort of each generation is about the same, the reasonable supposition that the distribution of relevant characteristics is much the same for one generation as for another impels us to the view that no generation deserves a right to enjoy a higher standard than any other.[15]

Irrespective, therefore, of the way each generation chooses to distribute its own outputs among its members, and irrespective also of the way we think any generation ought to distribute its outputs among them, we can agree on each generation's right to a natural resource and capital endowment that, with the same average effort, will produce for it the same per capita real consumption as that of any other generation. In sum, the ethical appeal of equality of per capita consumption over generational time is independent of a belief in the justice of an equal division of the product in any existing society, and is far more compelling.

Other approaches to this problem tend to reinforce this conclusion. One of the interesting aspects of the Arrow axioms, when placed within an intergenerational context, is that they define the class of nondictatorial social choice rules. All these rules have a common characteristic: if, in a finite number of generations all the others prefer option one to option two, then intergenerational social choice rules consistent with Arrow's axioms say that the first alternative should be chosen. As an abstract principle, this is not attractive. After all, the finite number of generations may be the next thousand generations, and an infinite majority may be all generations that follow. Yet the common sense of this idea may have appeal. Suppose this generation, the present, prefers A to B and, for the foreseeable future, every other generation prefers B to A, then consistent with the class of nondictatorial choice rules, B should be chosen. Roughly speaking this is like majority voting among a succession of generations. A single generation which imposes its will irreversibly in disregard of the preferences of all generations to follow is clearly acting as a dictator.

In a trivial sense the DPV, as a rule of intertemporal choice, is a dictatorship of the present. The present, after all, must choose in the absence of the future. In this trivial sense every decision rule is a dictatorship of the present. But suppose the present wishes to be fair to the future's interests, which may differ from the interests of the present because of the difference in vantage points in time, among other things. The present can estimate the future's interests concerning a decision made in the present, such as the control or noncontrol of ozone depletion. Moreover, the present can try to build its ideas of intertemporal fairness into the aggregation rules which combine the present's preferences with those of the future into a single decision or ranking of alternatives. And in considering the fairness or unfairness of intertemporal aggregation rules, some things can be said without any knowledge of the future's actual preferences. Some aggregation rules are so time biased to be considered unfair no matter what the actual pattern of intertemporal preferences.

In this latter sense, which accords with Arrow's technical definition of a dictator, we have just seen an example of an (incomplete) intergenerational social choice rule which is not a dictatorship of the present. This rule, which says that infinite majorities should be decisive over finite minorities, is illustrated in figure 7. In this case, the present generation prefers having project I to not having it, but every other generation prefers not having it. If the present abides by this rule, on the grounds that it values this version of intertemporal fairness more highly than the particular benefits associated with the project—convenience of freon hairsprays for example—the decision by the present—say to forgo from hairsprays—is clearly not a dictatorship of the present in the Arrow sense.

This aggregation rule may be called the "overtaking rule" because when it applies, eventually there comes a time when unanimously every later generation agrees on some course of action. The rule by itself is not time biased in the sense that a switch in time of one generation with another does not affect the outcome of any decision. However, the rule is clearly very future oriented. It is interesting to note that this rule follows from Arrow's axioms of transitivity, independence of irrelevant alternatives, and binary Pareto, none of which are future oriented in themselves, once these axioms are set in an intergenerational framework. The future orientation comes from the natural ordering of generations.

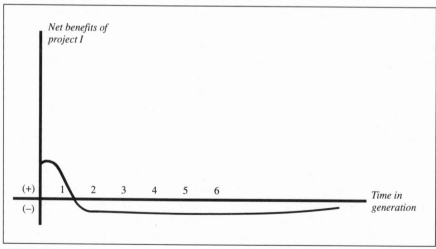

FIGURE 7

How, we may ask, does a discount rule (DPV) fit into this framework? In figure 7 it would be easy to draw a stream of net benefits such that for a discount rate greater than 2 percent the discounted net benefits were positive. Then the DPV would indicate acceptance of the project, even though only the present generation prefers it to its absence. This indeed appears to be a dictatorship of the present. Is this just a happenstance of the way figure 7 is drawn and the interpretation of "benefit"? Ferejohn and Page (1978) have shown that there is a close connection between a discount rule, with any interpretation and any non-zero discount rate, and dictatorship of the present in the Arrow sense. A necessary property of a discount rule is stationarity and this property added to transitivity, independence of irrelevant alternatives, and binary Pareto forces any resulting intertemporal social choice rule not only to be a dictatorship, but it picks out the present as the dictator. Further, a discount rule, through its property of stationarity, is not only time asymmetric; it is also time biased in the sense that switching one generation with another affects the outcome of the rule.

It appears that the proper procedure is to face the distributional problem directly. Only if the equity issue is to be otherwise ignored, does it make sense to consider a lower rate of discount as a kind of ad hoc palliative. One may surmise that some economists are a little uneasy about the possibility of intergenerational inequities resulting from the application of DPV to the time stream of a long-lived public project since, by way of apology to the future, so to speak, they sometimes propose a low rate of discount to be employed. But such a proposal is the sort of concession that springs from doubt. It does not rest on justifiable principle.

It seems to us that a proper and justifiable role for the discount rate is to help define the feasible set of intertemporal paths, from which one must choose an equitable resolution of intertemporal conflicts of interest. We have suggested that the simple procedure of discounting costs and benefits at the current opportunity cost of capital, about 11 percent, for long periods of a century or more, can lead to absurd results. Care must be taken to apply realistic behavioral assumptions when using a discount approach to defining the intertemporal opportunity set.

Once the intertemporal opportunity set is defined, an equitable intertemporal choice rule need not involve a further discounting procedure. For example, a promising procedure is to make a decision on the basis of net current benefits once a transition period is completed. This approach is virtually the same as following the overtaking principle and has been used by the Council on Wage and Price Stability (Broder, 1978) for its analysis of drinking water regulations affecting cancer risk. The approach is particularly suited for cases where there are long-term irreversibilities and long-term latencies, and where there appears to be at most a single switch in current net benefits once the project start-up costs and latencies are passed in time. Both the problems of ozone depletion and carcinogens in drinking water appear to share these characteristics.

5. The Treatment of Risk and Uncertainty

The uncertainty of a future event may be split into two phases, that of assessing, where possible, the risk in terms of probability and severity of an event occurring—whether the probability is objective (based on a statistical sample) or subjective (based on personal estimates of likelihood)—and that of determining a method of evaluating the risk of the event in question. The latter phase may be extended to include the choice of an appropriate technique for decision making when there is no known way of assessing the probability of the event occurring.

Wherever the statistics of a chance or risk of an event occurring are known, then *in principle* it is possible to place a value on the consequent increase or decrease in the welfare of each person subjected to that chance or risk, on an ex ante basis. Under these conditions, the Pareto criterion, where its application is justified, can be extended to cover changes in chance and risk.[16] There will, of course, always be the problem not only of assessing the magnitude of the risk but that of ensuring that persons affected by it are aware of it also. Although this consideration raises the question of further investment in gathering and disseminating information, the recognition of possible net benefits of such investment has never prevented economists engaged in allocative techniques from accepting individual valuations of goods or bads as the relevant data at the time of calculation notwithstanding the prevalence of imperfect knowledge.

Where, however, the risk in question is not known, and no agreement can be reached on the likelihood of its occurrence, techniques designed to deal with the resultant problem go beyond the bounds of allocative economics as described earlier. Such techniques, whatever their virtues, remain without social sanction unless they can be assumed to be understood and approved by society at large.

We may briefly describe some of the popular techniques proposed by economists and others for dealing with risk and uncertainty, bearing in mind the nature of the ozone problem.

1. Raising the discount rate. The notion of adding some arbitrary percentage points to the rate of discount may be defended as a crude way of coping with uncertainty, wherever the uncertainty refers to the magnitudes of the benefits over the future. It would be hard to justify for cases in which the events themselves, or the side effects of the projects in question, are as yet quite unknown.

Moreover, tampering with the discount rate is obviously an awkward form of recourse when employed simultaneously to cope with uncertainty (usually by raising the rate) and with the problem of intergenerational equity (usually by lowering the rate).

2. Building a probability distribution of net benefits from experts' guesses about future prices is an alternative way of dealing with the same kind of uncertainty. In an extremely simplified example in which there is uncertainty only about future input prices p_1 and p_2 and about output prices p_3 and p_4, experts confined to triple values for each price may agree that for each of these four prices the most likely price in the future has a 60 percent chance of occurring. As a result, the most likely estimate of the resulting net benefit has only a $(0.6)^4$ or (roughly) a 13 percent chance of occurring. As for the most optimistic and the most pessimistic net benefit, they will obviously have a much smaller than 13 percent chance of occurring. If, for example, experts agree that there is a 20 percent chance of each of the more optimistic prices occurring, there will be a $(0.2)^4$ or a 1.6 percent chance of the most optimistic net benefit outcome occurring. Similarly for the most pessimistic net benefit in this case.

For a triple value of each of the four future prices, there are as many as 3^4 or 81 possible net benefit outcomes, each with its own subjective probability. Such a distribution is likely to have a normal shape, but it cannot be more accurate than the guesses made by the experts.

In general, there will be far more than four uncertain prices over the future and, sometimes, more than three estimates for each price. Possible net benefit outcomes can then run into many millions. Nevertheless, a sample distribution can be simulated with the aid of a computer set to select at random a number of combinations consisting of each of the prices along with one of the prices' subjective probabilities, each such combination corresponding with a net benefit figure. A sample of some 200 or 300 combinations usually suffice to produce a reliable enough distribution to work with.

Such a technique might usefully be employed in evaluating the opportunity cost involved in controlling output of products believed to damage the ozone layer. In other words, it might be useful for estimating a distribution of net benefits forgone for each of a number of proposals for reducing the outputs of the suspect activities. No comparable calculations, however, can be made for the value of the benefits arising from a reduction of outputs of such activities inasmuch as existing knowledge of the effects of such activities on the ozone layer, and of the ecological and other consequences of its depletion over time, is too meager to permit of intelligent guesses.

3. The uses of game theory. Game theory is a technique applicable to cases in which there is complete ignorance about the probability of each of the possible outcomes of an uncertain event or combination of events. As such, it might seem to lend itself to decision making in this instance.

Restricting ourselves to a two-person zero-sum game (in which one person is "nature") and in which the game can be played but once, allows a choice of a single strategy among a given number, say n, where each strategy is deemed to produce a known result for each of the possible m outcomes. In consequence, there is an n × m matrix of possible results, each element having a value corresponding to the combination of one possible strategy and one possible outcome of the uncertain event.

The choice of the strategy to adopt, which is the object of the exercise, depends upon the rules or method adopted in the first place, the more popular being the "maximin" method, associated with a prudent decision maker and the "minimax regret" method, associated with a more enterprising decision maker. The maximin method selects a strategy that forgoes possibilities of greater gains in order to ensure that the resulting value, whatever it is, does not fall below some minimum, which value, however, cannot be made larger by the choice of any alternative strategy. A general criticism of this method is that, by so restricting itself, it can sometimes forgo the possibility of substantially greater gains.

The minimax method meets this criticism by estimating the potential loss from choosing every strategy other than the best for each of the possible outcomes. The original matrix of resultant values is thereby transformed into one of potential losses from not choosing a best strategy. In the event, the strategy that is chosen is that which, whatever the outcome happens to be, minimizes the potential loss as compared with the choice of any other strategy. The defect of the minimax method is, not surprisingly, the opposite of the more prudent maximin method. It is the risk of losing the certainty of a good gain for the chance of making just a little more.

There can be other criticisms of game theory and, indeed, the arbitrariness of the decision whether to adopt maximin or minimax (or some other rules) is itself a weakness of the technique. The chief factor in our rejection of game theory as a decision technique for the case under consideration, however, is the extent of our current ignorance of the ozone problem. The number of alternative strategies that may be adopted is, of course, unlimited although, as a practical matter, it can be reduced to a limited number. But, since we are almost wholly ignorant of the phenomenon, there can be no limit to the number of possible outcomes. Even were we able to guess at the nature of some of the results from adopting strategies involving little reduction of current activities, the placing of monetary values at various points of time on a number of the more disastrous of them would be arbitrary and highly controversial.

4. Other techniques such as risk-benefit analysis (which is, in fact, no more than a variant of cost-benefit analysis where the risk entailed is part of the cost), and the use of strategies based upon conditional probability (in which prior events associated from experience with the likelihood of specific outcomes occurring) have also to be precluded since they, too,

depend upon some knowledge of the nature of the risk and upon the social value or cost of the event should it occur.

The ozone problem in fact falls into the category of externalities or spillover effects that has grown rapidly since World War II, being the product of recent technical innovation, and having in common certain features that separate them from the more conventional spillover effects—effluent, noise, fume, congestion, and the like—which feature so large in the economic literature.[17] The chief distinguishing features of this new category of spillovers that appear to render them untractable to familiar economic methods are as follows:

First, since the industrial processes and/or products are novel to this planet, there is very limited experience of the nature or incidence of their side effects. The consequences for humanity of the continuance and spread of these new activities and/or products are, therefore, as yet under a gigantic question mark. Specific effects are sometimes suspect and give rise to controversy and speculation. For the rest, it is expected, and feared, that other side effects will emerge over time.

Secondly, there is in such cases an intelligent apprehension that the spillovers associated with these new activities may well take the form of large-scale disasters, possibly having global dimensions. In particular, the damage caused may be irreversible, and possibly fatal, to humanity or to all forms of life on earth.

Thirdly, some part or all of the as yet imperfectly understood damage or hazard of pursuing these new activities may fall on future generations. And there can be general presumption that safe technological methods for dealing with them will be discovered in time.

The question, then, is whether the economist or any kind of scientist can produce meaningful figures purporting to be an economic contribution to the decision-making process when the problem under consideration involves spillovers having the singular features mentioned above.

Thus, in the particular problem under consideration, of ozone depletion, the possibility of a number of catastrophic outcomes cannot, at present, be dismissed as being beyond the pale of likelihood. One such outcome is that of so much additional ultraviolet light reaching the earth as significantly to increase the incidence of melanoma and other skin cancers. Alternatively, or simultaneously, temperature and rainfall patterns over the earth may become so altered as to produce disastrous effects on agricultural output. At least as great a disaster could arise from a critical change in the amount of ultraviolet light reaching the ocean surface so as to interfere with the plankton photosynthesis cycle which both absorbs carbon dioxide and releases oxygen. This latter possibility deserves far more attention than it receives, for the oceans are the largest sinks for carbon dioxide. In general, it is important to take account not only of what are currently believed to be the more likely effects of ozone depletion but also of the potentially worst effects; and to try to estimate not only the probabilities of these worst effects but also to measure the degree of confidence with which they are held.

IX. Conclusions and Recommendations

In the circumstances surrounding the ozone problem, the conscientious economist has to recognize that the conventional tools may be only of limited service. Nonetheless, some proposals can be made by economists and others for coping with products or processes, the introduction of which involves the local or global community in some, as yet, unknown degree of hazard. The following are illustrative:

(1) Thinking in terms, not of the prohibition of a project, but of its public regulation, a prudent maxim would have it that the larger the possible catastrophe and the higher the probability of its occurrence the stricter should be the details of its regulation. Such a maxim, however, is not very useful where the conditions are so novel that we virtually know nothing of the nature of the catastrophes and/or of the probability of their occurrence.

(2) Still thinking in terms of government regulation, it might seem reasonable to suppose that the burden should be placed on the regulatory agency to show—in the words of the Toxic Substances Control Act—that there is a "reasonable basis for concluding that there may be an unreasonable risk." The regulatory agency would then have to demonstrate that something like a large-scale catastrophe is a possibility that cannot be lightly dismissed.

The trouble with this seemingly reasonable proposal, however, is that there may be no way of demonstrating the credibility of one or more possible large-scale catastrophes and, in default of such demonstration, the project in question would be adopted with the possible result that the suspicion of some dreadful calamity would, alas, be vindicated within the lifetime of the existing generation or of some future generation. Thus, while such a rule of procedure might be acceptable enough for a spectrum of limited risks, it is manifestly unacceptable wherever there is a risk of a major and irreversible disaster, even where the degree of risk cannot be calculated and even where there is reason to believe it is small.

(3) Arrow and Fisher (1974) have discussed the problem of irreversibility in terms of the growth of information over time. On the supposition that information improves continuously with time, they introduce a simple model designed to indicate the conditions under which there is a balance of advantage in not foreclosing irreversible options. Although their paper is indeed a contribution to the subject within their chosen context, and their conclusion that caution should be exercised in the presence of irre-

versibility is entirely acceptable, the extent of the caution envisaged has to be increased substantially when the problem is placed within an intergeneration context (one in which their conventional procedure of using a discount rate to maximize present value is no longer valid) and when the problem is raised in a situation in which the irreversibility contemplated has reference not so much to the loss, say, of some unique wilderness area but rather to the ecological viability of the planet earth.

(4) Another possible way of proceeding in the face of uncertainty with respect both to the range of outcomes and to their associated probabilities is to compare, for each possible or credible outcome, the consequences on the one hand, of acting on the basis of what, in the event, turns out to be unwarranted alarm with the consequences, on the other hand, of acting on the basis of what turns out to be unwarranted complacency. For there may well be close agreement among scientists that for each credible outcome, or for most of them, or at least for all the worst outcomes, the damaging consequences for humankind of adopting policies based on unwarranted complacency far exceed in magnitude the consequences, in terms of loss of social gain, of adopting policies based on unwarranted alarm.

Should this agreement exist, it might seem to follow that strict regulation of all suspect activities and products (which regulation may include a ban on the activities or products) should be enforced until our knowledge of their range of effects on the planet has increased to the point of consensus in detail and a high degree of confidence. Only in the fullness of time, then, should it become evident whether our apprehensions of possible disasters were justified, more than justified, or less than justified.

At this point, however, a caveat should be entered. However it is measured, the growth of knowledge, like any other index, is not likely to take the form of a smooth upward trend. Within short periods of time, say decades, we can now recognize with the benefit of hindsight that what was once believed to be new knowledge, or an advance in our understanding, turned out to be erroneous or misleading. Thus, in the near future, we may come to believe the action of certain items on the biosphere to be less dangerous than we originally thought it was, only to discover later that it was more dangerous. What is more, persistent research may eventually bring to light hitherto unsuspected consequences of these same items that may be potentially more dangerous than those currently suspected.

Issues touched upon in the above proposals combine to raise a crucial question. For the problems of the sort the economist has recently had to face are distinguished by three features: (a) although there are grounds for suspicion of a possible major disaster, there is an absence of dependable knowledge with respect both to the nature of, and the probability of, the worst outcomes. (b) Credible worst outcomes are marked by global irreversibility. (c) Recognition that such worst outcomes are as likely, or are more likely, to fall on some future generation as on the present.

The crucial question referred to, then, is that of the policy to be pursued during the period necessary for knowledge to accumulate to the extent needed for a decision with respect to the project to be taken with confidence. This question is clearly related to that which faces the pure scientist whenever he is presented with a new hypothesis. His traditional response in these circumstances can be interpreted as one of methodological conservatism: of resisting novelty until it has survived a long gauntlet of attack and opposition.

At all events, for the economist faced with problems having the aforementioned features it is appropriate to consider, first, two alternative and diametrically opposed social responses, or rules of action, wherever an existing or proposed economic activity may legitimately be suspected of generating dangerous and incalculable spillover effects.

Rule A would countenance the initiation or continuance of an economic activity until the evidence that it is harmful or risky has been established beyond reasonable doubt. Rule B, in contrast, would debar the economic activity in question until evidence that it is safe has been established beyond reasonable doubt. The phrase "beyond reasonable doubt" can excite much controversy, but whatever the interpretation agreed upon, the distinction between the two rules is of the essence.

Which rule tends to prevail depends upon the institutions and attitudes which reflect the ethos of a particular society. Which rule *ought to* prevail, however, depends upon the state of material well-being and *inter alia* upon a recognition of features of the spillover effects associated with the activities in question.

Concerning the existing tendency, the A rule has generally prevailed with respect to commercial enterprise in the West, at least since the Industrial Revolution, in the belief that the progress of industry, although it inevitably occasions inconvenience, eventually promotes the welfare of society as a whole. Whether or not this presumption could be justified by a sophisticated examination of the evidence is a matter of conjecture. However, it must be conceded that the spillovers which most concerned the public in earlier days were of the more conventional kind and, therefore, in a crude way at least, subject to economic calculation.

Since World War II, many authoritative voices have challenged this general presumption of economic progress though without making much impression on the mind of public until the last few years. For the seeming success, scientific and industrial, of the past 200 years has given rise to an establishment of technocrats, bureaucrats, and enterprises, steeped in the belief that science and technology, given the freedom and the funds, will eventually solve all the problems that have been and are being created by science and technology. Yet that immaculate faith in the omnipotence of the scientific method to overcome all obstacles has begun, slightly but discernibly, to waver. The subsequent history of acclaimed scientific discoveries or technological feats over the last 30 years do not read off like a success story. In recognition of the new type of spillovers referred to, the wisdom of being guided by the A rule is no longer self-evident.

If spillovers were such as to be restricted to a single country, and that country, perilously poor, could not depend on outside aid to mitigate the poverty and malnutrition of the bulk of its population, a case could be made for the adoption of the A rule wherever the benefits of introducing an innovation were expected to be substantial. After all, the incurring of some risk of uncertain and possibly irreversible damage to existing and future generations could arguably be justified if, in the absence of the new process and the dissemination of its products, millions of people would be almost certain to die of malnutrition or exposure.

The position is quite different, however, for a country such as the United States which, in comparison with a country such as India, is a goods-saturated economy. The continued use of freon and other gases is far from urgent in terms of the saving of life. The present value of the net benefits to be sacrificed from dispensing altogether with such luxuries can hardly be an impressive magnitude. And even if it were reckoned at some outlandish figure, say $100 billion or more, application of the A rule to the case in issue would be difficult to support in view of the possible danger and the possible irreversibility of the ecological disaster envisaged. We might well ask, just how large the value of the net benefits to be forgone has to be in order to warrant the incurring of a risk of that order. If there were some finite figure for these forgone benefits that would indeed warrant exposing the country's population to such a risk, it is virtually certain to be many times any plausible estimate of the present value of such benefits.

The above methodological maxim, if adopted, is sure to offend some commercial and consumer interests. But political sensitivity to these immediate interests on so momentous an issue for the future of mankind would be unforgivable and would amount, in effect, to clear proof of the utter inadequacy of our system of democratic government in the face of crisis.

In the circumstances surrounding the ozone problem, however, the commercial and consumer interests can hardly be very strong. Regulation or prohibition of the items in question would surely be more acceptable even to the less environmentally concerned or less informed segment of the public if they were to be replaced by substitutes that could not seriously be held to occasion much loss of welfare. A policy of replacing push-button aerosols by hand sprays, for instance, can hardly be described as one causing hardship or discomfort. Neither, for that matter, would increased regulation of refrigerant units or control of their disposal be regarded as imposing much of a sacrifice on the consuming public.

The response in the United States to the potential risks of supersonic transport and recombinant DNA suggest a shift toward the B rule. Development of the U.S. SST was suspended in part because the burden of proof that the SST would not deplete the ozone shield was shifted, in the public mind, toward the proponents of the SST. In subsequent years the extent of the risk has not been fully resolved, but it now appears that the risk is considered by scientists to be somewhat lower than first estimated. Some might argue that the later turn of events showed that the SST development should not have been slowed down because the risk proved smaller than originally thought. But even if it were known for sure that the risk of supersonic transport is less than originally estimated it would appear to us that the partial reliance on the B rule was the correct decision. Subsequent events have shown that the costs of delay are not nearly as high as proponents of the SST claimed. More important, some false positives are the price to be paid for controlling false negatives. Similarly it now appears that the risks of recombinant DNA are more manageable than originally thought. Application of the B rule at the Asimilar Conference led to a few years' delay of research development, but with the benefits of a greater understanding of the risks and institution of better laboratory controls. In this case as well, the costs of the B rule, in terms of delay, have been small in comparison with the benefits, in terms of precautionary management of potentially irreversible and catastrophic risk. On the other side, where the B rule has not been applied and where later estimates of risk have proved higher than earlier estimates there is likely to be an enormous amount of unnecessary suffering, as in the cases of *Tris* and PPBs. *Tris* is now known to be one of the most potent carcinogens the National Cancer Institute ever tested, yet it was used for several years as a flame retardant for children's sleepwear, with exposure to millions. During the period of regulation, burden of proof as to the potential toxicity was not shifted to the proponents of *Tris*, even though there was information existing as to the long-term toxicity of related chemicals. Similarly the tragedy of PPB contamination in Michigan could perhaps have been prevented or reduced with application of the B rule, at the beginning and throughout the legal and regulatory process.

Final Reflections

We are impelled to conclude that a valid cost-benefit calculation of actions to protect the earth's ozone shield cannot be undertaken in the present state of our ignorance concerning the relevant physical relationships and, therefore, in the present state of any ignorance concerning the nature and magnitude of the risks posed by existing economic activities. Nor can the decision techniques devised by economists and others for problems involving future uncertainty shed much light on the issue. It is, of course, proper that continued research into all aspects of the ozone problem should continue. But until such time as there is basic agreement on the range of consequences flowing from the use of all suspects goods and activities, or until such time as processes for recycling all substances suspected of affecting, directly or indirectly, the stratospheric ozone have been perfected, any society having a sense of obligation toward its citizens, and a sense of responsibility for generations yet to come, should adopt the prudent course entailed by the B rule.

The question of the instruments by which to implement action in constraint of such suspect activities is a secondary matter and one open to debate. Although economists by training tend to favor taxes rather than blanket prohibitions, there are political advantages in having recourse, in circumstances of such gravity, to the latter and more dramatic instrument and, indeed, for making the period of adjustment as short as possible. Public support tends to rally to a government that is manifestly in earnest about a declared clear and present danger. In contrast, prolonged debates about taxes and subsidies, about possible exemptions and extensions of the status quo, are apt to weaken the resolve both of governments and citizens, and to detract from the gravity of the situation.

Finally, although the problem is clearly an international one and the United States should seek ways of persuading other countries to act in concert in the interests of mankind as a whole, any initial failure to achieve international or multinational agreement ought not to deter her from taking unilateral action in an endeavor to diminish the existing risks being run. The United States is, in any case, by far the greatest user of spray cans, accounting for about half the world's total. Her unilateral action in this respect would therefore make a substantial difference to the global risk while serving also to enhance her moral influence in the world and, thereby to encourage other countries to follow her example.

NOTES

1. See Mishan (1969).
2. See Mishan (1976a), Meade (1972), and Mishan (1976b) for further discussion.
3. See Dasgupta, Marglin, and Sen (1972), p. 5.
4. See Georgescu-Roegen (1975), Daly (1977), Solow (1974b), Page (1977a), Sen (1977), Price (1973), Neher (1976), and Burness and Lewis (1977).
5. More precisely, the value "grows" in the sense that an individual in time zero is indifferent between B now and the anticipation of $B(1+r)^t$ t years from now.
6. See Marglin (1963).
7. For further discussion see the investment section of Mishan (1976a).
8. See Mishan (1976a).
9. From what vantage point in time is this indifference relation to be defined? Presumably for A the vantage point is at time zero, at which time it is plausible

that the future is valued less highly than the present. At a vantage point of year 20, figure 2 suggests that A values the past (years 0–19) more than the present (year 20), which is hardly plausible. For a discussion of intertemporal decision problems where vantage points shift and the present is more highly valued than either the past or the future, see Page (1977b) and for related discussion see Solow (1974) and Strotz (1955). In this section we consider some of the implications of the implicit assumption most commonly found in the literature, that time preference relationships do not change with changes in the vantage point of time. We find this assumption unrealistic, but to relax it would lead to questions of inconsistent planning and intertemporal equity, for the individual planner. As the issue of intertemporal equity can be understood most clearly across generations, rather than for a single individual, discussion of the equity issue is postponed until the following section. The implicit assumption that there is no intertemporal equity problem for this individual—that figure 2 describes A's time preference structure for any time in A's life—can be viewed as an intertemporal version of "conflation" in the utilitarian tradition. See John Rawls (1972), for further discussion of conflation.

10. Under the willingness-to-pay approach it has been estimated that workers are willing to accept a 1/1000 increase in the annual probability of death by accident for about $200 annual wage premium which translates to $200,000 per life, in actuarial terms. This empirical estimate does not by itself imply that individuals would be willing to accept a 1/100 increase in the chance of death per year for a compensation of $2,000, which would also translate into $200,000 per life. However, the time dimension of the empirical study is not clearly focused on risks of one-year duration. If workers viewed the decision to work in a mine as a decision to work for 10 years with a total risk of early accidental death of 1/100 and total premium of $2,000, then the figure of $200,000 per life would be appropriate as the actuarial equivalent of the "value of life" for risks in the range of 1 percent. We will not go into the important qualifications here of this approach but simply offer the figure of $500,000 as a "generous" estimate of what might be found in the risk-benefit literature using a discounting approach. See Linerooth (1975) and Bailey (1978) for further discussion. Some estimates of the value of life are a good deal higher; see also Page, Harris, and Bruser (1979), appendix D.

11. There is the valid question of whether a collective risk involving the entire world population should be treated as equivalent to 20 billion times the individual risk, where 20 billion is the assumed population. But resolution of this question is not essential for the observation made below.

12. For further discussion see Dasgupta (1977).

13. See Page (1977a).

14. See Mishan (1977).

15. These remarks define a base case in which secular declines are ruled out as long as steady states are feasible. They do not rule out advances, if the present is altruistic toward the future, or if some criterion like Rawls' "golden rule of saving effort" is adopted. Rawls' golden rule requires a saving effort of the present equal to what it would have liked its immediate predecessor to have made.

16. But see footnote 9 concerning intertemporal conflicts of interest for the individual. Society does not allow voluntary contracts made in the present leading to slavery at a future date, thus protecting the future interests of the individual

against present interests. The same ethical concern applies to lotteries for future slavery such as the exposure to carcinogens or other irreversible environmental risks. This ethical concern must be balanced against the supposition underlying methodological individualism, that the individual is better able to look out for his future interests than the government.

17. See Page (1978) for a more complete discussion of these differences and some of the implications of these differences.

REFERENCES

Arrow, K. J. and Fisher, A. C. (1974) "Environmental Preservation, Uncertainty, and Irreversibility," *Quarterly Journal of Economics,* V. 88, May 1974.

Arrow, K. J. and Lind, R. C. (1970) "Uncertainty and the Evaluation of Public Investment Decisions," *American Economic Review,* June 1970.

Arrow, K. J. and Lind, R. C. (1972) "Reply," *American Economic Review,* March 1972.

Bailey, Martin (1978) "The Discount Rate for Environmental Programs," appendix C of "Costs and Benefits of CFM Control," University of Maryland Conference on Ozone Management, John Cumberland, director, July 1978.

Baumol, W. J. (1969) "On the Social Rate for Public Projects" in *The Analysis and Evaluation of Public Expenditures: The PBB System,* V. I, Joint Economic Committee. Washington, D.C.

——— (1968) "On the Social Discount Rate," *American Economic Review,* September 1968.

Broder, Ivy (1978) "Analysis of Proposed EPA Drinking Water Regulations," Washington, D.C., September 1978.

Burness, H. S. and Lewis, T. R. (1977) "Democratic Exploitation of a Non-Replenishable Resource," Social Science Working Paper No. 161, California Institute of Technology, Pasadena, CA.

Choi, K. (1978) "Summary of Technical Information on Sources and Effects of Ozone Depletion," University of Maryland Conference on Ozone Management, John Cumberland, director. July 1978.

Daly, H. (1977) *Steady State Economics,* W. H. Freeman Co., San Francisco.

Dasgupta, A. K. and Pearce, D. W. (1972) *Cost Benefit Analysis, Theory and Practice.* London: Macmillan.

Dasgupta, P. (1977) "Resource Depletion, Research and Development and the Social Rate of Discount," Conference paper, Resources for the Future, Washington, D.C.

Dasgupta, P., Marglin, S., and Sen, A. (1972) *Guidelines for Project Evaluation.* New York: United Nations.

Eckstein, O. (1957) "Investment Criteria for Economic Development," *Quarterly Journal of Economics,* June 1957.

Ferejohn, J. and Page, T. (1978) "On the Foundations of Intertemporal Choice," *American Journal of Agricultural Economics,* V. 60, No. 2, May 1978.

Freeman, M. (1977) "Why We Should Discount Intergenerational Effects," *Futures,* V. 9, No. 5, Oct. 1977, pp. 375–76.

Georgescu-Roegen, N. (1975) "Energy and Economic Myths," *Southern Economic Journal,* V. 41.

Harberger, A. C. (1972) "The Opportunity Costs of Public Investment Financed by Borrowing," (1966) in R. Layard, ed., *Cost-Benefit Analysis.* London: Penguin Books Ltd.

Haveman, R. N. and Krutilla, J. V. (1968) *Unemployment, Idle Capacity, and the Evaluation of Public Expenditures,* Washington, D.C. Ref.

Hirshleifer, J., et al. (1961) *Water Supply: Economics, Technology, and Policy,* Princeton, Princeton University.

Kaldor, N. (1939) "Welfare Propositions of Economics and Interpersonal Comparisons of Utility," *Economics Journal.*

Krutilla, J. and Eckstein, O. (1958) *Multiple Purpose River Development,* Baltimore: The Johns Hopkins Press.

Linerooth, J. (1975) "The Evaluation of Life-Saving: A Survey," International Institute for Applied Systems Analysis, Laxonburg, Austria.

Marglin, S. (1963) The Opportunity Cost of Public Investment," *Quarterly Journal of Economics,* V. 77, pp. 274–89.

Meade, J. E. (1972) Review of *Cost-Benefit Analysis* by E. J. Mishan, *Economic Journal,* V. 82, pp. 244–46.

Mishan, E. J. (1977) "Economic Criteria for Intergenerational Comparisons," *Futures,* V. 9, No. 5, pp. 383–403.

——— (1976a) *Cost-Benefit Analysis* (2nd Edition). New York: Praeger.

——— (1976b) "The Use of CV and EV in CBA," *Economica,* May 1976.

——— (1974) "Consistency and Flexibility in Cost-Benefit Analysis," *Economica,* February 1974.

——— (1969) "Welfare Economics," deVries Memorial Lectures, Nath Holland.

——— (1967a) "Criteria for Public Investment: Some Simplifying Suggestions," *Journal of Political Economy,* September 1967.

——— (1967b) "A Proposed Normalization Procedure for Public Investment Criteria," *Economic Journal,* V. 77, pp. 777–96.

Nath, S. K. (1969) *A Reappraisal of Welfare Economics,* London: Routledge and Kegan Paul.

Neher, P. (1976) "Democratic Exploitation of a Replenishable Resource," *Journal of Public Economics,* V. 5, pp. 361–71.

Page, T. (1978) "A Generic View of Toxic Chemicals and Similar Risks," *Ecology Law Quarterly,* V. 7, No. 2, pp. 207–44.

——— (1977a) *Conservation and Economic Efficiency,* Baltimore: Johns Hopkins Press.

——— (1977b) "Equitable Use of the Resource Base," *Environment and Planning,* V. 9, pp. 15–22.

Page, T., Harris, R., and Bruser, J. (1979) "Removal of Carcinogens from Drinking Water: A Cost-Benefit Analysis," Social Science Working Paper No. 230, California Institute of Technology, Pasadena, CA.

Price, C. (1973) "To the Future: With Indifference or Concern?—The Social Discount Rate and Its Implications for Land Use," *Journal of Agricultural Economics,* V. 24, No. 2.

Rawls, J. (1972) *A Theory of Justice,* Cambridge, Mass.: Harvard University Press.

Sen, A. (1977) "Approaches to the Choice of Discount Rates for Social Cost-Benefit Analysis," Conference paper, Resources for the Future, Washington, D.C.

Smith, K. and d'Arge, R. (1978) "Managing an Uncertain Natural Environment: The Stratosphere," University of Maryland Conference on Ozone Management, John Cumberland, director. July 1978.

Solow, R. H. (1974a) "Intergenerational Equity," *Review of Economic Studies,* V. 41, Supplement, pp. 29–45.

——— (1974b) "The Economics of Resources or the Resources of Economics," *American Economic Review,* V. 64, May 1974.

Strotz, R. H. (1955) "Myopia and Inconsistency in Dynamic Utility Maximization," *Review of Economic Studies,* V. 23, pp. 165–180.

Weisbrod, B. (1968) "Income Redistributive Effects and Benefit-Cost Analysis," in *Problems in Public Expenditure Analysis* (S. B. Chase, ed.), pp. 177–208. Washington, D.C.: Brookings Institution.

3 Policy Science: Analysis or Ideology?

Laurence H. Tribe

IN THE 1960s it was fashionable to believe that Ideology, like God, was dead. In postindustrial society, it was said, man would increasingly live by reason rather than conviction. Because significant differences would center less on ends than means, it followed that the crucial choices would be essentially technical in character, the crucial techniques those of rational choice among competing means to largely settled ends. And in the limited sphere where ends themselves would still conflict, the task would be reduced to that of behavioral conditioning and reasoned accommodation—the largely managerial and technological province of a mature legal order.

Surely this diagnosis was greatly overdrawn. There are no doubt many explanations for its remarkable appeal, but one in particular seems noteworthy: perhaps passion was simply learning to pose as reason. After all, ideology has often sought to masquerade as analysis, deriving a power it could never justly claim from the garb of neutrality it has at times contrived to wear. In the past decade, I believe, the masquerade has reached new levels of sophistication and effectiveness.

My aim here is to embark on a sustained exploration of this problem and its possible solutions in several different sectors of human thought, including legal theory, welfare economics, moral philosophy, and decision analysis. In this initial essay I intend to focus on the latter area—that is, on the techniques and principles of problem-solving variously referred to as policy science, cost-benefit analysis, operations research, systems analysis, and decision theory.

I do not mean to suggest by this enumeration that the techniques listed are coextensive with a single, readily identifiable mode of problem-solving, or even that the difficulties they as a whole pose are unique, absent from the areas that I mean to turn to later. On the contrary, one of my theses will be that the policy sciences in certain important ways present difficulties shared by dominant or emerging styles of thought in a wide variety of disciplines. My overall aims will be (1) to elucidate the respects in which particular modes of analysis in a number of different fields— particular approaches to formulating questions, organizing information, and developing answers—entail fundamental (if often unwitting) commitments to substantive conclusions shaped in characteristic and often unfortunate ways; (2) to study the patterns of distortion that appear to recur in various distinct areas of thought; and (3) to search for possible remedies to the problems thereby identified. I begin with the policy sciences here not because they are necessarily more vulnerable than other fields to the sort of critique I wish to advance, but rather because their weaknesses are so typical of ones I expect to encounter elsewhere, because the claims they make so often include a consciously asserted immunity from the difficulties in question, and because those claims may come to be accepted in areas where unfortunate consequences can readily result.

I. The Basic Tools

Space permits only a brief description of the principal techniques I have in mind—their history, theory, and current practice.

Although many of the techniques which were to become the methodological component of the policy sciences already existed in the 1930s and earlier, their systematic development had its start in British and American responses to the onset of World War II. In particular, the successes achieved by groups of British and American physical scientists working in areas outside their professional interests to solve well-defined tactical problems led to governmental recognition, on both sides of the Atlantic, of the value of operations research.[1] Following the war, in an attempt to keep together some of the operations research teams, the U.S. Air Force contracted with Douglas Aircraft to set up a civilian research group to work on military problems. By 1948 this group had split from Douglas and had organized itself as the nonprofit RAND Corporation. Early RAND research, like wartime operations research, dealt with the mathematical and statistical treatment of well-defined lower-level tactical decision problems. By the early 1950s, however, RAND had come to emphasize what is now called systems analysis, focusing on problems in which there were no clearly defined objectives to be rigorously maximized. Systems analysis does not abandon quantitative techniques altogether, but reserves their use for selected aspects of each problem; its practitioners see it as an attempt to apply systematic, common-sense reasoning to the structuring of complex decision situations.[2]

Even as RAND was shifting from operations research to systems analysis, policy analysis in general was being taken over by economists. Sparked partly by the 1944 success of von Neumann and Morgenstern in demonstrating how economic modes of reasoning could be applied to seemingly noneconomic problems,[3] this trend had important implications. When the policy sciences came to be applied to the problems of government on a large scale in the 1960s, first in the Defense Department and then throughout the federal government, they would be characterized by a fundamentally economic approach to problems—an approach that retained much of the quantitative emphasis and mathematical rigor of early operations research but which structured situations in terms of the traditional economic model of social reality.

With the market as a central paradigm, that model takes as its starting point the idea of individual man as a rational maximizer of satisfactions operating self-interestedly (i.e., typically motivated neither by altruism nor by envy) in a world of relative scarcity. Problems of choice, whether individual or social, are perceived essentially as problems of marginal "trade-off" or "exchange" among desired outputs, attributes, or ingredients of welfare. Inasmuch as gains with respect to some outputs (or the welfare of some individuals) may occasionally be achieved at the expense of other outputs (or individuals), there arises quite naturally the notion of the production-possibility frontier (or transformation curve) as the locus of all those combinations of relevant outputs (or attributes or individual states of welfare) which have the property that no gain in any one output can be realized without some loss in another.[4] To decide which point on the production-possibility frontier (the so-called "efficient set") he prefers to all others, a satisfaction-maximizing individual in effect constructs a set of indifference curves (or surfaces), each defined by the property that the individual is indifferent among the combinations of outputs represented by the various points of any given indifference curve. The indifference curves are treated as varying continuously with each output, so that arbitrarily small increments of any output can be "traded off" for sufficiently small decrements of any other; and such continuous substitutability is assumed to hold over the entire range of each output, so that arbitrarily low levels of any given output (i.e., levels arbitrarily close to zero) can be compensated for by sufficiently high levels of another output.[5] Having constructed his indifference curves in this way, the rational individual chooses that point on the production-possibility frontier which lies on the highest of all those of his indifference curves that intersect the frontier, typically a point of tangency.[6]

If a large number of satisfaction-maximizing individuals are put into a perfectly competitive market situation (that is, a situation where all participants have complete information, all can bargain at no cost, and none can independently influence group behavior), classical economic theory dictates that the individuals will adjust their patterns of production, and will trade among themselves the goods they have produced, until all have identical marginal rates of substitution for all goods; until that point is reached, exchanges will be made moving each individual to a higher indifference curve. Prices—or more accurately, relative prices—serve as a common denominator defining the relative values different individuals place on different alternatives, providing a measure of the ratio of the rates of substitution between alternatives.

A market in equilibrium, when all marginal rates of substitution are equal, yields a Pareto-optimal result R in the sense that there is no alternative state S such that (1) some individuals would prefer S to R and (2) none would prefer R to S. This conclusion says nothing, of course, about how equitably goods are distributed in the equilibrium state; it merely asserts that the equilibrium is "efficient" in the limited sense defined above.

Classical economics treats such efficiency as the basic criterion of acceptability. Until a situation is Pareto-optimal, clear improvements can be made; once Pareto-optimality is achieved, no unambiguous (and hence unanimously acceptable) gains are possible. Pareto-optimality thus amounts to a specific, though indeterminate and incomplete, social welfare criterion—indeterminate because there will typically be a wide range of Pareto-optimal solutions, and incomplete because the criterion provides no way of making comparisons among any but a highly limited set of situations. In the late 1930s and early 1940s, representatives of the "new welfare economics" believed they could defend as wholly "objective" and free from either interpersonal comparisons of utility or personal (and hence controversial) value choices the "Kaldor-Hicks" criterion, a variant of the Pareto criterion under which a change from social state S to social state T would be deemed desirable whenever those who gained from the change could so compensate the losers that, *after* compensation, the Pareto criterion would be met. This criterion does not require that compensation actually take place; it posits a change to be unambiguously desirable whenever it generates enough "net gain" to make compensation possible.[7]

Either in its original form or as supplemented by a distributional constraint, the Kaldor-Hicks criterion provides the crucial intellectual underpinning for cost-benefit analysis. This technique, which marks the effective socialization of the policy sciences' market origins, assumes that it is possible for the policy analyst to estimate the quantities of benefits stemming from a (usually governmental) project under alternative designs, the quantities of things used up or reduced, and the prices that should be associated with both ends of this equation. Given this information, the analyst is to choose that design which maximizes the difference between benefits and costs.[8] Put this way, the problem seems largely to be one of measurement, the conversion of costs and benefits into some common denominator; correspondingly, the role of the analyst becomes that of simulator, determining the prices that would have been attached to the various goods if a perfectly competitive market had existed.[9]

Alternatively, the analytical problem may be seen as one of determining which attributes of the various outcomes, among both costs and benefits, to take into account, and with what weights.[10] Traditionally, the practice has been to focus on those costs and benefits accruing to the persons associated with the decision maker, leaving "externalities" out of the analysis. Further, in keeping with the implications of the Kaldor-Hicks criterion, there has generally been an attempt to separate costs and benefits related to efficiency (those bearing on "total" welfare or income) from distributional and other supposedly "intangible" considerations. Whatever cannot be expressed in terms of the common-denominator metric at the heart of the analysis is either excluded from consideration, simply noted outside of the analysis itself for the decision maker's possible use, or at most incorporated into the analysis in the form of a constraint—a qualitative requirement, subject to which the project is designed so as to maximize benefits minus costs.[11]

Once the analysis focuses explicitly on the definition and weighting of the key attributes in a decision problem, it may take the form of an explicit definition of an "objective function," a rule that associates with each outcome a single mathematically determined value by means of which it may be compared with other outcomes. In practice, an objective function is rarely used to develop a complete ranking of all alternatives; instead the rule is used to select an optimal alternative—one that either minimizes or maximizes the value of the objective function.[12] The complexity of the objective function depends upon the kind of policy analysis undertaken. For a cost-benefit analysis, the function may be of the apparently simple form: maximize "benefits" minus "costs." For a linear programming problem, the general form of the objective function is $C_1X_1 + C_2X_2 + \ldots + C_NX_N = Z$, where Z is the value to be maximized, $X_1, X_2, \ldots, X_N$ are the relevant attributes, and $C_1, C_2, \ldots, C_N$ are the weights assigned to each. Whatever the formal complexity, however, certain critical decisions—which attributes to regard as relevant and what weights to attach to each—must always be made by someone.[13]

Thus far, the techniques explored assume complete information as to the outcomes of various alternatives. Indeed, largely because institutional arrangements to force a confrontation with the *lack* of complete data have rarely been designed, the techniques are often employed with remarkable disregard for underlying uncertainties (of description or prediction) that render their conclusions indeterminate in critical respects. The theoretical apparatus for the inclusion of uncertainty, however, has not been lacking. Systematic efforts to incorporate uncertainty into policy analysis began with the publication in 1944 of von Neumann and Morgenstern's *Theory of Games and Economic Behavior,* which provided a technique whereby a decision maker could assign numbers (so-called "utilities"), unique up to a positive linear transformation, to the set of all outcomes under consideration in such a way that (a) in the absence of any uncertainty the utilities express the decision maker's ordinal ranking of the outcomes; and (b) given uncertainty, the utilities so incorporate the decision maker's attitude toward risk that, under certain axioms resembling those of classical economic theory, the decision maker will choose alternatives in a way that maximizes the expected utility of his choice.

The von Neumann-Morgenstern procedure (or VN-M procedure) is particularly simple:

(1) Assign arbitrary utility values, M and N, to the most favored and least favored outcomes, here called X and Y respectively. (M<N.)

(2) For any other outcome Z, determine the probability P_z such that the individual is indifferent between two lottery tickets, one of which offers Z for certain, and the other of which offers X with probability P_z and Y with probability $1-P_z$.

(3) Assign to Z a utility value U(Z) equal to the expected value of the lottery with which the individual judges Z to be indifferent:

$$U(Z)=[P_z \cdot M]+[(1-P_z) \cdot N].^{14}$$

Decision analysis applies this procedure to sequential decision problems, seeking that series of choices which maximizes the expected values of the outcomes.[15] It does so by (i) beginning with an explicit description of the set of alternative actions available by displaying in the form of a so-called "decision tree" the unfolding sequence of choices open to the decision maker and the chance contingencies confronting him; (ii) obtaining the decision maker's utilities for the entire set of possible outcomes at the tips of the tree's branches (using his utilities for the "best" and "worst" outcomes, plus VN-M theory); (iii) obtaining the decision maker's subjective probability assessments for each of the contingency forks in the tree;[16] and (iv) applying a straightforward mathematical computation to determine which "decision path" through the tree has the maximum expected utility. The decision maker is then advised to choose the sequence of alternative actions (the "strategy") embodied in this path.

Taken together, the family of techniques considered here have all been conceived as ways of improving decision making by broadening the role of logic and empirical inquiry. While policy analysts themselves have begun to qualify their claims by making increasingly explicit the interests and values they believe any particular analysis includes or excludes, other disciplines, attracted by the theoretical rigor that remains, seek to employ the policy sciences with an enthusiasm that stands in growing contrast to the analysts' own circumspection.

II. Through a Slide Rule Darkly

One of the most persistent beliefs about the techniques discussed above is a conviction of their transparency to considerations of value and their neutrality with respect to fundamental world views and to more or less ultimate ends. Although it is by now widely recognized that such techniques can be abused as tools in a disguised play for power, the myth endures that the techniques *in themselves* lack substantive content, that intrinsically they provide nothing beyond value-free devices for organizing thought in rational ways—methods for sorting out issues and objectively clarifying the empirical relationships among alternative actions and their likely consequences. The user of such techniques, the myth continues, may turn them to whatever ends he seeks. Ends and values, goals and ideologies are seen as mere "inputs" to a machinelike, and hence inherently unbiased, process of solving problems consistent with the facts known and the values posited. The machine itself, like all machines, is said to be subject to misuse but to have no imperatives of its own; only animistic thinking, we are told, can obscure its essential neutrality.

How are such claims to be approached? From the start, some degree of skepticism would seem appropriate, inasmuch as every other language (and the policy sciences are surely languages, at least in part) imposes its own categories and paradigms on the world of experience, every other system of thought its own tendencies on the world of aspiration. I am reminded here of a passage quoted by Michel Foucault, in which Borges refers to the assertion of a certain Chinese encyclopedia that "animals are divided into: (a) belonging to the Emperor, (b) embalmed, (c) tame, (d) sucking pigs, (e) sirens, (f) fabulous, (g) stray dogs, (h) included in the present classification, (i) frenzied, (j) innumerable, (k) drawn with a very fine camelhair brush, (l) et cetera, (m) having just broken the water pitcher, (n) that from a long way off look like flies." As Foucault observes, what we "apprehend in one great leap" in "the wonderment of this taxonomy" is not only "the exotic charm of another system of thought" but—even more pointedly—"the limitation of our own, the stark impossibility of thinking *that*."[17]

To each "system of thought," each distinctive approach to stating and solving problems, at least presumptively there should correspond important versions of Foucault's unthinkable—perspectives and possibilities hidden if not entirely obscured by the system's basic design and by its fundamental presuppositions. The policy sciences (and their analogues in law and other fields), one can hypothesize, are unlikely to be different in this respect. But because their language has not (yet) become fully our own—because it is still possible for most of us to stand outside their frame of reference—we are in a position to perceive, in rough outline, the ways in which the policy sciences structure our world: the gaps they leave and the distortions they promote in that world as we might otherwise perceive it, or as we might otherwise wish to approach it.

In attempting to understand the sort of lens through which the policy sciences view their subject matter, it is helpful to begin by noting the extreme importance that the social sciences as a whole (of which the policy sciences represent a subcategory) have long given to objectivity—to detached, deliberately impersonal, empirically verifiable, and purportedly value-free analysis. Undoubtedly deriving in part from insecurity about the intellectual credentials (and hence the political power) of social science, this compulsion to imitate the exact sciences has been coupled with the premise that in those fields the accepted methodology has in fact been a wholly impersonal one, resting on purely "objective" modes of relation between the observer and the object of observation. It is because of this premise, for example, that necessarily "personal" judgments about values have long been deemed improper (because "unscientific") subjects for economic discourse.[18]

This entire emphasis, however, is based on a profoundly misguided (albeit widely held) conception of how even the most "exact" of the sciences approaches the world. As Michael Polanyi convincingly showed some time ago, deeply personal appraisals play a crucial role in the evolution and testing of any scientific theory.[19] Polanyi's insight that such theories must rest on fundamental personal orientations toward the world—individual human appraisals of order, connection, probability that cannot be accounted for in purely empiricist, value-free terms[20]—parallels Russell's realization that the very existence of a meaningful science presupposes some knowledge independent of experience;[21] and it derives added support from the arguments of investigators like Noam Chomsky that each living organism possesses "a primitive, neurologically given analytic system . . . which . . . provides a specific interpretation of experience."[22] Thus "the objectivist urge to depersonalize our intelligent mental processes,"[23] which has its roots in the anti-Augustinian reaction culminating in the eighteenth century, may well be false to the biological character of knowing itself as well as to the historical truth of how bodies of scientific knowledge have in fact evolved. There are good reasons, therefore, to suppose that the social sciences' passion for objectivity (in the sense of impersonal, detached, and purely empirical modes of investigation) is seriously misplaced.

But one need not accept this analysis in order to study the consequences, for particular enterprises within the social sciences, of pursuing a relentlessly objectivist position. Even if one rejects, for example, Polanyi's epistemological attack on the disjunction of subjectivity and objectivity,[24] one can still find it worthwhile to explore the system of effects that may follow from constructing a theory or a methodology upon that disjunction—to investigate the ways in which a self-consciously objectivist ideal may substantively structure the characteristics and the conclusions of a given mode of thought.[25]

The central claim of the policy sciences, of course, has been their asserted capacity to enlarge the role of explicit, logical reasoning, of empirical knowledge, and of consensual discourse in realms of decision making otherwise dominated by supposedly less trustworthy sources of choice. Insofar as this claim rests on the sort of objectivist ideal I have been discussing, it presents a special case of the general question posed above: How might objectivism itself shape the conclusions of a theory or method in the social sciences?

Before attempting to address that question directly, I would make one further comment. When I describe the several respects in which I believe objectivism distorts the perspectives afforded by the policy sciences, I do not mean to assert that there is some sort of necessary or even "causal" connection between the objectivist ideal, on the one hand, and each of the categories of distortion I will outline, on the other. I mean to argue only that objectivism as an ideal is related in a natural and reciprocal way to the entire collection of distortions taken as a whole—that it provides a central vantage point from which to observe the system of which each individual category of distortions forms an important part.[26]

1. Collapsing Process into Result

From many perspectives, the *procedures* that shape individual and social activity have significance independent of the final products they generate. Yet the traditional approach of both moral philosophy and welfare economics has been to focus exclusively on the end results of social and institutional processes in assessing their value. Thus classical utilitarianism, for example, has asked simply whether a particular process or distribution produces the greatest net balance of satisfaction; still other teleological doctrines have asked whether a process maximizes some other independently defined good (in the case of Aristotelian or Nietzschean perfectionism, for instance, human excellence); and classical welfare economics has asked whether a process or distribution (that of the market, for example) is Pareto-optimal in the sense that its results could not be altered to the benefit of some without detriment to others. Such "end-result" theories have great appeal, for the notion of maximizing some desired end may seem the very essence of rationality.[27] Indeed, even the recent (and in many ways magnificent) effort by John Rawls to formulate a coherent theory of justice as an alternative to utilitarianism in major respects yields an end-result conception. For although Rawls argues that a "distribution cannot be judged in isolation from the system of which it is the outcome,"[28] his procedural method of defining a just *system*—by asking what system would be chosen by rational, self-interested persons knowing only the most general facts about the world but nothing about their own personal characteristics or values[29]—leads quite naturally to a scheme described by each person wholly in terms of its ultimate distribution of liberties and goods. Rawls concludes that a just system of institutions, the one that would be chosen in the "original position" described above, is one that assures (1) an equal right to the most extensive basic liberty compatible with a like liberty for all, and (2) only such deviations from social and economic equality as can be shown to maximize the share of the least advantaged (the "maximin" principle).[30]

In his initial statement of the maximin principle, Rawls adds the qualification that social and economic inequalities must be "attached to positions and offices open to all."[31] He later argues that the role of this "principle of fair opportunity is to insure that the system of cooperation is one of pure procedural justice"[32] in the sense that "there is no independent criterion for the right result."[33] But ultimately Rawls formulates an end-result rule even here, for he argues that inequalities of opportunity too are allowable as long as they satisfy a maximin rule of their own.[34] Hence the Kantian principles of justice derived by Rawls, like the quite different (and clearly less satisfactory) principles derived by the utilitarians before him, are indeed end-result principles after all. And arguably, at least, *only* principles of this sort can be generated by a choice in Rawls's "original position." For even if elements of time-bound procedural justice were to be included in the system that a rational, self-interested person chose under a veil of ignorance as to who he was, such elements would—by the very hypothesis of wholly self-interested choice—have to be selected solely as means to the satisfaction of the random person's chosen pattern of outcomes. Procedural requirements *as such* could not be chosen for *their own* sake by rational, purely self-interested persons (without prior moral conceptions) in Rawls's original position.[35]

I have dwelt at such length on the extent to which arguments from the original position *must* yield end-result principles for the reason that the *choice* of the "original position" as an intellectual device is ultimately motivated by a form of objectivism. Rawls asks what would be chosen by persons in an original position of ignorance because he wishes to derive principles in a manner he calls "objective," nullifying *personal* conceptions and circumstances that might tempt the participants to make divergent choices.[36] In a similar vein, other philosophers and economists have long been attracted to end-result modes of thought by an objectivist desire to avoid what seemed to them the more obviously personal and hence controversial assessments that any evaluation of process as such appeared to entail.

The history of American legal thought in this regard is only superficially different. Early notions of law as the objective expression of transcendent reason, successfully attacked by legal realism and sociological jurisprudence, have been re-formed into less mechanical, but no less rationalist, theories of law as process—but as process typically justified either in purely formal, positivist terms or in terms of a supposed tendency to maximize aggregate satisfaction in the end, rather than in terms intrinsic to the process itself in its constitutive function of defining substantive human roles, rights, and relationships and structuring their evolution over time. Paradoxically enough, therefore, proceduralism in legal thought has served largely as an "economic" vehicle of concern for end-result maximization.[37]

In the light of their intellectual origins in the same broad tradition, it should not be surprising that the policy sciences too have taken an end-result position, focusing almost exclusively on ultimate outcomes, with no independent concern for the *procedure* whereby those outcomes are produced or for the *history* out of which they evolve. This lack of concern for process comes about partly because procedures for choice must include processes to resolve conflicts among persons and their interests, and most policy analysts believe that methods which rank as "objective" within their intellectual heritage[38] can never settle how true conflicts should be resolved. But other factors also appear to play a role. Thus, as I have argued more fully elsewhere,[39] the characteristic obsession of policy analysis with end results may stem in part from the difficulty of always treating procedures as purely instrumental—and the resulting difficulty of reducing them to variables chosen mechanically (i.e., in an objective, impersonal way) so as to maximize some appropriately defined objective function. Finally, there may be intrinsic difficulties of self-reference (akin to those encountered in set theory, logic, and transformational linguistics) that arise when an analytic technique is focused on a process of choice that, if fully specified, would include reliance on the technique itself, rather than entirely upon some "detachable" subject matter. It appears, therefore, that the objectivist ideal lies close to the source of a major distortion in the policy sciences' perspective.

Nor can it be doubted that the distortion is a significant one. In most areas of human endeavor—from performing a symphony to orchestrating a society—the processes and rules that constitute the enterprise and define the roles of its participants matter quite apart from any identifiable "end state" that is ultimately produced. Indeed, in many cases it is the process itself that matters *most* to those who take part in it. Thus, when coupled with the policy analyst's characteristically passive role in accepting problems as formulated by a client,[40] the reduction of all process to result virtually assures that the advice offered by the analyst will often be wide of the mark. For example, if an agency asks "Where should we build this highway?" the best answer would often be "Don't ask me that; ask me to help you design a procedure for consultation and bargaining to help decide where." But the mode of thought engendered by objectivist policy science greatly reduces the probability that any such answer will be offered.[41]

2. Reducing Wholes and Blending Parts

Just as the policy sciences are driven (in part by the search for "objectivity") to collapse process into result, so too, and for closely linked reasons, they are driven to collapse results into structureless mass. Seeking to limit himself to matters about which he can be "completely objective," the policy analyst who must compare two alternative courses of action first focuses on the *consequences* of each alternative (the initial or "process" reduction) and then on *objectively comparable features* of those consequences (the second or "substance" reduction), a task that suggests either (1) finding a common denominator to which all can be reduced, or (2) at least establishing "substitution rates" or "exchange ratios" (e.g., in the form of smooth indifference curves) for the comparison by pairs of the key attributes of each consequence.[42]

To offer a crude but instructive analogy, the comparison of a particular painting by Rembrandt with one by Picasso (to help decide, for example, whether it would be desirable to sell one in order to buy the other) in terms true to the objectivist ideal might proceed first by disregarding the history of each work (the "process" reduction), in order to focus exclusively on what appears on the canvas; and second by considering each work (the "substance" reduction) as just so much paint of various specifiable colors, in order to focus on features that can be impersonally compared (e.g., the Picasso might contain more of certain pigments than the Rembrandt). Such "structural" features as balance, movement, composition, and the like would be left out of account; for how could one "objectively" compare or even "analyze" them?

As Rawls has demonstrated in the field of moral philosophy, any teleological theory—needing a way to compare the diverse good of different individuals so that the total good might be maximized—must seek "a common denominator among the plurality of persons, an interpersonal currency as it were, by means of which the social ordering can be specified."[43] The tendency of teleological theories, as Rawls shows, is thus to arrive at some form of hedonism, the maximization of the net balance of pleasure over pain, whether as the principle of rational action for an individual person or as the more extended principle of rational choice for a society of persons.[44] The classical utilitarian, for example, can be best understood as conceiving of "separate individuals . . . as so many different lines along which rights and duties are to be assigned and scarce means of satisfaction allocated . . . so as to give the greatest fulfillment of wants. The nature of the decision . . . is not, therefore, materially different from that of an entrepreneur deciding how to maximize his profit by producing this or that commodity, or that of a consumer deciding how to maximize his satisfaction by the purchase of this or that collection of goods. In each case there is a single person whose system of desires determines the best allocation of limited means. The correct decision is essentially a question of efficient administration."[45] Thus the classical utilitarian, seeking an objective basis for social choice, conflates all persons into one (often through the device of an imagined "impartial spectator")[46] and all goods into the production of a single good—individual satisfaction—whose maximization over the sum of all persons becomes the sole end of rational policy. Such a vision is an inescapably ideological one and lies at the core of "cost-benefit" analysis, with "total net benefits" serving to replace the concept of total individual satisfaction.[47]

I believe that Rawls is correct when he argues that this program is radically misconceived, and that "there is no [single] dominant end the pursuit of which accords with our considered judgments of value."[48] But more than that, I believe that the entire conception of reducing complex structures to their separate parts, and then making key features of those parts comparable by establishing rates of exchange among them, is in many contexts a profoundly limiting and distorting mode of analysis.

Consider, for the sake of illustration, the now almost traditional application of such analysis to the legal problem of how to assign "rights" and "liabilities"—for example, between polluters and breathers. The currently popular analysis, traceable to the work of Ronald Coase[49] and Guido Calabresi,[50] is roughly as follows: In an ideal world of free transactions, free competition, and full information, economic efficiency (in the sense of Pareto-optimality) would be achieved without regard to how rights (enforceable by injunction, tort liability, or positive sanction) are assigned by law; in the real world, where transactions (for instance, coalitions of breathers to bribe polluters to reduce pollution) are far from free, the only rational way to assign rights or entitlements is to do so in the way that best approximates the efficiency that would have been achieved by free bargains in the ideal world. As most recently summarized by Calabresi, this breaks down into a sequence of propositions: "(1) that economic efficiency standing alone would dictate that set of entitlements which favors knowledgeable choices between social benefits and the social costs of obtaining them, and between social costs and the social costs of avoiding them; (2) that this implies . . . that the cost should be put on the party or activity best located to make such a cost-benefit analysis; (3) that in particular contexts like accidents or pollution this suggests putting costs on the party or activity which can most cheaply avoid them; (4) that in the absence of certainty as to who that party or activity is, the costs should be put on the party or activity which can with the lowest transaction costs act in the market to correct an error in entitlements by inducing the party who can avoid social costs most cheaply to do so; and (5) that since we are in an area where by hypothesis markets do not work perfectly—there are transaction costs—a decision will often have to be made on whether market transactions or collective fiat is most likely to bring us closer to the Pareto

optimal result the 'perfect' market would reach."[51] If the resulting overall
distribution of wealth is deemed inequitable (evidently according to some
noneconomic, "nonobjective" criterion), the best way to deal with this
inequity is ordinarily through lump-sum transfers of income (through taxation and subsidies) that leave the allocation of rights unaltered: rights,
then, to maximize efficiency, with lump-sum transfers to produce a proper
distribution of wealth.[52]

I would remark first that this obviously states an end-result conception
of a proper theory of rights—and is in that respect subject to the sort of
critique sketched above.[53] But the difficulty with the conception goes
deeper, for even as an end-result theory it provides a perfect illustration of
the tendency in economics and policy analysis to reduce complex structures to an unstructured set of components rendered comparable by simple exchange rates or indifference functions. Specifically, the theory must
assume either that individual preferences may be expressed as simple
summations of the total bundle of goods the individual enjoys; or that
social preferences should be arrived at through some continuous aggregation of individual satisfactions.[54]

If, however, individual preferences have a more complex structure, then
the theory begins to crumble. Suppose, for example, that individuals would
not trade breathing rights for pollution rights (even *infinite* pollution rights)
below a certain point. That is, suppose individuals would insist on a certain
minimal quantity and quality B of "breathing opportunities" *as a matter of
right* before they would consider exchanging any part of their bundle of such
breathing rights for *any* quantity of polluting opportunities—or indeed for
any quantity of any other good. If certain interests have this discontinuous
character, then one simply cannot in such cases assign rights so as to maximize efficiency while relying on lump-sum transfers to achieve a proper
distribution of wealth, for the very concept of a proper distribution must
now be defined not with respect to the single homogeneous entity called
"wealth" but with respect to *the enjoyment of these rights as such*. More
precisely, in the case posited the *reasons* for recognizing in person X an
entitlement to B would in all likelihood be incompatible with making X's
enjoyment of B contingent upon his having to pay others to refrain from
depriving him of B, *even if X were given enough resources to make such
bribes.* For X's sense of self and of autonomy may be intimately bound up
not just with the bare fact of having B (or with having any other capacity or
good, such as eyes or limbs), but with *a shared social and legal understanding* that B belongs to X ab initio, as a matter of *right.*[55] And to the extent that
this is so, the Coasian analysis would fail even if it were ultimately to assign
B to X on grounds of efficiency, for being "assigned" B *on such grounds*
cannot satisfy the particular need met by a recognized *right* to B in the
special sense developed here.

The only way to escape from this conclusion would be to argue that, despite the complex discontinuities *within* individual preference order-ings, the proper way to arrive at social preferences *across* individuals is to treat a continuously varying quantity representing total welfare, utility, or some other measure of well-being as the sole end to be maximized, so that *any* imposition upon a particular individual, however extreme, could in theory be justified by a large enough total of gains to others. Even if this argument deserves to be accepted, the policy analyst who advances it is obviously advocating a particular social welfare function—more the role of an ideologue than that of a detached analyst. And if one believes that a just social ordering principle entails discontinuities that put limits on what sorts (or degrees) of losses to some can be offset by *any* gains to others, then the analyst's proposed route of escape (and the utilitarian ideology that shapes it) must be deemed unacceptable.[56]

That there are indeed such limits, and that the discontinuities posited above within individual preference orderings are also quite pervasive, has been convincingly argued by Rawls.[57] In brief, he makes a persuasive case for the view (1) that individuals in the original position[58] would impose a lexical ordering on at least some of the principles (P_1, P_2, . . . , etc.) that they would select to govern their basic institutions, demanding that P_1 be fully satisfied before moving on to P_{i+1};[59] (2) that the principles they would select would in turn impose a lexical ordering on the classes of individuals (C_1, C_2, . . . , etc.) in their society, perhaps demanding that the welfare of a representative individual in class C_i be maximized before that of a representative individual in better-off class C_{i+1} be considered;[60] and finally, (3) that rational individuals themselves have complex pluralities of ends that cannot be reduced to the maximization of any more or less homogeneous quality or attribute of experience.[61]

At this point, three quite different sets of observations seem in order: the first relating to the degree to which one could criticize the Coase-Calabresi approach on assumptions somewhat less rigid than those of Rawls; the second to the respects in which even Rawls appears to adopt something of the reductionist approach criticized here; and the third to the implications of this discussion for the policy sciences as such.

A. ENRICHING THE LEXICAL-ORDERING CONCEPT

A lexical, or lexicographic, ordering is one that effectively ranks alterna-tives with regard to one attribute at a time; only if alternatives A_1 and A_2 are equally satisfactory with respect to attribute a_1 is attribute a_{i+1} rele-vant for the ordering.[62] To use a vivid example, "[a] man would not agree to have his arms and legs cut off in exchange for any number of des-serts. . . ."[63] Despite the plausibility of this particular illustration, the en-tire tradition of economics flies in the face of any lexical analysis. If it is said that a list of goods L_1, L_2, . . . , etc., is lexically ordered (in the sense that a consumer would rank his needs with respect to L_i ahead of his needs with respect to L_{i+1}), the classic economic response is that such a list is useless because it neither tells the consumer to "spend all of his funds on [any particular L_i]" nor gives him any guidance as to exactly how "to allocate his budget among [the various L_i's]."[64] The consumer's problem, as the classical economist conceives it, is to "choose the allocation such that an extra dollar on [each L_i] is just as important to him as an extra dollar on [each other L_j]," so that at "the margin, . . . the objects of expenditure would be equally important."[65] What this position overlooks, however, is that if each L_i were coupled with a description of how much of L_i the ordering demands before moving on to L_i+_1, then the ordering would indeed tell the consumer exactly how to allocate his budget among the items in question.[66]

One might regard it as intuitively plausible that *some* sufficiently basic "rights" (such as, perhaps, the right to vote or the right freely to express one's views) would (or at least should) be given lexical priority over all other interests by a rational person.[67] But suppose one does *not* regard a particular right R as "unique" in this respect, so that one is not prepared to say that entitlement to the right, even in some minimal amount or form, is (or should be) given lexical priority over the enjoyment of certain other distinct interests S, T, and U. Must one then conclude that R is now "up for grabs" in a homogeneous pool of enjoyments and interests whose only organizing principle is "the more the merrier"? I think not.

A person might regard the right to his eyesight E (the "right to see") as wholly expendable in exchange for enough other pleasures, and he might feel the same way about his hearing H or his sense of touch T; but he might nonetheless regard the combined interest in preserving "E *or* H *or* T" as lexically prior to all other enjoyments. Indeed, he might require, in the absence of *any* E or H, some quite substantial level of T (perhaps defined in complex, partly qualitative and partly quantitative, terms)[68] as a good lexically prior to all others. Similarly, the case for a person's giving absolute lexical priority to any particular right of bodily movement M might prove unconvincing without ruling out the possibility that the person gives (or ought to give) lexical priority (1) to one, possibly quite high, level L_1 of M unless a certain minimal combination of P, S, and I (privacy, solitude, and information-manipulating capacity) has been provided; (2) to another, and lower, level L_2 of M once certain higher minimums with respect to P, S, and I have been independently satisfied; and perhaps (3) to *no* level of M once some still higher standard has been satisfied—in addition to (2)—with respect to I.[69]

Likewise, it might be that an acceptable principle of social ordering (an acceptable "social welfare function") would reject Rawls's strict formulation of the lexical difference principle[70] (which says, intuitively, that no person is ever to be benefited at the expense of any worse-off person) while still refusing to accept the utilitarian premise that *any* reduction in the welfare of an individual person can be justified by a large enough total gain for others. Instead one might believe, for example, that certain gains in equality (perhaps as reflecting some measure of the gross dispersion of certain fundamental goods) or even in cultural excellence (perhaps as reflected in the heritage left to succeeding generations), but *only* such gains, can justify some (but not all) kinds or degrees of reductions in the welfare of even the least well-off members of a society.

In short, both individual and societal preference orderings might well display significant discontinuities and structural features of the general form sketched above without any strictly lexical principle ever operating, or (alternatively) in addition to such lexical principles as might also operate. And as long as both individual and societal preference orderings display this sort of "lumpiness," the entire scheme of assigning rights and liabilities so as to maximize efficiency, while using transfers of income to smooth out the distribution of wealth conceived as a homogeneous good, is doomed to failure.

Indeed, this criticism goes further: it challenges the coherence of *any* methodology of social choice that seeks (1) to arrange entities with respect to which individual and social preference orderings are discontinuous or structured (in the sense used above); (2) in such a way as to maximize some single good (e.g., total income, or total benefits less total costs); and then (3) to take all distributional values into account by relying on transfers of some homogeneous good (usually money). What the preceding discussion has shown, I believe, is that (1) and (3) are fundamentally inconsistent.

A major task for further research, which I have begun but have not nearly completed, is to unravel the different sorts of structured orderings that rationality might suggest among various sorts of entities. Mathematical structures are typically relational, algebraic, or topological. Which of these might correspond to various aspects of the human condition? And might it not be necessary to study *peculiarly* human structures, such as those that characterize the capacity of a mature speaker of any language to recognize well-formed sentences?[71] Is it not plausible that features of man analogous to the "deep structures" of contemporary linguistics might directly impose some form of ordering on the exercise of various human capacities—not only with respect to the principles by which various combinations of such capacities would (should) be preferred to others,[72] but also with respect to the patterns in which such combinations can in fact occur?[73] Finally, might there not also exist analogous "deep structures" of an organic, communitywide (societywide? ecosystemwide?) nature that impose certain conditions on social orderings? Even knowing how to think about such questions—what to count as acceptable evidence, what to regard as criteria of truth—is by no means easy. But that *trying* to think about them should prove illuminating seems to me very clear.

B. The Deeply Entrenched Character of Reductionist Thought

In some quite obvious respects even Rawls approaches his intellectual task as a reductionist. He reduces wholes to parts: first, when he seeks to reason about human society only,[74] leaving aside all questions of what might be called "ecological morality"[75] despite the possible (and indeed plausible) inseparability of the two at some important levels; and second, when he reasons about human societies as aggregations of individuals and the good as individual self-realization, arguably disregarding important communitarian ends and structures entirely consistent with individual fulfillment.[76] And even at the level of the individual, Rawls reduces to the single homogeneous category of "wealth" many (though, unlike utilitarians, not all) personal rights such as the right to enjoyment of basic physical capacities, or the right to protection of integrity;[77] regards the distribution of "natural talents" as a common asset;[78] and seemingly accepts at least the main outlines of the Coase-Calabresi argument.[79] In each of these respects, Rawls appears to follow much the same prescription for which he so justly criticizes the utilitarians: he reduces complex, structured entities to essentially homogeneous, or at least smoothly exchangeable, characteristics.[80] The fallacy, then—if we are to regard it as one—is deeply ingrained in an intellectual tradition much broader than those of classical economics and teleological moral theory alone.

C. Reductionism in the Policy Sciences

As I indicated at the outset of this section, the policy sciences appear to be driven, partly by the objectivist ideal, to reduce the outcomes of decision problems to structureless masses, expressing the results of alternative courses of action in terms of greater or lesser amounts of certain qualities among which standards of commensurability are clearly established. Moreover, we have seen both how pervasive this reductionist approach has been in our intellectual tradition and how unacceptable its conclusions can be when certain structural features or discontinuities are posited.

There is a strong tendency, in this general mode of thought, to treat any indication of discontinuous or structured attributes in one of two ways. The first response is simply to treat the matter in question as involving a qualitative constraint—which usually means relegating it to the status of a mere afterthought in any full analysis or, equally significant, regarding it as an externally (and often politically) "given" feature of the situation rather than one amenable to analysis and rational discussion.[81] The second response is to overlook or deny the existence of the discontinuity altogether, often confusing the assertion of discontinuity with an assertion of absolute dominance.[82] For example, when it is argued that man may owe something to nature for reasons beyond his own future well-being, and that avoiding at least *some* incursions into nature may have lexical priority over certain other human goods, a frequent response is that man clearly owes *nothing* to nature as such, because it is implausible "that the preservation of every extant biological species is an absolute good to be set above any conceivable human benefit that might come as a by-product of its extinction."[83] This seems to me a non sequitur.[84] It might well be the case that there is no species whose complete preservation should have lexical priority over all human goods; but it simply does not follow that *no* minimal level (or perhaps some "overall" level) of species survival or diversity should receive lexical priority over at least *some* kinds of human benefits. Nor would it seem peculiar to insist, for example, that a lower limit be established on especially cruel treatment of animals, whatever the economic gains this cruelty brings to persons in general. The formulation of an appropriate moral theory in this regard must await further developments,[85] but it already seems clear that the objectivist tendency to deny discontinuities by reducing everything to varying levels of smoothly interchangeable attributes (inevitably related to human satisfaction) seriously limits the capacity of the policy sciences to accommodate certain kinds of values.

Three categories of values that are particularly vulnerable or "fragile" in this regard suggest themselves. The first category encompasses those values that are intrinsically incommensurable, in at least some of their salient dimensions, with the human satisfactions that are bound to play a central role in any policy analysis; here I would include values related to ecological balance, unspoiled wilderness, species diversity, and the like.

The second category encompasses values with inherently global, holistic, or structural features that cannot be reduced to any finite listing or combination of independent attributes.[86] Here I would again include ecological balance but also urban aesthetics, community cohesion, and the like.

The third and final category encompasses values that have an "on-off" character, and usually also a deeply evocative and emotional aspect. Under this heading I would include such values as the integrity of the body (threatened, for example, by chemical intrusion) or the integrity of the community or neighborhood (threatened, for example, by all influx of little-understood "outsiders").[87]

Whenever values in any of these major categories appear to be involved, at least potentially, in a given problem, one should recognize that the techniques of policy analysis as currently conceived will tend either to filter them out of the investigation altogether or to treat them in ways inconsistent with their special character.[88]

I have elsewhere referred to a closely related phenomenon as the "dwarfing of soft variables,"[89] arguing that quantitative decision-making

techniques are likely to bias conclusions in the direction of the considerations they can most readily incorporate. But the problem here goes
deeper. It relates not merely to undervaluing certain factors but to *reducing entire problems to terms that misstate their underlying structure,* typically collapsing into the task of maximizing some simple quantity an enterprise whose ordering principle is not one of maximization at all.

3. Anesthetizing Moral Feeling

It is increasingly remarked that the antiseptic terminology of systems
analysis and related techniques, particularly in their wartime applications
but elsewhere as well (for instance in the economics of poverty), has
helped to mask the moral reality of much that the techniques have touched. I say nothing new when I observe that talking of gruesomely burned
human beings as part of a "body count" hideously masks the truth, just as
talking of the "Phillips curve trade-off between employment and inflation"
conceals the anguish of joblessness, or talking of the "collapse mode in a
world resource model" obscures what global starvation would mean.

What seems to be less often recognized, however, are two facts about
this phenomenon. First, at least in most cases, it flows quite naturally not
from any Orwellian desire to corrupt language in order to deceive, but
from the policy sciences' objectivist ideal. To facilitate detached thought
and impersonal deliberation, what more plausible path could there be
than to employ a bloodless idiom, one as drained as possible of all emotion? Second, the phenomenon rests on an elementary fallacy: it presupposes that the task of identifying and naming categories can in fact be
wholly neutral. But one need only recall the passage from Borges quoted
earlier[90] to be reminded how false that is. The very choice of so deliberately emotionless a category as "body count" in which to place the dead
incorporates certain premises about the enterprise in which they died and
encourages perceptions and criteria of success framed in the terms of the
ideology those premises define.[91] Objectivism thus tends to generate a
policy jargon and a frame of reference that may be many things—but
surely cannot be called "objective."

4. Narrowing the Role of Rationality

I would suggest, finally, that the objectivist ideal in policy analysis dangerously (and paradoxically) constricts the role played by rationality in the
process of choice. The frame of mind engendered by the policy analyst's
concern to remain fully objective and detached leads him, at least in the
paradigm case, to formulate his function in terribly cramped terms. He
insists that his proper role is essentially to answer questions of fact as
formulated by a particular decision maker who seeks the policy analyst's

advice. Were he to go further, the analyst believes, he could fatally compromise his detachment and objectivity. Thus matters of value (as distinguished from fact) are beyond his province, and choosing what question to ask (as distinguished from providing an answer) is not his task. I am aware that deviations from this supposed "ideal" are not unknown in the practice of the policy sciences, but such deviations are typically regarded as instances of tempering objective analysis with "wisdom," "intuition," or "human sensitivity." As a general proposition, it remains true, despite these deviations, that the nether regions of values and question-formulation are treated by the policy sciences as beyond the reach of systematic intellectual inquiry, although their importance is rarely denied.

A. FACTS AND VALUES

As to the supposed fundamental distinction between fact and value in this context, one must recognize that it is an exceedingly troublesome one at best. "Values" as perceived by one who holds them are often nothing more than predictions referable to even more fundamental values.[92] "Facts" as perceived by one who believes in their truth are often inseparable from the values held by the believer, particularly when the facts in question refer to predictions of likely consequences in a highly uncertain environment. Moreover, both the relations within a set of values[93] and the internal structure of a particular value are amenable to much the same sort of disciplined insight and rational inquiry that can characterize discussions of "factual" questions. Finally, and perhaps most importantly, the whole point of personal or social choice in many situations is not to implement a given system of values in the light of the perceived facts, but rather to define, and sometimes deliberately to reshape, the values—and hence the identity—of the individual or community that is engaged in the process of choosing. The decision maker, in short, often chooses not merely how to achieve his ends, but what they are to be and who he is to become. The fact-value dichotomy and the perception of values as fixed rather than fluid thus impoverishes significantly the potential contribution of intellect to problems of choice.[94]

The analyst might reply that the sort of exploration of value structures contemplated here is not truly incompatible with objective, impersonal inquiry; and although this would take him well beyond the conventional conception of policy analysis, I cannot claim that objectivism, however misguided in other respects, would clearly preclude such a response. But I do believe that it would preclude any reply not ultimately referable to a posited dichotomy between facts and values and to a posited imperative that the two be treated differently.

So long as such a dichotomy is insistently maintained, however, the analyst's perspective will remain skewed. To offer one concrete if limited illustration, I would focus on the frequently stressed tenet of decision theorists that one of the analyst's main functions is to help the decision maker separate clearly (1) how he feels about various possible outcomes of his decision (this preference being a matter of personal value) from (2) his best assessment of the probability of each such outcome (this probability being a matter of impersonal fact).[95] Such separation, it is said, represents an essential prerequisite for rational choice. But a strong argument can be made that in many contexts this very separation tends to obscure an essential feature of the choice that the decision maker confronts. As I have tried to show elsewhere, for example, the value a rational person should attach to each of the several possible outcomes of a criminal trial depends in significant part on the probabilities of those outcomes as they appear to the jury at the time of decision; in particular, convicting an innocent person should be deemed a worse outcome when the jury feels very unsure of the person's guilt (but chooses to convict anyway) than when the jury feels fully confident of guilt (but simply happens to be mistaken).[96] What is being done to the accused in the two cases differs just as surely as kicking a child differs from tripping over it, and the consequences for society of permitting each of these practices differs as well. Similarly, destroying a species of wildlife should probably be regarded as a worse outcome when it results from the disregard of a high known risk than when it results from the materialization of a highly unlikely contingency. The tradition in many legal systems of distinguishing among acts in terms of the mental state accompanying them (treating murder differently from manslaughter, for example) rests on this sort of proposition. Yet the objectivist's fact-value dichotomy, leading to an insistence on separating assessments of probability from the valuation of outcomes, tends to exclude this important dimension of human choice.[97]

The same result can be arrived at, incidentally, by a quite different route. Even if the analyst were to drop his demand that probabilities and preferences be assessed separately, his objectivist ideal might nonetheless impel him to focus on those features of a situation that seem reducible to empirically verifiable propositions to the exclusion of those that cannot easily be discussed in a purely empiricist frame. Thus the "outcomes" a policy analyst allows himself to discuss are likely to be events stripped of such personal elements as reasons and intentions—elements without which the events in question may lose much if not all of their significance.[98]

It should be noted here that this distortion is not the sort that can be compensated for by the decision maker once he has received the policy analyst's supposedly "objective" input. For in the cases posited that input is fundamentally irrelevant, resting as it does on the decision maker's values with respect to a radically misspecified set of outcomes. Informing person D, for example, that he should choose alternative A_1 over alternative A_2 if and only if D believes the probability P of event X to exceed a particular value P_0 is useless if the analyst's calculation of P_0 rests on how

D values in the abstract the four possible outcomes[99] when in fact the values that D would attach to each outcome are themselves functions of D's assessment of P.[100] In such a situation, it will not do to inform D of P_0 and then expect D to "adjust" P_0 somehow (without the analyst's aid) to reflect the functional dependence in question, for the necessary adjustment will itself require a highly complex analytic operation.[101] The systematic truncations occasioned by the fact-value dichotomy thus represent weaknesses that cannot be overcome without fundamentally loosening the constraints on analysis typically engendered by the objectivist ideal.

B. Questions and Answers

But even if those constraints were loosened, there would remain the analytic posture of answering the decision maker's question rather than suggesting to the decision maker what question he should have asked. The very title "policy *analysis*" reveals a great deal in this regard. For analysis is not *synthesis,* and deciding what question to address—choosing the problem to solve—seems very much a synthetic task, and in any event is a task that can hardly be carried out in a wholly mechanical, and hence assuredly "objective," manner.

The first danger arising from this sort of posture is the danger of all literal-minded devices: they grant what you asked for and not what you *meant* to ask for. Norbert Wiener recalls in this connection a tale in which an English working couple comes into possession of a talisman, a monkey's paw said to have been endowed by an Indian holy man with the virtue of granting its owner three wishes.[102] The couple first wish for §200; shortly thereafter a messenger arrives to inform them that their son has been killed in a factory accident and that his employer has offered §200 out of sympathy. Their second wish is that their son return; it is answered by a strange knocking at the door that the parents somehow know to be their son—but not in the flesh. The tale ends with the couple's third wish, that the ghost go away. The moral that Wiener draws from this tale is that all magic—including the "magic" of automation—"is singularly literal-minded, that if it grants you anything at all it grants what you ask for, not what you should have asked for or what you intend."[103] The risk is that the resulting flaw in what you get may be less obvious than it was in the case of the monkey's paw—until it is too late. And the lesson, for policy analysis no less than for automatic computers, is that there must be a system of closely linked and frequent interactions between the decision maker and his "answering device" which employs to the full whatever capacity can be built into that device for identifying and expressing tacit assumptions and for exploring alternatives not envisioned by the decision maker at all.[104] Insofar as this needed degree of interaction and this required capacity are thought to be inconsistent with the detached, objectivist frame of reference, that frame must obviously yield to a broader conception.

But there are limits to how far it can in fact be broadened without wholly exceeding the intrinsic bounds of the concept of policy analysis. Basic to that concept, certainly, is the requirement that the analyst accept as given the values of the decision maker he is advising; to substitute others in the course of redefining or reformulating the problem put to the analyst by the decision maker would violate the notion of detached, impersonal analysis so radically as to inaugurate an altogether different technique, if indeed it could be called a "technique" at all. This very fact, however, imposes severe limits on the sorts of values that the policy sciences can realistically be expected to serve. Quite obviously, the only values that can be served will be those strongly held by persons who seek a policy analyst's aid. The point may seem too trivial to make, but its consequences are anything but minor. For at least three categories of values and interests are likely to be excluded on this basis:[105] those too widely diffused over space (or too incrementally affected over time) to be strongly championed by any single client of a policy analyst; those associated only with persons not yet existing (future generations); and those not associated with persons at all (for example, the "rights" of wild animals).[106]

And more generally, one must expect that *all* values peripheral to those centrally held by the analyst's client will be understated by the analysis. In this sense, policy analysis is afflicted with congenital tunnel vision—tied as it must remain (if it is to be "objective") to the mission, often single-minded, of its user.

One might reply that this is not a problem at all, inasmuch as a multitude of tunnel-visioned analyses for a multitude of clients will somehow leave all important values properly accounted for.[107] But there is no adequate ground for assuming the operation of any such invisible hand,[108] at least with respect to collective goods, future interests, and values not congruent with any directly human concern. The only remaining reply would have to be that the use of policy analysis need not be limited to individual decision makers with narrow interests to advance but can be extended instead to collective groups of decision makers and to decision makers representing a broad public constituency. But the consistency of any such extension with the intrinsically reductionist characteristics of the policy sciences remains at this point an open question, and we are at least entitled to be skeptical about the answer in light of what has been said above.[109]

We have thus seen that an objectivist framework can significantly color the sorts of conclusions one should expect of the policy sciences, not only because of its reductionist and anesthetizing characteristics but also because of the dichotomy such a framework presupposes and tends to reinforce between fact and value and the passivity it tends to impose on the act of analysis itself.

III. Policy Science as Ideology

Insofar as I set out to establish that the policy sciences as a whole embody a fully developed ideology of their own (beyond that of exalting instrumental [means-end] rationality and objectivity), I have obviously failed. At various times and places, particular branches of the policy sciences have taken what must be regarded as ideological positions (and narrow ones at that) in the name of objectivity and value-free analysis (as, for example, in the adoption of the Kaldor-Hicks criterion), but this hardly establishes a universal proposition, particularly as applied to anything as protean as policy analysis. To be sure, the policy sciences' intellectual and social heritage in the classical economics of unfettered contract, consumer sovereignty, and perfect markets both brings them within a paradigm of conscious choice guided by values[110] and inclines them, within that paradigm, toward the exaltation of utilitarian and self-interested individualism, efficiency, and maximized production as against distributive ends, procedural and historical principles, and the values (often nonmonetizable, discontinuous, and of complex structure) associated with personal rights, public goods, and communitarian and ecological goals. And one might even venture the speculation that the policy sciences' partial origins in (and repeated forays into) military planning did little to humanize the methodologies involved, or to counteract the anesthetizing quality of such stunningly detached terminology as "body counts," "kill ratios," or "utilities." But exposing these tendencies falls short of completely displaying policy science as ideology—or indeed even of fully baring its intellectual foundations. Ultimately the policy sciences—and the larger fabric of liberal thought of which much of contemporary economics, moral philosophy, and legal analysis are all integral parts—might stand revealed as the all but inevitable manifestations (and the all but invincible perpetuators) of the modern technocratic state. But that would require an investigation that has here been only begun.[111]

On the other hand, I believe that I have succeeded in making plausible the more modest claim that, in part because of their particular form of commitment to a posture of detached and impersonal objectivity, the policy sciences tend to partition and warp reality in certain patterned ways, generating a fairly understandable, and sometimes quite unfortunate, system of blind spots and distortions.

I do not rule out the possibility that a more intensive examination of the policy sciences as actually practiced, and of analogues of policy analysis in other disciplines such as law, might yet lead to a stronger conclusion—perhaps even to a conclusion that suggests the complete restructuring of systems analysis and related techniques over a wide range of policy contexts.[112] But nothing I have demonstrated here goes so far. Apart from uncovering the ideological structure of particular errors that I believe have flowed from the basic axioms of policy analysis and related techniques (as applied, for example, in the economic theory of how to assign legal rights), I have simply explicated certain types of distorting tendencies that might, at least in theory, be overcome by relatively modest changes in the assumptions, emphases, and approaches of policy analysis methods. Whether the required changes would so transform those methods as to make them into something other than "policy science" presents problems of meaning that I have not fully considered.

IV. Possible First Steps

At one level, a starting set of prescriptions for the policy sciences might be devised simply by outlining the converse of each major proposition developed above. Thus, insofar as the policy sciences have paid insufficient attention to conflict-resolving procedures, one would counsel greater emphasis on process. Insofar as the policy sciences have taken a reductionist approach, either ignoring structural features and discontinuities or treating them as externally "given" constraints, one would propose closer intellectual attention to structural aspects of decision problems and deeper investigation of what systems of related constraints such structural features or discontinuities might entail. Insofar as the policy sciences have masked moral realities in their search for a detached and emotionless vocabulary, one would suggest a reduced aversion to frankly evocative terminology. Insofar as the policy sciences have unduly separated facts from values, and treated the latter as fixed, one would urge more study of their interactions and of the rationally discernible structures within values and value systems as they are shaped over time. Finally, insofar as the policy sciences have too passively accepted as given the decision maker's formulation of what he wishes to accomplish, one would call for more sustained attention to the problem of how to frame questions, greater efforts in modeling and simulation aimed at yielding alternatives not yet conceived by the decision maker, and even a willingness to challenge the values that the decision maker posits.

All of these proposals appear to point in the general direction of a subtler, more holistic, and more complex style of problem-solving, undoubtedly involving several iterations between problem-formulation and problem-solution and relying at each stage on the careful articulation of a wide range of interrelated values and constraints through the development of several distinct "perspectives" on a given problem, each couched in an idiom true to its internal structure rather than translated into some "common denominator."[113] Needless to say, conceptual schemes as well as operational details remain to be developed; the result seems unlikely to bear much resemblance to the economic model with which we began.

Whatever else is done, it would seem essential that some effort be directed to reexamining what appears, from several different perspectives, to lie close to the center of the policy sciences' many limitations: their elusive ideal of wholly objective, impersonal, and detached instrumental analysis. As I have argued throughout, that ideal is not only unattainable but destructive—in that the very act of striving for it tends to warp the perspective of policy analyst and decision maker alike in the characteristic ways already outlined.

If there is to be a partial solution at this level, it must obviously involve the fuller engagement of the policy analyst (or indeed of any "expert" adviser) as a whole person—revealing his own values and biases to the extent that he is aware of them (subject to appropriately designed rules of evidence), but then proceeding to give advice not on the claim that he is acting as a detached, "objective" spirit but in the recognition that he is counseling as a complete, committed, human being, applying to the best of his capacity whatever disciplined insight he is able to bring to the entire task at hand. This means neither that the policy analyst (or the "expert") is to be given the ultimate responsibility for choice nor that his views are to be reduced to mere votes, counting as naked expressions of preference. It means only that the supposedly "expert" views of any adviser, policy scientist or otherwise, are to be offered and received as a mixed form of counsel, at once both objective and subjective, both learned and merely expressive of one man's vote, but always and ineluctably *personal*.

V. Postscript: Some Steps Beyond

In some ways a particularly illuminating test of the policy sciences—both as now practiced and as reformed along the lines sketched above—might be provided by juxtaposing their methods with those of legal theory, ecology, and moral philosophy (in some variant of each) with respect to the general problem of how human societies should treat nature—a problem rich with structural considerations and sharp discontinuities.

Recognizing that his theory of justice deals solely with relations among persons, Rawls argues that "cruelty to animals is . . . certainly . . . wrong," that destroying a species "can be a great evil," and that a correct conception of man's relations to nature "would seem to depend upon a theory of the natural order and our place in it." Rawls accordingly exhorts metaphysics to work out a world view suited to this purpose, identifying and systematizing "the truths decisive for these, questions."[114] There is surely much both in the ecological literature and in the considered judgments of many rational individuals that would suggest the fruitfulness of the task of formulating, in rational terms beyond anthropocentric self-interest, a convincing moral philosophy of ecological obligation. At the same time, there is both a substantial legal tradition of protecting the interests of animals and a growing body of scholarship investigating the possibilities of doctrinal and institutional innovations along these lines.[115] Much could be learned from a systematic effort to elaborate the possible nonanthropocentric foundations, in some coherent legal theory, for legislation to protect nature.[116]

By comparing the perspectives provided by philosophy, ecology, and law with those afforded by the policy sciences, preferably in the context of a concrete situation involving a clear conflict of interests (for example, a particular controversy about land use), I suspect that one could usefully test, refine, and in some instances greatly revise or supplement the sorts of hypotheses offered here.

Although my attention has been focused on the policy sciences and on the ways in which their allegedly neutral assumptions structure substantive conclusions, I have digressed often to note parallels and contrasts with the perspectives and tendencies of welfare economics, moral philosophy, and law. I intend in further work to pursue such comparisons more systematically, and to think about ways of developing coherent styles of legal thought (and problem-oriented thought in general) sharply distinguishable from the approach of policy analysis, and perhaps distinguishable from *all* instrumental rationality.

Some of these inquiries may seem to take me far afield from the topic with which I began. But I believe that a critique of so pervasive a mode of thought as that embodied in the policy sciences, and certainly a program for their reform or replacement, cannot be carried forward without constructive attempts to define an alternative methodology and to apply it to some of the problems with which policy analysts have at times grappled. By selecting such problems from among those that have also engaged (and often baffled) lawyers, I would hope to arrive at a methodology that might yield better ways of organizing thought about the legal order, which in turn might yield insight into better ways of thinking about policy choice. And if the result is simply the discovery that certain frustrations are inherent in the very categories and divisions we have been employing here (legal thought versus policy analysis, for instance), that should be justification enough for the effort.

NOTES

This article, first published in *Philosophy and Public Affairs* 2 (1972): 66–110, copyright © 1972 by Princeton University Press, is reprinted by permission. It was written under the auspices of the American Academy of Arts and Sciences, with support from the Ford Foundation and the Environmental Quality Laboratory of the California Institute of Technology.

1. For a history of wartime operations research see Florence N. Trefethen, "A History of Operations Research," in *Operations Research for Management,* ed. Joseph F. McCloskey and Florence N. Trefethen (Baltimore, Md., 1954), pp. 3–35.

2. Bruce L. B. Smith, *The RAND Corporation* (Cambridge, Mass., 1966), passim. The description of systems analysis is from Smith, esp. pp. 8–14, and from Howard Raiffa, *Decision Analysis: Introductory Lectures on Choices Under Uncertainty* (Reading, Mass., 1968), p. 296.

3. John von Neumann and Oscar Morgenstern, *Theory of Games and Economic Behavior* (Princeton, N.J., 1944).

4. The structural similarity between (1) this frontier for a single individual and (2) the curve of Pareto-optimal points (points where no one can gain unless someone else loses) where each "output" represents a different individual's welfare, should be obvious. Less obvious, perhaps, is the ultimate consequence of this structural congruence: the reduction of social rationality to the managerial goal of efficient resource deployment.

5. For a typical statement of a slightly weaker assumption see Richard Zeckhauser and Elmer Schaefer, "Public Policy and Normative Economic Theory," in *The Study of Policy Formation,* ed. Raymond A. Bauer and Kenneth J. Gergen (New York, 1968), pp. 37–38.

6. The situation may be described in another way. As an individual moves along the production-possibility frontier he continually gives up some of one alternative in order to produce more of another. The measure of this trade-off is the rate of transformation. As the slope of the curve changes, this rate changes also. At any point on the curve the rate is defined marginally, as the slope between two points separated by a distance tending toward zero. This slope is called the marginal rate of transformation. Much the same can be said for indifference curves; the corresponding terms are rate of substitution and marginal rate of substitution. Transforming the language of plane geometry into that of analytic geometry, we say: at the point of tangency between the production-possibility curve and the indifference curve, the marginal rate of transformation equals the marginal rate of substitution.

7. See the excellent discussion in Amartya K. Sen, *Collective Choice and Social Welfare* (San Francisco, Cal., 1970), pp. 56–57. Responding to the insensitivity of the Kaldor-Hicks criterion to distributional concerns, some critics have proposed supplementing it with the constraint that the redistributive effects of the change in question must be beneficial. See I.M.D. Little, *A Critique of Welfare Economics,* 2nd ed. (London, 1960), p. 94. The Kaldor-Hicks criterion, like Pareto-optimality, does not claim to generate a complete ordering of all alternative social states. Such an ordering would be a social welfare function. Called "individualistic" if it depends only on the welfare functions of individual members of the community, a social welfare function can be shown to be a logical impossibility if, in addition to being individualistic, it is required that the function also be transitive, be able to combine every possible configuration of individual preferences, be nondictatorial, and be independent of irrelevant alternatives (no inter-

personal comparisons of utility). See Kenneth J. Arrow, *Social Choice and Individual Values,* 2nd ed. (New Haven, 1963).

8. A. Myrick Freeman III, "Project Design and Evaluation with Multiple Objectives," in *Public Expenditures and Policy Analysis,* ed. Robert H. Haveman and Julius Margolis (Chicago, 1970), p. 351.

9. Julius Margolis, "Shadow Prices for Incorrect or Nonexistent Market Values," ibid., p. 315.

10. Roland N. McKean, *Efficiency in Government Through Systems Analysis* (New York, 1958), pp. 27–28. For a discussion of the early history of cost-benefit analysis, see pp. 18–20. A description of more recent use of cost-benefit analysis in Defense Department program budgeting is to be found in Alain C. Enthoven and K. Wayne Smith, "The Planning, Programming, and Budgeting System in the Department of Defense: An Overview from Experience," *Public Expenditures,* ed. Haveman and Margolis, pp. 485–501.

11. Burton A. Weisbrod, "Appendix: Concepts of Costs and Benefits," in *Problems in Public Expenditure Analysis,* ed. Samuel B. Chase (Washington, D.C., 1968), pp. 257–262. Also, McKean, *Efficiency in Government,* pp. 58–64. On the use of constraints, see Arthur Maass et al., *Design of Water Resource Systems* (Cambridge, Mass., 1962), pp. 62–86. It should be noted that if individual utility functions were allowed to assume strongly interdependent forms (in violation of the assumption of self-interested rationality), then any artempt to separate efficiency concerns from distributional concerns would quickly collapse; indeed, even the concept of Pareto-optimality could then be rendered vacuous (inasmuch as *every* situation might become Pareto-optimal).

12. "Maximizing" may not be strictly correct; taking into account the extent of a decision-maker's uncertainty and the high costs of fully evaluating all conceivable alternatives, he may do best simply by "satisficing" within a model of "bounded rationality." See Herbert A. Simon, *Models of Man: Social and Rational* (New York, 1967), pp. 241–260. This model employs a simplified objective function (perhaps classifying outcomes only as poor and good), a highly limited set of alternatives, and a sequential choice process including selection of the first "satisfactory" alternative encountered, adjusting the definition of "satisfactory" upward if the choice proves easy and downward if the choice proves diificult. See also Howard Raiffa and Robert Schlaifer, *Applied Statistical Decision Theory* (Cambridge, Mass., 1961), p. viii.

13. See Robert Dorfman, Paul Samuelson, and Robert Solow, *Linear Programming and Economic Analysis* (New York, 1958), pp. 30–31. The general form of the linear programming equation is that found in George B. Dantzig, *Linear Programming and Extensions* (Princeton, N.J., 1963), p. 61.

14. Not only does the VN-M procedure allow the policy analyst to incorporate a treatment of uncertainty into his study, but it provides at least a formal way of dealing with multi-attribute problems. For it is obviously possible to assign utilities to outcome vectors (where each component represents an attribute) by means of a reference lottery based on the best and worst of outcomes, as long as one assumes continuity (see note 42, below).

15. See Raiffa, *Decision Analysis,* passim.

16. To deal formally with probability assessments involving unique events, Bayesian decision theory (see ibid.) construes probability statements as express-

ing subjective degrees of confidence. Thus, to say that X attaches a subjective probability of 30 percent to proposition S means that X would be indifferent between (a) betting that S is true and (b) betting on a lottery (with the same stakes) having a known 30 percent chance of winning.

17. Michel Foucault, *The Order of Things* (New York, 1970), p. xv.

18. See, e.g., Lionel Robbins, *An Essay on the Nature and Significance of Economic Science,* 2nd ed. (London, 1935), pp. 142–143, 148–149.

19. *Personal Knowledge* (Chicago, 1958). See also Thomas S. Kuhn, *The Structure of Scientific Revolutions* (Chicago, 1962).

20. Even probability statements, as Polanyi stresses, can never be "strictly contradicted by experience" (*Personal Knowledge,* p. 21).

21. Bertrand Russell, *Human Knowledge: Its Scope and Limits* (New York, 1948), pp. 522, 524, 526–527.

22. Noam Chomsky, *Problems of Knowledge and Freedom* (New York, 1971), p. 13. See also Jean Piaget, *Biology and Knowledge,* trans. Beatrik Walsh (Chicago, 1971).

23. *Personal Knowledge,* p. 257.

24. For Polanyi, the concept of "personal knowledge" transcends the objective-subjective dichotomy by embodying both an irreducibly nonobjective dimension, insofar as it rests on an individual's appraisal and passion, and an irreducibly nonsubjective dimension, insofar as it rests on a commitment to obey requirements acknowledged by the individual to be independent of the self (*Personal Knowledge,* p. 300).

25. Obviously, more must be said to specify the exact functions and features of the "objectivist ideal" posited here (see note 36, below), but I trust that the general shape of the concept is clear enough for our purposes without further elaboration.

26. It might prove even more illuminating to view the system of distortions from the substantive perspective of the policy sciences' underlying axiom of individual satisfaction-maximizing behavior, but I leave that possibility for later study. Another and quite different approach to this entire subject (an approach I intend to explore in subsequent work) would be to investigate not so much the *consequences* of the policy sciences' axioms and criteria as the underlying *pattern* they reveal, to study how that pattern "interlocks" with other contemporaneously developed areas of thought (cf. Foucault's *The Order of Things*), and to examine what underlying *purposes* the pattern and its history reveal. See section III of this essay.

27. Compare the discussion of the deep intuitive appeal of teleological theories in John Rawls, *A Theory of Justice* (Cambridge, Mass., 1971), pp. 24–25. I first criticized the tendency of economics and policy analysis to focus on results to the exclusion of process in "Trial by Mathematics: Precision and Ritual in the Legal Process," *Harvard Law Review* 84 (1971): 1329, 1381–1383, 1391–1392. End-result theories are, of course, natural outgrowths of all instrumental (means-end) concepts of the rational.

28. *A Theory of Justice,* p. 88.

29. This notion of the "original position" was first put forth by Rawls in "Justice as Fairness," *Philosophical Review* 67 (1958): 164. But it appears to have been hit upon independently by Sidney Alexander in his RAND paper, "The

Public Interest in Public Television" (P-3676, September 1957), pp. 34–35. I am indebted to Robert Dorfman for calling Alexander's work to my attention.

30. This statement is necessarily a simplification of Rawls's far richer development of his two principles, but it suffices, I think, to convey their flavor here. I should add that, despite my great admiration for Rawls's work, its defense of the maximin principle (*A Theory of Justice,* pp. 150–192, 315–325) seems to me uncharacteristically unconvincing.

31. Ibid., p. 60.

32. Ibid., p. 87.

33. Ibid., p. 86.

34. "An inequality of opportunity must enhance the opportunity of those with the lesser opportunity" (ibid., p. 303).

35. Since writing this essay, I have learned that Robert Nozick advances a similar critique of Rawls's theory in chapter 7 of his *Anarchy, State, and Utopia.* As Nozick tellingly argues, purely end-state theories of distributive justice proceed as though "things fell from heaven like manna," naturally posing the question "how are all these things to be distributed?" without regard to any conception of the actual history of the things in question (e.g., who made what?) or any notion of entitlements to them based on that history coupled with procedural rules for how entitlements may justly arise or shift.

36. *A Theory of Justice,* pp. 516–517. Cf. Alexander's choice in "The Public Interest in Public Television" of a similar mode of argument in order to make normative judgments "impersonal." See Sidney Alexander, "The Impersonality of Normative Judgments," in *Induction, Growth and Trade,* ed. W. A. Eltis, M. F. Scott, and J. N. Wolfe (London, 1970), pp. 63–64. See also Rawls on intuitionism, *A Theory of Justice,* pp. 34–40, 317–320. The tendency to equate the "objective," the "impersonal," and the "consensual" is central to a certain style of thought characteristic of the policy sciences, classical economics, and much of moral philosophy and even law; the core of that style is purely instrumental rationality.

37. This underlying convergence of legal and economic thought in the instrumental rationality of end-result maximization may account for the paucity of attention within both law and economics to problems of distribution, with the result that *neither* of the two major intellectual pillars of politics in the United States has evolved a coherent framework in which to discuss distributive justice— a circumstance that has hardly helped to alleviate the inequities that demand lucid articulation in our system.

38. See, e.g., Zeckhauser and Schaefer, "Public Policy and Normative Economic Theory," pp. 60–64.

39. "Trial by Mathematics," pp. 1391–1392.

40. See pp. 137–38.

41. On the rare occasions when such an answer is given, the persisting tendency of the policy sciences is to overlook the significance of procedure *as such,* treating a process of choice or coordination as nothing more than a machine for generating outcomes. To use an instructive parable suggested to me by Robert Nozick, if a policy analyst were consulted by the members of an orchestra who wished to coordinate their efforts to play a Brahms concerto, he might advise them to use a special stylus he had invented to etch the optimal outcome (the ideal "sound of music") on a plastic disk, completely missing the point that the pro-

cesses of interaction, coordination, and participation according to defined rules are themselves of overriding importance to the players.

42. An assumption of continuous substitutability is implicit even in the least obviously market-oriented method, that of VN-M. See R. Duncan Luce and Howard Raiffa, *Games and Decisions* (New York, 1957), p. 27. When the continuity assumption is dropped, it turns out that substantial parts of VN-M theory can be constructed on the basis of n-dimensional utilities (see, e.g., Melvin Hausner, "Multidimensional Utilities," in *Decision Processes*, ed. R. M. Thrall, C. H. Coombs, and R. L. Davis [New York, 1954], pp. 167–180), but the characteristic invocation of the continuity axiom is itself significant, and the axiom is needed for many (although not all) of the typical applications of policy analysis techniques.

43. *A Theory of Justice*, pp. 559–560.

44. Ibid., pp. 554–555, 560–561.

45. Ibid., p. 27.

46. Ibid.

47. See note 4, above.

48. *A Theory of Justice*, p. 558.

49. "The Problem of Social Cost," *Journal of Law and Economics* 3 (1960): 1–44.

50. *The Costs of Accidents* (New Haven, Conn., 1970).

51. Guido Calabresi and A. Douglas Melamed, "Property Rules, Liability Rules, and Inalienability: One View of the Cathedral," *Harvard Law Review* 85 (1972): 1089, 1096–1097 (footnotes omitted).

52. Cf. the Kaldor-Hicks criterion, note 7.

53. See pp. 123–25 of this essay. A concern for the rootedness of substantive rights in the history and structure of corporeal persons and human communities would yield a notion very different from the end-result concept, even when their bare conclusions might coincide. There is a vast difference between saying "X has a right to his arms and legs because giving him the right maximizes aggregate welfare" and saying "X has a right to his arms and legs because they are organically and historically part of the person that he is, and his entitlement to them has not justly shifted to anyone else." See pp. 128–29.

54. I discuss this problem in a somewhat wider context in my book *Channeling Technology Through Law* (Chicago, 1972), chap. 6, sec. B. The second of the two assumptions noted above is the basis for the occasional efforts to incorporate distributive aspects of a policy choice in cost-benefit analysis by assigning various interpersonal weights to different individuals and then maximizing the weighted sum. See, e.g., J. E. Meade, *The Theory of International Economic Policy* (New York, 1954), vol. 2, *Trade and Welfare*, chapters V and VII; cf. Burton A. Weisbrod, "Income Redistributive Effects and Benefit Cost Analysis," *Problems in Public Expenditure Analysis*, ed. Chase, pp. 177, 179–180, 181–182, 184.

55. It is this sort of consideration, and not the notion that breathers should be richer than polluters because they are "worthier," that I believe underlies the decision that, say, the "right to breathe" should be properly distributed *as such*. Contrast Calabresi and Melamed, "Property Rules, Liability Rules, and Inalienability," p. 1098 (silence lovers versus noise lovers). In this connection, it would obviously be absurd to allocate rights between breathers and polluters so as to deny individual X his minimal breathing demand B in the interest of efficiency,

and then give X enough cash to buy B back again by bribing polluters. If, as we have hypothesized, B is the breathing demand X would insist on satisfying before moving on to satisfy other goals, then such compensation would merely represent a way of moving dollars in a circle. Assigning rights so as to maximize efficiency avoids this absurdity only if the lump-sum distributions at the end are such as to lead their recipients to find activities that substitute for the enjoyment of the rights that in the name of efficiency have been assigned elsewhere.

56. Portions of the argument of these two paragraphs, which I initially developed in connection with *Channeling Technology Through Law,* parallel a more formal demonstration independently advanced by Charles Fried in his forthcoming article "Rights." It should be noted that the references to "discontinuities," which I retain for reasons of intuitive appeal, might be technically misleading; for even if the orderings in question display no *discontinuities* in the strict mathematical sense, the argument made above holds as long as the orderings embody threshold characteristics precluding substitutions or trade-offs below certain positive levels—e.g., if the indifference curves asymptotically (albeit continuously) approach levels other than zero—and the argument remains particularly significant, with or without discontinuities, as long as such thresholds relate to needs that can only be met by the social acknowledgment of entitlements. See preceding paragraph.

57. *A Theory of Justice,* pp. 42–43.

58. See note 29, above

59. For example, he argues that the principle of maximum equal liberty with respect to basic political rights would be given lexical priority over the maximin principle with respect to the distribution of social and economic goods (*A Theory of Justice,* pp. 541–548).

60. See ibid., p. 83, for a statement of this "lexical difference principle." The "perhaps" in the text expresses my own doubts on this point. See note 30, above.

61. *A Theory of Justice,* p. 566.

62. The classic treatment is that of John S. Chipman, "The Foundations of Utility," *Econometrica* 28 (1960): 193.

63. Zeckhauser and Schaefer, "Public Policy and Normative Economic Theory," p. 38.

64. Charles J. Hitch and Roland N. McKean, *The Economics of Defense in the Nuclear Age* (Cambridge, Mass., 1960), p. 123.

65. Ibid.

66. Of course, the ordering might also be lexical at various points and continuous in between.

67. Again, this should not be confused with the proposition that lexical priority attaches to the mere exercise of the underlying activities (voting or speaking); the priority is likely to attach instead to the socially and legally recognized *right* to engage in such activities. See pp. 128–29.

68. Like most capacities and values, the sense of touch cannot properly be conceived on a zero to one continuum; below some minimal point, it simply is no longer a "sense of touch."

69. The structure described here has two tiers (with M on one tier and P, S, and I on the other), but one could just as well imagine n-tiered structures for any positive integer n. Moreover, the structure might employ some wholly nonquantitative ordering scheme, conceivably involving an essentially topological feature of how the critical entities are arrayed or related.

70. See note 60, above.

71. See Noam Chomsky, *Aspects of the Theory of Syntax* (Cambridge, Mass., 1965); and Jean Piaget, *Le Structuralisme* (Paris, 1968). Cf. Robert Nozick, "Moral Complications and Moral Structures," *Natural Law Forum* 13 (1968): 1.

72. I.e., structured and discontinuous preference orderings or indifference curves, in the economist's terminology.

73. I.e., structured and discontinuous choice sets or production-possibility frontiers, again borrowing the vocabulary of economics.

74. He concedes that even his "wider theory fails to embrace all moral relationships, since it would seem to include only our relations with other persons and to leave out of account how we are to conduct ourselves toward animals and the rest of nature" (*A Theory of Justice*, p. 17; see also p. 512).

75. See section V of this essay.

76. But see *A Theory of Justice*, pp. 262–265, 520–529, 581–586.

77. This point is also noted critically by Charles Fried in his review of Rawls's book in *Harvard Law Review* 85 (1972): 1691, 1697.

78. *A Theory of Justice*, p. 101.

79. Ibid, pp. 274–284. Perhaps it is Rawls's failure to posit a mode of ordering less rigid than the lexical (though still structured) that leads him to reduce all nonpolitical rights in this way.

80. We have also seen earlier that Rawls's reductionism encompasses "collapsing process into result."

81. Cf. pp. 137–38. At most the policy analyst may manipulate the objective function by estimating its value under each of several hypothetical constraints so as to convey a sense of what "price" imposing the constraints at various levels might entail; but this is not always attempted, and even it falls far short of a full examination of the structures in question and how they are formed.

82. Cf. pp. 129–30.

83. Address by Dean Harvey Brooks, Harvard Division of Engineering and Applied Physics, "What Can Technology Do About Technology?" delivered 14 October 1970 at the Industrial Research Institute, Washington, D.C.

84. Cf. pp. 129–30 and notes 64–66.

85. See section V of this essay.

86. Compare Gödel's famous demonstration that any sufficiently "rich" formal system S_1 must generate propositions whose validity is undecidable without constructing a still "higher" system S_2 that includes S_1. For an excellent nontechnical account of Gödel's 1931 paper "On Formally Undecidable Propositions of Principia Mathematica and Related Systems" see Ernest Nagel and James R. Newman, *Gödel's Proof* (New York, 1958).

87. For the perception that bodily, communal, and even global "integrity" in this sense may constitute related, deeply felt, and yet particularly fragile "on-off" values, I am indebted to Robert Socolow. I emphasize that my argument is not that the policy sciences have not been used (or cannot be used) to address such values, but rather that the *methods* of conventional policy science have been ill-suited to the elaboration of these values in any satisfactory way.

88. It should be noted that I have not included as a separate category of values intrinsically refractory to the techniques of policy analysis those that are "hard to quantify" (to order cardinally) or "difficult to rank" (to arrange ordinally). It seems to me unhelpful to talk about values in such terms, inasmuch as what

usually matters is not the *existence* of some sort of ordering relating to the value in question but its *significance*. The reason "ecological balance" tends to be filtered out by the policy scientist's lens is not that the number of birds, ferns, and trees cannot be determined but rather that the value in question is too "structural" in character to be captured by such enumerations.

89. "Trial by Mathematics," pp. 1361–1365.

90. See p. 121.

91. I do not, of course, blame the policy sciences as such for Vietnam. But the terms used by military spokesmen to describe that conflict do furnish dramatic illustrations of the paradoxical lack of neutrality that results from deliberately seeking to frame "objective" categories for policy discourse.

92. The values expressed by such notions as ecological balance, for example, represent for some not ultimate ends but hedges against risks to human well-being. See generally Sen, *Collective Choice and Social Welfare,* pp. 59–64. A similar point can be made as to the supposed distinction between means and ends.

93. For example, it might be that acting on value V_1 precludes subsequently realizing value V_2 but not the reverse—as where V_1 would permit the periodic use of a lake for toxic waste disposal and V_2 would permit the occasional use of the lake for swimming. See James Krier, "The Pollution Problem and Legal Institutions: A Conceptual Overview," *UCLA Law Review* 18 (1972): 429, 455–456. Or it might be that unless value V_3 is given priority over value V_4, values V_5 and V_6 cannot both be realized.

94. Whatever else may be said of the axioms underlying the policy sciences, and indeed underlying most of what might be called secular, pluralistic liberal thought (see note 26, above), it should at least be observed here that the objectivist fact-value (or means-end) dichotomy implicit in their structure (cf. note 36) leads to a deep internal inconsistency. Typically starting from the premise that human ends and moral values are wholly subjective and personal and hence not derivable from reality by the "objective" methods of analytic reason and empirical investigation, these theories purport to reach conclusions (sometimes utilitarian and sometimes contractarian) about how society *ought* to be organized or how social choices *should* be made (e.g., so as to maximize the sum of individual satisfactions); but if the starting premise is correct, then conclusions of this normative form can never be more than arbitrary expressions of personal preference, opaque to rational discourse—hardly the status to which they must aspire.

95. The "correct" probability is thought to be a matter of impersonal fact even though any particular assessment of it will invariably be personal and subjective. See note 16, above.

96. "Trial by Mathematics," pp. 1381–1382, 1390.

97. I say "tends to exclude" rather than "excludes" because a sufficiently careful policy analyst could define the "outcomes" in question so as to include information about the associated probability assessments. The objectivist perspective does not preclude such a step, but does make it far less likely.

98. Cf. "Trial by Mathematics," p. 1366. Note how parallel is the economic tendency to equate goods with rights, ignoring the fact that the very concept of a right entails certain assumptions as to the *reasons* given for its recognition. See pp. 128–29, above.

99. O_1 if A_1 is chosen and X is the case; O_2 if A_1 is chosen and X is not the case; O_3 if A_2 is chosen and X is the case; O_4 if A_2 is chosen and X is not the case.

100. See "Trial by Mathematics," pp. 1382–1383.

101. Ibid., p. 1383, note 168.

102. See Norbert Wiener, *God & Golem, Inc.*, (Cambridge, Mass., 1964), pp. 58–59.

103. Ibid., p. 59.

104. Far more attention should be paid to the possible uses of model-building and simulation for this explicit purpose—not merely to predict the consequences of already specified alternatives, but to aid in the choice of what alternatives to consider. Among other things, what appears to be an irreconcilable conflict of values will turn out in selected cases to pose no ultimate problem once a properly "synergistic" alternative has been imagined.

105. Cf. p. 133.

106. See section V of this essay. I have not explored in this essay the degree to which such problems might be overcome by encouraging the development of independent policy analyses responsive to no client at all, or at least responsive to no client on a problem-oriented basis.

107. Cf. Charles Lindblom, *The Intelligence of Democracy* (New York, 1965).

108. The very *tendency* to assume it may betray the policy sciences' debt to their economic heritage.

109. See pp. 126–33.

110. Karl Mannheim has observed that the entire notion of "value" in the setting of such "choice" arose from and was diffused by economics (*Ideology and Utopia,* trans. Louis Wirth and Edward Shils [New York, 1936] p. 82).

111. See notes 26 and 94 for one direction such an investigation might take.

112. In any event, quite apart from whether any such conclusion might follow, I believe that historical and empirical research is required, particularly to illuminate with greater precision the sources and functions of the premises implicit in the habitual procedures and "rules of thumb" of policy analyses as actually conducted and implemented (or ignored) in various institutional settings. In this respect, it must be stressed that the present essay relies quite heavily on the articulated *theories* of the policy sciences, and on relatively impressiontic conclusions as to their application. One would expect that their application *at its best* is subject to less criticism.

113. Compare Ian McHarg's technique of land use planning through the use of superimposed transparencies, each one indicating degrees of suitability for various uses and degrees of compatibility among these uses from a particular perspective, historic, ecological, economic, and so on. (*Design with Nature* [New York, 1969]).

114. *A Theory of Justice,* p. 512.

115. See, e.g., Clarence Morris, "The Rights and Duties of Beasts and Trees: A Law Teacher's Essay for Landscape Architects," *Journal of Legal Education* 17 (1964): 185; Christopher D. Stone, "Should Trees Have Standing?—Toward Legal Rights for Natural Objects," *Southern California Law Review* 45 (1972): 450–501.

116. As always in such cases, the anthropocentric justifications alone might, but need not, suffice to justify a particular rule, given man's profound dependence on the ecosystem as a whole.

4   Cost-Benefit Analysis: An Ethical Critique

Steven Kelman

At THE BROADEST and vaguest level, cost-benefit analysis may be regarded simply as systematic thinking about decision making. Who can oppose, economists sometimes ask, efforts to think in a systematic way about the consequences of different courses of action? The alternative, it would appear, is unexamined decision making. But defining cost-benefit analysis so simply leaves it with few implications for actual regulatory decision making. Presumably, therefore, those who urge regulators to make greater use of the technique have a more extensive prescription in mind. I assume here that their prescription includes the following views:

(1) There exists a strong presumption that an act should not be undertaken unless its benefits outweigh its costs.

(2) In order to determine whether benefits outweigh costs, it is desirable to attempt to express all benefits and costs in a common scale or denominator, so that they can be compared with each other, even when some benefits and costs are not traded on markets and hence have no established dollar values.

(3) Getting decision makers to make more use of cost-benefit techniques is important enough to warrant both the expense required to gather the data for improved cost-benefit estimation and the political efforts needed to give the activity higher priority compared to other activities, also valuable in and of themselves.

My focus is on cost-benefit analysis as applied to environmental, safety, and health regulation. In that context, I examine each of the above propositions from the perspective of formal ethical theory, that is, the study of what actions it is morally right to undertake. My conclusions are:

(1) In areas of environmental, safety, and health regulation, there may

be many instances where a certain decision might be right even though its benefits do not outweigh its costs.

(2) There are good reasons to oppose efforts to put dollar values on nonmarketed benefits and costs.

(3) Given the relative frequency of occasions in the areas of environmental, safety, and health regulation where one would not wish to use a benefits-outweigh-costs test as a decision rule, and given the reasons to oppose the monetizing of nonmarketed benefits or costs that is a prerequisite for cost-benefit analysis, it is not justifiable to devote major resources to the generation of data for cost-benefit calculations or to undertake efforts to "spread the gospel" of cost-benefit analysis further.

I

How do we decide whether a given action is morally right or wrong and hence, assuming the desire to act morally, why it should be undertaken or refrained from? Like the Molière character who spoke prose without knowing it, economists who advocate use of cost-benefit analysis for public decisions are philosophers without knowing it: the answer given by cost-benefit analysis, that actions should be undertaken so as to maximize net benefits, represents one of the classic answers given by moral philosophers—that given by utilitarians. To determine whether an action is right or wrong, utilitarians tote up all the positive consequences of the action in terms of human satisfaction. The act that maximizes attainment of satisfaction under the circumstances is the right act. That the economists' answer is also the answer of one school of philosophers should not be surprising. Early on, economics was a branch of moral philosophy, and only later did it become an independent discipline.

Before proceeding further, the subtlety of the utilitarian position should be noted. The positive and negative consequences of an act for satisfaction may go beyond the act's immediate consequences. A facile version of utilitarianism would give moral sanction to a lie, for instance, if the satisfaction of an individual attained by telling the lie was greater than the suffering imposed on the lie's victim. Few utilitarians would agree. Most of them would add to the list of negative consequences the effect of the one lie on the tendency of the person who lies to tell other lies, even in instances when the lying produced less satisfaction for him than dissatisfaction for others. They would also add the negative effects of the lie on the general level of social regard for truth telling, which has many consequences for future utility. A further consequence may be added as well. It is sometimes said that we should include in a utilitarian calculation the feeling of dissatisfaction produced in the liar (and perhaps in others) because, by telling a lie, one has "done the wrong thing." Correspondingly, in this view, among the positive consequences to be weighed into a utilitarian calculation of truth telling is satisfaction arising from "doing the right thing." This view rests on an error, however, because it *assumes* what it is the purpose of the calculation to *determine*—that telling the truth in the instance in question is indeed the right thing to do. Economists are likely to object to this point, arguing that no feeling ought "arbitrarily" to be excluded from a complete cost-benefit calculation, including a feeling of dissatisfaction at doing the wrong thing. Indeed, the economists' cost-benefit calculations would, at least ideally, include such feelings. Note the difference between the economist's and the philosopher's cost-benefit calculations, however. The economist may choose to include feelings of dissatisfaction in his cost-benefit calculation, but what happens if somebody asks the economist, "Why is it right to evaluate an action on the basis of a cost-benefit test?" If an answer is to be given to that question (which does not normally preoccupy economists but which does concern both philosophers and the rest of us who need to be persuaded that cost-benefit analysis is right), then the circularity problem reemerges. And there is also another difficulty with counting feelings of dissatisfaction at doing the wrong thing in a cost-benefit calculation. It leads to the perverse result that under certain circumstances a lie, for example, might be morally right if the individual contemplating the lie felt no compunction about lying and morally wrong only if the individual felt such a compunction!

This error is revealing, however, because it begins to suggest a critique of utilitarianism. Utilitarianism is an important and powerful moral doctrine. But it is probably a minority position among contemporary moral philosophers. It is amazing that economists can proceed in unanimous endorsement of cost-benefit analysis as if unaware that their conceptual framework is highly controversial in the discipline from which it arose— moral philosophy.

Let us explore the critique of utilitarianism. The logical error discussed before appears to suggest that we have a notion of certain things being right or wrong that *predates* our calculation of costs and benefits. Imagine the case of an old man in Nazi Germany who is hostile to the regime. He is wondering whether he should speak out against Hitler. If he speaks out, he will lose his pension. And his action will have done nothing to increase the chances that the Nazi regime will be overthrown: He is regarded as somewhat eccentric by those around him, and nobody has ever consulted his views on political questions. Recall that one cannot add to the benefits of speaking out any satisfaction from doing "the right thing," because the purpose of the exercise is to determine whether speaking out *is* the right thing. How would the utilitarian calculation go? The benefits of the old man's speaking out would, as the example is presented, be nil, while the costs would be his loss of his pension. So the costs of the action would outweigh the benefits. By the utilitarians' cost-benefit calculation, it would be *morally wrong* for the man to speak out.

Another example: Two very close friends are on an Arctic expedition together. One of them falls very sick in the snow and bitter cold, and sinks quickly before anything can be done to help him. As he is dying, he asks his friend one thing, "Please, make me a solemn promise that ten years from today you will come back to this spot and place a lighted candle here to remember me." The friend solemnly promises to do so, but does not tell a soul. Now, ten years later, the friend must decide whether to keep his promise. It would be inconvenient for him to make the long trip. Since he told nobody, his failure to go will not affect the general social faith in promise keeping. And the incident was unique enough so that it is safe to assume that his failure to go will not encourage him to break other promises. Again, the costs of the act outweigh the benefits. A utilitarian would need to believe that it would be *morally wrong* to travel to the Arctic to light the candle.

A third example: A wave of thefts has hit a city and the police are having trouble finding any of the thieves. But they believe, correctly, that punishing someone for theft will have some deterrent effect and will decrease the number of crimes. Unable to arrest any actual perpetrator, the police chief and the prosecutor arrest a person whom they know to be innocent and, in cahoots with each other, fabricate a convincing case against him. The police chief and the prosecutor are about to retire, so the act has no effect on any future actions of theirs. The fabrication is perfectly executed, so nobody finds out about it. Is the *only* question involved in judging the act of framing the innocent man that of whether his suffering from conviction and imprisonment will be greater than the suffering avoided among potential crime victims when some crimes are deterred? A utilitarian would need to believe that it is *morally right to punish the innocent man* as long as it can be demonstrated that the suffering prevented outweighs his suffering.

And a final example: Imagine two worlds, each containing the same sum total of happiness. In the first world, this total of happiness came about from a series of acts that included a number of lies and injustices (that is, the total consisted of the immediate gross sum of happiness created by certain acts, minus any long-term unhappiness occasioned by the lies and injustices). In the second world the same amount of happiness was produced by a different series of acts, none of which involved lies or injustices. Do we have any reason to prefer the one world to the other? A utilitarian would need to believe that the choice between the two worlds is a *matter of indifference.*

To those who believe that it would not be morally wrong for the old man to speak out in Nazi Germany or for the explorer to return to the

Arctic to light a candle for his deceased friend, that it would not be morally right to convict the innocent man, or that the choice between the two worlds is not a matter of indifference—to those of us who believe these things, utilitarianism is insufficient as a moral view. We believe that some acts whose costs are greater than their benefits may be morally right and, contrariwise, some acts whose benefits are greater than their costs may be morally wrong.

This does not mean that the question whether benefits are greater than costs is morally irrelevant. Few would claim such. Indeed, for a broad range of individual and social decisions, whether an act's benefits outweigh its costs is a sufficient question to ask. But not for all such decisions. These may involve situations where certain duties—duties not to lie, break promises, or kill, for example—make an act wrong, even if it would result in an excess of benefits over costs. Or they may involve instances where people's rights are at stake. We would not permit rape even if it could be demonstrated that the rapist derived enormous happiness from his act, while the victim experienced only minor displeasure. We do not do cost-benefit analyses of freedom of speech or trial by jury. The Bill of Rights was not RARGed. As the United Steelworkers noted in a comment on the Occupational Safety and Health Administration's economic analysis of its proposed rule to reduce worker exposure to carcinogenic coke-oven emissions, the Emancipation Proclamation was not subjected to an inflationary impact statement. The notion of human rights involves the idea that people may make certain claims to be allowed to act in certain ways or to be treated in certain ways, even if the sum of benefits achieved thereby does not outweigh the sum of costs. It is this view that underlies the statement that "workers have a right to a safe and healthy work place" and the expectation that OSHA's decisions will reflect that judgment.

In the most convincing versions of nonutilitarian ethics, various duties or rights are not absolute. But each has a *prima facie* moral validity so that, if duties or rights do not conflict, the morally right act is the act that reflects a duty or respects a right. If duties or rights do conflict, a moral judgment, based on conscious deliberation, must be made. Since one of the duties nonutilitarian philosophers enumerate is the duty of beneficence (the duty to maximize happiness), which in effect incorporates all of utilitarianism by reference, a nonutilitarian who is faced with conflicts between the results of cost-benefit analysis and non-utility-based considerations will need to undertake such deliberation. But in that deliberation, additional elements, which cannot be reduced to a question of whether benefits outweigh costs, have been introduced. Indeed, depending on the moral importance we attach to the right or duty involved, cost-benefit questions may, within wide ranges, become irrelevant to the outcome of the moral judgment.

In addition to questions involving duties and rights, there is a final sort of question where, in my view, the issue of whether benefits outweigh costs should not govern moral judgment. I noted earlier that, for the common run of questions facing individuals and societies, it is possible to begin and end our judgment simply by finding out if the benefits of the contemplated act outweigh the costs. This very fact means that one way to show the great importance, or value, attached to an area is to say that decisions involving the area should not be determined by cost-benefit calculations. This applies, I think, to the view many environmentalists have of decisions involving our natural environment. When officials are deciding what level of pollution will harm certain vulnerable people—such as asthmatics or the elderly—while not harming others, one issue involved may be the right of those people not to be sacrificed on the altar of somewhat higher living standards for the rest of us. But more broadly than this, many environmentalists fear that subjecting decisions about clean air or water to the cost-benefit tests that determine the general run of decisions removes those matters from the realm of specially valued things.

II

In order for cost-benefit calculations to be performed the way they are supposed to be, all costs and benefits must be expressed in a common measure, typically dollars, including things not normally bought and sold on markets, and to which dollar prices are therefore not attached. The most dramatic example of such things is human life itself; but many of the other benefits achieved or preserved by environmental policy—such as peace and quiet, fresh-smelling air, swimmable rivers, spectacular vistas— are not traded on markets either.

Economists who do cost-benefit analysis regard the quest after dollar values for nonmarket things as a difficult challenge—but one to be met with relish. They have tried to develop methods for imputing a person's "willingness to pay" for such things, their approach generally involving a search for bundled goods that *are* traded on markets and that vary as to whether they include a feature that is, *by itself,* not marketed. Thus, fresh air is not marketed, but houses in different parts of Los Angeles that are similar except for the degree of smog are. Peace and quiet is not marketed, but similar houses inside and outside airport flight paths are. The risk of death is not marketed, but similar jobs that have different levels of risk are. Economists have produced many often ingenious efforts to impute dollar prices to nonmarketed things by observing the premiums accorded homes in clean air areas over similar homes in dirty areas or the premiums paid for risky jobs over similar nonrisky jobs.

These ingenious efforts are subject to criticism on a number of technical grounds. It may be difficult to control for all the dimensions of quality other than the presence or absence of the nonmarketed thing. More important, in a world where people have different preferences and are subject to different constraints as they make their choices, the dollar value imputed to the nonmarket things that most people would wish to avoid will be lower than otherwise, because people with unusually weak aversion to those things or unusually strong constraints on their choices will be willing to take the bundled good in question at less of a discount than the average person. Thus, to use the property value discount of homes near airports as a measure of people's willingness to pay for quiet means to accept as a proxy for the rest of us the behavior of those least sensitive to noise, of airport employees (who value the convenience of a near-airport location) or of others who are susceptible to an agent's assurances that "it's not so bad." To use the wage premiums accorded hazardous work as a measure of the value of life means to accept as proxies for the rest of us the choices of people who do not have many choices or who are exceptional risk seekers.

A second problem is that the attempts of economists to measure people's willingness to pay for nonmarketed things assume that there is no difference between the price a person would require for *giving up* something to which he has a preexisting right and the price he would pay to *gain* something to which he enjoys no right. Thus, the analysis assumes no difference between how much a homeowner would need to be paid in order to give up an unobstructed mountain view that he already enjoys and how much he would be willing to pay to get an obstruction moved once it is already in place. Available evidence suggests that most people would insist on being paid far more to assent to a worsening of their situation than they would be willing to pay to improve their situation. The difference arises from such factors as being accustomed to and psychologically attached to that which one believes one enjoys by right. But this creates a circularity problem for any attempt to use cost-benefit analysis to determine *whether* to assign to, say, the homeowner the right to an unobstructed mountain view. For willingness to pay will be different depending on whether the right is assigned initially or not. The value judgment about whether to assign the right must thus be made first. (In order to set an upper bound on the value of the benefit, one might hypothetically assign the right to the person and determine how much he would need to be paid to give it up.)

Third, the efforts of economists to impute willingness to pay invariably involve bundled goods exchanged in *private* transactions. Those who use figures garnered from such analysis to provide guidance for public decisions assume no difference between how people value certain things in private individual transactions and how they would wish those same things to be valued in public collective decisions. In making such assumptions, economists insidiously slip into their analysis an important and controversial value judgment, growing naturally out of the highly individualistic microeconomic tradition—namely, the view that there should be no difference between private behavior and the behavior we display in public social life. An alternative view—one that enjoys, I would suggest, wide resonance among citizens—would be that public, social decisions provide an opportunity to give certain things a higher valuation than we choose, for one reason or another, to give them in our private activities.

Thus, opponents of stricter regulation of health risks often argue that we show by our daily risk-taking behavior that we do not value life infinitely, and therefore our public decisions should not reflect the high value of life that proponents of strict regulation propose. However, an alternative view is equally plausible. Precisely because we fail, for whatever reasons, to give life saving the value in everyday personal decisions that we in some general terms believe we should give it, we may wish our social decisions to provide us the occasion to display the reverence for life that we espouse but do not always show. By this view, people do not have fixed unambiguous "preferences" to which they give expression through private activities and which therefore should be given expression in public decisions. Rather, they may have what they themselves regard as "higher" and "lower" preferences. The latter may come to the fore in private decisions, but people may want the former to come to the fore in public decisions. They may sometimes display racial prejudice, but support antidiscrimination laws. They may buy a certain product after seeing a seductive ad, but be skeptical enough of advertising to want the government to keep a close eye on it. In such cases, the use of private behavior to impute the values that should be entered for public decisions, as is done by using willingness to pay in private transactions, commits grievous offense against a view of the behavior of the citizen that is deeply ingrained in our democratic tradition. It is a view that denudes politics of any independent role in society, reducing it to a mechanistic, mimicking recalculation based on private behavior.

Finally, one may oppose the effort to place prices on a nonmarket thing and hence in effect incorporate it into the market system out of a fear that the very act of doing so will reduce the thing's perceived value. To place a price on the benefit may, in other words, reduce the value of that benefit. Cost-benefit analysis thus may be like the thermometer that, when placed in a liquid to be measured, itself changes the liquid's temperature.

Examples of the perceived cheapening of a thing's value by the very act of buying and selling it abound in everyday life and language. The disgust that accompanies the idea of buying and selling human beings is based on the sense that this would dramatically diminish human worth. Epithets such as "he prostituted himself," applied as linguistic analogies to people who have sold something, reflect the view that certain things should not be sold because doing so diminishes their value. Praise that is bought is worth little, even to the person buying it. A true anecdote is told of an economist who retired to another university community and complained that he was having difficulty making friends. The laconic response of a critical colleague—"If you want a friend why don't you buy ourself one"—illustrates in a pithy way the intuition that, for some things, the very act of placing a price on them reduces their perceived value.

The first reason that pricing something decreases its perceived value is that, in many circumstances, nonmarket exchange is associated with the production of certain values not associated with market exchange. These may include spontaneity and various other feelings that come from personal relationships. If a good becomes less associated with the production of positively valued feelings because of market exchange, the perceived value of the good declines to the extent that those feelings are valued. This can be seen clearly in instances where a thing may be transferred both by market and by nonmarket mechanisms. The willingness to pay for sex bought from a prostitute is less than the perceived value of the sex consummating love. (Imagine the reaction if a practitioner of cost-benefit analysis computed the benefits of sex based on the price of prostitute services.)

Furthermore, if one values in a general sense the existence of a nonmarket sector because of its connection with the production of certain valued feelings, then one ascribes added value to any nonmarketed good simply as a repository of values represented by the nonmarket sector one wishes to preserve. This seems certainly to be the case for things in nature, such as pristine streams or undisturbed forests: For many people who value them, part of their value comes from their position as repositories of values the nonmarket sector represents.

The second way in which placing a market price on a thing decreases its perceived value is by removing the possibility of proclaiming that the thing is "not for sale," since things on the market by definition are for sale. The very statement that something is not for sale affirms, enhances, and protects a thing's value in a number of ways. To begin with, the statement is a way of showing that a thing is valued for its own sake, whereas selling a thing for money demonstrates that it was valued only instrumentally. Furthermore, to say that something cannot be transferred in that way places it in the exceptional category—which requires the person interested in obtaining that thing to be able to offer something else that is exceptional, rather than allowing him the easier alternative of obtaining the thing for money that could have been obtained in an infinity of ways. This enhances its value. If I am willing to say "You're a really kind person" to whoever pays me to do so, my praise loses the value that attaches to it from being exchangeable only for an act of kindness.

In addition, if we have already decided we value something highly, one way of stamping it with a cachet affirming its high value is to announce that it is "not for sale." Such an announcement does more, however, than just reflect a preexisting high valuation. It signals a thing's distinctive value to others and helps us persuade them to value the thing more highly than they otherwise might. It also expresses our resolution to safeguard that distinctive value. To state that something is not for sale is thus also a source of value for that thing, since if a thing's value is easy to affirm or protect, it will be worth more than an otherwise similar thing without such attributes.

If we proclaim that something is not for sale, we make a once-and-for-all judgment of its special value. When something is priced, the issue of its perceived value is constantly coming up, as a standing invitation to reconsider that original judgment. Were people constantly faced with questions such as "how much money could get you to give up your freedom of speech?" or "how much would you sell your vote for if you could?", the perceived value of the freedom to speak or the right to vote would soon become devastated as, in moments of weakness, people started saying "maybe it's not worth *so much* after all." Better not to be faced with the constant questioning in the first place. Something similar did in fact occur when the slogan "better red than dead" was launched by some pacifists during the Cold War. Critics pointed out that the very posing of this stark choice—in effect, "would you really be willing to give up your life in exchange for not living under communism?"—reduced the value people attached to freedom and thus diminished resistance to attacks on freedom.

Finally, of some things valued very highly it is stated that they are "priceless" or that they have "infinite value." Such expressions are reserved for a subset of things not for sale, such as life or health. Economists tend to scoff at talk of pricelessness. For them, saying that something is priceless is to state a willingness to trade off an infinite quantity of all other goods for one unit of the priceless good, a situation that empirically appears highly unlikely. For most people, however, the word priceless is pregnant with meaning. Its value-affirming and value-protecting functions cannot be bestowed on expressions that merely denote a determinate, albeit high, valuation. John Kennedy in his inaugural address proclaimed that the nation was ready to "pay any price [and] bear any burden . . . to assure the survival and the success of liberty." Had he said instead that we were willing to "pay a high price" or "bear a large burden" for liberty, the statement would have rung hollow.

III

An objection that advocates of cost-benefit analysis might well make to the preceding argument should be considered. I noted earlier that, in cases where various non-utility-based duties or rights conflict with the maximization of utility, it is necessary to make a deliberative judgment about what act is finally right. I also argued earlier that the search for commensurability might not always be a desirable one, that the attempt to go beyond expressing benefits in terms of (say) lives saved and costs in terms of dollars is not something devoutly to be wished.

In situations involving things that are not expressed in a common measure, advocates of cost-benefit analysis argue that people making judgments "in effect" perform cost-benefit calculations anyway. If government regulators promulgate a regulation that saves 100 lives at a cost of $1 billion, they are "in effect" valuing a life at (a minimum of) $10 million, whether or not they say that they are willing to place a dollar value on a human life. Since, in this view, cost-benefit analysis "in effect" is inevitable, it might as well be made specific.

This argument misconstrues the real difference in the reasoning processes involved. In cost-benefit analysis, equivalencies are established *in advance* as one of the raw materials for the calculation. One determines costs and benefits, one determines equivalencies (to be able to put various costs and benefits into a common measure), and then one sets to toting things up—waiting, as it were, with bated breath for the results of the calculation to come out. The outcome is determine by the arithmetic; if the outcome is a close call or if one is not good at long division, one does not know how it will turn out until the calculation is finished. In the kind of deliberative judgment that is performed without a common measure, no establishment of equivalencies occurs in advance. Equivalencies are not aids to the decision process. In fact, the decision maker might not even be aware of what the "in effect" equivalencies were, at least before they are revealed to him afterwards by someone pointing out what he had "in effect" done. The decision maker would see himself as simply having made a deliberative judgment; the "in effect" equivalency number did not play a causal role in the decision but at most merely reflects it. Given this, the argument against making the process explicit is the one discussed earlier in the discussion of problems with putting specific quantified values on things that are not normally quantified—that the very act of doing so may serve to reduce the value of those things.

My own judgment is that modest efforts to assess levels of benefits and costs are justified, although I do not believe that government agencies ought to sponsor efforts to put dollar prices on nonmarket things. I also do not believe that the cry for more cost-benefit analysis in regulation is, on the whole, justified. If regulatory officials were so insensitive about regulatory costs that they did not provide acceptable raw material for deliberative judgments (even if not of a strictly cost-benefit nature), my conclusion might be different. But a good deal of research into costs and benefits already occurs—actually, far more in the U.S. regulatory process than in that of any other industrial society. The danger now would seem to come more from the other side.

NOTE

This article, first published in *Regulation* 10 (1981): 33–40, is reprinted by permission of the American Enterprise Institute for Public Policy Research.

5 Efficiency and Utility

Mark Sagoff

ALL OTHER THINGS being equal, one could contend that a more efficient allocation of resources is better than a less efficient one.[1] The notion of "better," however, has no meaning in this context.

Efficiency and Utilitarianism

If the efficiency criterion had a normative basis in the ethical theory of utilitarianism, it would have a demonstrable connection with happiness or a related normative conception of the good, and it would judge the value of actions and decisions according to their consequences. The efficiency criterion and the theory of welfare economics from which it is developed possess neither of these attributes, however, and they therefore have no justification in the ethical theory of utilitarianism.

Sophisticated economic analysts do not try to connect the efficiency norm with the classical utilitarianism of Bentham, Mill, and Sidgwick, or with the goal of maximizing pleasure or happiness that those philosophers proposed.[2] As Richard Posner correctly points out, "The most important thing to bear in mind about the concept of value [in the welfare economist's sense] is that it is based on what people are willing to pay for something rather than the happiness they would derive from having it."[3]

Some policy analysts, however, believe that the satisfaction of consumer and other personal preferences has a moral foundation as a policy goal because it leads to or produces satisfaction in the sense of pleasure or happiness.[4] This belief rests on nothing more than a pun on the word "satisfaction." Preferences are *satisfied* in the sense of "met" or "fulfilled"; this is also the sense in which conditions and equations are satisfied. "Satisfaction" of this sort has no necessary connection with "satisfaction" in the sense of pleasure or happiness.

The evidence indicates, in fact, that the satisfaction of preferences does not promote or cause satisfaction in the sense of happiness.[5] Empirical research confirms what ordinary wisdom suggests: happiness depends more on the quality and pursuit of preferences than on the degree to which they are satisfied.[6]

It is useful to recognize, moreover, that the contemporary "utilitarianism" represented by current welfare economic theory is not concerned with what happens to people as a result of their choices. Instead, it is concerned with the beliefs and expectations revealed in those choices. The focus is on the amount people are willing to pay for things rather than on the consequences of those decisions, except insofar as these consequences are defined tautologically in terms of willingness to pay.

Whereas economists thus evaluate actions according to the preferences people reveal when they act, ethical utilitarians judge the value of actions according to their consequences. Thus, utilitarians, to prevent what were unconscionable levels of death and injury, have supported humanitarian legislation to improve unsafe conditions in the nation's mills and mines. Humanitarian legislation of this kind cannot be justified on an *expected* utility basis, however, for whenever workers voluntarily and knowingly take unsafe jobs, which they often do,[7] the market operates efficiently to that extent, even if they all die as a result.[8] The efficiency norm in public policy has no connection, other than a historical one, with the ethical theory of utilitarianism. To think otherwise is to confuse the satisfaction of preference, which many economists favor, with the utilitarian's preference for satisfaction.

Satisfaction of Personal Preferences

Conceding that utilitarianism does not provide a normative basis for the efficiency criterion, resource economists generally attempt to support their position by referring to a central value premise. "The value premise is that the personal wants of the individuals in the society should guide the use of resources in production, distribution, and exchange, and those personal wants can most efficiently be met through the seeking of maximum profits by all producers."[9]

Such assertions, however, provoke one to ask why individuals' personal wants should guide—indeed, along with equity considerations, determine—the government's natural resources management policy. Although an individual's preference may give him a reason to try to satisfy that preference, it does not necessarily follow that the government has a reason to try to satisfy that preference. To the contrary, the government in many instances strives to keep people from satisfying their preferences, as evidenced by laws prohibiting narcotics, prostitution, and gambling. The question thus remains why it should be the government's policy to satisfy personal preferences without regard to the values these preferences express.[10]

In posing this question, one may assume that the government generally should not interfere with the efforts citizens make to satisfy their own preferences, except insofar as necessary to protect the rights or freedoms of others. One may agree, moreover, that the government should guarantee citizens the background conditions of freedom and equality necessary for those citizens to have a fair basis on which to form their personal wants and to compete to satisfy those wants. Freedom, equality of opportunity, autonomy, and neutrality are all important values and the government ought to protect them. No one has yet explained, however, why efficiency in the allocation of resources is a value, or why the satisfaction of personal preferences *per se* should be recognized as a goal of public policy.[11]

Public policy as it stands is based on impersonal values chosen by the community through the political process. These values have survived a process of public deliberation and, on the merits, have gained the respect of at least a majority of the legislature. In the political process, partisans offer to support their positions with reasons they suppose to be publicly or intersubjectively valid for impersonal or public values.[12] These values, at least formally, address not what I want but rather what *we* should do; they take the community in general as their logical subject.[13]

Such values are logically different from personal preferences, which express only how the individual wants to live his own life, about which liberals believe the government should be as neutral as possible.[14] Why should environmental policy strive to satisfy personal preferences rather than respond to these public values?[15]

Some might reply that the government ought to try to satisfy personal preferences because this is what the people who have those preferences want. This reply would start an infinite regress if it were true. It is, however, mistaken. People want their preferences satisfied at the moment they have them, but they constantly reevaluate and revise their preferences. Over the long run, people may regret that many preferences were satisfied or be grateful that others were not. Besides, even if people want their preferences satisfied at the moment they have them, it by no means follows that they wish the government to adopt preference-satisfaction as a major policy objective. On the contrary, this goal has achieved credibility with hardly anyone beyond the academics who invented it.[16]

The ultimate question is why it should be a value premise "that the personal wants of the individuals in the society should guide the use of resources . . . ."[17] Markets are supposed to satisfy these personal preferences, and the government should guarantee individuals the liberty to pursue the satisfaction of their wants under conditions that are neutral among them and fair to all. The question why the government itself should try to satisfy these preferences, however, remains to be answered.

Welfare Maximization

Some might reply that the government should try to maximize the satisfaction of personal wants and preferences because this will increase the welfare or utility of those who possess those preferences. This reply, however, states a definition, not a fact.

The concepts of "welfare" and "utility," as policy analysts use them, are simply defined in terms of the satisfaction of preferences.[18] Thus, such an analyst might say that government should strive to maximize the satisfaction of personal preferences on a willingness-to-pay basis because this will increase overall social welfare or utility. Government should increase overall social welfare or utility, such reasoning continues, to maximize the satisfaction of personal preferences on a willingness-to-pay basis over society as a whole.

The same circular reasoning affects "normative" arguments for efficiency as a goal of public policy. Why maximize efficiency? Because this maximizes the satisfaction of preferences. Why maximize the satisfaction of preferences? Because this, in turn, maximizes welfare. Why maximize welfare? To allocate resources efficiently. And so there is a perfect circle on earth as there is in heaven.

Those who favor the efficiency norm in public policy often make the point that "not just one but both parties to an exchange are better off after the exchange is executed than they were before."[19] What this means is that the *expected utility* of both parties is increased. This, again, is tautologically true, because this kind of utility is inferred as a logical consequence from the willingness of the parties to enter into the exchange. To break out of this circle, analysts must explain how satisfying preferences, and thus how allocating resources efficiently, makes people better off in some normative, nontautological sense. This has never been done.[20]

Economic Prosperity

According to two observers, "The primary justification the Reagan administration gave for . . . regulatory relief was that regulation was one of the principal factors responsible for the nation's poor economic performance during the 1970s."[21] The social costs of pollution control, for example, are easily exaggerated. The efficiency norm in pollution control legislation, moreover, cannot be justified on the ground that microeconomic efficiency is related to the important normative goal of economic prosperity.

Speculations on the amount that governmental regulations "cost" society, of course, are part of political campaigning. In 1975, for example, President Ford, speaking in New Hampshire, declared that "some estimates that I have seen place the combined cost to consumers of Government relation and restrictive practices, in the private sector at more than the Federal Government actually collects in personal income taxes each year—or something on the order of $2,000 per family—unbelievable."[22] In the same year, the President's Council of Economic Advisors announced that "precise estimates of the total costs of regulation are not available, but existing evidence suggests that this may range up to 1 percent of gross national product, or approximately $66 per person per year."[23] And when the Reagan administration took office, one of its principal economic advisors, Murray Weidenbaum, estimated the then current social cost of governmental regulation, without regard to the benefits, at $100 billion per year.[24]

Serious attempts to estimate the social costs of pollution control regulation, again without regard to the benefits, during the period between 1972 and 1980, were conducted by Chase Econometric Associates (Chase)[25] and Data Resources Incorporated (DRI).[26] These studies "are in agreement as to the apparent size of the impacts of pollution control," namely that the cost of pollution control contributes between 0.2 and 0.6 percent to the inflation rate.[27] Both the Chase and the DRI studies "find the direct price, output, employment, and other macroeconomic effects of pollution control to be relatively small."[28]

The results of a 1976 Weidenbaum and DeFina study appear to be roughly consistent with these earlier studies.[29] Weidenbaum's famous $100 billion estimate of the annual cost of federal regulation in 1976 covers not simply pollution control but most major areas of regulation, including consumer, workplace, energy, and financial regulation.[30] For regulation of "energy and the environment," Weidenbaum and DeFina estimated administrative costs in 1976 at $612 million and compliance costs at $7.7 billion.[31] The 1976 total represents a cost of roughly $307 per American.[32] Total regulatory costs in 1979, on Weidenbaum's estimate, moreover, would come to $66 billion, not $100 billion.[33] Of this total regulatory cost, paperwork costs accounted for approximately 40 percent.[34]

The EPA and the Council for Environmental Quality have sponsored studies of regulatory impact based on large-scale macroeconomic models.[35] The results of these studies are generally consistent with a study published by the Conservation Foundation in 1982.[36] This latter study found that pollution control programs, which are labor-intensive, decreased the GNP by a modest 0.2 percent, but also decreased unemployment by 0.3 percent.[37] Eads and Fix caution that these large-scale macroeconomic simulations tell us *either* that regulation has relatively little impact on the variables that most economists watch as indicators of the health of the economy *or* that large-scale macromodels are not sensitive enough to reliably indicate the impact of such complex phenomena as a mass of individual programs that, when lumped together, might be called "regulation."[38]

It is important also to note the theoretical relationship between allocative efficiency, a microeconomic concept, and various desirable macroeconomic goals, such as growth and prosperity. In general, economists recognize that macroeconomic problems have macroeconomic causes and solutions.[39] Economists understand that there is no clear or straightforward relation between microeconomic efficiency and macroeconomic performance.[40]

Policy analysts, therefore, generally have not urged prosperity, economic growth, or any such macroeconomic goal as a justification for a cost-benefit approach to public policy. This is to their credit. For example, Edward Gramlich, in his basic text on cost-benefit analysis and government programs, acknowledges that "benefit-cost analyses of individual projects will for the most part not involve macroeconomic questions."[41]

Community Consent

The final argument supporting efficiency as a goal or criterion in pollution control policy is based not on ethical but political theory. Some analysts, recognizing that the efficiency norm in public policy has no basis in utilitarianism, argue that normative support may be found in the "hypothetical" or "counterfactual" consent of the community. Richard Posner, for example, proposes that consent "is the operational basis"[42] of the efficiency norm and, therefore, "consent to efficient solutions can be presumed."[43] Likewise, in discussing the regulation of risk, Herman Leonard and Richard Zeckhauser write: "Cost-benefit analysis . . . is the appropriate way to determine which public decisions affecting risk levels would gain the hypothetical consent of the citizenry. We know of no other mechanism for making [policy] choices that has an ethical underpinning."[44]

The argument these analysts give is an ingenious one. First, they assume the truth of a familiar, if metaphysical, view of human nature. They believe people are essentially self-interested maximizers intent on satisfying their interests and preferences. Leonard and Zeckhauser then argue: "What mechanism for making decisions would individuals choose if they had to contract before they knew their identities in society or the kinds of problems they would confront? Our answer is that, on an expected-value basis, cost-benefit analysis would serve them best, and hence would be chosen."[45]

It is important to see that the conclusion of this argument does indeed follow from the premises. A group of persons who are essentially self-interested maximizers, "economic persons" anxious only to satisfy desires, who did not know what their desires would be, would rationally choose a cost-benefit approach, because it promises to maximize the satisfaction of desire across society as a whole. Accordingly, these authors argue that, given the truth of their description of the essence or nature of persons, the cost-benefit approach in public policy has society's implicit or hypothetical consent.[46]

To see what is wrong with this argument, imagine how a Moslem fundamentalist might alter it. In his view, the essential nature of man is to be defined in religious rather than in economic terms. Man is essentially a creature of Allah meant to praise His name and comply with His laws. Given this conception of human nature, it is easy to show that society gives its hypothetical or counterfactual consent to fundamentalist Moslem laws rather than to the principles of microeconomic theory.

Likewise, a Marxist might argue that individuals, were they ignorant of their social identities, would base regulation on this principle: "From each according to his abilities, to each according to his needs."[47] This is because people would recognize their communal nature and assume the truth of dialectical materialism as the accurate metaphysics of history. The Marxist might then argue that the "apparent" will of the citizenry, as expressed by its legitimate political representatives, can be ignored because it is corrupted by bourgeois ideology, irrationality, heresy, or stupidity. The "real" social will is known to those in the forefront of society who have the right philosophy, analysis, religion, social theory, ideology, or understanding of human nature. This kind of argument speaks for itself.[48]

Long before it was written, the Leonard-Zeckhauser "hypothetical consent" argument had been refuted by John Rawls, whose "veil of ignorance" technique it ironically parodies. The point of Rawls' A Theory of Justice[49] is that, in liberalism, justice is a political, not a metaphysical concept. It depends on a reflective equilibrium of values brought to bear in politics, partly as a result of history, experience, and culture. The point of the Rawlsian approach is its independence from and neutrality among competing metaphysical views of history and of the person. Policy analysts, by using the "veil of ignorance" argument as they have, replace a reflective equilibrium among normative principles with a metaphysical theory of the person, and thus they make the same mistake from the right as communitarian critics of Rawls make from the left.[50]

It is thus clear that the efficiency criterion in environmental policy has no normative basis. It is a mistake to think that efficiency is to be "balanced" or "traded off" against some other conflicting value, such as equity. Efficiency in the allocation of resources has no inherent worth or merit against which such a value may be weighed.

This is not to deny the common sense view that the benefits of any regulation should outweigh its costs to society as a whole. It is only to say that the efficiency criterion fails to measure, much less to maximize, benefits; the latter must be assessed through the political process and cannot be determined on the basis of individual willingness-to-pay. Thus, meaningful cost-benefit balancing is necessarily a *result* of, rather than a desideratum in, legislation and the larger political process in which public officials at various levels deliberate over good and evil, right and wrong. This is a completely different process from anything that could take place within, or be inferred from, consumer markets.

NOTES

This article, excerpted from "The Principles of Federal Pollution Control Law," *Minnesota Law Review* 71 (1986): 55–68, is reprinted by permission of the author and the *Minnesota Law Review.*

1. A sophisticated defense of preference-satisfaction as a basis for both common law and social policy may be found in R. Posner, *The Economics of Justice* (1981). Posner defines the "wealth of society" as "the aggregate satisfaction of those preferences (the only ones that have ethical weight in a system of wealth maximization) that are backed up by money, that is, that are registered in a market." Id. at 61.

For a good introduction to the concepts of efficiency, welfare, wealth, Pareto optimality, and potential Pareto improvement, see Coleman, "Economics and the Law: A Critical Review of the Foundations of the Economic Approach to Law," 94 *Ethics* 649 (1984) and articles cited therein; Michelman, "Norms and Normativity in the Economic Theory of Law," 62 *Minn. L. Rev.* 1015, 1019–21, 1032–34 (1978).

2. Sidgwick defines the value to be maximized not as *consumer surplus* but as "the greatest possible surplus of pleasure over pain." H. Sidgwick, *The Methods of Ethics* 412 (7th ed. 1907). No connection between these two concepts, conceptual or empirical, has ever been demonstrated.

For a standard account of the utilitarian basis of welfare economics, see, e.g., I.M.D. Little, *A Critique of Welfare Economics* 42 (2d ed. 1957); A. C. Pigou, *The Economics of Welfare* (4th ed. 1960).

3. Posner, note 1 above, at 60. Posner is aware of the familiar objections against utilitarianism as an ethical theory. He believes reasonably that "normative" or welfare economics would benefit if it were *not* founded on classical utilitarianism. Posner, therefore, proposes economic analysis not as a consequence of utilitarianism but as an alternative basis for ethical theory. Id. at 48.

4. William Baxter writes:

The first and most fundamental step toward solution of our environmental problems is a clear recognition that our objective is not pure air or water but rather some optimal state of pollution. That step immediately suggests the question: How do we define and attain the level of pollution that will yield the maximum possible amount of human satisfaction?

W. Baxter, *People or Penguins: The Case for Optimal Pollution* (1974).

5. That efficiency, wealth, potential Pareto improvement, and the like, do not lead to happiness but, if anything, to its opposite, is the burden or number of important studies. See, e.g., F. Hirsch, *The Social Limits to Growth* (1976); A. O. Hirschman, *Shifting Involvements: Private Interest and Public Action* (1982); T. Scitovsky, *The Joyless Economy* (1976). For surveys and other empirical evidence that people do not become happier when they have more of the things they want to buy (but instead are frustrated by rising expectations or dissatisfied by those things) see A. Campbell, P. Converse, & W. Rodgers, *The Quality of American Life: Perceptions, Evaluations, and Satisfactions* (1976), and Erskine, "The Polls: Some Thoughts About Life and People," 28 *Pub. Opinion Q.* 517 (1964). These studies confirm the old saw of common wisdom that the way to achieve happiness is to overcome desires rather than to satisfy them.

6. It is possible that the satisfaction of preferences leads often to frustration and disillusionment (as divorce statistics suggest) while the *attempt* to satisfy desires, as long as they remain unfulfilled, is satisfying. See J. Keats, "Ode on a Grecian Urn," in *Complete Poems and Selected Letters* 352 (C. Thorpe ed. 1935).

7. For documentation of hazards in the workplace, see C. Gersuny, *Work Hazards and Industrial Conflict* (1981). For example, fatalities among railroad workers reached 28 per 10,000 per year in 1904 and in 1916 one in ten were seriously injured. Id. at 20. "War is safe compared to railroading in this country," said one railroad worker early this century. Id. See also W. K. Viscusi, *Risk by Choice: Regulatory Health and Safety in the Workplace* 76–77 (1983) ("The widespread evidence that the market does provide risk premiums suggests that workers are quite aware of job hazards."); L. White, *Human Debris: The Injured Worker in America* (1983) (documenting the lives of injured workers and discussing the problems of industrial injury, disease, and workers' compensation).

8. Kip Viscusi, recognizing that workers are generally aware of the extent of the hazards they face, argues that humanitarian workplace legislation, "While perhaps well intended . . . will necessarily reduce the welfare of the poorer workers in society, as perceived by them." W.K. Viscusi, note 7 above, at 80. The welfare of workers "as perceived by them" refers to their expected utility which is determined entirely by their willingness to take the risky job at a particular wage. This kind of "welfare" or "utility" remains the same no matter what actually happens to these workers. For example, it remains the same if they all die hideous deaths. This kind of "utility," since it is determined independently of consequences, has nothing to do with utilitarian ethics.

Thomas Schelling falsely claims that "economic theory evaluates actions by their consequences and by the way the consequences are valued by the people who benefit or suffer." Schelling, "Prices as Regulatory Instruments," in *Incentives for Environmental Protection* 3 (T. C. Schelling ed. 1983).

9. A. Kneese & B. Bower, *Environmental Quality and Residuals Management* 4–5 (1979). This value premise is related to a free market economy only if we assume that corporate executives are concerned with maximizing long-run

profits rather than, e.g., promoting their own short-term personal interests. Were the latter true, a centralized, planned economy, e.g., a socialist one, that makes use of cost-benefit analysis, might conform to the value premise better than a capitalist one.

10. Those who believe that preference-satisfaction should be a goal of public policy are faced with the problem of ugly preferences, e.g., those that are racist, vicious, self-destructive, adaptive to circumstances beyond the agent's control, or simply stupid. To save the general policy goal, analysts have to invent ad hoc reasons for discounting or dismissing these various kinds of preferences which plainly do not merit societal respect. For discussion, see Elster, "Sour Grapes— Utilitarianism and the Genesis of Wants," in *Utilitarianism and Beyond* (A. Sen and B. Williams, eds., 1982); Goodin, "Laundering Preferences" in *Foundations of Social Choice Theory* (J. Elster and A. Hylland, eds., 1986).

11. For additional discussion of this question, see Dworkin, "Is Wealth a Value?" 9 *J. Legal Stud.* 191, 194 (1980); Dworkin, "Why Efficiency? A Response to Professors Calabresi and Posner," 8 *Hofstra L. Rev.* 563, 563 (1980).

12. People should debate public policy in public terms, that is, from the point of view of what *we* stand for, desire or believe in as a community, not from the point of view of personal wants or preferences. As is evident in the now famous remark of former General Motors head Charles Wilson that what's good for General Motors is good for the country, even he recognized that public policy must be discussed in public terms, however self-serving the motivation. See E. Schattschneider, *The Semisovereign People* 27 (1960).

13. Kant argued that in making a moral judgment, the individual legislates for all, that is, she expresses a view about what *any* rational being would do in similar circumstances. See I. Kant, *Grounding for the Metaphysics of Morals* 14 (J. Ellington trans. 1980). In environmental policy, we must consider the relevant community to be the nation; law then respects the views individuals defend concerning what we, as a nation, ought to do. This is different from the wants or preferences the individual has for himself and may reveal in markets. For a good discussion of these distinctions in their Kantian context, see W. Sellars, *Science and Metaphysics: Variations on Kantian Themes* ch. 7 (1968).

14. For one version of the distinction between personal and impersonal preferences, see Dworkin, "What is Equality? Part 1: Equality of Welfare," 10 *Phil. & Pub. Aff.* 185 (1981). For example, Dworkin states:

> [P]eople have what I shall call impersonal preferences, which are preferences about things other than their own or other people's lives or situations. Some people care very much about the advance of scientific knowledge, for example, even though it will not be they (or any person they know) who make the advance, while others care deeply about the conservation of certain kinds of beauty they will never see. Id. at 192.

Dworkin is correct here in distinguishing environmental values from personal (i.e., self-regarding) preferences and from distributional considerations. To view all values as either personal preferences or distributional norms is to exclude the community-based or public values on which much of our environmental legislation rests. Community-based values are consistent with a liberal theory of legislation because they concern conceptions of the good society rather than conceptions of the good life, about which liberal policy is to be neutral. See also Dworkin, "Neutrality, Equality, and Liberalism," in *Liberalism Reconsidered* 1, 8 (D. Mac-Lean & C. Mills eds. 1983) (distinguishing between passive and active membership in a community).

15. There is a plethora of literature on the distinction between personal (self-regarding) preferences and public (group-regarding) values. See, e.g., Maass, "Benefit-Cost Analysis: Its Relevance to Public Investment Decisions," 80 *Q. J. Econ.* 208, 216–17 (1966); Marglin, "The Social Rate of Discount and the Optimal Rate of Investment," 77 *Q. J. Econ.* 95, 98 (1963).

16. See S. Kelman, *What Price Incentives? Economists and the Environment* ch. 3 (1981).

17. Kneese & Bower, note 9 above, at 4.

18. The underlying Paretian standard holds that a move from state A to state B increases social welfare or utility if at least one person prefers B to A and no one prefers A to B. This standard is generalized to more complex cases by the Kaldor-Hicks principle which holds that A's social welfare is increased if those who prefer B can compensate those who want A and still maintain their preference. Thus the notion of social welfare or overall utility is defined strictly in terms of satisfaction of preferences insofar as these preferences are measured in terms of willingness to pay. It has no independent, normative significance. For a clear discussion of these concepts in relation to current regulatory concerns, see Coleman, note 1 above, at 649.

19. Baxter, note 4 above, at 19.

20. Contemporary economic theory assumes that if a preference of any individual is satisfied, that individual and society as a whole is "better off" as a result. This, indeed, is the basis of the concept of a Pareto improvement—a change in social state that at least one person prefers and no one opposes. This is not an improvement in any normative sense. It is an improvement, if at all, from that individual's point of view. There is no "point of view of society as a whole" from which it can be viewed as a *social* improvement.

Gunnar Myrdal observed in 1953 that contemporary "utilitarianism" resembles communism in presupposing a "harmony of interests" and tends "to be forced into an untenable 'communistic fiction' about the unity of society." G. Myrdal, *The Political Element in the Development of Economic Theory* (1954), at 54. This fiction amounts to the assertion that society can be conceived as a single subject capable of having a single interest, called the general welfare or the common good, and consenting as one person to the policies that serve that interest. Id. at 194–95.

21. G. Eads & M. Fix, *Relief or Reform? Reagan's Regulatory Dilemma* 17 (1984).

22. White House Conference on Domestic and Economic Affairs: The President's Remarks at the Conference in Concord, New Hampshire, 11 *Weekly Comp. Pres. Doc.* 404 (Apr. 25, 1975). The President stated that "even if the real costs are only a fraction of this amount, this is an intolerable burden on our pocketbooks." Id.

23. *Economic Report of the President Transmitted to Congress February 1975*, at 159 (1975).

24. Weidenbaum, "On Estimating Regulatory Costs," *Regulation,* May-June 1978, at 14, 17.

25. For a detailed analysis of the 1976 Chase study, see Haveman & Smith, "Investment, Inflation, Unemployment, and the Environment," in *Current issues in U.S. Environmental Policy* 164, 175 (P. Portney ed. 1978).

26. Data Resources, Inc., *The Macroeconomic Impact of Federal Pollution Control Programs: 1978 Assessment* (Jan. 29, 1979) (report submitted to the Environmental Protection Agency and the Council on Environmental Quality).

27. Portney, "The Macroeconomic Impacts of Federal Environmental Regulation," in *Environmental Regulation and the U.S. Economy* 25, 47 (H. Peskin, P. Portnoy, & A. Kneese eds. 1981).

28. Id. at 47.

29. M. Weidenbaum & R. DeFina, *The Cost of Federal Regulation of Economic Activity* (The American Enterprise Institute Reprint No. 88, May, 1978).

30. Id. at 2.

31. Id.

32. Id. at 3.

33. The familiar $100 billion figure is reached by an odd method. Weidenbaum notes that administrative costs would increase in 1979 from the 1976 figure and that, in 1976, the ratio between administrative and compliance costs ran roughly 20 to 1. "With administrative costs estimated at $4.8 billion, the estimated total costs of federal regulation would exceed $100 billion." Weidenbaum, note 24 above, at 17.

34. In their 1976 study, Weidenbaum and DeFina rely on figures generated by a senate subcommittee which had studied paperwork costs in 1972. Weidenbaum & DeFina, note 29 above, at 29. They adjusted the figure to $25 billion in 1976 dollars. Id. at 2. This figure suggests that society could save a lot more money by controlling and reducing paperwork than it might gain by cutting back on programs to control pollution. For a discussion of this and other aspects of the Weidenbaum study, see Eads & Fix, note 21 above, at 28–31.

35. For a discussion of these studies, see Portney, note 27 above, at 39.

36. The Conservation Foundation, *The State of the Environment in 1982: A Report from the Conservation Foundation* (1982).

37. Id. at 35.

38. Eads & Fix, note 21 above, at 41.

39. There are two prominent exceptions to this general rule. First, "supply-side" economists, frustrated by the apparent failure of Keynesian demand management to keep down inflation and the apparent failure of monetary policy with respect to unemployment, have argued that microeconomic inefficiencies prevent full employment and maximum productivity. The supply-side argument does not attract many mainstream Ph.D. economists, but it has achieved a good deal of political attention, especially as formulated by George Gilder, who had no formal training in economics. G. Gilder, *Wealth and Poverty* (1981).

Second, "rational expectations" economists also tie macroeconomic performance to microeconomic efficiency, but unlike the supply siders, these economists believe that markets quickly discount governmental policies, which therefore make little difference. The government therefore cannot really improve matters by monetary or other policy; indeed, rational expectationists see poor economic performance as caused by random shocks, mistakes, and failures of information which cannot he controlled. For a survey, see Schoemaker, "The Expected Utility Model: Its Variants, Purposes, Evidence and Limitations," 20 *J. Econ. Lit.* 529 (1982).

For a good assessment of these two schools, see L. Thurow, *Dangerous Currents: The State of Economics* chs. 5, 6 (1983).

40. For a good collection or papers making this point, see *Microeconomic Efficiency and Macroeconomic Performance* (D. Shepherd, J. Turk, & A. Silberston eds. 1983).

41. E. Gramlich, *Benefit-Cost Analysis of Government Programs* (1981), at 17.

42. Posner, "The Ethical and Political Basis of the Efficiency Norm in Common Law Adjudication," 8 *Hofstra L. Rev.* 490 (1980).

43. Id. at 488.

44. Leonard & Zeckhauser, "Cost-Benefit Analysis Applied to Risks: Its Philosophy and Legitimacy," in *Values at Risk* 31, 33 (D. MacLean ed. 1986).

45. Id.

46. Id at 33–36.

47. K. Marx, *The Criticism of the Gotha Program* (1875).

48. It should be emphasized that the "hypothetical consent" argument used by Posner and Zeckhauser has no connection whatsoever with the legitimate use of social contract theory found, for example, in J. Rawls, *A Theory of Justice* (1971). Rawls is concerned with establishing the basic structure of institutions within a just society in which rational individuals may legitimately pursue incommensurable conceptions of the good. See Rawls, "The Basic Structure as Subject," 14 *Am. Phil. Q.* 159 (1977). On the contrary, Posner and Zeckhauser argue that a single conception of the good exists (e.g., preference-satisfaction, wealth-maximization, etc.) upon which all rational individuals would agree and, therefore, which may be assumed to have the hypothetical consent of the community. It is precisely because every ideologue, zealot, and academic-with-a-theory-of-the-common-good believes he is right and, therefore, that any rational and informed agent will necessarily agree with him (or not be rational or informed) that the Rawlsian argument is necessary. It aims at establishing social structures in which all these individuals, each with his own conception of what rationality and morality demand, can live peaceably together and secure the benefits of social cooperation.

49. J. Rawls, *A Theory of Justice* (1971).

50. See note 48 above.

6 Utilitarianism and Cost-Benefit Analysis: An Essay on the Relevance of Moral Philosophy to Bureaucratic Theory

Alasdair MacIntyre

THE PRACTICAL WORLD of business and government is haunted by unrecognized theoretical ghosts. One of the tasks of moral philosophy is to help us to recognize and, if possible, to exorcise such ghosts. For so long as philosophical theories in fact inform and guide the actions of men who take themselves to be hard-headed, pragmatically oriented, free of theory, and guided by common sense, such theories enjoy an undeserved power. Being unrecognized they go uncriticized. At the same time the illusion is encouraged that philosophy is an irrelevant, abstract subject—part of the decoration of a cultured life perhaps, but unnecessary in and even distracting from the activities of the practical world. The truth is, however, that all nontrivial activity presupposes some philosophical point of view and that not to recognize this is to make oneself the ready victim of bad or at the very least inadequate philosophy.

Consider for example, the way in which the business executive or the civil servant characteristically defines and conceptualizes the activities of himself, his colleagues and his clients. He or she does so in a way which appears to exclude both moral and philosophical considerations from arising within his everyday decision-making tasks. Certainly some large moral considerations may have been involved in the executive's choice of a corporation; some might not be prepared to work for an armaments firm or in the making of pornographic movies. And certainly there may have been moral grounds for some of the legal constraints imposed by government—the imposition of safety regulations, for example. But once the executive is at work the aims of the public or private corporation must be taken as given. Within the boundaries imposed by corporate goals and legal constraints the executive's own tasks characteristically appear to him

as merely technical. He has to calculate the most efficient, the most economical way of mobilizing the existing resources to produce the benefits of
power at the lowest costs. The weighing of costs against benefits is not just
his business, it is business.

The business executive does not differ in this view of his task from
other bureaucrats. Bureaucracies have been conceived, since Weber, as
impersonal instruments for the realization of ends which characteristically
they themselves do not determine. A bureaucracy is set the task of achieving within the limits set by certain legal and physical constraints the most
efficient solution of the problems of realizing such ends with the means
available.

The impersonality of bureaucracy has two closely related aspects. The
first is that those who deal with a bureaucracy over time must be able to
have continuous relationships of an intelligible kind with it, no matter
which individuals within the bureaucracy retire, die or are replaced during
that relationship. Correspondence is correspondence with the organization rather than with the individuals who dictate the letters. Hence the
existence of files or of computerized records is essential to bureaucratic
organizations. From this aspect of impersonality a second emerges. Reasons cited as explanations for or justifications of actions in correspondence
or in other external or internal transactions must hold as good reasons for
the members of the organization independently of whoever actually on a
particular occasion enunciates them. Thus established and agreed criteria
of sound reasoning are presupposed in the successful functioning of all
bureaucratic organizations. This is the point at which their impersonality
and their commitment to means-ends rationality can be understood as two
aspects of the same phenomenon.

The presupposed agreement on ends allows all disagreement within the
organization to take place on questions of means, that is on the merits of
rival policies for achieving the agreed ends. If these arguments are to be
settlable, then there must also be preestablished methods both for isolat-
ing all the relevant elements in each situation and for estimating the costs
and the benefits of proceeding by this route rather than that. In other
words, the norms of rationality, which on a Weberian or a neo-Weberian
view of bureaucracies must govern public discourse within bureaucracies
and between bureaucracies and their masters, clients, customers, or other
external agents, are such that the cost-benefit analysis provides the essential normative form of argument.

The effect of this is that questions of alternative policies appear to
become settlable in the same way that relatively simple questions of fact
are. For the question of whether these particular means will or will not
bring about that particular end with less expenditure of this or that resource than some other means is of course a question of fact.

The moral philosopher will at once recognize that the discourse of bureaucracy thus conceived reproduces the argumentative forms of utilitarianism. Not perhaps those of utilitarianism largely conceived as a morality capable of dealing with every area of life, but those reflecting acceptance of J. S. Mill's judgment upon "what a philosophy like Bentham's can do. It can teach the means of organizing and regulating the merely *business* part of the social arrangements." (Leavis, 1950, p. 73). Poetry, music, friendship, and family life, as Mill sees it may not be captured by the Benthamite calculus; but there is a part of life which may be so captured, and which therefore may be rendered calculable.

If it is correct that corporate activity embodies the argumentative forms of utilitarianism, then we ought to be able to identify the key features of utilitarianism, including its central errors and distortions, within corporate activity. The guide that I shall use to identify the argumentative forms of corporate activity will be the text-book versions of cost-benefit analysis (e.g., Mishan, 1971), which not only form the mind of the corporate executive but provide paradigmatic examples from practice. The question is whether we discover in the texts the same lacunae and incoherences as in classical utilitarianism. First we must characterize these deficiencies.

Utilitarianism and Its Deficiencies

The doctrines of classical utilitarianism appear to first sight simple and elegant. Every proposed course of action is to be subjected to the test: Will it produce a greater balance of pleasure over pain, of happiness over unhappiness, of benefits over harms, than any alternative course of action? It is right to perform that action which will be productive of "the greatest happiness of the greatest number," which will have the greatest utility. In calculating the greatest happiness, everybody is to count for one and nobody for more than one. Utilitarianism sometimes has entangled itself, but perhaps need not entangle itself, in questions about the meaning of such words as *right* and *good*. Bentham at least made no pretence that his doctrine was an analysis of what moral agents had hitherto meant in using such words; he proposed it instead as a rational substitute for the confusions and superstitions of earlier moral theory and it is as such that I shall examine it.

Two main versions of utilitarianism have been advanced: that which holds that the utilitarian test is a test of actions and that which holds that it is a test of rules. On the former view, generally known as act-utilitarianism, rules simply summarize our findings to date about what classes of action generally tend to produce the greatest happiness of the greatest number; they are rough and ready guides to action, but if it appears on a given occasion that an action which transgresses a rule hitherto employed will produce a greater balance of pleasure or pain than one which conforms to that rule then the former action ought to be preferred to the latter. On the other rule-utilitarian view, we perform those actions which the best moral rules we have prescribe; and we decide which moral rules are best by applying the "greatest happiness" test. But David Lyons (1965) has argued cogently that any case in which an act-utilitarian would have a good reason for breaking a rule would be a case in which a rule-utilitarian would have an equally good reason for emending his rule. Hence in practice they come to the same theory and our discussion can safely ignore their differences.

About any version of utilitarian doctrine five major questions arise. The first concerns the range of alternative courses of action which are to be subjected to the utilitarian test. For clearly at any moment an indefinitely large range of alternative courses of action are open to most agents. In practice I may consider a very limited set of alternatives: Shall I use this money to paint my house or to educate my child? But perhaps I ought to weigh every proposed expenditure of energy, time or money against the benefit that might accrue from devoting it to the solution of world population problems or the invention of labor-saving devices or the discovery of new methods to teaching music to young children. . . . If I try to construct a list of this kind of indefinite length, all decision making will in fact be paralyzed. I must therefore find some principle of restriction in the construction of my list of alternatives. But this principle cannot itself be utilitarian; for if it were to be justified by the test of beneficial and harmful consequences as against alternative proposed principles of restriction, we should have to find some principle of restriction in order to avoid paralysis by the construction of an indefinitely long list of principles of restriction. And so on.

Utilitarian tests therefore always presuppose the application of some prior nonutilitarian principle which sets limits upon the range of alternatives to be considered. But this is not all that they presuppose. Bentham believed that there was one single, simple concept of pleasure or of happiness. It did not matter what you called it.

Indeed Bentham believed that there were no less than fifty-eight synonyms for pleasure of which *happiness* is one. Nor is there any good which is not either pleasure itself or a means to pleasure. Moreover the difference between pleasures is only quantitative. Given these beliefs the notion of summing pleasures on the one hand and pains on the other, in calculating which course of action will produce the greatest happiness of the greatest number, is not mysterious. But Bentham's beliefs are of course false and were recognized as false even by his immediate utilitarian heirs.

Consider for the moment only genuine pleasures. It is clear that the pleasure of climbing a mountain, the pleasure of listening to Bartok and the pleasure of drinking Guinness stout are three very disputable things. There is not some one state to the production of which the climbing, the listening and the drinking are merely alternative means. Nor is there any scale on which they can be weighed against each other. But if this is true of pleasures, how much more complex must matters become when we seek to weigh against each other such goods as those of restoring health to the sick, of scientific enquiry or of friendship. A politician has to decide whether to propose spending a given sum of money on a new clinic for aged patients or on a new infant school; a student has to decide between embarking on a career as a musician or becoming an engineer. Both wish to promote the greatest happiness of the greatest number, but they are being called upon to decide between incommensurables—unless they can provide some prior scheme of values by means of which goods and evils, pleasures and pains, benefits and harms are to be ranked in some particular way. Such a method of rank-ordering will however have to be nonutilitarian. For like the principle which specified the range of alternatives to be considered it has to be adopted before any utilitarian test can be applied.

Third, there is the question of whose assessment of harms and benefits is to be considered by the agent making his assessment. For it is clear not only that there are alternative methods of rank-ordering, but also that different types of people will adopt and argue for different methods. The old do not weigh harms and benefits in the same way as the young; the poor have a different perspective from the rich; the healthy and the sick often weigh pain and suffering differently. "Everybody is to count for one and nobody for more than one," declared Bentham; but others—Sir Karl Popper (Popper, 1966 chapter 5, n. 6) , for one—have suggested that the relief of pain or suffering always should take precedence over the promotion of pleasure or happiness. So we have at least two contingently incompatible proposals immediately, for the outcome of Bentham's rule clearly will often conflict with the results of applying Popper's maxim.

Fourth, there is the question of what is to count as a consequence of a given action. We might be tempted to suppose this a very straightforward question, but it is not. For the apparently straightforward answer "All the predictable effects of my action are to be counted as consequences of my action" at once raises the question, "What are reasonable standards of prediction?" How much care and effort am I required to exert before I make my decision? Once again certain maxims must be adopted prior to the utilitarian test. But this is not the only difficulty which arises over the notion of a consequence. In the Anglo-Saxon legal tradition chains of cause-and-effect arising from an action are often thought to be modified when they pass through another responsible agent in such a way that the later effects are no longer held to be consequences of my action. I am a teacher grading a student's examination. I give him a well-deserved *C-*. The student who has hoped for an *A* goes home and in his anger beats his wife. Suppose that I could somehow or other have reasonably predicted this outcome; ought I to have counted the wifebeating as a consequence of my action in grading the paper? Ought I to have weighed this consequence against others before deciding on what grade to give the paper? Classical utilitarianism appears to be committed to the answer "Yes," the Anglo-Saxon legal tradition by and large to the answer "No." About what are they disagreeing? Obviously it is about the range of effects of an action for which the agent can be held responsible. Thus it turns out that some particular theory of responsibility must be adopted before we can have a criterion for deciding what effects are to count as consequences.

Fifth, a decision must be made about the time scale which is to be used in assessing consequences. Clearly if we adopt a longer time scale we have to reckon with a much less predictable future than if we adopt a shorter one. Our assessment of long-term risks and of long-term probabilities is generally more liable to error than our assessment of short-term risks and probabilities. Moreover, it is not clear how we ought to weigh short-term harms and benefits against long-term contingencies; are our responsibilities the same to future generations as they are to the present one or to our own children? How far ought the present to be sacrificed to the future? Here again we have a range of questions to which nonutilitarian answers have to be given or at least presupposed before any utilitarian test can be applied.

Utilitarianism thus requires a background of beliefs and of evaluative commitments, a fact that has usually gone unnoticed by utilitarians themselves. They are able to apply the test of utility only because they have already implicitly decided that the world ought to be viewed in one way rather than another, that experience ought to be structured and evaluated in one way rather than another. The world which they inhabit is one of discrete variables, of a reasonably high degree of predictability; it is one in which questions of value have become questions of fact and in which the aim and the vindication of theory is its success in increasing our manipulative powers. The utilitarian vision of the world and the bureaucratic vision of the world match each other closely.

Yet this is not just a matter of resemblance; the bureaucratic world contains a number of devices for ensuring that thought, perception and action are organized in a utilitarian way. The most important of such devices in contemporary bureaucracy is probably the cost-benefit analysis.

Cost-benefit Analysis and Bureaucratic Decision Making

The cost-benefit analysis is an instrument of practical reason, and it is one of the central features of practical reason that it operates under time constraints in a way that theoretical reason does not. Nothing counts as a solution of a practical problem which does not meet a required deadline; it is no good achieving a perfect solution for defeating Wellington at Waterloo on June 19, if the battle had to be fought on June 18. Hence problems cannot be left unsolved to await future solutions. But problems of a cost-benefit kind—of a utilitarian kind in general—can only be solved when all the elements of the problems are treated as belonging to the realm of the calculable and the predictable. Hence the executive is always under pressure to treat the social world as predictable and calculable and to ignore any arbitrariness involved in so doing. This pressure may operate in either of two opposite ways. It may appear in a tendency to restrict our operations to what is genuinely predictable and calculable; one manifestation of this will be a tendency to prefer short-term to long-term planning, since clearly the near future is generally more predictable than the more distant future. But the same pressure may equally appear in an opposite tendency to try to present all that we encounter as calculable and predictable, a tendency to overcome apparent difficulties in calculation by adopting *ad hoc* devices of various kinds. These conflicting pressures may appear in the way in which decisions are taken or evaluative commitments are made in any of the five areas which define the background of utilitarianism and which in a precisely parallel way define the background of cost-benefit analyses.

There is first of all the restriction of alternatives so that the benefits and the costs of doing this rather than that are weighed against one another, but neither alternative is assessed against an indeterminately large range of other alternatives. Yet ever so often in corporate or governmental or private life the range of alternatives for which cost-benefit analyses are sought changes; and this change always signals a change in underlying evaluative commitments. Up to a certain point in the history of a marriage, divorce remains an unthinkable alternative; up to a certain point in the history of a foreign policy, embarking on an aggressive war remains an unthinkable alternative; up to a certain point in the history of a war, truce or withdrawal remains unthinkable. Corporate parallels are not difficult to think of. The history of publishing or of automobile manufacture abound with them. The one-volume novel or the cheap intellectually substantial paperback were once unthinkable; so was the car which could be advertised primarily for safety factors.

Corporate executives may respond to this by saying that what restricts the range of alternatives which they consider is simply profitability. They can attend only to those alternatives which in the shorter or longer run will yield their stockholders a competitive return in the market. What this reply fails to notice is that what is profitable is partly determined by the range of evaluative commitments shared in the community. Sir Allen had to *make* the intellectual paperback profitable for the very first time and for that a firm conviction about intellectual values was required. What attitude both automobile manufacturers and the public take to death on the roads *changes* what is profitable. Consumer markets are *made*, not just given. Underlying the restricted range of alternatives considered by corporate executives we may therefore find both covert evaluative commitments and also unspelled-out assumptions about human wants and needs.

It is not at all mysterious why these commitments and assumptions should go unnoticed. For in the vast majority of cases the devices which presupposed the commitments and assumptions and which delimited the range of thinkable alternatives were not made by the executives themselves, but were simply imposed upon them as a defining part of the environment in which they are to carry out their task. This is especially so in the case of public utility companies, such as the telephone company or power companies, where the company is legally chartered for certain specific public ends. What is fascinating is that such companies are dominated not by the legal charter itself, but by an orthodox, taken-for-granted, interpretation of that charter which each generation of executives inherits from its predecessors and transmits to its successors. It is interpretations of this kind, unrecognized as interpretations, which limit the thinkable alternatives in many government bureaucracies as well as in public utility companies.

Second, the use of cost-benefit analyses clearly presupposes a prior decision as to what is a cost and what a benefit; but more than that it presupposes some method of ordering costs and benefits so that what otherwise would be incommensurable becomes commensurable. How are we to weigh the benefits of slightly cheaper power against the loss forever of just one beautiful landscape? How are we to weigh the benefits of increased employment and lessened poverty in Detroit against a marginal increase in deaths from automobile accidents? Once somebody has to consider both factors within a cost-benefit analysis framework these questions have to be answered. Considerable ingenuity has in fact been exercised in answering them.

Consider for example how we may carry through a calculation where one of the costs we may have to take into account is the shortening of human life. One recent example occurred in the argument over whether the Anglo-French supersonic aircraft *Concorde* should be allowed to land at United States airports. It is reasonably clear that the greater the use of *Concorde* the greater—as a result of the effects on those layers of the atmosphere which filter the sun's rays—the number of cases of skin cancer. How are we to include such deaths in our calculations?

Writers on cost-benefit analysis techniques have devised four alternative methods for computing the cost of a person's life. One is that of discounting to the present the person's expected future earnings; a second is that of computing the losses to others from the person's death so as to calculate their present discounted value; a third is that of examining the value placed on an individual life by presently established social policies and practices, e.g. the benefits in increased motor traffic which society at the present moment is prepared to exchange for a higher fatal accident rate; and a fourth is to ask what value a person placed on his or her own life, by looking at the risks which that person is or was prepared to take and the insurance premiums which he or she was prepared to pay. Clearly, those four criteria will yield very different answers on occasion; the range of possible different answers to one and the same question that you can extract from the same techniques of cost-benefit analysis makes it clear that all the mathematical sophistication and rigor that may go into the modes of computation may be undermined by the arbitrariness (relative to the mathematics) of the choice to adopt one principle for quantifying rather than another. Thus there once more appears behind the ordered world of discrete, calculable, variable elements in which the cost-benefit analysis is at home, a range of relatively arbitrary decisions presupposed—and sometimes actually made—by the analyst himself.

Third, once more as with utilitarianism in general, the application of cost-benefit analysis presupposes a decision as to *whose* values and preferences are to be taken into account in assessing costs and benefits. Indeed the choice of a method for weighing costs against benefits, the adoption of the type of principle discussed immediately above, will often involve equally a decision as to which voices are to be heard. Consider once again the different methods employed to estimate the cost of a human death. One of these considers the individual's own earnings, one the losses to others, one certain socially established norms, and one the individual's own risk taking. The last is an attempt to give the individual the value which he sets on himself; the second gives him the value he has to others; the third the value he has in the eyes of "society"; the fourth perhaps the value that he has in the eyes of the taxation system. To adopt one of these methods rather than another is precisely to decide *who* is to decide what counts as a cost and what counts as a benefit.

Consider the range of possible decision makers with whom a corporate executive might be concerned: his superiors, the consumers of his product, the stockholders, the labor force, the other members of his profession (if he is, say, a lawyer or an actuary), the community in which the corporation is cited, the government, and the public at large. What makes the question "Who decides?" so crucial is another feature of cost-benefit analyses. Very often, perhaps characteristically, neither future costs nor future benefits can be restricted to identifiable individuals. After the event we can say who died in the road deaths accompanying an increase in automobile traffic, or which children were deformed by the side effects of a new drug, or who in fact got skin cancer after an increase in use of higher flying jet airplanes. But beforehand all that is predictable at best is what proportion of a given population will be harmed (or will benefit). It is a chance of harm or benefit which is assigned now to each member of the population. Therefore the question is: Who should decide how the chances are distributed over a population?

There are some alien cultures where a family's ancestors are given an important voice in decision making; so it is in traditional Vietnamese culture, for example. There are cultures where the old have a very special voice. In our own culture our explicit beliefs label the former as a superstition and our dominant practices show that we implicitly label the latter a superstition too. This is directly relevant to, for example, the policies of public utility companies. Light and heat are peculiarly important to old people; ought therefore the old to receive special consideration from public utility corporation executives in determining what is to count as a cost and what as a benefit? Implicitly or explicitly a decision will have been taken on this point whenever a cost-benefit analysis is offered in a relevant context.

Fourth, the parallel with utilitarianism is maintained in the way in which the questions of what is to count as a consequence of some particular action or course of action arises for cost-benefit analyses. Any answer to this question, as I suggested earlier, presupposes a prior answer to the question: For what range of effects of his actions is an agent to be considered liable or responsible? What answer to this latter question is in fact presupposed by corporate practice? A necessary starting point is to recognize that in advanced societies today, and most notably in the United States, individuals often see their moral lives as parceled out between the different roles which one and the same individual plays. Parts of his moral self are allocated to each sphere of activity, and within each sphere responsibilities—and therefore consequences—are understood in very different ways. So the individual *qua* father or husband has one role and one way of envisaging responsibilities and consequences; but *qua* consumer, *qua* citizen or *qua* corporate executive he may see matters quite differently. The effects of the division of the self are characteristically to exempt the individual in any one role from considering those responsibilities which he is prepared to acknowledge only too readily in other roles. The individual learns to confine different aspects of his evaluative commitments to different spheres. Consider in particular how this may define the situation of the executive in a public utility company. For what is to some degree present in the situation of many corporate managers in America is present in his situation in a highly explicit form. Public utility companies . . . from the outset accepted public governmental regulation as the price to be paid for the privilege of monopoly. The case for monopoly is quite simply that competition involves extremely expensive reduplication of equipment and—especially in the case of rival . . . companies, each of whom serves only a portion of the subscribers—grave inconvenience for consumers. But if monopoly is permitted, then the consumer must find elsewhere the protection which otherwise would (in theory, at least) be provided by competition. Hence the activities of public utility companies are to be regulated and restricted by government-designated agencies.

The company's is the sphere of activity; the government's is the sphere of restriction.

The executive himself inhabits both spheres: *qua* corporate executive he represents the company; *qua* citizen and consumer the government represents him. Parts of his self are allocated to each area.

Other types of corporate executive have often come to embrace government regulation in a similar way; but the executive in the public utility company was forced to seek it out for himself. His acknowledgement of restriction, in that sphere at least, must not appear even to himself reluctant. He operates thereafter under a quasi-legal mandate which prescribes this definition of spheres. I say "quasi-legal," because in the case of . . . power companies [and other public utility companies] . . . , the various statutes which govern the operation of the company do not exhaust the mandate as the executives understand it. For that mandate is one to supply individual and corporate consumers with a good—electrical power. Hence, it is not after all only the statutory restrictions on their activities which define a moral dimension in their activities; there is also a goal conceived of as a goal of public service. (Chester Barnard who wrote what is still the single most influential—even if now usually unread—book on management theory [Barnard, 1938] laid it down that service is the true goal of corporate activity; it is, I think, no coincidence that he spent his entire working life with the telephone company.)

Morally then the executive faces in at least two directions: toward the morality of restriction where it is the duty of others and not himself—or if you like, his duty *qua* citizen and not *qua* executive—to discipline his activities, and also toward the morality of service which defines a goal external to, but justifying his day-to-day activity. What do I mean when I call this goal external?

The power company executive is able at this point to avail himself of a picture of his activities which has nothing particular to do with his serving a public utility company, but is one common to many executives in many industries. This picture is one of a moral contract, prior to and providing warrant for all legal contracts, between an autonomous supplier and an autonomous client. Their autonomy entails that each is the sole authority as to his own needs and wants. The acts of production by the supplier are undertaken for the sake of the client's consumption. Everyone is both in one aspect supplier and in the other client. A simple model of economic value informs their exchanges (something very like a labor theory of value is presupposed). The moral contract has replaced the crude rule of *caveat emptor*. Autonomy also entails that the supplier has no responsibility for the use that the client makes of the goods which he supplies. Moreover since the contract is between individuals no transactions transcend one generation. The supplier is morally bound to give the client what *he* wants; for the nature of the client's wants and the consequences of the act of supply he is not answerable. To make him so would be to injure the autonomy necessary for such a contract.

Only one kind of moral distinction needs to be made by the supplier: that which divides off genuine goods from dubious commodities. Many suppliers will not worry over this distinction except insofar as it is enforced by law; but many do. Goodrich and Goodyear clearly take pride in as well as make profit from producing first-rate tires; and many persons would not wish to involve themselves in selling second-hand napalm or pornographic movies. But once a businessman is assured of the goodness of what he supplies he has a sanction for what he does that leaves him free not to think about this aspect of his activity any more. In his dealings with consumers, in his investment policies, and in his dealings with his labor force he can press ahead exactly as he would do with any other product (except for technological considerations). The wants of the consumer for the good supplied are to be taken as given; whatever is asked for in the form of market demand will, so far as possible, be supplied. It is only as creators of demand that consumers appear in this picture.

It follows that the consequences of any course of action terminate for such an executive when the consumer has been successfully supplied. The further consequences of supplying demand—the trivialization of the culture by the major television networks, for example—are beyond the scope of any consideration by those who supply the electric power for such enterprises. Once again the cost-benefit analysis is not an evaluatively neutral instrument of choice.

The fifth and last parallel with utilitarianism concerns the time scale on which costs and benefits are to be assessed. When we make a decision— implicitly or explicitly, recognizing it or failing to recognize it—about the time span within which we are going to reckon up costs and benefits, at least three different kinds of consideration will affect our decision. The first of these concerns the fact that both types and rates of change for different cost and benefit factors may vary so that by choosing one time length rather than another the relation of costs to benefits will appear quite differently. If I am deciding how to transport commodities from one place to another (by building a road, building a railway, maintaining a canal or whatever) changes in the price of land, the prices of raw materials, the size of the labor force, the demand for utilization of surplus carrying capacity, the technologies involved, the alternative uses to which each type of resource might be put, will all change in such a way that, even if I am a perfect predictor, the choice of dates within which costs and benefits are to be assessed may give strikingly different results. Of course in a private profit-seeking corporation the current rates of return expected on investment will place constraints on such a choice of dates; and in public corporations the need to vindicate policies within terms ultimately specified by electoral laws will set not dissimilar constraints. Nonetheless, even within such limits a certain arbitrariness is likely to appear.

Second, it is not just that the different factors in a situation will be subject to different types and different rates of change; they will also differ in the degree to which they are predictable. Three key types of unpredictability are likely to be generated in the relevant types of situation. One springs from the sheer complexity of so many of the relevant types of situation and their vulnerability to contingencies of an in-practice unpredictable kind: earthquakes, viruses, panics. A second springs from the systematic unpredictability of all innovation that involves radical conceptual invention. We could not before the event have predicted Einstein's definition of "simultaneity" or Kant's doctrine of the transcendental ego or Turing's proof of the effective computability theorem, just because to have predicted these we would have had to specify their character and to have specified their character would be to have anticipated Einstein or Kant or Turing and so prevented their being the discoverers that they were.

It may be said that the author of a cost-benefit analysis simply cannot be expected to deal with unpredictability at all. If this were indeed so it would be equivalent to saying that he must exclude from his view a central feature of social reality—as in fact seems to happen with many studies of organization and management as well as with many conventional texts on the methodology of the social sciences. But of course this consciously or unconsciously willed blindness is not necessary. Reasoning of a cost-benefit analysis kind may include—often does include—some provision for unforseen contingencies. But once again how much and what types of unpredictability are allowed for will rest upon judgments independent of and prior to the cost-benefit analysis itself. Among these judgments will once again be those as to the length of time within which costs and benefits are to be reckoned; and once again there is, relative to the cost-benefit analysis, an element that seems purely arbitrary.

A less arbitrary consideration, but one perhaps no less difficult to handle, appears if we turn to the third factor impinging upon judgments about time scales. This concerns the view taken by individuals of the existence, identity, interests and responsibilities through time of the organization for which they are working. Let me make an initial point about the interests of individuals. We know that individuals vary in the degree to which their identification of their own interests ranges beyond their individual selves and their present state in time. A man may see his interests as being those of a man with a future of a certain kind rather than a present of a certain kind. So a man may for considerations of interest vote for a measure which benefits the aged, although he himself is young, because it is in his family's interest that the aged be supported. Or he may vote for a tax measure which benefits forty-five-year-old married men with high incomes, although he himself is a low-paid, unmarried, twenty-five-year-old, because he votes on the basis of the interests of his predicted future self rather than his present self. As with individuals acting for themselves *qua* individuals, so also for individuals acting in their organizational roles. What time span is assumed to be appropriate for determining costs and benefits will depend on how the organization's interests are envisaged through time and on how the interests of related institutions—the state, the local community, the profession or whatever—are envisaged through time. This becomes very clear if we look at the limiting case, that of organizations constructed and maintained only for some temporary purpose, such as a relief mission whose task is to feed and provide schooling for three thousand children for a period of four months.

The reason why the time scale within which costs and benefits are to be assessed is much less arbitrary and debatable in such cases is *not* merely that the time within which the project is to be completed is specified; for even with projects whose duration is specified, costs and benefits may range in time far beyond the actual duration of the project. What limits the time scale in a nonarbitrary way is rather the clear restraints placed on goals, tasks and resources in this kind of temporary organization and the consequent ease in identifying both the interests and the responsibilities of the organization. This limitation is, as it were, part of the legal or quasi-legal charter of the organization. But with permanent or at least long-term organizations the criteria for imputing responsibility for and defining interests in a variety of consequences are not assigned in this clear way; and the adoption of different time scales for the assessment of costs and benefits may presuppose the adoption of different views of how organizational responsibility is to be imputed and how organizational interests are to be defined.

Consider the example of a university. What counts as a cost or a benefit to a university may—and, it is to be hoped, characteristically will—depend upon a distinction between the essential and long-term purposes which a university serves and the short-term *ad hoc* projects with which universities necessarily become involved. A university which undertakes remedial teaching of adolescents from deprived groups in a situation of social and educational crises, or which organizes some of its research in terms of the immediate practical needs of its community, may and often does pay costs in terms of the damage done to its contract with those long dead and those yet to be born in the distant future to whom it is committed to transmit in living form to the unborn the cultural tradition of the dead. A public utility company or a country club is committed to no such contract; and this means that the appropriate time scale for assessing costs and benefits will be a different one from that appropriate to a university. But *any* time scale may presuppose some view of its identity.

Note that I have written "may" and not "will." For those who inhabit organizations are often unclear and confused as to what precisely they are doing, and the implicit presuppositions of their actions may be similarly unclear. Sometimes what appears arbitrary in choice of time scale just *is* arbitrary; but not always.

Any cost-benefit analysis therefore has to be understood against *some* background of assumptions about identity and time; and because it is impossible to speak of the identity of organizations except in terms of some evaluative commitment, these assumptions will be in part evaluative. Consider the concept of the university embodied in my remarks in the last paragraph but one. The concept in terms of which I wrote may have been the dominant one in the Western world, but it is far from being without rivals. What concept of the university you adopt will involve one out of a set of rival views of the place of knowledge and education in human life. There is no way to employ the concept of a university without adopting some such value-laden conception. And what is true in the case of universities is equally true, if less often noticed, in the case of such organizations as public utility companies and indeed in the case of private and public corporations in general.

Less often noticed? In fact of course not usually noticed at all. The moral structure underlying the corporate executive's thinking is one of which he remains almost entirely unaware. He does not recognize himself as a classical utilitarian; and he cannot therefore recognize that the presuppositions of classical utilitarianism which he shares—which the utilitarians themselves did not recognize—must go doubly unrecognized by himself and his colleagues. His vision of himself remains that of a man engaged in the exercise of a purely technical competence to whom moral concerns are at best marginal, engaging him rather *qua* citizen or *qua* consumer than *qua* executive. Does this false consciousness of the executive, whether in the private corporation or in government, itself have a function? It is plausible to suppose that it does. To consider what that function is, imagine what would occur if all these considerations became manifest rather than latent.

The executive would then be presented with a set of moral problems, or moral conflicts, on which he would have to make overt decisions, over which he would have to take sides in the course of his work. What sort of issues are these? The claims of the environment *versus* the claims of cheaper power, the claims of need (for example, of the old) against those of the urgent present, the claims of rival institutions—government, church, school—in certain respects, the claims of rival judgments of intelligence, integrity and courage. Now it is a crucial feature of our moral culture that we have no established way of deciding between radically different moral views. Moral arguments are in our culture generally unsettable. This is not just a matter of one party to a dispute generally being unable to find any natural method to convince other contending parties. It is also the case that we seem unable to settle these matters within ourselves without a certain arbitrary taking of sides.

It follows that to allow moral issues to become overt and explicit is to create at least the risk of and more probably the fact of open and rationally unmanageable conflict both between executives and within each executive. The avoidance of such conflict necessitates two kinds of device. Where the recognition of moral considerations is avoidable they must be apportioned out between the different areas of the self and its social life, so that what is done and thought in one area will not impinge upon, let alone conflict with, what is done and thought in another. Boundaries must be drawn between areas of social action whose effectiveness will depend upon them not being recognized for what they are.

Where however it is unavoidable that moral issues arise *within* one and the same area, then they must be disguised from the agent so that he can deal with them, so far as is humanly possible, as merely technical issues. Their moral and evaluative character must be relegated to a realm of latent presuppositions. But it is obvious at once that both these devices are central to the structures of life of the corporate executive, as I described them earlier. The morality of contract with the autonomous consumer and the morality of governmental regulation operate in carefully defined areas so that questions of their coherence or conflict with each other or with other moral considerations are prevented from arising. The moral considerations are prevented from arising. The moral considerations underlying cost-benefit analysis are simply suppressed.

NOTE

This article, first published in *Values in the Electric Power Industry,* ed. Kenneth Sayre (Notre Dame, Ind.: Notre Dame University Press, 1977), pp. 217–37, is reprinted by permission.

REFERENCES

Barnard, Chester I. (1938), *The Functions of the Executive,* Harvard University Press, Cambridge.
Leavis, F. R. (ed.) (1950), *Mill on Bentham and Coleridge,* Chatto and Windus, London.
Lyons, David (1964), *Forms and Limits of Utilitarianism,* Clarendon Press, Oxford.
Mishan, E. J. (1971), *Cost-Benefit Analysis,* Praeger, New York.
Popper, Sir Karl (1966), *The Open Society and its Enemies,* 5th ed., Routledge & Kegan Paul, London, Vol. 1.

7 The Ethical Poverty of Cost-Benefit Methods: Autonomy, Efficiency, and Public Policy Choice

John Martin Gillroy

Is EFFICIENCY A MORAL PRINCIPLE that can be balanced against others like freedom, equality, or benevolence, and is therefore adequate, in itself, to judge the ends of public policy, or is it only an economic precept that must be justified in terms of such ethical principles and therefore is adequate only to the judging of efficient means to public ends otherwise arrived at? Those who would propose that the assumptions of the competitive market are adequate to the decision process in public policy, and who recommend cost-benefit methodology as the test of a policy's adequacy, must also assume that efficiency has a deeper moral validity than merely its "rational" economic nature in order for it to hold sway outside of the pure market context.[1] In order for market decision and evaluation criteria to transfer into the realm of political decision making, its justification can no longer be based solely on efficiency as an economic standard, but an argument must be made that efficiency has moral weight, as a more universal and necessary ethical standard or principle. It is the claim, therefore, of those who would recommend cost-benefit methods, for policy making, that this moral weight exists at a more primitive level than the rational argument for efficiency. The two most probable bases for this moral weight are in the concepts of utility and autonomy. I will concentrate on the latter.[2]

Autonomy is a complex moral standard that has many definitions and that has found a place in both consequentialist and nonconsequentialist ethical thought from Mill to Kant to Hegel (Christman 1989). For the purposes of this essay I will categorize three theoretical orientations to autonomy, divide them into "thick" and "thin" theories of autonomy, and

195

claim that it is only the latter variety that can be claimed by efficiency as cost-benefit methods.

A "thick" theory of autonomy is one that has three components where the first two are logical entailments of the third. First, it defines what is important about the person (will or choice). Second, it describes what distinguishes between autonomous and nonautonomous behavior (a theory of the "good" or the "right"), and third, it provides a location for the moral worth of an act (the internal character of the act or its consequences).

There are two categories of autonomy theory that can be called "thick" by this definition. The first alternative is nonconsequentialist in nature and defines autonomy as the internal capacity of the human will in control of the agency of the individual. Here it is not the choices of the individual that matter the most nor their consequences, but the freedom of the will of the individual and one's intent, that is prior to, and conditions choice. It is critical, within this alternative concept of autonomy that one's will is controlled by an idea of human reason and that this in turn creates a full concept of the "self" that defines what is "right"—that is, what is necessary to enable or empower the will of the individual to legislate for himself and be autonomous.

The second "thick" alternative is consequentialist in nature and focuses on the choices individuals make for themselves. Here the internal will is not as important as the desires and wants that are revealed in the empirical choices individuals make and the moral worth of these choices is defined by the consequences produced by them. Essential to this approach to autonomy, as a moral standard, is a definition of the "good" that is rational and adequate to the decision environment in which the standard of autonomy is applied. By this I mean that since, to avoid tautology, all choices made by the individual cannot be considered autonomous; a definition of the "good" is necessary to distinguish that which consequentially affirms the autonomy of the individual. This distinctive standard must be adequate to provide for a complete sense of what the "good" autonomous individual is and what is of utility to his autonomy, so that it can be argued that the consequences of choice reaffirm the individual's autonomy. This definition of the "good" cannot do this if it does not reflect the complexity (economic, moral, political, social) of the environment within which the individual exists.

Although the "thick" theories have both a consequentialist and nonconsequentialist face, the "thin" theory is represented by a hybrid category that attempts to combine the use of empirical preferences and choice with a nonconsequentialist focus on rights that sanctify these choices.

Autonomy, as a nonconsequentialist ethical concept, is normally thought of in terms of one's control over one's own will (Kant 1786; 1788) as a "kind of higher order control over the moral quality of one's life" (Kuflik 1984, 273). But within philosophy, there is a split between nonconsequentialists who define autonomy as an internal qualitative consideration and those (Wolf 1970; Nozick 1974) who consider autonomy as the act of revealed choice, based on preference, and in terms of the noninterference of third parties in the act of consenting. Here what is important about a person is consequentialist (their empirical choices),[3] what distinguishes between autonomous and nonautonomous choice is nonconsequentialist (the "right" to have one's empirical choices respected by others), and the location of the moral worth of the act is also nonconsequentialist (the intent and desire of the individual). The problem is that by combining approaches to autonomy one is left with a theory that cannot tell autonomous from nonautonomous choice for it neither has the rich sense of "self" necessary to define the metaphysical standards of the nonconsequentialist "thick" theory nor the enriched theory of "good" consequences that would support a consequentialist vision.

The purpose of this essay is to explore the contention that there exists a *moral* justification for the use of cost-benefit method, based in a concept of individual moral freedom or autonomy, that carries more ethical weight than the economic arguments for rational efficiency and the teleological satisfaction of preferences for welfare.

First, I will assume that since cost-benefit criteria cannot support an ethical concept of the utility of consequences (Sagoff, this volume: Efficiency and Utility, pp. 165–77), it also fails to lend support for a consequentialist "thick" theory of autonomy. Second, I will contend that no rich sense of internal capacity is alive in the market definition of autonomy that would allow a standard of autonomy on the nonconsequentialist "thick" alternative to lay as a foundation for efficiency either inside a market or in making public choices. Last, I will show that the only autonomy argument accessible to cost-benefit methods is based on the "thin" alternative which I will call "autonomy as consent." Here, although this may be an adequate "thick" basis for a theory of autonomy within markets (where its theory of the "good" is coextensive with its economic concerns), its "thin" nature is revealed when the use of Pareto efficiency in the market context is replaced by Kaldor or potential Pareto criteria in the public realm. I will contend that outside of a market the idea of voluntary consent to trade based solely on economic criteria is inadequate to the task of defining the autonomy of the individual. We shall see that while the requirements of a concept of "good" have been expanded in the shift from markets to include political, social, and moral considerations in public policy, this is without an adequate expansion of the concept of individual welfare within cost-benefit methods to account for the shift. Nor is there an adequate metaphysics of the "self" that could accomplish the transition from markets to public choice and make distinctions between autonomous and nonautonomous behavior in a nonconsequentialist manner.

I will claim that the *"moral high ground"* for cost-benefit analysis is therefore coextensive with and no more powerful than, the "rational" or narrowly economic justification of cost benefit, and that at best the autonomy of individual public choice outside of a market is an impoverished and morally *"thin"* theory of autonomy, unable to stand on its own, or justify the use of an efficiency standard, outside of a competitive economic market, in a political context choosing public ends.

II

According to Mishan (1982), a cost-benefit criterion for public policy does what a market would do, but with externalities internalized. In turn, the ethical appeal of markets has been traced to notions of freedom, consent, and autonomy. "It is only under a system of voluntary exchange that freedom is maximized" (Director 1964, 7). The aim is to justify the market, efficiency standards, and a cost-benefit perspective toward policy decision making, on a more fundamental basis than the efficient aggregation of preferences.[4] The ability of the market to respect individuals, and their liberty to maximize their own personal welfare, provides this basis. In defining markets, Richard Posner appeals to Kant.

> It is also possible to locate Pareto ethics in a different philosophical tradition . . . broadly Kantian, which attaches a value . . . to individual autonomy; . . . highly congenial to the Kantian emphasis on autonomy is consent. And consent is the operational basis of the concept of Pareto superiority. Suppose we consider consent an ethically attractive basis for permitting changes in the allocation of resources, on Kantian grounds. . . . We are led . . . to an ethical defense of market transactions that is unrelated to their effect in promoting efficiency . . . In the setting of the market . . . it is clear that forbidding transactions would reduce both the wealth of society and personal autonomy, so that maximizing wealth and protecting autonomy coincide. (Posner 1983, 89–90)

Leonard and Zeckhauser have made the link between the ethical appeal of markets (without externalities) and the allocations of cost-benefit analysis (integrating externalities). They argue that "no [other] method that has a sound ethical basis . . . can deal with all issues equally well" (1986).

A cost-benefit test for policy therefore can be said to claim two levels of justification. *Rationally,* it is justified teleologically by the idea of efficient preference aggregation where a Paretian standard (the potential Pareto improvement)[5] acts as the primitive concept. In this justification, a cost-benefit approach has its foundation in the end of preference satisfaction. Each person is a maximizer of his/her welfare where individual rationality, in its efforts to provide for one's self-interest, can be aggregated by the policy maker (using cost-benefit methods to mimic the market) to produce a social ordering that, simultaneously over all persons, renders an efficient collective allocation of goods.

Ethically, a cost-benefit criterion is justified, on the basis of consent where autonomy is the primitive moral idea. In the realm of public policy, efficient allocation, on the surface, is a formal economic argument for the use of cost-benefit procedures that has no independent moral weight, but must be justified in terms of other moral principles (Gramlich 1981; Boadway 1979; Layard 1972; Lave 1981). The choice of cost-benefit methods rather than cost-effectiveness analysis in policy evaluation comes from the belief that the market assumptions about individuals, their consent and autonomy are true ex ante, for public choices. The "moral high ground" argument for cost-benefit procedures works or fails to the degree the market justification system of "autonomy as consent," that motivates the use of cost-benefit evaluation in nonmarket situations, has ethical strength in the public realm.[6] The ethical justification for cost-benefit analysis, its claim to "ethical propriety" (Leonard and Zeckhauser 1986, 15), and the "moral high ground" as an evaluative technique for policy making, is the central concern of the remainder of this essay.

The argument for the "moral high ground" which is purported to have autonomy as its ethically primitive concept is in actuality an argument based on the concepts of market consent and preference, which are expected to carry the weight for both the rational and ethical justifications. Therefore to understand the internal workings of the argument for the "moral high ground," I will examine the two concepts that are used in the economic literature to define and support the idea of autonomy as it comes up against the demands of morality in making policy choices: *consent* (which defines the theory of the "good") and *preference* (which acts as the theory of the "self").

III

Autonomy, as an independent concept, is rarely mentioned in the cost-benefit literature. The exception to this rule, as we have seen, is Richard Posner who uses the term as a Kantian justification for wealth maximization (Posner 1983, 80–95).

I will contend, however, that the economic idea of autonomy permeates the writings on the competitive market, and is wrongly used to support the transition from market to nonmarket decision making. Autonomy, in the guise of consent and consumer sovereignty in the market, is one of the basic normative assumptions of cost-benefit methods.

According to the literature, the individual is the sole repository of utility and welfare in the market mechanism. He is assumed to know his mind, what is best for him, and to have sovereignty over all judgments of welfare which will serve, primarily, his self-interest. The concept of sovereignty disallows any but the most basic collective (third-party) interference in one's affairs, limiting government policy to the role of protecting and encouraging wealth-maximizing transactions. Exchange is an individual choice motivated by subjective preferences that are the point of departure for all judgments of welfare.

The market operates on the assumption that individuals are self-sufficient, and sanctions transactions only on the basis of individual voluntary consent. Webster's *New World Dictionary* defines autonomy as "functioning independently without the control of others" (2d ed., s.v. autonomy). In the sphere of economic concerns this has come to mean the free exchange between individuals on the basis of their mutual consent, which is voluntary and without the negative interference of any collective entity. Here a definition of "autonomy as consent" is created for the market. But can this idea of the autonomous trader in the market be transferred, without further foundation, into the realm of public choice?

To answer this question we must begin with the economic definition of the "good" which supports "autonomy as consent" and is claimed as the moral primitive of cost-benefit evaluation. This concept of the "good" draws its normative power from the components of consent: the idea of voluntary choice, the connection of choice to consideration of welfare improvement, and the preferences that inform and motivate one's sovereign choices.

Choice

The central concern of "autonomy as consent" in a market is the voluntary *choice* of individuals and respect for that choice. The normative ramifications of choice are centered on the assumption of individual self-sufficiency, while the respect for these choices defines justice in a specific way that influences the role played by the status quo in market allocations.

First, in order for a choice to be voluntary, it must not be interfered with. The market approach is interested primarily in the interference of collective authorities in the individual maximization of wealth, but when considering public choices, there is the possibility that other individuals and their externalities, can be as interfering as any government. If one is enslaved or routinely exploited by another, then one's wealth maximization will be curtailed, as his utility function, and autonomous choices, become more and more part of the person who controls his life. When stuck on a bridge jammed with traffic, it is other individuals who have interfered with one's voluntary choices, not any collective authority, whose regulation may in fact be the only way out of the jam. In the public context the moral assumptions at the base of cost-benefit evaluation focus on the state as location of all principal interference, and therefore place maximum pressure on the noninterference of policy makers in the voluntary exchange of consumers. This blinds the policy maker to concern for the externalities of some as they affect the freedom of others. These externalities are assumed to be internalized and free of transaction costs (Page 1973; Coase 1963).

Voluntary choice, even in isolation, is still a function of the endowment of the fungible goods one has, with which he begins trade, and the opportunity set of which he can take advantage. One's entitlement is the sole basis on which his welfare improvements are judged and will constrain his power to maximize his own wealth in trade. If it is the case that the initial endowments of the individuals involved in an exchange are greatly asymmetric (which is very possible within a policy framework), then it is the case that voluntary choice is also asymmetrically distributed.

Even if endowments are not asymmetrically distributed, opportunity may be, so that individuals have the economic power to improve their lot but no occasion to make the actual exchange. In the public context, one may therefore be strategically exploited in two ways: by beginning with an asymmetrically small endowment, which puts one at a disadvantage to others because it restricts one's freedom to make voluntary choices, or by having an asymmetrically small opportunity set that does not allow one to take advantage of the choices that he would wish to. Both of these complicate the meaning of voluntary action for the policy maker and blur its connection to the ideal of consent as a moral concept (Barry 1992).

The market has no necessary guidelines to define the status quo point from which exchange begins and its results are evaluated. Although this may be an acceptable dimension of autonomy within the market, the policy maker must assume that the first distribution has an affect on the degree of freedom and voluntarism of his constituents and therefore the autonomy with which their consent to policy is framed. It is therefore the case that an important element in the definition of freedom, voluntary consent (autonomy in the economic sense), has no mechanism to ensure its fair distribution.

What public policy might consider to be an unfair distribution in the initial status quo does not morally cloud the capacity of individual consumer's choices to be reflected fairly in the results of potential Pareto improvements. The individual valuations (v_i) that the cost-benefit analyst will aggregate must be counted equally, regardless of the state of the individual's endowment or opportunity set, unless an argument can be made that the discrepancies are morally relevant. With the potential Pareto improvement, it does not matter to whom the benefit falls, only that the net welfare benefits exceed loss. The cost-benefit evaluation depends on the market assumption that allocation is based on protecting

individual autonomy that is violated by any central authority's involvement in distributive matters.

The policy analyst using the market approach is not actually concerned
with real autonomous choice but with attributing such choice to individuals,
assuming, whatever their condition or environment, that they are self-
sufficient and free to trade. However, autonomy, especially concerning
public policy, is not necessarily equivalent to individual self-sufficiency.
One could assume that individuals require assistance, through distribution
of entitlements, to empower their capacities for equal political/economic
participation. In other cases one may not know what is best, and his autonomy would not be a function of self-sufficiency, but would require the
involvement of others in one's life to assure a morally relevant decision.

> Autonomy is not to be equated with self-sufficiency. Indeed, in a complex
> world it is difficult to believe that anyone is always the best judge of every
> possible matter. Thus the morally reflective person is prepared to acknowl-
> edge that in certain cases someone else may be in a better position to gather
> morally relevant information or even to give disinterested attention to the
> facts, once they have been assembled. (Kuflik 1981, 273)

Autonomy, under this definition, is the ultimate power over one's
capacity to be a moral person, which may require the assistance of collective authorities in the definition and regulation of a fair first distribution.
A deeper sense of justice than what self-sufficient individuals choose for
themselves, given their lot, may be a necessary ingredient in a moral
definition of autonomy adequate to justifying public policy decisions.

Any sense of justice connected with the market definition of "autonomy as consent" does not supplement the concerns one might have with
the idea of voluntary choice but sets them in concrete within cost-benefit
methodology. The cost-benefit procedure requires that the choices and
valuations of individuals be respected as is and, at that point, defines the
role of the state in terms of the authority necessary to assure that "from
each as they choose, to each as they are chosen" (Nozick 1974, 160; Hayek
1976). This definition of justice grants the status quo entitlement the
moral validity of a just endowment and narrows the possible range of
redistribution to that which is voluntarily undertaken by those with the
wealth.

The probability is that any asymmetry that exists in the initial entitlement will be perpetuated into the future, where no government interference to redistribute will be allowed by "autonomy as consent" and those
with wealth will set the terms of trade to maintain their advantage. Under
these conditions, the first distribution, upon which all future allocations
will be based, gains moral sanction, and de facto right to its contents
becomes real and controlled by the owner. In reality, de facto right has
gained moral respect as the proper basis upon which voluntary choice will

define autonomy. One's entitlement will now dictate the degree to which one's freedom or autonomy will be expressed. "Autonomy as consent," however, with the assumption of self-sufficiency, will judge all exchanges as if they were made by voluntary consent. Cost-benefit evaluation will in no way interfere or compensate for this assumption, but will build on its basis as a fit point of departure for government-sanctioned public policy decisions.

Consent and Welfare

It is an inherent assumption in the economic analysis of policy decision making that autonomous individuals will always consent to that allocation that will improve their welfare relative to their initial endowment. Each consumer is said to be interested in maximizing his personal welfare and, to this end, will seek allocative alternatives that improve his economic position. The most important consideration concerning "autonomy as consent" is the necessary connection of autonomous choice with welfare improvements. Is this a sufficiently generous concept of "good" considering the various possible motivations of the individual within a policy context?

The first consideration, in evaluating policy ends, is that there may be other variables, of moral importance, connected with a public choice that override whether or not there has been an increase in welfare. It is possible, for example, that one may be involved in a transaction where, in the end, he is better off (in welfare terms) than he was to begin with, but where the transaction involved extortion or exploitation of power or strategic advantage. In these cases, where one can be said to have a gun at one's head, the fact of the extortion has no effect on the judgment of consumer autonomy or the welfare improvement for the cost-benefit analyst. All that defines consent is that there was a trade and that the gains from the trade out-weighed the net social loss. One may object to being in a position where exploitation causes trade, but this fact in itself does not affect the assumptions about autonomy in a market. It is not counted as a cost, and therefore cannot devalue the welfare increase that is the basis of assumed consent.

In addition, there are times at which one is motivated to act from motives other than wealth maximization that are morally relevant to a definition of autonomous choice in the public realm. One may decide to cooperate in a prisoner's dilemma even though he knows that he will lose welfare (at least initially), or he may lower his personal time preference and save more for the future than is efficient, being concerned less with his own well-being and more with the welfare of others. One who must aggregate individual considerations into public policy cannot always make the assumption that welfare maximization is the most morally relevant concern in a person's autonomous actions. Even assuming self-interested behavior, one may not always consent to those transactions that improve his wealth; in the end it is a subjective decision that is unpredictable, but a nonwealth choice option is nonetheless an important moral dimension of one's autonomy for the policy decision maker.

With cost-benefit analysis, there is also the reality that no real choice is being made in the market. A central decision maker is imputing the connection between consent and welfare as a sound base for public choice. This is especially suspect in a situation where the potential Pareto improvement will ensure that there will be welfare losers as well as winners.[7]

By assuming that all wealth-maximizing allocations would gain the consent of all consumers who benefit, the policy decision maker is, in reality, taking sovereignty over subjective valuations and decisions away from the individual. If it is possible that welfare improvements could gain consent, it may also be possible that welfare loss might gain or lose consent, or that consent and welfare are unconnected in any policy sense.

Hypothetical Consent

It is critical to remember that with cost-benefit analysis, we are not concerned with real market Pareto improvements, but only with potential Pareto improvements. Consequently, we are also faced, not with real consent to guaranteed welfare improvements over the collective, but with hypothetical consent to overall social benefits outweighing costs, where many might suffer welfare losses. This has certain entailments that compound the assumptive structure of the policy decision and place stress on "autonomy as consent" outside markets.

The first factor of concern is that, with the potential Pareto improvement, consent loses most of its power as a real moral expression of voluntary choice to maximize subjective welfare. Because all will not receive a welfare improvement, the decision maker cannot count on the voluntary consent of all unless the possible compensation is made actual, which is not necessary to cost-benefit efficiency.[8]

The decision maker is in a position where he must rely on the assumptions that voluntary choice and consent are connected, and that consent and welfare are also interdependent, to carry the weight of his policy decision. Only with these assumptions can he assure himself that individual autonomy is the basis of the public choice. With these assumptions he can assure himself that autonomy means consent to welfare improvements (potential or real) and that these are the choices that moral individuals would make to ensure their continued personal autonomy or freedom.

At this point a cycle develops in the moral argument as one concept is defined in terms of the other.[9] That allocation which would render a potential Pareto improvement is assumed to gain the autonomous consent of the people, while autonomous choice is considered protected and revealed in those policies that render potential Pareto improvements. But can one assume consent without compensating the losers? Yes, for there also exists a powerful sense of ex ante compensated consent within the concept of a potential Pareto improvement. If one is assumed to consent to such an allocation he is also said to consent to all outcomes of that new allocation, even if these turn out to be negative. Ex ante consent is then used as an assumption of prior compensation that relieves the potential Pareto improvement of dependence on real ex post compensation to turn a potential into a real Pareto improvement.

> It is my contention that a person who buys a lottery ticket and then loses the lottery has "consented" to the loss. . . . Many of the involuntary, and seemingly uncompensated, losses experienced in the market or tolerated by the institutions that take the place of the market . . . are fully compensated [for] ex ante and hence are consented to in the above sense. (Posner 1983, 94)

Again, the policy decision maker using an economic definition of autonomy outside of a market is conflating self-interest, subjective welfare, and consent, assuming that any fair lottery which is even potentially a benefit to one, gains one's consent, which is compensated ex ante, whatever the outcome.

If it is the case, however, that welfare and consent have no necessary ethical connection, then it must be true that counterfactual consent (Dworkin 1980; 123–42) cannot be used as justification for a potential Pareto improvement. In no case, even if consent and welfare are connected, can it be said that individual consent is compensated ex ante to an allocation that has uncertain outcomes. For, though one may choose to be part of a lottery, one does not simultaneously consent to the outcome whatever it is; this is a separate moral consideration requiring independent ethical justification to act.[10]

This distinction is especially true when the character of the choices at each stage of the lottery have distinct ramifications. For example, although one may agree that to buy a $1 lottery ticket for a chance at $1 million implies consent to win or lose the million, this is because both the cost of the ticket and the win or loss have a distinctly narrow and economic character. The same economic calculations are used to decide both the spending of the $1 and the probability of winning the $1 million. This is not necessarily the case in lotteries that are part of the public sector. One may participate in the military draft lottery, for instance, because one feels that *politically* one has a general obligation to his country, and his fellow citizens, to participate in the chance of nonvoluntary service. This does not *morally* obligate one to serve or fight if drafted. Each stage of the lottery has a distinct character that has political and moral ramifications that demand separate calculation and choice on the basis of distinct criteria. A duty to participate in a fair lottery to serve my country as an abstract political consideration does not imply a moral duty to serve in any war, any place, any time. The decision to serve would have to take into account the social, political, and moral particulars of the situation for which one was called up, their disposition of service and whether the conditions of their lives and the nation's plight necessitated their service. This distinction was even used by the Selective Service Commission, after the draft was canceled, to encourage signing up for the lottery as a distinct act, not implying service. The moral distinction is between registering for the draft lottery and actually being drafted: the former is the duty of all, the latter will be the duty of only some, under specific circumstances.

Overall, consent seems to have some inherent flaws as a definition of autonomy. It rests on an impoverished theory of the "good" that is solely concerned with wealth maximization as the extent of autonomous expression. Specifically, self-sufficiency is not morally necessary to autonomy in public policy choice, and it is a bad ethical assumption in a social reality where individual endowments and opportunity sets will dictate degrees of freedom and voluntarism. The sense of justice in the market definition of autonomy grants moral validity to de facto possession and places any asymmetric initial endowments in cement as a sanctioned point of departure for all judgments of "socially better." There is no necessary connection between welfare and consent, and the addition of the idea of hypothetical consent leaves the policy maker in an even less coherent justificatory argument cycling between autonomy and the potential Pareto improvement.

Cost-benefit analysis is a centralized decision process that is based on a definition of autonomy that is antithetical to centralized regulation, describing it as necessary only to protect and mimic market allocations, with no independent justification of its own. In addition, it is the case that no real choices are being made by consumers, but that connections are being assumed between welfare and consent and imputed to all social valuations (V) by the decision maker.

IV

The market argument for the "moral high ground" with autonomy as its moral primitive can be further broken down in terms of the preferences that form the basis of consent and the only definition of the "self" in the market theory of autonomy. Preference is therefore the most basic concept in the autonomy-based moral defense of cost-benefit analysis and could compensate for an impoverished theory of the "good" with a more complex theory of the "self" that could support a "thick" version of autonomy.

In order to understand the idea of consent as personal autonomy, one must first realize that all choices are based on subjective preference. I am interested in the assumptions made about the self, the normative ramifications of the inability to distinguish between preferences (on an ethical plane), and the problems with reliance on revealed preference. I contend that preference is the common primitive of both the rational and ethical arguments for the use of cost-benefit procedures, and that it adds nothing of moral importance to the market sense of "autonomy as consent" that gives an independent argument for its ethical significance outside of the market.

The Unified Mind

Basic to any discussion of preference as a moral primitive of the argument for cost-benefit methods is the capability of the individual self as related by the model. The assumption, on the part of the economic model, of a unified mind and unidirectional human goals dedicated to the satisfaction of subjective desire for welfare maximization, although perhaps adequate to autonomy within the market, is a very restrictive vision of these capabilities for a policy maker to assume when choosing public ends.

One might want to admit that individuals do have policy preferences for things that do increase their welfare, preferences that they may wish to satisfy, and which a policy maker might take for granted in policy choice. But it seems less than realistic to imagine that this is the extent of the human intellect, or its most basic moral capacity that ought to define the public decision maker's responsibility. If man's priorities are more complex than the theory that describes him, it would seem that his behavior will be hard to explain, and harder to predict, understand, or take into account in policy choice.

The market reduces the individual to a rational maximizer of his personal welfare where reason has no separate operation from desire satisfaction. It may be that it is important in making collective decisions to assume, contrary to market assumptions, that the mind has the internal capacity to originate a preference or at least distinguish between "proper" and "improper" preferences and recognize when a choice involves morality, and when it does not.

The internal decision process that results in one's personal cost-benefit valuation (v_i) is one where an end is defined that increases the person's welfare by matching it with one's subjective preferences. Here one's mind is used in an effort to judge a public policy alternative as a means to the fulfillment of the desire that motivates a preference. This economic means-end rationality prescribes hypothetical imperatives (Hill 1973, 429–450), but limits the mind to processing only those desires that produce the highest personal welfare. In reality "economic rationality" betrays the fact that the mental processes of economic man must be more complex than assumed, if indeed he is capable of thinking in terms of hypothetical imperatives. Defining a hypothetical imperative as an elective imperative to do A if you desire B, it is necessary to presuppose that the individual is capable of more than mere desire maximization.

> Reason cannot be, in practice, the mere instrument of wants and desires. For the hypothetical imperative, which must be valid if reason is to have a practical function in the service of desire, itself imposes choices, which are often undesired, between adopting means and relinquishing ends. In short, nobody whose action really is determined by himself as a result of deliberation (i.e., willed), even if he embarks on a deliberation with nothing else in mind than to gratify desire, can be subject to those desires, for his deliberation can lead him not to gratify them. (Donagan 1977, 230)

If the individual is assumed by the policy maker to have the ability to think morally, one might want to expand the concept of imperatives past the full use of the hypothetical variety and describe the individual making decisions independently of the influence of his desires, on the basis of intellectually approved principles, arrived at through reflection. If one is able to reason practically, and know when desire ought to play a role in decision making and when it ought not, then we have a more complex mental model that has a distinct ethical component. However, this dualistic mind, with both ethical and nonethical properties, is beyond the scope of the market model and cost-benefit methods, which prescribe policy for the one-dimensional man only.

Moral Preferences

The standard by which the economic market justification distinguishes between which preferences will count in cost-benefit evaluations and which will not, is the *willingness to pay* criterion. This distinction however is identical to that made in the rational justification and, in support of the concept of autonomy as a more powerful "moral high ground," adds nothing to the stature of cost-benefit evaluation. There is no way within the market structure of the concept of autonomy to "ethically" distinguish between preferences (Sen 1974) which is critical outside of markets where more than "economic preferences" compete for attention.

It would seem necessary for a public decision maker to be able to make a distinction between preferences that support or fit the accepted value system and those that do not. However, the only use which the willingness to pay standard has is as a means to decipher an economic preference and distinguish it. This sheds light on the fact that the sole distinction a market-based analysis exhibits is between economic and noneconomic preferences. But this distinction seems less than adequate from a public policy point of view, and grants no "moral high ground" to cost-benefit analysis as a method of choice in this realm.

Willingness to pay allows a preference for cocaine to be as acceptable as one for water, in terms of an efficient allocation of goods. Both are commodities, with consumer markets where preferences are fulfilled, making the recipient more satisfied than in his initial condition and therefore rendering a net benefit to him.

In order to make a "moral" distinction between these two preferences, one would have to go beyond the concept of preference, describing a standard that (in addition to the economic standard of willingness to pay) makes a moral distinction between human desires. There is however no sense of "right" or "good" in the economic model that is capable of such a distinction (Sagoff 1988; Page 1973; 1983). Therefore, the willingness-to-pay standard is the limit of the market justification in distinguishing between "proper" and "improper" preferences and is the most a policy maker using cost-benefit procedures can depend upon.

The market approach allows consumer sovereignty to preclude further distinctions among preferences in a cost-benefit analysis (at least by the collective decision maker who must take v_i as given), after the willingness to pay criterion has been applied. Whatever preferences fit into the economic exchange model, or can be quantified into costs and benefits and exist in individual valuations, are part of the subjective calculation of welfare, the satisfaction of which, without alteration, is the job of the policy maker.

There is no way of distinguishing between individual and collective preferences for policy alternatives from within a market justification system. Mark Sagoff (1988, chaps. 3 and 5) has suggested that there might be such a thing as a "citizen preference" that is held in common by a group of citizens and involves their collective interest in the provision and protection of a certain good. According to Sagoff, citizen preferences have the power to override individual preferences when they conflict. The market and its surrogate, cost-benefit evaluation, recognize no strata of preferences or standards except the individual and his valuations. Therefore there exists no basis for policy choice at a political or group level, not one that could override a subjective welfare preference without simultaneously violating the autonomy of individual citizens.

The cost-benefit analyst wants to locate a morally sanctioned collective policy choice that supports individual rationality, but only through the aggregation of individual economic preferences. The pertinent concern is only to identify individual welfare preferences so that the collective choice is efficient in response to them.

Revealed Preference

The major concern of the policy maker who must use individual preferences to define policy choice is that he accurately represent the true welfare preferences of these individuals in his eventual decision. "The crux of the question lies in the interpretation of underlying preferences from observations of behavior" (Sen 1982, 54). The only data readily available to the policy maker is the observed behavior of individual consumers. These preferences are the primitive and necessary basis of all policy choices. But do these empirical choices reveal autonomous policy choice (true preferences)? Can one make this judgment from within the concept of preference itself, as the moral primitive of the argument? Remember, there is no independent nonpreference standard within the definition of the "self" or the "good" by which to judge the real interests of the individuals involved.

As a representative of a collective third-party that must translate preferences into policy, the cost-benefit analyst functions on the basis of two assumptions. First, he assumes that one's valuation (v_i) or choice function reflects one's autonomous preferences (i.e., that what is manifested is a true representation of preference), and therefore is worthy of respect. Second, he assumes that there is a connection between preferences and welfare.

> This dual link between choice and preference on the one hand and preference and welfare on the other is crucial to the normative aspects of general equilibrium theory. All the important results in this field depend on this relationship between behavior and welfare through the intermediary of preference (Sen 1982, 66–67).

The problem arises when one discovers a situation, common in policy decisions, where the expressed behavior does not fit in with the choice that would produce the higher welfare increment.

It may be the case that an individual is motivated by principles different from that which encourages him to maximize welfare. In these cases (e.g., cooperating in a prisoner's dilemma), one cannot fit his revealed preference with other economic assumptions basic to the market model. At this time, one can assume that true preference is connected to personal welfare improvements and separate from that preference made manifest, or that a revealed preference is not necessarily welfarist but nevertheless decisive. One way or the other, however, a gap has developed between preference, behavior, and welfare that makes revealed preference a shaky ground for theoretical investigation and/or moral justification of policy.

The possibility that individuals live in a policy environment where a sense of political responsibility or moral duty may lead one to choose an outcome that does not reflect economic assumptions, illustrates the fact that all revealed preference cannot be accounted for by "autonomy as consent" used outside its proper context.

The reality of the situation is that the policy maker faced with a complex society, and without the possibility of getting at the distinction between true and manifest preferences (without a moral standard), will make assumptions about preferences to make his job easier. If he is convinced that the market provides a "moral high ground" for the justification of policy, he will adopt a cost-benefit analysis relying on the assumptions that preferences, choice, and the potential Pareto improvement are all related. In effect, he will ignore the myriad of problems and the moral poverty of this assumption and proceed to set up a cyclical argument as a justification for the application of cost-benefit evaluation.

Specifically, it will be maintained that a potential Pareto improvement is a moral policy because it satisfies the preferences of the individuals involved; that is, its efficiency respects the preferences or the autonomy of individuals who would only consent to an efficient allocation of welfare.

Autonomy is therefore defined in terms of individual preference for welfare improvements with little or no time spent in gathering real empirical evidence or in making an argument that a connection between preference, choice, and welfare really exists. In this way, the problems with subjective evaluations, true and/or manifest preference, and the consent of the individual, are assumed away in the axioms that preferences are the basis of all welfare calculations, that these involve welfare improvements, and that one would always consent on the basis of one's preferences for welfare improvements to a policy that renders an efficient potential Pareto improvement (even if one turns out to be a loser). In effect, the aggregation problem of the policy maker is assumed away and autonomy co-opted to the search for wealth maximization.

Overall, preference is the primitive of the economic argument for efficiency but has no distinct moral character from a policy maker's viewpoint. Preferences are an unstable and ineligible basis for autonomous consent as a moral concept prescriptive to policy. The theory of the "self" contained in this definition of autonomy is one dimensional and tied only to economic welfare maximization; but from the perspective of the policy maker one's preferences cannot be assumed to tie neatly into the desire for wealth maximization or any other single goal. The market framework does not have a theory of the "self" and its choices that can make any moral distinctions between preferences that would establish a deeper foundation for the potential Pareto improvement than already exists as a rational/formal concept and would compensate for the impoverished vision of the "good" and turn its theory of autonomy from "thin" to "thick."

V

When a rich sense of human reason informing a three-dimensional concept of the "self" is not considered applicable to ends, then preferences are all that is left as a basis for the setting and attainment of these ends. Morality becomes rationality, and ethics is reduced to efficient preference satisfaction. Autonomy is not a distinct moral foundation for cost-benefit methods and requires either a richer sense of what is consequentially "good" by way of policy that supports individual autonomy or a richer concept of the "self" which could describe what is necessary for a policy to respect the rights of autonomous persons.

Cost-benefit evaluation has no independent moral justification distinct from its rational claims as a formal model of economic analysis with a foundation in efficiency and the potential Pareto improvement and is based on the primitive concepts of consent and preference within markets. It is therefore wrong to think of autonomy as a more fundamental normative base for cost-benefit analysis or as a moral reason to justify the movement of market assumptions into the making of public policy decisions. There is no distinction between the "moral high ground" and the "moral low ground" of the rational efficiency justification. Autonomy, in the market ideal, is put into the service of economic assumptions connecting preference to choice and choice to welfare improvements which may be adequate to the market context but not to the judging of public *ends* in a policy context. Autonomy within cost-benefit methods is not a more primitive moral foundation for policy argument, but another economic argument for the goal of wealth maximization which is capable of placing only the means of policy under scrutiny.

I will call this the *thin theory of autonomy* and contend that, to the degree autonomy is not (or ought not to be) defined by the potential Pareto improvement and the rational justification for the application of cost-benefit procedures, it will fail to provide any ethical justification for cost-benefit as an evaluative technique for public policy choice.

Cost-benefit analysis presupposes that welfare improvements define consent and preferences, and that these in turn define the breadth of autonomy. This "thin" theory however is weighted by this contention, so that the ends of economic efficiency and allocation automatically become the overriding ends of all public policy, to the demise of ideas like equality, distribution and political or ethical responsibility which would seem necessary to a definition of autonomy outside the market context.

To say that costs and benefits, in welfare terms, are all that "morally" count in making a public decision, is to say that any ethical variable that is not directly translatable into a monetary equivalent is of consequentially less importance to the outcome. To treat individuals strictly as consumers (rather than as citizens, for example) limits the evaluation system to questions of consumption, when the real moral concern might demand that the case be considered from the angle of obligation or protection.

The weight in autonomy by the thin theory, is given to efficient allocation, when we have seen that the pretrade distribution is politically critical to all eventual allocative outcomes. Distribution is a critical problem for public policy, but it is ignored. Equality becomes less valuable as a principle when cost-benefit analysis can define autonomy and cooperation in exchange without any reference to it.

Efficiency is an economic precept, not a moral principle, and therefore is not competition for, but must be justified in terms of, moral principles like autonomy, equality or benevolence. Considering the complexity and conflict present in the environment within which political choices are made, it is necessary to justify and evaluate these decisions in a way that does not presuppose that efficiency is the primary principle. Public policy must address the ethical questions of obligation, equality, cooperation, and distribution as prior to considerations of efficiency. If autonomy is important as an independent moral ground for judging the ends of public policy, then it must be defined and justified for its context outside the market, for cost-benefit methods will reduce autonomy to a rational argument for efficiency based on assumed consent and personal preference.

NOTES

This article, first published in *Policy Sciences* (1992): 83–102, is reprinted by permission of Kluwer Academic Publishers. It was originally prepared for the annual meeting of the American Political Science Association in 1989, and I wish to thank all those who read and commented on my work at that time. In addition, I would like to thank those who participated in its evolution to this form: Douglas MacLean, Mark Sagoff, Russell Hardin, Maurice Wade, Andy Gold, Thomas Reilly, Diana Evans, an anonymous reviewer at *Policy Sciences,* and its editor, William Ascher.

1. Here one must distinguish between the use of cost-benefit method and its reputation. This procedure can be used only to judge both the means and ends of a particular public policy and is therefore a comprehensive standard that is distinct from cost-effectiveness analysis. However, economists frequently maintain that cost benefit is not a comprehensive analysis and that it leaves room for other types of more morally sensitive analysis. As can be seen in the chapters that lead to this one, this is simply not the case. Cost-benefit methods are meant to be, and are used as, a comprehensive standard for policy choice raised on an ethical consensus.

2. There has been much written on the moral basis of efficiency in utilitarianism. See, for example, Page (1983, 38–58; chap. 20, this volume); and Amartya Sen and Bernard Williams, eds. *Utilitarianism and Beyond* (Cambridge: Cambridge University Press, 1982). An especially devastating attack on efficiency as a consequentialist moral principle is given by Sagoff (1986, 55–73; chap. 5, this volume). Here the consequentialist moral argument for efficiency as utility proves to be circular.

3. Here I agree with Rosenberg (1988, 72): "Revealed preference theory in effect tells us that the starting point of economics is the consequences of, and not the causes of, individual choice."

4. I assume that the task of a decision maker, using cost-benefit methods, is to take each individual's personal valuation of a policy (v_i) as revealed to him and aggregate them into a social valuation (V). If this social valuation is a net positive, then he can say that the benefits outweigh the costs and recommend the policy as a potential Pareto improvement; if not, then the policy fails to provide more social benefits than costs and should be rejected.

5. When economic market assumptions are transferred into the public sector as a basis for public policy decisions, one is no longer talking about real Pareto optimality, where all those involved in a transaction improve their lot. One is then concerned with a potential Pareto improvement or Kaldor efficiency. The potential Pareto improvement has both winners and losers within its concept of efficiency which only assumes that the benefits of the winners will be enough that they could compensate the losers, turning the potential into a real Pareto improvement. This compensation however need not even actually take place for efficiency to be maintained under this definition.

6. The Rational justification of cost-benefit methods is only that, and has no moral independence or weight. Efficiency as a "rational" and economic argument must be justified in terms of other moral concepts (freedom, equality) if it cannot show that it has an independent moral justification of its own. See Sagoff (1986).

7. The reality that policy decisions result in winners as well as losers puts greater moral pressure on the policy maker to take more than wealth maximization as a basis for his choices. If one is to be a loser, it must be for a morally justifiable reason that his rights are being transgressed.

8. Some of the moral complexity of the public decision is lost if one assumes that all citizens consent to any outcome simply by their participation in the society. In the same way to assume that a consumer consents to any outcome of a transaction in which he is involved is to simplify the aggregation problem without solving it.

9. Sagoff finds a cycle in the·utilitarian argument for the morality of efficiency. See Sagoff (1986).

10. For a supporting argument on this point, see Fishkin (1979, 70–71).

REFERENCES

Barry, Brian. 1992. "Welfare Economics and the Liberal Tradition," chap. 13, this volume.

Boadway, Robin W. 1979. *Public Sector Economics*. Cambridge, Mass.: Winthrop Press.

Christman, John, ed. 1989. *The Inner Citadel: Essays on Individual Autonomy*. New York: Oxford.

Coase, R. H. 1960. "The Problem of Social Cost" *Journal of Law and Economics* 3: 1–44.

Director, Aaron. 1964. "The Parity of the Economic Market Place" *Journal of Law and Economics* 7: 1–10.

Donagan, Alan. 1977. *The Theory of Morality*. Chicago: University of Chicago Press.

Dworkin, Ronald. 1980. "Why Efficiency." In *Law, Economics and Philosophy*, ed. M. Kuperberg and C. Beitz, pp. 123–42. Totowa, N.J.: Rowman and Allenheld.

Fishkin, James S. 1979. *Tyranny and Legitimacy.* Baltimore: Johns Hopkins University Press.

Gramlich, Edward M. 1981. *Benefit-Cost Analysis of Government Programs.* Englewood Cliffs, N.J.: Prentice-Hall.

Hayek, Friedrich. 1976. *Law, Legislation and Liberty.* Vol. 2: *The Mirage of Social Justice.* Chicago: University of Chicago Press.

Hill, Thomas E. 1973. "The Hypothetical Imperative." *Philosophical Review* 82: 429–50.

Kant, Immanuel. 1786. *Foundations of the Metaphysics of Morals.* Berlin: Prussian Academy of Sciences.

———. 1788. *Critique of Practical Reason.* Berlin: Prussian Academy of Sciences.

Kuflik, Arthur. 1984. "The Inalienability of Autonomy." *Philosophy and Public Affairs* 13: 271–98 (chap. 21, this volume).

Lave, Lester B. 1981. *The Strategy of Social Regulation: Decision Frameworks for Policy.* Washington, D.C.: Brookings.

Layard, Richard, ed. 1972. *Cost-Benefit Analysis.* Harmondsworth, Middlesex: Penguin.

Leonard, Herman B., and Richard J. Zeckhauser, "Cost-Benefit Analysis Applied to Risk: Its Philosophy and Legitimacy" Working Paper, Institute for Philosophy and Public Policy. University of Maryland. Rpt. in *Values at Risk.*, ed. Douglas MacLean, pp. 31–48. Totowa, N.J.: Rowman and Allenheld.

Mishan, E. J. 1981. *Introduction to Normative Economics.* New York: Oxford University Press.

———. 1982. *Cost-Benefit Analysis.* London: George Allen and Unwin.

Mishan, E. J., and Talbot Page. 1992. "The Methodology of Cost-Benefit Methods as Applied to the Ozone Problem," chap. 2, this volume.

Nozick, Robert. 1974. *Anarchy, State and Utopia.* New York: Basic Books.

Okun, Arthur M. 1975. *Equality and Efficiency: The Big Tradeoff.* Washington D.C.: Brookings.

Page, Talbot. 1973. *Economics of Involuntary Transfers.* Berlin: Springer-Verlag.

———. 1983. "Intergenerational Justice as Opportunity." In *Energy and the Future*, ed. Douglas MacLean and Peter Brown, pp. 38–58. Totowa, N.J.: Rowman and Littlefield (chap. 20, this volume).

Posner, Richard. 1983. *The Economics of Justice.* Cambridge, Mass.: Harvard University Press.

Rosenberg, Alexander. 1988. *Philosophy of Social Science.* Boulder: Westview.

Sagoff, Mark. 1986. "The Principles of Federal Pollution Control Law." *Minnesota Law Review* 71: 55–73 (chap. 5, this volume).

———. 1988. *The Economy of the Earth.* Cambridge: Cambridge University Press.

Sen, Amartya K. 1974. "Choice, Orderings and Morality" in *Practical Reason*, ed. S. Korner, pp. 54–67. New Haven, Conn.: Yale University Press.

———. 1982. "Behaviour and the Concept of Preference." In *Choice, Welfare and Measurement.* Cambridge, Mass.: Harvard University Press.

Wolff, Robert Paul. 1970. *In Defense of Anarchism.* New York: Harper and Row.

8 Difficulties in the Economic Analysis of Rights

Charles Fried

THE EXAGGERATED CLAIMS that economic analysis in general and the market model in particular provide the key to the science of morals (to paraphrase John Austin's phrase) are obviously preposterous.[1] One would have thought that the sustained barrage of objections to the coherence and empirical soundness of such views, since Bentham (1780/ 1970) put forward his moral calculus, would have had its effect by now. That these objections have not had much inhibiting effect outside of academic moral theory is itself an interesting chapter in the sociology of knowledge. The latter day adherents of the moral calculus might perhaps find the situation quite natural, emphasizing as they do the differences between their position and Bentham's rather crude hedonism. But the differences are not nearly as great as they imagine. Indeed, one might say that what has been gained since the days of the classical utilitarians in invulnerability to obvious empirical objections has been purchased only at the price of increasing emptiness of the theory. As one economist, commenting on the currently voguish view of rights growing out of the work of Ronald Coase, has put it, there is almost no distance between the conclusions and the premises. Certainly the brilliant formal complexity with which some of the analyses in this mode are characterized accounts for much of its continued fascination. So, I suspect, and less flatteringly, does the fact that the practitioners of this mode of analysis tend to be relatively ignorant of arguments and traditions outside their own disciplines. They persist in the face of philosophical refutations that are unknown to them. For these reasons, one feels a certain diffidence in launching into this subject yet another time. Nevertheless, that diffidence should not be mistaken for timidity. It is not that one doubts that the job can be done, but rather that one wonders why it has to be done.

In this chapter, rather than review the familiar (but not for that reason less valid) general objections, I shall focus on the concept of rights, and more specifically apply it to the notion of health as a right. In the first part of the chapter, I will review the currently fashionable view of rights propagated by such writers as Coase (1960), Demsetz (1957, 1964, 1966), Calabresi (1970), and Posner (1973) and will offer some criticisms. I will then apply those criticisms to the area of health as an example of how alternative and more morally plausible ways of thinking would proceed.

The Economic Analysis—A Critique

Bargaining and Moral Foundations

The general concept of rights[2] in law and morals is important to my critique of the economic model of social analysis because rights represent the starting points from which bargaining takes place, the counters that are exchanged in bargaining, and the rules or constraints under which bargaining goes forward. Whether my false teeth or my blood are my property (Fried, 1970, 1974; Williams, 1962, p. 125)—i.e., whether I have rights in them—will determine whether in bargaining I must pay to keep them or others must pay to get them. Whether fraud and force are to be admitted as techniques of bargaining, and indeed whether bargains themselves will be enforced, also crucially determine what the net effect of the bargaining process will be.[3] All these determinants or constraints can be viewed as permanent, secure rights.

For a time, these problems and their implications for the economic analysis of social welfare were overlooked. It seemed to go without saying that the person who takes affirmative action, who imposes on others, who disturbs the status quo is the one who must purchase the right to do so (Mishan, 1967). The person in passive possession of this or that right was obviously the one whose cooperation had to be suborned. It is the great virtue of writers such as Ronald Coase and those who have followed him to have noticed the radical reciprocity in all these situations: the homemaker who hangs her laundry may be thought of as imposing on the soot-producing factory just as much as the factory imposes on her; deception in bargaining relates simply to having and communicating knowledge, and knowledge, of course, is a prime subject for bargaining or economic exchange; and violence is a term of opprobrium, but in fact freedom from physical imposition is something that can be purchased, as—reciprocally—can be the right to impose physically. Moreover, the mechanisms of justice by which contracts are enforced can be seen as goods that we may or may not wish to procure. Finally, in this view, the capacity to bind oneself or others simply provides a further strategic advantage or counter in dealing in a bargaining situation (Schelling, 1960, 1968, 1973).

Why, then, do we have such strong ethical intuitions about these matters? Why do we believe that intentional bodily harm, deception, and the breaking of promises are wrong? Why do we believe that correlative with this sense of wrong are rights to security, property, honesty, and perhaps to goods such as medical care or subsistence levels of clothing and housing? The analysts I am considering point out that in a frictionless world, free of bargaining costs, an efficient result must occur, irrespective of whether, say, rapists or their victims must pay for the right to have their way.[4] (The conclusion, at first surprising, should not be. It follows immediately on the definition of efficiency: the outcome of bargaining by rational agents in a world free of transaction costs.) How do we account, then, for these strongly held, persistent intuitions of right? The argument would have it that in our real world in which not all bargains are free of cost, imperfections will be corrected and bargaining is more likely to attain efficiency if one, rather than the other, point of departure obtains. If the bargain could really be struck and enforced without cost, the use of land for planting crops or the exploitation of hunting grounds would be optimal. But since some bargains are more costly than others, efficient solutions are more likely to be attained if farmers are given property rights in the fields they cultivate or tribes are given exclusive rights to trap fur-bearing animals in particular territories.[5] But the basis of such rights is no more fundamental or intrinsic than that.

These theories push the economic analysis to further, more startling limits. Rather than representing a structure built upon a foundation of common-sense ethical presuppositions, these more recent inquiries purport to supplant, explain, and thus call into question that foundation of common sense. Indeed, for the first time in a radical way, the market is proposed as the fundamental mode for morals. To put the point differently, as long as moral institutions or tradition accorded us our rights and defined the limits of bargaining, the pretensions of the market model were limited, harmless, and perhaps useful. But by this new critique, the market model seeks to replace or provide the analysis of that moral foundation.

Unfortunately, this critique is too radical. If the morality of bargaining is itself to be the subject of bargaining, then one must still ask under what constraints this second-order bargaining is to take place. Indeed, to the extent that force, fraud, and the honoring of bargains are themselves seen as the subject of bargaining, the model necessarily loses any normative power and becomes at best a purely descriptive model. It becomes a model of how "rational" people do in fact behave, but it loses any semblance of plausibility as an account of how they should behave. Of course, this may reveal a fundamental misunderstanding by these analysts of the nature of ethics. Ethics is certainly not a description of behavior, not even a description of "rational" behavior, and not even the description of the "rationality" of behavior that some people consider ethical. By contrast, if we have a firm theory of rights (both property rights defining what is ours to bargain with, and procedural rights setting forth the acceptable modes of bargaining), then it is plausible—perhaps more than plausible—that the bargaining procedures built up on a moral foundation will have significant moral content.

Distribution

One repeated, standard response to this criticism is the introduction of distribution as a further factor in the analysis. Before I show how this factor is included in the analysis of rights, a distinction must be made between two kinds of distributive ethical judgments—those that accept the premise of consumer sovereignty and those that do not.[6] Those that do not are judgments that would override the operation of the market, not in the name of realizing individual preferences as they actually are, but out of some sense that certain results are good in spite of or in addition to those preferences. If a solution nobody wanted were imposed on the grounds that it was "good," this would be anti-individualistic. These forms of judgment would extend further. The solution that is adopted may happen to be the preference of some portion of the relevant group; the result is still anti–individualistic if it is adopted, not on the basis of realizing the preferences of the members of the groups (conflicts being determined in terms of either number or intensity), but rather by some judgment as to the intrinsic value of those preferences. This form of judgment shades over into paternalism when the adoption of a solution is based, not on any judgment that a certain state of affairs is better irrespective of whether it serves the interests of the individual members of the groups, but rather on the supposition that it does indeed serve the interests of some or all of those members, but they do not know it.

Consumer sovereignty criteria determine the distribution of satisfaction (welfare) or scarce resources within the group by one of a class of rules expressed, not in terms of the intrinsic value of the satisfaction, but rather in terms of the value of the persons whose interests are realized. The most familiar example of such a distributive norm is equality, which posits the equal value of all members of the group and makes no judgment as to the things that the individuals prefer, only that each has an equal right to have whatever it is that he or she prefers.

Distributive judgments are admitted to be normative, ethical, and (it is usually added in the literature) subjective. It is generally recognized that such distributional judgments are inevitable. Even to accept the status quo and not to make judgments is implicitly to make a normative judgment that the status quo represents an ethically tolerable point of departure, or at least one that one is not ethically entitled to change. But what is done with this concession to ethics is in fact entirely unsatisfactory.

Distribution, Efficiency, and Rights

The model (greatly simplified) takes the following form: ethical judgments relate to distribution, while the function of the market in bargaining is allocative efficiency. As I have indicated, the analysis would have it that in an ideal, frictionless world, the free market would be allowed to operate without impediment. In our actual friction-fraught world, rights are assigned so as to approximate as closely as possible the workings of a frictionless market (Calabresi, 1970; Coase, 1960; Demsetz, 1957, 1964, 1966; and Polinsky, 1974). Since it is recognized that how rights are assigned (i.e., what the starting point for bargaining and the constraints on it are to be) makes a difference to distribution and to the relative welfare of individuals, the outcome is adjusted to accord with our ethical, distributive norm by a separate process of lump sum transfers that is effected outside of the market bargaining process. Once again, any systematic connection between rights and ethics is denied.

One might put the matter this way: According to the modern economic analysis of rights, the only right of an individual that is independent of the contingencies of what is needed to attain efficiency in that particular state of affairs (one might say the only moral or pre-economic right one has) is the right to whatever distributional share of the efficient total our ethical norm assigns to that person. But there are no rights in particular, concrete goods—at least not pre-economic or moral rights.

It is well known that it is difficult, if not impossible, to design mechanisms for lump sum transfers that do not interfere with efficiency, for instance by distorting incentives and thus leading to a suboptimal allocation between leisure and work (Samuelson, 1947), but I shall ignore these difficulties. My criticism is of a different order: I maintain that a large— and it seems to me better—class of social welfare distributive criteria determines the distribution of at least some rights directly. If this is so, then in respect to those criteria and those rights, at least it is not a question of defining rights so as to obtain efficiency, with distributional adjustments being made by lump sum transfers that leave the allocation of rights unchanged. In other words, in respect to some aspects of social welfare, the criterion and currency is the enjoyment of certain rights as such. And although economic analysis can tell us what might be the effect on allocation of recognizing these rights, it cannot pretend to provide the means for deriving these rights from economic premises.

Absolute Preferences

The economic analysis is intuitively unappealing, insofar as it suggests that all rights, even such basic rights as liberty of conscience, political rights, or the right to be free of deliberate physical incursions, are themselves not moral rights but contingent derivations of an optimizing mechanism. In any case, where the individuals concerned have systems of preferences that cannot be said to describe a utility function, for instance wherever an individual would prefer a certain good absolutely over some or all other goods, then there may be no other way to assure him his morally entitled distributive share without according him only that good. Or, to put the matter differently, if individuals have lexicographically[7] ordered individual values, then the only lump sum redistribution that would assure them their distributive shares would simply be whatever distribution would allow them to purchase the very goods that might have been taken away from them under the efficiency leg of the argument.

Now this difficulty not only undermines the economic analysis of rights, but also argues for a wholly indeterminate situation if these "poorly behaved" preference functions are also different for different persons. In such a case, we may be unable to maintain our distributional commitment to some of the members of the society. In other words, we had all better agree in respect to these fiercely held preferences, or if we do not agree, then the only way to account for the solution we arrive at is by putting forward ethical norms that do not pretend to seek merely the aggregation of actual preferences. For our ethical norm as to what is the correct distribution of welfare will have to permit the overriding of the preferences of some discordant members of the society without any notion that this can be made up to them by any lump sum transfer. Once we assume that individuals can have what I call "absolute preferences," then any concern for their welfare must treat the realization of these preferences as rights, and we must free ourselves from the notion that there is only one moral right to one's distributive share. The reason is that the distributive share can be dealt out only by what I might call the "material recognition of the rights." Later in this chapter, I shall argue that it is plausible to consider certain interests in health as having for the individual this kind of status, and thus compelling this kind of material recognition.

Needs[8]

A further difficulty with the economic analysis of rights relates to the way in which the welfare that is distributionally required shall be measured: subjectively (in terms of money) or some other objective index. An objective index is acceptable only if we are prepared to assume either that such objective goods lead to the same level of welfare in all individuals, or if we have as part of our distributional norm the notion that the subjective welfare derived from objective resources is not a matter of normative concern. To some extent we do believe one or both of these things. Where basic needs have been met, we are prepared to say that it is fair to give people with expensive tastes and cheap tastes the same amount of money. Or, alternatively, if people (always assuming basic needs have been met) are somehow unhappy even though they have received their fair share of money, goods, or whatever, we say that this is not the concern of social ethics. But these positions are tolerable only if basic needs are met. If, however, an individual requires a large amount of money simply to maintain his health, there seems to be something wrong with a view that says that the reasonable distributive norm is one that gives him the same amount of money (if equality is our distributive norm) as everyone else, even though he must live at little more than a subsistence level after he has purchased the medicines he needs just to remain alive. A need for medicine stands on a different footing from a desire for caviar, race horses, or champagne, and people should not be allowed to change the status of luxury desires by arguing that these things represent as much a necessity to them as medicine represents to the dying. In short, our distributive norm cannot afford to be measured either wholly by the objective share of goods, or wholly subjectively in terms of what those goods represent to the recipient. Instead, we must have a theory that identifies certain preferences or values as what I shall call needs, so that welfare in respect to these is measured by the result for the individual. The individual cannot be allowed to determine for himself what will be placed in this category, nor can a person decide what constitutes the correct index of results. Once again I shall argue that health is an interest that must appropriately be placed in the category of needs, and the distribution of resources toward health must be determined by different criteria than the distribution of what I would call "elective goods."

Preferences Are Not Brute Facts

The economic analysis of rights, particularly as it relates to such areas as health, is inadequate for reasons of a different sort. The economic analysis, and the criticisms I have been making of it so far, takes preferences, values, and needs as given and sets itself the task of rationalizing them in a world of scarce resources and conflicting claims. Now one can proceed in the way on one of two assumptions: (1) that preferences, values, and needs are brute facts about which nothing more can be said, so that they must form the primitive data of the system; or (2) that there are moral reasons why society should take values, preferences, and needs as given, rather than going behind them in imposing social solutions. Although many working in the economic mode may believe the first assumption to be true, no reason for this belief is provided. If the argument shifts to the second assumption, philosophers and theorists are not precluded from discussing with each individual, on a personal basis, how he should perceive his values, preferences, and needs, even though for reasons of principle we leave him the last word when it comes to formulating a social rule.

Indeed, philosophy has traditionally engaged in that second enterprise, and as we think about markets and morals in general, and markets for things like health care in particular, we might ask whether the commitment to leaving the consumer the last word in the public arena has not obscured from philosophers (in the broad sense) the educational and philosophical task of debating with individuals about what their values should be as they enter the marketplace.

I would go even further. Not only must we be prepared to dispute with the individual "consumer" his system of preferences, but we must be willing to impose upon him "paternalistically" at least to this extent: We must recognize that the very concept of choice or preference, as it is used in an argument that social morality requires consumer sovereignty, presupposes a certain rationality, a certain stability, a certain degree of contact with reality on the part of the consumer. Otherwise, what we have cannot even be described as choice or as a system of preferences, but only as random behavior. If the consumer sovereignty model, and the market model built upon it, are to serve anything other than descriptive purposes, there must be some reason to think that the behavior entered into the model is something more than random behavior. Even when such a model is used to analyze bizarre and seemingly irrational behavior, its usefulness as a heuristic device resides only in the assumption that the behavior in question has a purpose and rationality after all. And when it is put forward as a normative tool, surely some stringency may be admitted in what will be allowed to count as a choice system.

The Self as the Unit of Choice

The Self as Substance: Identity and Continuity

In this section, I shall put together the critique I have offered of the economic analysis of rights, seeking to show how a more adequate conception emerges from it. All three objections—that some values or preferences cannot be smoothly traded off or compensated for by other values and preferences of the individual, that a sensible normative rule must take into account needs as measured by objective criteria, and that the very concept of preference structure implies some constraints on what should count as a preference structure—might all be seen as converging on the notion that any acceptable, normative scheme must build on a theory of the self. That is, our notion of choosing individuals cannot be a notion of persons as normatively dimensionless points without characteristics (like Lockeian substances), tastes, needs, and physical characteristics being ascribed merely as parameters in an equation that will determine what the level of satisfaction enjoyed by that "self" will be.[9]

Although I do not feel able to give either a formal or an elaborate account of the conception of a self that I have in mind, certain aspects seem important and relate to the three objections I have detailed in the first section. The most formal of the characteristics defining a self have to do with its identity and continuity. The kinds of entities to whom values, preferences, choices, and the realization of these can be attributed are human bodies that persist over time, the continuity of which is the continuity of the self. Thus, an entity that existed only momentarily, or indeed for a period of time shorter than that of the living body with which it is associated, would not form a recognizable unit for the ascription of our concepts. The idea, for instance, that four or more "selves" inhabit the same persistent living body, would be so problematical that our ethics would not know what to do with it. I suppose we would have an analogous difficulty with the claim that a single self is to be associated with more than one living body, either simultaneously or sequentially, as in some notion of the transmigration of souls.[10]

This relatively formal notion can be fleshed out by the introduction of certain, more contingent psychological assumptions regarding the persistence and unity of the self. I shall not go into these in detail, but I would say that those psychological laws that bear on the conditions necessary first for the development and then for the maintenance of a firm, consistent, and unitary concept of the self, must also stand as the basis for any ethical judgments regarding the satisfactions of such a self. It should not be taken for granted that such a concept of the self always has and must necessarily develop as a matter of fact along with a persistent human body. Radical departures from this usual course of development tend to be viewed as some kind of insanity or monstrosity. But such departures only prove that the development of such a concept of self requires the existence of certain conditions, a certain nurturance, and a certain reinforcement.

Conditions for the Realization of a Sense of Self

Moving one step further, but still from a purely formal notion of self, I would incorporate in my argument the concept of self-respect as developed by Rawls (1971, chap. 7). For present purposes, it is sufficient to recall that Rawls gives as one of the most important of his "primary goods" the good of self-respect, which is the providing of that system of support to an individual that is necessary for his belief in the worth and seriousness of his system of values and preferences. Two aspects of this account should be emphasized here. First, that the good of self-respect is not—like other goods, or even other primary goods—a material condition for the realization of this or that particular end or desire. Rather, it is a set of background conditions that establishes the whole system of an individual's ends and desires as significant. Second, self-respect is a radically relational and systematic kind of good, in that its realization consists of the adherence by others to certain principles of action. It cannot be provided to the individual just by giving him this or that thing. It requires that others treat him as an individual worthy of respect. And this requires a system of attitudes and actions to exemplify those attitudes.

These aspects of the concept of the self relate to the three objections to the economic analysis of rights. There are material conditions for the development and maintenance of the integrity of the self, just as there are material conditions for the maintenance of self-respect. Given the priority of the concept of self, it should not be surprising that the interest in those material conditions is of a wholly different order from the interest in other conditions for the realization of other goods. It should not be surprising that these conditions should be given the absolute status, which, however, destroys the workability of the economic analysis of rights. Moreover, the assertion of such an absolute priority does not entail the radical incoherence of social norms that I have said would result if some or all members of the society had preference structures containing such absolute priorities, with no convergence across individuals. The concept of the self being a general philosophical concept, it is reasonable to assume convergence among individuals of the material conditions necessary for the realization of each of their selves.

Further, the exigencies of the concept of self entail a social norm defined in terms of needs, objectively identified, rather than in terms either of objective goods irrespective of needs or of subjective satisfactions. What is needed is the fulfillment in each individual's circumstances of the preconditions of a coherent concept of self. As the circumstances of the individual vary, so will the material needed to satisfy those conditions vary; and thus the norm must be specified in terms of needs. On the other hand, the concept of self is philosophical and objective, and what constitutes the satisfaction of this need is properly the subject of objective inquiry.

Finally, it should be readily apparent how my last objection to the economic analysis of rights relates to the conception of the self I have sketched. If a satisfactory analysis of welfare based on preference and choice must assume the coherence and rationality of the preference structure, then this involves importing into the analysis whatever conditions emerge from the development of a theory of the self. For it is a self that has preference structures and systems of value. Only those things will count as choices or preferences that can be ascribed to entities meeting the substantive conditions of self, and the concept of a system of preferences will itself relate to the systematizing elements within such a conception of self.

Let me be explicit as to why these constraints and conditions imposed on the market model lead to a system of fundamental rights. Whatever interests are established or whatever limits on bargaining are imposed, can be seen as establishing rights in respect to those interests and limits. And since they logically precede the bargaining model, such rights do not depend on the contingencies of the outcome of the model once put into operation. If the theory of the self yields the conclusion that necessary to the integrity of the self is a firm sense that one's body is one's own and not social property, then it follows that bargaining must proceed from the starting point that our bodies are our own. And that is what I mean by a fundamental or pre-economic right.

The Case of Health

Material and Residual Rights

The right to health is not one of the categorical, negative rights such as are handed down in the Ten Commandments. The prohibitions against murder, theft, and deception, for instance, together with the correlative rights they imply, might be thought of existing extrasocially; if there had ever been a state of nature, these rights and duties would have been present within it. The right to a particular distributive share is a paradigm of a right that requires a social context, an institutional context. Political rights provide another set of paradigms. The right to health, if it exists at all, is plainly a social, institutional right. The interest in the case of the right to health is that it presents an example of an institutional right, which is neither political nor a contingent derivation from whatever distributive share this society's social welfare function recognizes as the particular individual's right. My claim will be that a social welfare function that speaks, say, of an equal distribution or of a maximum distribution must be taken to refer essentially to residual goods. Residual goods are the vast collection of things people want and from which they derive welfare, which are left over after essential needs have been supplied. It is my notion that health, education, food, housing, clothing, as well as access to the political and adjudicatory processes of the society, are all essential needs, which should not come under the terms of the social welfare function.[11] Rather, the social welfare function should govern the distribution of the vast, heterogeneous range of goods that people want once their essential needs have been satisfied.

In proposing such a dichotomy, I do not mean to suggest that these residual goods are somehow trivial or unworthy. They are residual in the sense that no material argument regarding their status of rights directly (rather than through the exercise of market power determined by the distributive share) can be put forward. No doubt the arguments for the derivation of a material right to, say, political participation or education show as well that there is a certain priority, a certain basic quality to such a right. But I do not wish to overstate this point of priority. After all, in any decent society these rights can generally be taken for granted so that the burden of economic and political concern will relate to the realization of the residual goods. These residual goods might be thought of as being those goods that free people in a situation of relative prosperity seek in the realization of their freedom. And there is nothing second-rate about that. If these material rights are taken as basic, let us be sure precisely what this status means. It is like saying, perhaps, that absence of deep political corruption is basic to a good society. It is basic only in the sense that in the presence of such corruption other social and political goods are insecure. Yet for that very reason, we hesitate to define a good society in terms of the presence or absence of political corruption. Rather, we would like to assume this absence, and then go on to other things.

Respecting an Embodied Self

The argument that the right to health is basic in this sense depends on our ability to show that health (or some aspects of it) have the quality of being necessary preconditions for the general enjoyment of a just distributive share. Though I shall not attempt to make that argument in detail, the concept of the self put forward in the second section provides the foundations for the argument. It is critical that the self is an embodied self. An individual cannot, consistently with the concept of the integrity of an embodied self, treat his body or its needs as an entity separate from himself, to which he can—if he chooses—allocate resources, provided that his preference structure dictates this as the most efficient use of those resources. For such a view of the body would imply that the self is one thing and the body another, having no more than a contingent or instrumental relation to the self. This is not to say that a person may not rationally encounter physical dangers, for instance. My point is only that, in endangering his body, he endangers himself—that there is no way to endanger one without endangering the other.

If the self is an embodied self, then it follows that some aspects at least of care for that physical substrate of the self are essential to the integrity of the self. Plainly, that interest is not absolute; rational people at all times have assumed the right, and have been thought to have the right, to endanger that physical integrity in the pursuit of one or another interest—

including riches. The only point is that, in using up the body, man uses up himself.

Health and the Integrity of Self

This shows both the sense in which health relates to generalized welfare or residual goods and the sense in which it might be viewed as providing the foundation for both the self and its pursuits. In this dual nature it differs from, let us say, the basic goods of self-respect or liberty. For we do not think that we use these up in the pursuit of our other goals, but rather we just use them. Evidently, both the psychology and the philosophy of health is complex and elusive. Perhaps, after all, we do not use up our health in the pursuit of our goods so much as we use it in much the same way as we use our liberty in choosing one of two ends, both of which we are free to choose.

In any event, the foundational aspect of the right to health is better seen not so much in its absolute priority to other goods—for I suspect we would have a hard time establishing this in any thoroughgoing way—but rather by our natural tendency to treat it as a need and not as a good. That is, I am inclined to suggest that just distributional schemes would not (if equality were our canon of just distribution) be satisfied by an equal distribution of money with which the chronically ill could purchase medicines while others purchased holidays, opera tickets, or other luxury goods. Good health is a need precisely in the sense that we have or we seek objective measures of good health. We try to assure this objective good, the satisfaction of this objective need apart from, or without prejudice to, the balance of an individual's distributive share. That we treat health in this way is precisely indicative of the status we accord it. It is in this sense that it may appropriately be considered a right.

There are very great complexities in working out the details of this notion. Plainly, we are prepared to do things as a society that will irremediably endanger the health of some of our citizens—environmental hazards offer the obvious example. Moreover, we are not willing to do everything we can to restore the health of those who are disadvantaged in this respect. Not only are we unwilling to make available the necessary resources to provide what is presently within our ability for all members of our society, but we also refrain from taking those steps that are likely to increase our capacities in the future. Finally, we are miles away from any notion that we should try to "compensate" those whose sufferings are beyond medical help. We are far from thinking that the hopelessly mentally retarded, the aged, and the mentally ill should be treated as the most favored members of the society, since in respect to a fundamental good (their health) they are doomed beyond hope. Which of these tendencies represents the true moral intuition of our society? Or, is there a way in which the two can be reconciled? My guess is that any analysis departing from acceptable moral principles will show that we do far too little for the chronically unfortunate, while perhaps we do too much to overcome the effects of some illnesses, those being the very illnesses that in the end must strike everybody. My guess would be that a truly just allocation in this respect would move away from those illnesses that will eventually kill us all and toward those that make an unfortunate minority miserable throughout their lifetimes. The reason seems quite clear. Those illnesses that are sufficiently widespread that people may think contracting them is probable, are precisely those illnesses that it is fair and reasonable for us to accept philosophically, and about which it is fair to say that we would rather spend our resources in pursuing other goods and take our chances with, for example, cancer and heart disease. But where the disease strikes at birth, during youth, or in some other way "out of season," then we have a special obligation because the victims of such diseases cannot be seen as having participated in the benefits of a societal choice to enrich life in other ways. Ironically, the same lack of community identification with such unfortunates is precisely what leads us to relegate them to the worst categories of care.[12]

NOTES

This article, first published in *Markets and Morals,* ed. G. Dworkin, G. Germantrand, and P. Brown (New York: Wiley, 1977), pp. 175–95, is reprinted by permission of Hemisphere Publishing Corporation, Taylor and Francis Publishers.

1. The immediate progenitor of this claim, as of the notion of utility in general, is, of course, Bentham (1970). This is not to say that the "felicific calculus" does not have significant roots in earlier philosophical writing, even among the Greeks. The tradition of what might be called the free market liberals, such as von Mises, Hayek, and Friedman continue this tradition, prescinding, however, from the Benthamic premises regarding the comparability and additivity of individual utilities. As the work of modern-day Benthamites such as Harsanyi (1955) shows, this is a less radical departure from classical utilitarian principles than might be thought. A most sophisticated form of utilitarianism as an analysis of social ethics arose out of game theory. For recent, lucid examples, see Schelling (1968, 1973). For two extreme and enthusiastic examples of the application of market theory to social policy, see Posner (1973) and Tullock (1971).

2. For a recent, excellent exposition of the concept of rights that I am assuming, see Dworkin (1977, chaps. 6 and 7) and Fried (1974).

3. On this point, both Posner (1973) and Tullock (1971) are explicit.

4. It has been suggested by Professor George Fletcher that the Coase theorem should not be applied to cases of intentional impositions but only to "externalities"—that is to say, unintended impositions incidental to the pursuit of

some other end. Although many of the initial examples used by Coase (1960) and Demsetz (1957, 1964, 1966) are of this latter sort, and indeed the Coase theorem was devised to deal with the traditional problem of externalities, there is nothing in the theorem itself that would limit it in this way. Moreover, it is the very point of the analysis that the distinction between intended impositions and side effects or externalities cannot be analytically maintained. This is clearly seen in Posner's (1973) and Tullock's (1971) application of it. If bargaining in the absence of transaction costs would produce efficiency in respect to unintended impositions—ordinary externalities—then what is there in the theory that prevents the same conclusion being reached in respect to intended impositions? That this might be seen as a reductio ad absurdum of the Coase theorem is hardly an argument against the reductio itself, but rather against the theorem.

5. These examples are drawn from Demsetz (1957, 1964, 1966).

6. For two excellent introductions to these subjects, see Graaff (1957) and Sen (1970).

7. Values $a, b, c, \ldots n$ are said to be ordered lexicographically when all a's are preferred to any b's, all b's to any c's, all i's to any j's. Thus, in a dictionary, words are ordered lexicographically. An index number is not assigned to each letter in the word and a weighted average taken. Instead, the words are arranged by their initial letters, and then by their second letters, and so on. For a full discussion of lexicographical orderings and their significance in moral theory, see Rawls (1971), Banerjee (1964), and Sen (1970).

8. In my book *Right and Wrong* [Cambridge, Mass.: Harvard University Press, 1978], I take a substantially different position on the matter in this and the last section of the present essay.

9. It would seem that, in the view I have just characterized, a self would in principle choose not only the realization of whatever preferences it happened to have, but also those preferences that, in the world as it is, promised the highest degree of realization. Indeed, even if for some reason the self would not or could not choose its preferences in this way, this theory would provide no basis for objecting if others imposed, not limits on realizations of actual preferences. but the preferences themselves, as long as the degree of satisfaction or "utility," however measured by the distributive norm, was higher than that attainable under the actual preferences of that self. Nor is it open to such analysts to argue that it is just part of the distributive norm or social welfare function, that no action be taken to alter (fundamentally?) the self's system of preferences. Why should this be part of the distributive norm? What is "distributive" about such a constraint? Surely, to import this constraint into the social welfare function is to do precisely what I am arguing for, i.e., to constrain our whole mode of argumentation by a material notion of the self. Finally, this objection does not entail an infinite regress: one can wish to be happy without wishing for the only things available to make one happy.

10. For further development of these notions, see Fried (1970. chap. 11; 1974).

11. See Arrow (1963) and Fried (1974). Michelman (1973) is a detailed and important argument for the general proposition that the kinds of basic needs discussed here constitute not only moral rights but constitutionally protected rights as well.

232   *Charles Fried*

12. It might be argued that the institution of the medical deduction in the federal income tax represents a recognition of some of these notions: medical expenditures are deductible on the theory that they are nonoptional and based on needs, not wants. Moreover, they are deductible only as they exceed 3 percent of income, in recognition of the fact that some medical expenses—like food or clothing—are general to all, and that it is only the excess that represents unusual needs. For a full examination of these views, see Andrews (1972).

REFERENCES

Andrews, W. (1972) "Personal Deductions in an Ideal Income Tax," *Harvard Law Review* 86, p. 309.

Arrow, K. (1963) "Uncertainty and the Welfare Economics of Medical Care," *American Economic Review* 53, p. 941.

Banerjee, D. (1964) "Choice and Order: Or First Things First," *Economica* (n.s. 158) 31, p. 158.

Bentham, J. (1970) *An Introduction to the Principles of Morals and Legislation* (H.L.A. Hart, ed.). London: Athlone. (Originally published 1780.)

Calabresi, G. (1970) *The Cost of Accidents*. New Haven, Conn.: Yale University Press.

Coase, R. (1960) "The Problem of Social Cost," *Journal of Law and Economics* 3, p. 67.

Demsetz, H. (1957) "Towards a Theory of Property Rights," *American Economic Review* (No. 2, Papers and Proceedings), 57, p. 347.

———. (1964) "The Exchange and Enforcement of Property Rights," *Journal of Law and Economics* 7, p. 11. Reprinted in chapter 10 of this volume.

———. (1966) "Some Aspects of Property Rights," *Journal of Law and Economics* 9, p. 61.

Dworkin, R. (1977) *Taking Rights Seriously*. Cambridge, Mass.: Harvard University Press.

Fried, C. (1970) *An Anatomy of Values*. Cambridge, Mass.: Harvard University Press.

———. (1974) *Human Experimentation: Personal Integrity and Social Policy*. Amsterdam: Elsevier.

Graaff, J. (1957) *Theoretical Welfare Economics*. Cambridge: Cambridge University Press.

Harsanyi, J. (1955) "Cardinal Welfare, Individualistic Ethics, and Interpersonal Comparisons of Utility," *Journal of Political Economy* 63, p. 309.

Michelman, F. (1973) "In Pursuit of Constitutional Welfare Rights," *University of Pennsylvania Law Review* 121, p. 962.

Mishan, E. (1967) "Pareto Optimality and the Law," *Oxford Economic Papers* 19, p. 285.

Polinsky, M. (1974) "Economic Analysis as a Potentially Defective Product: A Buyer's Guide to Posner's Economic Analysis of Law," *Harvard Law Review* 87, p. 1655.

Posner, R. (1973) *Economic Analyst of Law*. Boston: Little, Brown.

Rawls, J. (1971) *A Theory of Justice*. Cambridge, Mass.: Harvard University Press.

Samuelson, P. (1947) *Foundations of Economic Analysis*. Cambridge, Mass.: Harvard University Press.

Schelling, T. C. (1960) *The Strategy of Conflict*. Cambridge, Mass.: Harvard University Press.

————. (1968) "Game Theory and the Study of Ethical Systems," *Journal of Conflict Resolution* 12, p. 34.

————. (1973) "Hockey Helmets, Concealed Weapons, and Daylight Saving," *Journal of Conflict Resolution* 17, p. 381.

Sen, A. (1970) *Collective Choice and Social Welfare*. San Francisco: Holden-Day.

Tullock, G. (1971) *The Logic of the Law*. New York: Basic.

Williams, B. (1962) "The Idea of Equality," in P. Laslett and W. Runciman, ed., *Philosophy, Politics and Society*. New York: Barnes & Noble.

PART II

*The Ethical Demands
of Public Policy
as a Collective Action Problem*

Introduction

As THE ESSAYS in Part I have noted, public policy analysis is currently dominated by approaches that are fundamentally economistic in nature. Such approaches look to the market, above all else, for the standard by which public policy should be designed and assessed. According to mainstream, neoclassical microeconomic doctrine, the market, when functioning ideally, produces social outcomes that are efficient, i.e., outcomes that maximize individual preference satisfaction. Economistic theorists hold that public policy is successful to the degree that it mimics the market and so also generates efficient outcomes. The economistic perspective thus takes legitimate public policy to be nothing more than the pursuit of market-type outcomes by political means. Maximum satisfaction of individual wants is its sole proper aim.

This essay has three goals. The first is to provide an account of the basic elements of the economistic outlook and its conception of public policy. The second is to show what policy demands of political theory by sketching some of the most important moral and political limitations of the economistic outlook. We will thereby show why this perspective's current dominance in policy analysis is both unwarranted and undesirable. The third and final aim is to pose a series of questions that will assist readers in grasping the significance of the remaining chapters of this volume.

I. The Economistic Outlook

The economistic approach to public policy is grounded in the conception of rational individual choice which is central to neoclassical microeco-

237

nomic theory, the individual as *homo economicus*. According to this theory, individuals seek solely to maximize satisfaction of their preferences and are rational insofar as their choices are aimed at attaining this goal. The rational individual is one who chooses, from among her options, the one that provides her with the largest net balance of want satisfaction.[1]

It should also be noted that the economistic conception of the individual is thoroughly atomistic. That is, individuals are conceived to be concerned only with their own wants. The wants of others are of importance to *homo economicus* only to the extent that they affect his own. An individual thus views others solely in terms of their impact on his own preferences. Each of us is thereby conceived to be regarding others as either instruments of or obstacles to attainment of our own personal satisfactions. The notion that others may have value independent of one's preferences is entirely foreign to the individual as he is conceived from an economistic perspective. The rational individual, in this view, pursues only maximization of his own wants, nothing more and nothing less.

This conception of individual rationality is coupled with a subjectivist theory of value. Proponents of the economistic outlook contend that an individual's good consists in nothing more than satisfaction of her preferences, her wants, and that no one has better access to what the individual prefers than she herself does.[2] This is taken to entail that no one but the individual is entitled to or able to determine what constitutes her personal well-being. Thus, the aims and ends pursued by the individual are placed beyond rational criticism by others. Only the individual is in a position to know what she prefers and how much she prefers it.

This is not to say that whatever an individual believes she prefers or claims to prefer is what she genuinely prefers. The economistic perspective takes the individual's behavior to be the only trustworthy indicator of her preferences. In particular, she is regarded as having a preference for something only insofar as she is willing to devote her resources to acquiring or attaining it. She is regarded as preferring one state of affairs to another only insofar as she is willing pay more for the one than for the other. Thus, although the individual alone is the sole determinant of her preferences, only her behavior, specifically her willingness to pay, indicates what her preferences truly are. In effect, then, from an economistic point of view, to say that individuals are maximizers of personal preference satisfaction is equivalent to saying that individuals are maximizers of personal wealth.

Accordingly, the conception of rationality held by traditional neoclassical microeconomics and the economistic approaches to policy based upon it are purely instrumental. This observation follows fairly directly from the economistic outlook's subjectivist understanding of value. One cannot be mistaken in the ends one pursues—i.e., satisfaction of one's preferences. Hence, one's preferences cannot be irrational. Rationality must therefore take these preferences as given. Where an individual can be mistaken is in identifying what will lead to maximal attainment of his preferences—i.e., in identifying the correct means to his ends. Here and only here can he be said to be more or less rational. Rationality can do no more than assess the instruments, the means, by which preference satisfaction is pursued.

Given this conception of rational individual choice, the kinds of actions and interactions with others that individuals will rationally undertake are only those that each views as rendering him better off than he would be otherwise. A given course of action or social interaction will be voluntarily chosen by a rational individual only if it promises to increase his personal wealth. Whatever the rational individual does, he does as a means of maximally satisfying his preferences. Whether he acts alone or in concert with others, what he does fails to be rational only if it fails to serve this singular end.

A definite conception of the proper nature of society evidently follows from this economistic perspective. Society has no substance or standing beyond the individuals who comprise it, the interactions they undertake, and the consequences of their wealth-maximizing efforts. Accordingly, society is the product of the voluntary choices of rational maximizers of want satisfaction. Its value is wholly instrumental, and it exists solely because it is a means by which individuals can maximize their personal wealth. Because only the individual herself can determine what she prefers and how much she prefers it, only she can determine which actions and interactions are worth investment of her resources. This means that the appropriate organization of social life, the institutions that are formed, and the policies that are undertaken must be the product of the voluntary choices of wealth-maximizing individuals. Ideally, society should simply be the sum of the consequences of these choices.

The economistic perspective maintains that ideally the free operations of the market embody precisely this social ideal. In the market, rational wealth maximizers pursue only their individual self-interest (defined as maximal satisfaction of their wants) and voluntarily interact, cooperate, and exchange with others only when doing so serves this end. The kinds of institutions generated and policies pursued are just the aggregate consequences of the voluntary choices of these individuals. They exist only because of those choices.

When the market functions ideally, a given social situation will be voluntarily changed only if some individual can thereby increase his personal welfare, his personal wealth, without at the same time reducing the personal welfare of anyone else. And, to hold that the market is efficient is to hold that (when functioning ideally) it alters the social status quo only when doing so yields some increase in individual preference satisfaction and no decrease. Thus, when it functions properly, the market yields personal wealth winners but no personal wealth losers.

Notice the social ideal inherent in this outlook. A social outcome is rational to the extent that it is the product of the voluntary choices of rational maximizers of individual preference satisfaction. Of course, this is also to say that a social outcome is rational to the extent that its existence maximizes preference satisfaction for each and all. Accordingly, the economistic perspective denominates but one social goal as legitimate—namely, maximal satisfaction of individual preferences. The more fully this goal is realized, the closer to ideal social life is.

But even the kinds of interactions with others that a wealth-maximizing individual would enter into and sustain—those that are definitive of the market—require a stable background which itself cannot be maintained voluntarily. Individuals must know who owns what and must be protected in these property rights. Some initial specification of rights of action over resources must be made and enforced.[3] Otherwise, cooperation, should it ever arise in the first place, will degenerate (or continually threaten to degenerate) into a Hobbesian war of each against all as rational individuals seek to appropriate the possessions of others while protecting their own. In other words, as rational wealth maximizers, they must recognize that placing and enforcing limits on what each may do in pursuit of his ends and aims is itself a rational requirement of the ability of each to maximize his own well-being. The ideal of social life embodied in the market thus itself presupposes nonmarket forms of social organization. Market outcomes themselves require political means. This reasoning provides what economistic theorists take to be the only genuine justification of the existence of the state and the only criterion upon which its actions and policies should be based and evaluated—maximization of individual preference satisfaction. The existence of the state provides all individuals with greater opportunities for satisfaction of their personal preferences than would otherwise be available to them; this is why, as rational creatures, they would agree to its establishment.[4]

From this conception of the proper role of the state, the economistic viewpoint also derives a criterion for legitimate state actions that go beyond initial determination and subsequent enforcement of property rights. Notice that the argument in question makes the legitimacy of the state hinge upon *all* individuals being provided by its existence with greater preference satisfaction than would be available to them in a state of nature. No one's condition is worsened by the existence of the state, and everyone's condition is improved. Otherwise, it could not garner unanimous consent. Proponents of the economistic point of view necessarily derive from this a justification of further state action. Even when property rights are specified and enforced, opportunities for increased satisfaction of individual preferences will exist which are not available by means of the voluntary choices of rational utility maximizers. Although these social outcomes would be desired by all rational individuals, they would not be produced by the very choices that it would be rational for each to make.

Situations of this nature consist of social outcomes which, although produced by the market, fail to maximize individual want satisfaction. They occur for a number of reasons. In some cases, individuals may be constrained to making choices without adequate knowledge of how others similarly situated will choose and therefore may be in ignorance of how these independent choices will interact. As a result, the very strategies that are rational for each of them on personal wealth-maximizing grounds turn out to be self-defeating. In other cases, outcomes that maximize total individual preference satisfaction will be attainable only by means of cooperation, but each potential party to the proposed cooperation will be situated so that it will be rational for him to seek to obtain the benefits of cooperation while evading its costs. In other words, each will have reason to free-ride on the cooperation of others, and cooperation will not take place or will collapse should it somehow manage to get started. In yet other instances, individuals will have no rational incentive to free-ride, but they will refrain from cooperation out of fear of being exploited or otherwise dominated by others. They will cooperate only if given guarantees as to the behavior of others, guarantees that the market itself will not produce. Given, then, that the economistic perspective takes rational social outcomes to be those yielding maximal individual preference satisfaction, and given that some such outcomes cannot be produced by the market, the adoption of political means of generating them will be rationally recommended.

Here we find the basis for what the economistic perspective takes to be the overriding if not the sole proper function of public policy—the use of the coercive powers of the state to produce socially rational outcomes that the market itself cannot produce. Because such outcomes maximize individual wealth, policies that produce them can be presumed to have the unanimous consent of rational individuals. Thus, the economistic perspective views public policy as no more than the pursuit of essentially individual aims by collective means—the pursuit of private interests by use of political instruments. Politics is viewed as private life conducted by public means and is resorted to only when the market fails.

Before turning to our criticisms of the economistic perspective, we must note an important difference between public policy and the market. Whereas the market is taken to produce social outcomes in which there are winners but no losers, no one believes that public policy can achieve such outcomes. Consequently, economistic theorists hold public policy to an apparently less stringent standard of efficiency than the standard met by the market. Public policy is required to pursue outcomes in which net benefit, net wealth, is maximized. Policy makers are to choose those policy options that provide the greatest balance of benefits over costs. The idea is that when net benefit is maximized, if personal utility winners were to compensate personal welfare losers, the want satisfaction of each would be maximized. Personal welfare losses would be canceled and winners would still be better off than under the status quo. The economistic outlook does not require that such compensation actually be paid, only that it be possible in principle. In principle then—but only in principle—such public policy outcomes are equivalent to the kinds produced by the market.

II. Limitations of the Economistic Outlook

Despite its current domination of policy analysis, the economistic perspective is deficient in a number of important respects. One of these shortcomings is made evident by considering the kinds of changes in the social status quo which would be produced by the market. Market efficiency is always determined by the social status quo. When the market functions ideally, it alters the current distribution of resources and opportunities only if it thereby increases the personal want satisfaction of someone without also producing personal welfare losses for anyone else. If no such improvement is possible, if no one's level of preference satisfaction can be increased without incurring a reduction in someone else's level, the status quo will remain unchanged by the market and, on economistic grounds, must be deemed efficient. No rational maximizer of personal wealth would voluntarily agree to accept a loss in personal welfare no matter how much gain was produced for someone else. Market social outcomes will thus always reflect the social status quo, the given distribution of resources and opportunities. It will always narrowly limit the sorts of social outcomes the market can produce. The question that needs to be answered here is why should the status quo be accorded this privileged position? Why should acceptable social change be so limited? Any perspective that is offered as the proper basis on which to assess policy and determine its ends must provide a compelling answer to this question.

Suppose we have a society in which some people are the slaves of others. In this society, the market, when functioning properly, will yield abolition of slavery only if no losses in individual preference satisfaction are produced thereby. If the only means of achieving abolition impose personal losses in want satisfaction, then slavery in this situation must be deemed efficient and, hence, socially ideal. Slavery is widely and rightly regarded as a moral abomination of the highest order, but if we limit acceptable social change to the kind produced by the market, we have little prospect of eliminating it. It must be accepted until some means of attaining its abolition can be found which increases the personal welfare of at least someone without also producing personal welfare losses for anyone else, a remote possibility at best.

What about the apparently less stringent conception of efficiency to which the economistic perspective holds public policy? Recognizing that public policy outcomes will produce both personal gains and losses, the economistic perspective requires of public policy outcomes only that the gains produced be larger than the losses, so that losses could, in principle, be compensated. In our hypothetical slave-owning society, resort to political means of abolition would be recommended only if the personal gains produced would be greater than the losses. If losses outweigh gains, no matter how small the difference, slavery must be deemed efficient and socially ideal. Here, too, the levels of loss and gain that would be produced by abolition are a function of the social status quo.

Surely slavery is the kind of evil that should be ended even if abolition would not voluntarily be produced by the efforts of rational wealth maximizers and even if total personal wealth losses caused by abolition were greater than total personal gains. Although there may be limits on how much negative welfare can properly be imposed on individuals to end an evil, even one of the magnitude of slavery, it certainly cannot be the case that no negative personal welfare can be legitimately sustained in doing so. The quite reasonable and widely held judgment that ending an evil of the magnitude of slavery should be undertaken even in the face of such losses cannot be supported by the economistic perspective, and this ought to be reason enough for rejecting it as the primary social ideal. The fact that evils on the order of slavery can be efficient social situations from an economistic perspective—and there is no reason they cannot be—shows that the economistic perspective is woefully deficient. A society that abolishes this kind of evil betters itself even if in doing so it causes losses in personal preference satisfaction, uncompensable or otherwise. Any conception of the social good which is consistent with this conclusion recognizes what economistic theorists do not and cannot, that the social status quo is not privileged. It is but one possible baseline against which we can measure the acceptability of various options for social change. An adequate conception of public policy cannot simply assume, as economistic thinking does, that the baseline provided by the status quo is the correct one. Whether the status quo is correct is itself a matter of our assessment of its merits, and the economistic point of view can provide us with no resources at all for making such an assessment. Hence, we must look beyond efficiency to find a suitable criterion for determining and assessing the tasks of public policy.

A second important deficiency of the economistic perspective is evident in its failure to recognize that individuals can evaluate their preferences as proper or improper. Suppose I find the sight of blond people repulsive. I might therefore prefer that all such individuals be kept locked away and out of sight. Surely it does not follow from this that I am incapable of seeing the moral bankruptcy of this preference. I may recognize that an individual's right to freedom of movement has no connection to his physical appearance but instead is premised upon some other ground altogether. I can admit that my preference is wrong even while also admitting that it is truly my preference. Indeed I may berate myself for continuing to have this preference. I may seek to establish constraints upon my conduct which will make it impossible or difficult for me to act upon it. I may even make efforts to rid myself of the repugnant preference altogether. If I am successful in expunging the preference, and possession of this sort of capability seems to be one of the ways that human beings are fundamentally different from other creatures, then the economistic perspective would be shown to be incorrect in holding that what one values is entirely a matter of what one prefers. Quite the contrary, for in an instance of this sort, what one prefers will be determined by one's antecedent and independent values. In reducing us to creatures of our preferences, the economistic perspective simply ignores an extremely important human capacity, the capacity to stand apart from what we want, to ask whether what we want is what we should want, to ask whether what we want is what we should get, and to ask whether we should try to eliminate certain wants that we in fact do have.[5] This capacity enables us to offer reasons to ourselves and others on behalf of and in criticism of the ends we want to pursue. It is this capacity that is omitted when rationality is conceived wholly instrumentally, as it is from an economistic point of view. A satisfactory conception of the aims that policy should serve and the instruments it should employ must recognize this fact about human nature. Any conception that fails to do so will thereby be based in an impoverished and one-dimensional conception of individual life and will necessarily offer an equally impoverished and one-dimensional conception of public life and our collective ends.

This human, perhaps uniquely human, capacity to evaluate our preferences means that we need not take maximization of their satisfaction, maximization of wealth, to be our sole collective end. In at least some instances, whether we will seek some form of preference satisfaction, some gain in wealth, will depend on just this sort of assessment. This means that we are not the mere consumers to which the economistic perspective reduces us. And, if we as individuals can evaluate our preferences and choose to reject their satisfaction, then we need not take maximal preference satisfaction to be our overriding social ideal. We can recognize that a society in which preference satisfaction is maximized, a society in which wealth is maximized, is not therefore necessarily a good society. Whether we judge it to be good or not will depend upon the nature of the preferences satisfied. If the preferences at issue are, for example, racist, sexist, exploitative, or otherwise immoral, we can and should conclude that they should not be satisfied. We may even find that our values force us to conclude that a good society is one where preference satisfaction is not only not maximized but where some efforts at preference satisfaction are deliberately thwarted and where some means of increasing wealth are deliberately thwarted. We may even conclude that, with respect to some such preferences, the good society will do what it can to expunge them from its members. (This does not mean, of course, that any and all means of achieving this must be judged acceptable. Our values will also limit what we believe ought to be done about unacceptable preferences.)

The difficulty we face here is what to do when our assessments of our preferences are incompatible, when we differ as to which preferences a good society will allow individuals to satisfy, and when we differ over what, if anything, a good society should do about preferences that are deemed unacceptable. How does the good society resolve conflicts of this sort, conflicts that the economistic perspective must fail to recognize at all? A perspective on public policy which fails even to see this difficulty and which therefore offers us no resources for adequately handling it is not worthy of dominating policy analysis and thereby setting the tasks for our collective endeavors. Thus, to be even minimally acceptable, a notion of public policy must recognize that our collective ends have rational sources other than our preferences and that a crucial and recurrent dilemma of our public life will be conflict over the proper definition of those ends. An ideal conception of policy would, of course, go far beyond this recognition and would provide us with resources for satisfactorily resolving such conflicts. On these grounds, the economistic perspective is not even minimally acceptable.

Given that we can assess our preferences, why then should we accept the economistic claim that maximization of individual preference satisfaction is the metric by which all social outcomes should be judged? Why should all social change be judged solely in light of its effects on personal wealth? That maximization of preference satisfaction requires some justification has not entirely escaped economistic thinkers. At least some have argued that efficiency itself rests on one or both of two traditional moral values—maximization of aggregate utility and respect for individual autonomy.[6] Seeing that neither of these values will support efficiency as the overriding social ideal further shows why the current dominance of the economistic perspective is unwarranted.

Consider maximization of aggregate utility first. When the market produces a change in the social status quo, it does so because the change yields some gains in personal welfare but no losses. Thus, it is quite plausible to hold that any change in the social status quo produced by the market will also be an increase in aggregate utility. But in this regard we need to remember an earlier point. The social outcomes that the market will yield are very narrowly constrained by the status quo, by the existing distribution of resources and opportunities. What any rational wealth maximizer will voluntarily agree to, or at least have no rational grounds for opposing, will be a function of her present resources and opportunities. That is, the changes in the status quo that she would be willing to devote her resources to bring about, or unwilling to use her resources to block, will be a function of what her resources are. It is clear, then, that insofar as market outcomes are those that result from the voluntary agreement of rational wealth maximizers, these outcomes are a function of the social status quo.

It is quite possible, however, that there are changes in the status quo that would yield greater increases in aggregate utility than those that could be produced without imposing any losses in want satisfaction on any individual, those that would be voluntarily produced by rational wealth maximizers. On utilitarian grounds, those would be the very changes that should be brought about, changes that, from a market perspective, are inefficient. The social outcomes that would maximize the wealth of each individual, those that would be countenanced from a market perspective, are not necessarily those that would yield maximal aggregate utility.

This is made plain once it is realized that the conception of the good held by economistic theorists is at best a very impoverished version of the utilitarian conception. This can be illustrated simply by thinking of the conception of utility held by classical utilitarians, namely, happiness. What maximizes one's happiness is not necessarily what maximizes satisfaction of one's wants, what maximizes one's wealth. This would be true in the case of the kind of individual we would judge to be a slave to his desires. Such an individual might well miss the satisfactions attendant on assessing one's wants and choosing to satisfy or frustrate them in light of that assessment. Such satisfaction is surely not available to one who only seeks preference satisfaction, who seeks only to increase personal wealth. And, such satisfaction may be of a magnitude great enough to outweigh any loss in preference satisfaction. So maximal satisfaction of an individual's preferences is not the same as maximal individual happiness. Accordingly, even if we were to allow that maximal satisfaction of the preferences of all individuals is equivalent to maximizing aggregate preference satisfaction, it still would not follow that maximum aggregate preference satisfaction is equivalent to maximum happiness.

The same would hold if our conception of utility was something like realization of interests rather than happiness. That which provides maximum preference satisfaction is not necessarily that which fully realizes an individual's interests. In other words, what an individual is interested in is not necessarily what is in his interests. This is widely recognized to be true of children and is one reason we are so willing to constrain their efforts at satisfying their preferences. It is also true of adults, even of adults who are quite adept at deploying their resources in ways that give them maximum want satisfaction. Life teaches even adults that what one wants, what one prefers, what one is willing to pay for, is not necessarily what is in one's interests. So even if maximizing the preference satisfaction of each is the same as maximizing aggregate preference satisfaction, it does not follow that maximum aggregate preference satisfaction is equivalent to maximum realization of interests at the aggregate level. What has been said here will be true of any conception of utility that does not reduce to preference satisfaction, and economism provides us with no grounds for accepting such a reduction.

If efficiency stands in need of justification by some deeper ethical principle, utility simply will not serve this end. What then about autonomy? Is it true that social outcomes of the kind the market would produce or the kind in which costs (personal wealth losses) are outweighed by benefits (personal wealth gains) are better at protecting individual autonomy than any alternatives would be? This is taken to be true of market outcomes because they are the results of the voluntary choices of rational wealth maximizers. It is taken to be true of outcomes in which costs are outweighed by benefits because if compensation were paid to losers by winners these outcomes would secure the consent of all rational individuals. In both cases, though, efficiency can be regarded as grounded in respect for autonomy only if the choices that rational wealth maximizers do or would make are the substance of autonomy.

Without attempting here to give a fully developed account of the nature of autonomy, we can note that to be autonomous is not simply to be an uncoerced chooser. Autonomy is self-direction, self-legislation, self-government, where these terms all connote that one who is autonomous is not a mere creature of her wants, her preferences. In addition to being able to choose without coercion, being autonomous is being able to assess one's preferences, wants, inclinations, and any other sources of motivation and being able to determine which, if any, of these motives will come to fruition in one's conduct. It is being able to rationally assess one's ends and to act on the basis of that assessment even in the face of other motives to the contrary.

Again, the case of children is instructive. An important aspect of the process of maturation which we hope is carried through in the development of a child into an adult is development of the capacity to rationally scrutinize one's motives, to choose which ought to be acted out, and even, as a consequence of this scrutiny, to acquire new motives. That we believe this kind of maturation can and does occur is an important reason for refusing to limit adult conduct in the ways we limit juvenile conduct. Although social outcomes that pass the economistic efficiency tests are rooted in actual or hypothetical voluntary choice, there is no guarantee that they are rooted in or protect autonomy. Our hypothetical slave case is useful here as well. The social changes that efficiency would justify in this case may well be rooted in actual or hypothetical voluntary choice, but if those changes do not add up to abolition of slavery they certainly do not respect individual autonomy, certainly not for the slaves. That efficiency can denominate this kind of social situation as efficient shows that efficient outcomes are not necessarily rooted in autonomy or protective of it.

The case of the slave-owning society illustrates a further difference between autonomy and voluntary choice. One very important reason for rejecting slavery, for regarding it an evil of great magnitude, is that by its very nature it reduces some persons to mere instruments of the will of others. In short, slavery fails to accord to some persons the respect that they deserve as creatures capable of autonomy. That we regard abolition of slavery as an important improvement in a society even when it must be imposed on those for whom it means losses in personal wealth shows that the value of autonomy is itself grounds for thwarting voluntary choice. It cannot be then that a social scheme that allows only voluntarily chosen changes in the social status quo necessarily protects individual autonomy.

To sum up, we have seen that efficiency, the market ideal for public life, cannot justify its privileging of the social status quo, does not recognize that individuals have values that are independent of and that can take priority over their preferences, fails to see that utility cannot be reduced to preference satisfaction and maximization of wealth, and fails to recognize that there is more to individual autonomy than mere voluntary choice. Hence, insofar as policy analysis and choice are dominated by the economistic perspective, our ability to recognize and effectively move against important social evils is severely handicapped and, both as distinct individuals and as citizens pursuing a collective life, we are reduced to mere creatures of our preferences. Fortunately, as the essays comprising the remainder of this volume collectively show, in our search for acceptable bases for setting and pursuing our collective lives, our public life, there is more under the sun than efficiency. We do have alternatives to the economistic perspective's impoverishment of our collective life. We can be more than mere consumers.

III. Guiding Questions

The essays in Part II address the following questions—questions the reader should keep in mind when examining each essay:

1. How are public policy choices distinct from the purely private choices of individual consumers? Why is the rationality of policy not reducible to the instrumental rationality of homo economicus?

2. How are the central problems of collective action the result of allowing narrow preference satisfaction to function as the sole end worth attaining? Why does successful resolution of these problems require public regulation supported by sound moral argumentation?

3. How can utility and autonomy, when these are not reduced to mere preference satisfaction and voluntary choice, serve as the bases of such argumentation?

NOTES

1. Of course, the options available to her will be a function of the resources she possesses and the environment in which she finds herself.

2. On this perspective, to regard something as a source of utility or to otherwise value it is simply to prefer it. How much a state of affairs is valued relative to an alternative reduces to how much more it is preferred.

3. Obviously, how this specification is to be made is one of the most important and contentious issues facing proponents of an economistic understanding of social life. How rights of action over resources are specified will determine the set of options open to individuals and, thus, the levels of personal utility available to each of them. This in turn will significantly constrain the kinds of social outcomes the market can produce.

4. Economizers disagree as to whether this means that the state is justified only if individuals actually did agree to its creation and continuance or that all that need be true is that rational utility-maximizing individuals would agree to its establishment and continuance. Is hypothetical consent sufficient or is actual consent necessary?

5. Indeed, one of the tasks that we wish education to perform for us, especially for children, is to establish this capacity, if it is not innate, and to nurture and enhance it. Among the most important distinguishing features of maturity is the ability to stand apart from one's preferences and gain some measure of control over them and their influence on one's conduct.

6. Maximization of aggregate utility and respect for individual autonomy are, of course, not the only moral values that have been offered as bases for setting collective ends and assessing various means of attaining those ends. The point here is that while the economistic position is correct in recognizing that, as a social ideal, efficiency needs some deeper moral grounding and in looking to maximization of aggregate utility and respect for individual autonomy as bases for public policy, it is quite incorrect in its belief that either of these values can be fully realized simply by pursing mere efficiency.

9 Collective Action as an Agreeable *n*-Prisoners' Dilemma

Russell Hardin

IN *The Logic of Collective Action,* Mancur Olson (1968) has proposed a mathematical explanation for the notable failure of the memberships of large interest groups to work together to provide themselves with their mutually desired collective goods. He concludes that the success of a group in providing itself with a collective good depends on the logical structure of the group.

> In a small group in which a member gets such a large fraction of the total benefit that he would be better off if he paid the entire cost himself, rather than go without the good, there is some presumption that the collective good will be provided. In a group in which no member got such a large benefit from the collective good that he had an interest in providing it even if he had to pay all the cost, but in which the individual was still so important in terms of the whole group that his contribution or lack of contribution to the group objective had a noticeable effect on the costs or benefits of others in the group, the result is indeterminate. By contrast, in a large group in which no single individual's contribution makes a perceptible difference to the group as a whole . . . it is certain that a collective good will *not* be provided unless there is coercion or some outside inducements. (p. 44)

These three sorts of group can be distinguished as the privileged group (i.e., the group in which at least one member could justify his full payment for the provision of the good on the basis of his sufficiently great return), the intermediate group, and the latent group.

Common sense and experience seem to confirm Olson's conclusions, although they seem to suggest a logic counter to our expectations. They suggest that "rational, self-interested individuals will not act to achieve their common or group interests" (Olson, 1968, p. 2). To clarify the logic of collective action, therefore, Olson gives a mathematical demonstration, which can be easily summarized.

The advantage (A_i) which accrues to an individual member (i) of a group as the result of his contribution to the purchase of the group collective good is given by:

$$A_i = V_i - C,$$

where V_i is the value to i of his share of the total collective good provided to the group at cost C to i. Clearly, if A_i is to be positive, then V_i must be greater than C. But this implies that i will contribute toward the purchase of the group collective good on his own rational incentive only if his share of that part of the good purchased at his cost is worth more to him than it cost him (Olson, 1968, pp. 22–25). Hence, the collective good will be provided in a privileged group, where this condition is met, but not in a latent group, where it is not met.

Collective Action and Prisoners' Dilemma

As with the prisoners' dilemma, we have for the latent group a result that tells us that individual effort to achieve individual interests will preclude their achievement, because if the collective good is not provided, the individual member fails to receive a benefit that would have exceeded his cost in helping purchase that good for the whole group. It would be useful to perform a game theory analysis of collective action to demonstrate that the logic underlying it is the same as that of the prisoners' dilemma. First, however, since Olson's analysis was accomplished from the perspective of an individual in the group, let us consider a particular instance of collective action in the game of Individual vs. Collective.

Individual vs. Collective

Let us construct a game matrix in which the row entries will be the payoffs for Individual, and the column entries will be the per capita payoffs for Collective, where Collective will be the group less Individual. The payoffs will be calculated by the prescription for rational behavior: that is, the payoffs will be benefits less costs. The group will comprise ten members whose common interest is the provision of a collective good of value twice its cost. There are two possible results of having one member of the group decline to pay his share: either the total benefit will be proportionately reduced, or the costs to the members of the group will be proportionately increased. Let us assume the former, but either choice would yield the same analysis. For the sake of simplicity, assume also that there are no initial costs in providing the collective good and no differential costs as payments and resultant benefits rise, that is, assume exactly two units of the collective good will be provided for each unit paid by any member of the group.[1]

If all members of the group pay 1 unit (for a total cost of 10 units), the benefit to each member will be 2 units (for a collective good of 20). The individual payoffs will be benefit less cost, or 1 unit. In the matrix, the first row gives the payoffs to Individual if he contributes his share; the first column gives the per capita payoffs to the remaining members of the group, i.e., to Collective, if they pay. The second row gives the payoffs to Individual if he does not pay, and the second column gives those for Collective if it does not pay. The various payoffs are readily calculated, e.g., if Individual does not pay but Collective does, the total cost will be 9 units, the total benefit will be 18 units, and the per capita benefit will be 1.8 units (for Individual cannot be excluded from the provision of the collective good); consequently, Individual's payoff for this condition will be his benefit less his cost for a pleasant 1.8 units. From the payoffs for the game in Matrix 1, one can see that it is evidently in Individual's advantage to choose the strategy of not paying toward the purchase of the collective good.

MATRIX 1
Individual vs. Collective

		Collective	
		Pay	Not Pay
Individual	Pay	1, 1	−0, 8, 0.2
	Not Pay	1.8, 0.8	0.0

Since it is individuals who decide on actions, and since each member of the group sees the game matrix from the vantage point of Individual, we can assume that Collective's strategy will finally be whatever Individual's strategy is, irrespective of what Collective's payoffs suggest. The dynamic under which Individual performs is clearly the same as that for the prisoners' dilemma: his strategy of not paying dominates his strategy of paying. For no matter what Collective does, Individual's payoff is greater if he does not pay. This can be seen more clearly perhaps in Matrix 1a, which displays only the payoffs to Individual for each of his choices. As in prisoners' dilemma, not paying is invariably more lucrative than paying.

MATRIX 1a
Individual's Payoffs

Individual	Pay	1	−0.8
	Not Pay	1.8	0

The payoffs to the two players in a game of prisoners' dilemma are shown in Matrix 2, and Row's payoffs only are shown in Matrix 2a. In this classic game, the delight of game theoreticians, Row and Column will

MATRIX 2
Prisoners' Dilemma

Column

		Cooperate	Defect
Row	Cooperate	1, 1	−2, 2
	Defect	2, −2	−1, −1

MATRIX 2a
Row's Payoffs

Row	Cooperate	2	−2
	Defect	1	−1

both profit (1 unit each) if both cooperate, and both will lose (1 unit each) if both defect. But as is clear in Matrix 2a, Row is wise to defect no matter what Column does. The Matrices 1a and 2a are strategically equivalent; the preference orderings of the payoffs to Individual and to Row are identical as shown by the arrows in figure 8.

n-*prisoners' Dilemma*

For the theorist of *n*-person games, a more cogent analysis of the problem of collective action defined by the game of individual vs. Collective would require a 10-dimensional matrix pitting the payoffs of each individual against all others. The payoffs can easily be calculated. The cell defined by all players paying would be (1,1,1,1,1,1,1,1,1,1), and that defined by all players not paying would be (0, . . . , 0). Every other cell would have payoffs whose sum would be equal to the number (*m*) of players paying in that cell; each player would receive a payoff of $2m/10-1$ if he paid, or $2m/10$ if he did not pay. Anyone able to visualize a 10-dimensional matrix can readily see that each player's dominant strategy is not to pay, because it yields the best payoff for whatever the other players do. The rest of us can easily enough calculate that whereas the payoff to player *i* is $2m/10-1$ with *m* players including himself paying, the payoff to *i* with *m*−1 players not including himself paying would be the preferred $2(m-1)/10$. (In the latter case *i*'s payoff is 0.8 units greater than in the former.) Hence, for each player *i*, the strategy of not paying dominates the strategy of paying. But playing dominant strategies yields all players the poor payoff (0, . . . , 0), and this solution is the only equilibrium for the game.

The game now defined is simply the 10-prisoners' dilemma, to which any solution algorithm generalized from the 2-prisoners' dilemma can be applied. To generalize the game further, *n* prisoners can be substituted for 10, and a ratio *r* of benefits to costs (with cost being 1 unit to each player) for the ratio of 2 assumed in Individual vs. Collective. The result is analogous, with the choice of not paying always yielding a payoff $(n-r)/n$ units higher than the choice of paying (the bonus increases as *n* increases); and

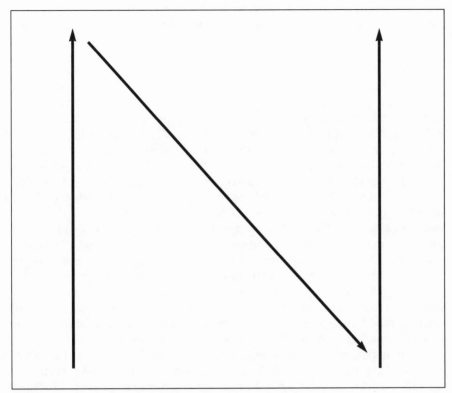

FIGURE 8.   Preference Ordering for Row and Individual

if all pay, all receive payoffs of $(r-1)$. Olson's privileged group would be the case in which r is greater than n in some player's perception (if costs are a matter of binary choice between paying a fixed sum for all players who pay, or paying nothing).

In this game there is only one (strongly stable) equilibrium (at the payoff of zero to every player, i.e., all players not paying); but this equilibrium solution is not Pareto-optimal. Moving from the equilibrium to the payoff of r to every player (i.e., all players paying) would improve the payoff to every player. Among the 78 strategically nonequivalent 2×2 games in the scheme of Rapoport and Guyer (1966), prisoners' dilemma is unique in its class. It is the only game defined by the condition that it has a single strongly stable equilibrium which, however, is Pareto-nonoptimal. Hence, the generalized game of collective action defined above is logically similar to prisoners' dilemma. (It should be clear that the reason for the equivalence of prisoners' dilemma and the game of collective action for a large, i.e., latent, group is precisely the condition that in such a group a player's contribution to the purchase of the collective good is of only marginal utility to himself. Hence, his payoff is increased by almost the amount he does not pay when he does not pay.)

Empirical Consequences

The significance of this result is that any analysis which prescribes a solution for prisoners' dilemma must prescribe a similar solution for the game of collective action. That means that the vast body of experimental and theoretical work on prisoners' dilemma is relevant to the study of collective action in general (and conversely that the growing body of work on collective action can be applied to the study of the prisoners' dilemma). In particular, any analysis of prisoners' dilemma which yielded the conclusion that the mutual loss payoff was not rational would, by implication, contravene Olson's (1968, p. 44) claim that, for logical reasons, in a latent group "it is certain that a collective good will *not* be provided unless there is coercion or some outside inducements." Considering the fact that there are arguments that the rational solution to prisoners' dilemma is the payoff which results from mutual cooperation, before turning to the rationale of group success, we should perhaps reconsider why it might be that, empirically, latent groups do generally seem to fail. Let us view the 10-prisoners' dilemma defined above in the light of some 2-prisoners' dilemma experimental results.

Some experimental data suggest that about one-half of bona fide players cooperate with and one-half exploit a noncontingent, 100 percent cooperative adversary-partner in 2-prisoners' dilemma (Rapoport, 1968). In the 10-prisoners' dilemma described above, let us assume that this result would mean that 5 of the players would not pay even if the other 5 did pay. In this circumstance, the benefit to each player would be 1 unit, and the cost to each of the 5 payers would be 1 unit: hence, the payoff to the payers would be zero. Consequently, even an analysis which prescribed cooperation, or paying, as the rational strategy under the assumption of all players rational would allow nonpayment as a rational strategy to players in a real world game in which habitual nonpayers drained off any positive payoff to the payers. Assuming the validity of the generalization from the prisoners' dilemma experimental data, in real world games in which the law of large numbers applies and in which the perceived benefits of the collective good are not more than twice the costs, one can expect no provision of the collective good for reasons different from Olson's logic. In the intermediate group (where the statistics of large numbers do not apply), even with benefits considerably less than twice the costs, there is some statistical chance that a collective good will be provided. In either case, the prospects for success decline as the ratio (or perceived ratio) of benefits to costs decreases, and as the differential perception of that ratio increases while the average perceived ratio remains constant.

As Olson (1968, p. 24) notes, the issue is not so much what an adversary-member's payoff will be, but rather whether anyone will choose to play the game at all. In the 10-prisoners' dilemma analysis here, by a different logic, it follows that one of the basic tenets of game theory is in one sense not useful in real world application. Ordinarily, in game theoretical analyses the actual values of payoffs are not important; the only consideration is the rank ordering of payoffs. But clearly, the normal inducement to play a real world game is the expectation of positive payoffs. Hence, a rational player in the game of collective action does not refuse to pay merely because his strategy of not paying is dominant and yields a higher payoff; rather he refuses to pay because enough others in the group do not pay that he would suffer a net cost if he did. Consequently, it would be irrational for him to play the game, and not playing means not paying. (However, this reasoning cannot be considered to give a proof that collective action will fail. That remains an empirical matter.)

The Condorcet Choice Solution of the Game of Collective Action

The usual analysis of prisoners' dilemma prescribes a strategy: the dominating strategy which in the 10-person game of collective action discussed above would be not to pay. Because the general employment of that strategy produces an undesirable outcome, and because many (roughly half) of the subjects in some 2-prisoners' dilemma experiments have not employed that strategy, it would be useful to analyze the outcomes (as opposed to the strategies) of the larger game of collective action. The matrix for the 10-person binary choice game has 2^{10} or 1,024 cells, each of which is a uniquely defined potential outcome of the game. Instead of considering the strategies of the players, let us view the game as though the 10 players were collectively choosing among the 1,024 outcomes. With a simple notation these 1,024 outcomes can be represented as 20 classes of outcomes. We can readily ascertain which among these classes are realizable outcomes, and can determine whether any among the realizable outcomes is a Condorcet choice. It will be a simple matter to demonstrate that in any game of collective action with n players and a ratio r, $r > 1$, of benefits to payments there is a Condorcet choice among the realizable outcomes, and it is the outcome defined by all players paying and all receiving payoffs of $r-1$ units.

2n *Classes of Outcomes*

In the 10-person game of collective action, the possible outcomes in the view of an Individual in the game are as in Matrix 3. The entries in the top

MATRIX 3

Pay	1.0	0.8	0.6	0.4	0.2	0	−0.2	−0.4	−0.6	−0.8
Not Pay	1.8	1.6	1.4	1.2	1.0	0.8	0.6	0.4	0.2	0

row are Individual's payoffs when all ten players pay, nine players including Individual pay, etc. Those in the bottom row are Individual's payoffs when he does not pay, ranging from the case in which all nine other players pay to the case in which no one pays. The upper left payoff results from only one outcome of the game: all pay. The upper row payoff of 0, however, results from 126 different outcomes of the game: all the possible combinations in which Individual and four other players pay while five players do not pay.

It will be useful to represent these classes of outcomes more generally. Let N_k represent any outcome in which exactly k players, including Individual, do not pay. And let P_k represent any outcome in which exactly k players, including Individual, pay. Matrix 3 can be rewritten as Matrix 3a.

MATRIX 3a

Pay	P_{10}	P_9	P_8	P_7	P_6	P_5	P_4	P_3	P_2	P_1
Not Pay	N_1	N_2	N_3	N_4	N_5	N_6	N_7	N_8	N_9	N_{10}

It is now a simple matter to rank order the outcomes according to Individual's preference; the position of an outcome P or N is determined by the payoff to Individual associated with it. Table 4 presents Individual's preference ordering and gives the total number of outcomes in the full 10-dimensional game matrix associated with each payoff class.

TABLE 4

Payoff Class	Number of Outcomes in this Class
N_1	1
N_2	9
N_3	36
N_4	84
P_{10}, N_5	1,126
P_9, N_6	9,126
P_8, N_7	36,84
P_7, N_8	84,36
P_6, N_9	126,9
P_5, N_{10}	126,1
P_4	84
P_3	36
P_2	9
P_1	1
Total	1,024

Clearly, Individual can guarantee himself his minimax payoff (N_{10} at the lower right in Matrix 3a). Those outcomes P_4, P_3, P_2, and P_1 which fall below the minimax line in Table 4, therefore, are outcomes which he can unilaterally prevent by not paying. Similarly, however, every other player in the game can prevent his own P_4, P_3, P_2, and P_1 outcomes, so that the complementary outcomes N_6, N_7, N_8, and N_9 of opposing players will be prevented (for instance, an N_9 can occur only if some player is willing to pay when no one else does, thus putting himself into a P_1 outcome). Hence, none of these outcomes is realizable, i.e., they would require that some player willingly recline below his minimax, as few of us are wont to do.[2] The only outcomes which can obtain in a play of the game are those of Table 5. It is from this set of realizable outcomes that the players must seek an agreeable outcome. If one of these outcomes is a Condorcet choice for the set, it is the prominently rational outcome of the game.

Condorcet Choice

We can define strong and weak Condorcet choices.[3] Let C be the collective (i.e., the group) of n members choosing among outcomes in the matrix of an n-person collective action game, and let j and k be outcomes from the set M of realizable outcomes in the game matrix (in the 10-prisoners' dilemma matrix there are 1,024 cells, of which 639 are realizable outcomes). Let c_{jk} be the number of those in C who prefer outcome j to outcome k, and let c'_{jk} be the number of those in C who are indifferent to whether outcome j or outcome k obtains. Clearly, $c_{jk} + c_{kj} + c'_{jk} = n$.

> *Definition:* j is a strong Condorcet choice if it is preferred by a majority in C to every k ($\neq j$) in M. Reduced to symbolic brevity, this condition is

$$c_{jk} > n/2 \text{ for all } k \neq j.$$

TABLE 5

N_1
N_2
N_3
N_4
P_{10}, N_5
P_9
P_8
P_7
P_6
P_5, N_{10}

Definition: j is a weak Condorcet choice if it is not a strong Condorcet choice but if, for each $k \neq j$, more of those in C prefer j to k than k to j. This condition is simply

$$c_{jk} > c_{kj} \text{ for all } k \neq j.$$

It should be clear that there can be at most one Condorcet choice.

From the definition of the game of collective action for n players the following theorem for the existence of a Condorcet choice among the set of realizable outcomes can be derived.

Theorem: For an n-person game of collective action, P_n is a Condorcet choice from the set of realizable outcomes for the game; it is a strong Condorcet choice except in a game in which n is even and $r = 2$, in which case P_n is a weak Condorcet choice from the set of realizable outcomes.

The proof of this theorem, which is not difficult but is tedious, is left to the appendix. However, it will be instructive to see that it holds for the case of 10-prisoners' dilemma. We need only to compare the outcome P_{10} to each of the other realizable outcomes listed in Table 5 to show that P_{10} is preferred to each of these others. Given an outcome of the class N_1, nine players will prefer P_{10}. Similarly, given an outcome of the class N_2, N_3, or N_4, eight, seven, or six players, respectively, will prefer P_{10}. And nine, eight, seven, or six players will prefer P_{10} to any outcome of the class P_9, P_8, P_7, or P_6, respectively. Finally, given an outcome of the class N_5, the five players whose outcomes are of the class P_5 will prefer outcome P_{10}; and the five players whose outcomes are of the class N_5 will be indifferent to the choice between N_5 and P_{10}. Consequently, a clear majority of the players will prefer P_{10} to any outcome except N_5, in which case all of those with a preference will prefer P_{10}. It follows that P_{10} is a weak Condorcet choice. It is weak because the game has an even number of players and a ratio of benefits to contributions of 2.[4]

Degeneracy—Back to the Prisoners' Dilemma

At the limits of the preceding analysis there occur several classes of degenerate games of collective action. These result when $r = 1$ or $n = 2$.

In the degenerate case of $r = 1$, the realizable outcomes are P_n and N_n, and all players are indifferent as to which of these obtains. For all cases of $r > 1$, the only realizable outcome is N_n. The game will not be played.

In the degenerate case of $n = 2$ there are five possibilities: $r < 1$, $r = 1$, $1 < r < 2$, $r = 2$, $r > 2$. The first two of these are degenerate in r. In the case of $r = 2$, all outcomes are realizable and the outcome of both pay is a weak Condorcet choice. If $r > 2$, each player's return from his own contribution is greater than his contribution, so presumably both will pay and reap appropriate benefits. (Recall that in general $r > n$ implies that the group is a privileged group in Olson's terms.) The interesting cases remain. They are those for $1 < r < 2$. They are represented in Matrix 4.

MATRIX 4

$r-1, r-1$	$(r/2-1), r/2$
$r2, (r/2-1)$	$0,0$

The payoffs in the games of Matrix 4 are related according to the preference ordering (if $1 < r < 2$):

$$r/2 > (r - 1) > 0 > (r/2 - 1).$$

This condition meets the definition of the symmetric 2-prisoners' dilemma game. For example, Rapoport and Chammah (1965, pp. 33–34 define the symmetric prisoners' dilemma by the condition that the payoffs (as given in Matrix 5) satisfy the relation:

$$T > R > P > S,$$

in which the letters didactically stand for Temptation (to defect), Reward (for cooperating), Punishment (for defecting), and Sucker's payoff (for cooperating). Note that the preference ordering for row is as in Figure 8. From the preference ordering and Matrix 4, it can be seen that only the outcomes $(r - 1, r - 1)$ and $(0,0)$ are realizable, and that of these $(r - 1, r - 1)$ is a strong Condorcet choice.

Conclusion

It has been shown that the problem of collective action can be represented as a game with a strategic structure similar to that of prisoners' dilemma. The logic which prescribes that a member of a group should not contribute toward the purchase of his group collective interest is the same as that which prescribes that a player in a game of prisoners' dilemma should defect (i.e., should not cooperate). However, from the set of all realizable outcomes in a game of collective action in which the ratio of benefits to contributions exceeds 1, the outcome in which all contribute is a Condorcet choice. The existence of a Condorcet choice, which is by definition unique, implies that a real world group could decide in favor of the Condorcet choice over every other realizable outcome. Consequently, it is rational in a world in which distrust seems endemic to use sanctions to enforce all members of an interest group to contribute toward the purchase of the group interest (Olson, 1968, p. 51). In a world not quite Hobbesian a threat of all against all might, ironically, help overcome distrust.

However, the threat of all against all is not a logical necessity; rather, it is only a potentially useful device, given human psychology. For, there is debate in the literature on the prisoners' dilemma as to whether the co-operative or the noncooperative outcome is rational or logically determinate. Therefore, it can hardly be granted that, as Olson contends, in the absence of sanctions in a latent group "it is certain that a collective good will *not* be provided," whereas in an intermediate group the result is merely indeterminate. The clarity of the analogy between the logic of collective action and the strategic structure of the prisoners' dilemma game makes it seem likely (as suggested above) that the differences in the statistics of success for the intermediate and latent groups is a function of statistics on, for example, the social distribution of distrust; but in any case it is not a derivation from the logic inherent in the group interactions.

Appendix: Proof of Theorem

Assume a group of m player-members in a game of collective action as defined with a ratio r of benefits to payments. When an outcome of class P_k obtains for k players, its complementary outcome of class N_{m-k} obtains for the other players. Let (P_k, N_{m-k}) represent the k outcome set for the game: it is the set of all outcomes which are of class P_k for k players and of class N_{m-k} for $(m-k)$ players. (The total number of outcomes represented by this set is $m!/k!(m-k)!$. For instance, when $k = m$, all players are in the single outcome of class P_m.) Finally, let c_{mk} represent the number of players who prefer outcome P_m to an outcome of the set k.

In order to demonstrate that P_m is a Condorcet choice among the set of realizable outcomes of the m-person game of collective action, we need only show that, for each $k<m$,

(1a) $c_{mk} > m/2$, or
(1b) $c_{mk} > c_{km}$, or
(1c) the outcomes in set k are not realizable.

Let us note two general conditions before proving the theorem. The condition which renders an outcome not realizable is that in that outcome some player receives a payoff less than his minimax, i.e., less than zero. If P_k represents the payoff to a player in an outcome of class P_k, and N_{m-k} the payoff to a player in the complementary outcome of class N_{m-k}, then

(2) $p_k = kr/m - 1$, and
(3) $n_{m-k} = kr/m$.

By definition it follows that:

Condition 1. The outcomes of the k outcome set are not realizable if $p_k < 0$.

The payoff at P_m is $(r - 1)$. At P_k, $k < m$, the payoff is $p_k < (r - 1)$. It follows that:

Condition 2. The k players in an outcome of class P_k, $k < m$, prefer outcome P_m to P_k.

Proof of the Theorem

To prove the theorem, we must show that requirement (1) is met for three possible values of k: (I) $k > m/2$; (II) $k < m/2$; and (III) $k = m/2$.

Region (I)
$$k > m/2$$

By Condition 2, P_m is preferred to P_k by k players, so that $c_{mk} > m/2$. Requirement (1a) is met.

Region (II)
$$(4)\ k < m/2$$

There are three regions in the value of the payoff to the players not paying: (a) $kr/m < (r - 1)$; (b) $kr/m = (r - 1)$; and (c) $kr/m > (r - 1)$. We must show that requirement (1) is met in each of these regions.

$$kr/m < (r - 1) \tag{a}$$

In this region, it is clear from (2) and (3) that all players prefer P_m to the set (P_k, N_{m-k}). Hence, requirement (1a) is met.

$$kr/m = (r - 1) \tag{b}$$

It follows that

$$kr = mr - m, \text{ or}$$

$$(5) \quad (m - k)r = m.$$

But from (4), we have

$$(6) \quad m > 2k$$

From (5) and (6) we have

$$(2k - k)r < m, \text{ or}$$

$$(7) \quad kr/m < 1.$$

But the payoff to those who pay is, according to (2),

$$p_k = kr/m - 1.$$

From (7) it follows that

$$p_k < 1 - 1, \text{ or}$$

$$p_k < 0.$$

From Condition 1 it follows that the outcomes of the k outcome set are not realizable. Hence, requirement (1c) is met.

$$kr/m > (r - 1). \tag{c}$$

By an argument almost identical to that for the condition of (b) above, we have

$$kr > mr - m, \text{ or}$$

$$(m - k)r < m.$$

From (6) it follows that

$$kr < m, \text{ or}$$

$$kr/m < 1.$$

This is the same as (7); from the argument above it follows that requirement (1c) is met.

> Region (III)
> $$k = m/2.$$

It follows from (2) and (3) that

(8) $p_k = r/2 - 1$, and

(9) $n_{m-k} = r/2.$

As in (II), there are three possibilities: (a) $r/2 < r - 1$; (b) $r/2 = r - 1$; and (c) $r/2 > r - 1$.

$$r/2 < r - 1. \tag{a}$$

In this region, it is clear from (8) and (9) that all players prefer outcome P_m to the set $(P_k, N_{m}{}^-{}_k)$. Hence, requirement (1a) is met.

(10) $r/2 = r - 1.$ \hfill (b)

From Condition 2 it follows that $m/2$ players prefer P_m to the set (P_k, N_{m-k}); and from (9) it follows that the other $m/2$ players are indifferent in the choice between P_m and this set. Hence, $c_{mk} = m/2, c_{km} = 0$, so that $c_{mk} > c_{km}$. Requirement (1b) is met.

$$r/2 > r - 1. \tag{c}$$

It follows that

$$r/2 < 1.$$

Hence, from (8) we have

$$p_k < 1 - 1, \text{ or}$$

$$p_k < 0.$$

From Condition 1 it follows that the outcomes of the k outcome set are not realizable. Hence, requirement (1c) is met.

Requirement (1) is met for all values of r and m, so that there exists a Condorcet choice among the set of realizable outcomes in a game of collective action. Moreover, in almost every case, either (a) or (c) of requirement (1) is met; for all these cases, P_m is therefore a strong Condorcet choice. The only exception to this is case (IIIb), in which requirement (1b) is met; in this case, m is divisible by 2, and from (10) it can be seen that $r = 2$. Consequently, P_m is a weak Condorcet choice among the realizable outcomes in a game of collective action in which there is an even number of players and $r = 2$. The theorem is proved.

NOTES

This article, first published in *Behavioral Science* 16 (1971): 472–81, is reprinted by permission. I am pleased to thank Hayward R. Alker, Jr., Joan Rothchild, and Jean-Roger Vergnaud for the help and advice they gave in the preparation of this paper.

1. Within a broad range, this assumption entails only that the payoffs in the upper right and lower left cells in Matrix 1 will contain payoffs only slightly higher or lower than might have been the case for a real world problem. Consequently, the logical dynamics of the game are unaffected by the assumption.

2. The use of this term conforms with Howard (1967, p. 24), in whose metagama theory an outcome is metarational for all players if every player's payoff in that outcome is at least equal to his minimax payoff. Hence, the only realizable outcomes are those which are metarational for all players.

3. Named for the eighteenth-century French economist and intellectual in general, the Marquis de Condorcet, who studied the problem of electoral majorities, believed in man's capacity for unlimited progress, and chose to poison himself rather than meet the guillotine during the Terror.

4. It was noted above that prisoners' dilemma is the only one of the Rapoport-Guyer games with a strongly stable equilibrium that is not Pareto-optimal. This statement can be made stronger. Every outcome in the 2-prisoners' dilemma is Pareto-optimal except the outcome of mutual loss.

In a game of collective action this stronger statement also usually holds. However, if r divides n, then any outcome defined by N_{n-r} for n/r of the players is not Pareto-optimal. (This is because $n - n/r$ of the players would benefit in a shift from this outcome to P_n, and the other n/r players would be indifferent to the shift.) All other outcomes in any game of collective action are Pareto-optimal except the single dismal solution N_n.

REFERENCES

Howard, N. A Method for metagame analysis of political problems. Mimeographed working paper, Management Science Center, University of Pennsylvania, 1967.

Olson, M., Jr. *The Logic of Collective Action.* New York: Schocken, 1968 (first published, 1965).

Rapoport, A. Editorial Comments. *J. Conflict Resolut.,* 1968, 12, 222–23.

Rapoport, A., & Chammah, A. M. *Prisoner's Dilemma.* Ann Arbor, Mich.: Univ. of Michigan Press, 1965.

Rapoport, A., & Guyer, M. J. A Taxonomy of 2 X 2 Games. *General Systems,* 1966, 11, 203–14.

10 The Exchange and Enforcement of Property Rights

Harold Demsetz

OUR ECONOMIC SYSTEM, with its specialization of economic activities into separate ownership and decision units, requires both control over goods and exchange of goods if it is to cope with the diversity of wants of specialist producers. This paper is concerned with the fact that the exchange of goods and the maintenance of control over the use of goods impose costs on traders and owners. It is also concerned with the cost of government alternatives to the market place. We seek to establish both the importance and the wide role of these costs in economic life.

A large part of our argument will be illustrated by two important controversies in welfare economics in which we will show, on the one hand, that zero pricing of scarce goods need not result in inefficiency, and, on the other, that zero pricing of "public" goods may result in inefficiency. The standard criticisms of resource allocation by the market, which turn on the market's failure to price "external" effects and on its tendency to price "public" goods, are shown to be invalid. To do this we extend the well-known axiom that there is no such thing as a free scarce good by including such goods as markets, government bureaus, and policing devices.

Throughout this paper, our attention is confined to the problem of efficiency within the framework of smoothly running markets and governments, in the sense that we assume that persons, whether in their capacity as civil servants or as private citizens, do not make arithmetic errors in calculating, or, at least, that they do not tend to make more errors in one role than in another. We do not concern ourselves with problems of monopoly by either a firm or the government, but the problem of imperfect knowledge is treated.

Instead of "external effects" or "neighborhood effects" we will use the phrase "side effects" to identify those for which no account *seems* to be taken in the market place. This avoids the flavor of location and of being *necessarily* outside of the market place that seem to be associated with the more common names for these effects.

I. Exchange Cost

Recent Developments

R. H. Coase,[1] in an important article, demonstrates that there is, in general, nothing special about side effects that rules out the possibility of their being taken account of by the market. These effects can be taken into account by market transactions between the parties affected once the courts have established who has what right of action. Under competitive conditions and assuming zero exchange costs, these transactions will result in an efficient solution to the scarcity problem. Thus, if ranchers are given the right to allow their cattle to roam and the cattle stray accidentally onto unfenced farmland, it will be in the farmer's interest to bring the damage they cause to the rancher's attention by offering to pay the rancher to reduce the number of cattle foraging nearby. If the rancher disregards this offer, he sacrifices a potential receipt equal to the crop damage. Thus, the crop damage becomes a private cost to the rancher of raising additional cattle and will be taken account of in his calculations. Moreover, Coase points out the efficiency of the solution with respect to the number of cattle and the size of the crops in the absence of exchange costs is independent of whether the farmer or rancher is legally liable for the damage. The party not held liable, of course, acquires the right to act in ways which may have harmful side effects. The assignment of the liability for crop damage to the rancher would lead to a direct accounting for this cost in his operations and he would need to decide whether to reduce his herd or pay the farmer to reduce the crop he plants. Whether the farmer will find it worthwhile to pay enough to the rancher to reduce his herd or whether the rancher can pay enough to the farmer to reduce the area he cultivates depends on whether the value lost because of the crop reduction is greater or less than the value lost because the size of the herd is reduced. Whichever way the rights are initially assigned, the outcome of the subsequent bargaining will be that which maximizes the value of output.

Coase has advanced the analysis of the roles that can be played by the market and the government a step beyond its previous position. For now Coase has shown that if exchange costs are positive, it is necessary to ask whether government can take the harmful effects of an action into account at less cost than can the market or, indeed, if the resulting resource realignment is worth the cost of taking the side effects into account at all.

Misapplication of Optimality Theorems

The question which asks whether or not realignment is worthwhile brings to light an improper usage to which we frequently have put our optimality theorems. The cost of using the market relative to the cost of using a political mechanism has seldom been considered explicitly or in detail in the bulk of the theory of welfare economics. This has led to an improper usage of those theorems. As a consequence of the conventional approach to these problems, it has not been recognized that the very conditions under which side effects are believed to lead to inefficiency are those conditions for which the welfare theorems used are inapplicable.

The usual analysis of market inefficiency in such cases attributes the difficulty to the absence of markets in which "appropriate" prices for measuring side effects can be revealed.[2] But absence of a market or of a price can be consistent with efficiency when optimality theorems are appropriately interpreted. *For produced goods,* the optimality theorems require equalities among various marginal rates of substitution. These same optimality conditions, however, do not require such equalities for goods and services that are *not produced* in the final efficient equilibrium; for these we have corner solutions involving inequalities. Thus, a basic premise in requiring equalities is that we are talking about goods which we require to be produced in positive quantities.

We then turn to the competitive model and observe that market prices will often bring about the equalities required for produced commodities and services. But, we ask, what if some goods produce side effects which are not exchanged over a market? We answer that the market fails to provide us with incentives which will guide behavior to take account of the side effects and that, therefore, the required equalities will be absent. The allegation is that even perfectly competitive markets fail to achieve efficiency. But, this reasoning generally fails to take account of the fact that the provision of a market (for the side effect) is itself a valuable and costly service. Where a market, or the political action which would be its counterpart, does not exist, this service is not being produced. If this service is not being produced some *in*equalities (instead of the equalities required for produced goods) among our marginal rates of substitution and marginal rates of transformation may be consistent with efficiency, as will be the case if the cost of taking account of side effects through either the market or the government exceeds the value of realigning resources. In such cases zero amounts of market pricing or the government equivalent will be efficient. In asking the implications of the nonexistence of some markets, we seem to have forgotten the cost of providing market services or their government equivalent. The existence of prices to facilitate exchange between affected parties has been too much taken for granted. A price for every produced good or service is not a necessary condition for efficiency, so that the absence of a price does not imply that either market transactions or substitute government services are desirable. If we insist either that all actions (services or commodities) be priced in the market or that the government intervene, we are insisting that we do not economize on the cost of producing exchanges or government services. Thus, most welfare propositions concerned with side effects are based on an invalid use of the standard optimality theorems, i.e., they ignore the cost of some of the goods.

Some Examples

We shall consider two examples to illustrate our point. In the first rights of action are clearly defined; in the second they are not.

Our first example is zero-priced parking at shopping plazas in which unpaid-for benefits exist insofar as shoppers, in the prices they pay, confer benefits on nonshopping parkers. Most economists, regardless of their philosophical persuasion, would probably argue that the number of spaces is nonoptimal. But, when we say nonoptimal, we must have some idea of what is the optimal number of spaces. Assuming the absence of increasing returns, the less careful of us are apt to reply that the proper number of spaces is the number that would clear the market when a charge is levied to cover construction cost. A more careful reply would include exchange costs in the charge. *Neither* answer is necessarily correct.

It is true that the setting and collecting of appropriate shares of construction and exchange costs from each parker will reduce the number of parking spaces needed to allow ease of entry and exit. But while we have reduced the resources committed to constructing parking spaces, we have increased resources devoted to market exchange. We may end up by allocating more resources to the provision and control of parking than had we allowed free parking because of the resources needed to conduct transactions. By insisting that the commodity be priced, we may become less efficient than had we allowed persons to ration spaces on a first-come, first-serve basis. Similarly, rationing by government involves its own costs and may be no better. Those who purchase merchandise and indirectly pay for parking spaces may prefer to substitute the smaller total cost of constructing additional spaces to accommodate free-loaders rather than ration out the nonbuying parkers by paying the required exchange costs minus the savings of constructing fewer parking spaces. Since the cost of providing additional parking spaces depends largely on the price of land, it follows that we should expect to observe free parking allowed more frequently in suburbs than in the center of towns because of the differential prices of land. Given this differential, both methods of allocating parking may be efficient.

Is this example consistent with competition? Will not competing stores open nearby and charge lower prices because their customers use a free parking lot supplied by a competitor? Will they, thereby, force their competitor out of business? The desirability of providing parking spaces implies that we are dealing with a world of finite dimension in which all cars cannot be parked at zero cost on a dimensionless point. For this reason, differential land rent will be taken into account. Owners of land surrounding the free parking lot will enjoy windfall profits, a question of wealth redistribution, but potential competitors will have the advantages of the nearby lot capitalized and included in the rent they pay; they will enjoy no competitive advantage. The equilibrium is a stable competitive one although it gives rise to differential land rent. If the windfall is expected to be large enough to warrant the additional transactions required to purchase surrounding land, the (prospective) owners of the shopping plaza could take account of these gains in their calculations by purchasing the surrounding land before free parking is allowed. This option, which Coase refers to as extending the role of the firm, is alternative to both exchange and government action.[3]

In this particular example, the efficiency of producing this costly but zero-priced parking depends on the supplier being able to recoup the cost by other means, namely in the prices of his merchandise. This method of financing the parking lot becomes economically superior *only* if demand interrelations are such that a sale in combination arrangement reduces exchange costs sufficiently. Both the loose combination sale (not all parkers need to buy merchandise) as well as tighter tie-ins may, in fact, be methods which reduce the cost of allocating and which lead to optimal quantities of goods. We will have more to say on the relevance of this for the problems posed by public goods.

For contrast, our next example, one that has become a favorite, involves neither tie-in arrangements nor defined rights of action. It is the case in which market transactions do not take place in the use of nectar by bees, so that prices do not arise which reflect the beneficial effects of apple blossoms on the productivity of bees. Clearly, as Coase would probably point out, it is possible for beekeepers and apple growers to strike a bargain over how many trees are to be planted, the bargain taking account of an apple tree's contribution to honey production and a bee's contribution to cross-fertilization of trees. Further, were there significant predictable benefits from the interaction, significant enough to offset any diseconomies of underspecialization, beekeeping and apple growing would be carried on by the same farmer. However, the benefits may be small relative to the costs of forsaking specialization. Merger will not then be the solution. Suppose, also, that estimates of benefits are small relative to estimates of the cost of developing the science of the apple-bee interaction and to either the costs of transacting in the market or providing substitute government services.

Then efficiency requires that bees be allowed to "help themselves" on a first-come, first-serve basis, which is, after all, an alternative arrangement for settling scarcity problems.

Here no combination sales are directly involved. A valuable and costly good, nectar, is provided free of charge because it would be too costly to take account of the indirect benefits to beekeepers. In contrast to the parking and merchandising example, the separate marketing of the two products, apples and blossoms, is costly. Hence a zero-priced good may be efficient even though no combination sale is used. Since no low cost combination sale seems possible, the good (nectar) will be provided free if apples, *per se*, are worth producing. If apples are not worth producing, our recognition of the existence of a benefit to beekeepers will not make the production of apples desirable, for the cost of inducing the apple grower to take this benefit into account is too high to make it worthwhile.

II. Police Cost

Up to now we have largely limited our attention to situations in which direct bargaining between individuals requires an exchange cost that is larger than the benefits derived from the exchange. To take account of these side effects, the interested parties, therefore, resort to combination sales, to extensions of the firm, or they find it expedient not to modify these effects. All of these alternatives are consistent with efficiency and yet all fail to exhibit a market in the side effect. There are situations, however, which are somewhat different in that the cost of *policing* the effects of actions, rather than the cost of exchange, may be so high as to cause additional complications. The following discussion of these situations is designed to reveal the roles played by police cost and private property and to help clear up some public good problems.

Property Rights and the Valuation Problem

There are two tasks which must be handled well by any acceptable allocative mechanism. These are, first, that information must be generated about all the benefits of employing resources in alternative uses, and second, that persons be motivated to take account of this information. To the extent that both these tasks are solved by the allocative mechanism, the problem of attaining an efficient allocation of resources reduces to arithmetic. Setting aside the second problem, we turn to the first and, in particular to the necessity for protecting the right to use economically valuable resources if we are to obtain accurate information about benefits.

It is well known that prices can serve as guideposts to where resources are wanted most, and, in addition, that exchangeability of goods at these prices can provide incentives for people to follow these guideposts. However, analytical concentration on the price mechanism has kept us from closely examining what it is that is being traded. The value of what is being traded depends crucially on the rights of action over the physical commodity and on how economically these rights are enforced. The enforcement of the accompanying property rights has an important impact on the ability of prices to measure benefits. An emphasis on this aspect or view of the problem, in conjunction with our emphasis on exchange cost, will allow us to unify our treatment of what is now largely a collection of special cases in which our measures of benefits diverge from actual benefits. The petroleum and fishery "pool" problems are good examples of problems created by treating economic goods as free goods. The general conclusion reached by the analysis of pool problems is that a resource, be it petroleum, fish, or game, is too rapidly worked. This conclusion is correct and if we think in terms of producible inventories, the absence of property right enforcement also can be shown to result in too little production of the good, or in too small an increment to the pool or inventory of the good. This is because the prices which reflect private benefits, fail to measure the whole of the social benefit derived from the good. As a special case of this general proposition, if we assume that it costs nothing to police property rights, it follows that there exists a direct relationship between the degree to which private benefits approach social benefits and the degree to which the conveyed property rights are enforced. This relationship can be illustrated with two examples.

Given any definition of the rights that accompany ownership in an automobile, the price mechanism will ration the existing stock of automobiles. But the total private value of this stock will depend on the degree to which auto theft is reduced by our laws and police. If we pass a law *prohibiting* the arrest and prosecution of auto thieves, and also prohibiting the use of private protection devices, the bids that persons subsequently offer for the purchase of automobiles will fall below the social value of automobiles. The lower bids will result from the reduction in control that a purchaser can expect to exercise over the use of a purchased auto and, in addition, from his ability to "borrow" at no charge those autos which are purchased by others. The bids submitted after the passage of such a law will underestimate the social value of autos, for we can assume for our purposes that the usefulness of an auto remains the same whether it is used by the purchaser or by the legal thief. This is true even though the existing stock of autos is efficiently distributed among owners. The total value of autos will fall below social value and the subsequent increase in the stock of autos will be less than it should.

The lowering of bids that results from our law is similar to the lowering of bids that will take place when high police cost reduces the degree of private control that it is economical to guarantee owners. The provision of

national defense provides us with a classic example of the impact of high
police cost. Voluntarily submitted bids for defense will be lower than the
social value of defense because the bidder can count on being able to
enjoy (some of) the defense bought and also enjoyed by his fellow citizen.
The effect on bidding is similar to that which takes place in our example of
legalized auto theft except that the reason for lack of control is not merely
the absence of an appropriate law but, rather, it is the high cost of defending a purchaser from a foreign aggressor while at the same time preventing
his neighbors from enjoying protection. The cost of excluding those who
have not contracted for benefits from the enjoyment of some of these
benefits is so high that a general attitude of letting others bear the cost of
defense can be expected. Consequently, voluntarily submitted bids will
underestimate the social value of defense.

If a low-cost method is available and is used to prevent those who do
not contract for defense from benefiting from the defense bought by others, the market would reveal accurate information about the social value
of defense. Such information would be extremely useful if the market or
the planner is to allocate resources efficiently.

The institution of private property, which attempts to exclude nonpurchasers from the use of that which others have purchased, should, therefore, not be looked upon as either accidental or undesirable. On the
contrary, its existence is probably due in part to its great practicality in
revealing the social values upon which to base solutions to scarcity problems. This is precisely why we do not worry that bids for, say, candy will
fail to reveal the social value of candy. The price of candy is accurate in its
measure of social value because reflected in it is the ability of each purchaser to control the use of his purchase, whether that use be for resale or
for charity, for his children, or for his own consumption. This valuation
function is related to but distinct from the incentives to work provided by a
property system, for even in a society where work is viewed as a pleasurable activity, and, hence, where incentives to work are not needed, it
would still be necessary to properly value the varieties of alternative output that can be produced.

We have already observed that the value of what is being traded depends upon the allowed rights of action over the physical good and upon
the degree to which these rights are enforced. This statement at once
raises the question of which rights and which degrees of enforcement are
efficient. If changing the mix of property rights that accompany ownership
increases the value of property, such a change will be desirable from the
viewpoint of wealth maximizing. For example, if the problem is whether
to allow automobile owners to increase the speed at which they travel on
side streets, one could assess whether there would result an increase in the
total value of affected property. Would people be willing to pay higher
prices for automobiles? It is by no means clear that they would, for some

prospective owners may fear high speed more than they value it. And, if there would result an increase in the price of automobiles, would it be large enough to offset any increase in the cost of insuring life, limb, and home (i.e., the resulting decline in the value of other property)? If a net increase in the total value of property follows a change in the mix of rights, the change should be allowed if we seek to maximize wealth. Not to allow the change would be to refuse to generate a surplus of value sufficient to compensate those harmed by the change. The process of calculating the net change in value will, of course, involve the taking into account of side effects and this is a problem that we have already discussed. The enforcement of rights call be viewed in the same way. Indeed, we can insist that a proper definition of a right of action include the degree to which the owner or the community is allowed to enforce the right. Enforcement thus becomes the specification of additional rights and can be included in the above analytical framework. The conclusion we have reached depends, of course, upon the existence of competitive entry in the exercise of particular rights. It is therefore necessary to exclude rights which confer monopoly by restricting entry and to insist that all owners have the sane rights of action. There are some difficult problems which we do not take up here. For example, since everyone has the right to take out a patent or a copyright on "newly created" goods or ideas, does the granting of this right involve the granting of monopoly power?

It is, of course, necessary to economize on police cost, so that we will not always want to guarantee full control to the purchaser; more will be said below about this aspect of the problem. But, this aspect aside, it is essential to note that the valuation power of the institution of property is most effective when it is most *private*. It is ironic, therefore, that one of the strongest intellectual arguments for expanding the role of government has been based on the alleged necessity for eliminating exclusivity and for allowing free access to the use of certain types of resources. These resources have been given the name "public goods" and they are characterized by their alleged ability to confer benefits on additional persons without thereby reducing the benefits conferred on others. The provision of national defense is a well known example.

The Public Goods Problem

The relevance of what we have been discussing for public goods is that if the cost of policing the benefits derived from the use of these goods is low, there is an excellent reason for excluding those who do not pay from using these goods. By such exclusion we, or the market, can estimate accurately the value of diverting resources from other uses to the production of the public good. Thus, even though extending the use of an existing bridge to additional persons adds nothing to the direct cost of operating the bridge, there is good reason for charging persons for the right to cross the bridge. Excluding those who do not pay for the use of the bridge allows us to know whether a new bridge is likely to generate more benefit than it is likely to cost.[4] Why should we desire information about a new bridge if the direct marginal cost of using the existing bridge is zero? First, the bridge may depreciate with time rather than with traffic, so that the question of replacement remains relevant even though the marginal cost of use is zero. Second, there is a private marginal benefit to users of the bridge, at least in lessening their driving costs, and this benefit can be measured by pricing the use of the bridge. Such information would allow us to ascertain whether it is economic to have a new bridge closer to some persons than is the present bridge.

For some goods, air for example, the supply is so plentiful that diversion from some uses is not required to increase the intensity with which they are used elsewhere. Only where scarcity is absent is it *a priori* reasonable to charge a zero price. Superabundance is the only true *a priori* case for a zero-priced public good. All other goods are such that their provision forces us into resource allocation problems. To solve these problems efficiently, we need information which is obtained by excluding nonpurchasers, *provided that the additional information is worth more than the exchange and police costs necessitated.* In cases where the costs are greater, a zero price can be reconciled with efficiency requirements. If we must distinguish among goods, we had best do away with the "public goods" *vs.* private goods dichotomy and instead classify goods according to whether they are truly free .or economic and classify economic goods according to whether marketing costs are too high relative to the benefits of using markets and to the costs of substitute nonmarket allocation devices.

Alternative Devices

The use of taxation for the provision of scarce goods must be defended on grounds other than the usual rationale of their being public goods. As we have seen, insofar as efficiency is concerned, the fact that side benefits can be derived by nonpurchasers from the acquisition by others of these goods is inconclusive. If the planner's or the market's calculation of benefits can be improved by a small expenditure to protect or to confer property rights, the use of price rationing to measure these benefits may be justified. The problem can be viewed as that of determining the degree to which it is desirable to purchase valuation information through the competitive pricing process. A purchase of valuation information reduces the utilization of a public good below the levels that seem to be warranted by the direct cost of extending utilization. If the direct cost of, say, increasing the volume of traffic carried by an existing bridge is zero, it may nonetheless be *un*desirable to charge a zero price because of the indirect costs implied by zero pricing. These indirect costs are of two kinds.

First, and obviously, valuation information about the bridge is sacrificed. (Is not valuation information one of the most important public goods?) Second, the alternative methods of financing the building of bridges may also lead to inefficiency, especially by degrading valuation information elsewhere. This is most easily seen by supposing that an excise tax is levied on other goods to finance bridges. Such a tax will lead to inefficiently small rates of production of these other goods (assuming competitive markets). Alternatively, the levying of an income tax will inefficiently reduce the quantities of income-generating activities undertaken by those taxed. A tax on property values, even one on rent, would tend to discourage the seeking out of more valuable uses of property. A head tax would have the least effect because it is not concentrated on particular activities. Even a head tax, one could argue, would alter a person's choice of community, and, moreover, a resident who refused to pay the tax might be excluded from use of the bridge. Taxes exclude just as do prices, so that on grounds of exclusion there is not much principle to guide us. Given these indirect costs of alternative methods of financing the provision of public goods, the desirability of zero pricing is not at all clear, especially if the cost of policing is low.

For some goods, however, it must be recognized that police cost may seem too high to allow the market to generate accurate information on social benefits economically. In these cases taxation *may* be the most practical method of finance and zoning the most practical way of establishing rights, just as subsidies, excise taxes, and government nonprice rationing may be the most practical way of coping with high exchange costs. But it must be remembered that all these devices are "exclusionary" and have costs of their own. At best, they would be second-best alternatives to a market in which police and exchange costs are small and in which there is no bias in arithmetic mistakes as between civil servants and others, for these devices are not as likely to turn up correct estimates of the social values of alternative goods.

In a world in which exchange and police cost and the cost of providing alternative political devices are all zero, reliance on the political mechanism of a smoothly run democracy will result in less efficiency than will reliance on the market. Aside from problems of monopoly in government or of errors in calculation, in a one-man, one-vote democracy, where votes are not for sale, the polling place will generate information that is based on majoritarian principles rather than on maximum benefit principles. Thus, suppose some citizens prefer a stronger national defense but that a majority prefer a weaker defense. Left to a vote, the weaker defense will be our chosen policy even though the minority is willing to pay more than the additional cost required to bring defense up to the level they desire (and so, if possible, they may hire private police services). An error in the opposite direction is also possible. The majority of voters may approve of a large space effort even though they would not be able to bid high enough to acquire these resources for space in the absence of forced tax contributions. (Here, however, the minority cannot privately adjust.)

Although taxation is sometimes the most practical way of dealing with the provision of high police costs goods, there are other methods which are likely to arise in the market and which will lower the required police cost. As we have seen, extending the firm and the practice of sale-in-combination may overcome many instances of high exchange cost. These devices can also be used to reduce high police cost.

In the famous railway example, sparks from passing trains destroy some crops. The damage caused was believed to be adequate grounds for the government to take action through one or more of the political devices we have already mentioned. Direct contracting between the farmers and the railroad might take account of this side effect were it not that a bargain struck between a farmer and the railway would automatically confer benefits on all surrounding farmers by reducing spark fall-out on their land. Police costs are too high to allow benefits to be conferred on the contracting farmer without at the same time conferring them on noncontracting farmers. Therefore, it is believed that each farmer will wait for someone else to buy a reduction in spark output. (This conclusion requires two preliminary assumptions. The exchange cost of farmers getting together to submit a joint bid must be high relative to the benefits they will receive so that it is blocked by the expense it entails, and the exchange cost of their getting together to submit a joint bid must be higher than the cost of their organizing politically to lobby for antispark legislation.)

However, once the spatial aspects of the problem are admitted, we must again consider the phenomenon of differential land rent. Presumably, land rents on property adjacent to railways have been suitably depressed to allow farmers to compete with those not affected by sparks. The landowners, who find it in their interest to reduce the railroad's output of sparks, also find themselves not willing to enter into contracts through which other landowners will benefit. To some extent each would wait for the other to transact with the railway for a reduction in spark output. However, the analysis is not yet finished. The railway may realize a profit by purchasing the surrounding land at its depressed price. The purchase of a parcel of land does not confer benefits on neighbors to the same degree as would a purchase of spark curtailment so that this action would not hamper the concluding of similar contracts with other landowners as much as would the sale of a reduction in sparks. After the railroad purchases title to enough land to make it worthwhile, it could take into account the effect of its output of sparks on land values and profitably bring about an adjustment of this output to the socially optimal amount—that which maximizes the joint value of railroading and landowning. The land must, of course, be rented or resold with a contractual agreement requiring a continuance of reduced spark output. The low police cost associated with the purchase of land is substituted for the very high police cost that would be required to eliminate sparks on some land but not on other nearby land. The necessity for purchasing a reduction in spark output is obviated by substituting a purchase of land.

The extension of the firm together with the combination-sale devices that are associated with differential land rent are extremely important alternatives to government action. These devices can extend considerably the usefulness of markets for revealing and measuring the value of many side effects. The sale of land may entail much less exchange and policing cost than the direct exchange of whatever is producing the side effect. The smoke emitted from a nearby factory would, in principle, be subject to solution in the same manner. Now, of course, in many of these cases we do not observe such solutions taking place because exchange and police costs are not reduced sufficiently and because they may require too much underspecialization cost. Governmental devices, say, zoning laws, may help take account of such benefits, however inaccurately, at a lower cost (in which we should include those costs imposed by the rigidities of zoning laws). It may be, however, that both governmental and market solutions are too costly and that the most efficient alternative is not to attempt to take account of some side effects.[5]

There are other indirect devices for internalizing via combination sales. The activities of labeling, branding, and advertising allow for internalization of side effects by tying in the sale of information with other goods. Suppose persons would like their tuna boiled longer before canning. Each canner would find it in his interest to prepare the tuna more carefully except that, in a world without labels, all competitors would enjoy at no cost some of the benefits of the resulting increase in demand. Some, therefore, wait for competitors to act. Underinvestment in tuna boiling (or overinvestment in boiling tuna at home) takes place and government regulations governing canning procedures are instituted.

Suppose we allow each canner to state on the label both his name and the minimum boiling time. The name is required to establish responsibility and thereby to reduce policing cost, which is another way of saying that the cost of exercising the rights acquired by purchasers by reason of the purchase contract is reduced for the buyer. The sale of knowledge jointly with that of tuna allows the value of longer boiling to be taken into account by producers and buyers. Structural market imperfections of the monopolistic competition variety can be ruled out if both longer boiled and less boiled tuna have numerous producers. The demand for each producer's tuna will then be the going market price of the particular quality he produces.[6]

Still other institutional arrangements have been devised to combine extensions of the firm with the sale-in-combination device. Department stores and shopping plazas are organizational devices for overcoming high police cost. The owner of the department store or shopping plaza can provide a general environment that is conducive for shopping, such as pleasant plantings, escalators, and other customer services that merchants who owned their own land might hesitate to pay for, hoping instead that neighboring landowners would incur the necessary expenses from which all would benefit. The enclosing of the land into a single ownership entity which often undertakes to provide services usually provided by government from tax revenues, such as streets, sidewalks, refuse collection, and even police protection, allows the owner to exclude those who refuse to pay rentals which cover the cost of these services. The competition of various plazas and department stores will provide ample opportunity for merchants to select the services that they wish to buy without fearing or counting on free-loading. Apartment buildings can also be viewed in the same light, and especially the modern apartment building which combines office and recreational space with living space. The development of these institutional arrangements provides an interesting challenge to political institutions for the provision of many of the services generally presumed to be within the scope of the polling place.

The preceding discussion has taken as given the state of technical arts. The levels of exchange and police costs that are required for effective marketing and the costs of government substitute services depend on how well we master the technology of operating markets and governments. Attention is sometimes called to the fact that emerging technical developments will make the use of markets or governments more economic than they now are. There are surely many instances where this is true. However, our analysis suggests that technological developments can operate in the opposite direction. At the same time that technology is reducing the cost of using these alternative institutional arrangements for economizing, it is also reducing the cost of constructing parking spaces, of developing fire-resistant corn, and of mass producing automobiles. Whether or not it pays to increase the extent to which we exchange via markets, protect private property rights, or use alternative government devices depends on how much we will thereby reduce production cost and crop damage. Markets or their government alternatives should come into greater prominence only if technical developments lower the costs of these institutional arrangements more than they reduce the costs of producing parking spaces and cars and the cost of crop damage.

Essentially, we have argued in this paper that there exist no qualitative differences between side effects and what we may call "primary" effects. The only differences are those that are implicitly based on quantitative differences in exchange and police cost. Suppose a factory invents a new more efficient furnace which can burn a cheaper grade of coal than can existing furnaces. The burning of cheap coal, we will assume, dirties homes in the neighborhood. We label this effect as side or neighborhood or external, but its real economic implication is to reduce the wealth of nearby homeowners. If this same factory, by virtue of its new furnace, successfully forces a nearby competing firm out of business, and if the resulting decline in demand for housing reduces the wealth of neighborhood homeowners, we do not become concerned. Why the difference in our attitudes toward these two situations which have the same effect on homeowners?

The decline in wealth which results from the fall in demand for housing is more than offset by an increase in wealth elsewhere. This increase accrues primarily to other homeowners and to persons purchasing the lower priced product produced by the factory. We accept the reallocation, I conjecture, because we feel that the existence of a smoothly operating market will ensure that wealth is maximized. In the smoke case, exchange and police costs are high relative to the benefits of marketing smoke and, therefore, we do not have an existing market to rely on for the reallocation, although a potential one always stands ready. If the costs of exchanging and policing smoke contracts were zero (and if the cost of exchanging houses were zero) there would be no reason for distinguishing between the two cases insofar as "remedial" action is concerned. We have already argued that the most efficient arrangement may, in fact, require that nothing be done to prohibit smoke and we will not go into these matters again. Our present purpose is merely to emphasize that there is nothing special or qualitatively different about any of these effects, including the effects which stem from what we ineptly call public goods, and that any special treatment accorded to them cannot be justified merely by observing their presence.

NOTES

This article, first published in *Journal of Law and Economics* 7 (1964): 11–26, is reprinted by permission of the author and the University of Chicago Press. The author wishes to thank Armen A. Alchian, Gary S. Becker, William H. Meckling, Peter Pashigian, and George J. Stigler for their comments.

1. Coase, "The Problem of Social Cost," 3 *J. Law & Econ.*, 1–44 (1960).

2. *Cf.* Arrow, "Uncertainty and the Welfare Economics of Medical Care," 53 *Am. Econ. Rev.,* 944–45 (1963):

> An individual who fails to be immunized not only risks his own health, a disutility which presumably he has weighed against the utility of avoiding the procedure, but also that of others. In an ideal price system, there would be a price which he would have to pay to anyone whose health is endangered, a price sufficiently high so that the others would feel compensated; or, alternatively, there would be a price which would be paid to him by others to induce him to undergo the immunization procedure. . . . It is, of course, not hard to see that such price system could not, in fact, be practical; to approximate an optimal state it would be necessary to have collective intervention in the form of subsidy or tax or compulsion.

and Bator, "The Anatomy of Market Failure," 72 *Q. J. Econ.,* 351, 353–54 (1958):

> Pareto-efficient . . . points . . . are characterized by a complete set of marginal-rate-of-substitution . . . equalities (or limiting inequalities) which, in turn, yield a set of price-like constants. Where no such constants exist, reference will be to *failure of existence* [of prices, and hence, of efficiency]. [Parenthetical phrase added.]

3. The existence of unique locations does not necessarily imply the inefficiency usually associated with monopolistic competition. *Cf.* Demsetz, "The Welfare and Empirical Implications of Monopolistic Competition," 74 *Economic J.* 623–41 (1964). It should also be noted that if the landowners could know of the differential land rents that would result from the superior technology offered by free parking, they would be inclined to enter into an agreement sharing the differential rent accruing to land adjacent to the shopping plaza. If they did not enter into such an agreement there would be an inclination to let the free parking facility be built on the other man's property.

4. See Coase, "The Marginal Cost Controversy," 13 *Economica,* 169–82 (1946), for an early application of this point in reference to the use of multipart pricing in natural monopoly situations. See also Minasian, "Television Pricing and the Theory of Public Goods," 7 *J. Law & Econ.,* 71 (1964).

5. The ability of combination sales to take account of side benefits depends on how closely the value of the tied-in good reflects the value of the public good. There is a direct and exact correspondence between the value of land and the (negative to farmers) value of spark output. A less exact correspondence between the values of the tied goods, while not a perfect device, can nonetheless be useful for taking account of the value of public goods.

Even the stubborn classic case of providing for the national defense is amenable to some usable tie-in arrangements. The provision of defense again presents us with a situation in which it is in the interest of a beneficiary to let others buy defense since he will benefit from their purchases. Suppose, however, that instead of financing defense with taxes, the government resorts to the sale of insurance to citizens which covers their lives and property in the event of loss arising from war. The tied goods, insurance and defense, are substitutes, but they do not fully correspond in value fluctuations. For a stated premium per thousand dollars of insurance and a stated maximum, citizens would buy more insurance the more likely they thought war and the less able they thought our defense. Those having more at stake would buy more insurance. The premiums could then be used to finance the defense establishment. The side effect is not fully captured, however, because your purchase of insurance, although it fully internalizes your losses in the event of war, also decreases the likelihood of war, and, hence, reduces the amount of insurance others would volunteer to buy. This smaller remaining public aspect of the good could be accounted for by offering the insurance for premiums that are believed to be subsidized.

War, as well as other events, can topple governments, so that to make the insurance credible, the government might need to offer citizens the option of canceling their insurance and receiving all or some of the premiums they have paid. This cancellation option need be effective only up to the date before a war starts. The insurance device is not without dangers. By raising the maximum purchasable insurance (and lowering premiums), the government could induce a more aggressive attitude among the citizens than is warranted by actuarial fair insurance.

6. It is not really necessary for efficiency to obtain to require that producers take the product price as given and beyond their control. See Demsetz, op. cit. note 3 above.

11 Public Goods, Property Rights, and Political Organizations

Duncan Snidal

ONE OF THE CONCEPTS central to the study of the development and performance of international institutions is that of a "collective" or "public" good. Unfortunately, much of the research on this concept has been severely hampered by the uncritical acceptance of a narrow, economistic definition of the term. This definition may be satisfactory for the analysis of market phenomena, but it is unsatisfactory for the analysis of political issues. At a superficial level this problem is evidenced by unrealistic assumptions about transaction and exclusion costs in the market setting; but at a deeper level, it requires an understanding of how political factors affect the nature and publicness of goods. Therefore, it is important to examine and clarify the use of public goods terminology as it applies to political questions.

The terminology of public goods was developed in the economics tradition by Samuelson (1954) and has been expanded upon and revised by economists such as Head (1962) and Buchanan (1968). Olson (1965) can be given primary credit for the introduction of the concept into political science and sociology. Subsequently, there has been a proliferation of public goods analyses in all areas of political science, but particularly in the international relations literature (Burgess and Robinson, 1969; Frolich et al., 1971; Olson and Zeckhauser, 1966; Pryor, 1969; Ruggie, 1972; Russett, 1970; Russett and Sullivan, 1971; Snidal, 1979; Wagner, 1975).

Public goods are defined by two factors which distinguish them from private goods: (1) They are "joint in supply," so that consumption by one person does not diminish the amount available to others. (2) They are "nonexclusive," so that if the good is available to one person then it is automatically available to all others. The concern of the first two sections of this article is to clarify these properties as a step toward a better understanding of the relation of political arrangements to public goods developed later in the article. This is necessary because confusion has arisen from application of the concept to instances that do not approximate its two required conditions and, especially, from the attempt to force political phenomena into a definition designed for economic analysis. This is particularly true in applications to international politics, where political regimes differ dramatically from those of the market economy.

Thus, the goal of this article is not to arrive at a "true" or "correct" definition of public goods, but rather to indicate problems in applying the narrow economic interpretation and to point out useful directions for political public goods analysis. To this end a set of "clarifications" about public goods is presented. These serve to illuminate the key role of political factors in analyzing the two main problems of public goods provision. The first problem is that if one person purchases a public good for personal consumption, others also will be able to consume the good and thus take a "free ride" off this provision. This is often referred to as a form of "exploitation" and raises the issue of "fair distribution" of costs. Closely related to this is the second problem of suboptimal provision of the good. The possibility for a free ride gives consumers an incentive to misrepresent their own preferences for the public good in the hope that others will pay for its provision instead. This results in lower levels of production than are optimal from a societal viewpoint. The third and fourth sections of this article deal critically with the ill-defined problems of optimality and exploitation in terms of the role of political mechanisms of property rights and exclusion.

The concept of the *quasi-public good* (where exclusion mechanisms are imposed on a public good) is introduced in the final section in order to properly address the crucial role of (political) organizations in public goods provision. The discussion suggests that at the international level the lack of strong institutions and authority structures makes the provision of public goods (such as security or environmental quality) very difficult. Understanding these problems requires more than just an analysis of the "good" itself, but also an analysis of the broader political framework—including such factors as power relations, international organizations, interdependencies, and the like. Conversely, to understand fully the impact of international political institutions, we must appreciate the relationship of political organizations to public goods problems.

I. Jointness of Supply

Jointness of supply (nonrivalness) is the condition where, given a level of physical production, consumption by one person does not thereby diminish the supply of the good potentially available for consumption by others. Standard examples include national defense and lighthouses, provided that in the first instance one citizen's defense does not diminish the amount of defense provided to another, and in the second instance one ship's use of the lighthouse does not impede its use by another ship. Analytically counterpoised to this is the pure private good where one person's consumption diminishes the amount available to others by just the amount of his consumption (e.g., my slice of pie is exactly one less slice available to others). Around these "ideal types" lies a continuum of shades and degrees of jointness of supply. However, *it is in terms of these ideal types that we offer the following clarifications.*

Clarification I.1: Jointness of supply requires that we distinguish two variable properties: (1) physical quantities of the good being consumed and (2) the number of people consuming each unit.

Actual total consumption depends on the total physical quantity available, the number of consumers per unit, and some function—call it the "nature of the good"—relating the two together. Thus for any good there are two marginal costs of relevance: (1) *a marginal cost of production* (MC_{prod}), which is the cost to produce one additional physical unit of the good and (2) *a marginal cost of extension* (MC_{ext}), which is the cost of extending consumption of a given unit of the good to an additional consumer. The meaning of jointness of supply is that this second type of cost, MC_{ext}, is equal to zero.[1]

Clarification I.2: Public goods do not subsume all considerations of one party of consumption done by another party.

Extension of a good requires that it is the good itself and not some by-product that is extended. We need to distinguish "joint satisfaction," where consumption by one person provides satisfaction to another, from "joint consumption," where the same unit of good enters each utility function separately and directly. Neither altruistic pleasure in others' well-being nor perceptual effects such as "keeping up with the Joneses" are appropriately dealt with under the rubric of public goods.

Clarification I.3: Pure public goods do not have capacity constraints vis-à-vis consumers. Once produced they present no rationing problem since MC_{ext} remains zero regardless of how widely benefits are distributed.[2]

Even common examples of public goods only approximate this ideal condition. We have suggested that national defense has a near-zero MC_{ext}, but there are qualifications to this since extra expense is undoubtedly involved in protecting either citizens living abroad or other geographic domains. Similarly, inoculation of one person provides partial protection against disease to others living nearby, but is likely not to be fully joint in supply since others probably do not get as much protection as they would by being inoculated themselves. This jointness also extends only to people who are in close contact with the inoculated individual. Clearly, few goods are purely joint in supply and most goods lie on a continuum between public and private. (Again, it is to be emphasized that our discussion concentrates on the ideal type of a public good and that actual empirical instances will usefully be analyzed as if they were pure public goods, even though they deviate somewhat from the strict definition.)

Clarification I.4: Public goods are not the same as free goods.

Free goods exist in amounts so vast that the available natural supply exceeds demand so that additional consumers may partake in private consumption at no extra cost by drawing upon this excess supply. Often these appear as unpriced factors of production such as oil reserves, road space, or fishing grounds. However, the nonpublic nature of most free goods has been highlighted in recent environmental crises where this natural supply has been threatened. Sales of bottled water and even clean air (Tokyo) demonstrate the essentially private nature of these goods once scarcity is introduced. ;

Clarification I.5: Jointness in supply is not equivalent to increasing returns to scale (decreasing costs).

Decreasing costs are defined across production units by the condition of a falling MC_{prod} as production increases. Jointness refers to units of consumption with the defining characteristic $MC_{ext} = 0$ and is independent of any changes in MC_{prod}. Rapidly falling production costs may make it appear as if the good is joint in supply, but the two cases are analytically distinct. Even in the extreme case where MC_{prod} approaches zero, we would not properly refer to the good as public, but rather as free beyond some initial threshold level of production.[3]

Clarification I.6: "Lumpiness" is not the same as jointness.

Closely related to increasing returns to scale are problems of lumpiness or indivisibility. Although the basic units of production (e.g., hospital beds or theater seats) may be completely rival in character, actual production occurs in blocks so that production of the good for one person necessarily entails production sufficient for several. Members of this class of goods— which have high fixed costs but low or nonexistent MC_{prod} over some range—are frequently confused with public goods. To the extent that they have capacity constraints vis-à-vis consumers, they are not appropriately dealt with as public goods.[4]

Clarification I.7: Jointness is to be distinguished from excess capacity. Bearing upon this, we must avoid misinterpreting private goods as public goods by viewing them through time.[5]

For example, a group of farmers may own a tractor and agree to use it on a rotating schedule. If there is no conflict over which day each wishes to use it and each will have the tractor for a sufficient length of time, then there might seem to be a public element present. But such an interpretation confuses excess capacity with $MC_{ext} = 0$. Once the tractor is purchased (i.e., given some quantity of "tractor work" to be consumed), it can be used "publicly" up to its capacity constraints (i.e., by only one farmer at a time and no more than 24 hours a day). If desired usage passes through either of these capacity constraints and more people try to consume it than there are physical units to be consumed, then, rather than jointness in supply, there is complete rivalness in supply. Goods do not become joint in supply simply by being shared over time.

Clarification I.8: Public goods exhibit jointness in supply but should not be confused with joint goods.

Joint goods exist whenever the production of two or more outputs is technologically interdependent.[6] They may be either public or private and are joint over production, whereas public goods are joint over people. The distinction is made more apparent when we remember that although public goods provide a problem for achieving optimal provision, this is not true for joint goods where retrading ensures adjustment to optimality (Samuelson, 1969). Of course, public goods may also be joint goods, but the two terms are analytically distinct. The term "joint good" refers to a production process, while "jointness in supply" refers to a technology of consumption.

II. Nonexclusiveness Versus Noncontrol over Exclusion

The second standard property of public goods is the property of *nonexclusiveness: if the good is available to one person, then it is available to all others.* This property is often phrased in terms of availability to members of a particular group. But this begs the question, so that rather than nonexclusiveness we have a situation where the group itself defines limits for the exclusiveness of the good. This and related points need clarification because the notion of exclusion is central to understanding the political aspects of public goods analysis.

Clarification II.1: Nonexclusiveness implies jointness and is both a necessary and sufficient condition for a public good; jointness is a necessary but not sufficient condition for a public good.

Olson (1965: 14) maintains that the definition of public goods entails only nonexclusiveness and not jointness of supply. Head (1962: 209–211) argues that both characteristics are required and that they are logically distinct. Both of these positions are logically inconsistent. If a good is not joint in supply, then A's consumption must reduce the amount available to B. If so, then B necessarily has been excluded from this amount of the good (i.e., it is not available to B). Therefore, A cannot be allowed to consume the good if the property of nonexclusiveness is to be maintained. In effect, if there is no jointness of supply then nonexclusiveness implies no consumption of the good.[7] Thus nonexclusiveness is a sufficient definition for a public good and embodies the characteristic of jointness which is a necessary but not sufficient condition.[8]

Clarification II.2: Nonexclusiveness and the inability to control exclusion (i.e., noncontrol over exclusion) are conceptually distinct.

Peston (1972: 13) suggests as an example of a rival nonexcludable good (which is logically impossible by Clarification II.1) the case of a beekeeper who is unable to control which of his flower-growing neighbors will receive the fertilizing benefits of his bees. This does not mean that exclusion does not take place. Every flower of flower grower X's crop that a bee fertilizes means one less of Y's flowers will be attended. Similarly, if private goods were distributed by a random lottery system, we would not therefore conclude that private goods were nonexclusive, but only that we had no control over the process of exclusion.[9]

Nonexclusiveness also does not include the case where individuals cannot be denied their share of a private good. This difference seems straightforward but has been confused in the literature. Olson (1965: 31) ascribes as nonexclusive the case in which landlord and tenant share the produce of a farm in some fixed ratio.[10] The "nonexclusion" presumably arises because each respects the other's right to a share. But clearly this is not a situation of nonexclusion, since what the farmer receives the landlord does not and vice versa. Similar problems arise whenever scholars fail to discriminate between all individuals consuming the same amount of the good (which can happen for purely private goods) and consumption of the same units of the good.

Clarification II.3: Not all externalities are public goods.

Many examples of externalities (i.e., of one person's behavior affecting another's well-being) are problems of inadequate control over exclusion (e.g., straying cattle eating a farmer's crop) and involve no jointness. Others involve interdependence of utility functions (see Clarification I.2) and are not properly treated as public goods.[11]

Clarification II.4: Gains from a cooperative arrangement do not imply that the goods covered by the arrangement are public.

Both the externality issue and the sharing arrangement are examples of cooperative arrangements involving purely private goods. Perhaps the best illustration of this is the neoclassical marketplace, which ideally is an arrangement resulting in benefits to all participants but which is essentially a forum for private goods. The standard game-theoretic examples of positive sum games or Prisoner's Dilemma are comparable cases where player cooperation results in benefits to all parties but no public goods need be involved. Many so-called "free-rider" situations are of this sort.[12]

> Clarification II.5: Nonexclusiveness, as used in describing public goods, is a function both of a good's level of jointness and of the extent of noncontrol over its exclusion. The social context of a good is vital in determining the extent of noncontrol.

We have already seen that jointness is a prerequisite for nonexclusiveness (Clarification II.1). But while nonexclusiveness also requires noncontrol over exclusion, we have seen that this latter condition may hold for goods not having jointness (Clarification II.2). *Public goods can be characterized by the conjunction of jointness in supply with noncontrol over exclusion.* These two characteristics are analytically distinct.[13]

Noncontrol over exclusion can be defined in terms of MC_{exclus}, *the cost of excluding an individual from consumption of the good.* As MC_{exclus} ranges from zero to infinity, it moves from perfect control to complete noncontrol over exclusion. The level of MC_{exclus} will depend partly on the physical properties of the good itself (e.g., a car is easier to steal than a house). However, the social context of a good (i.e., the structure of societies, governments, and property rights) is far more important in establishing and maintaining the ownership (e.g., protection of property is greatly facilitated by a strong police force and enforced laws).

Now we can fully illustrate the relationship between public and private goods (fig. 9). The ideal-type public good is defined by $MC_{ext} = 0$ and $MC_{exclus} = \infty$; pure private goods are defined by $MC_{ext} = \infty$ and $MC_{exclus} = 0$. However, more practical definitions can be achieved in terms of MC_{prod}. If MC_{ext} exceeds MC_{prod}, then attempts to extend goods are counterproductive (i.e., entail a net loss in units of total consumption). Therefore all provision in this range will be in terms of private consumption. Similarly, if MC_{exclus} exceeds MC_{prod}, then no attempt will be made to exert exclusion over the good since control over exclusion is more costly than provision of the units themselves. Therefore all production in this range will be in terms of public provision. These two zones are represented by the northwest and southeast quadrants of figure 9, respectively. In the northeast quadrant (where $MC_{prod} < MC_{ext}$ and $MC_{prod} > MC_{exclus}$) attempts to both control exclusion and extend consumption units are counterproductive, and production is unlikely to occur in this range.[14] The southwest quadrant thus contains "mixed goods," which have varying degrees of public and private good properties.

Finally, we should note the special problems of putting free goods and

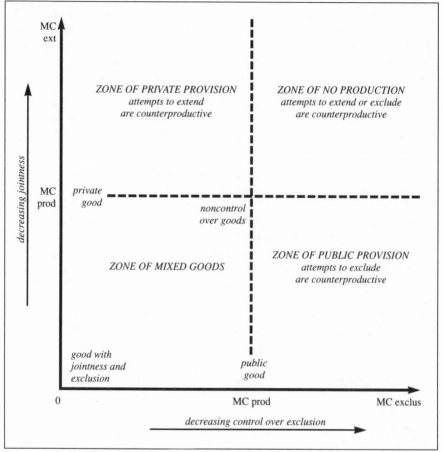

FIGURE 9.   The Relationship of Public and Private Goods

lumpy goods into this schema. Free goods represent the limiting case as MC_{prod} approaches zero. As this occurs the MC_{prod} lines approach the origin and all points move into the northeast quadrant. The situation thus becomes one of neither public nor private goods. The good will not be produced, although it will occur by virtue of natural supply. With lumpy goods MC_{prod} will appear to be very low as long as there is excess capacity, but very high once this excess is exhausted. In this case the discontinuous nature of MC_{prod} makes categorization by marginal properties inappropriate without reference to the level of capacity utilization.

Perhaps it would be wise to reiterate the basic distinction indicated by the title of this section: *Nonexclusiveness is different from noncontrol over exclusion.* Nonexclusiveness fully describes public goods and entails both jointness and noncontrol over exclusion. Noncontrol over exclusion (measured by MC_{exclus}) is a dimension which is logically independent of jointness and is the aspect of public goods which makes them of interest for political analysis, since many political phenomena can be explained in terms of the use of exclusion to achieve goals.

III. Jointness, Exclusion, and Optimality

We have now recast the definition of a public good in terms of jointness in supply and noncontrol over exclusion. It is now appropriate to determine if any goods fit these conditions. Jointness in supply is a necessary technological characteristic, whereas, given a level of jointness, the extent of noncontrol over exclusion is largely a function of social institutions in interaction with technological features. Generally, we might observe that greater degrees of publicness are often associated with less substantial physical manifestations of the good (e.g., "ideas" and "light-beams" are easier to extend and harder to restrict in consumption than cars or sheep). But very few goods are pure public goods. Ideas and their various manifestations (songs, scientific formulas, technology) seem to be very close, but patent and copyright laws are designed to add an element of control over exclusion to them and, hence, make them more like private goods. Shipping lanes, lighthouse beams, or TV signals seem to display extreme publicness. But techniques ranging from demands for tribute by Barbary Coast pirates to ship licenses to cable television reveal our ingenuity in assigning property rights and achieving some degree of exclusion.[15]

The notion of control over exclusion is fundamental to an understanding of public and private goods and may be discussed under the heading of property rights. *Property rights denote the existence of some system of mechanisms which serves to permit exclusion of goods and uniquely to determine the beneficiaries of (and losers from) that exclusion.* While one sometimes loses sight of these mechanisms in complex societies so that property seems more a result of shared values and tacit understanding ("That bicycle is Johnny's"), the mechanisms themselves usually lurk not too far in the background ("If Tommy doesn't return Johnny's bike, then Johnny will beat him up, and if that fails, Johnny will phone the police"). The examples in the preceding paragraph illustrate the variety of techniques available to establish exclusion. The Barbary Coast pirates demonstrate how this may be done by overt coercion. Patent rights are granted under the auspices of a much more sophisticated network of authority. Cable television is an interesting example in which the producer establishes property rights by changing the nature of the good itself from one where exclusion is difficult (i.e., transmission through the air) to one where exclusion is feasible (i.e., transmission through cables). Needless to say, there are innumerable other techniques by which property rights can be established.

Clarification III.1: Goods that are not joint in supply do not necessarily have $MC_{exclus} = 0$ (i.e., perfect property rights) and, indeed, exclusion may even be quite costly. Furthermore, price exclusion is possible only insofar as there exists an authority system to enforce it.

Whenever a good is not joint in supply, it must have some exclusive characteristics. (This follows as a direct result of the contrapositive formulation of Clarification II.1.) However, this exclusiveness implies only that each physical unit may have only one consumer and does not imply any unique determination of beneficiaries as is inherent in the notion of property rights (Clarification II.2).

So-called "private goods" analysis tends to ignore this distinction and assumes that perfect property rights exist so that $MC_{exclus} = 0$. However, as long as a good has not been consumed and remains of economic interest, then it is likely to have some exclusion costs associated with it. Vast resources are spent both to assert property claims (through devices ranging from labels to fences to armies) and punish violators of such rights (e.g., courts, prisons, and wars). In reality, neither the market nor prices are exclusionary devices. No thief was ever prevented from stealing something because its price was too high. (Indeed, higher prices may encourage theft.) Control over exclusion is only achieved through a system of property rights, and instead of price exclusion we should more appropriately speak of price inclusion: pricing as a criterion for inclusion in the consumption of a good through the (re)assignment of property rights.

Clarification III.2: Considerations of economic efficiency require explicit treatment of exclusion costs.

The standard Pareto-efficient private goods model deals with an abstraction where there are no costs of exclusion. In this imaginary world there are no locks, no police, and no prisons. At an absurd extreme we can see that crime itself is not Pareto optimal: Any world with crime can be bettered by a system in which stolen goods are simply redistributed to thieves and the savings in transaction costs (of crime and police) distributed in some manner among members of a society. Of course, in a more realistic world, such a regime would induce citizens to become criminals (or at least to misrepresent themselves as criminals), discourage production, and quickly reveal the sham of optimality. Although this example is an extreme case, we can see that completely ignoring the issue of exclusion gives optimality conditions for private goods that do not always reflect all of their costs.[16] But it is this very problem of imperfect property rights that is a key factor in making optimality impossible to achieve for public goods, in light of their jointness in supply. This suggests that the issue of optimality is not as different for the two types of goods as has been suggested.

> Clarification III.3: Viewed simply as a static allocation problem, any restriction on the distribution of goods having jointness in supply that serves to restrict the extent of distribution of already produced units of those goods is suboptimal.

This follows from the standard marginal conditions for optimality in markets. Whenever $MC_{ext} = 0$, then, if there exist any potential consumers who have positive evaluation for the good, optimality requires that the good be extended to them. Thus the Barbary Coast pirates are responsible for an economic inefficiency if the tribute they demand exceeds the value that a merchant places upon shipping goods through the waters. Ironically, if the pirates are perfectly discriminating monopolists who have knowledge of the preference functions of all shippers, then they could maximize their plunder while society as a whole simultaneously achieved a Pareto-optimal position. In the absence of such an imaginary centralized pricing system, any restriction on the distribution of already produced goods that are joint in supply is inefficient if it reduces consumption.

> Clarification III.4: For pure public goods the suboptimality problem is one of production and not distribution.

By definition, pure public goods have no restriction on their distribution and so fulfill the criterion of optimality in distribution (Clarification III.3). But it is a lack of exclusion which makes production of pure public goods infeasible for the profit-maximizing entrepreneur. Consumers have no incentive to pay to receive the good since they cannot be prevented from consuming it once it has been produced. Nor can they be properly induced to contribute to its production since the incentives point toward a "free ride" on the contributions of others.[17] This is the deficiency of the Samuelsonian condition of optimality which requires that once the good is produced it be extended freely to all consumers. Such a criterion fails to shed light on problems of resource allocation in getting the good provided. It tells how to ration a given output, but not how much total output to produce.

One way to achieve this optimal production would be to establish property rights over the good and provide it only to consumers prepared to pay an amount equal to their marginal evaluation of the good. Of course this requires heroic assumptions beyond just the establishment of property rights (i.e., that consumers do not conceal their true evaluation schedules for the good), but suggests that, in principle, property rights may be used to achieve a closer-to-optimal level of provision. In any event, the advent of property rights strengthens the bargaining power of producers vis-à-vis potential consumers. Now consumers who lie and maintain that they receive no benefit from the good (when in fact they really do) in order to avoid paying a share of the costs of production can easily be excluded from the good entirely. This danger of being totally excluded will encourage consumers to reveal more of their true preferences and contribute toward the cost of providing the good.

> Clarification III.5: Viewed as a dynamic production problem rather than just a static allocation problem, exclusion is not suboptimal for goods having jointness in supply.

Optimality implies some notion of the best possible state. Yet we must be careful to distinguish "possible" from "imaginable." The former term considers optimality in the context of resource and other constraints, whereas the latter deals in an ideal world where constraints seem to be eliminated by assumption. In standard "private goods" analysis we encounter this problem whenever we ignore the costs of exclusion (Clarification III.2).

In evaluating public goods optimality we are often deceived by gauging it against the situation in which all people reveal preferences and none cheats, rather than dealing with it in the context of how people really act (i.e., by including things like cheating or strategic bargaining as factors in the optimization problem). Viewed in this latter perspective, it is clear that the possibility for exclusion often increases optimality qua the best possible world.   ·

> Clarification III.6: Exclusionary devices that do not impede jointness are preferable to ones that do.

Optimality requires taking maximum possible advantage of any jointness in supply (i.e., the static distribution condition) consistent with exercising sufficient exclusion to encourage contributions toward costs of provision (i.e., the dynamic production condition). For a given level of exclusion, more jointness always allows the achievement of just as good a position and sometimes a better one (e.g., everyone who was previously induced to pay can still be induced to do so, in addition to a few of the new potential recipients). Thus it is preferable to have methods of exclusion that do not impede jointness. Cable transmission fails to meet this criterion because of the nonzero MC_{ext} involved in running cables to additional homes. Patents and copyrights are examples in which exclusion is imposed on goods without reducing jointness.

> Clarification III.7: Many so-called "public goods" problems are really cases where it is desirable to decrease exclusion on goods having jointness.

Whenever we have a good that is joint in supply and excludable (i.e., goods in the southwest corner of figure 9), there are strong incentives to take advantage of $MC_{ext} = 0$ by expanding the range of beneficiaries while simultaneously spreading the costs of production over a larger group. Defense alliances are an example of this (at least with respect to deterrence), since there are very low costs in protecting another ally but it is nevertheless often possible to exclude other countries. Viewed in a historical perspective, national defense reflects a very similar situation. The realization that the same army necessary to protect each of several units could provide nearly the same level of protection to the larger unit provides at least one incentive for the amalgamation of smaller territories into larger units. Over time this separability of units has been lost as the amalgamation of territories into single political units has solidified so that the exclusion property has been lost, and the good is nearly public within the boundaries of the state.

> Clarification III.8: Even when there is no control over exclusion of the good itself, a central agency capable of charging consumers for provision of the good can lead to more optimal provision of public goods.

For example, a national government is essentially incapable of discriminating among its citizens in providing defense. However, it also has the mechanism of tax collection to "force" all citizens to share in defense expenditure—though this mechanism is not necessarily tied to defense provision and money raised could be used for totally different purposes. But if this central assessing agency is able to charge consumers for approximately the defense benefits they receive, then this is likely to lead to a more optimal situation than if the good were not provided. Inaccuracy in the mechanism will detract from this optimality but may still provide for the achievement of a better position than without central involvement. Provision of this sort occurs when a nucleus group, organized to provide a good, agrees on a method of charging for it and establishes a way to enforce payment on all members of the group. The recent economic literature on "demand revealing processes" involves the use of such a mechanism (Groves and Ledyard, 1977a). It assumes the existence of a government able to allocate and enforce payment for the provision of public goods. Although consumers can misrepresent their preferences, they cannot evade paying some share of the costs associated with the public good. Many government services are implicitly provided on this rationale, although the schemes used to allocate costs are neither as accurate nor as elaborate as those proposed by the economists. The public good may be a governmental program, the group may include all the citizens of the nation, and the payment mechanism may be enforced through the tax system. Of course, many of the "groups" are so institutionalized as governments, alliances, or other organizations that provision and payment for the public good are greatly separated from the original establishment of the group itself.

Clarification III.9: Provision of and assessment for public goods by a central agency will necessarily involve issues of income distribution.

As the group becomes increasingly institutionalized, the connection between payments for and benefits from public goods may become increasingly tenuous. For example, taxes for defense may be based on income and wealth and only incidentally bear relation to the value that citizens place on defense. In such circumstances the proportion of costs borne by various consumers will bear little resemblance to benefits received. Pacifists will end up paying to support the army and pyromaniacs the fire department. Thus, in effect, the central assessing agency is likely to cause a redistribution of income between members of society, rather than merely an increase in income for all by moving provision of public goods to more optimal levels. This has been a problem even in the complicated mechanisms proposed in the "demand revealing processes" literature (Groves and Ledyard, 1977b). However, public goods provision also faces problems of "fair" distribution of costs and benefits at a more mundane level. In the next section we shall examine the problems of allocating costs even when there exists a perfect connection among individual preferences, the technology of production, and the mechanisms for assessing costs. Then we will return to the role of groups in public goods provision.

IV. Property Rights as Determinants of Income Distribution

A major concern has been the issue of "fairness" of sharing costs in public goods provision. However, conclusions such as "the small exploit the large" have been derived without an explicit statement of the normative model upon which the claim is based (Olson and Zeckhauser, 1966). Rather than attempt to impose such a model on the literature, we will instead focus upon the role of property rights in allocating gains to and costs of the provision of goods. This will reveal the inappropriateness of most of the "analytical" conclusions on "fairness" that have appeared.

Clarification IV.1: For private goods, different distributions of property rights will result in different distributions of gains from cooperative behavior, but the level of optimal production will be unaffected.[18]

Coase (1960) presents an interesting example in which one firm is engaged in an activity that is damaging to another firm. In figure 10, let E_1 and E_2 be the marginal evaluation schedules for the two firms respectively. Marginal considerations tell us that the optimal end result is at Q^*, since at any point to the right (left) of this, the second (first) firm would lose more from each marginal increase (decrease) in activity than the first (second) firm would gain. It would thus be prepared to pay compensation to reduce (increase) the level of activity.

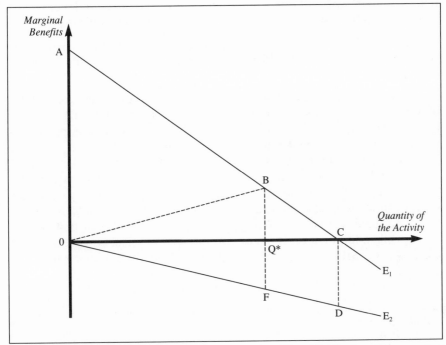

FIGURE 10.   Private Good Case—Property Rights Affect Distribution of Income but Not Level of Production

Following Coase, suppose that the first firm is legally allowed (i.e., has the property rights) to perform the activity at level C without restrictions. It would then be in firm two's interest to pay firm one to cut back its level of operation to Q^*. The minimum necessary compensation will be area BCQ^*, but if firm one bargains well it may get compensation of up to area $CDFQ^*$ and hence appropriate all the gains of cooperation. Firm two will lose at least area $OFQ^* + BCQ^*$ and perhaps as much as ODC. The precise distribution within this range is not determinate and would depend on the bargaining process employed.

If we reverse the property rights so that firm two has the right to ban the activity, then a very different distribution of income would result. Firm two would insist on at least breaking even or else would ban the activity. Efficient bargaining would again lead to production at Q^* as firm one would compensate firm two by an amount of at least $OQ^*F (=OQ^*B)$ to let it perform the activity. Area AOB would be divided in some manner between the firms as profit from reaching an agreement. The exact result is again indeterminate, but we can see that a drastic shift in the distribution of benefits has taken place. However, we cannot assess either situation as "unfair" without first stipulating a prior normative model of what a "just" distribution of property rights over this activity would be.

Clarification IV.2: For goods that are joint in supply, different property rights regimes will result in both different distributions of income and different levels of production.

Consider a group where members have agreed to provide a good that is joint in supply and to share costs according to some formula. The alternative property regimes we consider depend on whether the group can successfully exclude noncontributors (i.e., nonmembers) from enjoying the good. In figure 11 let E_g be the marginal evaluation curve for the group as a whole and let E_{fr} be the marginal evaluation curve for some nonmember of the group (FR) who will try to be a free rider, but who may become a paying group member if no free ride is available. Then E_{g+fr} is the sum of these marginal evaluations. MC_{prod} is the cost of additional units of the good, while additional units of consumption per physical unit are assumed costless (i.e., $MC_{ext} = 0$). Position Q_1 represents the optimal amount of

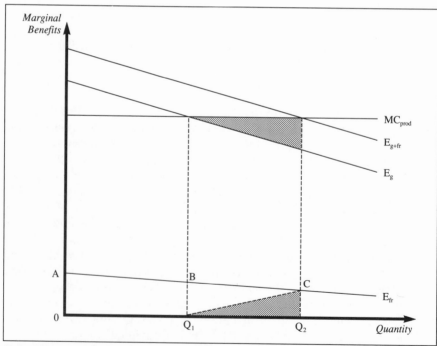

FIGURE 11.   Private Good Case—Property Rights Affect Both Distribution of Income and Level of Production

production for the group in isolation while Q_2 is optimal if FR is also taken into account.

If the group can exert no property rights over the good vis-à-vis FR, then FR will take a free ride and receive benefits equal to area OQ_1BA as a "gift" from the group. Of course, if the group can exert no property rights over the good vis-à-vis FR, then this may also be the case with respect to its own membership. This is the pure public good problem in which all individuals will try to "free ride" and none will contribute toward provision. However, a more realistic model would probably assume that there are some individuals who can receive benefits through a free ride but others who can be excluded if they attempt this. The "small exploiting the large" hypothesis probably fits this case to the extent that defense is a public good between nations. For example, small countries like Belgium and the Netherlands are geographically located so that it is hard to exclude them from NATO defense benefits if Germany and France are defended. Furthermore, the relative level of defense spending by larger alliance members has greater impact for the alliance as a whole than does that of smaller countries. Thus the alliance has further incentives to enforce contributions by the larger members. Finally, larger countries are more likely to experience private side-benefits from defense spending, and thus will spend more on defense for internal reasons.

The other extreme in property rights exists when the providing group can perfectly exclude noncontributors and charge FR as much as area ABQ_1O for admission to the group. But with FR included, the group optimum itself will be enlarged and expansion of production to Q_2 is warranted so that an amount up to area $ABQ_1O + CQ_2Q_1B$ can be extracted from FR. In this extreme case FR receives none of the consumer surplus achieved through group production. In other bargaining outcomes (e.g., as might be achieved if all individuals who joined the group were treated identically), FR would share in this surplus.

Clarification IV.3: Without the specification of a prior normative model, simple analysis of characteristics like "jointness" or "exclusion" does not allow us to evaluate a situation as "unfair" or "exploitative."

We have seen that both the distribution of property rights and the level of jointness will affect both total benefits and the distribution of these benefits. Economic analysis does not tell us how any increment in benefits from bargaining "should" be distributed except to say that cooperation will break down unless every participant remains at least as well off after the good is provided as before. Because of its popularity in the literature, we shall turn to the idea of marginal cost sharing and discuss its deficiencies both as an "equitable" way of allocating costs and as a technique for achieving more optimal levels of production.[19]

Clarification IV.4: Marginal cost sharing is of dubious value both as a normative standard of "fairness" and as a method of allocating costs of public good
provision.

Marginal cost sharing is a prescription only for how to allocate costs of
the last physical unit of the good (i.e., costs in proportion to benefits) and
is noninformative as to how to pay for the total costs of the good. It is a
standard economic result (by Euler's theorem) that such a system—if
applied to total production—will not raise the appropriate amount of
revenue except in the special case of constant returns to scale. There is no
viable argument that marginal cost sharing is particularly fair even in the
case of constant returns to scale.

In figure 12, under marginal cost sharing, X assumes the whole cost
and pays AEQ^*O for provision of the good. X gets a consumer surplus
of ACE, while Y, who pays nothing, receives a free bonus of BOF.
There is no economic argument that explains why, if there were power
to enforce it, it would be inequitable for X to charge Y an amount up to
ADFO for provision of the good. (Note that X cannot charge Y more
than ADFO or else it would benefit Y to produce amount AD on its
own.) As long as both consumers are just as well or better off after the

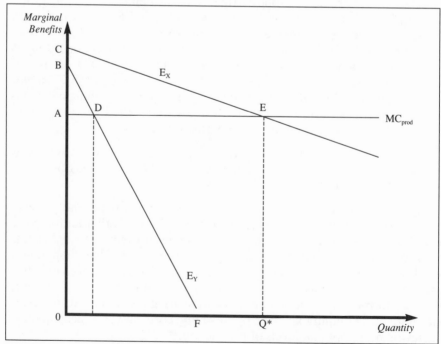

FIGURE 12.   The Deficiency of Marginal Cost Sharing

good is provided, then neoclassical economics gives us no criterion for gauging "exploitation."

Clarification IV.5: There is nothing special about marginal cost sharing in ensuring that the optimal level of provision will be attained.

Potential members of the providing group will not be more likely to pay assessments based on marginal benefits than assessments based on any other system. If exclusion (property rights) is infeasible, they will try not to contribute anything; if exclusion is possible, they will enter into the bargaining process and be willing, if necessary, to pay any amount up to the total benefit of being included. (Of course they will bargain to be admitted for less.) A similar point applies to attempts to collect payment for public goods by providing them in a package with private goods (e.g., unions providing both the public goods benefits of collective bargaining and such private goods as health programs). Since public benefits will be received in any case, the decision to contribute will depend only on the private goods benefits and no payment for public goods benefits will be induced by such an approach (see note 17). Thus, if we are to study goods which are joint in supply and over which we cannot assume perfect exclusion control, we must move beyond the standard tasks of microeconomics and examine the political and social context of the goods.

V. Political Organization and "Quasi-Public" Goods

We can now see the importance of political organizations as a way of achieving control over exclusion of a good without deleteriously affecting the inherent jointness of the good. These organizations may be formal governmental structures, treaties between governments, compacts between individuals, or other such arrangements. The crucial element is that power to enforce participation in payment (according to some set of ground rules) must be delegated to some central authority by the individual members. The central authority may operate directly by providing the good itself and allocating the costs through some sort of tax system, or it may operate indirectly by establishing and enforcing a system of property rights to facilitate decentralized production of public goods. In either approach the purpose is to ensure the provision of goods having jointness to group members while, at the same time, ensuring that beneficiaries of the good contribute to the costs of production. We may use the term *quasi-public good* to distinguish such a case in which an erstwhile public good has had payment and exclusion mechanisms attached to it by a central authority structure.

In order for a providing group to be stable and maintain itself against the incentives for individuals to take a "free ride," the group must be able to exert influence over the membership. In the case of centralized provision, it must be able to assess and enforce the collection of payment from members. The tax collecting branches of modern states illustrate how such mechanisms work. In the case of decentralized provision, property rights are assigned and enforced by complex legal and judicial procedures such as patent or copyright laws. Finally, the group either will have to restrict the extension of the good to nonmembers (as discussed in Section III above) or else use its power to force nonmembers to accept it as the central authority. While it may not be possible to do this with respect to all beneficiaries, the stability of the group requires that it be feasible with respect to a solid core of potential members. There is, of course, a vast literature on the establishment of such authority systems, but we will pursue the exact details of specific mechanisms no further here.[20] Instead, we will focus on the crucial role of the groups or organizations defined by these relations in providing quasi-public goods.

> Clarification V.1: For quasi-public goods, the relation of the individual to the group largely defines his relation to the good.

Understanding the nature of a good requires an analysis of the political relation of the individual to the group. For example, U.S. military defense is a quasi-public good to Hawaiians but not to New Zealanders. Hawaiians have delegated authority to the central government to extract a share of the costs of the defense which they receive. New Zealanders have not delegated such comprehensive authority to the U.S. government and thus receive fewer defense benefits. However, New Zealanders do receive some public good-like benefits from U.S. military expenditures. This is not because the United States cannot avoid defending New Zealand (i.e., it is not a prerequisite to its own defense), but because it has indicated its readiness to do so as part of a less comprehensive exchange of authority. This exchange of authority is formally reflected in common membership in international organizations (e.g., SEATO) and tacitly reflected in political, economic, and cultural ties. These latter factors are equally important in defining the limits of exclusion, even though their looser definition of the ties results in looser property rights and less well-defined boundaries of exclusion.

> Clarification V.2: The more effective a group is at establishing property rights, the more effectively it will perform in providing public goods.

The more effective a group is at establishing property rights, the harder it is to take a free ride and the greater the incentive for individuals to become paying members of the group. This will depend both on the properties of the good and on the extent to which members are able to delegate authority and power to the group. Thus the claim that small groups are more effective in providing public goods (Olson, 1965) is more appropriately restated as small groups are more effective at establishing exclusionary bounds around public goods, thus transforming them into quasi-public goods.[21] It is important to note that one group may be "nested" within another for purposes of exclusion. For example, a country club implicitly relies on the laws of larger society in keeping nonmembers off its premises.

> Clarification V.3: The optimal level of extension of quasi-public goods is likely to fall below the ideal optimality level of pure public goods (see Clarification III.5).

In terms of the Samuelsonian criterion for public goods efficiency, quasi-public goods provision is necessarily suboptimal since some individuals are excluded from the goods after production. The sole exception to this is the group in which property rights are so effectively enforced that no individuals can free ride and, thus, there is universal paying membership. In a more realistic world, further extension of a good will be efficient provided that induced contributions outweigh losses due to any increase in "cheating" by group members. Optimal group size will depend on the interaction of these effects.

> Clarification V.4: It is incorrect to assert that all outputs of governments and organizations are public goods or quasi-public goods.

It has been argued both that the adequate provision of public goods is the only proper function of governments and also that anything which produces public intervention in the supply of a good ensures its public quality.[22] However, in practice governments frequently deal in patently nonpublic goods. Income redistribution is an example of a governmental function which involves the purely rival transfer of private goods between citizens. Even many of the more "public" government functions actually involve goods that display severe rivalness. If police services are public goods, why do some areas of the city protest that they receive inferior services and why are the courts so overcrowded? Or why are the roads so crowded and why are students bused to better schools? In many instances government action is not just concerned with providing pure public goods, but also with arbitrating disputes entailed by the rivalness of goods.

> Clarification V.5: The most important set of quasi-public goods provided by organizations are property rights themselves.

Constitutions, laws, treaties, and other rules of conduct have important public qualities. On a superficial level it is easy to impute both jointness of supply and nonexclusion to them (e.g., one person following the law does not prevent another person from obeying the laws). More subtle aspects of the issue are revealed if we consider the phenomena usually classified under the rubric "protection of the laws." In the ab-

stract, jointness is ensured if the laws are such that all are potential beneficiaries of the restrictions or obligations placed on the actions of others.
Nonexclusion within the group is ensured by the agreement implicit in
establishing the laws that all members (i.e., those to whom the laws apply)
are to be protected by the laws. This nonexclusion may represent a technical inability to exclude due to the way the group is structured, but more
often it will reflect the establishment of mechanisms to prevent the exercise of any such exclusion vis-à-vis group members.[23]

In practice the mechanisms available to organizations are not purely
public in terms of either jointness or nonexclusion. For example, police
services clearly show rivalness and capacity constraints in the face of high
levels of lawbreaking. However, methods of enforcing laws agreed upon
by the group are often very effective and the marginal costs of extending
group size (MC_{ext}) relatively low. But this is not simply a function of
lumpiness in the supply of methods of control. New members entering the
group under agreements to respect the established rules involve essentially no marginal costs of extension except insofar as they violate this
covenant. That is to say, the costs of extension—and even the problem of
less than perfect jointness within the group—exist only insofar as the
voluntary nature of the group itself is not maintained and coercive mechanisms must be used.[24] With the potential for both coercion within the
group and exclusion from the group, the boundaries and property rights
defined by the group may indeed be quasi-public goods. Nevertheless, this
does not imply that the goods dealt with under the group's aegis need in
any way be public.

One of the most important examples of groups as quasi-public goods is
their capacity to regulate the production and exchange of both private and
other quasi-public goods. Not only goods like national defense (where the
property rights include every citizen's right to defense and the obligation
to share the costs), but even the neoclassical marketplace (where participants are required, or at least assumed, to observe property rights of
goods and the transfer of goods is restricted to instances of mutual and
voluntary consent) depends on the group for its provision. Groups can
serve as permanent frameworks for the mitigation "of cases in which
socially responsible behavior fails to receive anything like its just reward."[25] The actual solution of the individual problem may appear to be a
purely private exchange, but behind it will stand a very public framework
without which a solution would be impossible.

Clarification V.6: "Insuring groups" provide a quasi-public good.

When a group is formed for insurance or risk-spreading purposes, it is
clear that the physical good involved (premium payments and claim settlements) are rival in nature. Although the expected utilities of all individuals in the insuring group will increase with participation, the net sum of

actual gains and losses is always constant at zero. This apparent contradiction is due to the group's possession of public qualities: (1) It has greater than pure jointness in supply since additional participants raise the utility of all participants by spreading the risk further. (2) The insurance agreement defines the bounds of the exclusiveness and ensures both that no member of the group can be excluded and that only members of the group are included.[26] Thus a quasi-public good can be created by proper coordination of even purely private goods. A very similar parallel to this is the "deterrence" group in which members agree to share the burden of losses—partly in the belief that their agreement to do so will lessen the total losses faced by the group. A defensive alliance to deter and share the consequence of outside aggression is an example of this.

Conclusion

The political analysis of public goods problems is most appropriately viewed not as an analysis of the exchange of goods but as an analysis of the exchange of authority between actors.[27] The setting up of organizations or groups capable of imposing and enforcing property rights and of collecting payments for centrally provided services is crucial to understanding how public goods (or, more correctly, quasi-public goods) are provided. Conversely, an understanding of public good provision provides clues to the incentives for such exchanges in the first place.

Thus it is hardly surprising that public goods analysis undertaken in political science has been concentrated in international relations. It is at this level that institutions and authority structures are most deficient for the provision of public goods. At national or local levels these problems are mitigated by the existence of a central authority structure, although they still present important questions for public policy. Thus, "solving" public goods problems is a question of developing the appropriate political institutions. This may be done in the form of centralized provision (e.g., the world government approach), provision by a regional subgroup (e.g., regional groupings for economic goals), or decentralized provision after establishing appropriate exclusionary mechanisms (e.g., territorial division of the oceans).

Finally, we should emphasize that these quasi-public goods represent a distinct shift away from a pure public goods model. This shift is not surprising when we recall that public goods analysis developed in response to deficiencies in the private goods model. Blind acceptance of either model is inappropriate, although each provides a guidepost in a murky world of "mixed goods." But only by a detailed examination of both its technological characteristics and the political environment can we understand the true nature of a "good."

NOTES

This article, first published in *International Studies Quarterly* 23 (1972): 532–66, is reprinted by permission. An earlier draft of this article was presented at the annual meeting of the International Studies Association, Washington, D.C., February 1978. Raymond Duvall has been particularly helpful in his comments on this article; John Freeman, Steven Jackson, Gerald Kramer, Robert Hoyer, Henrik Madsen, Ian McKinnon, Joe Oppenheimer, and Bruce Russett also provided useful comments and criticisms.

1. In the standard private good model there is no need for this distinction, since every unit produced entails exactly one unit of consumption so that the relevant cost of providing the good to an additional consumer is the cost of producing another unit (MC_{prod}). Whereas MC_{prod} refers to the change in total costs entailed by producing an additional unit of the good, MC_{ext} typically refers to changes in total costs (including reduced quantity or quality of consumption) to existing consumers as an additional consumer is included.

2. We want to be careful not to confuse $MC_{ext} = 0$ with the very low proportional rise in total costs which may occur even in the provision of purely private goods to an additional consumer in a large collectivity. If a U.S. government program provided some private good to each citizen, then the inclusion of an additional citizen would increase costs by a proportion of only 1/200 million plus. The smallness of this proportion does not make the good joint in any sense.

3. The incorrect comparison of jointness to decreasing costs is pervasive. Examples include Head (1962), Millward (1970), and Samuelson (1958).

4. The whole notion of capacity is hard to pin down. It seems as if we can always squeeze one more person into an elevator, yet there is clearly some ultimate capacity constraint to elevators (as well as an additional person willing to cram in and try to find out exactly what it is). For purposes of exposition we will assume rigid capacity constraints, below which there is no congestion. The arguments in Buchanan (1965) skillfully develop the relationships between lumpy goods and public goods and parallel the discussion in this article. Bator (1958: 376) makes the distinction between lumpiness and public goods and correctly points out that "what is involved here is that most things are multidimensional and more than one dimension may matter."

5. Buchanan (1965) suggests that sharing a pair of shoes through time is a public good. Head (1962) treats peak and off-peak services as public goods.

6. The classic case of a joint good is Marshall's example of both meat and hides being produced by the process of raising cattle. Buchanan (1968: 34–36) is a prime offender in confusing these concepts. He fails to recognize the distinction between joint production of private goods and jointness in consumption of public goods.

7. Musgrave (1959: 10) correctly points out this relationship. Head (1962) attempts to refute this observation in his analysis and, unfortunately, his misconception has prevailed in the subsequent literature.

8. In logical notation we have $\sim A \rightarrow \sim B$ from which we conclude $B \rightarrow A$, where A = jointness in supply and B = nonexclusiveness.

9. This appears to explain how Head arrives at his erroneous conclusion

concerning the independence of jointness and nonexclusiveness. The example Head (1962: 210) uses is of an oil field with several wells drawing from the same pool so that "the firm which made the original strike [is] quite possibly unable to price exclude others from peacefully expropriating a significant part of its property." Here the problem is clearly one of inability to control exclusion, and the good fails to meet the criterion of nonexclusiveness as it is defined for public goods. For an example closer to international relations, see Ruggie (1972), who follows in the "law of the sea" tradition by failing to distinguish between nonexclusiveness and the inability to control exclusion vis-à-vis ocean resources.

10. This example clearly violates the requirement of jointness of supply.

11. The term "externality" is not well defined in the economics literature. Millward (1970) suggests that it involves situations in which "the utility function of a firm contains a variable in the control of some other person or firm."

12. See Wagner (1975), Schofield (1975), and Frolich and Oppenheimer (1972). All of these authors fail to make this distinction. A simple analogy is five people sitting around a table who agree to split $10 by taking $2 each. This does not make the $10 any more of a public good than if they pulled out guns and proceeded to shoot it out for the whole amount.

13. Thus, jointness and noncontrol over exclusion are necessary and sufficient conditions for nonexclusiveness.

14. Production is also increasingly less likely the closer a point in another quadrant lies to the northeast quadrant, since costs of extension and/or exclusion rise the closer a point moves in this direction.

15. For a discussion of the importance of this factor in economic theory see Furubotn and Pejovich (1972).

16. Millward (1970) demonstrates how the whole meaning of Pareto efficiency becomes blurred once we introduce exclusion costs. Minasian (1967: 73) points out that the same qualification applies to a public goods world: "A model of public goods which does not incorporate the costs of exclusion and the value of the information generated by the different signalling and incentive systems is *not* properly constrained for the purpose of solving real world problems."

17. Strategies that try to induce payment for public goods by attaching charges to related private goods also turn out to be a sham under closer analysis. All payments collected in this manner are for private goods benefits and provide no appropriate signals for public goods production.

18. Millward (1970: 160) shows that this latter conclusion is not strictly true if income effects are included.

19. Marginal cost sharing has been recommended by a number of authors. For example, see Olson (1971), Loehr (1973), and Frolich et al. (1971).

20. The relation of authority structures to economic goods is discussed thoroughly in Lindblom (1977).

21. A list of 10 strategies to provide public goods is presented in Russett and Sullivan (1971). These can be shown to depend implicitly on the enforcement of property rights around quasi-public goods or on the instillation of altruistic motives. The only exception to this is the case of the privileged group in which one member alone provides the good.

22. The underlying and faulty logic seems to be that since public goods imply a need for an organization, an organization must indicate a previously existing

public good. It is fallacious to argue from the premise that public goods imply a common interest to the conclusion that a common interest implies a public good. Not all instances in which cooperative action is appropriate are examples of public goods. This point is confused in Olson and Zeckhauser (1966) and Musgrave (1959).

23. The nature and extent of such mechanisms was one of the primary concerns of social contract theorists such as Hobbes, Locke, and Rousseau. Not surprisingly, they were writing at the time of the formation of such a quasi-public good: the modern nation-state.

24. Lindblom (1977) discusses the various ways to establish authority relations and the often extreme efficiency of such relations.

25. Head's discussion is somewhat confusing since he fails to recognize the distinction between nonexclusion and noncontrol over exclusion. He does give several examples, such as "beggar-my-neighbor" trade policies or inflation viewed from a Keynesian perspective, which are relevant here. Unfortunately, he confuses these as problems in dealing with public goods per se rather than as problems in the structure of the group.

26. Note that this is a case of one group being nested within another group. For example, most insurance groups rely on the laws and courts of a larger society to arbitrate disputes over settlements. One of the problems with defense alliances as insurance groups is that there is no such superior group to enforce agreements.

27. This problem is common to many attempts to formulate "exchange theories" of politics since it is authority whose "exchange" is really the interesting issue. However, many writers focus only on the exchange of "goods." See Lindblom (1977) for more on this point.

REFERENCES

Bator, F. M. (1958) "The anatomy of market failure." *Q. J. of Economics* 63 (August): 351–379.

Buchanan, J. (1968) *The Demand and Supply of Public Goods.* Chicago: Rand McNally.

——— (1965) "An economic theory of clubs." *Economica* 22 (February): 1–14.

Burgess, P. M., and J. A. Robinson (1969) "Alliances and the theory of collective action." *Midwest J. of Pol. Sci.* 13 (May): 194–218.

Chamberlin, J. (1974) "Provision of collective goods as a function of group size." *Amer. Pol. Sci. Rev.* 68 (June): 707–716.

Coase, R. H. (1960) "The problems of social cost." *J. of Law and Economics* III (October): 1–14.

Frolich, N., and J. Oppenheimer (1972) "Entrepreneurial politics and foreign policy." *World Politics* 24 (spring): 151–178.

Frolich, N., and O. R. Young (1971) *Political Leadership and Collective Goods.* Princeton, NJ: Princeton Univ. Press.

Furubotn, E. G., and S. Pejovich (1972) "Property rights and economic theory: a survey of recent literature." *J. of Econ. Literature* 10 (December): 1137–1162.

Groves, T., and J. Ledyard (1977a) "Optimal allocation of public goods: a solution to the 'free rider' problem." *Econometrica* 45 (May): 783–809.

—— (1977b) "Some limitations of demand revealing processes." *Public Choice* 29 (spring): 107–124.

Head, J. G. (1962) "Public goods and public policy." *Public Finance* 12 (3): 197–221.

K. Foglis, M. Z. (1961) "Welfare economics and subsidy programs." *University of Florida Monographs in the Social Sciences* 11 (summer).

Lindblom, C. E. (1977) *Politics and Markets: The World's Political Economic Systems.* New York: Basic Books.

Loehr, W. (1973) "Collective goods and international cooperation: comments." *Int. Organization* 27 (summer): 421–430.

Millward, R. (1970) "Exclusion costs, external economies and market failures." *Oxford Econ. Papers* 22 (March): 24–37.

Minasian, J. (1967) "Public goods in theory and practice revisited." *J. of Law and Econ.* 10 (October): 205–207.

Musgrave, R. A. (1959) *The Theory of Public Finance.* New York: McGraw-Hill.

Olson, M. (1971) "Increasing the incentives for international cooperation." *Int. Organization* 25 (autumn): 866–874.

—— (1965) *The Logic of Collective Action: Public Goods and the Theory of Groups.* Cambridge, MA: Harvard Univ. Press.

Olson, M., and R. Zeckhauser (1966) "An economic theory of alliances." *Rev. of Economics and Statistics* 48 (November): 266–279.

Peston, M. (1972) *Public Goods and the Public Sector.* New York: Macmillan.

Pryor, F. L. (1969) *Public Expenditure in Communist and Capitalist Nations.* Homewood, IL: Irwin.

Ruggie, J. G. (1972) "Collective goods and future international cooperation." *Amer. Pol. Sci. Rev.* 66 (September): 874–892.

Russett, B. M. (1970) *What Price Vigilance?* New Haven, CT: Yale Univ. Press.

Russett, B. M., and J. Sullivan (1971) "Collective goods and international organizations." *Int. Organization* 25 (autumn): 845–865.

Samuelson, P. A. (1969) "Contrast between welfare conditions for joint supply and public goods." *Rev. of Economics and Statistics* 51 (February): 26–30.

—— (1958) "Aspects of public expenditure theory." *Rev. of Economics and Statistics* 40 (November): 332–338.

—— (1954) "The pure theory of public expenditure." *Rev. of Economics and Statistics* 36 (November): 387–389.

Schofield, N. (1975) "A game theoretic analysis of Olson's game of collective action." *J. of Conflict Resolution* 19 (September): 441–461.

Snidal, D. (1979) "The arms race and public goods models of defense expenditure: common structure and impediments to cooperation." Presented at the annual meeting of the International Studies Association, Toronto, Ontario.

Wagner, R. H. (1975) "National defense as a collective good," in C. Liske et al. (eds.) *Comparative Public Policy: Issues, Theories and Methods.* New York: Halsted Press (a Sage Publications book).

12 Difficulties in the Notion of Economic Rationality

Russell Hardin

IN ECONOMIC THEORY and in discursive arguments and claims in the economic literature, rationality is a very simple notion. It is that people will choose more of what they value as opposed to less, all other things being equal. Since all other things are seldom equal, it is surprising that this assumption is often sufficient to explain behavior. But there are two major classes of problems in the notion of rationality assumed in economics and, increasingly, in social theory more generally. First, there are the problems of understanding what it is rational for an individual to do in situations involving strategic interactions with other similarly rational individuals. These problems are relatively well understood even if there are not always definitive solutions of them. Second, there is the massive problem of giving substantive content to the value theory or preference ordering on which an individual's choice of more over less will be based.

It is a striking fact of microeconomic theory that neither of these problems seems to matter. The first should not matter only in the extreme cases in which strategic interactions are of negligible significance, as in a one-person economy or in a market of large numbers of sellers and buyers. The most important results of modern economics concern large-number interactions in markets. The second should not matter only if there were great stability and predictability of what things people valued. In most economies, this problem is commonly resolved by the fact that there is money, which is a means to many ends and which virtually everyone values with great stability and predictability. Societies in which there is no money seem in fact to be societies in which things that are valued are few in number and are basic to almost everyone's well being, so that in these societies there is stability and predictability of the most direct kind. Hence one might argue that individuals in primitive societies have clear and stable preference orderings or value systems. But individuals in modern economies may not have. It is aggregates, not individuals, that display stability of preferences.

It is an irony—and the central issue of this paper—that the notion of economic rationality applies conceptually to the individual, to *homo economicus,* but that economic explanations based on that notion do not work well for individuals or even for small numbers of actors. The individual rationality that supposedly lies behind societal-level economic explanations is largely a chimera.

Strategic Interaction

That strategic interactions can complicate the explanation of rational behavior is very well understood since the development of game theory, and I will not rehearse the general issues. However, it is worth noting here that despite the advances of game theory economic vocabulary and analyses are still often grounded in prestrategic ways of thinking. I will do little more than illustrate this claim here by taking up a family of concepts, the Pareto criteria, that pervade economic analyses of policy issues. These criteria are important in large part because they are supposedly based on an unarguable assumption of individual rationality that is, I will argue, flawed just because it is unstrategic.

To overcome problems in comparing and aggregating values across people, Pareto introduced a set of notions that are now known as Pareto criteria. The first of these is Pareto optimality. A state of affairs is *Pareto optimal* if in it no one can be made better off without making someone else worse off. A related criterion is Pareto superiority—of all the Pareto criteria this one most transparently depends on a supposition of individual rationality, as will be discussed below. A state of affairs X is said to be *Pareto superior* to another state Y if at least one person is better off in X while no one is worse off in X. Through a series of Pareto-superior moves it should always be possible in principle to reach a Pareto-optimal state of affairs from which no further Pareto improvement could be made.

Before turning to the presumption of rationality on which the notion of Pareto superiority is based, note first that all the Pareto criteria are subject to strategic problems in practice. Indeed, Pareto optimality generally fails in actual contexts. It most obviously fails in cases in which the best state of affairs would require voluntary collective action. In these cases, the logic of individual rationality often implies that relevant groups will fail to act for their collective benefit. For example, if we all shovel our sidewalks of snow, we might all individually benefit enough to outweigh the individual burdens to us of shoveling. But I may not benefit enough from the shoveling of my own sidewalk alone to justify my shoveling it. Hence, we may all fail to shovel the walks and we will then all be worse off than in an alternative, reachable state of affairs—the result will not be Pareto optimal.

But Pareto optimality can fail in far simpler contexts as well, as the following strikingly simple problem in dyadic exchanges suggests. Consider a society in which all may enter into dyadic exchanges at will. The only constraint on the set of possible exchanges is that no one would ever trade something more valued for something less valued. Suppose x, y, and z are commodities and that A, B and C are persons with the following preference orderings (where xP_Ay means "A prefers × to y"):

$$xP_AyP_Az$$

$$yP_BzP_Bx$$

$$zP_CxP_Cy$$

Suppose also that A owns y, B owns z, and C owns x. Now A and B can make no mutually beneficial exchange because they both prefer what A owns (y) to what B owns. A and C can make no exchange because they both prefer what C owns to what A owns. Similarly, B and C can make no exchange. Yet all can be made better off if they pool their resources and let each take his or her most preferred commodity. Such cycles can be stretched out to thread their way through a numerous society. Strategic considerations therefore burden the notion of Pareto optimality at all levels, from the smallest group to the largest society.

Let us turn now to the rationality assumption in the notion of Pareto superiority. Moves to Pareto-superior states are supposedly rational since everyone would consent to them because under such moves there will be no losers, only gainers. Unfortunately, however, some might not consent. Why? Because any move will determine what states of affairs will then be Pareto superior to the newly reached state. Doing well on the first move raises the floor from which one maneuvers for the next and subsequent moves. Doing badly on the first move lowers the ceiling to which one can aspire on later moves. Figure 13 shows this point more clearly.

Figure 13 represents a distribution of resources between A and B beginning from the initial distribution at the origin. The Pareto frontier represents the set of distributions which are Pareto optimal: A and B can move from one point on the frontier only by harming one of them to help the other. Any point between the origin and the frontier is accessible from the origin with a Pareto-superior move. For example, the move from the origin at O to the point Q makes A better off without affecting B's holdings of the group's resources. A move from Q back to O, however, is not a Pareto-superior move because it reduces the holdings of A. But note what a move from O to Q does: it effectively defines a new Pareto frontier that

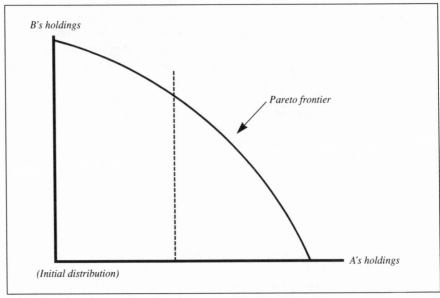

FIGURE 13.   Distribution of Resources and the Pareto Frontier

includes all points of the original frontier that are not to the left of Q. All of the points that have been eliminated would be preferred by B to any of the points which remain, while all of those that remain would be preferred by A to any that have been eliminated. In a meaningful sense, A has gained while B has lost in the move from O to Q.

Why then should we say that it is rational for B to consent to the Pareto-superior move from O to Q? It is self-evidently rational for B to consent to the move *only if* it is the *only move* available or is at least in the *only direction* in which it is possible to move. But this condition just means that the Pareto frontier must not be a curve as drawn but must be a point somewhere to the right of the origin. For B to consent to the move from O to Q, the Pareto frontier must be a point on the x-axis. If the Pareto frontier is as drawn, B cannot rationally consent to any move without considering its effect on potential other moves and hence its effect on an eventual Pareto-optimal distribution. Hence, Pareto superiority is not simply a rational criterion. If I am narrowly rational, I can be indifferent to what you receive only if it does not potentially interact with what I can receive. This condition may be met if, say, I live on one island and you live on another far away. For us, then, the Pareto frontier would be a square curve as in figure 14, and it would be pointless to apply Pareto criteria to aggregations of our welfare since there are no conflicts of value between us to be avoided. For A and B in the situation of figure 13, however, every

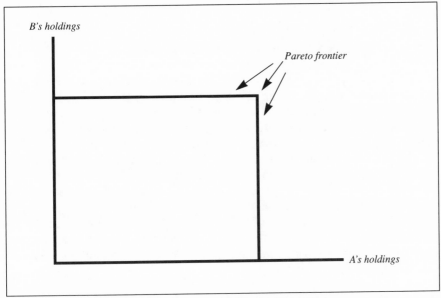

FIGURE 14.   Distribution of Resources with No Conflict of Value

Pareto-superior move involves opportunity costs for at least one of the two and often for both of them. That is to say, the move eliminates some attractive opportunities from the field of subsequent choice.

Hence, one cannot grant that the criterion of Pareto superiority is rational in general. It is rational only in contexts, such as that depicted in figure 14, in which it is pointless to apply it. In this respect it recalls Locke's assignment of rights of ownership over any natural object or parcel of land to the first person to make use of it. Locke argues that "every Man has a *Property* in his own *Person* . . . ." Hence,

> The *Labour* of his Body, and the *Work* of his Hands, we may say, are properly his. Whatsoever then he removes out of the State that Nature hath provided, and left in it, he hath mixed his *Labour* with, and joyned to it something that is his own, and thereby makes it his *Property*. . . . For this *Labour* being the unquestionable Property of the Labourer, no Man but he can have a right to what that is once joyned to, at least where there is enough and as good left in common for others. (*Second Treatise of Government,* par. 27)

The final proviso, the so-called Locke's proviso, may seem today to wreck the theory, but when "all the World was *America*" (ibid., par. 49) the "appropriation of any parcel of *Land,* by improving it," was no "prejudice to any other Man, since there was still enough, and as good left; and more than the yet unprovided could use. So that in effect, there was never the less left for others because of his inclosure for himself" (ibid., par. 33). In this state of affairs, the Pareto frontier was square, as in figure 14, and no one was in conflict for the basic good of unimproved land. The Pareto criteria would be rationally unobjectionable only in a world as primitive as that seen by Locke when all the world was America.

Note that the first objection on rational grounds to the Pareto criteria— in the discussion above of shoveling sidewalks of snow for mutual benefit— is an instance of the commonplace objection that Pareto optimality may be blocked by "market failures," as when there are external effects of some- one's actions. The external effect of my shoveling my sidewalk is that you benefit although you play no role in bearing the cost of the benefit. The objection to the notion of Pareto superiority—in, the discussion above of figure 13—is not a matter of market failure, however. The Pareto superior- ity criterion is rationally objectionable because it presumes consent in situa- tions in which conflict can arise over scarce or positional goods. When there is a shortage of arable parcels of land in the world, it may not be a matter of indifference to me whether others seize what parcels remain. Because my opportunities depend on what and how much land remains, my interest depends on whether it is taken.

Value Theory

Let us turn now to the more fundamental problem of the value theory behind the simple notion of economic rationality that one should prefer more to less. "The two main theorists of rationality in the social sciences are," Elster (1979, p. 68) suggests, "Max Weber and John von Neumann." Weber defined rationality as the choice of relevant means to given ends. Neumann contributed, with his theory of games, to our understanding of strategic interaction between two or more rational actors. Note that both are largely concerned with the rationality of actions (or choices) once ends have been assumed.

Harsanyi argues that

> classical economics has substantially increased the explanatory power of the concept of rational behavior by extending it from choices between alternative means to a given end, to choices between alternative ends. Under this more general concept, a person's behavior will be rational if he chooses among different goals according to a consistent scale of preferences, that is, according to the relative importance or utility he assigns to each particular goal. (Harsanyi, 1969, p. 515)

I wish to show that Harsanyi's claim is of only marginal significance— largely because the value theory in which it is implicitly grounded is, in a sense, only a marginal theory, that is, a theory of value at the margin.

The rationality of choices between ends to which Harsanyi refers is little more than a modest set of consistency requirements on individual preference orderings. For example, one ought not prefer × to y and also prefer y to x. But the crucial weakness of the implicit value theory for rational choice is its failure to define consistently what × or y can be. Unfortunately, the notion of rationality has no bite unless it is backed by a theory of value to tell us when there is more rather than less of what is valued. In some economic contexts this problem might seem to be resolved by the presumption that virtually everyone values money as a means to achieving various other values. Of course, the desire for money is not an adequate surrogate value theory in many economic contexts—for example, it would be hard to explain the high productivity of many people in terms of monetary incentives. But the greater problem with desire for money as a simple value theory is that money is clearly not generally an end but is merely a means. Hence, it is constantly traded off—at ever-increasing rates, it seems—for various goods and services. Since money will not do as a surrogate, we will have to go further to find a relevant value theory.

To get at the implicit value theory, let us consider first ordinal and then cardinal utility theory. Arrow's *Social Choice and Individual Values* is an instructive exemplar of the use of ordinal utility or preference theory. In setting up his conditions for his Impossibility Theorem, Arrow writes,

> In the present study the objects of choice are social states. The most precise definition of a social state would be a complete description of the amount of each type of commodity in the hands of each individual, the amount of each productive resource invested in each type of productive activity, and the amounts of various types of collective activity, such as municipal services, diplomacy and its continuation by other means, and the erection of statues to famous men. It is assumed that *each individual in the community has a definite ordering of all conceivable social states,* in terms of their desirability to him. It is not assumed here that an individual's attitude toward different social states is determined exclusively by the commodity bundles which accrue to his lot under each. It is simply assumed that the individual orders all social states by whatever standards he deems relevant. (Arrow, 1963, p. 17, emphasis added) ;

The principal point to note in Arrow's specification is how utterly fantastic it is. The individual surely does not have enough brain cells to record the preference orderings required or, likely, even to store rules from which to deduce them piecemeal. But there is a reason for Arrow's madness here. His complete ordering of whole states of affairs resolves a fundamental problem that any less holistic system faces. Suppose I say that I prefer × to y, where × and y are two objects or experiences I may enjoy. What I must mean is something roughly similar to this: I prefer "everything as it is otherwise plus x" to "everything as it is otherwise plus y." I cannot simply mean that I prefer × to y *tout court,* unless x and y are extraordinary alternatives (such as the destruction of the world versus its continuation as it is). Arrow's orderings over complete states of affairs as opposed to orderings of piecemeal aspects of states of affairs are meant to avoid the obvious difficulties in the latter. We may often be compelled to agree with Proust: "the absence of one part from a whole is not only that, it is not simply a partial omission, it is a disturbance of all the other parts, a new state which it was impossible to foresee from the old" (Proust, 1934, vol. 1, p. 234).

Of course, there may be large pragmatic implications in the claim that I prefer × to y with everything else as it is otherwise. It may not be possible to have everything else as it is plus x, but it may be very difficult to know whether this conjunction is possible. Recall the Saki tale of the couple who were given a magic monkey's paw good for three wishes. They wished for money, which came to them in the form of an insurance payment for their daughter's sudden accidental death. They then wished back their daughter, who returned home as a walking corpse. They then wished her back in the grave. In some sense, they preferred having the money to not having it—but not on the conditions under which that "preference" was fulfilled. But it is not the pragmatic implications of the possible causal relationships among the elements of whole states of affairs that are of interest here—rather it is the interactions among these elements in, determining the utility of whole states of affairs as in the quotation from Proust above.

Ordinal utility theory in part grew out of the recognition that utility is subjective—it is something in the mind of the user, not something stored in objects. This recognition itself stems, no doubt, from the obvious fact that utilities of objects interact. For example, a car without gasoline has little utility. Conversely, the possession of two identical cars may not offer twice the utility of the possession of one only. The first of these examples is a case of complementary goods, that is, goods for which, to speak crudely, the utility of both taken in combination is greater than the sum of their utilities taken separately. The second is a case of goods which are substitutes in an obvious sense. More generally Pareto concludes,

> if we are dealing with very wide variations, it is necessary, at least for the majority of goods, to consider the [utility] of a good as dependent, not only on the quantity of that good used or held, but also on the quantity of the many goods used or consumed at the same time. (Pareto, 1971, ch. 4, sect. 13)

That is to say, it is whole states of affairs, and not the piecemeal bits that make them up, that matter to us. This is, incidentally, a point which philosophers have long grasped. Although he calls it a paradox, Moore thinks it fundamentally important to recognize that the value of a whole "bears no regular proportion to the sum of the values of its parts" (Moore, 1903, ch. 1, sect. 18). Indeed, this principle of "organic wholes" is one of the four kinds of problems "with which it is the business of ethics to deal" (sect. 22). Yet, if the principle be granted, it is hard to imagine what can be meant by "the values of its parts."

Because of the ease with which we can weigh it arithmetically, money may seem to be nearly immune from the problems of dependent utilities, so that we might suppose we could consider its benefit to us even abstracting from its role in comprising whole states of affairs. That this may be a false supposition is suggested by Saki's tale of the monkey's paw discussed above. Admittedly, the problem in that tale is one of causal possibilities rather than of logical connections of the sort that seem to concern Proust, Moore, and Pareto. But it seems implausible that to keep everything else as it is otherwise while adding in $\times$ can be done—if $\times$ is of any significance, it will causally affect "everything else."

Ordinal utility theory was introduced to clear up apparent problems in the cardinal theory. Yet the latter has made a comeback as a result of its role in game theory as developed by Neumann and Morgenstern (1953). In order to solve certain two-person games of pure conflict, Neumann and Morgenstern imputed cardinal utilities to the various outcomes—indeed, they imputed transferable utility to the outcomes. With payoffs in the outcomes measured in such utility, they could generate a continuum of strategies for each player out of as few as two strategies. Hence, if the payoff pairs $(1,0)$ and $(0,1)$ are outcomes in a game, the pair $(\frac{1}{2}, \frac{1}{2})$ may also be generated as an outcome if the players mix their strategies by flipping an even coin to decide which strategy to play.

To meet objections against such a cardinal utility, Neumann and Morgenstern went on to show that, given one's ordinal indifference curves, one can attach cardinal weights to them in the following way. One selects curves B and C and curve A between these two. Now one should be able to say whether one prefers to be on curve A or to have a 50–50 chance of being on either curve B or C. At some mix, say 30–70, one should be indifferent. If B is arbitrarily assigned a utility of 0 and C a utility of 1, then at 30–70, A has a utility of 0.7.

For this cardinalization to work, it is necessary that the initial indifference curves make sense. But this means that they must represent, as in the stipulation of Arrow above, whole states of affairs. Neumann and Morgenstern (1953, p. 19) note that their "procedure for a numerical measurement of the utilities of the individual depends, of course, upon the hypothesis of completeness in the system of individual preferences." The indifference curves cannot represent, as in typical textbook economics, simple tradeoff functions between two goods, $\times$ and y, because, again, one cannot have preferences over various mixes of $\times$ and y *tout court*.

Hence, in the modern ordinal utility theory and in the cardinal theory of Neumann and Morgenstern the constituents of value are the same. What do economists thin these are? At the crucial point in his *Manual*,

Pareto relegates the issue of value theory to a footnote: "I consider the indifference curves as given, and deduce from them all that is necessary for the theory of equilibrium, without resorting to [utility]" (Pareto, 1971, ch. 3, sect. 54n). Later he adds, "The individual can disappear, provided he leaves us this photograph [his indifference curves] of his tastes" (ibid., sect. 57).

In some respects it makes perfectly good sense for the economist to leave people to stipulate their own values. But in one limited respect—that noted by Harsanyi above—it does not. Economists might, as Harsanyi supposes they do, stipulate certain rationality requirements on the relationships among values, including certain consistency requirements. In Arrow's system above, one should not prefer the whole state of affairs x to the whole state of affairs y and also prefer y to x. But notice what economists typically do: they speak not of whole states of affairs but only of particular incremental constituents of whole states. For example, Arrow himself supposes that his proof (based exclusively on orderings of whole states of affairs) has implications for whether there can be a reasonable voting system for choosing among candidates for public office (Arrow, 1963, pp. 26–27). In such a context, Arrow's requirement that the social ordering of whole states of affairs be generated from individual orderings of those states is blurred. And his so-called condition of "independence of irrelevant alternatives" may be utterly violated, since whether I prefer candidate X to candidate Y may turn on other facts, including such facts as whether Z is a candidate (see further, Barry and Hardin, 1982, pp. 224–227).

If we look at the works of economists more generally, we are unlikely to find many cases in which they follow through the full logic of Arrow's ordering of whole states of affairs. Rather, their indifference curves map the tradeoffs between, say, goods x and y *given that all else remains the same*. This is in fact also how Neumann and Morgenstern then use their cardinal utility in the theory of games. They apply it not to whole states of affairs but merely to payoffs in the various outcomes of a game, which itself is likely to be a marginal wrinkle on the players' existence. There is some reason for sticking to the evaluation of marginal changes of whole states of affairs. People will not be good at reasoning through lotteries over states radically outside their experience. Pareto (1971, ch. 4, sect. 26) notes that "if we were to ask a peasant woman who has never had any diamonds, 'if you were a millionaire, how many diamonds would you buy at such and such a given price?' we would get a reply at random and without any value." As with the physicists' problem of comparing angstroms to light years in actual measurements, if I am a cardinal utility theorist I cannot be sure that my supposedly cardinal scale, built up by marginal increments over a wide range of states of well-being, has any coherent meaning.

Conclusion

Perhaps what is required to make sense of the value theory needed for the assumption of economic rationality is to reconstruct it on arguments from the limits to reason, as Simon and others have reconstructed the theory of rational choice between given ends on arguments about the psychological and computational limits on our ability to decide. There is a difference between the two problems, however, that suggests that the value theory problem may be harder to resolve. It is commonly not unreasonable to assume that there is an objectively best means to a particular end to which, given computational and other limits, one at best merely approaches. It may be quite unreasonable to assume that there is any underlying value system to which one approximates in stating one's piecemeal preferences.

One short cut through the idealized value theories often implicit in economic reasoning is, again, to focus on money, a generalized means, rather than on ends, Dealings with such a means may often be very nearly detached from other considerations so that one can be piecemeal rational in acquiring it (if not so readily in exchanging it for various ends). Similarly, one might reconceive game theory in certain contexts as more nearly like serious poker than like life: the point of doing well in the game is to be able to do better thereafter in life. Payoffs then would not be in utility but in money or other assets, that is, in means. In more general contexts, we must often assume that the larger background against which we make our incremental choices remains approximately unaffected by these.

In acknowledging that our notion of rationality is orderly only at the margin, we are like Hume: confident of our grasp of practical reasoning while skeptical of its foundations. "Nothing is more certain," Hume writes, "than that men are, in a great measure, govern'd by interest" (*Treatise*, bk. 3, part 2, sect. 7, p. 534). The same Hume writes,

> I am uneasy to think I approve of one object, and disapprove of another; call one thing beautiful, and another deform'd; decide concerning truth and falsehood, reason and folly, without knowing upon what principles I proceed. I am concern'd for the condition of the learned world, which lies under such a deplorable ignorance in all these particulars. (*Treatise*, bk. 1, part 4, sect. 7, p. 271)

The rationality that underlies theories of economic equilibrium is not a property of individuals but is rather an emergent property of aggregates—it is the rationality of the average individual. Similarly, the rationality that governs individual choices between a bit of $\times$ and a bit of y is emergent from an underlying system of values that cannot be coherently characterized in terms comparable to those applied to the piecemeal choices. Neither of these conclusions can be entirely comfortable to anyone who wishes to explain individual behavior as rational.

NOTE

This article, first published in *Social Science Information* 23 (1984): 436–67, is reprinted by permission of the author and Sage Publications.

REFERENCES

Arrow, K. 1963. *Social choice and individual values.* New Haven, Conn., Yale University Press (second edition).

Barry, B.; Hardin, R. 1982. *Rational man and irrational society?* Beverly Hills, Calif., Sage.

Elster, J. 1979. "Anomalies of Rationality: Some Unresolved Problems in the Theory of Rational Behavior," pp. 65–85, in: L. Levy-Garboua (ed.). *Sociological economics.* London, Sage.

Harsanyi, J. 1969. "Rational-Choice Models of Political Behavior vs. Functionalist and Conformist Theories," *World politics* 21: 513–538.

Hume, D. 1739–1740. *A treatise of human nature.* London. (Ed. by L. A. Selby-Bigge and P. H. Nidditch, Oxford, Clarendon Press.)

Locke, J. 1963. *The second treatise of government* in: P. Laslett (ed.). *John Locke: Two treatises of government.* Cambridge, Cambridge University Press (amended edition).

Moore, G. 1903. *Principia ethica.* Cambridge, Cambridge University Press.

Neumann, J. von; Morgenstern, O. 1953. *Theory of games and economic behavior.* Princeton, N.J., Princeton University Press (third edition).

Pareto, V. 1971. *Manual of political economy.* New York, Kelley (translation of the 1927 French edition.

Proust, M. 1934. *Remembrance of things past,* vol. 1. New York, Random House.

13 Welfare Economics and the Liberal Tradition

Brian Barry

THE TASK THAT I have set myself in this paper is to examine the development of welfare economics in the past two hundred years: from *The Wealth of Nations* to the present day. I shall seek to analyze it less as a branch of economics than as a variant within the tradition of liberal political theory. I should add here that there are, of course, a number of liberal traditions: German liberalism, French liberalism and Italian liberalism, for example, are all distinctive from one another and from British and, later, Anglo-American liberalism. However, the welfare economics which is my subject has largely been created in Britain and the USA, and it is the Anglo-American tradition to which it is related—often most strongly when least self-consciously.

I think that the liberal affiliations of welfare economics can be established very easily. If we take John Locke, Jeremy Bentham, and John Stuart Mill as characteristically liberal thinkers, we can show that, at different times, welfare economics has been little more than the working out of the implications of premises supplied by them. What, however, makes things more interesting is that the two streams of thought—liberal political theory and welfare economics—have not always run parallel. In fact, it would be nearer the truth to say that welfare economics has gone backwards. More precisely, starting off in the eighteenth century, it progressed through the nineteenth century and the first quarter of the twentieth, and has since regressed to the seventeenth century.

In summary, my theme will be as follows. Beginning our survey with Adam Smith, we find that he has a conception of human history and society that is essentially Deistic. His economic ideas cannot be made sense of outside that context. With Bentham, we are still in the eighteenth century, though a different, rationalistic part of it. However, Bentham's principle of utility can be dissociated from his sociology; and as the nineteenth century wore on this increasingly happened, with a quasi-socialist line developing from John Stuart Mill through to A. C. Pigou. Then, in the 1930s, for a variety of reasons, the utilitarian tradition withered and postutilitarian welfare economics was born. To the extent, however, that it denies the possibility of comparing utilities yet remains committed to individualistic premises, it entails a reversion to seventeenth-century thinking, with all the weaknesses and limitations that, in every area of thought except economics, have been painfully transcended in the subsequent centuries. That is, at any rate, going to be my argument.

Adam Smith

I shall take *The Wealth of Nations* as the founding work in modern economics. (I know that there were predecessors but Smith overshadows them. More important, he does seem to have created a discipline defined by a distinctive subject matter and characteristic methods.) Now, Adam Smith is a figure firmly rooted in the eighteenth century, and specifically in the Scottish Enlightenment. In his work on moral philosophy, *The Theory of Moral Sentiments,* he continues the same line of thought as Hutcheson, Reid, and Hume. In *The Wealth of Nations* we can see the influence of the school of Scottish writers of "Philosophical History" such as Ferguson and Millar. The basic questions to which Smith's work constantly relates concern the conditions under which human beings can live together in society and the ways in which the institutions of societies evolve together. Like Marx, the members of this school identified the development of productive forces as the most important causal factor. As this indicates, Smith was a complex, broad-gauge thinker, quite unlike the single-minded (and simple-minded) enthusiast for the market that he is sometimes presented as in popularizations today.

What were Smith's normative views about economic systems in *The Wealth of Nations*? Because of his strong sense of the historical specificity of economic forms, Smith would clearly have denied that it made sense to put forward universally valid prescriptions. But for the England of his time, Smith advocated what he called, tendentiously, the "system of natural liberty." (How could anybody be against something combining those two potent words?) This is the now familiar idea that, except for providing certain public goods (defence, law and order, primary education and some public works) the role of the state should be to protect property and enforce contracts. In particular, it should not try to control prices, grant monopolies to particular companies, license entry into occupations, and so on.

But what exactly was Smith's rationale for this recommendation? I do not think that he ever sets out explicitly his criteria. It seems fair, however, to extract two from his discussion. The first can be drawn from the title: *An Inquiry into the Nature and Causes of the Wealth of Nations*. The market is an economically progressive force inasfar as it harnesses human self-interest behind social beneficial production, and in the long run the more a society allows free play to the market the more its level of overall prosperity will increase.

As a historical statement for the period until Smith was writing this has a lot to be said for it. If we ask why, beginning some time around the sixteenth century, some countries in western Europe began a slow but cumulative process of economic development that led us into the modern era, it seems quite plausible to answer that the key lay in the existence of states that were strong enough to suppress anarchy but not strong enough to suppress innovations in economic organization and in technology.

But Smith wished, I think, to make more than that kind of general claim. There is always a risk of reading back into earlier thinkers later doctrines which they lacked the apparatus even to contemplate. In the case of Smith, however, there is enough in the text to make it no anachronism to attribute to him at least an outline of the idea that would now be stated by saying that a competitive equilibrium is Pareto optimal, that is to say that when each economic agent is pursuing its self-interest with complete effectiveness in a perfectly competitive economy (ideally with an infinite number of producers and consumers) there is no way of shifting resources so as to make one person better off without making some other worse off.

This is a powerful result which, although it has been an article of faith among economists for over a century, has been proved rigorously only in the past thirty years. It underwrites, on a certain definition of efficiency, the efficiency of a market economy.

Smith, however, had a second criterion on the basis of which he commended a market economy, the criterion suggested by his calling it a system of "natural liberty." The concept of Nature played a central role in eighteenth century thought. For a Deist, as Smith was, Nature had its laws (like those discovered by Newton) but they were, in a way we now find it hard to empathize with, suffused with metaphysical significance in virtue of being the laws of Nature's God.

In the same way, when Smith talks about the system of "natural liberty," and of the "natural price" and the "natural wage" as the equilibrium prices and wages within that system, his words at once have an empirical referent and at the same time evoke what Wordsworth called "something far more deeply interfused." In following the system of Nature, Man is, as far as within him lies, cooperating in the half-hidden plans of Providence.

The natural price and the natural wage are not merely efficient, but in a deeper sense appropriate in that they are harmonious with the moral order of the universe.

If we secularize the "hidden hand," understood (as it should be in Smith) not just as working in the market but generally in history, to produce results that men could not have thought of or created by themselves, we can see that the closest contemporary figure to Smith is Hayek. And Hayek has indeed described himself as an "Old Whig"—a species of political figure already almost defunct by the turn of the (nineteenth) century.

Bentham

With Bentham, we move to another figure who could only have been born in the eighteenth century, but who occupied a very different intellectual world from that of Adam Smith. "In his most characteristic merits, as well as his most salient defects, Bentham is eminently a representative of this stirring and vehement age: in his unreserved devotion to the grandest and most comprehensive aims, his high and sustained confidence in their attainability, and the buoyant, indefatigable industry with which he sought the means for their attainment—no less than his exaggerated reliance on his own method, his ignorant contempt for the past, and his intolerant misinterpretation of all that opposed him in the present" (Henry Sidgwick, "Bentham and Benthamism in Politics and Ethics" [1877] in *Miscellaneous Essays and Addresses* [London: Macmillan, 1904], p. 137).

Whereas Smith was concerned with the reasons why countries were different in cultural, political, social, and economic respects, Bentham did not believe that different countries needed different institutions. It was said by critics that he had a stock of his legislative codes printed up with blanks left for the name of whatever country's government requested one. And the criticism was true in substance if false in detail. In this respect, Bentham was a more direct predecessor than Smith of the contemporary profession of economics, as represented, for example, by the officials from the IMF who tell every government that falls within their power—in Western Europe, the Caribbean or sub-Saharan Africa—to act on the latest orthodoxy: demand-management, monetarism, cutting the public sector, or whatever.

When it came to economic prescriptions, Bentham reached the same answers as Smith. Although he is not usually thought of as an economist, this is a reflection of the fact that his total output was so prodigious that a couple of books and various pamphlets and papers constitute only a tiny proportion. But he did write two books, a *Manual of Political Economy* and a *Defence of Usury*. Moreover, the rest of his work can be seen as an extension of the methods of economics to other areas. (Or, of course, vice versa, we can say that economics was a special case of a general approach.) He assumed that each person both must, as a matter of psychological necessity, and ought, to pursue his own happiness, but that the standard for a society was the maximization of the aggregate happiness of its members. The two could be reconciled in two ways: by the natural harmony of interests and the artificial harmony of interests. The idea of the natural harmony of interests is that if people understand their own individual interests correctly they will see that they are not incompatible with those of others. The idea of the artificial harmony of interests is that, where this fails, public institutions should provide sanctions so as to ensure that the pursuit of individual self-interest will in fact be led to conduce to the general happiness. We can see in both ideas Adam Smith's omnipresent "hidden hand," though stripped of its theological underpinnings.

As I said, Bentham in practice reached much the same economic prescriptions as Smith: that, within the sphere of divisible and excludable goods, the only need for state sanctions is to protect property and enforce contracts. (Thus, since the interest rate is the cost of borrowing money, the *Defence of Usury* is simply the application of Smith's strictures on attempts to regulate prices to the special case of interest rates.) However, although the conclusions are the same as those of Smith's, the method—the appeal to the single criterion of aggregate happiness—is different, and over the course of the nineteenth century this became of decisive importance.

Doctor Johnson once said of David Hume that he was "a Tory by chance," meaning that there was nothing in Hume's principles that led him inexorably towards Toryism, but that it was only because he attached great importance to political stability that he happened to end up as a Tory. (It had earlier been said of Hobbes, equally correctly, that he was a monarchist only by chance, in the same sense, and indeed Johnson acutely described Hume's principles as "Hobbist.") Now, in exactly the same sense, Bentham was an upholder of the untrammeled operation of the market only by chance. Given his assumptions about the basic compatibility of individual interest and general interest, it followed that the best plan was *laisser-faire*. But, whereas Smith, as we have seen, talked about "the system of natural liberty," Bentham had no time for liberty as such: liberty was important to the extent that it was a means of happiness and only to that extent.

Thus, although he thought slavery should be abolished this was on the ground of its inefficiency: "a free man produces more than a slave" and that slavery is as a matter of fact disliked by slaves. But if that dislike were overbalanced by the additional happiness of the owner, then slavery would be justifiable; and, indeed, Bentham said that if things could be arranged so that "there would be only one slave to one master," the sum of good would just about balance the sum of evil (Bhikhu Parekh, "Bentham's Theory of Equality," *Political Studies* 18 [1970], p. 489; Bowring I, p. 344).

And in defending his projected Panopticon, a prison for "grinding rogues into honest men and idle ones into industrious" by supervision and regimentation twenty-four hours a day, Bentham wrote: "Call them soldiers, call them monks, call them machines, so they were but happy ones, I should not care" (Parekh, p. 495; Bowring IV, p. 64).

Bentham's psychology, which he took over from the associationist psychologist David Hartley, was a forerunner of Skinnerian behaviorism. Extreme environmentalism of this kind seems to have as its inevitable concomitant the devaluation of freedom as an end in itself. For if everything is externally determined, the concept of autonomy has no meaning. If Bentham's Panopticon bears a certain resemblance to Skinner's *Walden Two*, this is not accidental. Both were, in Skinner's words, *Beyond Freedom and Dignity*.

Later Developments in Utilitarian Economics

Utilitarianism provides a standard for judging economic systems that is, at any rate in principle, quite definite: the best system is the one that maximizes the aggregate amount of happiness. As the earlier discussion of slavery indicated, there is nothing in the utilitarian principle that sets any constraints on the way in which happiness should be distributed. The right distribution simply is the one that maximizes aggregate happiness. Thus, there is no room for Smith's notion that the prices and incomes that arise in a competitive market have sort of ethically preferred status in virtue of being "natural." If it will increase happiness, prices and incomes can be manipulated in whatever way is required.

Suppose that we have a fixed amount of stuff—call it cake—to distribute. If we knew everybody's utility schedule (that is to say, the amount of pleasure each person derives from eating various amounts of cake), the utilitarian rule for dividing it up would be to give each person whatever share of the cake makes the marginal utility of cake the same for everybody. In other words, the maximizing condition is that the amount of pleasure or satisfaction each person gets from the last crumb of cake should be equal.

Now, this is not in general going to result in an equal distribution of cake, since there is no reason for expecting utility schedules to be identical. And the departure from equality will be in a direction that might be naturally regarded as perverse. For the implication of the rule for distribution that we deduced from the utilitarian principle is as follows. Suppose that there are two people, one of whom gets a higher marginal utility than the other for any given amount of cake consumption. Then the rule says that the one with the higher level of marginal utility should get more cake. Thus, the natural advantage of this person in getting more enjoyment out of any given amount of cake is compounded by the working of the utilitarian criterion. In addition to getting more pleasure per unit of cake he or she gets more cake!

This conclusion was embraced by one distinguished utilitarian economist, F. Y. Edgeworth (in *Mathematical Psychics* and *New and Old Methods of Ethics)* but most have been uncomfortable with it. The usual escape route has been to argue that, although the conclusion follows in theory, in practice the information required to give effect to it is not available. Clearly, if this line is pushed too far it is liable to lead to skeptical thoughts about the utilitarian principle itself. (Does it make much sense to set up as a criterion the maximization of something we can't recognize?) But it is possible to make a claim that falls short of that. It may be said that we do, indeed, have some rough idea of the differences between people, but that these differences are too subjective and the appearances are too open to manipulation by people to form a sound basis for social policy. And the discretionary power that would have to be entrusted to the officials charged with making the estimates would be something that, on utilitarian grounds, we would wish to avoid.

If then, for purposes of social policy we are going to decide to take no account of individual differences in utility schedules, what should be done about distribution? If we claimed total agnosticism, we would be able to say nothing about it. But if we make one quite weak assumption, that cake has diminishing marginal utility, then we can derive the conclusion that an equal distribution is more likely to maximize the total sum of happiness than any other. In other words, although we don't know that it *will* maximize it, and indeed have every reason to believe that some other would be better, we don't know what that other is. Thus, the situation is like that of the accounts manager who once said that he was sure that half of his advertising budget was wasted but had no idea which half. The point is, then, that any arbitrary deviation from equality has a greater probability of decreasing aggregate satisfaction than increasing it. So, in the absence of individualized information, the best we can do is divide the cake up equally.

Both the premises seem quite strong. It surely would be unpleasant to live in a society in which material things were allocated according to an individualized utilitarian calculus. And the idea of diminishing marginal utility is surely plausible. It does seem reasonable to suppose that the less you have of something the more pleasure you get from a bit more. However, it is worth noticing that the whole line of argument here could alternatively be seen as a backhanded way of transcending utilitarianism. We could thus regard it as an attempt to use the utilitarian framework to generate conclusions whose basic ethical underpinnings are nonutilitarian.

Let me explain what I have in mind here. One way of arguing against allocations of things—cake, income, or whatever—based on direct utility calculations is, as we have seen, that they would involve intrusive information gathering, arbitrary discretion, etc. But alternatively we might say that, even if this were not so, it would still be morally objectionable to make allocations depend on what people get out of the stuff they receive. The issue is still one of freedom but in a more subtle way. The point is, on this alternative view, that people should have a chance to control certain resources irrespective of the use they make of them. Even if they don't make productive felicific use of them that shouldn't be a reason, even in principle, for taking them away and giving them to someone else.

We can interpret along the same lines the argument that derives equal distribution from skepticism about individual differences plus knowledge of the general fact of diminishing marginal utility. What we will now say is that this is an obscure and convoluted way of putting forward a claim that is in essence nonutilitarian. The claim is that each person has his or her hierarchy of priorities in life, and should have an equal chance to get as far as possible down the list of them. And an "equal chance" here should be understood as an equal claim on resources. Thus, the underlying idea is not so much that we *can't* reduce the different ends that people have to a common measure, but rather that the result of our doing so is not ethically significant.

This idea, which I have barely sketched, is manifestly another liberal, individualist one, but it comes out of the tradition of rights doctrines rather than the utilitarian traditions. It underlies Rawls's conception of primary goods as the subjects of justice, and has recently been identified with liberalism by Ronald Dworkin under the name of "neutrality" ("Liberalism" in Stuart Hampshire [ed.], *Public and Private Morality* [Cambridge: Cambridge University Press, 1978]). And more recently still, Bruce Ackerman has made this same concept of neutrality the centerpiece of his book, *Social Justice in the Liberal State* (New Haven: Yale University Press, 1980).

So far I have been talking about the distribution of some quantity of material stuff that is assumed somehow already to be in existence. Even Bentham maintained that, in the absence of specific individualized information about utility schedules, the mode of distribution in that case should be an equal one, though his reasoning did not involve explicit reference to diminishing marginal utility.

It was in fact quite bogus. He argued that if you have two people with equal amounts, and take half away from one and give it to the other, you have reduced one person by a half but increased the other by only a third. Therefore there must be a net loss of utility. This is clearly incorrect: if utility were linear with income (or whatever) it would be unchanged by the transfer. The only way of making sense of Bentham here seems to me to be to assume that he is in a confused way arguing for diminishing marginal utility.

Bentham, in any case, regarded this egalitarian conclusion as having very little in the way of practical implications because he was so impressed with the importance of supporting the market and therefore accepting whatever distribution of income came out of its workings. It was in this respect that the later utilitarians diverged from Bentham. The tendency in later economists was to give the market its due as an efficient mechanism but to suggest that it would be possible to increase aggregate utility by redistributing income. We can see this move in utilitarian economics in John Stuart Mill's *Principles of Political Economy* in the mid-nineteenth century and, more systematically, in Pigou's *The Economics of Welfare*, first published in 1920.

Although Mill, in his *Autobiography*, looked forward to a time in which people would work for the common good without requiring material incentives, utilitarian analyses always actually continued with the assumption of individual self-interest. The problem for a utilitarian policy on economic distribution thus became to find the optimal level of redistribution, allowing for the need for incentives.

The considerations that arise here for a utilitarian (or indeed for others) are familiar enough. Taxes of the usual kind, whether on income or on consumption have the effect, at some point, of discouraging effort. (At one hundred per cent they obviously discourage it completely, if people dislike work and are motivated by self-interest. So by an assumption of continuity we must suppose that lesser rates do so too.) But these taxes provide the wherewithal for paying those who would otherwise have little or nothing, so that the money so disposed has high marginal utility, much higher than it would have left in the hands of highly productive people. Maximum utility thus requires some redistribution from the highly productive to the nonproductive (and also perhaps to able-bodied but relatively incompetent) but not too much.

As Pigou said, "The correct formal answer to our question is that economic welfare is best promoted by a minimum standard raised to such a level that the direct good resulting from the transference of the marginal pound transferred to the poor just balances the indirect evil brought about by the consequent reduction of the dividend" (Pigou, *The Economics of Welfare* [London: Macmillan, 1920; 4th edition, 1932], p. 761). But as Pigou himself admitted, this is entirely formal—indeed a simple tautology—and does not in itself give us any guidance on what to do. Clearly to get a complete answer we would need to know about each individual's consumption utility schedules and for the able-bodied their production disutility schedules, plus information on the way in which their actual production varied with the post-tax incentives they faced. We should then have to work out on different tax rates how much would be produced and how it would finish up by being distributed. We could then pick the tax rates that maximized aggregate utility. In practice, none of this information is available. However, it is possible to work out the implications of alternative assumptions, and it has been found that a utilitarian income tax would not have very high marginal rates of tax, on any vaguely plausible assumptions.

Although there is not much loss to aggregate utility by taking away high incomes, because the utility of a marginal dollar is low, by the same token the incentive provided to effort by a marginal dollar is also low. So the more one believes in declining marginal utility of money the more good the transfer from the rich does but the more serious the incentive problem. This, of course, presupposes that the efforts of high income earners are sensitive to variations in post-tax income. As far as directors of large companies are concerned it seems doubtful if there is any effect on their efforts of paying them a half a million rather than a quarter of a million dollars per year, so tax rates approaching one hundred per cent at this kind of level are probably almost pure gain for the aggregate utility.

The Anti-Utilitarian Movement in Economics

The view that "interpersonal comparisons of utility" are forever impossible was for many years an almost unquestioned dogma among economists, and it still claims the allegiance of many leaders of the profession such as Kenneth Arrow. Yet taken literally it seems absurd: surely, we can be in little doubt that being burned is more painful than being pricked with a pin, whether we are comparing the effects on the same person or different people. How then did the idea that interpersonal comparisons are "meaningless" come about?

The answer seems to be that Lionel Robbins studied with the Vienna Circle and contracted a severe case of naive verificationism, which subsequently infected the rest of the profession.[1] (Even today, economics textbooks continue to repeat the dogmas of logical positivism.) Thus, it was held that we can in principle give an operational definition of a preference, because we can observe people choosing between alternatives, and from this we can construct their "revealed preference" schedule. But we cannot observe pain or pleasure, and any imputation of pain or pleasure to people is "subjective." We can, indeed, develop a measure of strength of preference between alternatives for a single individual by presenting him with a series of lotteries. But these "cardinal utilities" do not give us a basis on which to compare the utilities of different people.

There are two lines of objection to this kind of view. The first is that the program of constructed "revealed preference" schedules cannot in fact be carried out in a coherent fashion (see especially Amartya Sen, "Behaviour and the Concept of Preference," Inaugural Lecture, London School of Economics and Political Science, 1973). The other is that we need not cry about this, because there is nothing much to be said for the verificationist criterion of meaning, construed so that interpersonal comparisons of utility are "meaningless." In fact, human behavior could not even be described in an intelligible way as a series of physical movements, noises, etc. Our vocabulary is designed for describing what people *do,* and describing what they do entails our having some ideas about what they intend, what they believe, and so on. But once we allow that, we are already well outside the sphere of naive verificationism and there is no reason why we should hesitate to say, for example, that A enjoyed the concert a lot more than did B. In many cases, the evidence for saying such a thing will be very strong.

At another level, the argument about "interpersonal comparisons of utility" may be seen as a piece of ideological skirmishing. As I have remarked, the classical utilitarians (a line which we may for this purpose regard as running up through Pigou) concluded from the rough similarity of human beings in their capacity to turn income into utility that an equal distribution of income would approximately maximize the aggregate utility derived from a given income stream. The extreme skepticism introduced into economics by Robbins undercut this egalitarian argument. Utilitarianism could no longer be defined in terms of maximizing the sum of individual utilities but must be redefined to make use only of ordinal utilities (i.e., individual preference orderings) as against interpersonally comparable cardinal utilities.

The utilitarian criterion expressed in ordinal utilities, however, reduces to the Pareto criterion, which reads that situation X is better than situation Y if and only if nobody prefers Y to X and at least one person prefers X to Y. As it stands, the Pareto principle is mute about almost any large-scale change that ever occurs or is ever proposed, since it is just about inconceivable that there would not be at least one person who loses from the change and at least one who gains from it. (Losses and gains are, it should be borne in mind, to be understood as defined in terms of preferences.)

One way of getting results out of the Pareto criterion has been to admit that in practice it is not feasible to arrange that in any change from one situation to another nobody will lose, but then to argue that as a second-best approximation we may say that a change is desirable if the gainers *could* more than compensate the losers, even if they never in fact do so. This was the leading idea of the so-called "new welfare economics" of the 1940s and 1950s. It survives now in the "economic analysis of law" associated particularly with the name of Richard Posner, who has proposed that the following should be the assignment principle for entitlements: "Confer the entitlement on that party who would have purchased it had the transaction costs not made it irrational for him to do so."

It seems to me that this modification of the Pareto principle has all the faults of classical utilitarianism without any of the virtues. It is completely indifferent to any questions of equity in distribution, like classical utilitarianism; but, unlike classical utilitarianism, it provides us with no reason for supposing that aggregate utility will be increased if its prescriptions are followed. A Pareto-superior situation may not maximize aggregate utility, and, if we go outside the utilitarian framework for a moment, we can add that it will tend to preserve any existing inequities that exist in the status quo. But we can at least be assured that, if some gain and none lose, aggregate utility must have increased. We no longer have any reason for such assurance if some actually lose, even if we believe that the gainers could have compensated the losers fully and still come out ahead. Indeed, on the assumption of the decreasing marginal utility of money, we have good reason to anticipate a loss of aggregate utility where the gainers are richer than the losers.

The other route is the one taken by James Buchanan and what we may call the Virginia school of political economy, who have in effect reinvented the social contract. It is this school to which I was referring when I said at the beginning that welfare economics, having started out in the eighteenth century and proceeded through the nineteenth and early twentieth centuries had now regressed to the seventeenth. It discards the painfully-won understanding of the past three centuries and substitutes an a priori theory of politics founded on the presumed interests of presocial individuals in a state of nature. There is no evidence that the members of this school have examined with care the reasons why this mode of proceeding has fallen into such universal contempt in the last couple of centuries and have, on mature reflection, found them wanting. Rather, they seem to me to display a kind of willful, arrogant ignorance about the entire history of historical and social thought.

The basic idea is as follows. It may be recalled that the Pareto principle, interpreted as saying only that a change from which everyone gains is an improvement, was forced to be agnostic about most changes. The Virginia school avoid this problem of indeterminacy by saying that Pareto superiority is not only a sufficient condition of a change's being an improvement but also a necessary condition.

The obvious problem that this raises—quite apart from the question whether there is any reason for accepting the criterion in this form—is that we have to have some baseline from which to reckon Pareto superiority. And this, it seems, is going to have to come out of some quite different sort of moral theory. At this point Buchanan invokes the notion of the social contract in the hopes that it will provide the foundation he needs. The idea put forward in *The Limits of Liberty* (Chicago: University of Chicago Press, 1975) is that we start from a Hobbesian "state of nature" and somehow derive Lockean conclusions. Buchanan's "state of nature" is super-Hobbesian in that there are no moral constraints operating within it. But, unlike Hobbes, Buchanan apparently does not believe in the approximate natural equality of all men, so he allows for the possibility that some will be able to dominate or (de facto) enslave others.

This unappetizing scenario constitutes Buchanan's baseline. He argues, again on Hobbesian lines, that the people in his "state of nature" would find it mutually advantageous (i.e., Pareto superior) to replace it with settled laws, enforced by a sovereign. But the shift to Locke occurs at this point. For, whereas Hobbes argues that everyone gains by setting up an absolute sovereign, who can make all the subsequent arrangements (including, for example, creating property rights by fiat), Buchanan insists that people should keep the specific advantages they had in the state of nature. The Pareto superiority consists in everybody keeping what they had but being secured in the possession of it. Thus, civil society, so far from operating so as to compensate for natural inequalities in physical and mental capacity puts the force of law behind the perpetuation of the material inequalities that would arise from them in the state of nature. We might think of this as an artificial analogue of the process whereby, in the Gombe Stream reserve, the dominance hierarchy is maintained without continuous fighting.

I won't spend time criticizing this as an ethical theory—the criticisms are obvious—because in any case Buchanan doesn't really use it. He never really asks what things would be like in a state of nature and then tries to see what allocations of rights and benefits would be Pareto superior to it. No doubt it is a sign of good sense that he does not, since the inquiry would be an absurd one. But it does, of course, mean that he is back with a criterion—Pareto superiority—that lacks a foundation.

At this point, Buchanan makes a prodigious leap, and says that as a second best to going back to the state of nature and starting from there, we should start from the *status quo* and freeze the distribution of rights and benefits we have now, or whatever modification of it would be generally agreed to, out of altruism or fear among those who would give things up. "We start from here," as Buchanan says. But this clearly raises equally serious ethical problems. Unless there is some independent basis for saying that the status quo is just, it is hard to see what the ethical attraction is of arranging things so that nobody can be adversely affected in relation to it.

Conclusion

The common feature of both the utilitarian and nonutilitarian versions of welfare economics has been their indifference to questions of distribution. This is explicit in classical utilitarianism and also in the hypothetical compensation criterion. The criterion of Pareto superiority as a necessary condition for something's counting as an improvement is, in one sense, strongly concerned with distribution. For it obviously has the implication that no gain, however large, to one person can counterbalance an uncompensated loss, however small, to another. But it is at the same time in another and more important sense sublimely unconcerned with distribution inasfar as it provides no basis on which to assess the status quo against which Pareto superiority is to be measured.

Out of the pantheon of economists whose work I have mentioned, only Adam Smith introduced distributive criteria into his analysis, and then only implicitly in the form of the claim that the market rate of return to factors of production was "natural" and thus somehow right. Writing in 1885, Henry Sidgwick was able to remark complacently that, although there had once been people who declared "the 'inalienable right of every man freely to exchange the result of his labour for the productions of other people,' " to be " 'one of the principles of eternal justice,' " English political economy had shaken off all connection with these "antiquated metaphysics" under the "more philosophic guidance of J. S. Mill" (Sidgwick, "Bentham and Benthamism," pp. 173–74).

Sidgwick spoke a good deal too soon. Almost a century after he addressed the Economics and Statistics section of the British Association for the Advancement of Science in those words, we are in the midst of an extraordinary revival of Lockean fundamentalism. As we have seen, James Buchanan's use of the criterion of Pareto superiority rests, at any rate in theory, upon the foundation of a curious kind of contract theory in which property rights are carried into civil society from a state of nature in which there are no rights but only de facto possessions. And, in political philosophy, as against welfare economics (if the two can any longer be distinguished) we have Robert Nozick's *Anarchy, State and Utopia* (New York: Basic Books, 1974), which is more Lockean than Locke himself, inasfar as it would render illegitimate the role that Locke left for majoritarian decision making in matters of property and taxation. It has to be said at once that Nozick does not appear to have made many converts among the ranks of Anglo-American philosophers, but the large amount of interest and the volume of response generated by this piece of archaism must itself be regarded as a significant cultural phenomenon.

My own view, as will probably be apparent from what has already been said, is that the concern with questions of distribution is to be welcomed— and distribution not merely in gross terms such as the overall dispersion of income levels, but also in terms of the claims on the basis of which income goes to one person rather than another. I do not think that it is at all helpful to answer such questions by bringing in a supposed state of nature. I think that the concepts already exist for criticizing the distribution of income (and of other benefits) in an existing society. In spite of all the problems in applying it, I believe that the principle that rewards should be related to contributions is a basic one on which widespread agreement is possible. It should not, indeed, be the only principle, but it can be supplemented by others, such as the principle that John Rawls placed at the foundation of his theory of justice: the "duty of fair play." This is the principle that tells us to play our part in arrangements for social cooperation that are of mutual benefit. One such arrangement is social insurance. All the members of a society gain from a scheme in which the unemployed, the incapacitated, the sick, and the old can make claims as of right on the rest of the society for assistance.

These are two elements in an arrangement that is explicitly distributive in that it defines justice in terms that discriminate between the claims of different individuals. At the same time, it does not involve interpersonal comparisons of utility, because "contribution" and "reward" can be denominated in nonutility terms (value created and income received) and the basis of social insurance is not to maximize any aggregate across a society but to provide a system beneficial (in prospect) to all. It thus avoids the two difficulties that we found in the ethical implications of welfare economics.

NOTE

1. [Lionel Robbins's] book, *The Nature and Significance of Economic Science,* was published in London by Macmillan's in 1932.

14 Public and Private Choice: A Philosophical Analysis

R. Paul Churchill

WHAT IS THE PROPER domain of public policy analysis; that is, to what sorts of problems are such techniques of rational decision theory as cost-benefit analysis applicable? For a student in a course in public policy analysis or for the authors of the standard textbooks in these courses, the answer might seem obvious: the domain of public policy encompasses every problem or conflict which concerns the interests of citizens collectively (the public) and for which solutions are not forthcoming from ordinary markets and private contractual trades (Leonard and Zeckhauser 1986: 46).

My purpose in this chapter is to challenge this notion that "public choice" is equivalent to "applying the economizing methods of rational decision theory." Thus I shall argue that the concept of public choice cannot be explicated entirely in terms of efforts to maximize the preference-satisfaction of individuals. I shall argue further that we should consider distinguishing between different categories of public policy problems and, therefore, should recognize two distinct "domains" of public choice. One category concerns problems of choice in which public interests can be interpreted as aggregates of personal preferences. For the sake of convenience, I will refer to the "domain of public preference" as comprising problems of this type; and I suggest that it is within this domain that the techniques of rational decision theory apply. But the other category concerns public choices that represent the expression of social values which play a central role in the definition, by people, of their community or society, and in the formation of their collective purposes and conceptions of meaningful life. I will speak of the "domain of social values" as comprising problems of this type; and I suggest that it is in this second domain of public choice that the economizing methods of policy analysis prove to be inappropriate.

Furthermore, because of these different categories of public choice, policy analysts should give more attention to the problem of "subsumption": the difficulty of finding a common metric with which to subsume, in a single analysis, all of the interests of all parties who will be affected by a policy decision. Thus my argument that we recognize two "domains" of public choice would support the claims of critics that techniques such as cost-benefit analysis often fail because they attempt to encompass incommensurable values. Moreover, it would challenge the view that analytic approaches to decision making are neutral devices that structure decision problems by encompassing all important considerations of value and giving them whatever weight we determine to be important. When they are misapplied to problems of public choice in the domain of social values, techniques such as cost-benefit analysis are hardly neutral; indeed, they promote efficiency as a social value that should take precedence over, or trump, competing social values.

My argument for the distinction between a domain of public preference and a domain of social values will proceed in two parts. In the first part I offer an analysis of interests that attempts to establish a significant difference between preferences and values, and hence, a difference between preferences shared by individuals collectively and social values. Following this analysis, I identify briefly the sorts of public policy problems that fall into these different categories. In addition I argue that, given this difference, it is not plausible to think that social values can be "reduced" to personal preferences; that is, interpreted as the aggregated preferences of the individuals who express them. In the second part of the paper I offer an explanation as to why policy analysts in general fail to understand that there are two different domains of public choice. This explanation draws upon historical evidence that in Western cultures there has been a major transformation in our understanding of what is "public," and hence, a major reversal of the public/private distinction. Understanding how this reversal has allowed traditionally private interests to come to dominate the "space" of public concern and decision will explain why it is so easy today to conceive of public interest as nothing more than an aggregate of individual preferences.

I. Personal Preferences and Social Values

I shall regard "interests" as referring to a broad category that includes both preferences and values as different types of interests. Attempts to distinguish between preferences and values may seem questionable or even suspect because ordinary English often reflects the indiscriminate use of the terms involved. Thus, common usage permits the word "value" to refer to anything deemed desirable, whatever the source, content, referent, or objective of the desire. This suggests that the verbs "value" and "desire" are interchangeable and that, as a noun, "value" is synonymous with "interest" or "preference." Substitutions of this kind in speech and writing are common and usually do not raise eyebrows. In addition, self-reflexive or recursive uses of the terms, as when one speaks of "preferring one value to another" reinforce our impressions that we are indeed on slippery linguistic terrain.

Nevertheless, those who have studied the way people tend to speak about their interests, or to defend their choices, call attention to certain recurrent patterns of expression and linguistic behavior. For instance, in conducting research for *Habits of the Heart,* Robert Bellah and his associates (1986) found that *values* are what people invoke when they try to define who they are as a people and what they accept as fundamental, orienting principles. Also, when people regard certain interests as absolute requirements or as non-negotiable demands, they tend to speak of them as values rather than as preferences.

In addition, values are associated with interests that exhibit stability over time and considerable resistance to change. By contrast, preferences are often unstable and are easily influenced by changes in mood and attitude, and vacillations of the opinions and preferences of others (Elster 1983: Ch. III). While values tend to influence perception and our interpretations of experience, preferences are highly adaptive and grow out of experience rather than predating it. We generally do not have very clear ideas of our preferences for things lying very far outside either our past experience or our present possibilities (Goodin 1980: 418).

Moreover, at an intuitive level we are all aware of the difference in significance and weight we attach to values over preferences. Thus, while each of us may be able to rank most of our preferences, and to explain why we have many of them, we don't feel that they require defense or justification. Nor do we regard mere preferences as warranting the respect of others. By contrast, we debate issues of value precisely because we presuppose that value judgments, unlike expressions of preference, are amenable to rational discourse. We presuppose, further, that discourse about value judgments is guided by a set of criteria according to which our respective values can be challenged or defended by appeal to reasons that can be recognized publicly as weighty or persuasive. And this shows not only that our thinking about values is similar, in important respects, to our thinking about moral judgments, obligations, and rights, but also that, far from being the products of lonely subjectivity, value judgments are predominantly interpersonal positions supported by reasons (Tong 1986: 9). As the philosopher Mark Sagoff notes, "When individuals participate in the political process to determine the common values and purposes that d them together as a community or as a nation, they regard themselves as judges of policy decisions, not merely as critics of their own welfare. . . . The application of a cost-benefit formula cannot replace the public discussion of ideas; it is not just what the individual *wants* but what he *thinks* that counts" (Sagoff 1986: 302).

The effort to treat preferences as if they had this additional dimension of weight and public consideration sometimes leads to some strained and awkward language. For example, commenting on what is said and debated on environmental issues, Ronald Dworkin refers to people as expressing "impersonal preferences" which he defines as preferences people have "about things other than their own or other people's lives or situations" (1982: 192). And in referring to controversies over sexual morality, Dworkin speaks of "external preferences" as "preferences people have about what others shall do or have" (1985: 196). But just because preferences concern our subjective feelings and desires, they are always personal and internal and never "personal" and "external." Indeed, by using this odd terminology, Dworkin must be trying to refer to things we prefer that are *not* reducible to our own subjective states; and therefore, referring, in this convoluted way, to people's choices of certain social values rather than others.

So far I have been discussing differences between personal preferences and values, but I believe the same distinction pertains to aggregates of preferences on one hand and social values on the other. In fact, the values I have been considering necessarily have a *social* dimension; they exist because members of a community have, through common goals and aspirations, *intersubjective* intentions. Douglas MacLean says, "We can characterize social values as the importance to members of the group of experiencing their public lives and social interactions in certain ways" (1986: 91), and Mark Sagoff says of social values (which he calls "communitarian," or "public values") "[p]ublic values are goals or intentions the individual ascribes to the group or community of which he is a member; they are his because he believes and argues that they should be ours; he pursues them not as an individual but as one of us" (1986: 302). (I leave open the question whether such so-called "personal values" as self-restraint or self-discipline could be desired by individuals if they were not identified and defined by various communities as admirable traits for human beings.)

This analysis of the difference between preferences and social values helps us understand why some conflicts, more than others, involve acrimonious debates in which many people act as if their fundamental moral or religious beliefs were being challenged, or as if their identity as Americans or as citizens was under attack. These disputes suggest the presence of public problems in the domain of social values. Examples include controversies over the following: the safety of nuclear reactors, the location of toxic waste sites, the location of MX missiles, occupational safety in the

workplace, consumer product safety, environmental quality and the protection of biological diversity, regulation of day care centers, teaching of
creationism or of sex education in the public schools, abortion, home-
lessness, and dignity for the terminally ill. (Some examples recently in the
news include the controversy over the fate of the Spotted Owl in the
Pacific Northwest, the political initiative to end the sale of furs in Aspen,
Colorado, and the conflict over the exhibition of Mapplethorpe's photog-
raphy in Cincinnati.) On an imaginary scale of public policy problems,
they are much closer to problems that revolve around attempts to extend
or limit human or constitutional rights. Hence, it is not surprising that
many of these problems involve controversies in constitutional law, and
that partial solutions are attempted through the extension of rights (e.g.,
the right to choose, the right to die). Just because rights function as trumps
in the political process, they are often effective constraints on alternative
"solutions" to public problems, including efforts to maximize preference-
satisfaction.

By contrast, problems in the domain of public preference usually involve tangible gains and losses that are perceived as having the same
dimension (and therefore as susceptible to analysis using a common metric). Examples of problems in this domain include controversies over utility rate setting, increases in postal rates, rezoning for business uses, allocation of water in arid regions, siting of a new highway in a suburban county,
regulation of savings and loans, regulation of the sale of junk bonds,
restructuring of tax rates, and the selection of a public transportation
system.

Of course, issues that concern the public do not come neatly bundled
up as either problems in the domain of preference or as problems in the
domain of social values. We know from experience that many "public
problems," for example, each of the controversies over "star wars," the
AIDS epidemic, and the "war on drugs" really consists of a cluster of
problems, some involving social values and others centering on the distribution of tangible gains or losses. This confusion is exacerbated by impre-
cise or even self-serving descriptions of "the problem" by the media, or by
politicians or citizen activists. It is to be hoped, therefore, that one consequence of the distinction made here will be greater clarity in the definition
and discussion of public problems.

But given the significance of the distinction between preferences and
social values, why has it not received more attention from policy analyses?
My main response to this question will come in the second part of this
paper where I explain how our understanding of public policy has been
affected by the reversal in Western culture of the traditional distinction
between the public and private spheres. Before turning to Part II [of this
chapter], however, I want to anticipate and respond to a possible objection to what I have said so far. No doubt some policy analysts might claim

that, despite the differences between preferences and values outlined above, all interests can be treated in rational decision theory *as if* they are all of the same type.

Thus, policy analysts might argue that, although social values are not the same thing as preferences, it is a *necessary* condition for the existence of social values that there be members of the community who *prefer* that certain conditions or states of the world be attained in society. Thus we can speak of preferences for different social values and we can even devise various measures of the intensity with which people express commitment to their values. Thus when a value, for example, the aesthetic value of a copse of woods, conflicts with a widely expressed preference for the convenience of a bridge that would destroy the woods, it seems reasonable for the majority who share the interest in convenience or efficiency to feel justified in proceeding to build the bridge if they are willing (or at least able) to compensate those whose interests in beauty will be sacrificed. Likewise, it should not be surprising if we find that some or even many of those who subscribe to the value agree to being "bought out" in this manner. Thus, for example, risk analysts like to point out that even most of those who value human life as "sacred" or "priceless" commonly accept low risks of the loss of life, for instance when they drive, in order to avoid paying for certain inconveniences or inefficiencies.

Phenomena of this sort are common enough, but why should this be regarded as proof that preferences and social values are essentially commensurable? It seems indisputable that if social values are to be effective in guiding behavior, then individuals must be able to express preferences for certain outcomes or conditions that embody or otherwise represent these values. Hence it seems incontrovertible that having social values must entail preferences for at least some actual or potential outcomes. But it does not follow from this that social values can be *reduced* to aggregated preferences. In the first place, because they conceive of goods as essentially individual, policy analysts fail to perceive that some public goods are not just shared but are "goods held in common" in the sense that they accrue only to persons in a relationship with each other (Briand 1990). Such "common goods" are not aggregates, or sums, of individual goods because they cannot be divided; they belong to members of a community who act collaboratively, but not to any of them individually. In addition, policy analysts often err in assuming that there is no difference between how people value certain things in private individual transactions and how they would wish those same things to be valued in public collective decisions. For example, Steven Kelman points out that in considering the regulation of health risks, we may wish our social decisions to provide us the occasion to display the reverence for life that we espouse but do not always show in our everyday personal decisions (1981:38).

Because social values come into being only through public agreement and cooperation, their continual existence will always be vulnerable to variations of the "assurance problem" and to free-riding. Often, however, when individuals proceed to "cash in" on social values or policy analysts make proposals to compensate losers, we find that the legitimacy or justification of this conversion process is itself called into question. There have been some controversies in which, because of public opposition, legislation has been passed to restrict compensation schemes or even to prohibit a cost-benefit test (Viscusi 1983: 162). And this seems to me to be a decisive consideration for the claim that social values are not equivalent to aggregated preferences. For if the two were equivalent, then I cannot understand why the efforts made by policy analysts to demonstrate this equivalency so often meet with strong opposition. But, of course, they often do; and what this opposition shows is that there is disagreement over the place to be given in public life to the *values* of efficiency or want satisfaction served by the conversion process, or the tradeoff, itself.

II. Transformation of the Public and Private Spheres

In this part of the chapter I seek to explain how insensitivity to the difference between preferences and values has arisen from confusion over what should be regarded as appropriately open to public scrutiny and decision in contrast to private behavior. And to understand this confusion we must try to recover what the public/private distinction has meant historically.

In his historical investigation of privacy, Barrington Moore traces the origins of the public/private distinction to classical Greece where it coincided with the distinction between the realm of politics—the affairs of the *polis*—and the realm of domestic life and household affairs (1984: 133). The words for public were *demios,* which means literally "having to do with the people," and *koinos,* which means "common" in the sense of shared in common. The word for private was *idios* (also the root for "idiot"), meaning "one's own, pertaining to one's self" (82). Moore notes that it was in classical Greece, and in the Roman world as well, that we find the origin of the view of private behavior as a realm protected against the intrusion of religious or secular authority: "many social obligations stopped quite literally at the front door of a citizen's house . . ." (196).

But the significance of these boundaries of social geography was greater than is suggested by the conflict between individual liberty and authority. Indeed, as the philosopher Hannah Arendt recognized, the public was a social and psychic "space" in which common values could develop; as a human creation, it was a realm of significance in which words and deeds could acquire a recognizable, "objective" meaning (Arendt 1958). And this was possible because, in public, individuals became related to (and differentiated from) each other through an intermediary world of objects, symbols, rituals, and conventions common to all members of the *polis*. The essential aspect of "the public" was precisely the sharing of the rituals, conventions, and artifices through which citizenship was defined and communal purposes were selected. While the historian, Linda Nicholson, claims that the public was the realm of "articulated reason, or law, in ordering social life" (1986: 25), Arendt goes further in averring that, by occurring publicly—by being seen and heard by others as well as by ourselves—some things acquire a special kind of reality. "The presence of others who see what we see and hear what we hear assures us of the reality of the world and ourselves" (50). While Arendt's claim may be extreme in some respects, she is certainly right that some desirable attributes, for example, fashion, style, reputation, fame, and honor can exist only in the presence of others.

Arendt argues that, in contrast to the public, the private realm has to be understood, in its origins, in the sense of "privative," as the area of activity, epitomized by family relations, in which every individual sought to satisfy the demands of nature. If the public was a human creation, then the private was the human condition (Sennett: 98), and it was identical with consumption and need gratification in the household and with related housekeeping activities. As such, the private was essentially a realm of undifferentiated activity and of inarticulate and incommunicable experience. Arendt points out that whatever is radically subjective—the intensely pleasurable and the intensely painful—are necessarily private. Because very intense sensations dominate consciousness, they dissolve and break down the structures of meaning needed to confer public significance on experience. Thus Arendt argues that intense pleasure and intense pain "cannot assume an appearance in public life" (51). We can certainly experience pleasure or pain collectively, but the experience is always an individual experience whether we are together or alone.

There seems today to be a common perception that the boundary separating the public and private domains has dissolved. This perception is reflected by the frequency with which people speak of the "politicization of the private." Linda Nicholson points out that, for radical feminists (among others), the "personal is political" because both gender and sexuality pertain to all of social life: "practices which take place between women and men acting *qua* women and men [do] not stand outside the domain of politics" (17). But, along with the politicization of the private, we might equally well talk about the "privatization of the public" because it has become increasingly common—and perhaps policy analysis has taken the lead in this—to conceive of public interest (even as social values or opinions about what ultimately matters) as mere aggregates of personal preferences and to aim for those policies that maximize expected preference satisfaction (Baier 1986: 51).

There are various explanations as to how this reversal of the public and private realms has come about. Both Arendt and Nicholson believe that the reversal was due chiefly to industrialization and the rise of market economies. Nicholson points out that in the past the family, as the primary unit for the production of food and objects needed for survival, was not differentiated from the sphere of economic activity as it is today. But with the rise of industrialization the production of consumable goods ceased to be governed by familial principles and instead became organized by the principles of the market (3). Arendt asserts that this admission of household and housekeeping activities to the public realm coincided historically with the transformation of private care for property into a public concern as property owners demanded legal protection for the accumulation of their wealth (45–47, 68). Arendt adds, however, that private property can never become common wealth in the sense of a common world, for, when concerns for property and livelihood are dominant, then only the government can be common to all and "the only thing people [will] have in common is their private interests" (69).

Richard Sennett agrees that the only thing individuals share in common today is the satisfaction of their private interests. The public interest therefore is nothing more than the aggregation of private interests. But Sennett identifies as the major cause of this phenomenon the rise of individual, subjective personality as the major "symbolic force" and organizing principle of society (108). Sennett points out that the existence of the *res publica* depends upon conventions, artifices, and rules that establish relatively stable but impersonal meanings (impersonal because they must be accessible to and intelligible to all). But the *res publica* has been effaced by widespread acceptance of the belief that all meanings are generated by the subjective feelings of individual human beings (340). Consequently, the classical vision of public life based on shared values is impossible in our excessively individualistic culture of autonomy.

Finally, several commentators have argued that the transformation in our understanding of the public and private realms was a result of the widespread acceptance of the ideology of liberalism (Sullivan 1989; Bellah 1990). Liberals have frequently characterized all conceptions of common ends as "metaphysical" commitments which necessarily imperil the freedom of those who do not subscribe to them (Berlin 1969). Hence defenders of classical liberalism frequently argue that public agreement concerning the ends of collective action must be tightly restricted to those agreements which do not "privilege" or benefit some conceptions of the ends of life over others. Consequently, public decision making should be guided by principles which are "neutral" among various conceptions of what is worth pursuing in life beyond the defense of the private freedom of individual choice.

Whatever the role of these several causes in shaping our modern sensibilities, the cumulative effect has been an almost complete reversal of the original understanding of the public and the private. Whereas "public" had connoted the activity of forming "objective" (or at least intersubjective) values and "private" had connoted subjective desires and preferences, today questions of value and purpose have been relegated to the private realm while the public interest is understood as the aggregation of personal preferences.

III. Conclusion

In this chapter I have argued that we should recognize two different types of problems of public choice, and thus, two distinct domains of public policy. My argument for this conclusion has involved two related strands: first, an analysis of interests that establishes the distinction between preferences and values; and second, an explanation of why public choice is so easily conceived as a problem of maximizing preference satisfaction rather than a problem of weighing and selecting the values by which a community chooses to define its way of life.

If this argument is correct, if there are indeed two different types of public choice, then some important implications follow for the way we understand public policy. In the first place, public policy as conceived of by professional policy analysts has a fairly limited scope. Techniques for the maximization of preference-satisfaction represent responses to what might be called "coordination problems;" they show how citizens can act collectively to produce an optimal satisfaction of private, individual preferences. But use of these analytical techniques is therefore restricted to those problems in which there is widespread agreement that a single metric can be used to weigh all relevant preferences; and, what is more important, only when there is general consensus that *efficiency,* the value that legitimizes these techniques, is the only social value at risk.

For this reason, the methods of rational decision theory are of very limited use in addressing the graver problems in the second domain of public policy. These problems concern the articulation and formation of social values themselves and solutions to conflicts in this domain depend on debating and choosing among "impersonal views" on their merits rather than on maximizing preference-satisfaction. Nothing is gained by forcing participants in these debates to disguise their values as personal wants or preferences. Indeed, when it comes to our "deep" public problems, we risk losing much by insisting on outcomes supplied by clumsy and one-sided analytical techniques, for we become increasingly forgetful that forging successful *public* solutions requires the development of our best capacities as social and political animals: our capacities for effective communication, rational discourse, and practical reasoning. For problems in this second domain of public policy, therefore, we need to develop what

Jurgen Habermas called our "communicative-moral rationality" and to remember that the "instrumental rationality" of policy analysis is only the means by which to attain the ends we *ought* to seek.

REFERENCES

Arendt, Hannah, 1958. *The Human Condition*. Chicago: University of Chicago Press.

Baier, Annette, 1986. "Poisoning the Wells." *Values at Risk*. Douglas MacLean, ed. Totowa, N.J.: Rowman & Allanheld.

Bellah, Robert, et al., 1986. *Habits of the Heart*. New York: Harper & Row.

———, 1990. *The Good Society*. Draft of Introduction for forthcoming book.

Berlin, Isaiah, 1969. *Four Essays on Liberty*. London: Oxford University Press.

Briand, Michael, 1990. "Conflicts of Values in Public Policymaking: Strategies for Dialogues on Social Problems." (unpublished).

Dworkin, Ronald, 1982. "What Is Equality? Part I: Equality of Welfare." 10 *Philosophy and Public Affairs*.

———, 1985. *A Matter of Principle*. Cambridge, Mass.: Harvard University Press.

Elster, Jon, 1983. *Sour Grapes: Studies in the Subversion of Rationality*. New York: Cambridge University Press.

Goodin, Robert, 1980. "No Moral Nukes." 90 *Ethics*.

Habermas, Jurgen, 1979: *Communication and the Evolution of Society*. Thomas McCarthy, trans. Boston: Beacon Press.

Kelman, Steven, 1981. "Cost-Benefit Analysis: An Ethical Critique." *Regulation* January/February; chap. 4, this volume.

Leonard, Herman and Zeckhauser, Richard, 1986. "Cost-Benefit Analysis Applied to Risks: Its Philosophy and Legitimacy." *Values at Risk*. Douglas MacLean, ed. Totowa, N.J.: Rowman & Allanheld.

MacLean, Douglas, 1986. "Social Values and the Distribution of Risk." *Values at Risk*. Douglas MacLean, ed. Totowa, N.J.: Rowman & Allanheld.

Moore, Barrington, 1984. *Privacy*. Armonk, NY: M. E. Sharpe.

Nicholson, Linda, 1986. *Gender and History*. New York: Columbia University Press.

Sagoff, Mark, 1986. "Values and Preferences." 96 *Ethics*.

Sennett, Richard, 1976. *The Fall of Public Man*. New York: Knopf.

Sullivan, William, 1989. "Bringing the Good Back In." (unpublished).

Tong, Rosemarie, 1986. *Ethics in Policy Analysis*. Englewood Cliffs, N.J.: Prentice-Hall.

Viscusi, Kip, 1983. "Presidential Oversight: Controlling the Regulators." 2 *Journal of Policy Analysis and Management*.

15 Economic and Political Rationality

Stephen L. Elkin

MUCH CONTEMPORARY POLITICAL debate focuses on the proper organization of the public sector. The central question is how best to regulate social activity and provide governmental goods and services. The merits of various institutional arrangements are compared, from the marketlike schemes relying on exchange processes to administrative agencies that are to enforce an elaborate set of regulatory directives. Virtually all parts of the public domain, from the environment and public health to transportation and education have been scrutinized in this fashion.

Perhaps the dominant view of these institutional arrangements is as instruments to achieve separately defined ends.[1] We may appropriately term this an economizing or economic rationality conception of institutional choice, applying a term commonly used for a view of rationality in which an instrumental relation between ends and means figures prominently.[2] Economizing embodies a widespread conception of the meaning of rational action in public affairs.

But, is it really appropriate to look at institutional arrangements, such as the traditional forms of regulation and the newer tax incentive schemes, as mere instruments? Can such an instrumental view capture what is fundamental to a consideration of their merits? Questions such as these prompt this paper. Anyone who shares the doubts implicit in these questions will want to look beyond economizing as a guide to selecting among institutional arrangements. The effort may be called a search for political rationality and that is my principal undertaking here.

I have two, more particular aims: (1) to demonstrate that sophisticated economizers can accommodate the criticisms typically aimed at them, and that if nothing else is offered beyond these criticisms, doubts such as those just noted can be put aside; and (2) to sketch an alternative view of choosing among institutional arrangements, namely, political rationality, and to outline a central feature of it that I will call a constitutive conception of political institutions.

Offering an alternative political conception of rationality is not in itself a decisive criticism of economizing. But an attempt to elaborate alternatives is a necessary step in accomplishing the purpose of such criticism, which is a proper understanding of what is at stake when we choose between types of political institutions. And a thorough-going critique of economizing will inevitably emerge once a plausible alternative is available. Such a searching evaluation of economizing will probably lead to its rejection as a comprehensive guide to choice among institutional arrangements, but that kind of discussion is beyond my purpose here. I should add that to sketch a conception of political rationality is not to mount an argument in its defense. That too will emerge from a comprehensive assessment of frameworks for understanding the choice among institutional arrangements.

I begin with a discussion of economizing, then turn to criticisms of it and indicate how economizers can meet them. Next, I discuss political rationality, particularly the constitutive conception of political institutions that is one of its fundamental features. I then examine how political rationality might be applied in selecting institutional arrangements. In conclusion I consider, among other things, the usefulness of political rationality in our present political context.

I. Economizing

McKean expresses the underlying idea of economizing when he says: "It should go without saying that all decision-making persons or groups attempt to economize, in the true sense of the word. That is, they try to make the 'most' as they conceive of the 'most' of whatever resources they have."[3] Economizers hold firmly to the belief that action should always aim at the best available balance between desired outputs and inputs.[4]

Many of the features of an economizing perspective turn up in studies of regulation.[5] Zeckhauser and Nichols,[6] for example, in their analysis of occupational safety and health, list a number of institutional arrangements, including reliance on a reformed market system, workmen's compensation, taxation and tort law schemes, and standard setting by administrative agencies. They consider each alternative in light of an efficiency objective ("minimize the sum of the cost of safety and health lost," p. 183), the distribution of costs and compensation, and administrative efficiency. These and other economizers see their job as defining a variety of instruments and evaluating each of them in light of sortie definition of the purposes to be achieved and the costs incurred in doing so. Institutions are instruments to produce a result and are interchangeable. Each is a potential substitute for the other.

Within economizing generally are two distinct approaches. Practitioners of the first we may call "narrow" economizers. They see ends or purposes as externally provided, by the "political process." Implicit in this view is the existence of a "decision maker" who has the authority to choose between instruments. The work of policy analysis is to provide him (or them) with evaluations of the alternatives. For narrow economizers efficiency is defined as choosing the alternative with the best ratio between the cost of the instrument and the extent to which policy objectives are achieved.

The second type of economizer attempts to take direct account of the multiple ends of the citizenry, rather than rely on a definition of ends provided by authoritative decision makers. These "broad" economizers evaluate institutional alternatives, at a minimum, in terms of "grand" efficiency,[7] by which they mean the efficiency of social states. They are concerned with how the choice of institutional arrangements affects society as a whole. Their particular definition of efficiency is one associated with Pareto[8] and may be formulated as follows: A state of affairs is efficient compared to another when at least one person is better off and nobody is worse off.[9] The terms, "better off" and "worse off," are defined by the persons involved so that efficiency deals with "want-satisfaction."[10] An increase in social well-being means that more wants are satisfied as defined by the persons involved.

If broad economizers attempted to evaluate alternative institutional arrangements by relying only on the Pareto criterion thus defined, they would have little to say, because virtually any institutional arrangement, when implemented, would make someone worse off. Such a move cannot be called efficient under the Pareto criterion, whatever else it might be. Economic theorists have therefore expanded the criterion to read: A policy change is desirable whenever those who gain from it "could so compensate the losers that *after* compensation the Pareto criterion could be met."[11] In practice, this has been interpreted to mean choosing the alternative with the best ratio between costs and benefits (in principle measured by the effects on want satisfaction).[12] Altogether, much of welfare economics and a good deal of the work in public choice theory fall in the category of broad economizing.[13]

II. Criticisms of Economizing

Economizing has been the target of a number of criticisms, each pointing to real deficiencies in the way it is typically practiced. Economizers can, however, provide adequate responses to each and so none is decisive.

Central to the first set of criticisms is the belief that economizing is deficient in its grasp of the actual characteristics of institutional arrangements. Economizers lack specificity and concreteness in their consideration of alternatives. As a result they do not have a clear view of how the institutional alternatives will actually operate, and regularly misjudge the cost of their operation and the degree to which they will be effective. Some illustrations drawn from the case of regulation will suffice to indicate what is at issue.

Economizers often argue for the relative efficiency of marketlike devices such as effluent charges or taxing schemes to promote occupational safety.[14] Firms that pollute or experience accidents will be charged on a scale that is tied to achieving some desired outcome. The firms may deal with these costs as they see fit, including the possibility of paying the charges on the assumption that they may be recouped in the marketplace. Economizers argue that these schemes will be less costly to run, require less information than ordinary standard setting, and provide incentives for the regulated to choose the most efficient means for dealing with the problem. The realities of such schemes are, however, likely to be very different. For when we consider information requirements, the presumed simplicity disappears. Most obviously, the complexity of the models necessary to calculate effluent charges, for example, is likely to be considerable and it is not at all clear that the modeling effort and the attendant calculations will be substantially easier than those required for a standards approach.[15]

More importantly, the lack of concreteness and specificity in the thinking of economizers is reflected in their assertion that we are dealing with alternatives that are quite different. In fact, what seem to be different institutional alternatives will likely end up in practice looking much alike. The idea of market versus nonmarket alternatives grows cloudy as do the grounds for preferring the former. Again, some regulatory examples will help.

Some economizing analyses recommend improving tort law to deal with market failures.[16] However, it may be argued that if consumers really were able to go to court—that is, if the cost and intricacy were not so great as virtually to exclude many people—the resulting organizational arrangements would resemble present regulatory agencies. Courts would become bureaucratized rule-promulgating bodies that reach deep into people's lives. For those less bold, who advocate replacing regulation by arrangements other than wholesale reliance on tort law, a similar problem arises. A seemingly straightforward market-oriented proposal like more labeling on food products will serve to make the point. Labeling comes under the heading of providing consumers with information in order to improve market functioning. Now the problem is not only the proper contents of the labels, but what the label *means*. The former can be settled by simple declaration. The latter, however, requires *very elaborate* definitions of various food items, additives, and other ingredients. We get, that is, regulations much like the present ones. This is all quite apart from the enforcement question: are the descriptions accurate? In short, what starts out as remedying market failures ends up looking a great deal like command and control regulation.

As important as these criticisms are, they merely challenge economizers to learn more about the proposals under consideration. This is something they can, in principle, do. Very much the same point applies to the next set of criticisms which imply political innocence on the part of economizers.

Economizers treat institutional alternatives as instruments to achieve ends, without seeing that they are also arenas of continuing conflict over purposes and methods. Any understanding of institutional alternatives that is confined to their instrumental qualities cannot fully grasp the reasons for their success or failure.[17] Now an understanding of and accommodation to political necessity in the form of political conflict is surely important in attempts to reach policy objectives. But, there is nothing here that economizers cannot accommodate since the primary mode of evaluation can still be whether institutional arrangements are effective instruments. Economizers may need an increased appreciation of the complexities of comparing instruments, but variation in the degree of political conflict across instruments can be taken into account by calculating its effects on goal achievement, by estimating the costs of reducing it, or by treating it as a constraint. In any case, there is nothing in such arguments about the political innocence of economizers that requires laying aside a weighing of the benefits and costs of each instrument.

A third, and seemingly more convincing, set of criticisms is that economizing is normatively deficient. Critics question whether the satisfaction of citizens' preferences, which is at the heart of broad economizing, ought to determine the ends of public policy. Some economizers simply ignore such charges and act as if economizing is a wholly instrumental science unrelated to normative matters. Their more reflective colleagues, however, dig a little deeper. What they offer from their expeditions is often some version of utilitarian moral theory.[18]

Now it is possible to mount powerful attacks on utilitarianism.[19] But there is little to gain from doing so if the real target is economizing since economizers need not be utilitarians. As Jules Coleman says, "even though satisfaction of the Pareto-superior standard does entail an increase in utility, it will not follow that the justification for its use is utilitarian."[20] Arguments from freedom and consent may also be employed, he says.[21] Economizers cannot perhaps be pure instrumentalists unconcerned with *any* justificatory scheme, but they are probably correct in thinking that they need not select a single brand of moral theory on which to rely.

In a less sweeping attack, some critics have contended also that economizers are too occupied with efficiency. To this charge economizers need reply only that they can and do take account of a variety of values beyond efficiency, including distributive justice and freedom. Even process values, the value of the way something is done, may be accommodated.[22] Economizers argue with some force that there is no reason in principle why they cannot employ a multivalue framework to evaluate alternative institutional arrangements,[23] to which I would add that, critics who contend that the problems of weighting each value are enormous typically fail to see that as long as a plurality of values is posited, economizers have no monopoly on the problem of weighting. Indeed, economizers have developed a number of techniques for clarifying relationships between values, including lexical orderings and various kinds of schemes for eliciting weights.[24]

Critics also argue that efforts to judge which institutional arrangement is Pareto-efficient or efficient according to the compensation test are unworkable. The valuation of lives, the appropriate rate of discount, and the estimation of benefits and costs in calculating the efficiency (and distributive qualities) of various institutional alternatives all present severe difficulties,[25] as does the compensation test itself. For example, to make the compensation test work, someone will need to gauge the extent of gains and losses barring actual negotiations between the affected parties. And if the compensation is not actually to be paid, as the advocates of the test say it need not,[26] the defense offered—that winners and losers will balance out over time—is too weak to stand up to data on the slow changes in income distribution.[27]

All of the just noted criticisms are valid. The difficulties are severe, but they are not decisive. Being inexact is not the same as being wrong. And that is an appropriate response to *all* the criticisms that have been considered so far (except the attacks on economizers' supposed utilitarianism). Economizers might reasonably reply that they need only sharpen their formulations in the face of what are, after all, complex problems of evaluation.

If the preceding criticisms could be said to represent the entire case against economizing, economizers would be seen as the true teachers of the study of public policy. To the extent that public policy is a central concern of political science, it would become a branch of economizing, contributing perhaps useful information on how types of policy strategies are likely to operate, or investigating the political costs and benefits of operating alternative institutional arrangements. But the underlying logic would be provided by economizing: institutional arrangements considered in terms of instrumental analysis. Is there in fact no other way of looking at institutional arrangements except as potentially interchangeable instruments?[28] If we can devise another way, we will have a central feature of an alternative view of rationality in public affairs.

III. Political Rationality

Political institutions such as legislative forums, courts, and regulatory commissions are not means to separately defined ends. In a manner of speaking, they are the ends. This is the central premise of a constitutive view of political institutions. The institutions are ways in which citizens experience one another. They are forms of activity in which citizens are brought into relation with one another and as such are themselves the ends with which we are concerned. The institutions are not aimed at some purpose extrinsic to themselves, that is, a way to get some place, but are there already.[29] Yet, they do not stand on their own as we shall see. Considered in this light, political institutions are not means to freedom, equality, or tyranny. They are egalitarian, free, or tyrannical institutions.[30]

The need to speak in this paradoxical manner—political institutions are not means to ends, but are the ends themselves—arises from the pervasiveness of means-ends language. It is perhaps more useful to say that political institutions are purpose- or end-creating activities, thereby cutting across the means-ends distinction. By helping to create or define the manner in which citizens are related to one another, political institutions constitute the citizenry in the sense of giving it an organized existence.

To understand a constitutive approach, we should first discard a common habit of mind that sees political institutions as primarily decision-making bodies that direct citizens to do some things and stop doing others. This is in fact the view of political institutions held by economizers: institutions are machines that produce commands designed to produce the desired ends. A constitutive view sees institutions first as relationships, as definitions of the manner in which members of a political community take account of each other. Thus, the primary importance of an institution lies not in what it decides but in what it is, that is, in how it gives shape to the citizenry by relating citizens to one another in a particular way.

We may say that political institutions are like constitutive rules. Such a rule both creates a certain sort of activity and says how it shall be performed if it is to be that kind of activity. It does more, that is, than regulate previously existing activity.[31] In much the same way, a political institution brings into being a form of activity in which the actions that compose the institution also constitute its purpose.

Consider the case of "rights." In a constitutive view rights are a certain form of relation between citizens. For a citizenry to have a right to free speech is to have in being institutional procedures that define how speakers and listeners stand in relation to each other. The same is true of property rights. A regulatory agency might thus be understood as creating a system of rights. What was once, for example, a matter of market transaction is that no longer. Previously, we might say, occupational safety was something a worker in effect purchased when he accepted a job, that is, it was something he received along with his wage. The relationship between employer and employee with regard to safety was then akin to that of producer and consumer. The creation of an occupational safety and health agency transforms what was a market transaction into a situation where workers are to be guaranteed a certain level of safety. If the level of safety is not provided, recourse of a certain kind is available. All of this adds up to the creation of rights. Employees and employers are now bound together in this particular regard by a system of obligations and by procedures to enforce them. In much the same way, to have equality, in a constitutive view, is to have institutions that create a certain set of activities, not produce a certain outcome.[32]

Political institutions are *purposive* then, but they are not primarily instruments. When we create a particular institutional arrangement, we are not merely, or most importantly, selecting machinery to produce results separate from it. Values such as freedom or equality are not *products* of an institution; they are part of its essential workings. Purposes and values are in important respects "in" politics.

In a constitutive view of political institutions, the distinction between means and ends, as separately defined categories, fades away. And with it fades the temptation to see institutions as having "intrinsic" value which must then be combined with values linked to the achievement of concrete purposes.

Again, a reference to rights may be useful. A typical way of talking about rights in the context of government regulation is to see them as something that can be assimilated to other values or benefits, which are in turn thought of as "produced" in the manner of a certain level of safety, for example. This is the way in which economizers characteris-tically proceed, if they talk of rights at all.[33] They offer judgments of efficiency or effectiveness focusing on aggregated "outputs," including rights, and compare the cost of producing various combinations. But in doing so they make the dubious assumption that rights are products rather than actual relationships engendered by the institutions. The idea of combining values—or trading them off against each other, which is what economizers most often have in mind—makes sense if indeed rights *are* products. But the idea becomes substantially less intelligible if it means trading off aspects of the people we are, as defined in part by our institutions, against our desire for a particular good or service.

When we speak about political institutions then, we talk of *acting* a certain way, of *being* a certain way, not *getting* to a certain place. We are speaking of "idioms of conduct."[34] It thus makes little sense to define a people and *then* indicate their preferences for doing things a certain way and getting to a certain place. How things are done is essential to the creation of the very preferences which on occasion we loosely suppose are "out there."[35] It may be exaggerative to say that without institutions there are no preferences or purposes. But it is not exaggerative to say that without political institutions there is no "people" to have preferences. The institutions say who the people are by defining their way of life, by creating a body of activities which helps to define their purposes.[36] We may call this political way of life the "regime," and political institutions are fundamental to its definition.[37]

As a way of summarizing the contrast between an economizing and a constitutive view of political institutions we can do no better than quote Lon Fuller's evocative juxtaposition of "pipelines" and institutions. Institutions are not like pipelines "discharging their diverse contents." An institution is rather "an active thing, projecting itself into a field of interacting forces, reshaping those forces." We cannot ask of an institution simply whether its end is good and whether it serves that end well. "Instead," says Fuller, "we have to ask a question at once more vague and more complicated—something like this: Does this institution, in a context of other institutions, create a pattern of living that is satisfying and worthy of man's capacities."[38] We must, that is, look to the regime for our evaluative bearings.

One might concede that a constitutive view is generally illuminating of political institutions and still wonder how such a conception helps us in the domain of public policy. Indeed, economizers might well allow that the particular organizational forms of legislatures and courts are not to be understood as means. But it is the realm of policy, facing a wide range of institutional alternatives from voucher schemes to administrative courts, that is our particular concern. Here is the ground that economizers claim as their special province. How then are we to make concrete the idea of policy choice as a selection among institutions understood constitutively?

IV. Political Rationality and Policy

Let us begin by taking another look at how economizers view the relationship between policy selection and politics. Probably the most common view is that their special competence lies in the selection of means,[39] while legitimate political authorities define values. That is *their* special competence. But to which authorities should economizers turn? They seem to imply that since economizing requires value statements precise enough to guide policy selection, its natural home is within the executive. Executive officials are more likely than the legislature to be in a position to offer relatively clear guidance. Or if not, they are at least in a better position to accept the economizers' advice about value selection. Moreover, executive officials are likely to view their job as instrumental—the execution of tasks to achieve some desired end. *If* executive officials could produce widely accepted values in a form suitable for guiding policy choice, the accommodation of economizing and politics would be a matter of simple division of labor built around the separation of ends and means. Under such conditions economizing would flourish.[40]

Political rationality on the other hand, being built around a constitutive view of political institution, finds its appropriate home in the legislature. Questions about what sort of people we are—that is, constitutive questions—arise whenever shaping and reshaping of the society's institutional arrangements are under consideration. Such matters are typically addressed, when they are at all, in the legislature.[41]

There is of course no compulsion to consider constitutive questions, whether in the legislature or elsewhere, but they will be settled by default if in no other way. We continue to say who we are by defining the activities that create our purposes, even if we do so in ignorance. For this reason constitutive questions are preeminent. Persons attempting to act efficiently are never just a mass of unrelated individuals. They are a people, a body politic. Constitutive questions come first, then, because the question always is: what sort of people is acting.[42]

How then might the legislature actually proceed? It is reasonable to assume that policy discussions cannot take place without some concern for the instrumental qualities of institutions. Economizers are surely right that efficiency considerations cannot be brushed aside. I have just argued that constitutive questions, and by extension a constitutive understanding of political institutions, are preeminent. This suggests that efficiency concerns must somehow be accommodated within an overall constitutive view. A useful starting point in bringing about this accommodation is to recognize that individuals who try to utilize their resources efficiently in pursuit of their own purposes stand in some particular relation to one another.[43] They may stand, for example, as bearers of rights, as superiors and subordinates in a hierarchy, as clients "mediated" by agency officials, as constituents served in some fashion by representatives, as equals in a participatory arena, or as producers and consumers in a market arrangement. The preeminence of these relationships suggests that efficiency concerns can best be handled by the legislature working to see that individual citizens are in a position to devise instrumentally rational ways of solving their own problems. The legislature has then the following tasks: employing a constitutive perspective to choose among alternative institutional arrangements; facilitating the efforts to be efficient of individuals whose standing in relation to one another will have been decided on constitutive grounds.

Now the question immediately arises as to why the legislature might select a particular form of relation. Even if it adopts a constitutive approach toward institutional alternatives—and that is by no means certain, as we shall see—the legislature must still decide what it wishes to constitute. As I have already suggested, its choice will depend on what is appropriate to the larger regime. If particular institutions are ways in which citizens experience each other, they must be part of a larger complex of such modes of experience, parts of the overall way of life that is the regime. This relationship between part and whole invites judgments based on what is necessary for the regime to flourish. There are at least two kinds of judgments at issue here. The first focuses on failures in ongoing institutional relationships. Here we look to what is "intimated" or incoherent in these relationships.[44] Reference to the larger way of life serves to tell us why we ought to care about seeking out those intimations.[45] Alternatively, and more ambitiously, the focus might be on "imbalances" in the mix of institutional arrangements that make up the regime.

Now, if we label the American regime as "liberal democratic," we need to understand the particular forms of relations or practices that are associated with this label and the mix between them. Whether such an understanding would lead a legislature that was acting constitutively to alter existing institutional arrangements in a participatory direction is difficult to say since no authentic and undisputed understanding of the American regime is readily available.[46] Moreover, the continuing ability of our political way of life to offer guidance is itself in doubt, a matter to which we will return.

A brief example drawn from the regulatory domain will help bring the preceding discussion together. If on constitutive grounds, the legislature decides in favor of a regulatory institution that relates citizens to each other in a participatory manner, the legislature should not devise arrangements that will actively hinder citizen problem solving. Over and above this, the legislative enactment may provide citizens who are acting in this participatory manner with access to economizers who can help in choosing efficient means. Similarly, if the relationship between citizens is to be that of consumers and producers, economizing considerations can be served by insuring that market participants are not prevented from engaging in mutually beneficial exchanges.

It is worth emphasizing that none of the foregoing requires political judgments that shore up existing institutional arrangements. To say that institutions are purpose-creating does not preclude the sort of critical reflection we have just sketched.[47] What *does* follow is that our manner of reasoning and our conception of the relation between institution and value will no longer be those characteristic of economizing.

The reasoning of someone employing political rationality is, on a larger scale, very much the kind displayed in judgments of good practice in professional disciplines or in aesthetic matters. It looks to "standards . . . which are appropriate to and partially definitive of a form of activity."[48] It is of the same order as when we say that something is "for the sake of" something else instead of being chosen "in order to" bring about some result. The reason of economizing is appropriate when we are referring to something that can be consumed. Political rationality is not primarily concerned with scarcity in the sense of something being subject to consumption. Unlike economizing which promises to be a universal abstract science, political rationality is in great part particularistic because it focuses on a *specific* regime.

Thus, underlying the differences between economic and political rationality is a different conception of the relationship between means and ends. Economic rationality relies on an "external" conception, where means and ends are causally and contingently related. Political rationality relies on an "internal" relationship where the end resides in having some activity done well.[49]

Having outlined some features of political rationality, we must finally ask whether, even in principle, a legislature can address constitutive questions. We should first note that there is nothing new in defining legislation as a collective effort to determine which relations among citizens are appropriate to the regime. A number of additional points are relevant. That relationships among citizens can be amended means that legislative activity need not start from scratch. The principal effort may well be (and most often is) an adjustment of what has already been done. Nor need effort to create or amend forms of relation be confined to the state. Neither is there any presumption that all adjustment is conscious: institutions evolve quite apart from conscious effort. Policy is the handmaiden of evolution, not a substitute for it. Moreover, there is no presumption that the legislative process must deal with all matters that come before it. Matters that are not greatly relevant to the constitution of the regime can be laid aside, perhaps until other questions arise which taken together are amenable to the exercise of political rationality. Altogether, the strongest point in this context is simply that whatever shortcomings the legislature may display in attempting to act constitutively, these failings are minor compared to those which result when it acts only as an economizer.

Still, we must add that the legislature may employ political rationality only intermittently or feebly. Indeed it may regularly do its work in the manner of an economizer. This is especially true given the present internal organization of Congress, which suggests that significant reforms will be required if it is to act constitutively in a consistent fashion. But we may say that defining and amending relations among citizens is what the legislature at its best does. Legislation is a principal way in which societies like ours provide answers to the question of how we shall be constituted.[50]

V. Conclusion

Political institutions are not severable from the political community, instruments to be deployed without marked effect on the character of the community itself. In selecting among institutional arrangements we directly constructing the sort of community we are. Ends and means are thus joined. It is important for us to care about political institutions in ways that cannot be reduced to, and must take precedence over the outcomes they produce. This is the core of political rationality.

But the attractions of economizing as a comprehensive view of rationality should not be underestimated. It builds on a deeply held conception of rational action and it seems particularly appealing in an interest-driven commercial republic such as ours where instrumental calculation is valued and the centrality of interests displaces concern or the relation between politics and the good life. Moreover, because government has taken on a large number of tasks which hitherto were dealt with in the marketplace and in the private sphere, the concern with producing "results" is a prominent theme in public discussion. Government is to be a policy machine that must be made to work efficiently. The danger is that in the pursuit of results we may consume the ingredients of a satisfactory political life. An inquiry into political rationality is animated by the sense that a satisfactory political life cannot rest on instrumental effectiveness alone.

Even if the discussion of political rationality presented here is compelling, it rests on the assumption that a political way of life exists that is vital enough to guide political judgment. Concern about the continuing vitality of the regime is manifest in a number of discussions that deal with the decline of liberalism, the onset of moral relativism, and the Nietzschean critique of philosophy.[51] Political institutions can do little if our political way of life has lost its meaning; they cannot by themselves remake the society. If this is our condition, then discussions of public policy are beside the point. The problem lies much deeper, and a much broader critique of instrumental reason may be required than what have attempted here. The case against economizing might then simply be that economizing is incoherent—it undermines its own basis because it helps to dissolve the way of life on which it depends. Economizers make the easy assumption that the foundations on which their want-regarding principles rest are secure. But a people tutored in the pursuit of wants may come to think that no foundations other than the serving of desire are justifiable.

Even if our political way of life is in such disrepair that it can offer little or no guidance, a constitutive view of political institutions is still fundamental. The sort of people we want to be must be an achievement of our politics, even if a precarious one. Once having seen the force of the constitutive argument, we cannot return to the view that political institutions respond to the ends of a people already formed. This is so even if we have no clear idea how to judge what sort of people we wish to be.

NOTES

This article, first published in *Polity* 18 (1983): 253–71, is reprinted by permission of the author and *Polity*. I am grateful to Diana Elkin, Ed Haefele, and Clarence Stone for their help in making this a more orderly discussion.

1. Robert Dahl and Charles Lindblom, *Politics, Economics and Welfare* (New York: Harper and Brothers, 1953); Robert A. Levine, *Public Planning* (New York: Basic, 1972); Charles Schultze, *The Public Use of Private Interest* (Washington, D.C.: Brookings, 1977).

2. Ludwig von Mises, *Epistemological Problems of Economics* (Princeton: Van Nostrand, 1960); Roland N. McKean, "The Role of Analytical Aids," in Lewis Gawthrop, ed., *Administrative Process and Democratic Theory* (Boston: Houghton Mifflin, 1970).

3. Roland N. McKean, "The Role of Analytical Aids," in Gawthrop, ed., *Administrative Process*, p. 253. See also von Mises, *Epistemological Problems*, especially p. 148, and Lionel Robbins, *An Essay on the Nature and Significance of Economic Science*, 2nd ed. (London: Macmillan, 1962). chap. 2.

4. Robbins, *An Essay*, p. 14.

5. See, for example, the studies cited in U.S. Senate, Committee on Governmental Affairs, *Study on Federal Regulation*, 6 Volumes, 95th Congress, Committee Print, 1977–78.

6. Richard Zeckhauser and Albert Nichols, "The Occupational Safety and Health Administration," U.S. Senate Committee on Governmental Affairs, *Study on Federal Regulation*, Appendix to Vol. VI, 95th Congress, Committee Print, 1977–78.

7. Otto A. Davis and Morton J. Kamien, "Externalities, Information and Alternative Collective Action," in Robert Havemen and Julius Margolis, eds., *Public Expenditures and Policy Analysis* (Chicago: Markham, 1970); Peter O. Steiner, "The Public Sector and the Public Interest," in Haveman and Margolis, eds., *Public Expenditures*.

8. V. Pareto, *Cours d'economie politique* (Lausanne: Rouge, 1897).

9. Brian Barry, *Political Argument* (London: Routledge and Kegan Paul, 1965), p. 50. See, more generally, Jules Coleman, "Economics and the Law: A Critical Review of the Foundations of the Economic Approach to the Law," *Ethics* 94, no. 4 (July 1984).

10. Barry, *Political Argument*, chap. 3.

11. Laurence H. Tribe, "Policy Science: Analysis or Ideology," *Policy and Public Affairs* 2, no. 1 (Fall 1972): 71 (chap. 3, this volume). See also Amartya K. Sen, *Collective Choice and Social Welfare* (San Francisco: Holden-Day, 1970), pp. 56–57, where the original formulations by Kaldor and Hicks are cited, and Kenneth J. Arrow, *Social Choice and Individual Values*, 2nd ed. (New Haven: Yale University Press, 1963), chap. 4.

12. Leonard Merewitz and Stephen H. Sosnick, *The Budget's New Clothes* (Chicago: Markham, 1971).

13. See Arrow, *Social Choice and Individual Values*, particularly p. 106. To be precise, public choice theory emphasizes that various kinds of bargaining processes may be more effective devices to promote preference or want satisfaction than institutions operating according to other principles. Institutions are, at least implicitly, still understood as interchangeable means to grand efficiency and other ends. But the emphasis has now shifted from an insistence on their instrumental qualities to showing two other things: that various kinds of preference aggregation schemes will or will not serve the posited ends; and that preference aggregation through exchange, bargaining, and the like is superior to alternative decision principles. Public choice theorists typically then have an aggregative view of politics. Although some violence is being done, we may say for present purposes that an aggregative view of politics is a version of economizing, but that not all economizers are aggregators.

14. Alan V. Knese and Charles L. Schultze, *Pollution, Prices, and Public Policy* (Washington, D.C.: Brookings, 1975).

15. Susan Rose-Ackerman, "Effluent Charges: A Critique," *Canadian Journal of Economics* 6, no. 4 (November 1973): 512–528.

16. American Bar Association, Commission on Law and the Economy, *Federal Regulation: Roads to Reform,* 1979, Introduction; Richard Posner, *Economic Analysis of Law,* 2nd ed. (Boston: Little, Brown, 1977).

17. Clarence Stone, "The Implementation of Social Programs: Two Perspectives," *Journal of Social Issues* 36, no. 4 (February 1980): 13–33.

18. Jules L. Coleman, "Efficiency, Utility and Wealthy Maximization," *Hofstra Law Review* 8 (Spring 1980): 508–551; Partha Dasgupta, Amartya Sen, and Stephen Marglin, *Guidelines for Project Evaluations* (New York: United Nations Industrial Development Organization, 1972); Stephen L. Elkin, "Political Science and the Analysis of Public Policy," *Public Policy* 22, no. 3 (Summer 1974): 399–422, and I.M.D. Little, *A Critique of Welfare Economics,* 2nd ed. (London: Oxford University Press, 1957), chap. 2.

19. C. B. MacPherson, *The Political Theory of Possessive Individualism* (New York: Oxford University Press, 1962); Laurence H. Tribe, "Ways Not to Think About Plastic Trees: New Foundations for Environmental Law," *The Yale Law Journal* 83, no. 7 (June 1974): 1315–1348; Roberto Unger, *Knowledge and Politics* (New York: Free Press, 1975); and Bernard Williams, "A Critique of Utilitarianism," in J.J.C. Smart and Bernard Williams, *Utilitarianism . . . For and Against* (Cambridge: Cambridge University Press, 1973).

20. Jules L. Coleman, "The Economic Analysis of Law," in J. Roland Pennock and John W. Chapman, eds., *Ethics, Economics and the Law* (Nomos XXIV) (New York: New York University Press, 1982), p. 88.

21. Coleman, "The Economic Analysis of Law."

22. Oliver P. Williamson, *Markets and Hierarchies* (New York: Free Press, 1975), chap. 3.

23. Peter O. Steiner, "The Public Sector and the Public Interest"; Burton A. Weisbrod, "Collective Action and the Distribution of Income: A Conceptual Approach," both in Haveman and Margolis, eds., *Public Expenditures.*

24. See Tribe, "Policy Science"; Julius Margolis, "Shadow Prices for Incorrect or Nonexistent Market Values," in Haveman and Margolis, eds., *Public Expenditures*; and John Rawls, *A Theory of Justice* (Cambridge, Mass.: Harvard University Press, 1971), part 1.

25. Nina W. Cornell, Roger G. Noll, and Barry Weingast, "Safety Regulation," in Henry Owen and Charles L. Schultze, eds., *Setting National Priorities* (Washington, D.C.: Brookings Institution, 1976); Mark Green and Norman Waitzman, *Business War on the Law: An Analysis of the Benefits of Federal Health/Safety Enforcement* (Washington, D.C.: Corporate Accountability Research Group, 1979); Bertrand de Jouvenel, "Efficiency and Amenity," in Kenneth Arrow and Tibor Scitovsky, eds., *Readings in Welfare Economics* (London: Allen and Unwin, 1969); Tribe, "Policy Science"; and Laurence H. Tribe, "Technology Assessment and the Fourth Discontinuity: The Limits of Instrumental Rationality," *Southern California Law Review* 46, no. 3 (June 1973): 617–660.

26. Laurence H. Tribe, "Policy Science."

27. A. B. Atkinson, *The Economics of Inequality* (London: Oxford University Press, 1975).

28. The premier contemporary statement of an alternative to economizing is Paul Diesing, *Reason in Society* (Westport, Conn.: Greenwood, 1973). His theme is echoed by Aaron Wildavsky ("The Political Economy of Efficiency: Cost Benefit Analysis, Systems Analysis, and Program Budgeting," in Austin Ranney, ed., *Political Science and Public Policy* (Chicago: Markham, 1968)). Both present views of political activity as having a noninstrumental character and Diesing, in particular, anticipates some of the arguments advanced below in his discussion of social rationality.

29. Alasdair MacIntyre, *After Virtue* (Notre Dame: University of Notre Dame Press, 1981), p. 211, says "Politics, as Aristotle conceives it, is a practice with goods internal to itself. Politics as James Mill conceives it, is not."

30. For some useful parallel discussions, see John Ladd, "The Place of Practical Reason in Judicial Decision," in Carl Friedrich, ed., *Rational Decision* (New York: Atherton, 1964), and Walter Lippman, *The Good Society* (Boston: Little, Brown, 1943), chap. 12.

31. On constitutive rules, see John Rawls, "Two Concepts of Rules," *Philosophical Review* 64 (January 1955): 3–32; John Searle, *Speech Acts* (London: Cambridge University Press, 1969), pp. 33–42; Hanna Pitkin, *Wittgenstein and Justice* (Berkeley: University of California Press, 1972), chap. 2; and George von Wright, *Norm and Action* (Highlands, N.J.: Humanities Press, 1964), pp. 6–16. See also Tribe, "Technology Assessment"; and Anthony Giddens, *Central Problems in Social Theory* (Berkeley: University of California Press, 1979), pp. 82–83. In general see Ludwig Wittgenstein, *Philosophical Investigations,* 3rd ed. (New York: Macmillan, 1968).

32. See Barry's comment on how English socialists such as Tawney viewed equality as a matter of "right relationship." Brian Barry, *The Liberal Theory of Justice* (Oxford: Oxford University Press, 1973), p. 168. Cf. also Fuller's remark that "Until we find some means by which equal treatment can be defined and administered, we do not know the meaning of equality itself." Lon Fuller, "Means and Ends," in Kenneth I. Winston, ed., *The Principles of Social Order* (Durham: Duke University Press, 1981), p. 62.

33. Charles L. Schultze, *The Public Use of Private Interest*, pp. 72–75.

34. Michael Oakeshott, "Political Education," in *Rationalism in Politics and Other Essays* (New York: Basic Books, 1962), p. 105.

35. By way of contrast, consider Arrow, *Social Choice*, particularly Chapter 7 where he comments that "in the present study . . . individual values are taken as data and are not capable of being altered by the nature of the decision process itself."

36. Cf. Duncan Kennedy's comment: "It is simply wrong to imagine the state as a means to the pre-existing ends of the citizens. Ends are collective and in the process of development. . . . . Good judging [i.e., good administration of justice] . . . means the creation and development of values, not just the more efficient attainment of whatever we may want." Kennedy, "Form and Substance," *Harvard Law Review* 89 (1976): 1772.

37. Cf. Joseph Cropsey, "The United States as Regime and the Sources of the American Way of Life," in Robert Horowitz, ed., *The Moral Foundations of the American Republic* (Charlottesville: University of Virginia Press, 1977), and Giddens, *Central Problems*, p. 65.

38. Lon Fuller, "Means and Ends," pp. 54ff.

39. Schultze, *The Public Use of Private Interest*; and Levine, *Public Planning*.

40. Leaving aside the nontrivial question of whether in our form of government it is the task of executive officials to resolve value conflicts—see Edwin T. Haefele, *Representative Government and Environmental Management* (Baltimore: Johns Hopkins University Press, 1973)—even on their own terms economizers face great difficulties. They themselves argue that a desirable outcome of economizing is precisely that initial value premises get substantially altered as the analysis of means comes up against the exigencies of the real world of choice. See E. S. Quade, "Principles and Procedures of Systems Analysis," in Quade and W. I. Boucher, eds., *Systems Analysis and Policy Planning* (New York: American Elsevier, 1968), for example. To this we may add the doubt that public officials are in fact particularly equipped or inclined to render orderings of social value as an exercise separated from concrete policy selection. See, generally, David Braybrooke and Charles E. Lindblom, *Strategy of Decision* (New York: Free Press, 1963).

41. The discussion here is not meant to imply that constitutive matters will or should be addressed only by the legislative process. The courts have always played a role. Complex questions of institutional competence are at stake, as is the connection between the rationality appropriate to legislatures and courts. Fuller for one has made a start on this subject. See the set of essays collected in his *Principles of Social Order*, 1981.

42. For a helpful discussion, see Sotorios A. Barber, *On What the Constitution Means* (Baltimore: Johns Hopkins University Press, 1984), pp. 30–32.

43. A reading of both Friedrich A. Hayek, *Law, Legislation, and Liberty* vol. 1, *Rules and Order* (Chicago: University of Chicago Press, 1973); and James Buchanan, "What Should Economists Do," in Buchanan, *What Should Economists Do* (Indianapolis: Liberty Press, 1979) is helpful here even though neither would agree with my general argument. See also Charles E. Lindblom and David K. Cohen, *Usable Knowledge* (New Haven: Yale University Press, 1979).

44. Oakeshott, "Political Education," p. 124. Michael Walzer, *Spheres of*

Justice (New York: Basic Books, 1983), pp. 6–10, makes a parallel point, focusing on "goods" as opposed to institutions. He argues that the social meanings latent in these goods help define appropriate relationships for their creation and distribution.

45. Or honor the social meaning of goods.

46. For distinguished efforts to discuss the American regime see Barber, *Constitution*; Theodore Lowi, *The End of Liberalism* (New York: Norton, 1979); and Herbert Storing, "American Statesmanship Old and New," in Robert A. Goldwin, ed., *Bureaucrats, Policy Analysts, Statesmen: Who Leads* (Washington, D.C.: American Enterprise Institute, 1980).

47. While political rationality is of a conserving nature then, it is not conservative in the popular use of that term. Indeed its prescriptions for what is appropriate to preserve a liberal democratic regime may be quite radical.

48. MacIntyre, *After Virtue*, p. 175. For another contemporary discussion see Donald Schon, *The Reflective Practitioner* (New York: Basic Books, 1982).

49. To attempt to say more is to open up the long-standing (and very vexed) discussion of the character of practical activity generally. See Aristotle, *Nichomachean Ethics,* book VI; and David Wiggins, "Deliberation and Practical Reason," in Amelie Oksenberg Rorty, ed., *Essays on Aristotle's Ethics* (Berkeley: University of California Press, 1980).

50. For some evidence that even contemporary legislatures can sometimes act in at least something like the manner described here, see Arthur Maass, *Congress and the Common Good* (New York: Basic Books, 1983), and William K. Muir, Jr., *Legislature: California's School for Politics* (Chicago: University of Chicago Press, 1983) and Philip Selznick, *Law, Society and Industrial Justice* (New Brunswick, N.J.: Transaction Books, 1980), especially pp. 137–154 on "The Constitutive Contract."

51. Cropsey, "The United States as Regime"; Jurgen Habermas, *Theory and Practice* (London: Heineman, 1974), especially chap. 7; and Jurgen Habermas, *Legitimation Crisis* (Boston: Beacon Press, 1975).

16 At the Shrine of Our Lady of Fatima *or* Why Political Questions Are Not All Economic

Mark Sagoff

LEWISTON, NEW YORK, a well-to-do community near Buffalo, is the site of the Lake Ontario Ordinance Works, where years ago the federal government disposed of the residues of the Manhattan Project. These radioactive wastes are buried but are not forgotten by the residents who say that when the wind is southerly, radon gas blows through the town. Several parents at a recent Lewiston conference I attended described their terror on learning that cases of leukemia had been found among area children. They feared for their own lives as well. On the other side of the table, officials from New York State and from local corporations replied that these fears were ungrounded. People who smoke, they said, take greater risks than people who live close to waste disposal sites. One speaker talked in terms of "rational methodologies of decision making." This aggravated the parents' rage and frustration.

The speaker suggested that the townspeople, were they to make their decision in a free market and if they knew the scientific facts, would choose to live near the hazardous waste facility. He told me later they were irrational—"neurotic"—because they refused to recognize or to act upon their own interests. The residents of Lewiston were unimpressed with his analysis of their "willingness to pay" to avoid this risk or that. They did not see what risk-benefit analysis had to do with the issues they raised.

If you take the Military Highway (as I did) from Buffalo to Lewiston, you will pass through a formidable wasteland. Landfills stretch in all directions and enormous trucks—tiny in that landscape—incessantly deposit sludge which great bulldozers then push into the ground. These machines are the only signs of life, for in the miasma that hangs in the air, no birds, not even scavengers, are seen. Along colossal power lines which criss-

371

cross this dismal land, the dynamos at Niagara send electric power south, where factories have fled, leaving their remains to decay. To drive along this road is to feel, oddly, the mystery and awe one experiences in the presence of so much power and decadence.

Henry Adams had a similar response to the dynamos on display at the Paris Exposition of 1900. To him, "the dynamo became a symbol of infinity."[1] To Adams, the dynamo functioned as the modem equivalent of the Virgin, that is, the center and focus of power. "Before the end, one began to pray to it; inherited instinct taught the natural expression of men before silent and infinite force."[2] Adams asks in his essay "The Dynamo and the Virgin" how the products of modern industrial civilization will compare with those of the religious culture of the Middle Ages. If he could see the landfills and hazardous waste facilities bordering the power stations and honeymoon hotels of Niagara Falls he would know the answer. He would understand what happens when efficiency replaces infinity as the central conception of value. The dynamos at Niagara will not produce another Mont-Saint-Michel. "All the steam in the world," Adams wrote, "could not, like the Virgin, build Chartres."[3]

At the Shrine of Our Lady of Fatima, on a plateau north of the Military Highway, a larger than life sculpture of Mary looks into the chemical air. The original of this shrine stands in central Portugal where in May 1917, three children said they saw a Lady, brighter than the sun, raised on a cloud in an evergreen tree.[4] Five months later, on a wet and chilly October day, the Lady again appeared, this time before a large crowd. Some who were skeptical did not see the miracle. Others in the crowd reported, however, that "the sun appeared and seemed to tremble, rotate violently and fall, dancing over the heads of the throng."[5]

The Shrine was empty when I visited it. The cult of Our Lady of Fatima, I imagine, has only a few devotees. The cult of Pareto optimality, however, has many. Where some people see only environmental devastation, its devotees perceive efficiency, utility, and the maximization of wealth. They see the satisfaction of wants. They envision the good life. As I looked over the smudged and ruined terrain I tried to share that vision. I hoped that Our Lady of Fatima, worker of miracles, might serve, at least for the moment, as the Patroness of cost-benefit analysis. I thought of all the wants and needs that are satisfied in a landscape of honeymoon cottages, commercial strips, and dumps for hazardous waste. I saw the miracle of efficiency. The prospect, however, looked only darker in that light.

Political and Economic Decision Making

This essay concerns the economic decisions we make about the environment. It also concerns our political decisions about the environment.

Some people have suggested that ideally these should be the same, that all environmental problems are problems in distribution. According to this view, there is an environmental problem only when some resource is not allocated in equitable and efficient ways.[6]

This approach to environmental policy is pitched entirely at the level of the consumer. It is his or her values that count, and the measure of these values is the individual's willingness to pay. The problem of justice or fairness in society becomes, then, the problem of distributing goods and services so that more people get more of what they want to buy: a condo on the beach, a snowmobile for the mountains, a tank full of gas, a day of labor. The only values we have, according to this view, are those that a market can price.[7]

How much do you value open space, a stand of trees, an "unspoiled" landscape? Fifty dollars? A hundred? A thousand? This is one way to measure value. You could compare the amount consumers would pay for a townhouse or coal or a landfill to the amount they would pay to preserve an area in its "natural" state. If users would pay more for the land with the house, the coal mine, or the landfill, than without—less construction and other costs of development—then the efficient thing to do is to improve the land and thus increase its value. That is why we have so many tract developments, pizza stands, and gas stations. How much did you spend last year to preserve open space? How much for pizza and gas? "In principle, the ultimate measure of environmental quality," as one basic text assures us, "is the value people place on these . . . services or their *willingness to pay.*"[8]

Willingness to pay: what is wrong with that? The rub is this: not all of us think of ourselves simply as *consumers*. Many of us regard ourselves *as citizens* as well. We act as consumers to get what we want *for ourselves*. We act as citizens to achieve what we think is right or best *for the community*. The question arises, then, whether what we want for ourselves individually as consumers is consistent with the goals we would set for ourselves collectively as citizens. Would I vote for the sort of things I shop for? Are my preferences as a consumer consistent with my judgments as a citizen?

They are not. I am schizophrenic. Last year, I fixed a couple of tickets and was happy to do so since I saved $50. Yet, at election time, I helped to vote the corrupt judge out of office. I speed on the highway; yet I want the police to enforce laws against speeding. I used to buy mixers in returnable bottles—but who can bother to return them? I buy only disposables now, but to soothe my conscience, I urge my state senator to outlaw one-way containers. I love my car; I hate the bus. Yet I vote for candidates who promise to tax gasoline to pay for public transportation. And of course I applaud the Endangered Species Act, although I have no earthly use for the Colorado squawfish or the Indiana bat. I support almost any political cause that I think will defeat my consumer interests. This is because I have contempt for—although I act upon—those interests. I have an "Ecology Now" sticker on a car that leaks oil everywhere it's parked.

The distinction between consumer and citizen preferences has long vexed the theory of public finance. Should the public economy serve the same goals as the household economy? May it serve, instead, goals emerging from our association as citizens? The question asks if we may collectively strive for and achieve only those items we individually compete for and consume. Should we aspire, instead, to public goals we may legislate as a nation?

The problem, insofar as it concerns public finance, is stated as follows by R. A. Musgrave, who reports a conversation he had with Gerhard Colm:

> He [Colm] holds that the individual voter dealing with political issues has a frame of reference quite distinct from that which underlies his allocation of income as a consumer. In the latter situation the voter acts as a private individual determined by self-interest and deals with his personal wants; in the former, he acts as a political being guided by his image of a good society. The two, Colm holds, are different things.[9]

Are these two different things? Stephen Marglin suggests that they are. He writes:

> The preferences that govern one's unilateral market actions no longer govern his actions when the form of reference is shifted from the market to the political arena. The Economic Man and the Citizen are for all intents and purposes two different individuals. It is not a question, therefore, of rejecting individual . . . preference maps; it is, rather, that market and political preference maps are inconsistent.[10]

Marglin observes that if this were true, social choices optimal under one set of preferences would not be optimal under another. What, then, is the meaning of "optimality"? He notices that if we take a person's true preferences to be those expressed in the market, we may neglect or reject the preferences that person reveals in advocating a political cause or position. "One might argue on welfare grounds," Marglin speculates, "for authoritarian rejection of individuals' politically revealed preferences in favor of their market revealed preferences!"[11]

Cost-Benefit Analysis vs. Regulation

On February 19, 1981, President Reagan published Executive Order 12,291[12] requiring all administrative agencies and departments to support every new major regulation with a cost-benefit analysis establishing that the benefits of the regulation to society outweigh its costs. The order directs the Office of Management and Budget (OMB) to review every such regulation on the basis of the adequacy of the cost-benefit analysis supporting it. This is a departure from tradition. Historically, regulations have been reviewed not by OMB but by the courts on the basis of the relation of the regulation to authorizing legislation, not to cost-benefit analysis.

A month earlier, in January 1981, the Supreme Court heard lawyers for the American Textile Manufacturers Institute argue against a proposed Occupational Safety and Health Administration (OSHA) regulation which would have severely restricted the acceptable levels of cotton dust in textile plants.[13] The lawyers for industry argued that the benefits of the regulation would not equal the costs.[14] The lawyers for the government contended that the law required the tough standard.[15] OSHA, acting consistently with Executive Order 12,291, asked the Court not to decide the cotton dust case in order to give the agency time to complete the cost-benefit analysis required by the textile industry.[16] The Court declined to accept OSHA's request and handed down its opinion in *American Textile Manufacturers* v. *Donovan* on June 17, 1981.[17]

The Supreme Court, in a 5–3 decision, found that the actions of regulatory agencies which conform to the OSHA law need not be supported by cost-benefit analysis.[18] In addition, the Court asserted that Congress, in writing a statute, rather than the agencies in applying it, has the primary responsibility for balancing benefits and costs.[19] The Court said:

> When Congress passed the Occupational Health and Safety Act in 1970, it chose to place pre-eminent value on assuring employees a safe and healthful working environment, limited only by the feasibility of achieving such an environment. We must measure the validity of the Secretary's actions against the requirements of that Act.[20]

The opinion upheld the finding of the District of Columbia Court of Appeals that "Congress itself struck the balance between costs and benefits in the mandate to the agency."[21]

The Appeals Court opinion in *American Textile Manufacturers* v. *Donovan* supports the principle that legislatures are not necessarily bound to a particular conception of regulatory policy. Agencies that apply the law therefore may not need to justify on cost-benefit grounds the standards they set. These standards may conflict with the goal of efficiency and still express our political will as a nation. That is, they may reflect not the personal choices of self-interested individuals, but the collective judgments we make on historical, cultural, aesthetic, moral, and ideological grounds.[22]

The appeal of the Reagan Administration to cost-benefit analysis, however, may arise more from political than economic considerations. The intention, seen in the most favorable light, may not be to replace political or ideological goals with economic ones, but to make economic goals more apparent in regulation. This is not to say that Congress should function to reveal a collective willingness-to-pay just as markets reveal an individual willingness-to-pay. It is to suggest that Congress should do more to balance economic with ideological, aesthetic, and moral goals. To think that environmental or worker safety policy can be based exclusively on aspiration for a "natural" and "safe" world is as foolish as to hold that environmental law can be reduced to cost-benefit accounting. The more we move to one extreme, as I found in Lewiston, the more likely we are to hear from the other.

Substituting Efficiency for Safety

The labor unions won an important political victory when Congress passed the Occupational Safety and Health Act of 1970.[23] That Act, among other things, severely restricts worker exposure to toxic substances. It instructs the Secretary of Labor to set "the standard which most adequately assures, to the extent feasible . . . that no employee will suffer material impairment of health or functional capacity even if such employee has regular exposure to the hazard . . . for the period of his working life."[24]

Pursuant to this law, the Secretary of Labor in 1977 reduced from ten to one part per million (ppm) the permissible ambient exposure level for benzene, a carcinogen for which no safe threshold is known. The American Petroleum Institute thereupon challenged the new standard in court.[25] It argued, with much evidence in its favor, that the benefits (to workers) of the one ppm standard did not equal the costs (to industry).[26] The standard therefore did not appear to be a rational response to a market failure in that it did not strike an efficient balance between the interests of workers in safety and the interests of industry and consumers in keeping prices down.

The Secretary of Labor defended the tough safety standard on the ground that the law demanded it.[27] An efficient standard might have required safety until it cost industry more to prevent a risk than it cost workers to accept it. Had Congress adopted this vision of public policy—one which can be found in many economics texts[28]—it would have treated workers not as ends-in-themselves but as means for the production of overall utility. This, as the Secretary saw it, was what Congress refused to do.[29]

The United States Court of Appeals for the Fifth Circuit agreed with the American Petroleum Institute and invalidated the one ppm benzene standard.[30] On July 2, 1980, the Supreme Court affirmed the decision in *American Petroleum Institute* v. *Marshall*[31] and remanded the benzene standard back to OSHA for revision. The narrowly based Supreme Court decision was divided over the role economic considerations should play in judicial review. Justice Marshall, joined in dissent by three other justices, argued that the Court had undone on the basis of its own theory of regulatory policy an act of Congress inconsistent with that theory.[32] He concluded that the plurality decision of the Court "requires the American worker to return to the political arena to win a victory that he won before in 1970."[33]

The decision of the Supreme Court is important not because of its consequences, which are likely to be minimal, but because of the fascinating questions it raises. Shall the courts uphold only those political decisions that can be defended on economic grounds? Shall we allow democracy only to the extent that it can be construed either as a rational response to a market failure or as an attempt to redistribute wealth? Should the courts say that a regulation is not "feasible" or "reasonable"—terms that occur in the OSHA law[34]—unless it is supported by a cost-benefit analysis?

The problem is this: An efficiency criterion, as it is used to evaluate public policy, assumes that the goals of our society are contained in the preferences individuals reveal or would reveal in markets. Such an approach may appear attractive, even just, because it treats everyone as equal, at least theoretically, by according to each person's preferences the same respect and concern. To treat a person with respect, however, is also to listen and to respond intelligently to his or her views and opinions. This is not the same thing as to ask how much he or she is willing to pay for them. The cost-benefit analyst does not ask economists how much they are willing to pay for what they believe, that is, that the workplace and the environment should be made efficient. Why, then, does the analyst ask workers, environmentalists, and others how much they are willing to pay for what they believe is right? Are economists the only ones who can back their ideas with reasons while the rest of us can only pay a price? The cost-benefit approach treats people as of equal worth because it treats them as of no worth, but only as places or channels at which willingness to pay is found.[35]

Liberty: Ancient and Modern

When efficiency is the criterion of public safety and health, one tends to conceive of social relations on the model of a market, ignoring competing visions of what we as a society should be like. Yet it is obvious that there are competing conceptions of what we should be as a society. There are some who believe on principle that worker safety and environmental quality ought to be protected only insofar as the benefits of protection balance the costs. On the other hand, people argue—also on principle—that neither worker safety nor environmental quality should be treated merely as a commodity to be traded at the margin for other commodities, but rather each should be valued for its own sake. The conflict between these two principles is logical or moral, to be resolved by argument or debate. The question whether cost-benefit analysis should play a decisive role in policy making is not to be decided by cost-benefit analysis. A contradiction between principles—between contending visions of the good society— cannot be settled by asking how much partisans are willing to pay for their beliefs.

The role of the *legislator,* the political role, may be more important to the individual than the role of *consumer.* The person, in other words, is not to be treated merely as a bundle of preferences to be juggled in cost-benefit analyses. The individual is to be respected as an advocate of ideas which are to be judged according to the reasons for them. If health and environmental statutes reflect a vision of society as something other than a market by requiring protections beyond what are efficient, then this may express not legislative ineptitude but legislative responsiveness to public values. To deny this vision because it is economically inefficient is simply to replace it with another vision. It is to insist that the ideas of the citizen be sacrificed to the psychology of the consumer.

We hear on all sides that government is routinized, mechanical, entrenched, and bureaucratized; the jargon alone is enough to dissuade the most mettlesome meddler. Who can make a difference? It is plain that for many of us the idea of a national political community has an abstract and suppositious quality. We have only our private conceptions of the good, if no way exists to arrive at a public one. This is only to note the continuation, in our time, of the trend Benjamin Constant described in the essay *De la liberte des anciens comparee a celle des modernes.*[36] Constant observes that the modern world, as opposed to the ancient, emphasizes civil over political liberties, the rights of privacy and property over those of community and participation. "Lost in the multitude," Constant writes, "the individual rarely perceives the influence that he exercises," and, therefore, must be content with "the peaceful enjoyment of private independence."[37] The individual asks only to be protected by laws common to all in his pursuit of his own self-interest. The citizen has been replaced by the consumer; the tradition of Rousseau has been supplanted by that of Locke and Mill.

Nowhere are the rights of the moderns, particularly the rights of privacy and property, less helpful than in the area of the natural environment. Here the values we wish to protect—cultural, historical, aesthetic, and moral—are public values. They depend not so much upon what each person wants individually as upon what he or she thinks is right for the community. We refuse to regard worker health and safety as commodities; we regulate hazards as a matter of right. Likewise, we refuse to treat environmental resources simply as public goods in the economist's sense.

Instead, we prevent significant deterioration of air quality not only as a matter of individual self-interest but also as a matter of collective self-respect. How shall we balance efficiency against moral, cultural, and aesthetic values in policy for the workplace and the environment? No better way has been devised to do this than by legislative debate ending in a vote. This is very different from a cost-benefit analysis terminating in a bottom line.

Values Are Not Subjective

It is the characteristic of cost-benefit analysis that it treats all value judgments other than those made on its behalf as nothing but statements of preference, attitude, or emotion, insofar as they are value judgments. The cost-benefit analyst regards as true the judgment that we should maximize efficiency or wealth. The analyst believes that this view can be backed by reasons,[38] but does not regard it as a preference or want for which he or she must be willing to pay. The cost-benefit analyst tends to treat all other normative views and recommendations as if they were nothing but subjective reports of mental states. The analyst supposes in all such cases that "this is right" and "this is what we ought to do" are equivalent to "I want this" and "this is what I prefer." Value judgments are beyond criticism if, indeed, they are nothing but expressions of personal preference; they are incorrigible since every person is in the best position to know what he or she wants. All valuation, according to this approach, happens *in foro interno*; debate *in foro publico* has no point. With this approach, the reasons that people give for their views do not count; what does count is how much they are willing to pay to satisfy their wants. Those who are willing to pay the most, for all intents and purposes, have the right view; theirs is the more informed opinion, the better aesthetic judgment, and the deeper moral insight.

The assumption that valuation is subjective, that judgments of good and evil are nothing but expressions of desire and aversion, is not unique to economic theory.[39] There are psychotherapists—Carl Rogers is an example—who likewise deny the objectivity or cognitivity of valuation.[40] For Rogers, there is only one criterion of worth: it lies in "the subjective world of the individual. Only he knows it fully."[41] The therapist shows his or her client that a "value system is not necessarily something imposed from without, but is something experienced."[42] Therapy succeeds when the client "perceives himself in such a way that no self-experience can be discriminated as more or less worthy of positive self-regard than any other . . . ."[43] The client then "tends to place the basis of standards within himself, recognizing that the 'goodness' or 'badness' of any experience or perceptual object is not something inherent in that object, but is a value placed in it by himself."[44]

Rogers points out that "some clients make strenuous efforts to have the therapist exercise the valuing function, so as to provide them with guides for action."[45] The therapist, however, "consistently keeps the locus of evaluation with the client."[46] As long as the therapist refuses to "exercise the valuing function" and as long as he or she practices an "unconditional positive regard"[47] for all the affective states of the client, then the therapist remains neutral among the client's values or "sensory and visceral experiences."[48] The role of the therapist is legitimate, Rogers suggests, because of this value neutrality. The therapist accepts all felt preferences as valid and imposes none on the client.

Economists likewise argue that their role as policy makers is legitimate because they are neutral among competing values in the client society. The political economist, according to James Buchanan, "is or should be ethically neutral: the indicated results are influenced by his own value scale only insofar as this reflects his membership in a larger group."[49] The economist might be most confident of the impartiality of his or her policy recommendations if he or she could derive them formally or mathematically from individual preferences. If theoretical difficulties make such a social welfare function impossible,[50] however, the next best thing, to preserve neutrality, is to let markets function to transform individual preference orderings into a collective ordering of social states. The analyst is able then to base policy on preferences that exist in society and are not necessarily his own.

Economists have used this impartial approach to offer solutions to many significant social problems, for example, the controversy over abortion. An economist argues that "there is an optimal number of abortions, just as there is an optimal level of pollution, or purity . . . . Those who oppose abortion could eliminate it entirely, if their intensity of feeling were so strong as to lead to payments that were greater at the margin than the price anyone would pay to have an abortion."[51] Likewise, economists, in order to determine whether the war in Vietnam was justified, have estimated the willingness to pay of those who demonstrated against it.[52] Following the same line of reasoning, it should be possible to decide whether creationism should be taught in the public schools, whether black and white people should be segregated, whether the death penalty should be enforced, and whether the square root of six is three. All of these questions arguably depend upon how much people are willing to pay for their subjective preferences or wants. This is the beauty of cost-benefit analysis: no matter how relevant or irrelevant, wise or stupid, informed or uninformed, responsible or silly, defensible or indefensible wants may be, the analyst is able to derive a policy from them—a policy which is legitimate because, in theory, it treats all of these preferences as equally valid and good.

Preference or Principle?

In contrast, consider a Kantian conception of value.[53] The individual, for Kant, is a judge of values, not a mere haver of wants, and the individual judges not for himself or herself merely, but as a member of a relevant community or group. The central idea in a Kantian approach to ethics is that some values are more reasonable than others and therefore have a better claim upon the assent of members of the community as such.[54] The world of obligation, like the world of mathematics or the world of empirical fact, is public not private, and objective standards of argument and criticism apply. Kant recognized that values, like beliefs, are subjective states of mind which have an objective content as well. Therefore, both values and beliefs are either correct or mistaken. A value judgment is like an empirical or theoretical judgment in that it claims to be *true* not merely to be *felt*.

We have, then, two approaches to public policy before us. The first, the approach associated with normative versions of welfare economics, asserts that the only policy recommendation that can or need be defended on objective grounds is efficiency or wealth maximization. The Kantian approach, on the other hand, assumes that many policy recommendations may be justified or refuted on objective grounds. It would concede that the approach of welfare economics applies adequately to some questions, for example, those which ordinary consumer markets typically settle. How many yo-yos should be produced as compared to how many frisbees? Shall pens have black ink or blue? Matters such as these are so trivial it is plain that markets should handle them. It does not follow, however, that we should adopt a market or quasi-market approach to every public question.

A market or quasi-market approach to arithmetic, for example, is plainly inadequate. No matter how much people are willing to pay, three will never be the square root of six. Similarly, segregation is a national curse and the fact that we are willing to pay for it does not make it better, but only us worse. The case for abortion must stand on the merits; it cannot be priced at the margin. Our failures to make the right decisions in these matters are failures in arithmetic, failures in wisdom, failures in taste, failures in morality—but not market failures. There are no relevant markets which have failed.

What separates these questions from those for which markets are appropriate is that they involve matters of knowledge, wisdom, morality, and taste that admit of better or worse, right or wrong, true or false, and not mere economic optimality. Surely environmental questions—the protection of wilderness, habitats, water, land, and air as well as policy toward environmental safety and health—involve moral and aesthetic principles and not just economic ones. This is consistent, of course, with cost-effectiveness and with a sensible recognition of economic constraints.

The neutrality of the economist is legitimate if private preferences or subjective wants are the only values in question. A person should be left free to choose the color of his or her necktie or necklace, but we cannot justify a theory of public policy or private therapy on that basis. If the patient seeks moral advice or tries to find reasons to justify a choice, the therapist, according to Rogers' model, would remind him or her to trust his visceral and sensory experiences. The result of this is to deny the individual status as a cognitive being capable of responding intelligently to reasons; it reduces him or her to a bundle of affective states. What Rogers' therapist does to the patient the cost-benefit analyst, does to society as a whole. The analyst is neutral among our "values"—having first imposed a theory of what value is. This is a theory that is impartial among values and for that reason fails to treat the persons who have them with respect or concern. It does not treat them even as persons but only as locations at which wants may be found. The neutrality of economics is not a basis for its legitimacy. We recognize it as an indifference toward value—an indifference so deep, so studied, and so assured that at first one hesitates to call it by its right name.

The Citizen as Joseph K.

The residents of Lewiston at the conference I attended demanded to know the truth about the dangers that confronted them and the reasons for those dangers. They wanted to be convinced that the sacrifice asked of them was legitimate even if it served interests other than their own. One official from a large chemical company dumping wastes in the area told them in reply that corporations were people and that people could talk to people about their feelings, interests, and needs. This sent a shiver through the audience. Like Joseph K. in *The Trial*,[55] the residents of Lewiston asked for an explanation, justice, and truth, and they were told that their wants would be taken care of. They demanded to know the reasons for what was continually happening to them. They were given a personalized response instead.

This response, that corporations are "just people serving people," is consistent with a particular view of power. This is the view that identifies power with the ability to get what one wants as an individual, that is, to satisfy one's personal preferences. When people in official positions in corporations or in the government put aside their personal interests, it would follow that they put aside their power as well. Their neutrality then justifies them in directing the resources of society in ways they determine to be best. This managerial role serves not their own interests but those of their clients. Cost-benefit analysis may be seen as a pervasive form of this paternalism. Behind this paternalism, as William Simon observes of the lawyer-client relationship, lies a theory of value that tends to personalize power. "It resists understanding power as a product of class, property, or institutions and collapses power into the personal needs and dispositions of the individuals who command and obey."[56] Once the economist, the therapist, the lawyer, or the manager abjures his own interests and acts wholly on behalf of client individuals, he appears to have no power of his own and thus justifiably manipulates and controls everything. "From this perspective it becomes difficult to distinguish the powerful from the powerless. In every case, both the exercise of power and submission to it are portrayed as a matter of personal accommodation and adjustment."[57]

The key to the personal interest or emotive theory of value, as one commentator has rightly said, "is the fact that emotivism entails the obliteration of any genuine distinction between manipulative and nonmanipulative social relations."[58] The reason is that once the affective self is made the source of all value, the public self cannot participate in the exercise of power. As Philip Reiff remarks, "the public world is constituted as one vast stranger who appears at inconvenient times and makes demands viewed as purely external and therefore with no power to elicit a moral response."[59] There is no way to distinguish the legitimate authority that public values and public law create from tyranny.[60]

"At the rate of progress since 1900," Henry Adams speculates in his *Education,* "every American who lived into the year 2000 would know how to control unlimited power."[61] Adams thought that the Dynamo would organize and release as much energy as the Virgin. Yet in the 1980s, the citizens of Lewiston, surrounded by dynamos, high tension lines, and nuclear wastes, are powerless. They do not know how to criticize power, resist power, or justify power—for to do so depends on making distinctions between good and evil, right and wrong, innocence and guilt, justice and injustice, truth and lies. These distinctions cannot be made out and have no significance within an emotive or psychological theory of value. To adopt this theory is to imagine society as a market in which individuals trade voluntarily and without coercion. No individual, no belief, no faith has authority over them. To have power to act as a nation we must be able to act, at least at times, on a public philosophy, conviction, or faith. We cannot abandon the moral function of public law. The antinomianism of cost-benefit analysis is not enough.

NOTES

This article, first published in *Arizona Law Review* 23 (1981): 1283–98, is reprinted by permission of the author and the *Arizona Law Review.*

The author is Director and Research Scholar, Center for Philosophy and Public Policy and Center for Environmental and Estuarine Studies (Horn Point

Laboratories), University of Maryland. A.B. 1963, Harvard College; Ph.D. 1970, University of Rochester. Work on this article was supported by the National Science Foundation and National Endowment for the Humanities, Grant No. OSS 8018096. Views expressed are the author's, not necessarily those of the NSF or NEH. The author is grateful for criticism received from colleagues, especially David Luban.

1. H. Adams, *The Education of Henry Adams* 380 (2d ed. 1970).

2. Id.

3. Id. at 388.

4. For an account, see generally J. Pelletier, *The Sun Danced at Fatima* (1951).

5. 5 *New Catholic Encyclopedia* 856 (1967).

6. See, e.g, W. Baxter, *People or Penguins: The Case for Optimal Pollution* ch. 1 (1974). See generally A. Freeman, R. Haveman, A. Kneese, *The Economics of Environmental Policy* (1973) [Hereinafter A. Freeman].

7. Posner makes this point well in discussing wealth maximization as an ethical concept. "The only kind of preference that counts in a system of wealth-maximization," he writes, "is . . . one that is backed up by money—in other words, that is registered in a market." Posner, "Utilitarianism, Economics, and Legal Theory," 8 *J. Legal Stud.* 103, 119 (1979).

8. A. Freeman, note 6 above, at 23.

9. R. Musgrave *The Theory of Public Finance* 87–88 (1959).

10. Marglin, "The Social Rate of Discount and the Optimal Rate of Investment," 77 *Q. J. Econ.* 95, 98 (1963).

11. Id.

12. 46 Fed. Reg. 13,193 (1981). The order specifies that the cost-benefit requirement shall apply "to the extent permitted by law."

13. *American Fed'n of Labor, etc.* v. *Marshall,* 617 F.2d 636 (D.C. Cir. 1979), cert. granted sub nom. *American Textile Mfrs. Inst., Inc.* v. *Marshall,* 49 U.S.L.W. 3208 (1981).

14. 49 U.S.L.W. 3523–24.

15. Id.

16. Id.

17. *American Textile Mfrs. Inst., Inc.* v. *Donovan,* 49 U.S.L.W. 4720 (1981).

18. Id. at 4724–29.

19. Id. at 4726–29.

20. Id. at 4733–34.

21. Id. at 4726–29.

22. To reject cost-benefit analysis as a basis for policy making is not necessarily to reject cost-effectiveness analysis which is an altogether different thing. For this difference, see Baram, "Cost-Benefit Analysis: An Inadequate Basis for Health, Safety, and Environmental Regulatory Decision-making," 8 *Ecology L. Q.* 473 (1980). "*Cost-benefit analysis* . . . is used by the decisionmaker to establish societal goals as well as the means for achieving these goals, whereas *cost-effectiveness analysis* only compares alternative means for achieving 'given' goals." Id. at 478 (footnote omitted). In practice, regulatory uses of cost-benefit analysis stifle and obstruct the achievement of legislated health, safety, and environmental goals. Id.

at 473. Further, to the extent that economic factors are permissible considerations under enabling statutes, agencies should engage in cost-effectiveness analysis, which aids in determining the least costly means to designated goals, rather than cost-benefit analysis, which improperly determines regulatory ends as well as means. Id. at 474.

23. Pub. L. No. 91–596, 84 Stat. 1596 (1970) (codified at 29 U.S.C. §§ 651–678 [1970]).

24. 29 U.S.C. § 655(b)(5) (1970).

25. *American Petroleum Inst.* v. *Marshall.* 581 F.2d 493 (5th Cir. 1978), aff'd, 448 U.S. 607 (1980).

26. 581 F.2d at 501–05.

27. Id. at 501.

28. See, e.g., R. Posner, *Economic Analysis of Law I & II* (1973). In G. Calabresi, *The Costs of Accidents* passim (1970), the author argues that accident law balances two goals, "efficiency" and "equality" or "justice."

29. *American Petroleum Inst.* v. *Marshall,* 581 F.2d 493, 503–05 (5th Cir. 1978).

30. Id. at 505.

31. 448 U.S. 607 (1980).

32. Id. at 719.

33. Id.

34. 29 U.S.C. §§ 655(b)(5) & 652(8) (1975).

35. For a similar argument against utilitarianism, see Hart, "Between Utility and Rights," 79 *Colum. L. Rev.* 828, 829–31 (1979).

36. B. Constant, *de la Liberte des Anciens Comparee a Celle des Modernes* (1819).

37. "Oeuvres politiques de Benjamin Constant," 269 (C. Louandre, ed. 1874), quoted in S. Wolin, *Politics and Vision* 281 (1960).

38. There are arguments that whatever reasons may be given are not good. See generally Dworkin, "Why Efficiency?" 8 *Hofstra L. Rev.* 563 (1980); Dworkin, "Is Wealth a Value?" 9 *J. Legal Stud.* 191 (1980); Kennedy, "Cost-Benefit Analysis of Entitlement Problems: A Critique," 33 *Stan. L. Rev.* 387 (1980); Rizzo, "The Mirage of Efficiency," 8 *Hofstra L. Rev.* 641 (1980); Sagoff, "Economic Theory and Environmental Law," 79 *Mich. L. Rev.* 1393 (1981).

39. This is the emotive theory of value. For the classic statement, see C. Stevenson, *Ethics and Language* chs. 1 & 2 (144). For criticism, see Blanshard, "The New Subjectivism in Ethics," 9 *Philosophy & Phenomenological Research* 504 (1949). For a statement of the related interest theory of value, see generally R. Perry, *General Theory of Value* (1926); E. Westermarck, *Ethical Relativity* chs. 3–5 (1932). For criticisms of subjectivism in ethics and a case for the objective theory presupposed here, see generally P. Edwards, *The Logic of Moral Discourse* (1955) and W. Ross, *The Right and the Good* (1930).

40. My account is based on C. Rogers, *On Becoming a Person* (1961); C. Rogers, *Client Centered Therapy* (1965); and Rogers, "A Theory of Therapy, Personality, and Interpersonal Relationships, as Developed in the Client Centered Framework," 3 *Psychology: A Study of a Science* 184 (1959). For a similar account used as a critique of the lawyer-client relation, see Simon, "Homo Psychologicus: Notes on a New Legal Formalism," 32 *Stan. L. Rev.* 487 (1980).

41. Rogers, note 40 above, at 210.

42. C. Rogers, *Client Centered Therapy* 150 (1965).

43. Rogers, note 40 above, at 208.

44. C. Rogers, note 42 above, at 139.

45. Id. at 150.

46. Id.

47. Rogers, note 40 above, at 208.

48. Id. at 523–24.

49. Buchanan, "Positive Economics, Welfare Economics, and Political Economy" 2 *J. L. & Econ.* 124, 127 (1959).

50. K. Arrow, *Social Choice and Individual Values I–V* (2d ed. 1963).

51. H. Macaulay & B. Yandle, *Environmental Use and the Market* 120–21 (1978).

52. See generally Cicchetti, Freeman, Haveman, & Knetsch, "On the Economics of Mass Demonstrations: A Case Study of the November 1969 March on Washington," 61 *Am. Econ. Rev.* 719 (1971).

53. I. Kant, *Foundations of the Metaphysics of Morals* (1969). I follow the interpretation of Kantian ethics of W. Sellars, *Science and Metaphysics* ch. vii (1968) and Sellars, "On Reasoning About Values," 17 *Am. Phil. Q.* 81 (1980).

54. See A. MacIntyre, *After Virtue* 22 (1981).

55. F. Kafka, *The Trial* (rev. ed. trans. 1957). Simon applies this analogy to the lawyer-client relationship. Simon, note 40 above, at 524.

56. Simon, note 40 above, at 495.

57. Id.

58. A. MacIntyre, note 54 above, at 22.

59. P. Reiff, *The Triumph of the Therapeutic: Uses of Faith After Freud* 52 (1966).

60. That public law regimes inevitably lead to tyranny seems to be the conclusion of H. Arendt, *The Human Condition* (1958); K. Popper, *The Open Society and Its Enemies* (1966): L. Strauss, *Natural Right and History* (1953). For an important criticism of this conclusion in these authors, see generally Holmes, "Aristippus In and Out of Athens," 73 *Am. Pol. Sci. Rev.* 113 (1979).

61. H. Adams, note 1 above, at 476.

17 The Place of Principles in Policy Analysis

Charles W. Anderson

IN ORDER TO MAKE a policy decision, one must invoke some criteria of evaluation. We cannot decide whether a proposal for public action is desirable or undesirable, whether the results of a public program are to be adjudged a success or a failure, except in the light of a standard. We have to make a decision on some basis, for some reason. We can favor a specific program for the reason that the benefits seem to outweigh the costs. We can base our decision on the grounds of legality, or on the grounds that one option appears more politically feasible than the rest. We can decide on the basis of majority will or fundamental fairness or because of self-interest, organizational interest or the interest of some group whose cause we are trying to advance. We can decide on instrumental grounds, that this policy would rectify a balance of payments disequilibrium or provide a consistent, low-cost energy supply. Failing all else, we can make a decision because heads came up rather than tails.

All of these are potential criteria for choice, and all identify standards for public judgment. One could incorporate any or all of them into a model of the decision-making process, and each, except perhaps for the last, has been highlighted somewhere in the policy-making literature as constituting the essence of decision. Nonetheless, the essential question is not how we can decide, or how we in fact do decide, but how we ought to decide. What counts as a good reason for a policy decision and what is an inappropriate basis for political judgment?

Any theory of policy evaluation[1] has to address the problem of the choice of criteria for decision making. This is as true for those who would propose models to explain the behavior of policy makers as it is for those whose interest is in trying to clarify what "policy rationality" or "good judgment" entails. However, it is probably fair to say that even purely "empirical" theories of policy process cannot escape the normative implications of policy evaluation. The move from the empirical to the prescriptive is easy and natural for the consumers of policy theory, and in the eyes of students and practitioners, current models of policy making readily become standards for the craft of policy analysis. Such has been the fate both of pluralist interest-group theory and incrementalist models of the budgetary process. (It is very easy for those who look upon political science as a repository of practical wisdom to conclude that it is "good practice" to inflate a budget request by approximately the amount of the anticipated legislative cut.) In any event, the "fact-value distinction" is not a profound stumbling block in policy theory. There are few enough students of policy analysis who are not concerned with the implications of different modes of policy choice and many significant works in the field— those of Dror, Lindblom and Simon, for example—are overt arguments for preferred strategies of decision.

Logically, the choice of criteria is the first element in any theory of policy evaluation. How we perceive a problem depends on how we propose to evaluate it. Problems are not just "out there" waiting to be resolved. The first act of evaluation is to make a distinction between "problems" and "the way things are." Poverty is not a problem for a society that believes that "the poor are always with us"—or that they get precisely what they deserve. Inflation can be regarded as a "condition" rather than a "problem," for it means no more than a rise in the price structure. Inflation has to be regarded as a problem for a reason, as, for example, that it affects business confidence, or represents an illegitimate confiscation of some forms of property, or redistributes income in socially undesirable ways. A policy problem, in short, is a political condition that does not meet some standard.

It is not merely in the phase of problem identification that the choice of standards is important. Each step in the process of decision making depends on the initial stipulation of values to be served. We cannot just "weigh" or "compare" policy alternatives. We must weigh and compare them against something. At the end of analysis, we cannot merely make decisions. We also have to justify them. However whimsically or equivocally we *came* to our conclusions, good reasons have to be given for our policy preferences if they are to be taken seriously in the forums of policy deliberation. Ultimately, policy analysis has less to do with problem solving than with the process of argument. The better metaphor for policy analysis may not be the mathematical equation but the legal brief—it is a reasoned case for a preferred course of public action.

The Stipulation and Ranking of Values

Like the famous recipe for rabbit stew that begins, "Catch the rabbit," most formulas for rational policy choice begin with the admonition, "Identify and rank your values."[2] The problem for any theory of policy evaluation is how this should be done. Contemporary policy theory tends to side-step the issue. Either the selection of criteria is treated in a highly formal and abstract manner or policy rationality is regarded as a kind of economizing activity and a utilitarian conception of political judgment is implicitly or explicitly endorsed. A third alternative is to rely on a "political" conception of evaluation, in which feasibility or social agreement become overriding norms. In any event, in most contemporary formulations of the problem the stipulation and ranking of values is regarded as more or less arbitrary, as a "given" in the appraisal of policy. The specification of values is not itself part of the process of rational choice. Rationality is defined in a purely instrumental sense, as "goal-directed behavior" (Riker and Ordeshook, 1973, p. 10). As Dahl and Lindblom write (1953, p. 38), "An action is rational to the extent that it is 'correctly' designed to maximize goal achievement, given the goal in question and the real world as it exists."

What virtually all contemporary policy theories have in common is a positivist or "emotivist" theory of evaluation. Values cannot be justified in terms of objective criteria. Hence, they must be regarded as "preferences" on the part of the policy maker. "Technical" or "rational" policy analysis can only begin once relevant values have been stipulated, either by an authoritative decision maker or through the statement of citizen preferences in a democratic political process. It is impossible to specify what standards ought to be taken into account in rendering a policy evaluation.

This, of course, is not the case. To be regarded as "reasonable," a policy recommendation must be justified as lawful; it must be plausibly argued that it is equitable and that it entails an efficient use of resources. Else it is subject to legitimate criticism.

It does appear that there are certain fundamental considerations that must be accounted for in any policy evaluation, a set of problems that can be identified with the classic concerns of political theory and with a repertoire of basic concepts including authority, the public interest, rights, justice, equality, and efficiency. As standards of policy evaluation, these are not simply preferences. They are, in some sense, *obligatory* criteria of political judgment. To justify any policy recommendation, one must argue that it is within the legitimate powers of government, that it is, in some sense, "in the public interest," that it is consistent with lawful rights, that it is fair, and efficient in the use of resources.

The view that "comprehensive" policy rationality is impossible, as argued by Braybrooke and Lindblom (1963), March and Simon (1958), and others, then might not be precisely correct. While there may be an "infinite number of evaluations" for any policy question (as Lindblom argues in criticism of the classic rational model), it may be the case that there are only a limited number of values appropriate to address in rendering a policy evaluation. All policy argument leads back, eventually, to a finite and bounded set of classic principles and problems of political evaluation.

Furthermore, it may be that instrumental rationality is not the only conception of rationality pertinent to policy theory. The sense of rationality as "goal-directed behavior" is perfectly formal; it applies to *any* type of decision and not in any specific sense to *policy* decisions. It is an ideal of formal, logical validity that a given conclusion can be shown to derive from a given set of premises. However, formal validity is not the only tenable meaning of rationality in modern theories of logic. In the spirit of Wittgenstein's *Philosophical Investigations,* modern logicians like Stephen Toulmin (1969, p. 188) have argued that the problem of rational assessment—of telling sound arguments from untrustworthy ones—depends on the characteristics of an arena of discourse and the standards that are pertinent to it; or they have argued with Friedrich Waismann (1951, p. 117) that the known relations of logic can only hold between statements which belong to a homogeneous field of discourse. Thus, it may be possible to say more about policy rationality than about rational choice in general, and it may be that certain standards of judgment are necessary to rational policy choice because of the very nature of what we do when we make, and appraise, public decisions.

In the development of contemporary policy theory, what happened was that the ideal of the utility-maximizing individual was simply taken from positive economic theory and applied to the role of the policy maker. Policy rationality then becomes efficiency in the pursuit of any set of utilities. However influential this instrumental conception of rationality may have been in defining the dominant models of contemporary policy analysis, it is by no means the only acceptable use of the term. In modern analytic philosophy, it is also possible to conceive of rationality as performing an action for reasons that an individual correctly or reasonably regards as good reasons (Benn and Mortimore, 1976, p. 2). This conception of rationality as acting for good reasons leads to two related senses in which an action can be called rational. Either we ascribe rationality to individuals who act for reasons which they regard as good, or we call actions rational when we judge that there are reasons to support them, as when we say, "That seemed a rational thing to do." This conception of rationality seems particularly germane to the process of policy discourse and policy argument. And when we consider what would count as a good reason in policy discourse, it would seem that we are inevitably led back to the classic concerns of political evaluation and the classic principles of political thought.

However, merely to invoke the "classic principles" as criteria for policy evaluation is not to have done very much. To talk about "justifying" decisions in the light of such principles seems to lead us down a familiar and none-too-promising path. We begin to ask questions like "What is justice?" and "What is the public interest?" seeking an essentialist definition that would serve as a conclusive test of the propriety or impropriety of public action. It is not my intention to propose an idealist theory of policy evaluation. I want to stay safely within the positivist and pragmatic tradition that has been dominant within this field of political theory, though perhaps to reveal some unexpected implications of what is possible within that tradition. To this end, we must be quite clear about the kind of problem involved in the selection of criteria for policy making and in defining the logical status of the classic principles in any theory of policy evaluation.

The Pluralism of Policy Languages

We can begin from a consideration of a practical problem of policy appraisal. If, as I have argued, standards of evaluation are embedded in specific fields of discourse, if they arise from specific paradigms of inquiry and analysis, then our sense for what counts as a good reason and as a mistake depends on the ideological, disciplinary, or cultural context within which we are operating. This is a familiar problem, both of the sociology of knowledge and of the philosophy of science, that our "plausibility structures" have much to do with social context and social reinforcement. However, the crucial difficulty is not merely the relativity and contingency of standards that such a view entails. The significant issue is how we should proceed when we are aware that public issues can be perceived and appraised through multiple frameworks of evaluation. Given the diversity of the policy sciences in our times, this has become a characteristic dilemma of policy choice and policy rationality.

The proliferation of "policy professions" in the past generation or so has created a great variety of languages and logics of policy evaluation and justification. In such a field as energy policy, for example, the policy maker or citizen must somehow decide what to make of the various arguments and analyses presented by economists, environmentalists, engineers, scientists, lawyers, and so on, each claiming to be authoritative for a specific aspect of the problem, each justified by its own premises of inquiry and rigorous logic of analysis, each containing imperatives for definitive public action.

In the conventional wisdom of policy making, policy makers specify objectives and policy professionals deal only with means to politically designated ends. However, the conventional wisdom may have the matter almost precisely backwards. The actual role of policy professionalism in contemporary government is probably more prescriptive than instrumental. The setting of standards of good practice is a large part of what professionalism means. Most policy professions are such precisely because they provide standards for public policy. In such diverse fields as forestry, public health, nutrition, and welfare, the essential function of the expert is often that of setting criteria for the definition of public objectives and the appraisal of public programs.

Policy evaluation takes place within and between such languages of policy analysis. Like scientific disciplines, policy languages constitute a realm of discourse and of argument. What counts as a "problem," and a "good reason," and as a "mistake" in judgment depends on the normative standards embedded in a specific framework of analysis. The process of policy evaluation and argument is different in law, macroeconomics, diplomacy, environmental planning and civil engineering. In each of these professions, different rules exist for the identification of the problematic; there are different norms of evaluation and different criteria for what would count as a "solution" to a public problem, for how we would distinguish a "successful" public venture from a policy "failure."

This pluralism of policy languages does not pose any ultimate problems of justification in itself. All arguments trail back eventually to certain normative postulates and assumptions widely shared in liberal political discourse (and arguably, by Marxian and Catholic corporatist thought as well). When we *justify* a policy standard (address the question of why it is appropriately invoked as definitive in making judgments about alternative public projects and purposes) we generally appeal to some higher-order principle with which the criterion of choice is deemed to be consistent (Taylor, 1961, pp. 45–46). Thus, the neoclassical economist, when asked why "market failure" is an appropriate (and perhaps exclusive) test of the propriety of government intervention in the economy, will refer back to the values of freedom and efficiency served by the market mechanism and behind this perhaps to some notion of the moral autonomy of the individual and to a nominalist skepticism toward the possibility of objective standards of public judgment apart from individual preference and wants. Similarly, if one inquired of the committed conservationist why it might not be a plausible energy policy alternative to simply use up all fossil fuels in one generation of grand bacchanalian extravagance and let the future fend for itself, appeal would probably be made, in the final analysis, to some notion of justice between generations (Barry, 1977).

It is not then that the diverse policy professions do not rest on a shared set of justificatory principles. Rather, the problem is that the weight, emphasis, and significance given to the various fundamental principles is different in each. Because they endorse different standards of argument (what counts as a good reason) and because they are organized to account for different facets of experience, they entail different orderings of relevant values. Thus, the central normative construct of law is rights, while that of economics is efficiency. While it might be possible to argue considerations of efficiency in delimiting the scope of an established right (a court might plausibly argue potential bankruptcy as a ground for denying counsel to indigent defendants), in legal reasoning, the ordinary procedure for establishing the categories and scope of rights is not that of a calculus of individual utilities. Conversely, while the logic of economic reasoning may rest on certain postulates of rights (such as property rights), the purpose of a calculation of alternative utility functions is not to stipulate a system of rights.

Hence, it makes a great deal of difference whether we choose to adopt the rules of rational discourse of one of these policy professions rather than another in evaluating a policy problem. We may come to very different conclusions if we choose to regard a specific issue as falling in the domain of law rather than economics. As Arthur Okun (1975) suggests, it makes a difference whether we regard a problem like income distribution from the point of view of rights rather than that of efficiency. There is, he suggests, a "big trade-off" between these two considerations, either of which can be regarded as definitive for policy making.

In such a pluralistic universe of policy discourse and policy rationality, the crucial problem for a theory of policy evaluation becomes that of identifying standards by which we may weigh the claims of various languages of policy analysis. On what grounds should we choose to regard a problem from the point of view of one of the policy professions rather than another? What justifies the choice among the several logics of policy evaluation?

This is to put the "metapolitical" problem in applied form. Consider the following situation. A labor leader is deciding whether to declare an illegal strike. If the decision is made to strike on the grounds that the probable benefits would be greater than the probable costs, we would say that the decision was based on economic reasoning. If the strike is not called because of its illegality, we would say that the decision was based on legal grounds. But what guidance can be given as to whether the leader ought to decide for economic or legal reasons?

Hence, the problem that must be faced in constructing a theory of policy evaluation is also a characteristic practical problem of policy making in our times. How do we judge a judgment? What standards must any system of policy evaluation meet? The problem concerns the justification of the procedures of policy analysis, but it also addresses the concrete question of how we weigh the rival claims and considerations adduced by different "rationalities" of policy appraisal.

The Metapolitics of Policy Evaluation

A few political scientists have begun the process of trying to extend the idea of policy rationality, asking what is logically required in any stipulation of criteria for policy evaluation. For example, Brian Barry and Douglas Rae (1975, pp. 337–401) set forth seven requirements that any system of political evaluation must meet. Their standards derive largely from formal decision theory. They are rules that must be followed if we are to judge rationally among alternatives in the light of standards.

For Barry and Rae, the formal tests of adequacy are these. The standards by which a policy is judged must be *internally consistent,* that is, transitive. It is logically impossible to come to conclusions about preferred policy unless the criteria are clear and hierarchically ranked. Standards must be *interpretable:* we must be able to tell what a standard means in policy discourse, to judge when it has been met or fails to be met. It must be possible to *aggregate criteria,* to rank them, for a variety of standards might be relevant to choice; yet we cannot simply say, for example, that we favor both, say, equity and efficiency, for no alternative may satisfy both criteria equally.

Any theory of policy evaluation, for Barry and Rae, must also account for the problem of forced choice, that not to decide is in fact a policy choice, and there is no a priori reason why the status quo should have a privileged position in policy appraisal. A system of political evaluation must acknowledge *risk and uncertainty* (we cannot say with confidence, that a given choice will actually meet standards) and it must deal with *time* (policies will have both proximate and distant consequences). Finally, choices must be logically justified in terms of some conception of *individual welfare.*[3]

Duncan MacRae (1976) has attempted to develop a "metaethics" for normative policy discourse on the basis of an analogy between the logic of policy evaluation and the rules of scientific inquiry. MacRae suggests that normative discourse can be as rigorous as empirical investigation in politics, that it is not mere assertion, but can be seen as disciplined inquiry to be judged by "higher-order" standards of appropriate procedure. MacRae envisions normative discourse as debate between the proponents of rival evaluative systems. The standards that any system must meet, the grounds of appropriate criticism of any normative judgment, include (1) generality, if the proposed system fails to apply to a choice about which both discussants have moral convictions and to which the critic's system does apply; (2) *internal consistency,* in which the proponent's system yields contradictory recommendations where the critic's does not; (3) *inconsistency with shared convictions,* that the proposed system leads to conclusions at odds with presumably shared evaluations.

I offer no critique of the position of either Barry and Rae or MacRae.

Both have extended and clarified the domain of rationality in policy evaluation. Yet, I think the logic of their analysis can be carried further. They emphasize procedural norms, formal rules of consistency, and logical rules of validity in rational choice and ethical judgment. However, it seems possible to continue this line of logic to assimilate certain substantive principles that distinguish policy judgment from the more general language regions of rational choice or normative discourse. Barry and Rae, to be sure, do take up the place of the classic principles in policy analysis. However, they view such concepts as justice, rights, the public interest, etc., primarily as "simplifying devices," culturally derived constructs that somehow pull together and focus attention on certain facets of our shared political experiences. The logical status of such principles is somehow different from that of the formal norms of rational decision making. My own view is that something more can be said for and about the place of such principles as "metapolitical" standards, as criteria for judging the worth of any system of policy evaluation.

The Place of Principles in Policy Analysis

It is not immediately apparent that any systematic relationship exists among the classic principles of political thought. Words like *right, the public interest, justice, freedom,* and *community* can seem to be no more than an array of discrete "good things." We are used to the idea that political argument can fasten arbitrarily on one or a few of these concepts and that they can be arranged in different patterns in ideological thinking, invested with a variety of meanings and given different degrees of emphasis.

To make the point that the criteria which enter into a policy evaluation are not merely preferences, but that certain substantive standards need be accounted for in any rationally defensible policy judgment, one must show that certain principles do form, in some sense, a finite and bounded set and one must establish in what specific way such criteria are mandatory in the activity of policy evaluation. It is also necessary to show that these principles can be stated in such a way as to be free from any partisan or ideological quality. They must reflect no more than the logical characteristics of any form of political judgment.

The essence of my argument is this: a defensible policy judgment must meet certain formal standards of rational choice—it must have regard for such problems as the transitivity of values and forced choice—but it must have other qualities as well. By virtue of the fact that these are policy judgments, certain political values must be taken into account. It is not that these values can be justified in any ultimate sense. I will not argue the Kantian position that there are certain normative propositions that any rational thinker must endorse to remain consistent, nor will I argue, with

Rawls, that there are certain principles that self-interested individuals would be led to accept if placed in the "original position" and called upon to formulate basic norms of political life. Rather, the argument is that certain criteria of choice are inherent in the activity of politics itself, that they are part of what we mean by "making a political judgment" or as Wittgenstein might have put it, that they are part of politics as a "form of life."

My case is that a specific set of principles is *obligatory* in political evaluation in a very special sense. It is important to be very clear about the logical status of such principles as criteria of "metapolitics"—standards for judging the adequacy of any system of political judgment. There is a difference between claiming that certain *concepts* are indispensable in political evaluation and that certain *propositions* are. To say that a comprehensive policy analysis must account for the problem of authority is not to say that a binding policy recommendation must be shown to "derive from the will of the people." As Stephen Toulmin says (1972, p. 418),

> It is one thing to argue that a certain concept is something that a rational thinker or agent cannot very well get along without; it is quite another to establish the necessary truth of certain substantive ethical or scientific principles.

As standards at the "second level," as criteria for evaluating a policy evaluation itself, the classic principles have a particular standing. They are not norms of conduct; rather, they identify those aspects of a policy recommendation that require justification. The status of such principles in normative policy theory is not unlike the standing of a hypothesis in scientific inquiry. As a hypothesis *requires* experimentation to test its validity, so "principles," in the sense I shall be using the term, require justification to demonstrate the rational plausibility of a policy recommendation.

Taken in this sense, it is possible to identify three of the classic principles that appear to be rationally requisite to the construction of a defensible policy evaluation. These are authority, justice, and efficiency. The relationship of these to other fundamental political ideas can also be specified. Nonetheless, this statement is to be taken as exploratory and provisional. While I think it is possible to demonstrate that these considerations, *at least,* have to be accounted for in the process of policy evaluation, it is possible that a similar case can be made for other principles as well.

Authority

In the most general sense, authority means that an exercise of power is rightful, which is to say, justifiable. This implies that good reasons can be given for the act of policy making, that an entitlement can be established to decide on the public behalf and a concomitant obligation to abide by such decisions. Thus understood, authority is a necessary characteristic of any legitimate policy decision and a requirement of any system of policy evaluation. A decision which cannot be justified in terms of this standard is simply an act of domination or coercion.

Put another way, as a logical characteristic of any system of policy evaluation, authority functions to structure the terms of the public debate. It locates the burden of proof in political argument. The logic of public policy making requires that the burden of proof rest always with the state (Neuman, 1953, p. 904). It is up to government to justify its actions; it is not up to citizens to demonstrate why policy makers should not do precisely as they please. It is hard to imagine how the presumption could be reversed and retain any meaningful sense of political discourse. If we were to accept that public action might just as well be whimsical and arbitrary, no problem of political evaluation really arises.

To justify a policy evaluation, then, reasons have to be given for regarding a problem as properly resolved through public action. In liberal political thought, the problem of authority is systematically related to such principles as individual freedom and consent. In liberal discourse, the problem of justification takes the form of giving good reasons for overriding the presumption in favor of individual autonomy. Any legitimate public action must be shown to derive, in some sense, from consent or individual wants and interests. However, the problem is not at all peculiar to liberalism. "Divine right" was, after all, a formally rationalized justification for the exercise of authority. Sixteenth-and seventeenth-century doctrines of sovereignty were an attempt to "give reasons" for unlimited authority. Marxism is an elaborate critique of the consistency of the liberal notion of authority and provides an alternative system of criteria for regarding public action as appropriate or inappropriate. (In fact, Marx, like Rousseau, can be regarded as doing no more than making the liberal presumption in favor of freedom a more stringent test of the legitimacy of public action.)

Even the so-called "irrationalist" political theories, those that *argue* that rationality is far from a definitive force in human affairs, rest paradoxically on a reasoned justification for a certain pattern of authority. Thus, A. James Gregor writes (1969, p. 19):

Adolf Hitler's *Mein Kampf* can, in no sense, be conceived as *simply* a statement of the author's personal emotional preferences. Suggestions, admonitions and imperatives are *argued*. The arguments may be elliptical—vital premises may be suppressed—or they may be invalid and their factual premises erroneous, but they are not simply assertions of personal preference. Hitler advocates, for example, the fulfillment of one of mankind's highest aspirations; man's continued evolutionary progress . . . . We raise objections when Hitler contends that the fulfillment of such an ideal demands the caste superordination of a specific biological race . . . . We demand evidence, for example, that would confirm that a given race is the sole repository of man's foremost creative capacities. But such objections raise questions of fact and definition and as such are subject to cognitive appraisal.

In any rational policy evaluation, then, good reasons have to be given for regarding a problem or project as appropriately the subject of public action. In the contemporary languages of the policy professions, this can be and is done in a variety of ways. The neoclassical political economist may argue that "market failure" or bona fide "public goods" are the only grounds for state intervention that legitimately override the presumption in favor of autonomous, individual choice. The utilitarian may appeal to some aggregate social welfare function as an appropriate test that "authorizes" a public action. The social democrat may argue from some need or desert-regarding conception of distributive justice. The legal positivist may simply hold that a policy option is legitimate if it is apt to be upheld by the courts, while the constitutionalist will admit the propriety of considering a policy option if it squares with the formal powers of government. Whatever the particular reasons offered, the essential point is that *some* justification on the grounds of authority has to be provided. Authority is not simply a "preference" of the policy maker that may be introduced as a criterion for the evaluation of public policy or not as one likes. One simply cannot say, in justifying a policy appraisal, "I don't care if it's blatantly illegal and rides roughshod over established rights; it's still the most efficient way of getting the job done."

There is an intimate connection between the principle of authority, thus understood, and such concepts as freedom, rights, and justice. These are grounds of argument, criteria that can be introduced to make claims about authority, or to test propositions about authority. Different conceptions of freedom—the distinction between the "freedom from" imperatives of the classic liberal and the more activist sense of "freedom to" (Berlin, 1969, pp. 118–72)—give rise to different images of legitimate authority. It might be argued that freedom is as much an obligatory consideration in any political judgment as is the concept of authority itself. (Certainly, the very notion of political argument implies a notion of the individual capable of judging the worth of rival claims.) Yet, it is such only in relation to the problem of authority, or justice. We make propositions about human freedom in order to arrive at a conception of legitimate authority. We do not make cases about authority so as to arrive at a conception of human freedom.

The concept of "the public interest" also bears a close relationship to the problem of authority. It is easy enough to demonstrate that there is no definition of the public interest to which all reasonable persons would necessarily repair. It is equally easy to show that any rational policy evaluation must give reasons for regarding a policy proposal as, in some sense, in the public interest. One cannot justify a policy recommendation on the grounds that "it would make me and my friends richer." However refreshing the candor of such an argument might be, it does not and cannot stand as a legitimate warrant for a public action. (When self-interest is argued as a legitimate basis for decision it is always in connection with some theory of how the public interest will arise from the competition or aggregation of individual interests.)

The concept of the public interest is itself logically dependent on other fundamental criteria of political evaluation, among them concepts of individual welfare and community. The connection between individual and collective welfare must somehow be accounted for in any comprehensive policy evaluation and it is necessary to specify precisely which "public's" interest is to be taken into account. Any policy appraisal entails a decision about who is properly regarded as "us" and "the others," whose interests are to be promoted and whose thwarted or ignored. It makes a considerable difference if the relevant community in whose "interest" policy is to be made excludes the adjoining class, county, nation, the rest of humanity, or the people who will live five centuries hence.

Thus, a rigorous and comprehensive policy analysis must touch a number of bases to establish the propriety of public action. This does not mean that every policy argument must contain a full-fledged case about authority going back to first principles and premises. To think of policy analysis and debate in this way would be tedious indeed. Authority may not be problematic in all exercises in policy evaluation. It may simply be assumed that the available array of alternatives passes the test of legitimacy. There are short cuts and simplifying devices in the ordinary language of any policy debate. What is certain, however, is that if a policy is controversial, it will be so in relation to one of the fundamental dimensions of evaluation. Implicitly or explicitly, a policy recommendation must be regarded as plausible in terms of each of these considerations.

Justice

John Rawls (1971, p. 3) states that "justice is the first virtue of social institutions, as truth is of systems of thought." It may or may not be the case that justice must rank first in any ordering of criteria for policy evaluation. Justice might be taken as the paramount criterion for policy evaluation, as a test, say, of rival conceptions of authority. This is the thrust of Marxian analysis and modern theories of civil disobedience, which suggest that a system of government is not rightful if it can be shown that prevailing standards of authority do not permit the consideration of the more equitable policy alternatives. On the other hand, one can argue, with Jimmy Carter, that "the world is unfair," that government should deal only with those cases of inequity that meet the tests of authority and efficiency (and therefore, that welfare funds need not be made available to pay for abortions). It does not seem possible to specify a *necessary* priority between the principles of authority and justice. However, this does not mean that the ranking of these standards of policy evaluation is simply a matter of the policy maker's preference. Good reasons must be given to justify assigning priority to one or the other of these values. Furthermore, it would seem possible to show that justice is not an optional but a necessary consideration in any system of policy evaluation.

This is the case not only because any public decision will have distributional consequences but also because it is inherent in the logic of policy making that rules must either be stated universally or so as to apply to particular cases and categories. The maxim of justice, "Treat like cases alike and different cases differently," stands then not as an ethical imperative but as a statement of a problem that requires justification: it raises the question of what counts as a good reason for regarding cases as alike or dissimilar. As Benn and Peters (1959, p. 99) put it: "If, for example, we believe in democratic rights for white men, we must show good grounds for denying them to black, and the simple criterion of skin color alone is not an obviously relevant ground of distinction. There may be other and better grounds—but the onus of proof rests on those who would limit the right, not on those who would give it universal scope."[2]

The concept of equality then is probably best regarded not as an independent consideration in policy evaluation, but as a proposition that stands in a logical relationship to the problem of justice (Perelman, 1963, pp. 1–60; Bedau, 1971; Benn and Peters, 1959, pp. 107–34). In liberal argument, equality locates the burden of proof in making cases about justice, as freedom does in relation to the problem of authority. All individuals are to be regarded as in the same position with regard to policy unless good reasons can be given for treating them differently. Grounds for differentiation may include need or desert, merit, compensation, or some public interest criterion (as in the familiar appeal to the need for incentives as a spur to productivity and economic growth, which stands as a proxy for aggregate social utility in most modern economic analysis). To my knowledge, there has never been a pure egalitarian argument that cases are to be treated alike regardless of circumstances. Most contemporary egalitarian arguments rest on the premise that existing inequalities are unjust, and that failing a reasonable justification for differential treatment, cases should be treated alike. Thus it seems appropriate to regard justice and not equality as the necessary consideration in any system of policy evaluation.

The point then is that any policy evaluation must include a justification of the categories of universal or differential treatment to be established (though liberals might argue that equality requires no justification) (Feinberg, 1973, pp. 98–102). Once again, it does not make sense to regard justice simply as a preference of policy makers, a consideration which they are free to incorporate into a policy evaluation or not as they wish. One cannot really vindicate a policy recommendation by asserting, "I know this program is unfair, but it is efficient, and we clearly have the authority to enact it."

Efficiency

It is easy enough to show that efficiency is a necessary consideration in any system of policy evaluation. Means must be appropriate to the ends chosen, and it is a legitimate criticism of any policy recommendation to demonstrate that there are better alternatives for achieving stipulated values. What is more important is to demonstrate that efficiency cannot be the exclusive consideration in rendering a policy appraisal.

In many models of policy evaluation, efficiency is regarded as tantamount to rationality. The problem of policy is "solved" when it can be demonstrated that one alternative yields an optimum level of benefits over costs. As we have noted, rationality is often defined in an instrumental sense, as "goal-directed behavior" in policy theory. Yet, some conceptions of policy rationality carry the matter even further. They argue that the efficient solution to a policy problem is also the solution that is necessarily in the public interest. In fact, latent in the logic of much of contemporary political economy, whether founded on neoclassical or utilitarian premises, is the notion that to solve for the problem of efficiency is simultaneously to solve for the problems of authority and of justice.

The cost-benefit analysis is a fundamental paradigm of much contemporary policy analysis. In the most general sense, any cost-benefit analysis rests on a utilitarian foundation. The only appropriate (or possible) criterion of policy is individual wants and interests, somehow aggregated to yield a social utility function. Any policy which reduces social costs or increases net social welfare is "beneficial." The standard of policy evaluation may be cast in terms of Pareto optimality: a desirable policy is one which makes someone better off without making anyone worse off (or in terms of the looser formulation, a desirable policy is one where winners could conceivably compensate losers through costless transfers). In either case, a solution to the problem of efficiency also yields a solution to the problem of the public interest.

Thus, it can be argued, as it has been, that cost-benefit analysis can be justified as a mode of policy evaluation, that it accounts for those considerations that are necessarily incorporated in any rational system of policy appraisal. However, this is not a necessary conclusion, and in fact most economists do not understand the force of cost-benefit analysis in this way. Efficiency is better identified as one element, but not the exclusive element in policy discourse. As E. J. Mishan says (1973, p. 13),

> It cannot be too strongly stressed, however, that even the result of an ideally conducted cost-benefit analysis does not, of itself, constitute a prescription for society. Since it simulates the effects of an ideal price-system, the ideal cost-benefit analysis is also subject to its limitations. Any adopted criterion of a cost-benefit analysis, that is, requires *inter alia* that all benefits exceed costs, and therefore can be vindicated by a social judgment that an economic rearrangement that *can* make everyone better off is an economic improvement. The reader's attention is drawn to the fact that such a judgment does not require that everyone is actually made better off, or even that nobody is actually worse off. The likelihood . . . that some people, occasionally most people, will be worse off . . . is tacitly acknowledged. A project that is adjudged feasible by reference to a cost-benefit analysis is, therefore, consistent with an economic arrangement that makes the rich richer and the poor poorer. It is also consistent with manifest inequity, for an enterprise that is an attractive proposition by the lights of a cost-benefit calculation may be one that offers opportunities for greater profits and pleasure by one group, in the pursuit of which substantial damages and suffering may be endured by other groups.
>
> In order, then, for a mooted enterprise to be socially approved, it is not enough that the outcome of an ideal cost-benefit analysis is positive. It must also be shown that the resulting distributional changes are not regressive, and no gross inequities are perpetrated.

Even an ideal cost-benefit analysis, then, is normatively incomplete; it cannot escape criticism on the grounds that are pertinent to any policy appraisal. However, this is not the only difficulty with the kind of utilitarian calculation that cost-benefit analysis represents. Since it is impossible in practice to know and to aggregate individual utilities, any concrete exercise in cost-benefit analysis requires a stipulation of the costs and benefits to be taken into account. The values postulated, and their ranking, has to be defended on *some* basis. Alasdair MacIntyre (1977, p. 226) points out that "the use of a cost-benefit analysis clearly presupposes a prior decision as to what is a cost and what a benefit" and that this decision has to rest on some ground other than utilitarianism itself.

It is not possible to derive a complete policy evaluation from any form of purely economic analysis. Efficiency is properly regarded as one ground of policy evaluation, a necessary one to be sure, but not as the exclusive consideration in policy appraisal. Efficiency is best regarded as an instrumental value, a tool for comparing policy options in terms of other values. In fact, in any cost-benefit analysis, we do not compare all alternatives but only those that have survived scrutiny on other evaluative grounds. In making an economic analysis of different road-building techniques, we do not draw up a neat comparison of the costs and benefits of corvee and slave labor in relation to more conventional methods. In terms of our standards of authority and justice, these options are simply out of bounds.

If efficiency is properly regarded in this instrumental sense, then it is a lower-order criterion of political judgment, basically a "tie-breaker" between policy options that have passed minimum tests of acceptability on grounds of authority and justice. If this is in fact the case, then it is possible to specify not only the values that have to be taken into account in any comprehensive policy evaluation but to advance certain propositions about their ranking as well. Though it is difficult to stipulate a logical priority between authority and justice (some would argue that justice is the supreme test of the propriety of any exercise of public authority, others that government should only act with regard to those forms of injustice that fall within its legitimate powers), it is possible to say that efficiency can never be assigned a higher priority than authority or justice in any plausible value ordering. Again, we simply cannot argue, "I realize that this policy is unjust; nonetheless, it is the most efficient way of achieving our objectives."

The propositions I have outlined would seem to raise problems of democratic theory. If individual wants, somehow aggregated into "public wants," are not to be regarded as a definitive test of policy, then neither, it would seem, is "majority will." To be sure, in any democratic polity majority will, expressed through prescribed constitutional mechanisms, is accepted as the definitive test of authority. A policy is legitimate insofar as it reflects the "will of the people." However, unless we are very dogmatic "absolute majoritarians" we do recognize that to regard majority will as the exclusive standard for the evaluation of policy is both paradoxical and unsatisfactory. Within most versions of democratic theory, it is an appropriate criticism of majority will to argue that what the majority wants is unjust (as, for example, if the majority wills genocide against a minority) or inefficient (if the policy preferred by the majority would lead to national bankruptcy). The puzzles and quandaries that arise in relation to any simplistic conception of democratic theory suggest that the majoritarian principle cannot be the exclusive ground of justification. In fact, of course, within any democratic polity, we do judge the worth of majoritarian policies on other grounds.

Conclusion

The problem for a theory of policy evaluation is not to discover the right policies but to establish the appropriate grounds for decision making. Not all reasons are good reasons for a policy decision. One cannot justify a public decision simply by invoking a schedule of personal preferences. A justifiable policy evaluation must meet certain standards; it must address specific problems that are characteristic of the activity and enterprise of politics itself.

To say that a policy is justifiable is not the same as saying that one will endorse it. Rather, it means that we regard the basis on which it was made to be plausible, or rationally defensible. A plausible policy argument is one worth taking seriously in the public debate. An impartial observer would weigh its claims and a critic would feel obliged to respond with careful counterargument.

There are in fact only a finite number of kinds of reasons that can and must be given in justification of a policy recommendation, a logically delimited set of grounds that are appropriate to the appraisal of public policy. It is possible to set standards of comprehensiveness in policy evaluation, to identify those questions that must at least be addressed if a policy appraisal is to appear "worthy of consideration" in our eyes.

It is not simply the stipulation of values to be served that requires reasoned justification but their ordering as well. One cannot state a transitive ranking of values simply as a matter of preference. If efficiency is to be regarded as more than an instrumental value, reasons will have to be given for regarding the most efficient solution as also within the range of "just" alternatives, and as in some sense "in the public interest."

It might be argued that this conception of policy rationality does not transcend our ordinary sense for what is at issue when we face dilemmas of public choice or when we criticize prevailing notions of how public issues ought to be perceived or analyzed. I admit that my discussion of the limitations of instrumental rationality is hardly novel and my conception of the critical political principles unexceptional. And that is precisely the point. There is something wrong when our dominant models of policy rationality are so obviously at odds with what we in fact take to be fundamental considerations in the deliberation of policy choices. My object has simply been to make explicit what we do regard as legitimate grounds of criticism of any framework for policy choice, and to suggest that our "ordinary language" is probably not deceptive, that certain standards are inherent in the logic of policy evaluation itself.

It can also be argued that this analysis has not "solved" the problem of policy choice, that it provides no prescriptive tests which the practitioner might apply in making decisions about desirable and undesirable public purposes or options for action. That, of course, was not in the cards. In order to reduce policy analysis to a routine, rather than an object of deliberation, one must state criteria of judgment in the form of rules. As Barry and Rae suggest, it is a requirement of any "first-order" system of evaluation that standards be interpretable, that we be able to gauge clearly when a policy meets the mark or fails to do so. The sense of policy rationality described here does not pertain to decisions of this type.

Rather, it comes into play at the second, or "metapolitical" level, when we are trying to decide how to decide, when we must face the decision of which system of standards to apply to a given situation.

We face a genuine dilemma of decision only when we are aware that public purposes can be perceived and appraised in more than one way. As I noted, given the proliferation of policy languages in our time, we increasingly face quandaries of this type. So long as we are operating within a bounded framework of policy evaluation, we face no such perplexity. We can "justify" first-order decision rules according to the higher-order value propositions with which they are deemed to be consistent. It is when we understand that different frameworks of evaluation could be applied to a given situation of policy choice that we face a decision of a different kind. The standards that apply to such a judgment have a different logical character from those that apply to first-order policy choices. We must invoke criteria that test the adequacy of any system of policy evaluation. The requirements of formal decision theory, as described by Barry and Rae, pertain to decisions of this type. So do the rules of normative consistency proposed by Duncan MacRae. My point has been that a certain conception of the classic political principles, understood as necessary considerations rather than as explicit normative propositions, is essential to complete this expanded sense of policy rationality.

The classic principles, then, have a place in policy theory that is very much like that of the norms of inquiry in scientific investigation. Thus, the sense of the concept "validity" in scientific discourse is not unlike that of "justification" in policy evaluation. Validity has no clear, incontestable meaning as a standard of science and different disciplines endorse different rules concerning what counts as a valid scientific argument and what does not. By the same token, different policy languages and professions endorse different notions of what counts as a justifiable policy proposal.

One basic norm of scientific inquiry is that propositions be stated in "operational" form, that one can at least imagine an objective procedure that would identify the presence or absence of a phenomenon. Again, different scientific disciplines endorse different standards regarding the kind of scientific evidence that is appropriate or obligatory, what kinds of reasons can or must be given to establish the plausibility of a scientific hypothesis. In the same way, the maxim of justice that "like cases be treated alike and different cases differently" establishes no necessary test of the justice of a public project. Different policy languages endorse different standards regarding the equity considerations that would establish the plausibility of a public proposal. Yet just as *any* scientific argument must account for the problem of experimental demonstration, so also *any* given policy argument must account for the problem of the propriety of universal or differential treatment of cases.

There is no final justification for the norms of scientific inquiry or for those of policy evaluation. There is no way of showing that a policy *must* be equitable any more than it can be shown that a proposition *must* be verifiable. What can be said instead is that just as there is nothing binding about the norms of scientific inquiry unless we are doing science, there is also nothing binding about the norms of political discourse unless we are engaged in policy evaluation.

Inevitably, the policy sciences will endorse some conception of how one ought to proceed when faced with a problem of public choice. The function of policy theory is not merely to explain why we get the kind of public policies that we do, but to provide guidance as to what is involved in thinking through a public problem to a reasonable conclusion. The very notion of policy evaluation implies that we will make judgments about desirable and undesirable public purposes and projects on some grounds.

The models of instrumental rationality that have provided our dominant strategies of decision do not adequately represent what we acknowledge to be at issue when we confront public decisions. Models of decision which place the stipulation and ordering of the values which will serve as objectives and constraints on choice outside the realm of policy rationality provide a truncated and unsatisfactory foundation for policy theory. They place the policy analyst in the position of an agent to an authoritative policy maker. The mission of policy analysis becomes that of maximizing the evaluative preferences of a particular client. Either that, or one invokes some equally problematic norm of "public responsiveness" which similarly evades the fact that in policy making we do debate the grounds on which public issues ought to be decided. However, it has generally been assumed that no other moves were possible without introducing some absolute criteria of decision, which would violate the fundamental norms of scientific neutrality and rational generality on which any comprehensive theory for the policy sciences would have to rest.

This analysis suggests that it is possible to treat the question of specifying the substantive standards that are properly introduced in any comprehensive policy evaluation as well as the rules that appropriately guide choice for any stipulated set of values along lines that are perfectly compatible with the fundamental norms of modern policy theory. In doing so, it opens up the possibility of an alternative model of policy rationality, one in which policy making is understood as a process of reasoned deliberation, argument, and criticism rather than a pragmatic calculus. However, this more comprehensive vision of policy choice does not displace but rather complements the formal requirements of instrumental rationality. Furthermore, it does not imply that institutional and sociological factors are unimportant elements in the calculus of choice. Rather, it is simply explicitly recognized that to follow dictates of situational or strategic necessity is not a sufficient criterion of good political judgement. Finally, by suggesting that normative political argument has its own strenuous rules and standards, one defines a rather precise relationship between the perennial concerns of political philosophy and the paradigms of practical reason which the policy sciences aspire to develop.

NOTES

This article, first published in the *American Political Science Review* 73 (1979): 711–23, is reprinted by permission of the author and the *APSA*. I gratefully acknowledge the helpful comments of Murray Edelman, Booth Fowler, Leon Lindberg, Ben Page, Gina Sapiro, and John Witte on earlier drafts of this manuscript.

1. Recently, the term "policy evaluation" has been appropriated to designate a subspecialty within the general field of policy analysis, denoting the technical appraisal of the impact of public programs. I want to reserve the concept for a broader, more essential use, to refer to the process of making deliberate judgments on the worth of proposals for public action as well as on the success or failure of projects that have been put into effect.

2. Charles E. Lindblom's formulation (1968, p. 13) of the idea of policy rationality will do for an example:

1. Faced with a given problem,
2. A rational man first clarifies his goals, values, or objectives, and then ranks or otherwise organizes them in his mind;
3. He then lists all important possible ways of—policies for—achieving his goals
4. And investigates all the important consequences that would follow from each of his alternative policies,
5. At which point he is in a position to compare consequences of each policy with his goals
6. And so choose the policy with consequences most closely matching his goals.

For similar formulations, see Dror, 1968, pp. 129–49; Downs, 1957, p. 6, and Zeckhauser and Schaefer, 1968, p. 29. Pragmatic and incrementalist theories differ only in that standards are to be identified and ordered after the fact, in the light of the consequences of policy. See Brecht, 1959, p. 192.

3. Barry and Rae also take up a rigorous critique of certain specific criteria of decision, including utilitarianism, equality, Pareto optimality, majority, minimax, and dominance and they do consider the place of principles in political evaluation, about which more further on.

REFERENCES

Barry, Brian, and Douglas W. Rae (1975). "Political Evaluation." In Fred I. Greenstein and Nelson W. Polsby (eds.), *Handbook of Political Science*, Vol. 1. Reading, Mass.: Addison-Wesley, pp. 337–401.

———— (1977). "Justice Between Generations." In P. M. S. Hacker and J. Raz (eds.), *Law, Morality and Society: Essays in Honour of H. L. A. Hart*. Oxford: Clarendon Press, pp. 268–84.

Bedau, Hugo, ed. (1971). *Justice and Equality*. Englewood Cliffs, N.J.: Prentice-Hall.

Benn, S. I., and R. S. Peters (1959). *Social Principles and the Democratic State*. London: George Allen and Unwin.

Benn, S. I., R. S. Peters, and G. W. Mortimore, eds. (1976). *Rationality and the Social Sciences*. Boston: Routledge and Kegan Paul.

Berlin, Isaiah (1969). *Four Essays on Liberty*. Oxford: Oxford University Press.

Braybooke, David, and Charles E. Lindblom (1963). *A Strategy of Decision*. New York: Free Press.

Brecht, Arnold (1959). *Political Theory*. Princeton, N.J.: Princeton University Press.

Dahl, Robert A., and Charles E. Lindblom (1953). *Politics, Economics and Welfare*. New York: Harper and Row.

Downs, Anthony (1957). *An Economic Theory of Democracy*. New York: Harper and Row.

Dror, Yehezkel (1968). *Public Policymaking Re-examined*. San Francisco: Chandler.

Feinberg, Joel (1973). *Social Philosophy*. Englewood Cliffs, N.J.: Prentice-Hall.

Gregor, A. James (1969). *The Ideology of Fascism*. New York: Free Press.

Lindblom, Charles E. (1968), *The Policy-Making Process*. Englewood Cliffs, N.J.: Prentice-Hall.

MacIntyre, Alasdair (1977). "Utilitarianism and Cost-Benefit Analysis: An Essay on the Relevance of Moral Philosophy to Bureaucratic Theory." In Kenneth Sayre (ed.), *Values in the Electric Power Industry*. Notre Dame, Ind.: Notre Dame University Press.

MacRae, Duncan (1976). *The Social Function of Social Science*. New Haven: Yale University Press.

March, James G., and Herbert A. Simon (1958). *Organization*. New York: John Wiley.

Mishan, E. J. (1973). *Economics for Social Decisions*. New York: Praeger.

Neuman, Franz L. (1953). "The Concept of Political Freedom." *Columbia Law Review* 53: 901–14.

Okun, Arthur M. (1975). *Equality and Efficiency: The Big Tradeoff*. Washington, D.C.: Brookings.

Perelman, Chaim (1963). *The Idea of Justice and the Problem of Argument*. New York: Humanities Press.

Rawls, John (1971). *A Theory of Justice*. Cambridge, Mass.: Harvard University Press.

Riker, William H., and Peter C. Ordeshook (1973). *An Introduction to Positive Political Theory*. Englewood Cliffs, N.J.: Prentice-Hall.

Taylor, Paul W. (1961). *Normative Discourse*. Englewood Cliffs, N.J.: Prentice-Hall.

Toulmin, Stephen (1969). *The Uses of Argument*. Cambridge: Cambridge University Press.

—— (1972). *Human Understanding*. Vol. 1. Princeton, N. J.: Princeton University Press.

Waismann, Friedrich (1951). "Verifiability." In G. N. Flew (ed.), *Logic and Language: First Series*. Oxford: Oxford University Press.

Zeckhauser, Richard, and Elmer Schafer (1968). "Public Policy and Normative Economic Theory." In Raymond A. Bauer and Kenneth J. Gergan (eds.), *The Study of Policy Formation*. New York: Free Press.

18 Ethical Principles for Environmental Protection

Robert E. Goodin

FOR PURPOSES OF PUBLIC policy making, subtle ethical doctrines are invariably translated into simple-minded principles. There are many reasons for this. Some seem to be inherent in the nature of public bureaucracies. Others derive from the nature of moral principles themselves.[1] But whatever its source, this tendency does exist and it powerfully constrains moral analysts of public issues: if their ethical advice is ever to be implemented, it must ultimately be reducible to some such rules of thumb, which can be stated simply yet applied widely. Ethical analysts of public policy, just as more ordinary policy analysts, must conduct and report their research in such ways that policy makers find it "usable."[2]

Here I shall canvass several such simple principles that might be applied in environmental, natural resource, and, most especially, energy policy making. One of the great advantages of focusing on specific policy issues in this way lies in the possibility of discovering important limits of and alternatives to rules of thumb, which look compellingly attractive in the general case. After surveying the orthodox "utilitarian/cost-benefit" rule and its shortcomings as a principle for environmental policy making, I shall survey six alternatives to that principle which might be better suited to this particular context.

Maximizing Expected Utility

The orthodox rule used in making public decisions generally and environmental ones especially is an updated version of utilitarianism. Each alternative course of action is evaluated according to the ratio of its costs to its

411

benefits, rendered commensurable most commonly through monetary equivalents. The option which "maximizes happiness" in the modern sense of having the highest cost-benefit ratio is recommended. Where costs and benefits of each option are probable rather than certain, their expected values (or certainty equivalents) are calculated by discounting each possible cost or benefit by the probability associated with its occurrence. Those who are indifferent to running risks decide strictly on the basis of these expected values, while those who either like or loath risks adjust these figures upwards or downwards, depending on the size of the risks and the intensity of their feelings about them. Such techniques are now widely used in deciding whether and where to pollute the air and water, build cities and dams and airports and power stations. The techniques are familiar, as are the objections to them.[3] Hence my own discussion of them can be rather perfunctory.

The first objection to "utilitarian/cost-benefit/expected-utility" rules is that they are based on individual preferences, which may provide infirm foundations for policy making in various ways. When stating their preferences, people always act at least partially in ignorance. Even if they "knew" all the relevant facts intellectually, they would often be psychologically incapable of conjuring up the sort of vivid image of what it would be like to *experience* that state of affairs which is necessary in order to form a proper preference for it, one way or the other. Furthermore, people's preferences do not predate experience but rather grow out of it. We do not have a very clear idea of our preferences for things lying very far outside either our past experiences or our present possibilities. Hare's proposal for a "trial-design" method of environmental planning—asking people to choose between alternative plans rather than just to state their preferences in the abstract—might go some way toward expanding people's vision, but it cannot go far enough to meet the real objection. The point remains that desires are powerfully adaptive, tailoring themselves to people's histories and possibilities; and if what people want is largely determined by what they get, then it is ludicrously circular and irrational to decide what they should get by asking what they want. My own view is that preferences and goods do come bundled together, but that we can still sensibly determine which bundle leaves people most satisfied. We can argue in that way, however, only if we accept "cardinal" notions of utility, which are an anathema to most economists.[4]

A second objection centers around the commensurability of values which this utilitarian principle presupposes. In one aspect, this is the famous problem of comparing the preferences, desires, and utilities of different individuals. Even if we had no qualms about basing policy on people's preferences, we would still need to aggregate their conflicting demands into a single social decision; although there are various ingenious techniques for such interpersonal comparisons, I am persuaded that none can provide an objective basis, and such comparisons must rest instead on ethical postulates.[5]

Another aspect of the commensurability problem, which is more central to the practice of cost-benefit/expected-utility analysis, is that not all goods are tradable for one another or able to be converted into monetary equivalents. The problem is partly with the instruments used to establish equivalence. It is, for example, absurd to suppose that the amount of insurance coverage carried on a life or a historic church represents its full value to society.[6] More fundamentally, the problem is that some things may not be tradable for one another. The stock philosophical example asks how many sweets it would take to induce you to kill your grandmother: the answer, presumably, is that you would not be willing to kill her, no matter how many sweets you were offered; and the reason is not just that you would be satiated before you ate them all but is, rather, that granny ranks lexicographically prior to sweets in your value system.[7] Similarly in environmentalist debates, old-line conservationists often argue that preserving a threatened species or wilderness should rank absolutely prior to economic growth. If there are any such commodities that are not cashable in terms of a common metric, then the summing up implicit in utilitarian/cost-benefit/expected-utility procedures is strictly impossible. It would be like adding apples and oranges.

The third and most common objection to utilitarianism, which also applies to its modern embodiments, is that it is impervious to distributions of happiness. Suppose utility could be maximized by giving everything to one person (a "super-efficient pleasure machine"), while leaving everyone else to starve. Then utilitarianism and its heirs recommend doing so, whereas our very strong moral intuitions dictate otherwise. Cost-benefit analysis has equally distressing implications: it would be better to dam up a river so as to displace a thousand families living in £20,000 houses rather than inconvenience one family living on a £21,000,000 estate.[8] That, of course, assumes crucially that all we care about is the value of the property flooded. We may, however, care not only how high the costs are but also who has to pay them. There is nothing in the logic of expected-utility calculations that forces us to take distributions into account, but neither is there anything that precludes us from doing so. If decision makers care about the distributive impact of their policies, they can—and there is some evidence that they do—build "distributive weights" into their assessments of policy options, boosting the expected utility of policies that allocate benefits to certain favored groups (e.g., the least advantaged).[9] Still, I take it to be a serious criticism of expected-utility procedures that they treat distributive adjustments merely as an option, whereas on most other principles they are morally obligatory.

This discussion is little more than a sketchy reminder of familiar problems associated with utilitarianism and, *pari passu,* with its modern instantiations, cost-benefit/expected-utility analysis. While these objections are perfectly general, they apply with particular force, given some of the peculiar features of environmental decisions. Taken together, they should suffice to motivate the search for alternative principles which can be used to guide decision making on environmental and analogous issues.

Keeping the Options Open (Reversibility)

Some of the most poignant pleas for environmental protection are couched in "forever more" terms. We are urged to prevent the *extinction* of certain species, or to prevent the destruction of *irreplaceable* historical landmarks or natural vistas. Many factors might contribute to the power of these appeals, but surely one of the more important is that they violate Arthur C. Clarke's rule, "Do not commit the irrevocable." The Study Group on Critical Environmental Problems explicitly defined its goal as being "to prevent irreversible global damage" and, along these lines, defined as among the most critical pollutants heavy metals such as mercury, which is "a nearly permanent poison once introduced into the environment."[10]

Similar "keep-the-options-open" rules are used in more mundane ways in energy policy making. Many analysts recommend "open-ended planning" in the sense that "any choice made now must be made in such a way that . . . a later generation, or the same generation at a later date, can reverse the choice and return to the original situation."[11] This is a principle endorsed even by the United Kingdom's Department of Energy, whose Energy Policy review argued that choices "should not prematurely close options" and whose deputy secretary testified at the Windscale Inquiry of the need to "establish a wide range of energy options and maintain a flexible energy strategy which can be reviewed and adjusted if necessary in light of subsequent developments."[12] Such suggestions parallel Barry's analysis of the demands of intergenerational justice "that the overall range of opportunities open to successor generations should not be narrowed."[13]

Keeping options open does not, of course, entail refusing to make any choices at all. Having chosen one path, it will always be costly to shift over to some other; but, while costly, the shift is at least possible. This is all that keeping the options open requires. Thus we may, consistent with that rule, pursue certain options provided our policy is *reversible*—provided we can backtrack if necessary. Such considerations must be superimposed on ordinary decision rules, since expected value calculations overproduce irreversible outcomes even among risk-neutral decision makers.[14]

For an example of the reversibility criterion explicitly at work in policy debates, consider the issue of nuclear power. As regards implementation of the nuclear option, Rochlin recommends "reversibility" as one of two "social criteria" to be used in selecting sites and techniques for disposing of radioactive wastes.[15] It is better, he argues, to place radioactive wastes in deep rock deposits, where we can recover them if something goes wrong and they begin leaking, than it would be to put them where we cannot get them back (letting them melt their way into the polar ice or slide between continental plates in the deep seabed or shooting them off into deep space).

The same sort of reversibility criterion can be used to guide our choice between nuclear and non-nuclear energy options. Elster supposes that such considerations make fossil fuels preferable to nuclear ones.[16] Both entail risks of catastrophic consequences: carbon dioxide discharges from coal- and oil-fired plants might alter the global climate; proliferation of nuclear weapons built with plutonium from nuclear power plants might hasten Armageddon. The difference is that the "hothouse" effect could be reversed. If it really does happen—which is far from certain—then by ceasing to burn fossil fuels we can gradually reverse the damage to the climate. It is a slow process and less certain of success than Elster supposes, perhaps; but at least reversibility looks possible here. Nuclear proliferation, in contrast, seems truly irreversible. Once nations have the technical capacity to build nuclear weapons, they have it forever. Nuclear reactors and their radioactive by-products themselves impose irreversible obligations. As the Oak Ridge team concedes, "One cannot simply abandon a nuclear reactor the way one can abandon a coal-fired plant." It is instead an "unforgiving" technology which, as Kneese worries, "will impose a burden of continuous monitoring and sophisticated management of dangerous material, essentially forever. The penalty of not bearing this burden may be unparalleled disaster. This irreversible burden would be imposed even if nuclear fission were used only for a few decades, a mere instant in the pertinent time scales."[17]

Although the expected-utility rule must obviously be modified to take better account of irreversibilities, it would be inadvisable and, indeed, impossible to make decisions strictly on the basis of the reversibility/keep-the-options-open rule. Usually some options can be kept open only by closing off some others. This, many argue, is the case with energy policy choices. Lovins maintains that "hard" and "soft" energy paths "are mutually exclusive . . . . Commitments to the first may foreclose the second." Other interveners at the Windscale Inquiry claimed that, although reprocessing was justified in terms of keeping the options open, it would actually foreclose them: given the immense capital investment, we will inevitably be stuck with using such plants once we have built them.[18] If some options can be kept open only by closing off others, we must look closely at the likely costs and benefits of each. It would be foolhardy to keep the second, third and fourth options open if the price is foreclosing the first. On the other side, there are surely some options that should be closed forever. One obvious example is the option to initiate a nuclear war.

Some, such as Farley, defend the expansion of "peaceful" nuclear programs on the grounds that "they constitute a hedge against failure of nonproliferation efforts, an assurance that countries which try the nonproliferation option will not be permanently disadvantaged if it fails."[19] But here reversibility looks singularly unattractive. Keeping the option of acquiring and using nuclear weapons open in this way would be clearly indefensible if we ever could find a way to close it irrevocably for everyone. Irreversibility in this case would be a virtue. Similarly, suppose we find a guaranteed way to dispose of radioactive wastes once and for all. Provided we can be absolutely sure of the technique, it would be far better to dispose of these wastes permanently and irreversibly instead of keeping them where we (along with saboteurs, thieves and careless miners) can get at them.[20]

Comparing the Alternatives

If forced to make irreversible choices, we should at least do so on the basis of a full survey of all advantages and disadvantages of all available alternatives. Cost-benefit/expected-utility analysis is one way of doing so, but not the only way. This "compare-the-alternatives" principle is enshrined in the economic notion of opportunity costs and was recently brought to the attention of political theorists by Fishkin's discussion of "tyrannical-decision" rules, defined as those which impose gratuitous suffering.[21] This principle of comparing the alternatives is clearly practiced in energy debates when various authors routinely compare costs, benefits, and risks arising from alternative strategies. And it clearly underlies their criticisms, each of the others, for failing to make *comprehensive* comparisons between *all* the alternatives which are available.[22]

Alongside these very ordinary applications of the compare-the-alternatives principle, we also find a rather more novel one. This assesses the riskiness of a policy in terms of the *increment* of risk it adds to those pre-existing in the status quo, rather than in terms of the absolute value of the risk associated with the policy. Føllesdal's paper on recombinant DNA research, for example, argues that we need not fear a "mad scientist" using these new techniques to unleash a deadly virus on the world, not because that could not happen but rather because there are already enough devastatingly lethal viral and chemical agents available to any given "mad scientist" to do the job. The "added risk" entailed in offering one more way to destroy all life on earth is effectively zero, although of course the absolute risk of that person doing so is frighteningly high.[23]

This principle emerges at various points in the nuclear-energy debate. In Cochran and Rotow's standards for an acceptable system for disposing of nuclear wastes, for example, the radiation hazard to future generations need not be eliminated altogether but only reduced to where it is "comparable to the cumulative risk to all future generations from the original uranium resources from which the radioactive wastes were derived, assuming these uranium resources were unmined."[24] Risk-added reasoning may also underlie our failure to protect future generations adequately from even rather larger risks of leaks of radioactive wastes. The present generation may be willing to forgo nuclear energy in light of such risks to successors "if that action would protect future societies forever. But it would be in no position to control the choices of future societies." And, as long as someone will contaminate their environment anyway, it might as well be us.[25] The risk-added argument is also used by the Oak Ridge team to brush aside concern with the proliferation of nuclear weapons: "We believe that the effect of a moratorium [on civilian uses of nuclear power] adopted only by the United States would be marginal . . . because reactors would be available from other countries," and these could supply plutonium for bomb building even if American-built reactors did not.[26]

Wohlstetter aptly replies that "to argue . . . that such restrictions would be irrelevant because there are other ways to get a bomb is like opposing inoculation for smallpox because one might also die of bubonic plague. Better to suggest protection against the plague."[27] That the status quo contains other ways for nuclear weapons to spread or for people to be poisoned or irradiated is a criticism of the status quo rather than a defence of policies only moderately increasing those risks. The general flaw of the risk-added approach is that it adopts the status quo as a baseline. Truly comprehensive risk-benefit analysis acknowledges no baseline. We must compare the profiles of *all* the alternatives, the status quo being just one option among many. The fact that an option is no worse than the status quo is irrelevant if there are options available that are significantly better than the status quo.

Finally, we can question the moral relevance of how bad one's alternative opportunities might be. Would we really feel comfortable buying up a bankrupt farmer's land at bargain-basement prices just because we know that there are no other bidders; would we not have a moral duty to pay a "fair market price," even if the market did not force us to do so?

The recent United States Supreme Court decision on the drug Laetrile, thought by some to cure cancer, offers a case in point. Those taking the drug are dying of cancer anyway—their alternatives are grim indeed. Still, we object to other people taking advantage of their sadly restricted opportunity set to peddle drugs which have never been shown safe and effective. The fact that cancer victims have little to lose is beside the point. The court held that the law's protection extends even to the terminally ill.[28] Judging from this case, we do seem to feel that certain things should or should not be done, whatever the competing alternatives look like. The injunction to "compare alternatives" or "inspect opportunity costs" might have distinctly limited applicability if many cases fit into this category.

Protecting the Vulnerable

A further rule, suggested by the last objection to the compare-the-alternatives rule, might require that we give special protection to those who are particularly vulnerable. Someone may be vulnerable to another's actions if he is strongly and directly affected by them; or he may, like the cancer victim or the bankrupt farmer, simply be vulnerable *tout court,* in that he has so restricted an opportunity set as to put him at the mercy of others in general.

Protecting the vulnerable might mean many things. Some environmentalists seem to play on this principle when pointing out that, given modern technology, seals and whales are utterly at our mercy and are enormously vulnerable to our choices. This principle also underlies the practice of judging the acceptability of pollution and radiation hazards by reference to the dose risked by the most exposed group. The most striking application, however, seems to be to future generations, who are peculiarly vulnerable to the effects of our choices, especially in the environmental or energy fields. They would, for example, be strongly and directly affected by our decision to leave them with the radioactive wastes from our nuclear power plants; and, once we have made that decision, they have very little choice but to live with it.

Intergenerational transactions are singularly one-way affairs. Later generations are extraordinarily vulnerable to the choices of earlier ones, but forebears are largely immune to the choices of their successors. This absence of reciprocal relations would, on Hobbesian or Humean accounts, imply that we have no moral obligations toward future generations.[29] But, on other understandings, such asymmetrical power relations are the very stuff of moral obligations: those in a position of dominance have a special obligation to protect those dependent upon them. Such codes clearly underlie the patronal arrangements of peasant societies. Similarly, in our own cultures special vulnerabilities underlie codes of professional ethics and form the basis of loving relationships.[30] Or, again, within the family, the very fact that children are dependent upon their parents gives them rights against the parents. Were we to extend such a principle to policy decisions more generally, we would have to cease discounting the interests of vulnerable future generations. Instead, we would have to count their suffering (from, e.g., our leaky nuclear-waste dumps) at least on a par with our own pains and pleasures.

Maximizing the Minimum Payoff

Protecting the vulnerable is recommended on ethical grounds alone. A related principle—maximin, or "maximize the minimum payoff"—is recommended on epistemic ones as well. This rule compares the "worst possible outcomes" of all alternative policies, selecting that policy with the least unbearable consequence should worse come to worst.[31] This decision rule, or something very much like it, is forced upon us whenever any of the three crucial steps in the expected-utility calculus is impossible. That procedure requires that we (a) list all the possible outcomes, and that we then set (b) values and (c) probabilities for each. One or more of these steps is often not feasible. It is often impossible to list all the possible scenarios and outcomes, especially where the "human factor" might be involved (as in the operation or sabotage of a nuclear reactor).[32] Furthermore, it is typically difficult to get reliable probability estimates: objective statistics are unavailable; theories are either too few or too numerous and contradictory; and subjective estimates are unreliable. Finally, it might even be difficult to get a good indicator of the value (or cost) of each of the consequences. Such problems might motivate our reluctance to let a smoker take any risks he wants—we just do not believe he fully appreciates the pains of lung cancer.

Where any of these steps cannot be performed, the expected-utility/cost-benefit/benefit-risk calculations cannot be performed. Instead we must rely upon other types of decision rule capable of functioning without those inputs. Two alternative rules are widely discussed. Føllesdal suggests that "in such cases we estimate the probability of the worst consequence to be 1, and act accordingly," which is the maximin (maximize the minimum payoff) rule. Closely related to this is Savage's "minimax regret rule," requiring us to choose the course of action which minimizes the maximum regret we might suffer.[33] Alternatively, we might follow the suggestion of Arrow and Hurwicz, adopted by the Swedish Energy Commission for assessing nuclear reactors, to choose policies upon the basis of a weighted combination of the best possible and worst possible outcomes which might result from each alternative policy option.[34] If, as Elster argues is the case with alternative energy strategies, all options have roughly the same best possible outcomes, then the Arrow-Hurwicz rule reduces to the maximin rule, and we need only worry about maximizing the minimum possible payoffs.[35] Either of these rules would go far towards avoiding the stringent preconditions for applying the expected-utility rule: while both do require that we know enough about the range of possible outcomes to pick out the worst (or best and worst, or most regrettable), none requires any more information about intermediate possibilities, their costs or benefits; and, most especially, none requires us to know anything whatsoever about probabilities.

Popular resistance to untried technologies with the potential for causing large-scale catastrophes—usually dismissed as a rational risk aversion—might therefore be a wholly rational response to irresolvable uncertainties. It is, I think, clear enough that such uncertainties plague energy choices and render expected-utility calculations impossible. What this may mean for the choice is, however, unclear. The British Department of Energy argued in favor of the nuclear option, saying that "our energy strategy should be robust, producing minimum regret whatever course future events take."[36] Apparently the most regrettable outcome they could imagine is running short of energy. Others draw attention to plausible scenarios with still more regrettable outcomes, ranging from altering the world climate (a possible result of burning oil and coal) to genetic mutations or proliferation of nuclear weapons (a possible result of nuclear power). On balance, it would seem that both nuclear and conventional fossil-fuel power plants are disqualified on this maximin criterion in favor of energy conservation combined with a range of "alternative" strategies relying on solar, wind, wave, geothermal, etc., power.

Maximizing Sustainable Benefits

Another rule directs us to opt for the policy producing the highest level of net benefits which can be *sustained* indefinitely. This contrasts with the directive of ordinary expected-utility maximization to go for the highest total payoff without regard to its distribution interpersonally or intertemporally. Utility maximization looks only to the sum total of benefits and is indifferent to whether they come in a steady stream or all bunched in one period. Considerations of intergenerational equity would demand instead that each generation be guaranteed roughly equal benefits and insist that one generation may justly enjoy certain benefits only if those advantages can be sustained for subsequent generations as well.[37] Following the "maximize-sustainable-benefits" rule would strongly encourage current decision makers to think in *maximin* terms also, since the lowest possible payoff is one that the initial generation must suffer along with everyone else.

The rule of maximizing sustainable benefits has clear and important applications to certain aspects of environmental policy, such as setting permissible levels of fish catches.[38] But it also has significant implications beyond these obvious applications. In the case of energy policy, for example, it decisively favors renewable sources (solar, geothermal, wind, wave, etc.) over utilization of scarce natural resources (such as oil and coal). Uranium falls into the category of scarce resources: "The amount of uranium available to the United States at costs that can be afforded in a LWR [light water reactor] is usually estimated to be 3×10^6 tons. Thus, prima facie, we have enough uranium to support about 25,000 reactor-years of LWRs—say 800 reactors for 30 years."[39] With the "fast breeder," of course, the supply of fissionable plutonium could be rendered virtually inexhaustible, transforming nuclear energy into a sustainable benefit. Then the question is simply which strategy, among those yielding sustainable benefits, yields maximal ones. But there is, more fundamentally, a question of whether the benefits of nuclear energy really are sustainable. The benefits must, remember, be net of costs, which will be increasing throughout time on the most plausible accounts.[40] Even if the energy flow remains constant, the benefits of nuclear power net of these constantly increasing costs will be steadily diminishing.

Avoiding Harm

In all the previous principles, harms and benefits are treated as symmetrical. To avoid a harm is to produce a benefit. We are indifferent between two plans, one generating positive benefits valued at §x and the other avoiding costs of §x which we would otherwise have had to suffer. Avoiding a harm of a certain magnitude is just as desirable (and, indeed, arguably equivalent to) producing a benefit of that same size. The "harm-avoidance" principle denies this symmetry, arguing instead that it is much worse to create costs than it is just to fail to produce equally large benefits.

Initially we might be inclined to run this together with the more familiar "acts/omissions" doctrine.[41] But, in truth, the harm-avoidance principle is not only distinct from that doctrine but is also part of what really underlies its appeal. People who are victims of an immoral *act*—of fraud or criminal assault, for example—are generally worse off than they would have been in the absence of such an act. Where someone merely *omits* to perform a morally desirable act, others are usually no worse off than they were before the omission—they have just lost out on some further benefits they might have enjoyed had the action been performed. Psychological studies show that individuals, when making decisions, generally do weigh losses more heavily than corresponding gains.[42] And ethically it does seem worse actually to harm someone than merely to fail to help him. This sentiment underlies "negative utilitarianism" and the distinction Foot draws between weaker "positive duties" to help people and stronger "negative duties" not to harm them.[43]

Harm avoidance is one of the more important components in environmentalist arguments against reckless interventions into natural processes. Consider, for example, the problem of seeding hurricanes. The hope is that they will thereby lose force before hitting land, and there is every reason to believe that such an action will save many lives and reduce property damage. But there is also a slight chance that seeding the hurricane will make it worse and increase the costs. Some decision-theoretical treatments of the problem, sensitive to the harm-avoidance principle, weight such potential costs more heavily than the costs resulting from just letting the hurricane take its natural course: the government bears more responsibility for causing such damage than for letting similar damage occur naturally.[44]

Applying this principle to the problem of energy choices would, I think, argue decisively in favor of alternative and renewable sources (solar, geothermal, wind, wave, etc.), combined with strenuous efforts at energy conservation, in preference to nuclear or fossil-fuel generation of power. The worst that can be said against alternative, renewable sources is that they may yield less energy—that they produce fewer benefits. Both nuclear and oil- or coal-fired plants, in contrast, run real risks of causing considerable harm. If we weight the harms much more heavily than the benefits forgone, as the harm-avoidance principle directs, both nuclear and conventional power plants will appear much less advantageous than reliance upon solar, geothermal, wind or wave power combined with energy-conservation programs.

Conclusion

The upshot of this discussion is that the standard maximize-expected-utility decision rule has very serious limitations. It is at best a partial response to the range of considerations that should be taken into account by policy makers, especially (but not exclusively) when environmental, natural resource or energy decisions are at issue. At the very least, we would want to modify the maximize-expected-utility rule to take these neglected considerations into account. We might, for example, want to weight outcomes in the expected utility calculus in such a way as:

1. to bias decisions against *irreversible* choices (which may sometimes be permissible, but only after much more careful scrutiny than they receive in the ordinary expected-utility calculus);
2. to bias decisions in favor of offering special protection to those who are especially *vulnerable* to our actions and choices;
3. to bias decisions in favor of *sustainable* rather than one-off benefits; and
4. to bias decisions against *causing harm,* as distinct from merely forgoing benefits.

Even after the expected-utility calculus has been modified to meet these further ethical demands, epistemological ones remain. When the logical preconditions for applying that rule are absent, we are logically compelled to fall back on other principles (such as "maximize the minimum payoff") that build on weaker premises altogether. Obviously it would be folly to suppose that all these new rules always converge in their recommendations on particular cases. But as a general rule they would all tend to strengthen the ethical case for environmental protection.

NOTES

This article, first published in *Environmental Philosophy,* ed. R. Elliot and A. Gare (University Park, Pa.: Penn State University Press, 1983), pp. 3–20, is reprinted by permission.

1. Robert E. Goodin, "Loose Laws," *Philosophica* 23 (1979): 79–96. For another application, see Marshall Cohen, Thomas Nagel, and Thomas Scanlon, eds., *War and Moral Responsibility* (Princeton: Princeton University Press, 1974).

2. See Charles E. Lindblom and David K. Cohen, *Usable Knowledge* (New Haven: Yale University Press, 1979); Carol H. Weiss, ed., *Using Social Research for Public Policy Making* (Lexington, Mass.: D. C. Heath, 1977).

3. On cost-benefit analysis generally, see: I.M.D. Little and J. A. Mirrlees, *Project Appraisal and Planning for Developing Countries* (New York: Basic, 1974); A. K. Dasgupta and D. W. Pearce, *Cost-Benefit Analysis* (London: Macmillan, 1972); and Richard Layard, ed., *Cost-Benefit Analysis* (Harmondsworth: Penguin, 1972). For environmental policy applications see: A. M. Freeman III, R. H. Haveman, and A. V. Kneese, *The Economics of Environmental Policy* (New York: Wiley, 1973); Lincoln Allison, *Environmental Planning. A Political and Philosophical Analysis* (London: Allen & Unwin, 1975); and Robert E. Goodin, *The Politics of Rational Man* (London: Wiley, 1976), pt. 4. For critiques, see: Peter Self, *Econocrats and the Policy Process* (London: Macmillan, 1975); Alan Coddington, " 'Cost-Benefit' as the New Utilitarianism," *Political Quarterly* 42 (1971): 320–25; and Laurence Tribe, "Policy Science: Analysis or Ideology?" *Philosophy and Public Affairs* 2 (1972): 66–110 (chap. 3, this volume).

4. R. M. Hare, "Contrasting Methods of Environmental Planning" and Jonathan Glover, "How Should We Decide What Sort of World Is Best?" In *Ethics and Problems of the 21st Century,* ed. K. E. Goodpaster and K. M. Sayre (Notre Dame, Ind.: University of Notre Dame Press, 1979), pp. 63–78 and 79–92, respectively. Jon Elster, "Sour Grapes: Utilitarianism and the Genesis of Wants," *Beyond Utilitarianism,* ed. A. K. Sen and B. Williams (Cambridge: Cambridge University Press, 1982). Robert E. Goodin, "Retrospective Rationality," *Social Science Information* 18 (1979): 967–90.

5. Robert E. Goodin, "How to Determine Who Should Get What," *Ethics* 85 (1975): 310–21.

6. Richard Zeckhauser, "Procedures for Valuing Lives," *Public Policy* 23 (1975): 454, concludes that "it would be quite rational" for a woman contemplating the threat of breast cancer "to insure no more than the medical expenses" of a mastectomy, since the insurance payment would not restore her breast should it have to be removed.

7. Cf. James Griffin, "Are There Incommensurable Values?" *Philosophy and Public Affairs* 7 (1977): 39–59.

8. Coddington, "New Utilitarianism"; Goodin, *Politics of Rational Man,* 16; Aaron Wildavsky, "The Political Economy of Efficiency," *Public Administration Review* 26 (1966): 292–310. This example further assumes that people will not be compensated for the loss of their homes, or that they cannot be fully compensated by monetary payments for moving from where they grew up.

9. Burton A. Weisbrod, "Deriving an Implicit Set of Governmental Weights for Income Classes," in *Cost-Benefit Analysis,* ed. Layard, pp. 395–428.

10. For further discussion of the reversibility rule, see (a) M. P. and N. H. Golding, "Why Preserve Landmarks? A Preliminary Inquiry," *Ethics and Problems of the 21st Century,* ed. Goodpaster and Sayre, pp. 175–90; (b) Clarke's maxim is quoted in Lynton Keith Caldwell, *Environment: A Challenge for Modern Society* (Garden City, N.Y.: Natural History Press, 1970), p. 214; (c) Carroll L. Wilson et al, *Man's Impact on the Global Environment,* Report of the Study of Critical Environmental Problems, vol. 4, sec. 138 (Cambridge, Mass.: MIT Press, 1970), pp. 259–63.

11. David W. Pearce, Lynne Edwards, and Geoff Beuret, *Decision Making for Energy Futures* (London: Macmillan, 1979), p. 26.

12. Ian Breach, *Windscale Fallout* (Harmondsworth: Penguin, 1978), pp. 27–28.

13. Brian Barry, "Circumstances of Justice and Future Generations," in *Obligations to Future Generations,* ed. Richard Sikora and Brian Barry (Philadelphia: Temple University Press, 1978), p. 243. See also, Barry, "Justice Between Generations," in *Law, Morality and Society,* ed. P.M.S. Hacker and J. Raz (Oxford: Clarendon Press, 1977), p. 275.

14. Kenneth J. Arrow and Anthony C. Fisher, "Environmental Preservation, Uncertainty and Irreversibility," *Quarterly Journal of Economics* 88 (1974): 312–19; Claude Henry, "Investment Decisions Under Uncertainty: The 'Irreversibility' Effect," *American Economic Review* 64 (1974): 1006–12.

15. Gene I. Rochlin, "Nuclear Waste Disposal: Two Social Criteria," *Science* 195 (1978): 23–31.

16. Jon Elster, "Risk, Uncertainty and Nuclear Power," *Social Science Information* 18 (1979): 371–400.

17. Alvin M. Weinberg et al., *Economic and Environmental Impacts of a U.S. Nuclear Moratorium, 1985–2010,* 2nd ed. (Cambridge, Mass.: MIT Press, 1979): 79. Allen V. Kneese, "The Faustian Bargain," *Resources* 44 (1973).

18. Amory B. Lovins, *Soft Energy Paths* (Harmondsworth: Penguin, 1977), pp. 26, 59–60; Breach, *Windscale Fallout.*

19. Philip J. Farley, "Nuclear Proliferation," *Setting National Priorities: The Next Ten Years,* ed. H. Owen and C. Schultze (Washington, D.C.: Brookings Institution, 1976), p. 160.

20. Robert E. Goodin and Ilmar Waldner, "Thinking Big, Thinking Small and Not Thinking at All," *Public Policy* 27 (1979): 1–24.

21. James Fishkin, "Tyranny and Democratic Theory," in *Philosophy, Politics and Society,* 5th series, ed. P. Laslett and J. Fishkin (Oxford: Blackwell, 1979), pp. 197–226.

22. Lovins, *Energy Paths*; Weinberg et al., *Economic & Environmental Impacts*; Herbert Inhaber, "Risk with Energy from Conventional and Nonconventional Sources," *Science* 203 (1979): 718–23.

23. Dagfinn Føllesdal, "Some Ethical Aspects of Recombinant DNA Research," *Social Science Information* 18 (1979): 401–19.

24. Thomas B. Cochran and Dimitri Rotow, "Radioactive Waste Management Criteria," mimeographed (Washington, D.C.: Natural Resources Defense Council 1979); Weinberg et al., *Economic and Environmental Impacts,* p. 94.

25. Zeckhauser, "Procedures" p. 439.

26. Weinberg et al., *Economic & Environmental Impacts,* p. 56.

27. Quoted by Czech Conroy, *What Choice Windscale?* (London: Friends of the Earth, 1978), p. 57. See further, Albert Wohlstetter, "Spreading the Bomb Without Quite Breaking the Rules," *Foreign Policy* 25 (1976–77): 145–79.

28. *United States* v. *Rutherford* 442 U.S. 544, 551, 555, 558 (1979) came to the U.S. Supreme Court on appeal from the Tenth Circuit Court of Appeals, which "held that the safety and effectiveness terms used in the statute have no reasonable application to terminally ill cancer patients." Since those patients, by definition, would "die of cancer regardless of what may be done," the court concluded that there were no realistic standards against which to measure the safety and effectiveness of a drug for that class of individuals. The Court of Appeals therefore approved the District Court's injunction permitting use of Laetrile by cancer patients certified as terminally ill. The U.S. Supreme Court unanimously overturned this ruling. Mr. Justice Marshall, for the Court, writes, "Only when a literal construction of a statute yields results so manifestly unreasonable that they could not fairly be attributed to congressional design will an exception to statutory language be judicially implied. Here, however, we have no license to depart from the plain language of the Act, for Congress could reasonably have intended to shield terminal patients from ineffectual or unsafe drugs . . . . Since the turn of the century, resourceful entrepreneurs have advertised a wide variety of purportedly simple and painless cures for cancer, including lineaments of turpentine, mustard, oil, eggs, and ammonia; peatmoss; arrangements of colored floodlamps; pastes made from glycerin and limburger cheese; mineral tablets; and "Fountain of Youth" mixtures of spices, oil, and suet . . . . This historical experience does suggest why Congress could reasonably have determined to protect the terminally ill, no less than other patients, from the vast range of self-styled panaceas that inventive minds can devise."

29. Barry, "Justice Between Generations," idem, "Circumstances of Justice."

30. James C. Scott, *The Moral Economy of the Peasant* (New Haven: Yale University Press, 1976); Bernard Williams, "Politics and Moral Character," in *Public and Private Morality,* ed. S. Hampshire (Cambridge: Cambridge University Press, 1978), p. 56; John R. S. Wilson, "In One Another's Power," *Ethics* 88 (1978): 299–315.

31. Maximin implies avoiding the worst state of the world all round, whereas protecting the vulnerable implies avoiding the worst consequences possible for certain target groups. It is, of course, possible to build a similar distributive focus into maximin (as does Rawls, for example): but it is important to realize that we *are* building something more into the rule when we do that.

32. Robert E. Goodin, "Uncertainty as an Excuse for Cheating Our Children," *Policy Sciences* 10 (1978): 25–43.

33. Føllesdal, "Ethical Aspects," p. 406; L. J. Savage, *The Foundations of Statistics* (New York: Wiley, 1954).

34. Kenneth J. Arrow and Leonid Hurwicz, "An Optimality Criterion for Decision-Making under Ignorance," in *Uncertainty and Expectations in Economics,* ed. C. F. Carter and J. L. Ford (Oxford: Blackwell, 1972), pp. 1–11; Swedish Energy Commission, *Mijöeffekter och risker vid utnyttjande av energie* (Stockholm: Liber Förlag, 1978).

35. Elster, "Risk, Uncertainty and Nuclear Power."

36. Breach, *Windscale Fallout,* p. 28.

37. Talbot Page, *Conservation and Economic Efficiency* (Baltimore: Johns Hopkins University Press for Resources for the Future, 1977). Even the goal of maximizing (undiscounted) utility usually—although not always—prohibits destruction of "interest-bearing resources . . . like crop species, fish species, draft animal species, topsoil, genetic variation, etc. . . . which are such that their capacity to supply energy for future consumption is not decreased by the utilization of some of the energy they supply . . . . Interest-bearing resources renew themselves and provide a bonus for us," and total utility derived from them is usually maximized by skimming off the interest and leaving the capital intact. This, once again, amounts to extracting the maximum sustainable yield from the resources, as argued in Mary B. Williams, "Discounting versus Maximum Sustainable Yield," in *Obligations to Future Generations,* ed. Sikora and Barry, p. 170.

38. Arild Underdal, *The Politics of International Fisheries Management* (Oslo: Universitetsforlaget, 1980).

39. Weinberg et al., *Economic and Environmental Impacts,* p. 82.

40. For a survey of these arguments, see Robert E. Goodin, "No Moral Nukes," *Ethics* 90 (1980): 417–49.

41. G. E. M. Anscombe, "War and Murder," in *War & Morality,* ed. R. A. Wasserstrom (Belmont, Calif.: Wadsworth, 1970), pp. 42–53, Jonathan Glover, *Causing Deaths and Saving Lives* (Harmondsworth: Penguin, 1977), pp. 86–112.

42. Frederick Mosteller and Philip Nogee, "An Experimental Measurement of Utility," *Journal of Political Economy* 59 (1951): 371–404, Anatol Rapaport and T. S. Wallsten, "Individual Decision Behavior," *Annual Review of Psychology* 23 (1972): 131–76.

43. Philippa Foot, *Virtues and Vices* (Oxford: Blackwell, 1978), pp. 28–30. Much the same distinction is drawn by Charles Fried, *Right and Wrong* (Cambridge, Mass.: Harvard University Press, 1978), Ch. 2, although he justifies it in terms of "intentions." On negative utilitarianism, see H. B. Acton, "Negative Utilitarianism," *Proceedings of the Aristotelian Society (Supplement)* 37 (1963): 83–94; and Barrington Moore, Jr., *Reflections on the Causes of Human Misery* (Boston: Beacon Press, 1970).

44. R. A. Howard, J. E. Matheson, and D. W. North, "The Decision to Seed Hurricanes," *Science* 176 (1972): 1191–1202.

19 Hume's Theory of Justice and the Role of Public Policy

Maurice L. Wade

HUME'S ANALYSIS OF CAUSATION, the epistemology upon which it is based, and the theory of human nature grounding that epistemology have received a great deal of attention and acclaim from philosophers and others seeking to understand the distinctive features of human life. However, Hume's theory of justice and the moral theory of which it is a part have received far less attention. This lack of attention is unfortunate, for Hume has much to say that is insightful and helpful on the subject of human social and political life. His theory of justice is grounded in an empirical and nonutopian understanding of human nature and the objective circumstances in which humankind finds itself. That theory also usefully illuminates some of the most fundamental problems of human society, as well as the roles that political institutions do and should play in addressing those problems. As such, Hume's theory of justice has much to say to contemporary students of political morality and public policy.

The aim of this essay is to explicate the central features of Hume's theory of justice, to draw out some of its more important implications for the tasks of public policy, and finally, to contrast a Humean conception of public policy with what has been referred to in the introduction to Part II of this volume as the economistic conception of public policy.

I. Hume on Justice

Perhaps the best place to begin in explaining Hume's theory of justice is by noting one of the ways it differs from most contemporary theorizing.

Unlike most contemporary theorists of justice, who are concerned with advancing criteria for the assessment of a society's distribution of the benefits and burdens of social cooperation, Hume's central concern is the role justice plays in enabling and maintaining social cooperation. Hume is concerned less with generating a standard on which to base and assess the distribution of liberty, wealth, power, and other social goods within a society than with explaining how justice solves humankind's most important collective action problem—a problem which, by Hume's lights, must be solved if human beings are to survive and flourish. That collective action problem is posed by the confluence of certain features of human nature with certain features of the environment in which humankind finds itself. Its solution is afforded by a particular human artifice, and this artifice Hume refers to as justice.

The Human Dilemma

What is this fundamental collective action problem to which justice is the answer? Hume begins to answer this question with the following words:

> Of all the animals, with which this globe is peopled, there is none towards whom nature seems, at first sight, to have exercis'd more cruelty than towards man, in the numberless wants and necessities, with which she has loaded him, and in the slender means, which she affords to relieving these necessities. (T. 484)

The human individual is endowed by nature with a wealth of needs and wants and a poverty of innate resources for satisfying them. Thus, the human individual is among nature's most vulnerable creatures. Alone, he or she has meager powers, productive capability, and means of personal security. For this reason, Hume argues, in agreement with many before and after him, that social cooperation—collective action—is crucial both to human survival and to individual flourishing. Human social life is accordingly firmly grounded in individual self-interest.

> 'Tis by society alone he [the human individual] is able to supply his defects, and raise himself up to an equality with his fellow-creatures, and even acquire a superiority over them. By society all his infirmities are compensated; and tho' in that situation his wants multiply every moment upon him, yet his abilities are still more augmented, and leave him in every respect more satisfied and happy, than 'tis possible for him to become in his savage and solitary condition, ever to become. . . . By the conjunction of forces, our power is augmented: By the partition of employments, our ability encreases: and by mutual succor we are less expos'd to fortune and accidents. 'Tis by this additional *force, ability,* and *security,* that society becomes advantageous. (T. 485)

Yet, although social cooperation is in the interest of each and every individual, the motives with which human beings are naturally endowed militate against this very cooperation. The limits of human nature make society necessary but also impel individuals to antisocial conduct. Hence, the fundamental collective action problem of human life is how to engender and maintain society. That which best serves the interests of everyone, social cooperation, will not be produced by the kinds of actions individuals are naturally inclined to undertake. Two features of human nature, selfishness and limited generosity, are particularly germane here, according to Hume.

No motive actuates human conduct more effectively than the individual's own happiness, Hume argues. No end has greater motivational force than one's own personal good. In the eyes of many, this writer included, recognition of this feature of the human psyche is one of the respects in which Hume is more realistic than many who describe human nature. Equally realistic is his recognition that much human conduct cannot be explained as the product of selfishness. Motives that are as natural to the individual as his own interests serve to spontaneously limit his selfishness.

> I am sensible, that, generally speaking, the representations of this quality [selfishness] have been carried too far; and that the descriptions, which certain philosophers delight so much to form of mankind in this particular, are as wide of nature as any accounts of monsters which we meet with in fables and romances. So far from thinking, that men have no affection for any thing beyond themselves, I am of the opinion, that tho' it be rare to meet with one, who loves any single person better than himself; yet 'tis as rare to meet with one, in whom all the affections, taken together, do not over-balance all the selfish. (T. 486–87)

Along with selfishness, human beings are naturally endowed with a motivating concern for the interests of others, a concern that is sufficient on occasion to limit the pursuit of self-interest and even to engender efforts to improve the lot of others. A realistic recognition of this limit to human selfishness must also recognize that it falls far short of total altruism. Human generosity, as a spontaneous concern for the welfare of others, is limited to only a very few others. In Hume's view, this concern focuses chiefly on an individual's family and friends. Beyond these persons, natural human generosity is very weak indeed.

In and of itself, this partiality to which all human individuals are subject would not be problematic "did it not concur with a peculiarity in our *outward circumstances,* which affords it an opportunity of exerting itself" (T. 487). This "outward circumstance" is the natural insecurity and scarcity of those external objects that are the focus of human desire. Among the most important sources of satisfaction of human interests are external possessions, "such possessions as we have acquir'd by our industry and good fortune." Whatever the source of our external possessions, hard labor or good luck, each of us is easily deprived of them by others. They are not in large enough supply for each to have as much as he or she desires and, as a consequence, each strongly covets those held by others. This natural and irremediable scarcity and insecurity converges with human partiality to induce individuals naturally to act in ways that are destructive of social cooperation. Hume refers to this convergence as the "circumstances of justice." This is the fundamental human dilemma in Hume's view, and justice is its solution.

Justice and Property

As noted earlier, Hume's conception of justice is less one of who should have what among society's benefits and burdens than it is one of what is necessary for the existence and sustenance of social cooperation. Justice is, for Hume, primarily a matter of a society's rules governing property, rules that determine what may be owned and how it may be transferred to others. Conformity with these rules is, he argues, precisely the means by which the central human dilemma is solved. Every society must have such rules. They are the means by which the antisocial nature of humankind's most efficacious motives, selfishness and limited generosity, are successfully blunted and social cooperation is made possible.

> When men, from their early education in society, have become sensible of the infinite advantages that result from it, and have besides acquir'd a new affection to company and conversation; and when they have observ'd, that the principle disturbance in society arises from those goods, which we call external, and from their looseness and easy transition from one person to another; they must seek for a remedy, by putting those goods, as far as possible, on the same footing with the fix'd and constant advantages of the mind and body. This can be done after no manner, than by a convention enter'd into by all the members of society to bestow stability on the possession of those external goods, and leave every one in the peaceable enjoyment of what he may acquire by his fortune and industry." (T. 489)

By having rules of property in place and conforming their conduct to those rules, individuals are able to feel secure about their possessions, peacefully arbitrate disputes over who rightfully owns what, and engage in mutually beneficial transactions. Furthermore, the security that effective property rules brings enables each to know what to expect from fellow humans and thereby to plan out future courses of action. In conforming to the rules of property, and thereby acting justly, individuals refrain from doing what they are otherwise naturally impelled to do by self-interest and limited generosity—namely, to enhance their own well-being and improve the welfare of their friends and family by seizing the possessions of others. Given that this kind of constraint does make every individual better off in the long run, conformity to the rules of property serves self-interest by limiting self-interest. Hume writes:

There is no passion . . . capable of controlling the interested affection, but the very affection itself, by an alteration of its direction. Now this alteration must necessarily take place upon the least reflection; since 'tis evident, that the passion is much better satisfy'd by its restraint, than by its liberty, and that by preserving society, we make much greater advances in acquiring possessions, than by running into the solitary and forlorn condition, which must follow upon violence and an universal licence (T. 492)

Like the social cooperation that it serves and facilitates, justice too is firmly grounded in individual self-interest.

The Conventional Nature of Justice

By conforming their conduct to the rules of property, individuals blunt the threat to social cooperation posed by their partiality to their own interests and the interests of their friends and kin. Such conformity compensates for the limited nature of the individual's natural endowment and enables the individual to satisfy many desires far better than he or she ever could hope to do alone. But how does conformity to the rules of justice arise? After all, abiding by the rules of justice is itself a form of social cooperation.

The security afforded by effective rules of justice enables individuals to magnify their abilities by coordinating them, gives them access to the many benefits of the division of labor, and provides them with the ability to mount a collective, and hence more effective, defense against various kinds of threats to their well-being. Yet this security and its many advantages require that all or nearly all obey the rules of property. Without such universal or nearly universal obedience, each individual will prey upon fellow humans as they will upon him or her. How does this fundamental form of social cooperation, upon which much of the rest of social life is based, arise? The best of all possibilities for any given individual is to be free to prey upon others while remaining secure that they will not prey upon him or her. If individual partiality militates against social cooperation in any case, it surely does so against conformity to the rules of property as well. Securing conformity to the rules of property poses the very same type of collective action problem to which justice itself is the solution. Hume gives evidence of his recognition of this when he writes:

From all this it follows, that we have naturally no real or universal motive for observing the laws of equity, but the very equity and merit of that observance; as no action can be equitable or meritorious, where it cannot arise from some separate motive, there is here an evident sophistry and reasoning in a circle. Unless, therefore, we will allow that nature has established a sophistry, and render'd it unnecessary and unavoidable, we must allow, that the sense of justice and injustice is not deriv'd from nature, but arise artificially, tho' necessarily from education and human conventions. (T. 483)

As the above remarks show, in Hume's view, justice is an artificial virtue, and the rules of justice are conventional in nature. Herein lies his answer to the question of how conformity to those rules is secured. What then does it mean to say that justice is an artificial virtue? As the very term implies, virtues of this kind are counterposed to natural virtues. Hume argues that empirical examination of all those forms of conduct that are denominated virtuous will reveal that they share two features. First, all forms of virtuous conduct are attended by moral approval. That is, when one regards a form of conduct as virtuous, one feels a distinct sort of pleasure at it, a sort of pleasure that is produced only in the contemplation of acts that conduce to the happiness of others. We feel this pleasure, according to Hume, because we are, by nature, sympathetic creatures. We naturally enter into and feel the happiness of creatures that resemble us. This gives us the second feature that Hume takes to be definitive of virtuous conduct. A form of conduct is denominated virtuous only when it benefits others.

To be virtuous is thus to be disposed to engage in behavior that conduces to the happiness of others and the nature of this disposition is crucial to Hume's distinction between natural and artificial virtues. Naturally virtuous conduct is conduct that we are spontaneously motivated to perform. Hume's paradigmatic example of a natural virtue is benevolence, our natural inclination to promote the good of particular others. Their well-being naturally moves us to forgo our own interests in some measure and to serve theirs. But as noted earlier, Hume takes our benevolence to be severely limited. Human beings are generous only up to a point. We are spontaneously moved only by those with whom we share some sort of relatively intimate relationship, namely, our family members and our friends. Our sympathy with them is quite strong.

The rules of property, and hence justice, do not directly conduce to the good of particular others. Conformity to those rules, just conduct, promotes the happiness of family and friends only indirectly and in the long run just as it serves individual self-interest only indirectly and in the long run. Just conduct benefits oneself and those for whom one has natural concern only by benefiting society as a whole. Indeed, if Hume is correct, the requirements of justice will surely contradict the requirements of benevolence on particular occasions just as they are sometimes inconsistent with individual self-interest. Justice is thus an artificial virtue in the sense that conformity to its dictates is not based on a spontaneous, natural motive, as is benevolent conduct. Some artifice is need to motivate just conduct and to inculcate a disposition to act justly.

Given that we are not naturally, i.e., spontaneously, moved to serve the welfare of society as a whole and that doing so will, with some frequency, clash with what we are naturally motivated to do, how do rules of property come into being, and how do we secure universal or near universal conformity to them? How does the collective action problem of securing justice get solved?

Hume writes:

> To extend man's generosity to include a larger group [than family and friends] requires the establishment of a convention. Convention is not a departure from one's self-interest but its long-term insurance. Instead of departing from our own interest, or from that of our nearest friends, by abstaining from the possessions of others we cannot better consult both these interests than by such a convention; because it is by that means we maintain society, which is so necessary to their well-being and subsistence, as well as our own. (T. 498)

Thus, to answer the question of how justice is established in the first place, we must look to Hume's notion of convention. Here we will see how virtuous conduct to which we are not spontaneously motivated is secured, how artificial virtue is enabled. As William Charron has noted, in Hume's definition (T. 490), three features are definitive of a convention. First, two or more individuals must have some common interest, some interest "which can be satisfied only through coordinated behavior so that they either gain together or lose together" (Charron 1980, 328). Second, each must be aware of this interest and the cooperation it necessitates. Third, this interest must be "mutually express'd" (T. 490). Each party to the common interest must be ". . . made aware that each of the other parties is aware of the interest all have in coordinated behavior" (Charron 1980, 328). Accordingly, we have a convention, in Hume's sense, when two or more individuals conform their conduct to some rule that each recognizes as serving the interests of all. When our common situation is such that we sink or swim together, we know this to be the case, and we manage to swim and so to avoid sinking only by coordinating our conduct, that coordination is a Humean convention. Virtues like justice are artificial precisely because they rely upon such conventions for their realization.

Conformity to the rules of property, just conduct, is a Humean convention. Given that *virtue* is that which promotes the well-being of others, we can see that acting in accord with this convention is virtuous action and that to possess the virtue of justice is have the kind of character that disposes one to so act. Yet, unlike other acts that are beneficial to others and hence are also virtuous—acts of benevolence for example—the motive that secures conformity to a convention is one's own interest, at least in the initial stages of the convention's existence. One cooperates in a convention not out of the kind of concern for others that is a natural concomitant of kinship and friendship. When acting justly, one places on oneself a constraint that is squarely focused on one's self-interest. It just so happens that doing so also serves the good of others. Here morality and self-interest happily converge. One is motivated to do what is virtuous, what benefits others, by the benefit it holds out for oneself.

Attaining and maintaining this sort of convention is relatively unproblematic when the parties to it are few in number, as when two people must row a boat if either is to reach shore. In such cases, the identity, the convergence, of the interests of the various parties is clear to each and each can see that none will succeed if all do not cooperate. Achievement of this sort of convention becomes rather more problematic, though, as society's membership increases and as a scheme of social cooperation comes to embrace greater numbers of people—an important difficulty, which Hume clearly recognizes.

> After men have found by their experience, that their selfishness and confin'd generosity, acting at their liberty, totally incapacitate them for society; and at the same time have observed that society is necessary to the satisfaction of those very passions, they are naturally induc'd to lay themselves under the restraint of such rules, both in general, and in every particular instance, they are first mov'd only by a regard to interest; and this motive, on the first formation of society, is sufficiently strong and forcible. But when society has become numerous, and has encreas'd to a tribe or a nation, this interest is more remote; nor do men so readily perceive, that disorder and confusion follow upon every breach of those rules, as in a narrow and contracted society. (T. 499)
>
> Two neighbors may agree to drain a meadow, which they possess in common; because 'tis easy for them to know each others mind; and each must perceive, that the immediate consequences of his failing in his part, is the abandoning of the whole project. But 'tis very difficult, and indeed impossible, that a thousand persons sho'd agree in any such action; it being difficult for them to concert so complicated a design, and still more difficult for them to execute it; while each seeks a pretext to free himself of the trouble and expense, and wou'd lay the whole burden on others. (T. 538)

The Basis and Role of Government

Hume regards government as the answer to the difficulties posed by the increases in size to which any but the most primitive societies will be prone. To clearly understand Hume's views on the role of government in human social life, the difficulties for maintaining conventional cooperation must be made clearer.

Three forces work to undermine a convention when the parties to it are sufficiently numerous. First, when a convention involves a large number of people, its benefits become more diffuse. In such a scheme of social cooperation, losing sight of the connection between it and one's own interests and between the interests of others and one's own is simply far easier. These connections are far less direct than when the convention at issue involves only a few people and, as a consequence, they are simply less easy to recognize. For this reason, individuals may strike out on their own and fail to stay within the constraints that maintain the convention.

Second, when a scheme of social cooperation is large, the benefits produced may be available to one only in the relatively distant future. Hume notes, quite correctly, that human beings are naturally prone to discount the value of future benefits rather heavily and thereby often to undervalue them severely.

> Now as every thing, that is contiguous to us, either in space or time, strikes upon us with such an idea, it has a proportional effect on the will and passions, and commonly operates with more force than any object, that like in a more distant and obscure light. Tho' we may be fully convinc'd, that the latter object excels the former, we are not able to regulate our actions by this judgment; but yield to the solicitations of our passions, which always plead in favour of whatever is near and contiguous. (T. 535)

This, too, can motivate uncooperative and antisocial behavior. Third, as the parties to a convention grow in number, each individual's contribution to the scheme of cooperation appears to be only marginally important to its maintenance. Individuals therefore see the possibility of the convention continuing unabated even without their participation. Thus, the best situation for each is when he or she forgoes cooperation but obtains its benefits nonetheless. So when considering his or her own interests, each finds that these interests can be maximized if the individual can manage to free-ride on the cooperation of others. This can keep large-scale schemes of cooperation from getting started altogether as well as cause them to collapse once started.

As a consequence, then, of these three attributes of large-scale conventions, government becomes a necessity in human social life. Whereas in very small societies, self-interest alone will be adequate to motivate conformity with the rules of property, unaided self-interest will not secure justice in larger, more complex social groups. Recognizing that without justice the kind of social cooperation that benefits every individual cannot be maintained, individuals are moved by self-interest to establish political institutions. The social peace and stability that presuppose justice thus come to presuppose government as society develops beyond its original primitive condition.

> When men have once perceiv'd the necessity of government to maintain peace, and execute justice, they wou'd naturally assemble together, wou'd chuse magistrates, determine their power, and promise them obedience. (T. 541)

Government can sustain conformity to justice both by tying the self-interest of individuals more directly to such conformity and by creating in them unselfish sources of conformity. One means by which government can tie just conduct more directly to self-interest is by attaching penalties to violation of the rules of property. The natural desire to escape such penalties will thus be a self-interested source of motivation to avoid doing

injustice. Government can also promote this sort of self-interested conformity with justice by making such conduct a matter of reputation. It can
make unjust conduct subject to public scorn and derision, while making
just conduct subject to public praise and honor.

Government can provide individuals with an unselfish basis for just
conduct by exploiting what Hume refers to as "sympathy with the public
interest." The moral approval we give to ethical conduct is based, according to Hume, in the distinctive pleasure we take in actions that conduce to
the happiness of others. This pleasure, in turn, derives from our naturally
sympathetic nature. Human beings naturally identify with the pleasures of
those who are like themselves—e.g., other human beings—and, Hume
claims, even come actually to feel those pleasures to some degree. This
pleasure itself can be a source of conformity to the rules of property. Of
course, to experience it, one must have a lively sense of the connection
between the public interest as it is served by justice and human happiness.
This connection surely exists since, in long term at least, the well-being of
society as a whole promotes the well-being of its members. By keeping
individuals aware of this connection and thereby aware of the fact that just
conduct is itself a source of the happiness of others, government can
provide individuals with a distinctly moral motive for conformity with the
rules of property. (Apparently, this is why Hume says that a "sense of duty
and obligation" motivates just conduct only when individuals are in a
"civiliz'd state") (T. 479).

II. Implications of Hume's Theory of Justice

The Role of Public Policy

What implications can we draw from Hume's theory of justice for public
policy? The first implications worth noticing follow from the conventional
character of justice. If justice is, as Hume says, a human invention, it does
not consist in a set of eternal and immutable standards. There is no one
particular set of rules of property which ought to be in place in all societies
at all times. A critical task of public policy, then, would be to determine
what the content of justice should be for a given society at a given time.
Should the prevailing rules of property remain unaltered? Should they be
modified in some respect? If so, what modifications are appropriate?
These will be crucial questions to be answered by public policy from a
perspective informed by a Humean conception of justice.

How should these question be answered? By what criterion should we
determine whether to preserve the status quo? From a Humean perspective, we must look to the nature of morality. Individuals and their actions
are deemed virtuous only insofar as they contribute to the happiness of
others. Political virtues like justice are distinguished from what we might

refer to as personal virtues by looking to the happiness of society as a whole rather than to the happiness of particular others. Accordingly, a set of property rules is appropriate to the degree that it serves the well-being of society. This is the Humean criterion by which the political status quo is to be judged and upon which it is to be maintained and or modified. Indeed, if Hume is correct, this criterion, the well-being of society, ought to be the *summum bonum* of public policy and all its means and ends should be derived therefrom.

As students of contemporary political philosophy will notice, in profer-ring this conception of morality, Hume rejects the conception currently referred to as *deontological liberalism*. Any conception of morality must have at least two parts, a theory of the good (a theory of what has value) and a theory of the right (a theory of morally appropriate conduct). Deontological liberalism holds that the right is independent of and takes priority over the good. This is to say that the constraints that are appropri-ately placed on human conduct, including public policies and institutions, are specified independently of the good and constrain what can properly be done in pursuit of the good, whatever it may be. From the standpoint of deontological liberalism, the means are not necessarily justified by the ends. Which means can legitimately be used in pursuit of even legitimate ends will depend on standards of right conduct which are not derived from those ends. The liberalism of deontological liberals resides in their com-mon belief that the proper constraints on human conduct must be based on an appreciation of the fundamental importance of individual auton-omy. (The two most widely read modern deontological liberals are John Rawls and Robert Nozick, each of whom cites Kant as the source of this particular perspective on morality.)

Hume apparently feels that the correct conception of morality must be derived from the study of actual human beings and societies. Such study, he insists, will reveal that, in fact, morality is conceived and practiced from a teleological point of view. That is, in Hume's view, human beings actu-ally do make the good prior to the right and define the right as that which produces the good. As noted above, Hume argues that examination of the kinds of conduct and characters in fact deemed virtuous in any society will show that all have in common the promotion of the happiness of others. This means that human beings take the good to be the well-being of others and the right to be whatever serves the well-being of others. Political virtues are seen to achieve this end by promoting the good of society as a whole and thereby to differ from the more personal virtues that focus on the good of particular others. Hume thus rejects deontology and embraces teleology because the latter is grounded in the facts of human conduct whereas the former is not.

A second implication of the Humean perspective concerns the particu-lar shape that governmental institutions should take. Above all else, the job of government is to secure universal or nearly universal adherence to the demands of justice, the rules of property. It is as means to this end that governmental institutions should be viewed; accordingly, the shape they should take ought to be whatever will best attain this end. This means that there no one form of government is necessarily best now and forever. As the circumstances of social life change and as the dispositions and sensibilities of individuals change, institutions that are effective today at securing adherence to the appropriate rules of property may become ineffective tomorrow. Public policy must then be attuned to such changes, aware of what they require by way of governmental reform, and capable of instituting such reform.

Since one means by which government is able to secure the requisite level of obedience to the demands of justice is by attaching penalties to disobedience, an important task of public policy will be to determine what penalties are effective. This, too, will be a matter that is subject to change as individuals and their circumstances change. Policy makers must know the nature and circumstances of their constituents and be able to determine from this knowledge the penalties that should be attached to infractions and the timing and type of change that may be necessary. Similarly, because shame and honor will also be self-interested motives for conforming to the rules of property, policy makers must know the sensibilities of citizens and even how and when to shape those sensibilities in service of the public interest. Of course, policy makers must be ever mindful, from a Humean perspective, that service to the public interest is itself ultimately grounded in the importance of the public interest to the long-term interests of all individuals and that it thus serves the ends of the two most powerful natural human motives, self-interest and benevolence. (Given that moral education in the form of parental socialization of children as well as in the form of formal institutions of education will be crucial to this task, policy makers will require expertise in facilitating such education.)

The ability of government to exploit the natural sympathy individuals have for their fellow humans also poses important tasks for public policy. As noted above, their sympathetic natures cause humans to take a distinctive pleasure in conduct that benefits others. This disinterested pleasure can itself be an unselfish source of just conduct. But for sympathy with the public interest to arise, individuals must have a lively awareness of the role that justice has in benefiting others. Individuals must know that just conduct provides social peace and stability and that these values are essential to the long-term happiness of all members of society. Keeping this knowledge and awareness sufficiently present in its populace is a means by which government can use natural human sympathy to assist self-interest in generating adequate obedience to the laws of property. Performing this job is yet another important role to be played by public policy from a Humean outlook.

A very important point to be taken from these Humean implications for public policy, particularly this last one concerning sympathy for the public interest, is the importance of what Steven Kelman refers to as "public spirit."

> "Public spirit" refers to an attitude on the part of the individual participants in the policy-making process. The behavior of public-spirited individuals is motivated by an honest effort to achieve good public policy. This contrasts with the behavior of the self-interested, who do not ask what policy would be right overall but rather simply what policy would be best for themselves. The standard of public spirit assumes, at least as an ideal, honest efforts to seek and work for the right policies. It demands, again as an ideal, disinterestedness: whether as a participant in the political process or someone working for a government organization charged with responsibilities for production, one should act to achieve policies that take everything into account, not just oneself. When public spirit is important in the political process, general ideas about what constitutes good policy are important in determining the results of the process. (Kelman 1987, 208)

These words of Kelman's could easily be Hume's. Hume recognizes that what makes conformity to the rules of property a matter of virtue, a matter of morality, is its impact on the interests of others. From a Humean point of view, public institutions and policies arose not to serve this or that individual or group of individuals but to serve all. It is because they serve others by serving all that justice and other political matters are, from this point of view, inherently moral matters as well as matters of individual self-interest. And, if Hume is correct, the circumstances of justice that constitute the fundamental human dilemma make this service essential to human survival. Accordingly, from a Humean point of view, public spiritedness, in Kelman's sense, on the part of policy makers and politicians is essential to good public policy—policy that is both morally sound and practically efficacious. Such policy will, if Hume's notion of human nature is broadly accurate, generate its own support by also producing public spiritedness, sympathy with the public interest, in the individuals it serves.

III. The Humean and Economistic Perspectives on Public Policy

Although a Humean approach to public policy shares much with the economistic perspective, its differences are important; seeing them will help clarify the nature of both points of view. Like the economistic theorists, Hume takes human rationality to be purely instrumental in nature. That is, like his economistic counterparts, Hume takes rationality to be a matter of determining which means will best attain given ends. Ends, in turn, are not themselves subject to rational assessment. (Unless, of course, they are only conditional ends, ends that apparently must be attained for some more important end to be attained.)

Unlike his economistic counterparts, though, Hume does not take individual self-interest to be the only ultimate end of human life. Hume recognizes that individuals are, by nature, equipped with motivating concern for the interests of others, particularly for family and friends. Hume also recognizes that human beings naturally take sympathetic pleasure in the happiness of others and can be moved to pursue even the public interest when it is linked to this pleasure. The ability to take such pleasure is not recognized by economistic thinkers. Hume's awareness of it allows him to see that human individuals are more than the mere consumers to which they are reduced by economistic theorizing and to see that there is more to the public interest than the narrow self-interest of such consumers. Concern for the public interest is at once compounded of individual self-interest, the interest that individuals take in their intimates, and the natural regard their sympathetic natures incline them to have for that which serves society as a whole. (This latter kind of regard requires, of course, awareness that the happiness of others is served by measures that are to the benefit of society as a whole, an awareness that political institutions, "political artifices," can be particularly useful in developing and maintaining in Hume's view.)

Given that sympathetic pleasure at the well-being of others is the core of moral approbation in his view, Hume recognizes a connection between morality and the collective interest served by public policy—a connection to which economistic thinkers appear to be entirely blind. He recognizes that individuals are capable of valuing the good of society in its own right, valuing it as a good that is not solely an instrument of their personal interests. This means that, although his conception of society and the public interest is individualistic, Hume's individualism does not reduce to the atomism of the economistic perspective. Individuals value the well-being of their fellows for its own sake and thus have a kind of noninstrumental connectedness with them, of which economistic thinkers seem to have no awareness. An important task for public policy, as noted above, is to exploit this natural other-directness of human beings to serve others (and themselves) by serving society as a whole. Consequently, a Humean perspective can see what economism cannot, the value of public spiritedness, and can see that this value is firmly rooted in human nature, even if it requires political artifice for its full expression.

This comparison of the Humean perspective with the economistic perspective is admittedly very cursory. Yet it should suffice to show that the Humean perspective is far richer than its economistic counterpart. This richness derives from its appreciation of the multidimensional nature of human individuals and provides the Humean perspective with an appreciation of how impoverished homo economicus is when compared with actual people. For this reason, the Humean perspective is a far better vantage point to take than the economistic outlook when considering the proper aims and ends of public policy.

Conclusion

The above list of implications for public policy of taking a Humean perspective is very far from being exhaustive. It should, however, provide a good idea of the kind of light it can shed on policy in the public interest. But why take a Humean perspective in the first place? Why should Hume's theory of justice be allowed to inform the tasks and ends of public policy? One very good reason may be the very nature of Hume's moral theorizing. Moral theorists often distinguish conceptions of morality into two broad classes. Jonathan Harrison explains this distinction in the following words:

> Very roughly speaking, it could be said that there are two attitudes toward morality. According to the first, there is the moral law, which is independent of men's wants, needs, and abilities, and it's the duty of men to force their wills to conform to it; they must make themselves ideally rational beings by obeying its dictates, regardless of the difficulty of doing so and the sacrifice it may involve. According to the second, there are men with certain wants and limited abilities, and it is the business of morality to regulate their behavior in such a way as to enable them to augment men's abilities and satisfy their wants. On this latter view it would be pointless of morality to enjoin sacrifices which were out of proportion to the benefits for which it was designed, or to impose demands on human beings which involve the neglect of human nature. On the first view man is the slave of morality, and is at his best and most perfect when his will is totally subjugated to its inexorable demands. On the second view morality is the servant of man, and can fulfil its office only by moulding itself to his needs, and taking account of his limitations. (Harrison 1981, 4–5)

As Harrison and others note, Hume's moral thinking fits into the second category. It is thus empirically grounded in a nonutopian appraisal of what human beings are and what human society can do for them. It views morality as a tool by means of which human beings can flourish and overcome their limits. This alone, at least in the eyes of this writer, makes it a particularly apt vantage point from which to see why public policy should be grounded in morality and how such grounding can be accomplished.

REFERENCES

Charron, William C. 1980. "Convention, Games of Strategy, and Hume's Philosophy of Law and Government" in *American Philosophical Quarterly* 17: 327–34.

Harrison, Jonathan. 1981. *Hume's Theory of Justice*. Oxford: At the Clarendon
    Press.
Hume, David. (T). 1975. *A Treatise of Human Nature*. (ed.) L. A. Selby Bigge.
    Oxford: At the Clarendon Press.
Kelman, Steven. 1987. *Making Public Policy: A Hopeful View of American Gov-
    ernment*. New York: Basic Books.

20 Intergenerational Justice as Opportunity

Talbot Page

IN MANAGING THE RESOURCE base we have to deal somehow with the potential of long-lived costs. For nuclear power a principal concern is the effects of radioactive material: for oil, depletion; for coal, cancer, climate modification, and ultimately depletion. How much emphasis we give to conservation and other alternatives depends on how we think about these long-term costs. I attempt [here] to distinguish between two views.

In the first, long-term energy costs should be discounted, in the same way as other future costs. When present and future energy costs are weighted and added together, with a positive discount rate future costs count less heavily than present costs. If, as a matter of equity or justice between generations, it is thought that future generations are going to be made to suffer too much from these costs (or any other costs imposed by the present generation), then this view allows for compensation by a transfer of aggregate wealth across generations. The usually recommended means to such a transfer, and a consensus view among neoclassical economists, is to lower the discount rate uniformly for all investments through the tax structure.[1] This is a *global* approach to handling long-term energy costs.[2]

As a special case, it is sometimes recommended as a matter of intergenerational justice that the intertemporal weights be made equal by setting the discount rate at zero. This recommendation, which is rarely if ever followed in practical decision making, is a special case of discounting because it still treats present and future costs as commensurable—to be combined by a simple (weighted) average. It is a global approach in the other sense as well, as it treats energy and other costs on the same footing.

443

In the second view, potentially large and very long-term costs of energy alternatives should be treated specially, partly because of their size and length, and partly because they have to do with the management of the resource base. In this view, the resource base should be preserved essentially intact, as a matter of justice between generations.

In succeeding sections I will (1) contrast the two views of long-term energy costs; (2) give conditions that define "neoclassical [economic] utilitarianism" (instead of attempting to maximize the sum of utilities over all people, as does his classical utilitarian forbear, a neoclassical utilitarian has each person maximize his own utility separately); (3) suggest that a global discounting approach fits naturally but not inevitably with the defining principles of utilitarianism, both classical and neoclassical; (4) consider what happens when the principles defining the neoclassical system are no longer viewed as obtaining; and (5) consider the principal objection to the second view that it is likely to lead to intergenerational inefficiency.

A preliminary caveat is in order. First, one does not need to abandon a notion of discounting if one accepts the second view. The traditional role remains for discounting once the prerequisites or constraints of intergenerational justice are met. But while the second view neither abandons discounting nor advocates zero discounting, the two views are fundamentally different. Second, in attempting to elucidate the two views, I have drawn a simplified picture of a neoclassical utilitarian and his theory of mind. I hope I have not done injustice to others' conceptions of a neoclassical utilitarian. As sketched, his theory of mind is simple, but simple theories have hard cutting edges. My purpose in making the characterization is to provide a perspective of the problem of intergenerational justice somewhat different from that of neoclassical utilitarianism.

I. Global versus Special Views of Long-Term Energy Costs

The most appealing argument for discounting long-term energy costs at the same rate as other costs is related only peripherally to a concept of intergenerational justice. Instead it is based on intergenerational Pareto optimality.[3] The argument: in markets, costs and benefits are discounted at a rate equal to the opportunity cost of capital, i.e., the value of alternative uses of invested capital. If energy costs are handled specially— discounted at a lower rate, discounted at a zero rate, or handled in some other way altogether—the resulting plan and resource use will be intergenerationally inefficient. It will be possible to modify the plan by discounting energy costs "just like" other costs and benefits, so that some or all generations are made better off without hurting others. Since a Pareto improvement is generally considered good, discounting, as the condition for it, must also be considered good.

An example illustrates the point. Suppose we are to choose among several possible uses of $100,000 worth of resources. The choices are: (a) use the $100,000 for a short-term safety program with the expectation of saving two lives this year; (b) invest the $100,000 at the prevailing market rate of interest, which we take for illustration at 7 percent; (c) spend $100,000 on incrementally improving the safety features of a nuclear plant with the expectation of saving four lives thirty years from now; and (d) a combination of the above. Suppose further that in thirty years it will still be possible to institute a short-term safety program for $100,000 worth of real resources with the expectation of saving two lives in that year. If we are to treat energy costs specially, particularly ones having to do with costs to life, we might not want to discount the four lives of (c). Treating the date of a life saved as morally irrelevant, the saving of four lives thirty years from now appears an even better bargain than saving two lives now, so (c) seems better than (a). Because we are treating lives and energy costs specially we might not even consider (b) and would choose (c).

But according to the argument for discounting this would be a mistake, as shown by a simple discount calculation. Discounting four lives thirty years from now at 7 percent per year, we have the equivalent of only 0.5 expected lives, at present. Thus (a), which saves two lives now, beats (c), and there must be an intergenerational inefficiency. So we must be able to find a way of making all generations better off, compared with plan (c). One way would be to follow (d). By devoting half the $100,000 to the short-term lifesaving program, we would expect to save one life in the present generation; i.e., plan (a) with half the resources. The other half is invested in (b) at 7 percent, where it grows to $381,000 in thirty years. The proceeds then are channeled into a short-term lifesaving program with the expectation of saving slightly more than seven lives in that generation. Thus all generations are made better off, compared with (c): the first generation by saving an extra life, the second by saving an extra three lives.

A well-known difficulty with this type of efficiency argument is that it sidesteps the equity issue—efficient allocations may not be fair or just. The present generation might be well off and future generations starving and cancer-ridden, from radioactive materials and other toxic chemicals, yet the situation could still be intergenerationally efficient in the sense that the future could not be made better off without making the present worse off. Justice is not efficiency: it may be possible to move from one efficient but unfair allocation to another efficient and fairer allocation. While Pareto improvements are to be desired, saying so does not deal fundamentally with the problem of intergenerational equity.

The across-the-board, aggregative aspect of the discounting approach is global in the sense that everything is subject to substitution and trade-off. This approach can be contrasted with the more specialized approach in a second illustration. Suppose you occupy a friend's house for a month, while the friend is away on vacation. In the course of your stay you make phone calls, eat staples, and drink beer from the refrigerator. At the end of your stay you restock the refrigerator, replenish the staples, mow the lawn, and generally put the house back into the condition in which you found it. This is a piecemeal approach. You are not primarily concerned with maximizing the sum of your and your friend's utility, nor are you concerned with an efficient allocation between you and your friend. You are interested in putting things, *particular* things, back where you found them. Of course the rice you buy is not the identical rice that you ate—it may not even be rice if you can't find it—but it will be a close physical substitute. You might leave some flowers or a house present, but that would be a gift, not a requirement. What is required, on this view, is to leave intact physically what is not yours to run down.

It is also possible to take a more global view. "Why should I mow the lawn?" you might say. "Perhaps my friend will want to reseed the lawn. Why should I do the laundry? Perhaps my friend will want to buy some new sheets. Instead I will leave a generalized transfer, money enough to compensate him if he wants to mow the lawn and do the laundry himself, or hire someone, or help finance some other choice if he prefers." In this view the range of choice is increased and efficiency improved.

Putting the house back into its original condition is like keeping the resource base intact intergenerationally. Taking the more global perspective and letting the house run down but trading off with generalized compensation illustrates the discounting approach, but somewhat abstracted from it because I have abstracted from time, productivity, and discounting itself. I will suggest that the specialized approach is more appropriate than the global one, as a matter of intergenerational justice. But I will not argue for it within the framework of utilitarianism underlying modern neoclassical economics because (1) in this framework there is little room for a concept of justice; and (2) when we depart from the neoclassical system by modifying its defining principles, the specialized view of resource preservation as a notion of intergenerational justice fits nicely with the modified principles. Thus the next step is to define the central features of the neoclassical system.

II. Defining Neoclassical Utilitarianism

An economist's definition of utilitarianism starts with the notion of maximizing behavior. This definition, of course, is too vague and inclusive. To some extent we are all self-serving, and we all practice maximizing behavior. In a sense, even inanimate objects practice maximizing (or minimizing) behavior: soap films minimize surface area; light bends to minimize travel time through different media; water flows in a way to minimize potential energy. If some form of maximizing behavior is the defining characteristic of utilitarianism, then we are all utilitarians by definition.

But the important thing for utilitarianism is not that we maximize; it is the pervasive nature and the particular conception of utilitarian maximizing behavior. Thus it is useful to define utilitarianism by the principles that make the maximization process universal.

Maximization is difficult when many distinctions are drawn, because it is generally impossible to maximize separate things at the same time. The principles, or conflations,[4] set out below serve to clear away or collapse distinctions that might otherwise interfere with the maximization process. My approach is to take conflations as the defining characteristics of utilitarianism. Clearly there are advantages to abstracting from detail and blurring distinctions. In the case of mathematical argument, abstracting and generalizing often lead to deeper and more powerful insights into structures of ideas. But there can be disadvantages, too. When the distinctions are important, glossing them over can lead to a structure of ideas quite different from the world we are trying to describe.

Principles of Neoclassical Utilitarianism

Some utilitarian principles can be seen as defining a theory of mind, and a very simple one at that. The neoclassical utilitarian is drawn to this theory for two important reasons. The first is to portray all a person's values as generally comparable, so that some general maximization can make sense. The second is to base the theory in observable behavior.

The first aspect of this theory of mind can be expressed as a view of how values are formed. What might otherwise be considered heterogeneous things (for example, decision processes, descriptions of conceivable states of affairs, the present and the future) are treated as unified, homogeneous objects. I will call attention to five ways in which distinctions are collapsed.

1. Only Preferences Matter.

There seem to be several ways of making decisions. For some questions the process of decision might follow moral reasoning; for others it follows a maximization calculus. Some decisions might be made on the basis of religious concerns, others on the basis of habit, still others on the basic of some automatic code of behavior. Or we might posit two entire preference structures: one appropriate for normal decisions, the other for moral choices, as was done by Plott.[5] If we make such distinctions we have to explain when each one applies; we need, at least in principle, some way of defining the boundaries among the processes; and we have to be able to say how one process shifts into another. But if we conflate all decision processes into a single process, that of ordering preferences, such difficulties are cleared away. A preference conflation implies that all these processes are fundamentally the same process and can be modeled as though they were just one process, that of preference ordering.[6] For the classical utilitarian this first conflation can be stated by saying that each person has just one utility function; for the neoclassical utilitarian, just one preference ordering.

2. ALL STATES ARE COMPARABLE.

The idea of a "state" is a very general concept. It is a complete description of reality. This description can include such morally laden possibilities as "John was murdered." The second conflation says that any complete description of reality is directly comparable with any other in the sense that each individual is assumed able to judge whether he prefers the first to the second, the second to the first, or is indifferent between the two. The classical utilitarian states the second conflation by saying that the domain of the utility function is all conceivable states. The neoclassical utilitarian would say that preference orderings are complete over all conceivable states for the world.

3. FUTURE AND PRESENT STATES ARE DIRECTLY COMPARABLE.

Now we turn to a matter that was left open by the second principle: whether a complete description of the world—a state—includes a description of the future as well as the present. The third conflation says that a state is a description not only of a conceivable present, but also of a conceivable entire future. We can think of a state as a whole movie film where the first frame is a complete description of the present, and each successive frame is a complete description of a possible future day, or generation. Thus the utilitarian chooses among whole possible movie films, not just single frames of the movie, which are snapshots of the present moments.[7]

A logical implication of this conflation is that if we are really choosing among whole movie films there is really just one choice, now, for all time. Many economic models are of this form. Dynamic programming models, or control theory models, collapse the future and the present together into a single-shot choice. This point is clear when we realize that for control theory problems there is a single-valued functional, ranging over all time, being maximized just once, from the vantage point of the present moment. Thus a value is being put on the entire movie film, and not on just a single frame.

The collapse of time is held across the life of the individual as well as across generations. It is as though one could put a thermometer into a person's mouth and out would pop rankings of entire life plans. These plans would, of course, be made from the vantage point of the present moment. In many models, the only problem is to find the top element of the ranking—it is one of maximization. It seems apparent, however, that in ten or fifteen years a person's interests will differ from those of today (because he has grown and changed, or perhaps merely because of the shift in vantage point in time). If we accept the third conflation, we concern ourselves only with what the thermometer says today, because today's reading includes today's preferences about future states.[8] Backing off from this collapse of time, we might be concerned with the different readings of the thermometer in different vantage points in time. Then we would have the problem of "justly" taking into account potentially conflicting interests. In the language of social choice, there is an "aggregation" problem (the problem of resolving conflicting interests), in addition to the maximization problem (the problem of picking off the top element once the aggregation problem is solved). The framework of intertemporal social choice, which later will be used to discuss justice across generations, can also be applied to justice between the earlier and later selves of a particular individual. For a classical utilitarian, the third conflation says that time-dated states are legitimate arguments for each individual's utility function. For the neoclassical utilitarian, preference orderings are complete over time-dated states.

4. UTILITIES OF DIFFERENT INDIVIDUALS ARE NOT DIRECTLY COMPARABLE.

This principle expresses the second feature of what I call the neoclassical utilitarian theory of mind—the inclination to behaviorism—and can be stated as a conflation that divides classical and neoclassical utilitarianism. The classical utilitarian accepts comparability, but the neoclassical utilitarian does not (except sometimes in the intertemporal case). For the classical utilitarian, utility is a measurable quantity, at least in principle, and a quantity of utility from one individual can be added to a quantity of utility from another individual. For a neoclassical utilitarian, utility is not a "real" quantity—it cannot be measured even in principle—and thus there is no way to add one person's utility to another's.

It is interesting, however, that in the intergenerational case, neoclassical utilitarians often cross the line and act like classical utilitarians. While economists are greatly reluctant to add one person's utility to another's within a generation, utilities of different people are commonly added across time. One way to avoid adding utilities across time is to assume that each person lives forever, and this counterfactual assumption is sometimes invoked. Another approach that permits adding utilities across generations is to assume that our heirs are "just like" ourselves. They are extensions of ourselves, sharing the same interests, and one utility function fits all (per extended family). Neither approach is very satisfying.

A colorful way of stating how the neoclassical utilitarian came to reject the fourth conflation is to say that it was killed by the possibility of a utility monster, a sensitive fellow who can squeeze more utility out of a given resource than can an ordinary person. Classical utilitarians attempting to maximize the sum of utilities across people should give a larger share of a resource to the one who can squeeze the most utility out of it. But many economists are unwilling to give the largest shares of the economic pie to those most efficient in converting utility. (One might even argue to the contrary, that the less efficient converters should be given larger shares in compensation.) Added to this is the incentive problem, of great concern to modern economists. Even if utility "existed" it would be nonobservable, and if we were to maximize the sum of utilities each of us would have obvious incentives to claim to be a utility monster (the youngest child of each family is sometimes tempted toward such claims).

To state the matter a little more soberly, many economists rejected classical utilitarianism in favor of its neoclassical version when they decided that utility was entirely nonobservable. At the same time it became clear that most of the structure in economics could be preserved by thinking in terms of preference orderings instead of quantitative utilities. Preference orderings have the advantage of being, at least in principle, observable by choices actually made. This rejection of classical, quantitative utility has two repercussions noteworthy for our purposes.

First, if interpersonal comparisons of utility are impossible, then we are no longer able to maximize the sum of utilities across people. So the neoclassical utilitarian defends a weaker kind of maximization process in which each one maximizes his own utility. The classical utilitarian's moral principle, which says to maximize the sum of utilities, is strong in the sense that it sometimes directs people to act against their own selfish interests. The corresponding, weaker neoclassical utilitarian's moral principle says that we should move toward Pareto optimality. This principle is weaker in not requiring individuals to act against their own selfish interests. It is also weaker because in many situations it does not tell us what to do (it is a partial ordering).

Second, the rejection of unobservable utilities leads toward a behaviorist or a black-box theory of the mind. The only evidence allowed for inferences about happiness or satisfaction is observable behavior: for example, actual purchases in markets. Evidence from introspection is looked upon with suspicion, as are surveys of stated preferences. The situation is a little like trying to infer the structure of a car's motor by observing the car's operation. With this black-box approach it is not surprising that we might be limited to simple concepts of the motor.

The neoclassical utilitarian's theory of mind may be a very primitive theory, but the overall view is consistent and coherent so there is little chance of refuting it internally. In that sense it is a comprehensive theory and can explain almost anything.[9] It is similar in this respect to other comprehensive theories of mind and human behavior. For example, another alternative explains every human action by "God willed it." The theories are different but each is difficult to refute. The mere fact that things are explainable within a system is not an argument for that system. Another way of choosing among systems involves the appeal to some outside criterion—for example, Occam's razor, predictive success, introspection, or ethical considerations.

The view of the mind presupposed by an economic theory will of course be very important in assessing the moral implications of using that theory for making choices. In addition, one explicitly moral principle is central to neoclassical utilitarianism. It is a thesis about rights.

5. PROPERTY RIGHTS MUST BE WELL SPECIFIED.

This principle tends also to be a conflation because, in its extreme version, it can be taken to mean that the only important rights for the neoclassical utilitarian are property rights, and that anything that can be valued should be privately owned.[10]

The motivation here is that free transactions through the market are the best way of revealing preference orderings and also of arriving at allocations of goods and services—states of affairs—that are Pareto optimal. A primary way to lower transaction costs and reduce conflicts among various individual rights is to completely specify ownership rights and make them tradeable.

III. Discounting Within Both Utilitarian Systems

Discounting fits easily but not inevitably with principles 1 through 5 or a subset of 1–5. Indeed, one is struck by the number and variety of the arguments that take these principles as background and lead to discounting. (The impression is that all roads lead to Rome.) I will discuss four of these arguments, all of which incorporate principles 1 through 3. Two approaches are in the classical utilitarian tradition and incorporate principle 4; the two in the neoclassical tradition reject principle 4.

All four approaches are "institution free": they define criteria, but not institutions for achieving the criteria. Conflation 5 concerns property rights, an institutional structure. Thus the four approaches below are compatible with but do not directly incorporate the notion that all rights should be construed as property rights.

For purposes of this chapter as a whole, it is more important to show that discounting does not inevitably fit than to show it fits easily into the landscape of principles 1 through 5. A single counterexample will prove that some roads do *not* lead to Rome. The counterexample below shows that the choice of intergenerational decision rules, even within the confines of principles 1 through 5, is much broader than that of choosing between discounting at a positive rate or discounting at a zero rate (adding up utilities or some other measure across time). Nevertheless, principles 1 through 5 do shape a perspective, and they do not appear to be a compatible background for a specialized conception of justice as opportunity. In the following section, I attempt to modify 1 through 5 to develop a background more conformable to this latter notion.

Four Roads That Lead to Rome

The four arguments leading to discounting involve a "planner" who trades off present and future generations' utilities somewhat as he would trade off his own present and future utilities in the third conflation. But here the planner is assumed to be, in some sense, intertemporally neutral, or sympathetic with the interests of all generations.[11]

A. The planner who maximizes the sum of present and future utilities is not selfish, because he weights other generations' utilities as heavily as his own generation's. To do this the planner must accept the 4th conflation (he is a classical utilitarian). But he sees no sense in allocating equal weight to a distant generation, since it may never exist. So he discounts each generation's utility by the probability that it will not exist. To arrive at a constant discount rate (Rome) it need only be assumed that the probability of extinction during the course of one year, given that extinction has not already taken place, equals the probability of extinction during the course of another year, given that extinction has not already taken place before that other year.[12]

From the point of view of this discussion, the most fundamental normative problem is that this approach treats the probability of extinction as a fixed parameter outside the system, unaffected by this generation's actions. But the probability of the next generation's survival is strongly affected by the present generation's actions, and a sufficient guarantee of an "adequate" level of survival is the central question of intergenerational justice.

B. The selfish planner whose self-serving tendencies are blocked by a veil of ignorance is looking out only for his own welfare and is not comparing it with others (he is a neoclassical utilitarian). But even though he wants to maximize only the utility of his own generation, he does not know to which generation he belongs. Thus he maximizes the expected value of his own utility, weighting each generation's utility by the probability that he attaches to being in that generation. (For simplicity we imagine that each generation contains only one person, who may or may not be the planner.) The planner's utility function takes into account his own (selfish) risk aversion to being caught short in a particularly barren generation. As in the previous argument, the planner posits the increasing likelihood of eventual extinction, and we end up again with utility discounting, by a different route and a different interpretation of the utility function. For this Rawlsian gambler or, more accurately, Harsanyian gambler as interpreted by Dasgupta and Heal, the key assumption leading to discounting is again the declining certainty of future existence.

C. *The egalitarian planner who is worried about productivity.* In simple models that allow for capital productivity, if we add up utilities across time (in the classical tradition) to achieve equal utilities across time, we then need to discount by the marginal productivity of capital. In this type of model, simply maximizing the sum of utilities, discounting at a zero rate, means that early generations would sacrifice to invest more so that later generations could feast off time-delayed yields of capital. To achieve an egalitarian sharing across time, the productivity of capital needs to be offset by discounting future utilities. In more complicated models egalitarianism is not achieved so simply, but the flavor of egalitarianism remains in allowing discounting to offset productivity.[13]

D. *The planner who is fair because his preferences are generated by fair axioms.* This more complicated path is based on some important work that attempts to find a social choice rule for aggregating individual utility orderings. If we allow, as a simplifying assumption, that each generation's utility can be treated as a separate preference ordering and then combined by an aggregative social choice rule, then the fairness of this rule would seem to be deducible from the fairness of each of the axioms that describe it. This is consistent with a neoclassical utilitarian perspective.

In a pioneering set of papers, Tjalling Koopmans proves a theorem which can be reinterpreted in an intergenerational context.[14] The theorem depends on a set of axioms, each of which appears neutral, innocuous, and fair. In its reinterpretation, the theorem proves that an intergenerational planner who adopted these axioms must be led to a social choice rule that discounts the utilities of future generations. The proof is mathematically complicated, and we will not recapitulate it here.[15]

It is possible, however, to choose a set of axioms also appearing neutral, innocuous, and fair, that leads to a different social choice rule. Kenneth Arrow's well-known axioms, applied to the intergenerational context, generate a social choice rule that strongly favors the future over the present. Arrow's collection of axioms are in some ways similar to majority rule voting, and the infinite majority of future generations dominates the minority of the present (with an infinite number of voters no single generation dictates). Yet Koopmans's axioms, which are also applied to an infinity of generations, yield a quite different time bias. Most interesting, if we take the crucial axiom from Koopmans's set, the axiom of stationarity, and combine it with Arrow's three axioms, we get a still different result: "dictatorship of the present."[16] This term has a technical meaning in social choice theory: whatever the first generation prefers is the intergenerational social choice.

Thus, an axiom that seems plausible can be combined with other plausible axioms to yield controversial results about discounting, and even to yield different results under different combinations. Time bias is not apparent from looking at axioms singly, but depends on sensitive interaction among the axioms.

A further observation is that the Koopmans axioms and the Arrow axioms illustrate the weakness of efficiency (Pareto optimality) as an ethical principle. Koopmans's axioms lead to discounting as a social choice rule; Arrow's do not. But both satisfy Pareto optimality. It is an axiom in both systems. Thus, the Pareto principle cannot be used to choose between them.

Finally, this social choice rule framework illustrates that discounting can take place at three possible levels. Each generation, individually, may discount to reflect its own time preference, because each generation determines its own preference ordering over the entire time path. This is true for both Koopmans's and Arrow's axioms. Second, discounting can also show up, in both systems, in the definition of the feasible states, by taking account of capital productivity in determining what is feasible. Thus, the opportunity costs of capital can be embedded in the definition of feasibility. The difference between the Koopmans and Arrow axioms appears at the third level. For the Koopmans axioms, discounting is also the form of the aggregation rule. For Arrow's axioms, it is not.

We conclude, then, that within the framework of neoclassical utilitarianism, many paths lead to a discounting formulation. They exhibit a rich variety of assumption and interpretation. But there are also paths that do not lead to discounting, *at the level of intergenerational choice*. This third level is the level of our main concern. Arrow's axioms, reinterpreted intergenerationally, show that it is possible to have Pareto optimality without discounting at the level of social choice, yet with discounting for personal time preference and the opportunity cost of capital at the other two levels.

IV. Outside the Neoclassical System

In the preceding section we looked inside the neoclassical system. We found room for aggregation of intergenerational interests without discounting them. In the neoclassical system, however, any notion of justice would have to be built on the utilitarian principles 1 through 3. Within this theory "preferences are all." They soak up and explain all forms of choice and behavior at the individual level. It may be possible to develop within this system a satisfactory notion of a fair or just aggregation of intergenerational preferences. Indeed, we have shown alternative conceptions of intergenerational fairness within the neoclassical system. But the utilitarian principles 1 through 3 are confining, as are 4 and 5. In this section we enlarge the inquiry.

To develop a conception of justice based on opportunity rather than utility, I must move outside the neoclassical system by modifying its defining principles. Why opportunity rather than utility? Inside the neoclassical system there is little room for a concept of justice at the individual level; outside the system there is no unified concept of utility (or preferences). A simple solution is to move outside the system and base a notion of justice on something other than utility (or preferences). Brian Barry suggests that opportunity is a more sensible base than utility (and I have put forward a similar suggestion).[17]

There is another reason for moving outside the neoclassical system: it may be "unrealistic," too simple to describe adequately how our values determine which choices are made and which actions undertaken, and too simple to incorporate our considered judgments about rights and property. If the world is "really" more complicated, then to capture the most important complications it becomes necessary to draw some distinctions.

So now we move outside both utilitarian systems and attempt to draw some distinctions that might be considered realistic and important. These distinctions lead toward a common sense notion of justice generally, intragenerationally as well as intergenerationally. But in the intergenerational context they appear to pick out the resource base as a special concern of justice. The conception of intergenerational justice constructed below is not "inevitable"; other conceptions are possible. But the idea is to base this intergenerational concept of justice on its relationship to a common sense notion of justice intragenerationally.

I will proceed by making some relevant distinctions in the neoclassical principles 1 through 5, as they lead toward a common sense concept of justice intragenerationally, and will then apply these distinctions to the intergenerational case. The appeal for this concept of justice is thus grounded in the independent reasonableness of the distinctions.

A. ALL OWNERSHIP RIGHTS ARE NOT ON A PAR.

I adopt here the Lockean notion of "just acquisition." The most absolute claim of just acquisition is an individual's claim to work wholly created by himself. Thus, Byron had a right to burn his books, but his wife did not, without his permission. (The *classical* utilitarian would not see the point of this distinction and might deny Byron the right to burn his own books.) The next strongest claim of just acquisition is by an individual who "produces" an object by mixing his labor with a resource of which there is "enough and as good" left for others. The least claim, in fact no claim at all, of just acquisition concerns the resource base passed into the hands of the present generation by the mere passage of time. Shakespeare's plays are an example of this resource base. They are not produced by the present generation, which has no right of ownership over them in a sense that would justify doing what it wants to the plays, including destroying all records of them.

By this distinction, ownership is a relative, not an absolute, concept and is based on a relative notion of just acquisition. This notion of acquisition sharply distinguishes the resource base, including the cultural and technological heritage of past generations, from the capital stock produced by this generation. The distinction between present capital and the resource base is not admitted in the neoclassical utilitarian system. In fact, within the neoclassical utilitarian system, it is likely to be argued that such a distinction will lead to large intertemporal inefficiencies. (I will discuss this in section V.)

The distinction between just and unjust acquisition is common to everyday life. Even if one innocently buys stolen goods, that ownership is not secure because the goods were not justly acquired by the thief and thus were not the thief's to sell or the purchaser's to own. In the United States we allow strong ownership rights over particular natural resources, for it has historically been believed that here resources are sufficiently extensive that "enough and as good" remains for others, including later generations. In other countries, where resources are more limited, ownership of natural resources is more circumscribed. With the growing concern that the Lockean proviso is not satisfied, there is growing concern about how absolute the ownership of natural resources *should* be. For example, the trend toward increasing severance taxes can be viewed in part as a limitation on the absolute ownership of materials extracted from the environment.

The distinction—between what is and is not acquired more or less through our own efforts—leads to a common sense notion of intergenerational justice. By this notion, it would be unjust to future generations if we were to run down the resource base, which was not justly acquired by us, when we have the opportunity to treat it on a sustainable basis. By the same token, it would be unjust to run down the previous generation's capital and cultural accumulation. It might be ungenerous if the present generation chose to add nothing to the future heritage, but it would not be considered unjust (like the house sitter's nonobligation to provide flowers). This common sense notion of justice is therefore a kind of minimum of moral responsibility.

Clearly, the idea of preserving what is not justly acquired needs to be made more practical. The present generation cannot be required to preserve every obscure, minor literary work produced in previous generations. Nor can it be required to preserve every tree, or deposit of oil and coal. In the example of our house guest, the replacement of the basic stocks was not precise. Little things need not be restored to their original condition, only the more essential. Thus, to make this notion of justice practical, we need some notion about what is more, or less, essential.

B. NOT ALL STATES OR GOODS ARE COMPARABLE.

Some things are more essential than others. Obvious candidates for essentiality are basic health and liberty. Essential goods appear to correspond with Rawls's primary goods. The idea of essentiality also appears in Adam Smith's diamond and water paradox. Smith thought it a paradox that although water was much more valuable (essential) than diamonds, diamonds had a much higher price per unit than water.

A way of distinguishing the essential from the nonessential is to note that we might consider trading essential goods near the margin, but not far inside the margin. For example, suppose you are wrongly convicted and imprisoned for a day, before the authorities realize their mistake and set you free. Unlike the current system, the authorities attempt to make complete restitution. They ask you how much money would make you feel completely indifferent between the day's imprisonment and the compensation and neither the imprisonment nor the compensation. Even though you are trading off liberty in this case, you might be able to name a figure that would indeed make you indifferent between the mistake and the compensation, and neither. (Whether or not you would honestly reveal this figure is another question.)

On the other hand, suppose you are falsely convicted and imprisoned for twenty years before the authorities realize their mistake. What compensation would make you feel indifferent between the twenty-year mistake and the compensation and neither the mistake nor the compensation? In this case, even if you attempt to address this question honestly, you might have no way of dealing with it, for you have no basis for the comparison and no way of naming such a figure. Similarly, what is the premium wage payment you are willing to accept in order to live with a slightly higher risk of cancer? You might be quite willing to make this trade-off on the margin. But suppose you, in fact, developed cancer. Is there then some compensation that could make you feel indifferent to it? Or suppose you are asked to work in a hazardous occupation with an 80 percent probability of cancer.

Turning to the intergenerational case, it is plausible to argue that the resource base as a whole is more essential than this generation's capital stock accumulation. For example, Japan and Germany survived the destruction of more than one generation's worth of capital stock, and both countries were able to rebuild their capital stock quickly. But neither country could have survived without energy, metals, and other materials from the resource base. A particular metal may not be essential, but metals as a group are. Similarly, a single source of energy may be unessential, but the entire energy sector is essential. A sufficient condition for sustainability, and one that is perhaps unnecessarily strong, is to keep roughly constant the cost of extraction from the resource base, major sector by major sector. This criterion allows substitution within sectors and destruction of some resources.

C. Offsetting Harms With Benefits.

Attitudes toward the distinction between doing good and avoiding harm provide a litmus test for utilitarians. Within the utilitarian system we can't distinguish between avoiding harm and doing good; one is the opportunity cost of the other. MacLean offers the example of randomly killing a person in order to extract two kidneys to save the lives of two renal disease sufferers.[18] Within utilitarian systems this might seem like a net gain, but most common sense notions of justice would consider it unjust to kill one person in order to save two.

In the intergenerational context, we are currently harming future generations by physical depletion of the resource base and by the dispersion of radioactive wastes and toxic chemicals. At the same time, we are benefiting the future by increases in the capital stock, technological understanding, and cultural accumulation. But under this distinction there is no simple one-to-one trade-off because of the asymmetrical treatment of the resource base. How do we draw a distinction between allowable harms and unallowable harms? We can't prevent all harms to the environment. But we can "protect" and "renew" essential goods. We can reduce our releases of radiation toward the levels of release that would occur through natural erosion; we can stabilize the population to help maintain the resource base on a constant per capita basis.

The ethical choice for the present generation is to move in one of two directions: the present can manage the resource base on a sustainable basis, or it can let the base slide into an irreversible decline. (If there were no way of preventing the latter option, the choice would lose its moral relevance.) Within the utilitarian system the former choice is viewed simply as a preference of the present generation which may or may not be automatically achieved by market interactions. The consequences of the latter path would of course be unfortunate for the future. In the alternative view the latter choice is unjust as well as unfortunate.

D. Opportunity vs. Utility.

It seems sensible to focus on and limit our responsibility to what we can foresee and control. As future opportunity is more in our control than future utility, it would seem that opportunity is a more sensible object of intergenerational justice. With some effort we can control the form of the heritage to be passed on to the next generation. It is beyond the control of the present generation to ensure that the next one will be happy or hardworking. It is beyond our control to increase their welfare; we can only assure them of certain opportunities for happiness that we foresee will be essential. But we *can* preserve certain essentials, such as the valuable parts of the cultural and natural resource base. If we cannot ensure that these will in fact be passed on to future generations, we can at least keep from ensuring that they will not be passed on.[19]

V. The Inefficiency Issue

From the perspective of neoclassical economics, the most obvious objection to a special treatment of the resource base is that attempting to preserve it essentially intact could conceivably lead to very large inefficiencies. A great deal of effort and sacrifice could be spent preserving some part of the resource base that no one in the future might want. The objection suggests both empirical and conceptual considerations.

Of course the possibility exists that the present will go to great effort to preserve something that the future does not want. But is this possible for essential goods—conditions of basic health, alternative provision of energy sources, water, soil, space per capita, etc.? In the case of radioactive waste, intergenerational justice suggests that aggregate exposure be kept near natural background levels, perhaps by diminishing natural releases to compensate for releases from energy production. Whether or not this standard can be met, and if so at what cost, is an empirical matter. But it is unlikely in the foreseeable future that people will come to be indifferent to the dangers of cancer. Even if a cure were found, it would not help many millions of people with little or no medical care.

As an empirical matter, it appears that with the present accumulation of man-made capital, dependence on the physical resource base is growing, not shrinking. If we should someday free ourselves from our dependence on (say) metals, metals would become inessential and their preservation, in an opportunity sense, would no longer be considered a matter of intergenerational justice. But annual rates of extraction for aggregate resource groups go up every year, not down.

Also as an empirical matter, we can ask how much it would cost to satisfy a notion of justice as equal opportunity. Consider a switch from present depletion allowances to severance taxes. Compared with the present tax system, such a switch appears to impose few or no aggregate costs upon the present and yet to produce net benefits to the future.[20] In other words, implementing this notion of justice may even coincide with a step toward intergenerational efficiency.

And finally, as a quite different and more conventional approach toward intergenerational efficiency, we may consider the kind of compensating investments contemplated in section I. Suppose, for example, we calculate that there is a 1 percent chance of large-scale radioactive contamination following uncontrolled nuclear proliferation, leading to a worldwide 10 percent excess risk of cancer 100 years from now. Suppose further that this risk could be eliminated by a present investment in safeguards of $5 billion. Are we to decide against the safeguards if the expected number of deaths, discounted at the marginal rate of productivity (say 10 percent), is less than the $5 billion? In this case the rationale for the comparison falls apart because the compensating investment is not sustainable for a century or more at a 10 percent marginal rate, when the entire economy is growing at substantially less than that. For such a long period a substantial marginal investment is not a real option, because it would dwarf the economy in a 100-year interval (as it would for this example if the economy as a whole were growing only 3 percent annually).

These empirical inquiries, by no means settled but at least partially identified, are useful but less fundamental than conceptual considerations. Suppose, for example, contrary to empirical likelihood, it is possible to make large compensating investments over a century or more. Obviously, if the compensating investment is not made in the present, compensation is not an option in the later period, because the investment has to grow in the intervening years to become available in the later years.

The impossibility of later compensation through redistribution stands in stark contrast to the conventional notion of potential Pareto improvement. In the standard example, a dam is constructed that floods the land of some farmers. But so much benefit is created from the dam as a whole that there are enough proceeds for the winners to compensate the losers and everyone comes out ahead. Actual Pareto improvement is possible in the second period, and thus the compensation choice does not have to be taken in the first period. But in the intergenerational case the compensating investment must be made in the first period or it will become irrelevant from the point of view of the second period, when it is no longer an option.

The standard argument for discounting says that it is permissible to harm the future, as long as it might be possible to benefit the future on net balance by a compensating investment, whether or not the investment is taken. To abstract from time, this is like saying that it is all right for me to harm you if I have the option, which I do not take, of aiding you. If the harms are minor, and there are many interactions, and on balance I am aiding you, then we may overlook the non sequitur. But when grave harms are involved the argument has less appeal.

When grave harms are involved, moreover, we may not be willing to trade off at all. If we reject the first and second conflations, and conclude that not all things are comparable, the demands of efficiency become weaker. For some cases there may be no way of deciding when someone or some generation is better or worse off. Perhaps nothing can be said on balance—only that in some ways a person or generation is better off, in some ways worse off.

And finally, neoclassical utilitarianism is unable to distinguish or choose between two very different intergenerational rules of choice (e.g., the implications of the Arrow and Koopmans axioms) because both satisfy the condition of intergenerational efficiency *in principle*. We should start with a notion of a just protection of fundamental opportunities and from this initial starting point encourage steps toward intergenerational efficiency. This would mean establishing institutions that in some sense permit one generation to "communicate" with another. Common law may be one such institution.

It is not possible to establish trades among generations in the same way that trades take place intragenerationally, but it is possible to establish institutions whereby one generation anticipates the needs of another. To the extent that we are successful in establishing such institutions, the efficiency cost of providing justice as equivalent opportunity can be diminished.

VI. Conclusion

Neoclassical utilitarians make no distinctions between natural resources and man-made capital. These are highly substitutable. The focus is on highly aggregative concepts—complete preference orderings for the neoclassical utilitarian; utility for his classical forbear.

In this essay we moved outside the utilitarian tradition to make several distinctions that appear to lead toward a common sense notion of intergenerational justice. These distinctions support a specialized notion of justice focused on the preservation of opportunities arising from the resource base and the accumulated cultural heritage. Not all opportunities demand preservation, only the most essential.

I suggest that if the present generation provides a resource base essentially the same as it inherited (including roughly the same lack of contamination), it has satisfied intergenerational justice. "Essential," of course, is the key word, and I construe it perhaps more narrowly than some others might. This notion of intergenerational justice appears to be sufficient in the sense that if the present generation gives the next an equal chance at what is jointly shared across time, the requirements of intergenerational justice will have been fulfilled.

NOTES

This article, first published in *Energy and the Future*, ed. Douglas MacLean and Peter G. Brown (Savage, Md.: Roman and Littlefield, 1983), pp. 38–58, is reprinted by permission. All the participants in the Working Group on Energy

Policy and Our Obligations to Future Generations contributed to my ideas in one way or another, and I would like to thank them all, especially Douglas MacLean and Claudia Mills, for their excellent editing. I would also like to thank Will Jones and Ed Green for helpful comments.

1. See, for example, Joseph Stiglitz: "The appropriate instruments to use for obtaining a more equitable distribution of welfare (if one believes that the present distribution is not equitable) are general instruments, for example, monetary instruments directed at changing the market rate of interest." "A Neoclassical Analysis of the Economics of Natural Resources," in *Scarcity and Growth Reconsidered,* edited by V. K. Smith (Baltimore: Johns Hopkins Press, 1979), p. 61.

2. How "the discount rate" and hence all interest rates are to be manipulated is usually left unclear. Presumably, adjustments are to be done through the tax structure, or perhaps through monetary policy. There does seem to be a "targets and instruments" problem, because manipulation of interest rates is suggested for several purposes (inflation control, stimulation of certain sectors of the economy, balance of trade, etc.)

3. An intergenerational Pareto improvement is a move in which at least one generation is made better off without making any other generation worse off. In a Pareto-optimal plan, no Pareto improvements are possible. "Intergenerationally efficient" is used synonymously with "intergenerationally Pareto optimal," and "inefficient" synonymously with "not Pareto optimal."

4. John Rawls uses this term in *A Theory of Justice* (Cambridge, Mass.: Harvard University Press, 1971), p. 27.

5. Charles Plott, "Ethics, Social Choice Theory and the Theory of Economic Policy," *Journal of Mathematical Sociology* 2 (1972): 181–208.

6. Stephen Marglin discusses the possibility of having two different types of valuation processes, one appropriate for market decisions and the other for the political arena. While he says he has strong sympathy for the distinction, which he calls the schizophrenic answer, he does not appeal to this approach in his paper. Instead he develops his argument on the basis of a single preference ordering both public and private, intertemporal and intratemporal. Stephen Marglin, "The Social Rate of Discount and the Optimal Rate of Investment," *Quarterly Journal of Economics* 77 (1963): 95–111.

7. We might imagine that the first frame, which describes the present, would be in much sharper detail than the other frames, which describe the future. But in most models the whole film is in equal color and detail. The film does not represent what we know or forecast about the present and future, in which case later frames would rapidly blur. The film represents a conceivable present and future, and each possible conception of the future can be in as much detail as a possible conception of the present.

8. Economic models become more difficult when we admit that in the future we can have different interests from our current ones, and that these differences in interests depend upon the shifting vantage point in time. In such models time really evolves. In a pioneering paper Strotz analyzes one of these problems, which is known as the problem of intertemporal consistency. Strotz notes that this problem of inconsistency disappears if individuals have utility functions of a discount-

ing form. Strotz believes that not everyone would have such a utility function, and there could be an "intertemporal tussle." But Strotz's resolution of the intertemporal tussle is really one of imposition by power as opposed to a solution by justice. The idea is that if a person's utility function is of a discounting form, he will constrain future opportunities in such a way that later there will be no way to depart from today's plan, to the advantage of the future self. Robert Strotz, "Myopia and Inconsistency in Dynamic Utility Maximization," *Review of Economic Studies* 23 (1955–56): 165–80.

9. It is not tautological, however. Preference theory usually includes axioms such as transitivity and the "weak axiom of revealed preferences," and with these or other axioms the theory is, in principle, refutable. For such counterevidence, see David Grether and Charles Plott, "Economic Theory of Choice and the Preference Reversal Phenomenon," *American Economic Review* 69, (September 1979): 623–38.

10. For some further discussion, see Hillel Steiner, "The Rights of Future Generations," in *Energy and the Future,* edited by Douglas MacLean and Peter G. Brown (Towota, N.J.: Rowman and Littlefield, 1983).

11. Three of the four approaches are discussed in P. S. Dasgupta and G. M. Heal, *Economic Theory and Exhaustible Resources* (Digswell Place, Welwyn: Cambridge University Press, 1979), chap. 9.

12. This is the condition defining a Poison process. See ibid., pp. 260–65, for further discussion: pp. 269–75, for discussion of B: pp. 275–81, for D.

13. This road combines Derek Parfit's third, fourth, and fifth arguments in "Energy Policy and the Further Future: The Social 'Discount Rate'," in *Energy and the Future,* edited by Douglas MacLean and Peter G. Brown (Towota, N.J.: Rowman and Littlefield, 1983).

14. This reinterpretation was made, independently, in Dasgupta and Heal, *Economic Theory and Exhaustible Resources,* and in John Ferejohn and Talbot Page, "On the Foundations of Intertemporal Choice," *American Journal of Agricultural Economics* 60, no. 2 (May 1978): 269–75.

15. The ambitious reader can consult Tjalling Koopmans, "Representation of Preference Orderings Over Time," in *Decision and Organizations,* edited by C. B. McGuire and R. Radner (Amsterdam: North Holland Publishing Co., 1972).

16. This proof can be found in Ferejohn and Page, "(On the Foundations of Intertemporal Choice."

17. See Brian Barry, "Intergenerational Justice in Energy Policy," in *Energy and the Future,* edited by Douglas MacLean and Peter G. Brown (Towota, N.J.: Rowman and Littlefield, 1983); Talbot Page, *Conservation and Economic Efficiency* (Baltimore: Johns Hopkins Press, 1977).

18. See Douglas MacLean, "Quantified Risk Assessment and the Quality of Life," in *Uncertain Power,* edited by Dorothy Zinberg (New York: Pergamon Press, 1982).

19. The same idea of foreseeability can be applied to the means of ensuring opportunity. To some extent, we can foresee ways that new capital and technology can substitute for inherited resources. But many conceivable substitutions (for example, the potential substitution of fusion energy for fossil fuel) are highly speculative. Similarly, we might speculate that there will be a cure for cancer so it

is not important to contain radioactive materials. But it is much easier to foresee that cancers from radiation will be prevented if the radioactive materials are contained. Thus our responsibilities are more direct to prevent radiation releases than to work for a cure, because of the greater uncertainties of the speculative cures for genotoxins.

20. See *Conservation and Economic Efficiency,* chap. 6, for further discussion of inefficiencies in the present taxation of the resource sector.

21 The Inalienability of Autonomy

Arthur Kuflik

PHILOSOPHERS OTHERWISE AS DIVERGENT in their views as Locke, Spinoza, Rousseau, and Kant, all subscribed, in one form or another, to the following thesis: no agreement by which a person places himself wholly and irrevocably at the disposition of someone else's will is valid and binding.[1] In this tradition, persons are thought to have the capacity to make morally rational choices and to take action accordingly. Moreover, that capacity not only commands the respect of others, but a special kind of self-respect as well. For if the tradition is correct, nobody can reasonably obligate himself not to function as a morally autonomous agent.

In this article, I address the question of whether moral autonomy, suitably conceived, is inalienable. The first section deals with three basic issues: what it could mean to say that someone is functioning as an autonomous moral agent; what would be involved in alienating or relinquishing moral autonomy; what is the force of saying that moral autonomy "cannot be" alienated. In the second section, I explore the extent to which something like the ideal of the inalienably autonomous moral agent has figured in the philosophies of Locke, Spinoza, Rousseau, and Kant and then critically assess certain arguments that have been advanced in behalf of the inalienability thesis. In the third and principal section, I defend the thesis against what I take to be the most serious objections to it. The final section contains a brief, programmatic discussion of the implications which the inalienability of autonomy might be expected to have for political life. I suggest that far from being incompatible with the existence of legal and political arrangements, the ideal of moral autonomy has a significant role to play in shaping them.

I. The Concept of Moral Autonomy

To be "autonomous" is (literally) to be self-legislating or self-regulating.[2] This strongly suggests that what matters, from the standpoint of autonomy, are the principles by which a person lives. A person who determines his actions in accordance with principles he has mindlessly borrowed from others is not *self*-regulating at a sufficiently deep level. A person who simply does whatever he happens to want to do is not self-*regulating* at all. The morally autonomous person subscribes to principles that have either been formed, or (more to the point) ratified, by his own moral scrutiny.[3] But moral scrutiny is not to be confused with "gut feeling," however intense or overwhelming the feeling may be. On the contrary, there is a very definite process of moral deliberation and it is only by engaging in that process that a person can be said to "decide for himself" what is right and wrong. Just as someone who is incapable of mathematical reasoning is incapable of grasping for himself the validity of an important proof, so also someone who is incapable of moral reflection—that is, of thinking impartially, empathetically, and the like—is incapable of appreciating for himself the validity of various principles of right and justice. If, as I believe, the soundness of the arguments to follow is independent of the details of moral epistemology, it is unnecessary to try to master those details now. But it is worth noting that respect for moral autonomy does not necessarily reflect the view that what is morally right is a matter of "purely subjective" preference.[4]

The morally autonomous person forms his everyday judgments about right and wrong in light of considerations that can bear the weight of his own critically reflective moral scrutiny. Moreover, he shapes his actions to accord with his judgments. It would be a mistake to infer from this that the autonomous life is one of ceaseless reflection, calculation, deliberation, and decision. For it is often quite unreasonable to deliberate at length, or even at all. If a person has good reason for not securing further information or entertaining further argument, then he is acting in a rationally self-acceptable way; his life accords with considerations he can "legislate" for himself. In addition, the ideal of autonomy is perfectly compatible with a "division of moral labor." Autonomy is not to be equated with self-sufficiency. Indeed, in a complex world it is difficult to believe that anyone is always the best judge of every possible matter. Thus the morally reflective person is prepared to acknowledge that in certain cases someone else may be in a better position to gather morally relevant information or even to give disinterested attention to the facts, once they have been assembled. The crucial point is that whatever the person does or does not do, whether he deliberates at length or not at all, whether he decides a particular matter directly or relies on the knowledge or judgment of another, he must be able to justify, on morally rational grounds, the direction he has taken. For only in this way can he be said to function as a rationally self-accountable moral agent.

In essence, then, moral autonomy is a kind of higher-order control over the moral quality of one's life. Still there may be some question about how it is possible to maintain that control without becoming hopelessly lost in thought and deliberation. It is plausible to suppose that the autonomous agent will preserve his autonomy in two ways: (a) by a more or less continuous but essentially passive receptivity to particularly significant developments that might warrant a change in his moral course; (b) by periodic full-scale reviews of his life and the principles on which it is based. On the one hand, then, the autonomous person is almost always "alive to" prominent signs or indicators that his life-course is not what it should be; and on the other hand, he is prepared to step back, though only from time to time, to engage in a more deliberate and thorough self-assessment. Thus he is able to monitor the moral quality of his life without having to defer life itself in favor of all-consuming reflection.[5]

Given this account of what it is to function as an autonomous moral agent, what would it mean to alienate one's autonomy? If to function autonomously is to live in accordance with one's own critically reflective moral judgment, and to alienate something is to transfer or relinquish it, then to alienate autonomy is to bind oneself to obey someone else, regardless of one's own critically reflective moral judgment. Thus, in alienating autonomy, one transfers the ultimate direction of one's moral life to someone (or something) other than oneself.[6]

What then does it mean to say that autonomy is inalienable? If to alienate autonomy is to assume a duty not to function autonomously, then to say that autonomy is inalienable is to say that it is never morally justifiable to assume a duty not to act in accordance with one's own, critically reflective moral judgment. To clarify this thesis we might do well to distinguish it from other claims with which it is likely to be confused:

1. To say that autonomy is inalienable is to make a normative, not a psychological, claim. The question is not whether it is possible to think of oneself as having given up one's autonomy and to carry on accordingly, but whether it is morally appropriate to do so. Indeed, normative notions enter twice: first, the force of saying that one "cannot" alienate autonomy is to indicate moral unjustifiability rather than psychological impossibility; second, what one cannot do, morally speaking, is to make a very special change in the structure of what one is obligated to do.

2. To say that autonomy cannot be alienated is not to imply that in special circumstances it cannot be forfeited. A person may lose through misconduct what it would be wrong for him to transfer or relinquish through consent or agreement.

3. To say that autonomy cannot be alienated is not to deny that under compulsion or duress a person may be excused for acceding to demands

that would not be worthy of his free, rational acceptance. In certain cases, threats may oblige a person to say that he will do whatever someone else tells him to do, but his own "consent" cannot *obligate* him to obey.

4. Finally, to say that autonomy cannot be alienated is not to deny that one human being can be legitimately subject to the guardianship of another. To function autonomously one must be able to take a critically reflective attitude toward one's life and the principles on which it is based; one must be able to survey alternatives, reach decisions, and make a sincere effort to act as one has decided one ought to do. Individuals who altogether lack, or have lost, the relevant capacities are prime candidates for paternalistic intervention. But the fact that some human beings—for example, infants, elderly people in advanced stages of senility, the severely brain-damaged—are placed completely in the care and direction of other human beings, does not necessarily run afoul either of the principle that autonomy must be respected or of the principle that it must not be alienated. Indeed, the question of autonomy-abdication can only arise with respect to someone who is capable of autonomous functioning in the first place.

Now suppose a person agrees to do what someone else tells him to do. If in making the agreement he agrees never to deploy his own critically reflective moral judgment, then, in light of all that has been said thus far, he has clearly abdicated (whether legitimately or not) his autonomy. Suppose, however, that in agreeing to obey someone else he remains prepared to weigh the evil of what he might be ordered to do against the good of keeping his agreement. Then he has not abdicated his autonomy after all, for he continues to be governed by his own critically reflective moral judgment.[7]

If someone were to reach, in advance, a morally reasonable decision to obey someone else regardless of his own critically reflective moral judgment, then he would be autonomously abdicating his autonomy. The fact that the decision had been made on critically reflective grounds would make it an autonomously generated decision; the fact that what was decided was to act contrary to his own critically reflective judgment (on subsequent occasions) would make it a decision to abdicate autonomy. I shall argue that a person who is capable of autonomous moral functioning cannot freely and rationally alienate his autonomy; in effect, there can be no genuinely autonomous decision to abdicate autonomy.

II. A Brief Historical Survey

The idea that we must not abdicate our status as rationally self-accountable moral agents has played, whether explicitly or implicitly, an important role in the political philosophies of Locke, Spinoza, Rousseau, and Kant. In this section, I briefly document that role and then critically evaluate some of the arguments that have been advanced in behalf of the claim that the right to function as an autonomous moral agent is inalienable.

On Locke's view, we have no right to subject ourselves to the "inconstant, uncertain, unknown, arbitrary will of another man"[8] or to submit to "absolute arbitrary power" (sec. 23). The fullest explanation for this position—a position which Locke affirms repeatedly—can be found in the following passage:

> For nobody can transfer to another more power than he has in himself; and nobody has an absolute arbitrary power over himself, or over any other to destroy his own life, or to take away the life or property of another . . . and having in the state of nature no arbitrary power over the life, liberty or possession of another, but only so much as the law of nature gave him for the preservation of himself, and the rest of mankind; this is all he doth, or can give up to the commonwealth, and by it to the legislative power. (sec. 135)

Because we do not have absolute arbitrary power over our own lives (whether in our self-regarding or other-regarding actions), we cannot rightfully transfer any such power to anybody else. We must live in accordance with the law of nature, that is, in accordance with fundamental moral requirements. In acknowledging the authority of a government our aim is only to remedy the moral problems that would arise in a world in which there were no settled positive law and no mechanism to provide regular and impartial adjudication of conflict. But if the officials of the state go well beyond the bounds of moral propriety and ignore the conscientious complaints of the citizens, the citizens must reserve the right to decide for themselves whether it is right to resist, by force if necessary, and thereby make their "appeal to Heaven":

> Should either the executive or the legislative, when they have got the power in their hands, design, or go about to enslave or destroy them, the people have no other remedy in this, as in all other cases where they have no judge on earth, but to appeal to Heaven . . . . And therefore, though the people cannot be judge, so as to have, by the constitution of that society, any superior power to determine and give effective sentence in the case, yet they have reserved that ultimate determination to themselves which belongs to all mankind, where there lies no appeal on earth, by a law antecedent and paramount to all positive laws of men, whether they have just cause to make their appeal to Heaven. And this judgment they cannot part with. (sec. 168)

Thus, while the people may, or indeed must, give up some of their natural liberty if they are to overcome the moral inconveniences of the state of nature, they can never abdicate their moral autonomy.

According to Spinoza, "No one can ever so utterly transfer to another his power and, consequently, his rights, as to cease to be a man."[9] On the contrary, we must "grant that every man retains part of his right, in dependence on his own decision, and no one else's" (p. 215). The case for democracy rests on the observation that of all forms of government "it is

the most consonant with natural liberty" (p. 207) for "In it no one transfers his natural right so absolutely that he has no further voice in affairs"
(p. 207). But whatever system of government prevails "no one can willingly transfer his natural right of free reason and judgment or be compelled so to do" (p. 257). If government did have the right, and the ability,
to determine what people think and how they reason, then "every subject
would shape his life according to the intentions of his rulers and would
esteem a thing . . . just or unjust in obedience to their dictates" (p. 257).
To abdicate freedom of reason and judgment would be, in effect, to turn
oneself into a slave since "he alone is free who lives with free consent
under the entire guidance of reason" (p. 206).

For Rousseau, the terms of the social contract must somehow resolve
the following problem: "How to find a form of association . . . under which
each individual, while uniting himself with the others, obeys no one but
himself, and remains as free as before."[10] The significance of the problem
can be best appreciated if we recall that "to renounce freedom" *is* "to
renounce one's humanity, one's rights as a man and equally one's duties."
Any agreement to do so "strips a man's actions of all moral significance"
and is "illogical and nugatory" (p. 55). When the terms of the social contract
are properly formulated people wisely exchange "natural liberty" for "civil
liberty." But more importantly, they "acquire moral freedom, which alone
makes man the master of himself; for to be governed by appetite alone is
slavery, while obedience to a law one prescribes to oneself is freedom" (p.
65). These remarks strongly suggest that the "freedom" which we cannot
renounce is not freedom in the Millian sphere of the self-regarding, but the
right to function as rationally self-accountable moral agents.

By his own acknowledgment, Kant's moral philosophy, with its emphasis upon the autonomy of the person, was inspired by his reading of
Rousseau. There is ample evidence, however, that the concern for autonomy is reflected in his political philosophy as well. In the introduction to
the *Metaphysics of Morals*, he tells us that what is right in matters of law
and public policy, just is "the sum total of those conditions within which
the will of one person can be reconciled with the will of another in accordance with a universal law of freedom."[11] In effect, the rules of a just
society must somehow reflect the equal status of the citizens as autonomous agents. Moreover, "No-one who lives within the lawful state of a
commonwealth can forfeit this equality other than through some crime of
his own, never by a contract. . . . For no legal transaction on his part or on
that of anyone else can make him cease to be his own master."[12] Concerning the duties that are imposed by law and enforced by government "each
person requires to be convinced by reason that the coercion which prevails
is lawful [i.e., morally lawful], otherwise he would be in contradiction with
himself."[13] If instead of trying to provide the necessary rational demonstration, government attempts to control men's actions by whatever means
are "expedient," then "since there is no appeal to right but only to force,

the people themselves may resort to force and thus make every legal constitution insecure."[14]

Granted that the inalienability thesis has figured prominently in the thinking of a number of important social philosophers, it is natural to wonder how, if at all, they would have defended the claim. Although Locke is clearly committed to the thesis, it is by no means clear that he has, or thinks he needs, an argument for it. An argument in the spirit of his position might be constructed along the following lines. Both reason, and the right to direct our lives in accordance with it, have been given to us by God. Because they are gifts from Him, they are not entirely ours to give up. If we may submit to the authority of others, it is only to achieve a more satisfactory application of the law of nature, that is, of principles which we can and do appreciate for ourselves. But in the last analysis, we must reserve the right to decide whether the authority thus granted is exercised within the proper bounds. Otherwise, we give up altogether what was given *to us*; we exercise a power we do not really have.

Of course, some would object from the outset to an argument couched so heavily in theological terms. But even if we grant that the power we have over our own lives has been given to us by God, there is a gap in the argument. For not all gifts have quite so many strings attached. In giving us the right to direct our lives in accordance with fundamental moral requirements, God might have given us the right to make a complete and permanent transfer of that right as well. In the absence of a further explanation or argument, to say that the moral authority which we have over our lives is a gift from God that cannot be altogether transferred to others is just another way—albeit for many a more beautiful and inspiring way—of saying that moral autonomy is inalienable. The challenge is not only to say this but in some way to demonstrate it. If there is good reason for the inalienability of autonomy, such reason needs to be made intelligible to the intelligent creatures God has created.[15]

To the extent that a demonstration can be found in Spinoza's text, it would seem to rest, not on special theological assumptions, but on the psychological claim that people will form their own opinions in their own way and do only what seems reasonable to themselves, regardless of the agreements they have made. For consider the following:

> Now it is a universal law that no one ever neglects anything which he judges to be good . . . everyone will, of two goods, choose that which he thinks is the greatest. . . . This law is so deeply implanted in the human mind that it ought to be counted among the eternal truths and axioms.
>
> As a necessary consequence of this principle just enumerated no one can honestly promise to forego the right which he has over all things (p. 203)

And

> No man's mind can possibly lie wholly at the disposition of another. (p. 257)

This suggests an argument of the following sort: because it is impossible to fulfill an autonomy-abdicating agreement, it is morally impermissible to make it. If somebody agrees to think and to do whatever somebody else tells him to, he makes an agreement he will be unable to keep. One has no right to incur an obligation one cannot discharge. Thus, one has no right to abdicate autonomy. (Indeed, since "ought" implies "can," not even the agent's apparent consent could be invoked against him to establish an alleged duty of obedience.)

Unfortunately, the psychological assumption that underlies this argument is simply not true. Nowadays, a measure of "mind-control" can be attained through psychosurgery, brainwashing techniques, mind-altering drugs, and the like. Someone could agree to have another person employ such devices to whatever ends the latter had chosen. In this way, he would not merely be promising obedience to the will of another; he would be taking effective steps to ensure compliance. Even in Spinoza's day, there were methods of indoctrination and censorship that had reasonably good prospects of success in rendering people incapable of independent, critically reflective judgment and ready to do someone else's bidding, regardless of how cruel or crazy it might be. A person could have deliberately immersed himself in a social environment which employed such methods with full expectation that if he remained there for a period of time his way of thinking would be reshaped to the point that he could only perceive as the greater good, whatever his superiors had intended. In short, whether or not a person can alter what he judges he ought to do in immediate response to another person's will, he can usually take indirect steps to accomplish the same end.

But even if the psychological claim could be established, there is reason to wonder if the argument that is based on it cuts deeply enough. To be sure, it is a valid argument; and it does establish an appropriately normative conclusion. For from the fact that one knows one will not be able to fulfill a proposed commitment, it does seem to follow that one ought not to make the commitment in the first place. The problem is this: one is inclined to suppose that even if someone were perfectly capable of complying with an agreement to abdicate autonomy, he would still be wrong to make it. This suggests that the impropriety of an autonomy-abdicating agreement has more to do with the impropriety of autonomy-abdication itself than with the more general fact that we have no right to make commitments we know we will be unable to keep. Of course, this raises the question of what makes autonomy so morally significant that we ought not to abdicate it even if we can. But given the fact that people do seem to be able to subordinate themselves to the will of another, that is a question which the opponent of autonomy-abdication may not be able to avoid altogether.

Perhaps more than any other philosopher, Rousseau works hard to provide a full-length argument for the inalienability thesis. His first move is to suggest that the terms of an autonomy-abdicating agreement are so patently irrational that nobody who made such an agreement "could be in his right mind" (p. 54). Of course, someone who is not in his right mind is not competent to make a contract in the first place and so the contract in question would be null and void. This argument is clever but it leaves off too soon. We still need to know what makes an autonomy-abdicating agreement so objectionable that nobody in possession of his rational faculties could find its terms acceptable. A bit later in his discussion, Rousseau seems to be supplying the missing argumentation. Claiming that "To renounce one's freedom is to renounce one's humanity, one's rights as a man and equally one's duties," he reasons that there can be "no quid pro quo" for that renunciation. Since it "strips a man's actions of all moral significance" he is no longer even a person; he has given up "everything" (p. 55). To put the point more plainly, when you abdicate autonomy, there is really no "you" left to be the recipient of whatever benefits might be offered in return; and that is why nothing could really repay you for your loss.

Offhand, this argument would seem to strike an excessively egoistic chord. The agent who agrees to become someone else's complete and permanent slave need not have his own welfare in mind at all; the concession he seeks in return might be a benefit that is to be bestowed upon loved ones or the promotion of a worthy cause. Perhaps the claim that to give up all one's freedom is to give up "everything" is really just a way of saying that the autonomy of the person—any person—is virtually infinite in (nonegoistic) value; hence no benefit, whether to oneself or to another, can compensate for the affront to human dignity which autonomy-abdication represents. If this is so, we have come full circle. To explain why autonomy cannot be legitimately abdicated we have to assume that autonomy is "everything," that is, infinitely valuable. But while the assumption does support the conclusion, it stands in as much (or more) need of argument itself.

In terms that seem to echo Rousseau, Kant maintains that nobody has the right to become a "mere instrument" of another person. His line of argument is that "No-one can enter by contract into such a state of dependence and thus cease to be a person; for only as a person is he able to make a contract."[16] In a parallel passage, he insists that nobody can make an agreement or other legal transaction "to the effect that he has no rights but only duties, for such a contract would deprive him of the right to make a contract and would thus invalidate the one he had already made."[17]

In either version, the argument falters on a temporal equivocation. Up to the moment that the contract is made, or more accurately, is to take effect, the agent retains both his status as a person and whatever rights that entails, including the right to make a contract. Only after the contract takes effect does the agent (putatively) "cease to be a person" and thereby lose all his rights. Thus if the contract to abdicate autonomy is valid, any further contract that the agent might wish to make is not. But it remains to be shown just how the contract in question invalidates itself.

Here it may seem that Mill's celebrated opposition to self-enslavement in the last chapter of *On Liberty* also addresses the point at hand, and that failure to mention him constitutes a significant omission. Closer inspection, however, suggests that his focus is narrower than that of the other writers we have considered. According to Mill, the person who proposes to sell himself into slavery would "defeat" by this one act the "very purpose which is the justification" for allowing him to dispose of his own lot in life.[18] But what is that purpose? Broadly speaking, personal happiness. People need a measure of liberty to experiment with different "modes of living"; they need liberty to review and revise the choices they have made. But slavery—construed as an arrangement which the slave has no right to revoke—has the following implication: even if experience should teach the agent that his personal happiness lies elsewhere, he has no right to change his direction. From these remarks, as well as from the more general context of his discussion, it seems apparent that Mill is primarily concerned with abdication of liberty in the so-called "sphere of the self-regarding." The question for him is whether a person has the right to give up his right to decide matters that primarily affect himself—to abdicate what might be called personal, rather than moral, autonomy. This is not to suggest that Mill would have found abdication of moral autonomy any more acceptable than abdication of personal autonomy—only that his argument in *On Liberty* addresses the latter, not the former, issue. Indeed, because his conception of self-enslavement is narrower, his task is more ambitious. "Not even in matters that are a person's own business only," we might say, "will Mill allow someone to subordinate himself to the will of another."

In contrast, the slavery contract which Rousseau opposes stipulates "absolute dominion for one party and absolute obedience for the other." The person who enters into such an agreement renounces "all rights *and* duties," save the duty to do whatever his master commands him. It is not surprising then that Rousseau would condemn such an agreement for stripping "all the moral significance from a man's actions." In a similar vein, Kant deplores any contract which relegates a person to the status of "property," a "mere instrument" of someone else's will. He claims that in making such an agreement, one "ceases to be a person."

There is no indication, in other words, that these writers were concerned with abdication of autonomy with respect to purely self-regarding matters. Their question was whether a person has the right to resign his status as a morally self-directing agent—to abdicate moral, rather than personal, autonomy. From the texts already cited, I believe we can infer that essentially the same preoccupation is fundamental to the thought of Locke and Spinoza.

In the remainder of this article, I shall be concerned with the question of whether persons can reasonably alienate moral, rather than personal, autonomy. There are at least two reasons for this emphasis. The thesis that moral autonomy is inalienable seems to be the more deeply entrenched in the philosophical tradition, yet the less seriously discussed in recent years; most contemporary philosophers either ignore it or assume it without argument. Of the two theses it is the one with the more far-reaching implications for social and political philosophy.

III. Objections to the Inalienability Thesis

The thesis that we must preserve our status as rationally self-accountable moral agents retains an air of plausibility which most of the reasons that have been advanced in its behalf seem to lack. There is something plainly right about the idea that as morally autonomous agents we have no right to "abdicate" freedom of "reason and judgment" (Spinoza), to submit to "absolute arbitrary power" (Locke), to renounce all rights and duties save the duty of "absolute obedience" (Rousseau), or to relegate ourselves to the status of "mere instruments" (Kant). Perhaps the very appeal of the inalienability thesis lulled its exponents into a state of argumentative complacency. Perhaps it is not the sort of claim for which proof, in the usual sense, can be given (since any proof we might provide is likely to rest on considerations less plausible and less fundamental to our way of thinking than the thesis itself). I suggest that we may yet be able to gain a greater appreciation for the thesis if we turn around and look more closely at what might be said in objection to it. Of course, there may be no way to prove that we have exhausted all that can be said on the other side of the issue. But if we can succeed in defusing the most potent objections thus far presented, we can at least claim to have provided a reasonable defense. And we can hope that in the process, our sense of what is at issue will have been sufficiently enhanced to enable us to handle further objections as they arise.

In what follows, I suggest that seemingly plausible counterexamples can be subsumed under one of two possible headings: (1) autonomy-abdication in exchange for significant benefits; (2) autonomy-abdication to protect against self-acknowledged irrationality. With respect to each class of cases, my argument takes the following form: insofar as the agent's decision is rationally defensible, it is not actually a decision to abdicate autonomy; insofar as it is a decision to abdicate autonomy, it is demonstrably irrational.

1. Autonomy-Abdication in Exchange for Significant Benefits

In an atmosphere that is free of threats and deceptions, a person proposes his own autonomy-abdication, that is, he agrees to do whatever another person tells him to do, regardless of his own critically reflective moral judgment. His goal is to achieve some highly desirable state of affairs—for example, the payment of a huge sum of money to his wife and children or to some worthy cause. The general idea behind such examples is clear enough. An agreement to become completely and irrevocably subject to the will of another person is thought to be just as reasonable as any other agreement, provided that the expected good consequences are sufficiently attractive to offset whatever is lost in the bargain.

Perhaps there is an absurdity in this supposition, even from the standpoint of the bargain itself. If one is not permitted, by the terms of a putatively legitimate agreement, to function as a critically reflective moral agent, then one is henceforth without the legitimate means to "monitor" the arrangement, to see to it that the other side is carrying through on its part of the deal. Suppose that to circumvent this difficulty one simply stipulates that whatever good is to be obtained in return, must be fully achieved by the time of the agreed-upon abdication. Here it is possible to take issue with the notion of a completed good work; what good is done can usually be undone later. But even waiving such doubt—as perhaps we should in special cases—we must still be careful not to equate autonomy-abdication with an ordinary agreement, even an agreement to work indefinitely many hours, without monetary reward, in return for some specified benefit.

For suppose that once the agreement has taken effect, the agent is ordered to commit an extremely evil deed—for example, to murder another man's wife and children. Now the agreement to abdicate autonomy is an agreement to become the mere tool of someone else's will. If it is valid, then the autonomy-abdicating agent has no right to object, let alone to refuse. He has only an unbounded, unconditional duty of obedience. Hence the agent has no assurance that he will not be ordered to commit an evil deed, or perhaps a series of such deeds, whose magnitude clearly overshadows any good he had sought to achieve beforehand. It is this open-ended, unconditional character which renders an autonomy-abdicating agreement irrational and irresponsible in any event.

In objection, it might be said that the reasonableness of autonomy-abdication merely depends on how likely it is that one will be ordered to do such evil things. The implication is that if the probability is very low, then an agreement to abdicate autonomy may be perfectly justifiable. Of course, nothing is absolutely certain; the person to whom one subordinates oneself might become senile or lazy or corrupt or subject to the coercive control of someone else. Unlikely though any of these developments might be, none can be totally discounted. So what shall we say about a case in which the unexpected does take place? Could the agent revoke the arrangement at that time on the ground that he "only agreed to do it in the expectation that orders of *this* sort would not be given"? To suppose that the agent would be entitled to disobey, or even merely to complain, in the event that he were ordered to do evil things which he had reasonably expected he would not be told to do, is to imply that he *does* have the right to function as a critically reflective moral agent and that the agreement was implicitly bounded by certain conditions. But this in turn is to deny that it was an autonomy-abdicating agreement after all. Evidently the appeal to probabilities is meant to play a different role. The thought seems to be that if orders of certain kinds are *not* likely to be given, then it *is* reasonable to make a strict commitment to full-fledged autonomy-abdication.

But this only produces a further puzzle. Presumably the low-probability assessment was based on knowledge of the other person's moral character. If it *is* so reasonable to expect that the agent will not be ordered to do unconscionably evil things, then it should be no problem to get actual assurances, to have the other party agree to a more limited and conditional authority. Of course, the other side might be unwilling to give assurances; it might refuse to settle for anything less than the complete and unconditional surrender of the agent's will. But if that is the case it would seem to belie the claim that there is virtually no chance of being ordered to do the things one could not in good conscience agree to do.

Let us suppose, for the sake of argument, that despite such bargaining behavior, it is reasonable to assign a low probability to the prospect of being directed to do profoundly unacceptable things. Just what follows from this fact? If it is very unlikely that one will be ordered to do things which one would have preponderant reason not to do, then it clearly follows that one can reasonably agree to do whatever *it is reasonable to expect* one is going to be asked to do. But does it follow that one can reasonably agree to do *whatever* one is ordered to do, *whether or not* it was reasonable to expect it? (The need to insert this last phrase was the lesson of the paragraph before the last.) Why should the fact, if it is indeed a fact, that unreasonable orders are not likely to be given make it reasonable to agree to obey any orders whatsoever? Perhaps the root idea is just this: since it is reasonable to expect that one won't be ordered to do evil or irrational things, the question of whether to disobey is not very likely to arise; if it is not very likely to arise, then it can for all practical purposes, be ignored. So there is really no need to worry about having to break the agreement. But if that is the case, then there should be no problem about making the agreement in the first place. In short, one can enter into it in good conscience.

This argument trades on a crucial ambiguity and an underlying misconception about what it means to be bound by an autonomy-abdicating agreement. Not disobeying the orders one actually receives is not equivalent to keeping an agreement to abdicate autonomy. If we observe a person who is following all the instructions he receives from some other individual, we still cannot conclude that he has abdicated autonomy until we find out what he *would* do if he were presented with instructions contrary to what he himself can plainly see there is reason to do. To abdicate autonomy is to be committed to doing whatever one is told to do, even if, unexpectedly, there is a preponderance of good reason not to do it. But then, how can it be reasonable to be obligated to do what one has preponderant reason not to do?

Here it might be said that what there is reason to do, all things considered, cannot be determined in abstraction from the agreements one has made; in this case, it cannot be determined in abstraction from the fact that one has made an agreement to abdicate autonomy. For (a) if one had good reason to make such an agreement—for example, the benefit to be secured in return, the low probability of being ordered to do unacceptable things that would overshadow the benefit—and (b) if one did actually agree—then the fact of agreement must now weigh in the scales of moral deliberation and tip the balance in favor of doing whatever one has been ordered to do.

The first and most obvious objection is to the suggestion that the scales would *always* be tipped in favor of obedience. The most plausible response, I take it, is this: even if the scales are not always tipped in the direction of obedience, the validity of the autonomy-abdicating agreement merely depends on whether the fact of the agreement must at least be weighed in the scales. Were we discussing any agreement other than an agreement to abdicate autonomy, this response would have real merit. For in the case of ordinary agreements, to say that the agreement is valid and binding is not to imply that it could never be right, all things considered, to break it. The crucial point is simply whether in the mere fact of having promised or agreed there is significant, additional reason to conform. At times, therefore, an agent will be bound to take a course which he would have sufficient reason to reject were it not for a valid agreement which he has made. At other times, the balance of good reasons will justify his departure from the terms of the agreement. But in any event, the fact of his having made the agreement will weigh in the scales. In the case of an agreement to abdicate autonomy, however, the matter is entirely different. If *that* agreement is valid, then the agent simply has no right to function as a critically reflective moral agent. In abdicating autonomy he alienates the right to weigh the evil of doing something he has been ordered to do against the evil of not observing the terms of the agreement. Thus someone who is judiciously engaged in a careful consideration of reasons for and against the course of conduct he has been ordered to take is already operating outside the bounds of an agreement to abdicate autonomy. And this is true even if among the considerations which he judiciously considers is the fact that he agreed to abdicate autonomy.

So to establish the validity of an agreement to abdicate autonomy one must show that the agent is thereby strictly obligated to do whatever he is told to do. Moreover, if the agent is to establish this for himself so that his acquiescence in the arrangement is fully reasonable, he would have to make all the relevant calculations *prior* to the time that the agreement is to take effect. How is he to do this? There are really only two things to which he can appeal: the good of achieving whatever condition was to be secured in advance; the evil of disappointing contractually induced expectations. We have already imagined cases in which the good to be achieved beforehand has been overshadowed by an unexpected, but also unprohibited evil order. So if one is still intent upon showing that obedience is the justifiable course *in any event,* one must come down rather heavily on the importance of keeping the agreements one has made. But now, since we can imagine orders that are evil to virtually any degree of magnitude, to establish that it would always be wrong to default on one's autonomy-abdicating agreement it would have to be argued that the evil of breaking the agreement is infinitely great. This shifts the burden of proof, and the onus of implausibility, to the other side—to those who would say that autonomy-abdication is perfectly reasonable. The discussion here makes an interesting contrast with Rousseau's treatment of the same subject. To argue against autonomy-abdication, Rousseau evidently thought he had to insist that autonomy is of infinite value, something beyond all price. As it turns out, the illegitimacy of autonomy-abdication merely turns on the denial that breaking one's agreement is infinitely disvaluable.[19]

It is sometimes said that an agreement to abdicate autonomy is, in principle, no different from other agreements; *any* agreement will tie down the agent's future life in ways that limit liberty and narrow his options. But the line of argument presented here does not turn on the proposition that we must always try to leave our options open, or on the (dubious) claim that we must never undertake irreversible enterprises. Any course of conduct—including what might be called "doing nothing at all"—inevitably closes off options that would have been open otherwise. If autonomy-abdication is objectionable it is not because it fails to do what cannot be done in any event. The argument here rests on a different point—one that clearly differentiates autonomy-abdication from other contractual arrangements.

With ordinary contractual arrangements, a person's future is tied down in fairly specific ways in return for certain benefits. The agent not only has a reasonably good idea of what is to be gained but at what price. In an autonomy-abdicating arrangement the gain may be clear, but the potential costs are, in principle, unbounded. Moreover, in the case of ordinary contractual arrangements—which are limited in duration or in scope, and which place definite constraints on the future behavior of others as well— it may be said that the ability to shape and direct his life course is actually enhanced. For by making at least certain aspects of the future more predictable, the agent can make further plans and decisions within a more clearly defined framework. In contrast, the agreement to abdicate autonomy strips the agent of the right to make any further choices while subordinating the whole future course of his life to the unconstrained will of another person.

2. Autonomy-Abdication to Protect Against Self-Acknowledged Irrationality

I have been arguing that autonomy-abdication cannot be regarded as a rational and responsible act. There is a type of case, however, in which it might be said that the failure to abdicate autonomy is irrational and irresponsible. This is the case of what might be called "self-imposed paternalism." Recognizing, with good reason, that someone else has morally better judgment, a person agrees to subordinate himself to the will of the other person. He authorizes him to manage his life on his behalf, and in particular, to guard against self-acknowledged, irrational tendencies. Has he autonomously abdicated his autonomy?

There are two sub-cases. The guardian's authority is either subject to the agent's review and revocation or it is not. If it is, then the agent has not abdicated autonomy after all. As already noted, to preserve autonomy it is hardly necessary to make each and every decision oneself. By making the arrangement subject to his own review and by reserving to himself the right to have the guardian's authority revoked, should he be in a position to demonstrate that the arrangement is not serving the purpose for which he constituted it, the agent maintains higher-order, rational control over the moral quality of his life.

Suppose instead that the agent relinquishes the right to have the guardian's authority revoked. Here we may grant that his authorization is tantamount to an abdication of moral autonomy, but could the decision to enter into such an arrangement bear the weight of morally rational self-scrutiny?[20] Now it is important to clarity what is at issue. The question of whether autonomy can be autonomously abdicated is not to be confused with the question of whether it is ever legitimate for one human being to be subject to the guardianship of another human being, contrary to his own wishes or desires. The question is whether an irrevocable guardianship arrangement draws its legitimacy from the fact that the agent himself opted for it. I shall argue that even under the circumstances in question, the decision to make an irrevocable grant of guardianship authority is unreasonable and irresponsible. Following Rousseau, we could then say that anyone who consented to such an arrangement would thereby exhibit a level of incompetence that deprived his "consent" of morally binding force.

To test the reasonableness of an irrevocable delegation of guardianship authority, let us suppose that at some future time it is the will of the person in question to be released from the guardianship arrangement which he authorized. We must consider two further cases. At the time the agent seeks to be released, either he is competent to decide if the arrangement fulfills the purpose for which he authorized it, or he is not. If the agent is no longer competent to decide such a matter then he has lost (perhaps not permanently) his capacity for rational self-management. His present volitions lack whatever moral authority would otherwise have to be assigned to them. From this, several things seem to follow. First, some guardianship arrangement is now perfectly appropriate, given his present condition. Second, if he had been in this condition when the present arrangement was first constituted, his consent to it at that time would have lacked moral force. And finally, so long as he remains incompetent to decide if the arrangement fulfills the purpose of shielding him and others from his own irrationality, neither his consent nor his refusal to grant consent, can be morally authoritative. Thus, a guardianship arrangement of some sort will be perfectly appropriate even in the face of his present desire to be rid of it. But its legitimacy is quite independent of any earlier "authorization" of a putatively irrevocable arrangement. What legitimates the arrangement is simply his present condition.[21]

Admittedly, the fact that the agent himself had thought that at a later time he would need to be placed in someone else's care, over and against his own pleas to the contrary, does seem to make the perpetuation of a guardianship arrangement somewhat more palatable to us. But the reason, I suggest, is this: when we try to assess the individual's present state of mind to determine if he is suffering from severely diminished rational capacity, the agent's own beliefs, both prior and present, are relevant data. In this connection, what he once thought would be his future condition is an interesting datum; but it carries evidentiary weight, not the authority of a morally binding command. Thus, if the arrangement is legitimate despite his pleas to be released from it, it is legitimate because the individual presently lacks the capacities of autonomous agency, not because he "authorized" an "irrevocable" arrangement.

But suppose instead that the agent is competent to decide if the arrangement is serving the purpose which warranted his authorization of it, and can make a reasonable demonstration that it is not. If, when he authorized the other person to be his moral guardian, he relinquished his right to have the guardian's authority revoked, then the commitment he made was indeed autonomy-abdicating. The question here is whether the decision to make such a commitment can be defended on morally reasonable grounds. To answer this question we must recall why it seemed plausible to suppose that the agent could legitimately authorize someone else to serve as his "moral guardian" in the first place. In order to represent his appointment of a guardian as a reasonable and responsible act we had to attribute to the agent certain very special *higher-order* judgments—the judgment that his own everyday moral judgments are deficient in certain respects, and the judgment that the proposed guardian can be counted on to make up that deficiency by providing morally sound governance. By appointing a guardian he was seeking to bring his daily conduct more into line with his own most considered convictions about right and wrong. In view of his diminished rational capacity at the level of ordinary, everyday judgment, this may have been the best he could do, at least in the short run, to control the moral quality of his own life. (In the long run, he might be better advised to aim for a more "internal" reform.)

Yet what gave the agent good reason to appoint a moral guardian did not, at the same time, give him good reason to give up the right to review and revoke the authority which he had thus delegated. For the point of the arrangement is to compensate for deficiencies in "first-order" moral judgment; an irrevocable grant of authority denies the agent the right to exercise his capacity for higher-order judgment as well. It is conceivable, of course, that when the agent "agreed" to guardianship, he was comparably deficient in his capacity to make morally sound higher-order judgments, and hence in need of more profound governance even at that level. But in that case he would have been incompetent to "authorize" such an arrangement in the first place. It is also possible that between the time he appointed the guardian and the time he sought to be released from the arrangement, the higher-order capacity that the agent once had has been lost and with it the right either to constitute or to revoke guardianship arrangements. But the question is not whether in losing the capacity he would have lost the right. This point has already been established and a person who acknowledges its potential applicability to his own case does not give up a right that would have been his otherwise. Nor does someone abdicate autonomy when, believing that he may lose even his highest-order capacity for morally rational reflection, he calls upon others to be particularly alert to that possibility and to be prepared, if his fears should come true, to act appropriately.

What makes a grant of guardianship authority autonomy-*abdicating* is that even if the agent remains competent to establish that the arrangement is not serving the purpose which warranted his authorization of it to begin with, he no longer has the right to sue for the guardian's dismissal. He has relieved anybody who would deny him that right of the burden of having to prove his incompetence to exercise it. This means that if the guardian should either order or approve just the sort of behavior which he had been authorized to guard against, the agent has no rightful recourse. The guardian's relation to the ward takes on the character of an absolute and arbitrary authority. The situation has deteriorated into a case of the sort we have already had reason to reject. Yet if the agent's authorization of a moral guardian had seemed more reasonable than submitting to arbitrary authority, it was because the authority in question was intended to serve the very definite and inherently limited purpose of correcting for self-recognizable errors in judgment. Alienating one's right to have the guardian's authority revoked is not only unsupported by, but inconsistent with that purpose. Thus while in special circumstances the decision to submit to the authority of a self-appointed moral guardian might have to be regarded as reasonable and responsible, the same cannot be said of the decision to *give up* one's right to have the guardian's authority revoked.

To summarize, either the individual remains capable of functioning as a critically reflective moral agent or he does not. If he does, then any purpose which might have warranted his authorization of a guardian is ill-served by his prior renunciation of the right to have the guardian's authority revoked. If, however, he no longer has the higher-order competence which qualified him to constitute the arrangement in the first place, others will be entitled to have him committed, in any event, to a more profound form of guardianship. Moreover, it is neither unreasonable nor autonomy-abdicating to acknowledge that possibility, and even, if it is appropriate, to give others an anticipatory warning of it. What there is no reason to do, and good reason not to do, is to go any further.

The argument here recalls some of the spirit, if not the letter, of the argument Kant advanced. It is not, as Kant supposed, that the contract somehow invalidates itself, but rather that if the arrangement into which the individual has putatively contracted (a guardianship arrangement not subject to the agent's review and revocation) is legitimate, then *his* having contracted into it is not. Of course, Kant's argument was aimed at autonomy-abdication in general; the argument here is concerned with the special case of abdication as self-imposed paternalism. But in narrowing the focus of attention in this way, we underscore an important point: a condition of the possibility of legitimately placing a person under a guardianship authority which he has no right to revoke is that he be incapable of *functioning* as a rationally self-accountable moral agent. (In Kant's phrase, he has "ceased to be a person.") Whether this condition obtains or not is a matter to be determined by disinterested inquiry, not stipulated by contractual agreement or prior "authorization." Thus Kant was right in thinking that there is something absurd in the idea of a person legitimating his own total subordination to another person's will by a mere contract. The right to function as a rationally self-accountable moral agent can be lost (if one loses the capacity to so function) or perhaps even forfeited (through criminal conduct), but it cannot be legitimately abdicated.

IV. Conclusion: Autonomy and Political Community

Human beings are social creatures; they need, and for the most part, want, one another's cooperation and companionship. But on what terms can they reasonably agree to coexist and cooperate? If autonomy is inalienable, then it serves as a "fixed point," so to speak, in the formulation of any morally acceptable social contract. The question becomes, "Are there ways of settling conflict and determining the conditions of community life to which all could submit, without thereby abdicating their essential status as autonomous moral agents?"[22] (Cf. Rousseau's question, "How to find a form of association . . . under which each individual while uniting himself with the others, obeys no one but himself, and remains as free as before?")

Perhaps it is true that virtually any known and established method for resolving disputes and facilitating social cooperation is better than none at all. But persons who are concerned to preserve their autonomy must surely demand more of the social order than regularity and stability. Otherwise their acquiescence in the "system" comes dangerously close to resembling an abdication of autonomy in exchange for significant benefits—an arrangement which we have rejected as demonstrably unacceptable. Thus from the ideal of the inalienably autonomous moral agent it is plausible to suppose that a number of specifically political rights derive significant support: the right to freedom of thought and speech, the right to be addressed by clearly stated prospective rules rather than manipulated by the latest techniques of behavioral engineering, psychosurgery, and the like; the right to participate, whether directly or indirectly, in the processes by which basic rules are made; the right to petition for redress of grievance and to engage mechanisms for the revocation of laws, policies, etc. The idea behind all this is that someone who has the capacity to judge for himself what is right and wrong must have a reasonable opportunity to ask for and to receive moral justification for whatever laws and policies are directed to him; and he must have a reasonable opportunity to register objections and to argue for whatever changes he believes ought to be made.[23]

Of course, other persons—insofar as they are also capable of thinking morally and deciding for themselves what is right and wrong—must have comparable opportunity as well. Thus nobody has the right to have his conscientious convictions automatically translated into official action; nobody has the right to be dictator. Indeed, in a system that meets conditions of the sort indicated above, everyone could be said to have a weighty prima facie duty to work in and through the system rather than around it. It is a duty grounded in respect *for one another* as equal, autonomous agents. The point, of course, is that a morally thoughtful person will not think himself automatically justified in disobeying any law or policy with which he finds himself in moral disagreement. He recognizes that in deciding what to do there may be more to consider than the law or policy itself—for instance, the degree to which the question of its moral propriety admits of reasonable disagreement, the moral seriousness and sincerity of those who hold opposing views, the extent to which the established framework genuinely fosters the settlement of differences through reason and argument rather than through threats and deceptions. Thus it is quite possible to reach the judgment, all things considered, that one ought to abide by a law or policy which, on its own merits, one would reject. This does not mean that one abandons either the judgment that the policy is wrong or the effort to get it revoked. Rather, one forms the more considered judgment that under the circumstances, the right way to proceed is to engage established mechanisms for bringing about change. It would be a mistake to suppose that persons who act on such a judgment thereby compromise their integrity as autonomous moral agents. Integrity is compromised when one elects *not* to act on one's most considered moral judgment. Moreover, in giving special weight to modes of interaction that involve reason and argument rather than force and cunning, we affirm our nature as morally rational beings.

Now the suggestion that autonomy provides grounding for several familiar features of the legal and political order by no means precludes additional lines of supporting argument. Indeed, it is in any event implausible to suppose that the whole of what is right and just can be deduced from the relatively formal ideal of a community whose members respect one another's inalienable status as rationally self-accountable moral agents. Yet while such practices as rule of law or freedom of thought and speech can be defended on more than one ground, the appeal to autonomy—if autonomy is indeed inalienable—is particularly helpful in explaining their special preeminence within a just social order. And though it hardly provides a complete account of political rectitude, respect for autonomy does serve to define a basic framework within which other, more substantive concerns can, and should, be addressed.

Of course, these remarks are no more than a sketch; a full treatment of such matters is beyond the scope of this article. But the important thing to note is that a theory which assigns a central place to the moral autonomy of persons does not commit us to philosophical anarchism. On the contrary, the very autonomy which we are unable to alienate requires a definite stage-setting of legal and political arrangements. And this helps to explain why, once such a system is in place, we have a prima facie duty to support it. In acknowledging that duty we show our respect for the autonomy of others even as we insist upon, and give fundamental expression to, our own.

NOTES

This article, first published in *Philosophy and Public Affairs* 13 (1984): 271–98, copyright © 1984 by Princeton University Press, is reprinted by permission. I am grateful to my colleagues, William Mann and Alan Wertheimer, for their careful reading of earlier drafts and to the editors of *Philosophy & Public Affairs* for very helpful commentary. I am especially indebted to George Sher for his skillful counsel and generous encouragement.

　　1. Cf. John Locke, Second Treatise, secs. 22, 23, 135, 137, 164, 168, 172, in *Two Treatises of Government* (Cambridge: Cambridge University Press, 1960); Benedict de Spinoza, *Theologico-Political Treatise,* chaps. 17 and 20, in *Works of Spinoza,* trans. R.H.M. Elwes (New York: Dover, 1951); Jean Jacques Rousseau, *The Social Contract,* Bk. I, chap. 4, trans. Maurice Cranston (Harmondsworth: Penguin, 1968); Immanuel Kant, *Theory and Practice,* II; *The Metaphysics of Morals: Introduction,* sec. B., and *The Theory of Right,* Pt. II, sec. 49, D, in *Kant's Political Writings,* ed. Hans Reiss and trans. H. B. Nisbet (Cambridge: Cambridge University Press, 1970). Subsequent page references are to these editions.

　　2. The predicate "is autonomous" is ambiguous. In saying that someone is an autonomous agent we could be saying any or all of the following: (a) that the person in question is capable of functioning autonomously; (b) that he actually does function autonomously; (c) that he is entitled to do so; and (d) that he is actually respected in his right to so function. I assume that in having the capacity one has the right. When I speak of "alienating autonomy" this is an abbreviated way of saying "alienating the right to function as a critically reflective moral agent."

　　3. Cf. Robert Paul Wolff, *In Defense of Anarchism* (New York: Harper & Row, 1970), p. 13: "He may learn from others about his moral obligations, but only in the sense that a mathematician learns from other mathematicians— namely, by hearing from them arguments whose validity he recognizes even though he did not think of them himself." Cf. also S. I. Benn, "Freedom, Autonomy and the Concept of a Person," *Proceedings of the Aristotelian Society* 76 (1975–76), p. 126: "To be autonomous one must have reasons for acting, and be capable of second thoughts in the light of new reasons; it is not to have a capacity for conjuring criteria out of nowhere."

　　4. I believe that this interpretation of "moral autonomy" accords with Kant's general position on the subject. Kant never suggested that a person should simply make up the moral principles upon which his life is to be based. Rather, he must be able to certify their validity for himself by reasoning in the appropriate way. Clearly there have to be standards governing the moral reasoning process. Otherwise, the contrast between autonomy and "heteronomy" is lost: the autonomous person simply believes whatever he believes. Now chief among the standards which Kant thought must characterize our thinking if it is to be morally rational is

the requirement that we reason in abstraction from the fact that certain interests happen to be our own; in short, that we reason disinterestedly. It is plausible to suggest that other conditions (e.g., knowledge, empathy) also govern the moral reasoning process. The crucial point is that the moral decision procedure is not arbitrary; it is a reasonable procedure for resolving certain very fundamental questions about human conduct. Because we are reasonable beings, it will not strike us as "alien" or imposed by others but rather as something whose force and relevance we can appreciate for ourselves.

5. From these observations it also follows, I think, that a person does not lose autonomy merely by submitting to various limitations on liberty. Everything depends on which liberties are limited and why. Indeed someone who refused to acknowledge any restrictions on conduct could be justly accused of not functioning autonomously, i.e., as a self-regulating moral agent, at all. But it does *not* follow that a person "acts autonomously" even when he is compelled to act, contrary to his present will, in accordance with rules for which there is a morally adequate justification. There is no need to say that a person can be "forced to be" autonomous. It would be more appropriate to say that insofar as his will is not determined by morally rational reflection he fails to act autonomously.

6. In saying that someone has alienated autonomy there is a certain ambiguity: this could simply mean that he and everyone else behave *as though it were* the case that he has assumed a duty not to deploy critically reflective moral judgment; or it could mean that, morally speaking, he really has assumed such a duty. If the arguments of this article are correct, alienation of autonomy is never morally legitimate and so in one sense, at least, no one ever does succeed in alienating his autonomy. It is useful, however, to preserve the notion of autonomy-alienation in its positive or de facto sense; for when we say that a person can't (i.e., is not morally permitted to) alienate his autonomy, we presumably have in mind something that he would be doing but should not.

7. In Scanlon's phrase, he continues to regard himself "as sovereign" over questions of what he morally ought to do (see "A Theory of Freedom of Expression," *Philosophy & Public Affairs* 1, no. 2 [Winter 1972]: 215); or as Locke might say, he "reserves" to himself the "ultimate determination" of his moral course (see Locke, op. cit., sec. 168).

8. Locke, *Second Treatise*, sec. 22.

9. Spinoza, *Theologico-Political Treatise*, p. 214.

10. Rousseau, *The Social Contract*, p. 60.

11. *Kant's Political Writings*, p. 133.

12. *Theory and Practice*, II, in *Kant's Political Writings*, p. 76.

13. Ibid., p. 85.

14. Ibid., p. 86. Although this is not the place to attempt a more extensive survey, I should note that in leaving off with Kant, I do not mean to imply that the tradition in question extends no farther in time. Of Hegel and Marx, for example, it has been said that "their ideal is also at bottom the ideal of Rousseau and Kant: that no man should be the mere instrument of other men and that all men should be able to live in accordance with principles they inwardly accept." John Plamenatz, *Man and Society: Political and Social Theory: Bentham through Marx* (New York: McGraw-Hill, 1963), p. 407.

15. A reader for *Philosophy & Public Affairs* has pointed out to me that

"some further explanation and argument" is available to Locke. For God's aim is the preservation of mankind and "it is allegedly contrary to that aim to allow some people to exercise arbitrary control over others."

16. *The Metaphysics of Morals,* sec. 49, p. 153.

17. *Theory and Practice,* II, p. 75. By the phrase "no rights but only duties" I take Kant to mean whatever duties shall be imposed by the will of the other party to the agreement, one's self-chosen "master," so to speak. This is a reasonable interpretation, I think, in light of the parallel passage in *The Metaphysics of Morals.* It would also follow from what I take to be the plausible suggestion that Kant is trying to make good on Rousseau's claim that an agreement which stipulated "absolute dominion for one party and absolute obedience for the other" would be "illogical and nugatory."

18. *On Liberty,* chap. 5 (Indianapolis: Library of Liberal Arts, 1956), p. 125.

19. The above argument can be reformulated in the vocabulary of "reasons" for and against courses of conduct, rather than in the vocabulary of "goods" and "evils." Thus the crucial embarrassment to the champion of autonomy-abdication can be stated as follows: if the agreement to abdicate autonomy is valid, one is bound to obey any order, even if the reasons that tell against it clearly outweigh (a) whatever reason there was for securing the benefit which was to be achieved in return, (b) whatever reason there is for keeping one's word.

Now it might be said that I have overlooked one important possibility: that some actions (besides autonomy-abdication) are wrong "no matter what." The suggestion is that "absolutism" in ethics yields a relatively simple demonstration of the inalienability of autonomy. For if certain conduct is absolutely forbidden, then a mere agreement could not possibly obligate a person to do whatever someone else told him to do. Indeed, no agreement which committed people to do what is absolutely impermissible would be valid. Moreover, anyone who didn't know which actions are absolutely impermissible would be incompetent to make a morally binding agreement in the first place.

I do not wish to reject this general way of thinking or the argument against autonomy-abdication that goes along with it. But it deserves at least two comments. (1) Most of the resistance to the idea that autonomy can never be legitimately abdicated comes from philosophers—whether they be utilitarians or intuitionists—who are extremely skeptical about "moral absolutes" of any sort. In arguing for the impermissibility of autonomy-abdication, without benefit of the initial assumption that some actions are wrong no matter what, I am trying to make the case in the very court of those who would provide the stiffest opposition to the thesis.

(2) The "absolutist" defense of inalienability is a bit more complicated than the argument above might suggest. For if the one and only absolute duty were the duty to keep one's agreements, absolutism would provide no bar to autonomy-abdication, at least for someone who had managed to discharge all his other contractual commitments. Thus even the absolutist argument must tacitly rely on a claim that is essentially equivalent to the view that the reasons which tell against promise breaking are not infinitely weighty (which in turn is isomorphic to the view that the disvalue of promise-breaking is not infinitely great). But so long as we are allowed to make an assumption of this sort, we are in a position to show that autonomy-abdication is "absolutely" impermissible, even if nothing else is.

20. I say "tantamount" to an abdication of autonomy because in some ways an arrangement of this sort is quite different from the arrangement we have been discussing thus far. On the one hand, the person in question relinquishes his right to function as a critically reflective moral agent and in that sense can be said to abdicate autonomy. But at the same time, the authority which he grants to the other party is not meant to be unlimited. (This point figures in the subsequent argument against the irrevocable delegation of such authority.)

21. It is worth noting that the question of who shall serve as guardian is distinct from the question of whether guardianship is appropriate in the first place. Thus to say that a person has no right to contract away his autonomy is not to deny that in the event of his total demise as a rationally self-managing moral agent, his previously expressed wishes should carry at least some weight in the selection of a suitable guardian. The inalienability of autonomy is unaffected by this acknowledgment.

22. In posing the question in this way, I do not mean to suggest that a society in which everyone functioned as a morally autonomous agent would be particularly strife-ridden. Following Hume, we might wish to argue that the conditions which characterize the moral thought-process are especially well-suited to the task of bringing the otherwise diverse judgments of different persons more nearly into line with one another. Cf. *An Inquiry Concerning the Principles of Morals*, sec. IX, Pt. 1 (Indianapolis: Library of Liberal Arts, 1957), p. 93. Thus it might be said that conflict in human affairs would be mitigated, rather than exacerbated, if only everyone were more, rather than less, morally self-scrutinizing. But the fact remains that in the ordinary course of human affairs, people will not always be guided by reflective moral judgment, and even when they are, many of the problems that confront them will carry enough uncertainty and complexity to generate honest moral disagreement. I discuss these matters at greater length in "Morality and Compromise," *NOMOS* 21, *Compromise in Ethics, Law and Politics*, particularly pp. 48–52.

23. These remarks are meant to recall Kant's insistence that "in all matters concerning universal human duties, each individual requires to be convinced by reason that the coercion which prevails is lawful. Otherwise he would be in contradiction with himself," *Theory and Practice*, p. 85. For Kant, this requires a "spirit of freedom" in political society. One might argue that respect for moral autonomy would require far more than the freedom of thought and speech which Kant seems to have had in mind in this particular passage. For an autonomy-grounded defense of one particular version of the free speech doctrine, see Scanlon, "A Theory of Freedom of Expression," pp. 204–26.

22 A Kantian Argument Supporting Public Policy Choice

John Martin Gillroy

IN THIS ESSAY, I will discuss Kant's political theory with refer-ence to how it might inform public policy choices.[1] I am most concerned with presenting an interpretation of the political theory of Immanuel Kant that will serve as a foundation for making and justifying public choices. Because Kant never completed a political treatise, but only a "metaphys-ics of morals" to underlie political decision, actions, and institutions, I will endeavor to accurately represent Kant's moral philosophy and to con-struct its political entailments from its ethical premises.

Currently, whether one can base any political theory in Kantian meta-physics is itself a subject of controversy.[2] The debate is generated from the nature of Kant's project, which, as I interpret it, is to understand how a moral (noumenal) self survives and prospers in a sociopolitical (phenome-nal) world.[3] It is true that at many junctures Kant is ambiguous and seems to maintain the tension between noumena and phenomena rather than resolve it. He seems to simultaneously maintain two contradictory points that make the use of Kant's metaphysics as a base for political theory difficult. These two points are, first, that the noumenal self is responsible for moral actions regardless of the empirical context, and second, that justice in the phenomenal world is necessary to ensure the survival and full actualization of the noumenal self.[4] This essay is an attempt to get beyond this ambiguity and to contest the claim that metaphysics ought not be a vital part of political theory. The attempt involves extrapolating from the essential premises of Kant's moral and political theory to the role of collective action and policy choice in creating a phenomenal world that supports the moral humanity of the noumenal self. I intend to take a combination of Kant's premises and extrapolate to their implications on

491

the basis of the argument that the principles expounded by Kant and the logic in which they nest are more important than the extent to which Kant himself would prosecute them.

First, I will assume that metaphysics has an essential place in politics. I will assert that political theory is better if it can say something about what is essential (necessary and universal) to the human being regardless of his social or cultural context.[5] Second, I will assume that it is possible to take the known parameters of Kant's philosophical position and to extrapolate the metaphysical elements of political action and decision— that is, to take the logic further than Kant did and draw conclusions about the political requirements of the noumenal self in a phenomenal world.

Specifically, within the context of this essay, I will take Kant's moral and political theory and show that it can provide a reasonable metaphysics for collective action and policy choice. I will describe Kant's exegesis and show how extrapolation from that exegesis gives one a metaphysical platform that specifies a duty to act collectively in the establishment of a redistributive state. In the following exegesis, I hope to establish a flow of logic, so that it will be hard to find the point at which Kant leaves off and my extrapolation begins. My aim is to get the reader to accept nontraditional conclusions from accepted Kantian premises while I maintain that the latter are logical entailments of the former.[6]

Standards and Policy Choice

The predominant methodology of policy choice involves the principle of efficiency in the deciphering and weighing of the costs and benefits of policy alternatives. The market analysis of costs and benefits has but one overriding normative principle, that of potential Pareto optimality. The Pareto rule judges between states of affairs by their total welfare and assumes that one person's free and voluntary trade in the market is backed up by a rough equality of opportunity, position, and strategic power in relation to the other actors. Welfare economics has no vocabulary for the problem that is basic to ethical and political discourse: conflicts of interest. When conflict of interest within or between generations can be assumed away without damage to the model of social interaction, there is no need for more than a Pareto rule to decide optimal allocation of resources within the model. However, in many cases, the policy decision involves distribution of goods where inherent conflicts of interest exist involving the nonexistence of a baseline of equality for fair transactions. In such cases, some new principle must be found on which the pre-exchange situation can be rearranged through positive redistribution of endowments, freedom, and risk, so that the conflict of interest can be resolved before the forces of the market are allowed to rule the social interrelationships.

One alternative is a Kantian system of justice as *Recht,* which takes as its central principle the freedom and dignity of each individual in harmony with all others. A Kantian theory of collective action is one that places the individual and that individual's human interest, in maximum scope for his moral agency, as the principle at one level of independent and necessary consideration, and describes politics as the working out of this principle in various forms of public institutions.

Recht (justice as right) is contrasted, by Kant, with *Gerechtigkeit* (justice as positive law) and is described as a system of external constraints that takes the primary idea of Kantian ethics—individual freedom—and harmonizes each person's freedom with that of all others. *Recht* builds politics on the foundation of an objective moral law (the categorical imperative), which is necessary to the full and equal realization of freedom for all rational beings. The first task of this essay, in its attempt to explore an alternative foundation for policy choice, is to inform our future discussion of *Recht* with the necessary preliminaries: Kant's ideas of rationality, freedom, and the categorical imperative.[7]

The Individual and the Moral Law

The process of reasoning that motivates individuals to action can be described in two basic ways (Nagel 1970). One can believe that all motivation is based on the satisfaction of exogenous desire, which selects means to the ends of inclination. The other possibility, and the definition of human reason more directly related to Kant, is to separate the influence of inclination from the power of the mind to will by intellectually approved principles, irrespective of what one believes the circumstances are or the consequences will be of what one chooses. In this case, reason has a reflective critical capacity unique yet common to humans, and it sets humankind off from other earthly creatures as "rational beings." It is my contention that Kant's project in his political ethics has two components. The first is to take this human capacity to will what is rationally approved, independent of what is desired, and build around and from it a system of political institutions that respect the dignity of this rational nature. The second is to foster public policy that protects and preserves it equally for all.

The currency of man's rational nature is the idea of freedom. Freedom is an idea the realization of which cannot be empirically proved or falsified but is an a priori condition of thinking of oneself as a responsible agent able to overcome the direct influence of sensation determining the will. To proceed on the assumption that freedom is part of rational behavior and investigate its ramifications, all we need assume is that humans are capable of decision making that is not always a direct response to the influence of desire.

To think of human beings as having the power to will (as distinct from being moved only by desire) is to think of them as willing freely. The will is free in two senses: negatively, humans can will free of desire; positively, they can will in accord with what is rationally required.

Wille is the capacity of the human will to legislate in accord with the demands of reason. *Willkür* is the capacity of the will to execute choices in the empirical world so that reason finds the proper external expression. *Wille* is the component of the human will that applies the moral law and defines rationality in its own terms. Imperatives of reason are then passed on to *Willkür* as the component of the will that deals with the choice of action in the empirical world. *Wille* is right calculation as *Willkür* is calculation. The failure of *Willkür* to heed *Wille*, or its dominance of *Wille*, causes the moral integrity and rationality of the willing process to be overcome with the influence of desire and inclination (filling the vacuum left by reason), which affects the freedom of will.[8]

Negative freedom is the capacity of *Wille* to operate without overwhelming pressure from the effects of inclination and desire on *Willkür*. Positive freedom is the full internal operation of *Wille* and its external manifestations through *Willkür*. Freedom as an a priori idea of reason is dependent on the will being negatively free before it can legislate as *Wille*, choose in line with the moral imperative as *Willkür*, and exercise its full range of internal and external positive freedom.

The moral law (categorical imperative) regulates freedom, and it is respect for your capacity to will and act freely and for the dignity of others as free persons that lays the foundation, the metaphysical foundation, for political institutions and policy decision making.

A. The Categorical Imperative

The moral law is that principle by which reason makes itself practical. Facing the empirical world and considering a decision problem with moral components, one uses the categorical imperative to decide, apart from circumstances and self-interest, whether any action in a particular situation is demanded by practical reason. The categorical imperative presents the formal requirements of the pure (a priori) part of rationality, and is, I will argue, really three principles in one. I will describe the three principles that are the categorical imperative so that "right" and rationality can be defined in Kantian terms and the moral basis of justice set up.

The first principle of the categorical imperative instructs one to "act only according to that maxim by which you can at the same time will that it should become a universal law" (G, A421). The moral law in Kantian ethics must be what is *universal* and *necessary* about human actions and incentives in order for them to carry moral worth. The first principle is primarily concerned with the first of these characteristics: universality. In moral decisions, one is not to act in a way that one could not internally sanction for everyone. The individual's immediate self-interest is not to be satisfied in such a way that the generalization of the behavior would lead to self-contradiction or the dissolution of morally permissible institutions. The first principle is the most formal of the three and is primarily negative in its application in that it informs the individual what morality does not allow, but it does not adequately define either the necessary and independent ground for the universal willing of a maxim or what one ought positively to do to act with respect for the moral law. Many theorists have taken this one "formula" as the complete construction of the categorical imperative and concluded that Kantian ethics are empty and formal (MacIntyre 1981, 43–45; Hegel 1821, sec. 135). However, with the addition of the second principle, Kant provides a necessary ground for the moral will. The addition of the third principle gives complete manifestation, a foundation for a theory of the just state, and a strong positive direction to one's willing the moral law.

Kant states that if there is to be "a categorical imperative for the human will, it must be one that forms an objective principle of the will from the conception of that which is necessarily an end for everyone because it is an end in itself" (G, A429). The ground of the precept is that "rational nature exists as an end in itself" (G, A429). From this deduction, Kant derives the second principle, which commands that one "act so that you treat humanity, whether in your own person or in that of another, always as an end and never as a means only" (G, A429). If there exist no ends in themselves, there can be no necessary end for everyone. Then the independent and necessary character of morality is gone, and there are no maxims that cannot be universalized.

The principle of the end in itself provides in one's rational nature what Kant believes is the only objective ground for the moral law. Negatively, it requires that one refrain from interfering with others while, positively, it directs one to promote one's own and others' ends. The dichotomy between noninterference and positive promotion is the first trace of what I will argue is Kant's distinction between the idea of freedom as coordinated by a theory of *Recht* and freedom actualized by a theory of *Tugend* (virtue). Here again, noumenal self in ethical legislation (virtue) meets phenomenal reality in juridical legislation (justice), and moral imperative is asked to shape the empirical reality to the needs of the moral self. The second principle is still insufficient, however, to the task of giving full definition to what it means to respect the moral law for one's self and in relation to others.[9]

Kant gives full characterization to his categorical imperative with the third principle, which directs that "the rational being must regard himself always as legislative in a realm of ends possible through the freedom of the will" (G, A434). The realm or kingdom of ends places the idea of each rational creature as an end in himself as "the supreme limiting condition on the freedom of actions of each man" (G, A431). Kant is concerned with the moral worth and necessity of each individual willing the universal moral law, not with the willing of subjective ends by particular actors. The third principle gives full characterization to the individual in terms of his collective milieu: It describes the full manifestation of an end in itself as a rational being legislating for himself autonomously, while it defines the concept of an end in itself as prescribing that each person (consider) one's freedom in relation to the potential freedom of all others with the aim of a system of common law and policy that respects each and every citizen with equal freedom and moral representation, prior to any and all subjective ends one may have.

I will argue that these considerations contradict the proposition that all individual decisions ought automatically to command moral respect from political authorities.[10] One's choices command respect in that one must be assumed to be an objective end for one's self as well as others; however, only decisions made autonomously, in line with the determination of one's will by the moral law, are worthy of public respect. A decision that contradicts the categorical imperative is immoral. Those decisions pertaining to one's particular subjective ends are for the most part amoral, unless they infringe on the freedom of others, in which case the moral law commands that one's choice be overruled by the just state.

A rational being functioning autonomously in a realm of ends is necessary to morality, which is necessary to human dignity, for humanity has dignity "only so far as it is capable of morality" (G, A435). Dignity in a realm of ends is a characteristic of individual freedom to self-legislate. As such, dignity has to do with the internal rational consistency of the will, which of itself is deserving of the respect of others. One's dignity is not granted by others but is native to the intellect and the process of willing— one is born with negative and positive freedom due to one's rational nature and therefore ought to be the subject of respect in a moral world. The freedom inherent in each rational being can never be taken away or fully plowed under by external forces. A "good will," a will free to respect the moral law, can "shine forth" under the most oppressive conditions. However, like an adult runner compared with a crawling infant, the full use and proper realization of one's free will can best be exercised when one's negative freedom has full scope that allows positive freedom its complete actualization.

The three principles that induce the categorical imperative give form (universality), objective material content (rational nature as an end), and full characterization (realm of ends) to the moral law and what is "right" for an individual making moral decisions. To be fully practical, one further problem must be overcome so that the commands of the imperative find application for the individual in the empirical world—that is, so autonomy can find actualization in a heteronomous reality.

Kant sets up the realm of ends as an ideal for the full realization of potential freedom that can be realized only to the extent that others act morally. However, no one can determine whether another wills morally; that decision is made solely by the agent himself. The problem then surfaces as to how I legislate as a rational agent in a kingdom of ends without being taken advantage of by those who flaunt the moral law when it is in their interest to do so. How can I make a situation real where morality and dignity can find secure and equal expression, when I cannot make any other person will morally?

I contend that the answer lies in the distinction between *Recht* and *Tugend*. *Tugend,* or virtue, is the condition where one's incentive, as well as the act that results, come from one's respect (*Achtung*) for the moral law. *Recht* or justice, on the other hand, is concerned only that the act and its external ramifications are in line with the demands of the civil law— that is, a civil law drafted in the light of the imperatives of the moral law. One cannot make others moral, but one can contribute to the construction of a *Rechtlicher Zustand* (just state) that will institutionalize the demands of the categorical imperative, as they affect external behavior, setting up the optimal political framework in which freedom is well distributed and the full scope of negative freedom is insured against the acts of others. My freedom to act as a potential member of a kingdom of ends is thus assured, and in addition others have the most perfect environment for the full growth and expression of their positive freedom as autonomous, rational beings in a heteronomous and irrational world.

In consideration of the vital role of politics as the empirical manifestation of the moral law, via practical reason, I will construct a political addition to the categorical imperative.[11] It will instruct the individual as a duty to oneself and others to

> establish and contribute to a just polity (*Rechtlicher Zustand*) in order to secure one's dignity as a rational legislator in a potential kingdom of ends and to provide the proper process and environment for the distribution and allocation of freedom via a system of external constraints and incentives that coordinate while they encourage the full and proper realization of others' autonomy in their respect for the moral law.[12]

B. Recht

Justice as *Recht* has to do with external coercion. It is concerned that one's action shows respect for a civil law that is the embodiment of the moral law. It begins by securing the moral baseline[13] of equal agency, without which full moral choice is made inaccessible to some by the power and fortune of others. It continues by establishing the processes necessary to distribute above this baseline in ways that continue to ensure that one person's moral agency (dignity) will not be sacrificed to another's arbitrarily.

Recht as collective action coerces the individual justly—that is, guided by the framework of the categorical imperative, where the moral law "will ultimately have to provide the justification for setting up a system or coercive state law" (Murphy 1970, 96). A slave society or a civil state in which one class of individuals is routinely exploited for the sake of another would not be just. Kant wants the coercive power of the state to be based on independent principle that will define what is necessary and rational from the standpoint of the critical morality (*Recht*), while it allows the particular manifestation of the positive law (*Gerechtigkeit*) to have various expressions on a social level.

The role of the moral law in defining justice as *Recht* makes Kant's theory of collective action different from either Hobbes's or Hume's (Hobbes 1651, Hume 1740) description of the origin of politics and the establishment of justice. All three use institutions and political process to settle conflicts of interest and regulate the behavior of individuals so that cooperation and nonviolence secure one person against all others. However, where politics and justice flow from the institutions of convention or contract relative to a specific population and its circumstances for both Hume and Hobbes, justice as *Recht*, for Kant, creates[14] the political institutions and defines the objective interest of individuals and collectives independent of circumstance. Kant separates the critical morality in *Recht* from the positive law as *Gerechtigkeit,* giving the former a prior and purely independent point of origin, distinct from the origins of convention and the positive law. Reflective reason is given a metaphysical point of objective standard, based on the moral law, from which all judgments of ethical matters can be made.

Recht does not presuppose as much as *Tugend* (i.e., that one is free to will for the sake of the moral law), but rather is concerned with what virtue (the application of the categorical imperative) demands of a system of political constraints and incentives. In order for an individual to seek virtue and will for the sake of the moral law, he must fully exercise his positive freedom—internally, in the determination of his will, and externally, in the action demanded for the expression of his freedom by the moral law. The assumption is that each person will want to express his positive freedom (as a noumenal self) and that to accomplish this he will use space and resources in the empirical (phenomenal) world. Because we live on a finite planet, the individual external expression of positive freedom will lead to a situation in which conflict of interest ensues. Conflict will allow fortune and natural discrepancies in power and circumstance to decide on the distribution of freedom and, consequently, the range of liberty allowed to each individual. In this case, the expression of positive freedom by some will infringe on the negative freedom of others, in that the circumstances of some (poverty, ill health, exploitation) will fuel the power of desire and inclination to influence the determination of their wills and limit the resulting growth and actualization of their positive freedom. The situation in which contingencies, rather than the moral law, decide on the scope of freedom for the individual is an unjust situation that inhibits the power of some individuals to provide for their moral integrity (MM,T A387–388).

In terms of the two capacities of the will,[15] an unjust society allows the acts or conditions of some to put their fellows in a situation in which humans are under abnormal pressure from desire and inclination to exercise their *Willkür* contrary to *Wille*. Under these conditions, *Wille* has its scope of negative freedom tightened; as a consequence, its power to be positively free and spontaneous is constrained. Remember that the moral law demands that persons determine the exercise of *Willkür* by use of reason (as given by *Wille*). Now external circumstance is constraining opportunity and the individual's choice set, so that *Willkür* is limited and therefore *Wille* inhibited in its full and spontaneous operation.[16] Without a positively free *Wille* with its full capacity intact, the individual cannot maintain her moral integrity and, as a consequence, her dignity as an autonomous legislator. When *Willkür* acts upon or disregards *Wille,* it is no longer a capacity of the will but an "incapacity."

The coordination of expressions of positive freedom so that the maximum equal scope of negative freedom is assured to all falls to *Recht*. Justice as *Recht* cannot and does not concern itself with the internal workings of *Wille* but can influence any affect *Willkür* might have on *Wille*. To establish *Recht* one need only assume that, by their rational nature, all individual *Wille* are worthy of respect and, hence, noninterference from unequal or arbitrary pressure from *Willkür*. At this point, *Recht* (through the just state) takes on the job of harmonizing the freedom of each with the freedom of all by maximizing the scope of each person's negative freedom of choice through an elimination of conflicts among their individual expressions of positive freedom.

Recht does not assume virtue but self-interest[17] on the part of each individual for a civil arrangement that will insure each against all others, in the personal (external) expression of their freedom. Kant describes the transition to a juridical state (*Rechtlicher Zustand*) as a duty of each person to himself (MM,R, A315–16) and to universal law. But I will argue that another reason to prefer freedom and security in a juridical state to "lawless" freedom in a state of nature begins with the individual compulsion to express his freedom, and the violence and conflict that ensues from the inability of nature, or of individuals themselves, to coordinate their degree of freedom and their behavior so that the moral integrity of each and every one is respected. The moral law therefore entails the collective action of all for the moral autonomy of each.

Kant defines *Recht* as the "aggregation of those conditions under which the choice [*Willkür*] of one person can be conjoined with the choice [*Willkür*] of another in accordance with the universal law of freedom" (MM,R, A230). I contend that under the "universal law of freedom," negative freedom is not the absence of external constraints. Rather, it is the presence of a just (juridical) state with political institutions that, through positive acts, coordinate behavior and shape the environment in such a way that a full and equal baseline distribution protects negative freedom of choice and allows one to develop and express one's positive freedom of will in one's own way. In his theory of the principles of virtue (*Tugendlehre*), Kant identifies two perfect duties that the moral law commands of each individual. The first is in regard to others and gives the imperative to provide for their happiness; the second is in terms of the individual himself and implores each toward his own perfection (MM,T A385). The first of these gives the imperative to aid in the establishment of a juridical state, and the second concerns the initiative within the framework of this state to see to the full expression of one's own autonomous nature. I would argue that the order of Kant's statement of duties is significant. The pursuit of personal perfection is an individual responsibility. The collective framework that will allow the maximum equal pursuit of happiness for all, however, is the primary and prerequisite moral responsibility of every rational being to all others.[18]

The Evolution of Collective Action

The question for this part of the essay is how *Recht* works itself out in the world. When Kant writes about virtue he maintains that the will legislating itself is an ideal toward which we, as rational beings, have a duty to strive toward via self-perfection. In the same way his idea of justice is practically applicable but utopian in character. *Recht* sets political goals: what "ought" to be the civil reality of all rational beings.[19] Kant's greater project is world peace and stability in unity under an international federation of just states. However, here we are concerned only with the political ramifications of the transition from a state of nature to a juridical or just state.

A. The State of Nature

The point of departure for Kantian collective action theory is the state of nature. It is conceived not as an historical reality but as a moral condition before the origin of a juridical state, where positive freedom is expressed and the private claim to property becomes a base for conflict of interest.

For Kant, the primary premise of the state of nature is that "all men are originally in common collective possession of the soil of the whole earth" (MM,R, S11, 13, 16). Kant's proposition that the earth originally belongs to everyone is in opposition to both Locke and Nozick. The importance here is Kant's reliance on the idea of a "united will a priori" as the basis for distributive considerations of property. Property is a common collective good that can be rightly (*mit Recht*) transferred into private hands only by acquisition along certain lines that ensure the transfer is legal and just (MM,R, S13, 15).

The transfer, to and between private ownership, takes place as part of the self-interest of individuals as they express their positive freedom. However, in a state of nature, acquisition does not always coincide with the freedom of the 'will of all,' and conflict results. Without the framework of a juridical state, the acquisition of property is unregulated and causes violence. Each desires use of the land but it is a scarce collective good and, in a state of nature, there are no just rules for its proper distribution (MM,R, S14).

Kant distinguishes between two forms of possession (*Mein und Dein*): there is *de jure* or intellectual possession and sensual or physical possession. Only the latter is possible in a state of nature. Consequently, a person who takes possession of property without a juridical state in operation must physically seize it to obtain possession; since there are no just rules of transfer, the person is always liable to counterclaims and violence by others. The insecurity of ownership compounded by potential physical danger, violence, and constant supervision of one's possessions causes individuals to give up their lawless freedom for a regulated but more complete and equal freedom in a just civil state (MM,R, S11, 14, 15).

In order to justly and legally maintain one's possessions without having constant physical control of them, one must obtain the cooperation of one's fellow rational beings through consideration of their freedom and wills. Then a system of distributive justice can be set up that fairly and equitably maintains freedom while regulating private ownership. Ownership will be set into law and maintained by a system of constraint, which, at the same time, will be an incentive to own possessions, since the problems of secure and just ownership have been solved (MM,R, S15).

Four things are important about Kant's theory of private right. First, property is necessary to one's freedom. Second, property is a relation between people and not between people and objects. Freedom and protection from violence are the matters of concern, not the objects of ownership. Third, the state of nature establishes original ownership as public and first (private) acquisition as subject to independent moral and political constraints, which are necessary to avoid instability of property and violence. Private acquisition beyond the restrictions of the moral law infringes on personal freedom and causes violence and exploitation to all parties who must live in a social situation without just ground rules. Finally, all allocations of private use are subject to these moral constraints that place the primary right of the "will of all" prior to first private acquisition. Private right is necessary to individual freedom, but it must be coordinated by a framework that exists prior to its de jure establishment (MM,R, S13, 15, 16).

Property right is therefore not, as Nozick believes, absolute to the individual who has primary physical possession. At the same time, because collective ownership has moral ground, the initial endowment of private possession has no independent moral force, as Nozick maintains it does (Nozick 1974, chap. 7). I would describe Kant as measuring the moral gravity of possession in terms of the constraints and incentives necessary to collective, equal freedom, without which private ownership is unjust and unstable, causing problems for those exploiting freedom as well as those exploited. Kant states, "Right as against every possible possessor of a Thing, means only the claim of a particular Will to the use of an object so far as it may be included in the All-comprehending universal Will, and can be thought as in harmony with its law" (MM,R, S17).

The self-interest of the individual and his expression of freedom in the possession of property and resources brings him to the point where the establishment of justice (*Recht*) is necessary to peace and any sense of real de jure private right. One does not have to act in accordance with the moral law to understand that without its application, through the first principle of justice, the expression of individual autonomy will be a creature of circumstance and fortune being arbitrarily denied (in full) to some at the hands of others, who will be in fear of losing possession due to the violence caused by their exploitation. As described within *Recht*, the freedom of each is dependent on the equal freedom of all. One does not need to be an altruist to acknowledge that a state of affairs in which individual freedom finds optimal and nonviolent expression is preferred to one in which the conflict of freedom and its unequal distribution by natural lottery, without a moral framework, causes exploitation, violence, and instability of possession that harms the rational agency of all participants.

B. Ideal Contract

The contract is the mechanism by which Kant establishes the ideal of the juridical state out of the instability of his state of nature. In this case, the contract is neither historical nor is it hypothetical consent under uncertainty (Rawls 1971, chap. 3). The Kantian contract is an ideal construction of reason that outlines the constitution of the new juridical state in line with the demands of the moral law that all rational beings would consent to were they canvassed (which they are not). The contract in this case is made necessary by the social chaos of a state of nature and is drawn along morally necessary lines that provide for the innate right, without which no constitutional process would be just.

The distinction, then, is between innate and acquired right, the former belonging "to everyone by nature independent of any juridical act" (MM,R, A237), and the latter requiring such an act. There is but one innate right, "Freedom (independence from the constraint of another's choice [*Willkür*]), insofar as it is compatible with the freedom of everyone else" in accordance with the moral law (MM,R, A231). This right is the "one sole and original right that belongs to every human being by virtue of his humanity" (MM,R, A237). Within the innate right to freedom there is the right to "innate equality" (MM,R, A238).[20]

The innate right to freedom is basic to the moral integrity of the rational nature of all human beings and is the origin of respect for the individual and his dignity. I would contend that only the move to a juridical state can secure this right in positive law through the influence of the principles of *Recht* on the statutes of *Gerechtigkeit*.

Kant's concept of the necessity of the state is not Hegel's (1821, Part 3 [iii]). I read Kant as supporting the proposition that the freedom of the individual is an innate capacity that does not require the sanction of the state to exist but requires it only to grow to its full potential. Man is endowed with his innate right to equality of freedom; the question is whether he will use his freedom to survive in an unjust environment or to flourish in a just one. The *Rechtlicher Zustand* is the only proper political environment for the rational human will. The just coercion of government is necessary for the full and equal scope of negative freedom to be distributed to all, without which, positive freedom will have great difficulty reaching its optimum general expression.

The distinction made by the ideal contract in Kantian ethics can be said to be not that between a state of nature (*Natürliche Zustand*) and society (*Gesellschaftliche Zustand*), but that between a state of nature and a certain type of civil society (*Bürgerliche Gesellschaft*): one with a system of distributive legal justice (*Rechlicher Zustand*) (MM,R, A306).[21] The ideal contract is that transition between an unjust state of affairs (nonjuridical) and one where the moral principles of *Recht* are being applied, through a constitution, to the positive law.

If we are to take this distinction seriously, then it calls into question the condition of a state that has a system of law but not one that respects the moral law as Kant sets it out. The state in such a condition cannot qualify as a juridical state because it is an unjust society. It would therefore have to be classified, in a Kantian system, as in a moral state of nature. Society does exist in this moral state of nature, as do those civil organizations that have not yet adopted the ideal contract and become juridical (MM,R, A306–07).

The real meaning of Kant's ideal contract may be better served by a three-way delineation among the state of nature, nonjuridical states, and juridical states. The ideal contract would have application between the second and third stages of classification, as Hobbes's contract applies between the first and second stages (Hobbes 1651, chap. 17). If this is indeed a way Kant thought about the matter, then his political theory must be seen as applying only to the juridical state where *Recht* plays the primary role. In particular, both his theory of punishment and his consideration of political dissent and revolution as strictures against collective action would have effect only with the adoption of the ideal contract and the processes of distribution native to a just (*mit Recht*) society. In all other sorts of civil organization, the harsh strictures connected with these Kantian theories would not hold allowing collective action, in line with the moral law, to take many forms, including revolution.

C. Collective Action and the Juridical State

What Kant calls "the juridical [*Rechtlichen*] state" (MM,R, A311) is that relationship between the moral law and the municipal law, where the latter reflects the imperatives for rational behavior in the former. *Recht* as the practical embodiment of the moral law ought to render a system of positive law that does not violate but promotes the harmonization of individual freedom according to the moral law. The constraints and incentives to external human behavior will, in this way, reflect the necessity of the moral law, which is the only ethical basis for political coordination.

The juridical state requires, via the ideal contract, "a condition of society under a Wille that unites them—a constitution" (MM,R, A311). The constitution contains the principle "circumscribing external freedom through laws" (MM,R, A312), without which coercion is unjust. However, with a just constitution, coercion is compatible with the universal law and is moral, contributing to the greater, equal freedom of each of citizen. Kant maintains "if a certain use of freedom is itself a hindrance to freedom according to universal laws . . . then the use of coercion to counteract it . . . is consistent with freedom . . . [and is] just" (MM,R, A231). I would argue that it is therefore the case that any coercion used to redistribute, in line with the demands of the moral law, is right and necessary to the persistence of a just society.

The united will in the constitution contains three authorities. The sovereign authority residing in "the person of the legislator," the executive authority residing in "the person of the ruler (in conformity to law)," and the judicial authority residing "in the person of the judge" (NM,R, A313).[22]

The sovereign authority is the central authority that creates the law by which the other two must conduct themselves. Right and justice proceed from the authority of the 'will of all,' which "united and consenting" creates a situation "by which each decides the same for all and all decide the same for each" (MM,R, A314). The individual by his autonomous nature is subject and sovereign concurrently and comes to a common and united will by the necessary imperatives of the moral law that set up the juridical state.

Members of a just society are called citizens and must have three "juridical attributes" (MM,R, A314) to qualify for full participation in legislative affairs. First, the individual must have autonomy or lawful freedom "to obey no law other than one to which he has given his consent." Second, civil equality demands a "power to morally bind" any other citizen, even in a superior power position. Third, civil independence requires that no one "owe his existence and support to the choice [*Willkür*] of another person . . . but to his own rights and powers as a member of the commonwealth" (MM,R, A314).

On the basis of these "juridical attributes," Kant makes the distinction between active and passive citizens. Active citizens have all three attributes and therefore, as full members of the commonwealth and not just uninvolved parts of it, can vote. In contrast, passive citizens "lack civil personality" (MM,R, A314) and cannot be given a vote in a just society.

The distinction between active and passive citizens is a call for collective action, but some critics (Hicks 1971, Goedecke 1973) have identified it as a type of political elitism that disenfranchises women, among others, from the political process. To claim this, however, one must ignore statements that Kant makes in the following paragraphs. The primary distinction between active and passive citizens relates to the former having property and the latter being without property and therefore without independence. Kant maintains that the natural laws of freedom, one's innate rights, still apply to passive citizens. In addition, Kant insists that the law of the land respect the innate rights of passive citizens by providing an environment within which equality of freedom allows "everyone [to] be able to work up from his passive status to an active status"—in other words, to acquire the juridical attributes (MM,R, A315). In describing the dependent condition of a passive citizen, Kant defines dependence only in relation to the choices of other person(s). He specifically (MM,R, A314) exempts arrangements by the state for support of the individual.

I argue that these three conditions—the exemption of the state from making citizens dependent, the imperative to construct a political environment in which passive citizens can make themselves independent and active, and the realization that property separates an active from a passive citizen—commit the Kantian state to full participation in the distribution (or redistribution) of goods in support of the freedom of all its citizens. On this reading, Kant distinguishes between active and passive citizens not to discriminate against the latter but to highlight their condition and give a responsibility to the political system to provide the necessary environment so these persons can become independent.[23]

Kant's concern is that only morally independent persons with their integrity intact can cast a true vote with a free will. Those who are economically, socially, or politically dependent on the will of others have less than a full scope of negative freedom; consequently, they lack full autonomy for the expression of positive freedom. By giving a vote to a passive citizen, one would in fact be giving that vote to the person on whose support the dependent person relies. Such action would grant those with power over others disproportionate political influence and freedom, which is both contrary to universal law and an injustice. The 'will of all' is no longer represented, just the will of the independent few.

The juridical state is "the idea of the state as it ought to be according to pure principles of justice," which provides an "internal guide and standard (norma) for every actual union of men in a commonwealth" (MM,R, A313). However, there are three organizational forms that can represent *Recht* as just political systems. These three options are autocracy, aristocracy, and democracy (MM,R, A338).

For Kant, the most complex and the ideal form of government is the democracy based on a republican constitution. In a democracy, the 'will of all' unites to "constitute a people." The will of all citizens forms a "commonwealth," and they place at the head of the commonwealth their united will in the form of a republican constitution (MM,R, A339).

The 'will of all' represented in a democracy with active independent citizens is Kant's "pure republic" (MM,R, A340). The democratic republic has less chance of slipping back into despotism than either of the other two organizational options (autocracy or aristocracy). The democratic republic also carries the mandate of the moral law to its evolutionary apex and fulfills the spirit of the ideal contract in the real world. In addition, it sets into law not only a baseline of equal freedom for all members of the commonwealth but also the political and public-choice mechanisms by which above-baseline allocations and distributions can be made justly.

The problem is the transition from an inferior stage of political organization to the pure republic. Kant contends that the spirit of the ideal contract carries with it an "obligation of the constituted authority to make the type of government conform to this ideal [republican] and, accordingly, to change the government gradually and continually, if it cannot be done at one time, so that it will effectively agree with the one and only legitimate constitution . . . a pure republic" (MM,R, A340).

Kant is contending that even an autocratic juridical state must provide the conduits of peaceful dissent that will cause social and political change in the direction of the pure republic. The juridical state is, in this way, providing for its full growth and perfection. To remain a just society and to give moral weight to its coercive structure, it must allow change and organizational evolution.

D. Collective Action and the Nonjuridical State

A problem arises, however, outside of the juridical state. If I am correct in assuming that a juridical state is one in which the ideal contract and the imperative to harmonize freedom have been institutionalized, then it would seem that a large class of cases in the real world do not measure up to Kant's ideal of a just society. Many societies and nations have systems of law that exploit many and distribute property and freedom to only a few. In many places, the negative freedom of persons has little scope, and government is used by the few to deny the innate rights and duties owed to the many. In such situations, no political conduits have been established to channel dissent for change, and the state, by Kantian definition, is nonjuridical and in violation of the moral law.

Many societies and states are therefore nonjuridical civil arrangements that still exist from a moral point of view in an unjust state of nature. On the basis of what I have said about contract and the applications of strictures only in a just state, I will argue that in the "moral" state of nature the Kantian prohibitions against revolution do not apply, and the possession of property is not real but only provisional.

In a moral state of nature there is an imperative of self-interest in the establishment of a juridical state, but there are no just political processes by which the change might come as a matter of evolution. The personal right to property lies not with the individual but with the collective will, which can transfer use only within the framework of a just constitution. The moral imperative of all persons is to gain the proper political environment for the exercise of their freedom, denied to all (exploited and exploiter) in a moral or civil state of nature. I contend that the means are not limited to peaceful and political acts—for these will find few avenues of expression—but include both civil disobedience and armed revolution to affect change in accordance with universal and necessary moral law.

The above extrapolation is supported by one possible interpretation of Kant's use of self-contradiction as the basis for his condemnation of revolution. He believes that to revolt would dissolve a constitution, which by definition is one that each and every member of the commonwealth had himself willed, in line with the moral law and his practical reason. In this case, the person would be revolting against autonomous legislation that is just and that has provided peaceful political outlets to effect change toward the pure republic. He would be contradicting his own will that as part of the 'will of all' gives moral legitimacy to his political authority (MM,R, A320).

However, if no such constitution existed, and if my freedom is being unjustly infringed by a nonjuridical environment, then in no way have I willed, or would the moral law ever move me to will, the political arrangement I am currently in. Because it is self-contradictory for me to allow an unequal distribution of freedom to remain in force, the absence of avenues for dissent and the presence of the imperatives of the moral law would impel me to revolt. The imperative is to leave the moral state of nature and forge a juridical state, even an autocratic one if necessary, so the evolution toward the pure republic can begin and the spirit of the ideal contract can be implemented. Remember that within and outside of a juridical state, the sovereign legislative authority rests with the 'will of all.' This sovereign is charged with the movement to a republic and the duty of the 'will of all' is collective in that it must strive toward justice (the moral law reflected in the civil law) by whatever means are at hand (MM,R, 321–22). If the ruler does not properly represent the sovereign (which can be assumed outside the juridical state), then reform is not possible and revolution becomes a moral imperative.

The juridical state replaces the French *fraternité* with the concept of *Selbständigkeit* (independence). The Kantian ideal is equal freedom and individual autonomy that, based on the moral law, gives the same principles to all. Principles give moral importance to the individual determining his will and his society (in equal concert with his fellow rational beings) in terms of what is universal and necessary: his freedom fully actualized and in social harmony with others.

Moral Context and the Imperatives for Policy

I will argue that the distinction Kant maintains between *Recht* and *Tugend* can be used as a basic distinction between the proper subjects for collective policy decisions and improper ones. The political institutions that come about within the juridical state (in any of its forms) have the primary responsibility to set up a system of law that gives legal sanction to one's innate right to equal freedom. On the basis of Kant's premises, I would argue that the scope of one's negative freedom and, as a result, of one's positive freedom, can be affected by social and economic discrepancies in the wealth and power of an unjust state (MM,R, A388).

Therefore, a juridical state does not set into opposition freedom and basic well-being; it defines a baseline distribution of goods and opportunities as a component of one's moral integrity and as a public responsibility (education, health care, job opportunity).[24] The state would institute a system of taxation (MM,R, A326) so that wealth distribution preserves the moral integrity of those who are "unable to provide the most necessary needs of nature for themselves." Beneficence and charity are unacceptable in a just society because charity insults the dignity of the individuals to whom it is given. The government of a juridical state is the only entity that can support the individual without circumventing or coopting his will. Government support has the intention of making the individual independent and autonomous, whereas dependence on the will of other individuals, through charity, has the effect of maintaining the recipient in a state of perpetual dependence (MM,R, A325–26, 327; T, A388, 448, 454).

Nozick maintains (1974, Part I) that this type of public intervention to redistribute wealth is a violation of freedom. However, the Kantian theory sets up a tax system as a necessary part of the moral responsibility of the just state and as critical to the harmony of individual freedom. I would say that it is not the case, as Nozick contends, that political distribution of wealth violates autonomy, but that, instead, imposing taxes is coercion in the name of justice to protect the autonomy of all the members of the commonwealth.[25] Violation of freedom from government distribution of wealth could occur only when one is taxed beyond the baseline property level necessary to maintain one's autonomy.

Autonomy in a Kantian context is not *Willkür*, the power to choose (Goodin 1982, 81–82); it is the freedom to exercise fully one's own rational will. Autonomy is therefore necessary to moral agency but can be restricted by environmental variables. Autonomy itself is the realm of *Tugend* and the *Wille*, whereas the environmental effects on *Wille* are the responsibility of politics as it protects *Willkür* against morally arbitrary and unequal influence from the economic and social environment. My argument is that those issue areas that pertain to the protection of the moral integrity of the individual (education, health, environmental risk, security and definition of property, opportunity for employment and self-reliance, public safety, etc.) are the proper sphere for government regulation. These issue areas need a coordinated collective effort to address problems that are beyond the individual's capacity to properly effect change.[26] Issues dealing with the perfection of the individual—the type of education, risks only to one's personal health, private moral choice, etc.—however, involve virtue, and such issues are only the business of the individual involved.

I contend that the distinction Kant makes is similar to an economist's distinction between public and private goods with one exception: Kant places moral responsibility on the political authority to handle externalities of private action that infringe on the freedom of others; the economist has full faith in the market.

In the establishment of the baseline of freedom, the basis of policy must be the result of the demands of the moral law, not the subjective preferences of the individual. The system of external constraints that is a juridical state is based on moral necessity and represents the long-term and timeless interests of all rational beings. Herein lies the objective standard of the critical morality and the independent sense of the collective interest which can provide a moral standard and a metaphysics for public policy choice.

In a just society, human beings have their worth measured in terms of dignity, not price. To try to price a rational nature would be like trying to measure distance in grams. My point, extrapolating from Kant, is that politics and policy should establish, in law, the equal dignity of all rational beings. The juridical state is necessary to the equal freedom of all, and, as such, is critical to the individual's moral capacity to have the agency necessary to establish independent preference orders and to execute them. Without individual freedom and the material baseline of property that acts as its prerequisite, preference orders, as a basis for welfare allocations, are mere reaction to exogenous desire and not the result of a full use of one's power to reason and will reflectively.

These preferences therefore do not represent the essential requirements of the individual will; they represent the subjective wants of the elective self, which hold no connection to moral freedom and therefore no imperative for the policy maker. Although a full investigation of the Kantian imperatives for policy choice must await another venue, I can state that as a standard of decision making, Kantian politics and public policy imperatives establish the common moral and material baseline as a public duty or political responsibility that assures that one individual's pursuit of the subjective ends necessary for her expression of positive freedom will not interfere with the freedom of others involved in the same pursuit.

NOTES

Versions of this chapter were given at various places, including the University of Chicago and the California Institute of Technology. I wish to thank many individuals for their help and comments, including Brian Barry, Russell Hardin, James Woodward, R. T. Page, and especially Alan Donagan, whose friendship and encouragement to look at Kant with an unorthodox eye gave me the energy to complete this essay.

1. All quotations from Kant are translated by the author and are given by Academy page (A), or section number (S). Kant's works are given the following short forms: *Grundlegung zur Metaphysik der Sitten* (The Groundwork, G); *Die Metaphysik der Sitten* (Metaphysics of Morals, MM), with its two parts on justice *Rechtslehre* (R) and virtue *Tugendlehre* (T).

2. There presently exists, on the border between philosophy and political theory, a discussion that centers around the connection between metaphysics and politics and that originates in a confrontation between John Rawls and his critics. (See MacIntyre 1981; and Sandel 1982.) Rawls's critics maintain that political theory ought not to involve metaphysics, especially not a Kantian metaphysics

that places the self before its community context. As the logic states: The self with no community is a self without ends, and a self without ends is no self at all (Sandel 1982, 55–65). This debate seems to be a call for the limitation of political theory and for giving up the idea that politics is not only about our social context (what we are) but also about what transcends that context and makes us human (who we are). These claims have led Rawls to retreat in the face of his critics on this issue and to reject the metaphysical roots of political action and decision. (See Rawls 1985; 1987.)

3. Kant's point is that the essential moral character of the individual, one's humanity, is in the noumenal self. This is the subject of his moral theory. However, it can also be argued that he recognizes that the noumenal self exists in the phenomenal world. Man is, after all, not a god nor an animal but a combination of both. As we will see the positive freedom (the will) of the moral noumenal self is conditioned by the negative freedom (the range of choice) of the physical phenomenal self.

4. The distortion of this project, which is drawn by Rawls's critics (Sandel 1982, 7–13), is one of a Kantian system that is entirely about a noumenal self that is impervious to the vagaries of the empirical world and, therefore, of no use in understanding political thought or action. I wish to argue that this characterization is wrong and that Kant's metaphysics considers the noumenal self because it is encased in the phenomenal world which affects it. Kant's point is that the essential moral character of the person as agent holds priority in considering the demands of each individual's humanity, not that this humanity exists in a vacuum. For a complete discussion and defense of Kant within the context of the debate between Rawls and his critics, see Hill (1989) and Doppelt (1989).

5. There are two claims that I understand the critics to be making against basing politics in metaphysics. (See [Baier 1989] and [Hampton 1989] for a complete discussion.) First, it is claimed that the job of political theory is to seek consensus, not truth. Second, it is inferred that a non-context-oriented metaphysics (which I take to be a necessary condition of metaphysics) cannot tell us anything about practical political reality. I interpret this second point to be that, without an historical or cultural content, political theory is impotent in its consideration of collective action or policy decision making. Combined with the first claim, it is being argued that there is no essential truth about humanity in the person and that if there were it would not tell us anything about the motivation to act collectively or set standards for public choice. These claims notwithstanding, I will proceed on the basis of the contention that we ought to see how far metaphysics can get us before we give up the possibility of saying something about the humanity of the moral person that is transcendent of culture and convention. Here I agree with Hampton (1989) and Buchanan (1989) that the criticisms leveled at metaphysics in political theory are not fatal.

6. To combine metaphysics and politics is to relate the noumenal and phenomenal world and to draw the logical entailments of moral theory to the political realm. The task with Kant's philosophy is to combine his moral theory, property theory, and concept of justice to create a phenomenal home for all noumenal selves. This requires that we begin with exegesis but that we are not limited to it. The task is to draw out logical entailments without contradicting Kant's premises.

Kant neither confirms nor denies collective action and the redistributive state. I contend that he implies them. He may not have made all the connections himself, but he left a map for us to do our own navigation.

7. This exegesis may seem detailed but is a walk through Kant's moral theory for the analytic purpose of constructing the proper platform for extrapolation.

8. I will argue that this is the first confrontation between the noumenal will and the phenomenal world where pressure can cause the moral self to be overruled by the empirical contingencies that are present.

9. Robert Nozick (1974, 32) has used the concept of the end in itself to deduce the proposition that all the decisions relating to one's own ends or property must be respected by all others as part of the imperative to treat each other as ends. Nozick and MacIntyre make the same mistake at different places along the logical extrapolation of the whole categorical imperative. As MacIntyre did not consider anything past the first principle, Nozick takes up the second without reference to the third and shows the range of error in application of the categorical imperative possible without a full reading that includes the principle of the kingdom of ends.

10. See, for example, (Nozick 1974, chap. 7, esp. 167–74). All that Nozick, as a Kantian, can actually claim is that one has a right to only that which does not interfere with the capability of others to function as autonomous ends in themselves.

11. Kant suggests that the duty to form the juridical state is an outgrowth of the categorical imperative; he refers to it in both the *Rechtslehre* and *Tugendlehre* but does not consolidate these statements in such a way that their importance is properly emphasized and succinctly stated. Because of the importance of the imperative to establish a just state to Kant's political theory I have composed a synthesis statement.

12. The state secures and supports the exercise of "good will" and its full realization.

13. Baseline is defined in terms of an ideal goal that should be the primary objective of government policy in a just society. It is not a strategic sense of baseline as noncooperation but a moral requirement for individual agency and autonomy. It requires positive acts of political regulation to achieve and replaces noncooperation with (at least) an externally enforced and ethically just cooperation among equals.

14. Kant, as a friend to the Enlightenment, describes reason and the a priori part of human intelligence as the primary force in the creation of the empirical world. Humans are not created by their environment as much as they have the power to create. Universal law rather than local convention or habit is the dominant factor in institution formation for a Kantian ethics.

15. L. W. Beck relates Kant's concepts of *Wille* and *Willkür* to different interpretations of Kantian political theory by first defining three common criticisms: empty individualism, empty universalism, and libertarianism; Beck then shows how the critics misunderstand Kant by assuming two wills instead of one. The "empty individualism" critics emphasize *Wille* and downplay *Willkür*. Those who see "empty universalism" as Kant's problem do the reverse and describe the power of individual *Willkür* defeating any common social harmony. The libertarians take the two capacities of the will and institutionalize *Wille* in the state,

leaving *Willkür* with no authority, "as something to be . . . eradicated." (See Beck 1981, 224–27.)

16. The point here is that both the exploited and exploiter lose the use of reason in determining their will—the former through constraints on negative freedom from environmental inequalities, and the latter from the improper use of their freedom and power, which is motivated by desire rather than reason.

17. Kant distinguishes between self-interest and rational self-love (*Critique of Practical Reason*, A, 73–75). The latter is a goal, not a starting point, and is not a necessary assumption to *Recht*. All we need assume is that even a primitive sense of self-interest is based on the need to express positive freedom and to handle its resulting conflicts collectively and justly. In order to assume self-interest as a prerequisite to the establishment of *Recht*, we do not have to assume that individuals will act with enlightened self-love (which is part of *Tugend*). We need only assume that a political system of incentives and constraints set up to foster the cooperative expression of rational self-love would be inherently more moral (*rechtlich*) than any other civil arrangement and, as such, rationally necessary in Kantian terms. *Recht* serves the long-term self-interest of each and the freedom of all simultaneously.

18. Kant assumes throughout that the individuals involved are humans and not "holy wills" who always act rationally. The system of coercion that is *Recht* is based on the assumption that all will not act morally or could not avoid the conflict of expressions of positive freedom without central guidance. The coordination by government provides the only sure means to the full and proper expression of each person's freedom equally with all others and, for this reason, freedom in the empirical world requires politics.

19. Kant states the universal principle of justice in the following way: "Every action is just/right when, itself or together with its maxim (etc.) it is such that the freedom of the choice [*Willkür*] of each can coexist with the freedom of everyone in accordance with a universal law" (MM,R, A230). The principle of justice is the basis for civil institutions and policy.

20. Instead of a variety of "primary rights," Kant has but one with two parts. Freedom and the equality of that freedom are basic to each person's potential autonomy and necessary to his moral character. All claims in the empirical world must contribute substantially to one's autonomy to be considered necessary to the innate right and therefore a proper acquired right. Kant is unique in that he encapsulates liberty, equality, and basic well-being under the heading of freedom. A baseline freedom then requires not just noninterference or no harm but positive balance of material goods in order for a rational agent to be free.

21. In his treatise on religion, Kant defines the step out of a state of nature as *Rechtichbürgerlicher (politischer) Zustand* [a just civil state] (*Religion Within the Limits of Reason Alone*, S, III, 1), supporting my distinction.

22. Beck (see note 15), defines Kant's two conceptions of the will in political terms when he describes *Wille* as a legislative power and *Willkür* as executive. This would lend support to the contention that *Willkür* and all executive authority is subject to reason through the legislative authority, whether within the person or in his external political relations.

23. Kant is not a paternalist and considers government that concerns itself with the individual's self-perfection as "the worst despotism" (MM,R, A317). The

role of government and policy is not to support or take care of the individual but to facilitate his attempts to provide for himself, through the distribution of equal freedom and opportunity and the security of a just state.

24. Unlike Rawls, Kant has no "priority of liberty" problem. In Kantian politics, liberty, equality, and well-being are all the basic concerns of a baseline of freedom (see note 20). A state that postponed full freedom of expression for a redistribution of property and wealth would not be compromising freedom or trading it off for material well-being but would be establishing freedom in one area before another. The imperative makes it necessary that the baseline include all three components. None is acceptable alone or complete without the others. Together, they are sufficient and necessary for a baseline of freedom.

25. One should consult section C, The Juridical State, above, to find Kant's statement on the use of coercion justly to counteract improper expression of freedom that "is itself a hindrance to freedom."

26. In *The Limits of Obligation,* James Fishkin contends that "at the large scale" positive general obligations and individual morality work at cross-purposes (Fishkin, 1982, 8). Kant coordinates the demands of individual morality and the positive general obligations of each to all with the introduction of the state. Politics and policy represent the individual in collective matters. The state collects taxes, protects and fosters freedom, and distributes to those in need, as an extension of the individual will based on universal law.

REFERENCES

Baier, Kurt. 1989. "Justice and the Aims of Political Philosophy." *Ethics* 99: 771–90.

Beck, Lewis W. 1981. "Kant's Conceptions of the Will in Their Political Context." In L. W. Beck (ed.) *Studies in the Philosophy of Kant.* Westport, Conn.: Greenwood Press, pp. 215–19.

Buchanan, Allen E. 1989. "Assessing the Communitarian Critique of Liberalism." *Ethics* 99: 852–82.

Doppelt, Gerald. 1989. "Is Rawls' Kantian Liberalism Coherent and Defensible?" *Ethics* 99: 815–51.

Fishkin, James S. 1982. *The Limits of Obligation.* New Haven: Yale University Press.

Goedecke, Robert. 1973. "Kant and the Radical Regrounding of the Norms of Politics." *Journal of Value Inquiry* 2: 81–95.

Goodin, Robert E. 1982. *Political Theory and Public Policy.* Chicago: University of Chicago Press.

Hampton, Jean. 1989. "Should Political Philosophy Be Done Without Metaphysics?" *Ethics* 99: 791–814.

Hill, Thomas E. Jr. 1989. "Kantian Constructionism in Ethics." *Ethics* 99: 752–70.

Hegel, G.W.F. 1821. *Grundlinien der Philosophie des Rechts.* Edited by Johannes Hoffmeister, Hamburg: Felix Meiner Verlag.

Hicks, Joe H. 1971. "Is Kant's Theory of Justice Self-Defeating?" *Southwestern Journal of Philosophy* 2: 205–17.

Hobbes, Thomas. 1651. *Leviathan*. C. B. Macpherson (ed.) Pelican Classic. Harmondsworth, Middlesex: Penguin Books.
Hume, David. 1740. *A Treatise of Human Nature*. L. A. Selby-Biggs (ed.) Oxford: The Clarendon Press.
MacIntyre, Alasdair. 1981. *After Virtue: A Study in Moral Theory*. Notre Dame: Notre Dame University Press.
Murphy, Jeffrie G. 1970. *Kant: The Philosophy of Right*. London: Macmillan.
Nagel, Thomas. 1970. *The Possibility of Altruism*. Princeton, N.J.: Princeton University Press.
Nozick, Robert. 1974. *Anarchy, State, and Utopia*. New York: Basic Books.
Rawls, John. 1971. *A Theory of Justice*. Cambridge, Mass.: Harvard University Press.
———. 1985. "Justice as Fairness: Political Not Metaphysical." *Philosophy and Public Affairs*. 14: 223–51.
———. 1987. "The Idea of an Overlapping Consensus." *Oxford Journal of Legal Studies* 7: 1–25.
Sandel, M. 1982. *Liberalism and the Limits of Justice*. Cambridge: Cambridge University Press.

Epilogue:
Normative Argument and
Public Policy Choice

HAROLD LASSWELL (Lerner and Lasswell 1951), the patriarch of the discipline of policy studies, encouraged the search for the "science" of policy analysis. Over the years, this task has grown and has been interpreted primarily as a search for quantitative and empirical methods (e.g., Dunn 1981; Portis and Levey 1988). Simultaneously, the discipline of economics has grown to be considered the most "scientific" of the social sciences for the same reason: its reliance on mathematical models and quantitative methods (e.g., Boadway 1979; Feldman 1980; Lave 1981; Pigou 1931).

The parallel evolution of these two disciplines has created, within policy sciences, a bias toward economic method that has also transported with it a dependence on the normative framework of the market paradigm (e.g., Gramlich 1981; Director 1964; Mishan 1981; 1982; Posner 1983). Those who attempt to synthesize new theory outside this "scientific" evolution and expand the idea of "policy science" are often eclipsed by the theoretical demands and conventions of the market paradigm. In this volume, we have attempted to expose the poverty of the dominant theoretical framework by bringing together, in a systematic way, nontraditional thought and exposition on policy studies and by setting this in juxtaposition to the market paradigm. Our intent was to free the reader to choose his or her own primary principles and justificatory arguments for policy analysis.

This anthology is a systemic organization of the seminal work that attempts to redefine policy science as a normative and not just an empirical field. This new paradigm of normative political analysis and public policy can grow and prosper within minds and schools of policy studies only if it emerges from the shadow of the predominant methodological orientation of the market paradigm. We do not maintain that efficiency is unimportant but rather that when efficiency is the first principle of policy

517

analysis it sets the terms of argument to the detriment of other competing principles.

In this anthology we have gathered together essays and arguments that show the inherent normative nature of public policy decision making. Our point is not to synthesize the authoritative theory that applies normative political analysis to policy but to analyze the market paradigm and show that it is inadequate to the task it sets for itself. We then suggest a number of requirements that a complete normative analysis of policy should encompass. Our first contention is that the normative dimension of public choice causes problems for the application of cost-benefit methods within the public sector. The second contention is that a more sophisticated analysis of policy choice would reveal alternative ways to apply normative political analysis to the subject of the public agenda so that more rigorous theory and better empirical policy can be created.

We have attempted to provide the reader with the resources, first, to fully examine the normative essence of economic method; and second— and more essential—to investigate public policy choice using normative political analysis. We perceive our efforts as creating a point of departure for a larger theoretical and applied project, which will take much more time and effort outside of this anthology.

With the normative, strategic, and political scrutiny of collective decision making, we hope we have shown that a wealth of concepts and ideas exists for the construction of competing and—one hopes—more adequate policy arguments than the market paradigm can provide. The nature and shape of this larger project is to use new and fuller concepts of rationality, self, utility, autonomy, the good, rights, human action, individual and collective interests, and ends and means to synthesize new frameworks and arguments that might help us to understand, evaluate, and predict our joint decisions more effectively.

We do not advocate a specific theory and its full application—this task we leave to our readers. It will be up to them to apply their theoretical acumen and to argue about the "socially better" option for each policy, given its particular circumstances and requirements. The possibilities here are many, as can be seen in the second part of this volume and in the following bibliography. In closing, however, we would like to point out some basic concerns that this anthology has attempted to identify and to suggest that all theoretical frameworks adequate to the analysis of policy must be able to handle these concerns:

1. The State Represents a Distinct Decision Paradigm

Policy argument must recognize the state as a separate and distinct decision-making entity that requires its own normative framework and theoretical paradigm to define its mission of responsibly solving collective problems. The first requirement of normative policy analysis is the recognition that policy is a collective action problem (Olson 1971; Hardin 1983; Elster 1979, 1983). Here the allocation of collective goods can be examined within a variety of game-theoretic formats, including the traditional prisoner's dilemma (covered in Part I of this volume), chicken (Taylor 1987; Taylor and Ward 1982), the assurance game (Sen 1967; Elster 1979; Taylor 1987), and the coordination game (Lewis 1969; Hardin 1983), to name only a few. Whatever its strategic format, policy analysis must cover or explain away the recognition that individuals and states have a relationship defined by responsibility as well as by efficiency.

2. The Individual Citizen Is More Than a Consumer

The policy maker must assume that each person is a strategic actor with both a moral dimension to his or her individual and collective life and the capacity to combine values and principles with preferences. For most areas of policy concern, the individual must be assumed able to do more than simply order preferences for personal property. The individual has the capacity to create a wide range of preferences and even to overrule them with a moral principle. The policy maker's point of departure must be that human beings function with a more sophisticated rationality than economists give them credit for.

3. All Policy Has a Normative Dimension

Because the individual who creates and is affected by public policy is a moral person, those who propose to evaluate an existing policy or to suggest a new one must construct an adequate theory of the "good" or the "right." If it means anything, adequacy in this context means that policy ends other than wealth must be part of the assumptions that justify the definition of the "public interest" lying at the base of collective choice. The moral character of the individual demands that policy must be able to incorporate more than *instrumental* economic values. Policy analysis must acknowledge *intrinsic* as well as instrumental values and must consider efficiency as a secondary and purely economic consideration. If the analysis cannot sustain, protect, and empower intrinsic value, then it must justify its exclusion from the analysis. In either case, policy argument cannot ignore the existence of such value or it will have ignored the most important aspect of its nature as a normative pursuit: the creation of a "better" environment for human beings.

BIBLIOGRAPHY

This bibliography of sources is not exhaustive. It provides only a basic group of useful books and articles for further study of the topics covered in this anthology. Readers should also consult the bibliographies following individual essays.

I. General Treatments of Policy Argument (Normative and Empirical)

Bobrow, Davis B., and John S. Dryzek. 1987. *Policy Analysis by Design.* Pittsburgh, Pa.: University of Pittsburgh Press.

deLeon, Peter. 1988. *Advice and Consent: The Development of the Policy Sciences.* New York: Russell Sage Foundation.

deHaven-Smith, Lance. 1988. *Philosophical Critiques of Policy Analysis.* Gainesville: University of Florida Press.

Dryzek, John S. 1983. *Conflict and Choice in Resource Management: The Case of Alaska.* Boulder, Colo.: Westview Press.

Dunn, William A. 1981. *Public Policy Analysis: An Introduction.* Englewood Cliffs, N.J.: Prentice-Hall.

Fischer, Frank, and John Forester, eds. 1987. *Confronting Values in Policy Analysis: The Politics of Criteria.* Newbury Park, Calif.: Sage Publications.

Goodin, Robert. 1982. *Political Theory and Public Policy.* Chicago: University of Chicago Press.

Hamlin, Alan, and Philip Pettit, eds. 1989. *The Good Polity: Normative Analysis of the State.* New York: Basil Blackwell.

Kelman, Steven. 1987. *Making Public Policy: A Hopeful View of American Government.* New York: Basic Books.

Lasswell, Harold D. 1971. *A Pre-View of Policy Sciences.* New York: Elsevier.

Lerner, Daniel, and Harold D. Lasswell, eds. 1951. *The Policy Sciences.* Stanford, Calif.: Stanford University Press.

Majone, Giandomenico. 1989. *Evidence, Argument, & Persuasion in the Policy Process.* New Haven, Conn.: Yale University Press.

McLaren, Ronald. 1989. *Solving Moral Problems: A Strategy for Practical Inquiry.* Mountain View, Calif.: Mayfield Publishing Co.

Meehan, Eugene J. 1990. *Ethics for Policymaking.* New York: Greenwood Press.

Nagel, Stuart. 1988. *Policy Studies: Integration and Evaluation.* New York: Praeger.

Portis, Edward Bryan, and Michael B. Levey. 1988. *Handbook of Political Theory and Policy Science.* New York: Greenwood Press.

Stone, Deborah A. 1988. *Policy Paradox and Political Reason.* Glenview, Ill.: Scott, Foresman.

II. The Market Approach to Policy and Its Critics

Boadway, Robin W. 1979. *Public Sector Economics.* Cambridge, Mass.: Winthrop Press.

Buchanan, James. 1975. *The Limits of Liberty.* Chicago: University of Chicago Press.

Coase, R. H. 1960. "The Problem of Social Cost." *Journal of Law and Economics* 3: 1–44.

Director, Aaron. 1964. "The Parity of the Economic Market Place." *Journal of Law and Economics* 7: 1–10.

Dworkin, Ronald. 1980. "Why Efficiency." In *Law, Economics and Philosophy,* ed. M. Kuperberg and C. Beitz. Totowa, N.J.: Rowman and Allanheld, pp. 123–42.

Feldman, Allen M. 1980. *Welfare Economics and Social Choice Theory.* Boston: Martinus Nijhoff.

Gramlich, Edward M. 1981. *Benefit-Cost Analysis of Government Programs.* Englewood Cliffs, N.J.: Prentice-Hall.

Hayek, Friedrich. 1976. *Law, Legislation and Liberty. Vol. 2: The Mirage of Social Justice.* Chicago: University of Chicago Press.

Kelman, Steven. 1981. *What Price Incentives? Economists and the Environment.* Boston: Auburn House.

Lave, Lester B. 1981. *The Strategy of Social Regulation: Decision Frameworks for Policy.* Washington D.C.: Brookings.

Layard, Richard, ed. 1972. *Cost-Benefit Analysis.* Harmondsworth, Middlesex: Penguin Books.

Leonard, Herman B., and Richard J. Zeckhauser. 1986. "Cost-Benefit Analysis Applied to Risk: Its Philosophy and Legitimacy." In *Values at Risk,* ed. Douglas MacLean, pp. 31–48. Totowa, N.J.: Rowman and Allanheld.

Mishan, E. J. 1981. *Introduction to Normative Economics.* New York: Oxford University Press.

———. 1982. *Cost-Benefit Analysis.* London: George Allen and Unwin.

Okun, Arthur M. 1975. *Equality and Efficiency: The Big Tradeoff.* Washington D.C.: Brookings.

Page, Talbot. 1973. *Economics of Involuntary Transfers.* Berlin: Springer-Verlag.

Pigou, A. C. 1932. *The Economics of Welfare.* London: Macmillan.

Posner, Richard. 1983. *The Economics of Justice.* Cambridge: Harvard University Press.

Sagoff, Mark. 1986. "Values and Preferences" *Ethics* 96: 301–16.

Sen, Amartya K. 1974. "Choice, Orderings and Morality." In *Practical Reason,* ed. S. Korner, pp. 54–67. New Haven, Conn.: Yale University Press.

———. 1982. "Behaviour and the Concept of Preference." In *Choice, Welfare and Measurement,* ed. A. K. Sen. Cambridge, Mass.: Harvard University Press.

III. The Strategic Analysis of Collective Action

Abrams, Robert. 1980. *Foundations of Political Analysis.* New York: Columbia University Press.

Barry, Brian, and Russell Hardin. 1982. *Rational Man and Irrational Society?* Newbury Park, Calif.: Sage Publications.

Elster, Jon. 1979. *Ulysses and the Sirens: Studies in Rationality and Irrationality.* Cambridge: Cambridge University Press.

———. 1983. *Sour Grapes.* Cambridge: Cambridge University Press.

Goodin, Robert. 1976. *The Politics of Rational Man.* London: John Wiley.

Hardin, Russell. 1983. *Collective Action.* Baltimore: Johns Hopkins University Press.

Harsanyi, John C. 1982. "Morality and the Theory of Rational Behavior." In *Utilitarianism and Beyond,* ed. Amartya Sen and Bernard Williams, pp. 39–62. Cambridge: Cambridge University Press.

Lewis, David. 1969. *Convention: A Philosophical Study.* Cambridge, Mass.: Harvard University Press.

Olson, Mancur. 1971. *The Logic of Collective Action.* 2d ed. Cambridge, Mass.: Harvard University Press.

Riker, William,. and Peter C. Ordeshook. 1973. *An Introduction to Positive Political Theory* Englewood Cliffs, N.J.: Prentice-Hall.

Sen, Amartya. 1967. "Isolation, Assurance and the Social Rate of Discount." *Quarterly Journal of Economics* 81: 112–24.

Taylor, Michael. 1987. *The Possibility of Cooperation.* Cambridge: Cambridge University Press.

Taylor, Michael, and Hugh Ward. 1982. "Chickens, Whales and Lumpy Goods: Alternative Models of Public Goods Provision." *Political Studies* 30: 350–70.

Ullmann-Margalit, Edna. 1977. *The Emergence of Norms.* Oxford: Clarendon Press.

IV. Utility, Autonomy, and Moral Principle in Public Policy Analysis

Barry, Brian. 1965. *Political Argument.* New York: Humanities Press.

Braybrooke, David. 1987. *Meeting Needs.* Princeton, N.J.: Princeton University Press.

Christman, John. 1989. *The Inner Citadel: Essays on Individual Autonomy.* New York: Oxford University Press.

Donagan, Alan. 1968. "Is There A Credible Form of Utilitarianism?" In *Contemporary Utilitarianism,* ed. Michael Bayles. Gloucester, Mass.: Peter Smith.

———. 1977. *The Theory of Morality.* Chicago: University of Chicago Press.

Feinberg, Joel. 1973. *Social Philosophy.* Englewood Cliffs, N.J.: Prentice-Hall.

Fishkin, James S. 1979. *Tyranny and Legitimacy: A Critique of Political Theories.* Baltimore: John Hopkins University Press.

———. 1984. *Beyond Subjective Morality: Ethical Reasoning and Political Philosophy.* New Haven, Conn.: Yale University Press.

Hampshire, Stuart. 1982. "Morality and Convention." In *Utilitarianism and Beyond,* ed. Amartya Sen and Bernard Williams. Cambridge: Cambridge University Press, pp. 145–58.

Hart, H.L.A. 1979. "Between Utility and Rights." *Columbia Law Review* 79: 828–46.

Hill, Thomas E., Jr. 1973. "The Hypothetical Imperative." *Philosophical Review* 82: 429–50.

———. 1980. "Humanity as an End in Itself." *Ethics* 91: 84–99.

Hobbes, Thomas. 1651. *Leviathan,* ed. C. B. Macpherson. Pelican Classics edition. Harmondsworth, Middlesex: Penguin Books.
Hume, David. 1740. *A Treatise of Human Nature,* ed. L. A. Selby-Bigge. Oxford: Clarendon Press.
Kant, Immanuel. *Gesammelte Schriften.* Berlin: Prussian Academy.
—— 1788. *Critique of Practical Reason.* [A translation is available by Lewis White Beck. Macmillan, Library of Liberal Arts, 1956.]
—— 1795. *Perpetual Peace.* [A translation is available by Ted Humphrey. Hackett, 1983.]
—— 1797. *Metaphysics of Morals: Principles of Right and Virtue.* [Translated as The Metaphysical Elements of Justice by John Ladd for Macmillan, Library of Liberal Arts, 1965, and the Elements of Virtue, translation available under title of "Ethical Philosophy" by James W. Ellington for Hackett, 1983.]
—— 1800. *The Anthropology.* [A translation is available by Mory Gregor for Martinus Nijhoff, 1974.]
Nozick, Robert. 1974. *Anarchy, State and Utopia.* New York: Basic Books.
Sen, Amartya, and Bernard Williams, eds. 1982. *Utilitarianism and Beyond.* Cambridge: Cambridge University Press.
Shue, Henry. 1980. *Basic Rights.* Princeton, N.J.: Princeton University Press.
Wolff, Robert Paul. 1970. *In Defense of Anarchism.* New York: Harper and Row.

V. Environmental Politics and Policy

Bosso, Christopher J. 1987. *Pesticides and Politics: The Life Cycle of a Public Issue.* Pittsburgh, Pa.: University of Pittsburgh Press.
Gillroy, John M., and Robert Y. Shapiro. 1986. "The Polls: Environmental Policy." *Public Opinion Quarterly.* 50: 270–79.
Paehlke, Robert C. 1989. *Environmentalism and the Future of Progressive Politics.* New Haven, Conn.: Yale University Press.
Page, Talbot. 1977. *Conservation and Economic Efficiency.* Baltimore: Johns Hopkins University Press.
——. 1978. "A Generic View of Toxic Chemicals and Similar Risks." *Ecology Law Quarterly* 7: 207–44.
Rabe, Barry. 1988. "The Politics of Environmental Dispute Resolution." *Policy Studies Journal* 16: 585–601.
Sagoff, Mark. 1982. "On Markets for Risk." *Maryland Law Review* 41: 755–73.
——. 1988. *The Economy of the Earth.* Cambridge: Cambridge University Press.
Tribe, Laurence. 1974. "Ways Not to Think About Plastic Trees: New Foundations for Environmental Law." *Yale Law Review* 83: 1326–1427.

Index of Names

525

Contributors

CHARLES W. ANDERSON is Professor of Political Science at the University of Wisconsin, Madison.

BRIAN BARRY is Professor of Political Science and Philosophy at the London School of Economics and Political Science.

R. PAUL CHURCHILL is Professor of Philosophy at George Washington University, Washington, D.C.

HAROLD DEMSETZ is Professor of Economics at the University of California, Los Angeles.

STEPHEN L. ELKIN is Professor of Government at the University of Maryland, College Park.

CHARLES FRIED is Carter Professor of General Jurisprudence at the Harvard University Law School.

JOHN MARTIN GILLROY is Assistant Professor of Political Science and Public Policy Studies at Trinity College.

ROBERT E. GOODIN is Professor of Philosophy at the Australian National University, Canberra.

JOHN A. HAIGH is with Temple, Barker & Sloane of Lexington, Massachusetts.

RUSSELL HARDIN is Professor of Political Science at the University of Chicago.

DAVID HARRISON JR. is with National Economic Research Associates, Cambridge, Massachusetts.

STEVEN KELMAN is Professor of Public Policy and Government at the John F. Kennedy School of Government, Harvard University.

ARTHUR KUFLIK is Associate Professor of Philosophy at the University of Vermont, Burlington.

ALASDAIR MACINTYRE is Professor of Philosophy at the University of Notre Dame.

EZRA J. MISHAN was formerly Professor of Economics at the London School of Economics and Political Science.

ALBERT L. NICHOLS is a Senior Consultant with National Economic Research Associates, Cambridge, Massachusetts.

528

TALBOT PAGE is Professor of Economics at Brown University.

MARK SAGOFF is Director of the Institute for Philosophy and Public Policy, University of Maryland, College Park.

DUNCAN SNIDAL is Associate Professor of Political Science at the University of Chicago.

LAURENCE H. TRIBE is Tyler Professor of Constitutional Law at Harvard University Law School.

MAURICE WADE is Associate Professor of Philosophy, Public Policy and Area Studies at Trinity College.

Pitt Series in Policy and Institutional Studies

Bert A. Rockman, Editor